The Foundations of Behavioral Economic Analysis:
Volume 7

The Foundations of Behavioral Economic Analysis is also available in seven newly revised volumes published by Oxford University Press

PRAISE FOR *"THE FOUNDATIONS OF BEHAVIORAL ECONOMIC ANALYSIS"*

"*The Foundations of Behavioral Economic Analysis* is a masterpiece. It covers the whole field of behavioral economics. And it is also an easy read, as beautiful examples throughout lead readers to appreciate behavioral decisions from the perspective of their own lifetime experience."

George A. Akerlof, University Professor, Georgetown University, and 2001 Nobel Laureate in Economics.

"The publication of this book is a landmark occasion for the field of behavioral economics. Until now there has been no comprehensive survey of the field suitable for graduate students. Professor Dhami has thoroughly and rigorously filled that gap. The book will be placed in a handy place in my office since I plan to consult it regularly."

Richard H. Thaler, Charles R Walgreen Distinguished Service Professor of Economics and Behavioral Science, University of Chicago, and 2017 Nobel Laureate in Economics.

"The seven volumes of *The Foundations of Behavioral Economic Analysis* offer a fascinating mix of theory and evidence and represent the most comprehensive synthesis of behavioral economics at an advanced level. They will be very useful for advanced researchers as well as for graduate students in behavioral economics and beyond."

Ernst Fehr, Professor of Economics, University of Zurich.

"This series of seven volumes is a tour de force, a literal encyclopedia of behavioral economics. Its extraordinary breadth and depth, spanning all aspects from psychological foundations to the most recent advances and seamlessly integrating theory with experiments, will make it the must-have reference for anyone interested in this field, and more generally in where economics is headed. It will quickly become the standard textbook for all graduate courses in behavioral economics, and a much-thumbed companion for all researchers working at the frontier."

Roland Benabou, Theodore A. Wells' 29 Professor of Economics and Public Affairs, Princeton University.

"In *The Foundations of Behavioral Economic Analysis*, Sanjit Dhami offers the first summary and exposition of research in this rapidly growing and increasingly influential subfield. The coverage is comprehensive, extending even to the recent subtopics of behavioral welfare economics and neuroeconomics. The book is distinguished by its detailed yet readable coverage of theory and evidence and its balanced discussion of the philosophical and methodological differences and similarities between 'behavioral' and neoclassical approaches to microeconomics. Select undergraduates, graduate students, and interested scholars will all gain from this masterful book."

Vincent P. Crawford, Drummond Professor of Political Economy, University of Oxford, and Research Professor, University of California, San Diego.

"Economic theory in the twentieth century developed an extremely powerful repertoire of analytical techniques for studying human behavior, but labored under the rather bizarre misconception that the postulates of rational choice were sufficient to characterize economic behavior. Behavioral economics from the late twentieth century to the present demonstrated the explanatory power of hitching these analytical techniques to empirical data gleaned from laboratory and field experiments. The result has radically transformed economics as a scientific discipline, and the best is surely yet to come. Sanjit Dhami has performed a monumental task in consolidating this research and explaining the results in a rigorous yet accessible manner, while highlighting major controversies and sketching the central research questions facing us today."

Herbert Gintis, Santa Fe Institute.

"Displaying wit and wisdom, in *The Foundations of Behavioral Economic Analysis* Professor Dhami conveys both the substance and the excitement of the burgeoning field of behavioral economics. These remarkable volumes will serve as a reference for practitioners and a compelling entry-point for the curious."

George Loewenstein, Herbert A. Simon Professor of Economics and Psychology, Carnegie Mellon University.

"In the development of any field there comes a moment where the results already established must be synthesized, explained and consolidated both for those in the field and those outside. In these amazing volumes Sanjit Dhami has done just that and far more. This book will serve as an encyclopedic must-have reference for anyone seeking to do work in this field or just curious about it. The coverage is exhaustive and the exposition extremely clear and at a level suitable for advanced undergraduates, graduates students, and professionals. This is truly an achievement."

Andrew Schotter, Professor of Economics, New York University and Director, Center for Experimental Social Science.

"For someone, like myself, who started by being ignorant of the richness of the conversation within behavioral economics on a variety of issues, this magisterial volume is the ideal introduction, at once lucid and sophisticated."

Abhijit V. Banerjee, Ford Foundation International Professor of Economics, M.I.T., and 2019 Nobel Laureate in Economics.

"These seven volumes cover all relevant theoretical aspects of behavioral economics in great depth. A great strength is their comprehensiveness: they cover the whole field in a unified manner. They thus are unique in bringing to the fore the unity and diversity of the behavioral approach. The material is well-organized and accessible to a wide audience. It is invaluable to anyone teaching or studying any topic in behavioral economics, showing how the topic fits into the whole."

Peter Wakker, Professor of Economics, Erasmus University Rotterdam.

"Sanjit Dhami's *The Foundations of Behavioral Economic Analysis* is a major and most impressive achievement. It provides an exhaustive account and a masterful synthesis of the state of the art after more than three decades of behavioral economics. It has proven to be an indispensable reference for researchers in economics and psychology. The second, updated edition comes in seven volumes, and it is bound to become the standard text in graduate and advanced undergraduate courses on behavioral and experimental economics for many years to come."

Klaus M. Schmidt, Professor of Economics, University of Munich.

"This is the most complete and stimulating series of books on behavioral economics. With elegance and unprecedented elaborateness, it ties together a wealth of experimental findings, rigorous theoretical insights and exciting applications across all relevant fields of behavioral research. Sanjit Dhami's work has been shaped by numerous comments of the leaders in the field. Now, in the years to come, it will be the standard that shapes how the next generation of students and researchers think about behavior and its science."

Axel Ockenfels, University of Cologne, Speaker of the Cologne Excellence Center of Social and Economic Behavior.

"The expansion of behavioral economics during the past quarter century has been remarkable, much of it concerning strategic interaction and using tools from game theory. Sanjit Dhami's amazing book, now available in a convenient multi-volume format, summarizes—and even defines—the field, broadly as well as in depth. His coverage of theory as well as of experiments is superb. *The Foundations of Behavioral Economic Analysis* will be an indispensable resource for students and scholars who wish to understand where the action is."

Martin Dufwenberg, Karl & Stevie Eller Professor and Director of the Institute for Behavioral Economics at the University of Arizona.

"*The Foundations of Behavioral Economic Analysis* will be a central textbook for behavioral economics. One key feature is its appealing focus on the interplay between theory and evidence. For researchers, it will be a great source of information, puzzles, and challenges for the many years to come. It is a major achievement."

Xavier Gabaix, Pershing Square Professor of Economics and Finance, Harvard University.

"This is a unique and truly remarkable achievement. It is a magnificent overview of behavioral economics, by far the best there is, and it should define the field for at least a generation. But it is much more than that. It is also a brilliant set of original discussions, with pathbreaking thinking on every important topic. An invaluable resource for policymakers, students, and professors— and if they want to try something really special, for everyone else."

Cass Sunstein, coauthor of Nudge and Founder and Director of the Program on Behavioral Economics and Public Policy, Harvard Law School.

"This is truly an amazing work. It is unique in both comprehensiveness and depth. The author is to be applauded for producing what will surely be the standard reference for both researchers and students. And breaking it into seven volumes will greatly enhance its usability. I highly recommend these volumes to any serious reader in behavioral economics."

Gary Charness, Professor of Economics, University of California, Santa Barbara.

The Foundations of Behavioral Economic Analysis: Volume 7

Further Topics in Behavioral Economics

SANJIT DHAMI

OXFORD
UNIVERSITY PRESS

Great Clarendon Street, Oxford, OX2 6DP,
United Kingdom

Oxford University Press is a department of the University of Oxford.
It furthers the University's objective of excellence in research, scholarship,
and education by publishing worldwide. Oxford is a registered trade mark of
Oxford University Press in the UK and in certain other countries

First Edition published in 2020

Published in the United States of America by Oxford University Press
198 Madison Avenue, New York, NY 10016, United States of America

British Library Cataloguing in Publication Data
Data available

Library of Congress Control Number: 2020938072

ISBN 978–0–19–886195–9

Printed and bound by
CPI Group (UK) Ltd, Croydon, CR0 4YY

To my Parents, wife Shammi, and son Sahaj

PREFACE TO VOLUME 7: FURTHER TOPICS IN BEHAVIORAL ECONOMICS

The Foundations of Behavioral Economic Analysis (henceforth, FBEA) was published by Oxford University Press in November 2016. It was the culmination of more than a decade of dedicated work. The book was quite well received and it was heartening to receive messages of support, encouragement, and appreciation from many quarters. Several reviews of FBEA have been published and they have praised the comprehensiveness, formal analysis, and the attention to empirical detail in the book. The book is increasingly taught around the world in behavioral and experimental economics courses in the leading economics departments. Encouragingly, it is also being used in more enlightened courses in economic theory, which was always an important objective of writing this book. The practice of ignoring the empirical evidence and the theoretical models in behavioral economics, in many courses in microeconomics, game theory, and contract theory, is one of the most retrogressive practices in the profession and a form of self-handicapping that is difficult to understand.

At 1,796 pages (including unnumbered pages), FBEA is probably one of the longest economics books ever to have been published in a single volume. Binding the book was a major challenge, which Oxford University Press accomplished with great competence. Some friends have written on a lighter note about the physical size and the weight of the book. Samuel Bowles wrote to say that Herbert Gintis had presented him with a copy of the book on Christmas and that he had to hire a truck to take it home. In one of his reviews, Daniel Read congratulated me on writing the "War and Peace" of behavioral economics. Andrew Schotter wrote to say that he keeps one copy at home and another in his office in NYU to avoid carrying it on the New York subway. A friend who had purchased the paperback version took the drastic step of physically separating Part 4 on behavioral game theory (a good 320 pages long) to carry around with him. Xavier Gabaix is one of many readers who prefers the electronic version that makes issues of the size of the book irrelevant. However, at least some readers, and I am part of this group, tend to be old fashioned and prefer the printed version.

We did explore the idea of splitting FBEA into two volumes before it was published and this was put to an informal vote among 30 of the leading behavioral economists. They were almost equally split. OUP took the casting vote to decide on a single volume, understandably because there are not too many multiple volume mainstream texts in economics. As more feedback from the users of the book emerged, Adam Swallow, the commissioning editor at OUP, began exploring with me the possibility of splitting the book into multiple volumes. Just as publishing such a long book and making it available for teaching to several instructors prior to its publication was a novel and bold experiment in publishing, so too is the proposal to split it into multiple volumes. After extensive discussions at OUP, I was given the go ahead to pursue this exciting and unprecedented opportunity.

What we present to you here, after considerable thought, is a seven-volume book on behavioral economics that splits the nine parts of FBEA into the following topics: Behavioral economics of risk uncertainty and ambiguity (Volume 1); Other-regarding preferences (Volume 2); Behavioral economics of time discounting (Volume 3); Behavioral game theory (Volume 4); Bounded rationality (Volume 5); Behavioral models of learning (Volume 6); Further topics in behavioral economics that include emotions, behavioral welfare economics, and neuroeconomics (Volume 7). Other possible splits of FBEA were possible (e.g., combining Volumes 1 and 3; and Volumes 2 and 4), but none of these proposals offers the clean separation into the main topics in behavioral economics that the current split offers.

We believe that these seven volumes improve on FBEA for several reasons aside from just better portability of the print edition. First, it is a welcome opportunity to correct several typos and errors, as well as to improve the clarity of the text in many places. Second, it allows the updating of some of the material to reflect important recent scholarship in the form of a "guide to further reading" at the end of each volume. This allows me to introduce several new concepts and tie them back to the discussion in the main text. Third, it gives readers the option to buy individual volumes, depending on their current research and teaching interests. However, those with a serious interest in economics, certainly all university academics, ought to consider reading all of the seven volumes. Fourth, given how daunting the prospect of revising the 1,800 page FBEA would have been, the split volumes increase the likelihood of a second edition to some, or all, of the volumes in due course.

For the benefit of readers who buy the separate volumes, or just a few of the volumes, we have taken several steps. Each of the volumes will have a new preface, a new introduction, and carry a reprint of the original preface in FBEA. This will give readers an opportunity to get acquainted with how and why this book came to be. The introductory chapter in FBEA covered important ground. In particular, the first 25 pages outlined the antecedents of behavioral economics, the role of scientific methodology, and the rationale for the experimental method. A lack of proper understanding and appreciation of these critical prerequisites may seriously hamper an understanding of the subject matter. For this reason, in each volume, we shall also print an edited version of the first 25 pages in FBEA. In these pages, I have also added a brief new subsection on replication of experiments. The remaining part of the introductory chapter in FBEA (pages 25–64) is printed only in Volume 1. I have taken care to remove as many typos and errors from the introduction of FBEA as I could find, and improved the clarity of the material in many places.

Readers will find that we have done many of the same things that we might have done in bringing out a second edition of FBEA in these seven volumes. We hope that our efforts in this direction will lead to a better understanding and appreciation of the subject matter of behavioral economics.

PREFACE TO THE FOUNDATIONS OF BEHAVIORAL ECONOMIC ANALYSIS

We print below the original preface to *The Foundations of Behavioral Economic Analysis* in Dhami (2016).

Neoclassical economics is a logically consistent and parsimonious framework of analysis that is based on a relatively small set of core assumptions, and it offers clear, testable, predictions. However, extensive and growing empirical evidence reveals human behavior that is difficult to reconcile within the typical neoclassical models. There has been a parallel development in rigorous theoretical models that explains better the emerging stylized facts on human behavior. These models have borrowed insights from psychology, sociology, anthropology, neuroscience, and evolutionary biology. Yet, these models maintain a distinct economic identity in terms of their approach, rigor, and parsimony. Collectively, these models form the subject matter of behavioral economics, which is possibly the fastest growing and most promising area in economics.

This book is an account of behavioral economics that starts with the basics and takes the reader to the research frontiers in the subject. Depending on how one chooses to use it, the book is suitable for courses at the advanced undergraduate, postgraduate, and research level in economics, and the related social sciences, including, but not restricted to, psychology, management, finance, political science, and sociology. The book should also serve as an essential reference book for anyone generally interested in behavioral economics at any level, and also serve to stimulate the interests of non-specialist academics, specialist academics who are looking for a bird's-eye view of the entire field, and policymakers looking for policy applications of behavioral economics. It would be desirable to assign this book as background reading to courses in economic theory. The book is also, in my view, the minimum subject matter that anyone who writes behavioral economics as their research interest, should be deeply familiar with.

In November 2003, two months after I joined the department of economics at the University of Leicester, I chanced upon an invitation to attend a talk by a colleague, Ali al-Nowaihi, on the subject of *prospect theory*. Ali, a mathematician by training, an economist by profession, and a keen student of the philosophy of science, put forward a Popperian view to evaluate economic theories. He argued that *expected utility theory* was decisively rejected by the evidence, and prospect theory was the most satisfactory decision theory currently available. As a purely neoclassically trained economist, I was troubled by the claims, but also extremely skeptical. For a start, prospect theory sounded like a strange name for a theory, and the evidence was largely "experimental," a data source, that I knew little about. As my defensive instincts started to kick in, I wondered if prospect theory really was so important, then surely my graduate courses, many taught by leading decision theorists, would have found some reason to mention it. Nor was there any mention of such a theory in conversations with colleagues at the two British universities where I had taught so far, or at seminars or conferences that I had attended.

However, rather than just dismiss Ali, a very likeable and respected figure in the department, I decided to put his seemingly extreme views to the test. One of my majors was in public economics, so I decided to conduct a prospect theory analysis of tax evasion in the hope of explaining the *tax evasion puzzles*, which had been outstanding for three decades (details in Part 1). There was already some preliminary work in this area that Ali had mentioned in passing, but none of the papers explained all the puzzles in one fell swoop, using all components of prospect theory. It took me just a few weeks to work out the results. To my utter amazement, prospect theory explained the qualitative and quantitative tax evasion puzzles. By contrast, the predictions based on an expected utility analysis were wrong by a factor of up to 100. This led to my first joint publication with Ali, with whom I have spent many years of fruitful collaboration since then.

This initial, and successful, encounter with prospect theory convinced me that I needed to explore behavioral economics in greater depth. Yet, around 2004, there was no definitive graduate text on behavioral economics. To be sure, there were many excellent sets of collected readings, and several insightful surveys and commentaries on selected aspects of behavioral economics that I eagerly read. In particular, while there were many excellent discussions of the experimental evidence, a full treatment of behavioral economic theory and its applications was missing. One could always pursue the journal articles, but the literature was already enormous, rapidly expanding, and scattered, which made it difficult to spot the links between the various models or to clearly visualize how the various pieces of the jigsaw fitted together. This book was motivated initially by the lack of a serious graduate book on the entire subject matter of behavioral economics, my desire to master behavioral economics, and to support my growing research agenda with Ali. In due course, and as the full range of the subject matter gradually dawned upon me, the scope of the book naturally became more ambitious and daring.

I strive to strike a balance between behavioral economic theory, the experimental evidence, and applications of behavioral economics. The choice of theoretical models in this book is dictated, first and foremost, by their ability to explain the empirical evidence. In some cases, where no decisive empirical evidence is available, I make a judgment on which models are more promising than others, although I give a wide berth to most models.

The main prerequisite for the book is training in the first two to three years of a reasonably good British or North American undergraduate degree in economics, or its equivalent. Any further concepts and techniques are introduced in the book, where needed. A prior course in behavioral economics is not a prerequisite for the book.

The book is divided into nine parts that cover decision making under risk, uncertainty, and ambiguity; other-regarding preferences; behavioral time discounting; models of behavioral game theory and learning; role of emotions in decision making; models of bounded rationality; judgment heuristics and mental accounting; behavioral welfare economics; and neuroeconomics. The book also considers a range of applications of the theory to most areas in economics that include microeconomics, contract theory, macroeconomics, industrial organization, labor economics, development economics, public economics, political economy, and finance. A set of exercises at the end of each part, except the part on neuroeconomics, serves to enhance the reader's understanding of the subject.

Behavioral economics is now a mainstream area in economics. One just has to look at the growing and large number of journal publications and Ph.D. theses every year; the Nobel Prizes to Herbert Simon, Daniel Kahneman, Robert Shiller, Alvin Roth, Vernon Smith, and George Akerlof; the John Bates Clarke medal to Matthew Rabin; the growing importance of behavioral economics among policymakers, as witnessed by the 2015 World Bank Development Report, and the formation of the behavioral insights team in the UK; and the choice of Richard Thaler as the incoming President of the American Economic Association.

It is fair to say that no self-respecting economics department can now afford to omit a course in behavioral economics from its undergraduate or graduate curriculum; indeed, doing so would be grossly unjust to its students and a retrogressive step. Nor can any academic economist, who wishes to retain professional honesty and a balanced opinion on the subject, afford to be unfamiliar with the subject matter of behavioral economics; I am often amused by the ignorance and arrogance of many who pass judgment on behavioral economics with supreme confidence, yet appear to have little understanding of it.

This book has taken more than ten years to write, and my debts are deep and profound. My first and foremost debt and gratitude is to my loving family without which this book could not have been written. To my parents, Manohar and Baljeet, for their unconditional lifelong love and support, and instilling in me the core values of honesty, commitment, and hard work. To my wife, Shammi, and my son, Sahaj, for their patience, sacrifice, unflinching support, and constant encouragement. When I started writing this book, Sahaj was in primary school, and in the month of its first publication, he could be packing his bags to join a university. I do not recommend this as the best template to encourage your son to write any books in the future. However, there are close parallels between Sahaj's educational journey from primary school to university, with my own journey in behavioral economics.

I owe a deep intellectual debt to my long-time coauthor and friend, Ali al-Nowaihi. I first learnt about prospect theory from him. I also owe my appreciation of methodology and the philosophy of science entirely to him. He has undertaken a larger burden of our joint research in the last few years, allowing me to be immersed in the book. For all these reasons, he is very much a coauthor of the book in spirit.

I am extremely grateful to many academics and Ph.D. students who unselfishly and generously contributed their time and efforts to reading drafts of various parts of the book. The participation of so many leading behavioral economists in the making of this book is unprecedented and has really made it into a public project for which I shall always be very grateful. Herbert Gintis, Martin Dufwenberg, and Vincent Crawford deserve special mention for being so very gracious with their inputs into most parts of the book, and very quickly responding to my queries.

Many others also played a critical role in the writing of this book and commented on material closer to their areas of interest, and/or offered valuable encouragement and advice. In particular, I wish to thank Mohammed Abdellaoui, Ali al-Nowaihi, Dan Ariely, Douglas Barrett, Björn Bartling, Karna Basu, Kaushik Basu, Pierpaolo Battigalli, Roland Bénabou, Florian Biermann, Gary Bolton, Subir Bose, David Colander, Andrew Colman, Patricio Dalton, Alexandra Dias, Florian Englmaier, Armin Falk, Ernst Fehr, Urs Fischbacher, Xavier Gabaix, Sayantan Ghosal, Uri Gneezy, Werner Güth, Shaun Hargreaves Heap, Fabian Herweg, Karla Hoff, Philippe Jehiel, David Laibson, George Loewenstein, Michel Marechal, Friederike Mengel, Joshua Miller, Axel Ockenfels, Amnon Rapoport, Ludovic Renou, Alvin Roth, Klaus Schmidt, Andrei Shleifer, Dennis Snower, Joe Stiglitz, Cass Sunstein, Richard Thaler, Jean-Robert Tyran, Klaus Waelde, Peter Wakker, Eyal Winter, and Peyton Young. I owe a profound intellectual debt to many others who did not read the book manuscript but whose work has greatly inspired me. These include Daniel Kahneman, Amos Tversky, Colin Camerer, Matthew Rabin, Herbert Simon, Robert Shiller, and George Akerlof. I am also very grateful to two successive Heads of the economics department at Leicester, Steve Hall and Chris Wallace, who tried to free up as much of my time as possible for writing the book.

I would like to specially acknowledge the enormous amount of work put in by two extremely conscientious and able Ph.D. students, Teimuraz Gogsadze and Junaid Arshad. They closely read and commented on successive drafts of the manuscript at all stages, offered very useful advice, and served as excellent sounding boards for new ideas. Jingyi Mao came up with a very nice cover for the book in a burst of creativity, for which I am very grateful. Other Ph.D. students who carefully read and commented on selected parts of the manuscript include: Ala Avoyan, Nino Dognohadze, Sneha Gaddam, Narges Hajimoladarvish, Emma Manifold, Jingyi Mao, Alexandros Rigos, David Tsirekidze, Yongli Wang, Mengxing Wei, and Mariam Zaldastanishvili.

I would be remiss not to thank the large number of other researchers whose work has made this book possible. I must also sincerely apologize to authors who feel that their work has been inadequately cited or not given the importance they feel that it deserves. To such authors, I say, omission of your papers does not mean that I necessarily viewed your papers as unimportant. In mitigation, I do not intend my book to be a survey of all the experimental results on all topics in behavioral economics; there are already excellent sources with this objective. And, quite possibly, I was simply unaware of your important work, which is in keeping with the evidence on limited attention and bounded rationality that plays an important role in this book.

I am very grateful to the team at Oxford University Press who have done an excellent job at all stages of this book. In particular, I would like to thank Adam Swallow, the commissioning editor for economics and finance at OUP for his patience, good cheer, organizational skills, and sound advice. Scott Parris, the economics editor at the US office of OUP, who retired just as this book was about to come out, was the first to spot the importance of this project. He offered very valuable advice and encouragement throughout the writing stage and played a key role in my decision to go with OUP. I must also thank Niko Pfund, the President of Oxford University Press USA, for his continued interest in the manuscript over several years, despite his many other responsibilities. The production and marketing teams at OUP were a pleasure to work with. Jon Billam took on the challenge of copy-editing an unusually large book with great enthusiasm. I am also very grateful to Emma Slaughter, the production editor for the book; Kim Stringer, the indexer; Kim Allen, the proofreader; Carla Hodge-Degler who took over as production editor from Emma; and to Leigh-Ann Bard, the marketing manager for the book.

CONTENTS

Part III NEUROECONOMICS

Part IV A GUIDE TO FURTHER READING

LIST OF FIGURES

LIST OF TABLES

Introduction to Volume 7

The final volume of this book deals with three topics, *emotions, behavioral welfare economics,* and *neuroeconomics*. The first two chapters are on emotions, followed by a chapter each on behavioral welfare economics and neuroeconomics. In keeping with the format of the other volumes, Chapter 5, the final chapter, gives a guide to further reading. We now give the broad outline of this volume.

Part I of the book deals with emotions in behavioral economics. In neoclassical economics, the standard practice is to focus on *emotionless deliberation* and assume that economic agents make cool, calculated, decisions in considering trade-offs between alternative choices. By contrast, evidence suggests that humans operate along the entire range of the emotional spectrum. Emotions are central to human behavior and affect economic outcomes in fundamental ways. Till fairly recently, economic theorists had little to say about emotions, and researchers working in the area of emotions, little to say about the effect of emotions on economic variables. However, in recent years, there has been an impressive spurt of research activity in this area.

One may give the following useful taxonomy of emotions (Elster, 1998). *Social emotions* include anger, hatred, guilt, shame, pride, admiration, and liking. *Counterfactual emotions* are generated by thinking about unrealized possibilities, e.g., regret, rejoicing, disappointment, and elation. *Anticipatory emotions* are caused by anxiety about what may happen, e.g., fear and hope. *Realized emotions*, e.g., grief and joy, are caused by events that have already been realized in the past. *Material emotions* are caused by the possession of material or non-material objects by others, e.g., envy, malice, indignation, and jealousy. There are other kinds of emotions that do not fall into any of these categories, e.g., contempt, disgust, and romantic love.

In this volume, we are mainly interested in the study of a limited number of emotions and their impact on economic behavior.[1] We also consider the interaction between emotions and cognition in shaping economic decisions. Indeed, as Elster (1998, p. 73) writes: "The more urgent task is to understand how emotions interact with other motivations to produce behavior."

There is a range of interesting questions that we cover somewhat selectively; however, these questions are more fully discussed in other sources.[2] For instance, are emotions culture-specific or universal? What hormonal or physiological changes are associated with emotions? What is

---

[1] There is a corresponding realization among emotion theorists about the importance of economic models. For instance, Rolls (2014) devotes a major part of his Chapter 9 to economic models, albeit the main focus is on neuroeconomics.

[2] The interested reader may consult Frank (1988), Elster (1998), Loewenstein (2000), Goldie (2009), Winter (2014), and Rolls (2014).

the valence, or location on a pleasure-pain scale, of different emotional states? Can emotions be called upon/avoided by individuals in a deliberate and rational manner, or are they passively undergone? Can we learn to avoid cues that trigger different emotional states? Can individuals successfully induce emotions in others?

We have already considered, elsewhere in the book, material that would also appear to be well situated for this chapter. Instructors who wish to teach a specialized course on the role of emotions in economics, or a behavioral economics course with special emphasis on emotions may wish to combine the following topics from different parts of the book. (i) Formal models of emotions such as guilt, anger and disappointment using *psychological game theory* (see Volume 4 of the book),[3] (ii) models of *disappointment aversion* and *regret* (see Volume 1 of the book), and, (iii) issues of *self-control* that arise from *present biased preferences* (see Volume 3 of the book). In order to avoid repetition, we omit a discussion of these issues here, and focus on the remaining issues in the role of emotions in economics.

Chapter 1 gives an introduction to some components of emotions and physiological states (moods, physical pain, hunger, thirst) that are of interest in economic models; collectively these are known as *visceral factors*. We briefly consider the question of the rationality of emotions. In Volume 1, we considered the role of *anticipated emotions* such as regret and disappointment that might be experienced at some future time, on account of decisions made today. Here, in Chapter 1, we introduce *anticipatory emotions* experienced at the time of making decisions, such as anxiety and dread. Volume 1 also considered various theories of risk. However, risk may also bring about feelings of dread, anxiety, and apprehension. Thus, it would appear that emotions ought to be inextricably linked to explanations of human behavior under risk. We explain the *risk as feelings hypothesis*, that is almost never taught in mainstream courses in economic theory, but it ought to be taken more seriously by economists.

Visceral factors are typically activated by external cues. We develop a model of *habit formation* in the presence of *stochastic cues* and discuss the role of active cue management. Anticipation of future pain or rewards can create anxiety or elation, thus, we also incorporate the role of *anticipal utility* into a simple life-cycle model. We develop a *preference representation of anxiety* and apply it to a problem of portfolio choice in a life-cycle model of consumption. It turns out that risky assets, whose uncertain returns create anxiety, may command an *anxiety premium* that could potentially explain the equity-premium puzzle.

When predicted future tastes differ from their actual realization, individuals are said to suffer from *projection-bias*. In this case, individuals might make time-inconsistent choices, and may end up making decisions in a hot state that they regret later. This explains the role of public policy and legal provisions that provide for various cooling-off periods, be it for the purchase of consumer durables or applying for marriage/divorce.

Volume 3 discussed issues of self control in the context of temporal present biased preferences. Here we discuss the Gul–Pesendorfer framework of *temptation preferences* that explains temptation and self-control problems in the classical revealed preference framework. In this framework, one response to temptation is to remove a tempting option from the menu of choices, even when one is sure that one could resist temptation in the future, because resisting temptation takes up costly willpower. However, in the presence of uncertainty about the future, there are costs and benefits from this option. For instance, removing a currently tempting option from the menu

---

[3] For a discussion of guilt inculcation in children by parents that does not rely on the machinery of pscyhological game theory, see Becker (1996) and Frank (1988), although they invoke very different mechanisms to each other.

may improve current savings, yet an adverse shock to marginal utility in the future may reduce the future enjoyment of these savings.

In the final section of this chapter we discuss the emerging literature on *happiness economics*. Unlike many other areas in economics, the evidence relies on self reported measures of well-being, health, and life satisfaction. However, there is a strong correlation between various measures of well-being and these, in turn, successfully predict job quits, suicides, productivity, and probability of a divorce among couples. We examine a celebrated result in this literature, the *Easterlin paradox*. The cross-sectional evidence in any country shows that richer people are happier. However, the time series evidence shows that growth in income is not associated with higher self-reported measures of well-being. A leading explanation is that as incomes increase over time, the reference point of individuals, as captured by their aspiration levels, moves upwards. Thus, an increase in income over time is not associated with greater happiness. In recent years, the data behind the Easterlin paradox has been increasingly questioned based on a longer time series and a more representative sample of poor countries.

Chapter 2 considers the interaction between emotions and cognition. This interaction has evolutionary origins. The cognitive system is associated with the development of the prefrontal cortex, 150,000 years ago. However, the cognitive system was built on top of an already existing emotional system that we share with other mammals. The result is that the objectives of the emotional and the cognitive systems can sometimes be in conflict, and at other times, in harmony. We also employ a System 1 (quick, reactive emotional system) and System 2 (slow, deliberative cognitive system) distinction as we did in Volume 5. However, here we are interested in examining a different set of issues.

We begin by presenting a promising model of the interaction between the two systems that can serve as a template for the development of future models. This model has the advantage of endogenously deriving several behavioral features of interest to economists such as reference dependence, loss aversion, social preferences, and hyperbolic discounting. In a formal model of *dual selves*, we show how the cognitive system can control the emotional system through the exercise of costly willpower. We derive the optimal solution in the presence and in the absence of a commitment technology.

People often try to discover themselves through their actions. For instance, charitable giving may be a self-signal that the individual has empathy and compassion for others. Withstanding extreme stress and successfully completing a timed task may self-signal abundant willpower to an individual. These issues can be modeled in several ways. A radical proposal is to model the interaction between the two systems using classical game theoretic asymmetric information models. However, this leaves open the question of how contracts are enforced between the two systems, and what does a participation constraint imply in this special case?

In the final two sections, we consider the *strategic transmission of information* in a multiple-selves model. In these models, if the current self chooses to acquire some information, it immediately becomes available to all future selves, who can use this information to the detriment of the current self. In this case, the current self may choose to be strategically uninformed. For instance, individuals vastly overestimate the effects of smoking on lung cancer, yet typically are not proactive in accessing easily available information that could inform them of the objective risks. There can be other equally plausible explanations for this phenomenon. For instance, individuals may procrastinate in the presence of hyperbolic discounting. However, here we study a different set of explanations that are based on *imperfect willpower, imperfect recall,* and *motivated cognition* (i.e., managing the degree to which subsequent selves can recall past events).

In Part II of this volume, which is limited to Chapter 3, we consider the hugely important topic of behavioral welfare economics; we discuss newer, significant, developments in the guide to further reading (Chapter 5). In neoclassical economics, rational individuals are considered to be the best judges of their own welfare, and their choices reflect informed judgment of their welfare. One can then use revealed preference arguments to derive an individual's preferences based on observed choices. The findings from behavioral economics show that individuals suffer from a range of biases and misperceptions. Here, and throughout the book, the terms *biases* and *misperceptions* only make sense, relative to the rational benchmark in neoclassical economics.[4] In the presence of biases and misperceptions, individuals can no longer be considered to be making informed judgments of their welfare. This calls for a modification of the methods of neoclassical welfare economics, because revealed preference analysis does not apply. These issues form the subject matter of Part II.

Libertarianism and *paternalism* are loaded words. Economists have typically used these terms to mean, respectively, respect for individual choices, and interference with individual choices in a direction that improves welfare. Relative to behavioral interventions, neoclassical forms of paternalism are sometimes referred to as *heavy-handed paternalism*. Examples include taxes and subsidies; banning of certain substances, such as narcotics; protection of the vulnerable against usury laws; health and safety regulations; regulation of the 'approval process' for drugs; regulations that make seat belts mandatory in cars, and mandatory car insurance.

The main approach advocated in behavioral economics is *soft paternalism*. This is an umbrella term that nests several kinds of interventions, such as *libertarian paternalism*, *asymmetric paternalism*, and *light paternalism*. The main thrust of these approaches is to design interventions, or *nudges*, that improve the welfare of boundedly rational individuals, as judged by themselves, but impose minimal costs on fully rational individuals. A leading example is *default options* that address a range of potential biases of boundedly rational individuals; these biases include, but are not limited to, present-biased preferences, temptations, and limited attention. Appropriate defaults improve the decisions of boundedly rational individuals, but impose small, if any, costs on rational individuals. How do we know that the welfare of individuals as judged by themselves, improves after the imposition of the nudge? Or if we cannot answer this question, then what is the appropriate scope of behavioral welfare economics? This question, which has philosophical and empirical dimensions, is taken up in Chapter 5.

We also consider a range of other important topics in this part that we now briefly note.

We examine the case for *mindless economics* versus the case for *mindful economics*. This debate is about the very scope of economics and addresses the question: Should economics be limited to choice data alone, or are non-choice data admissible too? The reader will not be surprised to learn that this book strongly advocates the use of choice and non-choice data, such as survey evidence, experimental evidence, and neuroeconomic and biometric evidence. The extreme view that economics ought to be restricted to choice data and revealed preference arguments only is overly restrictive.

We also consider formal models of choice-based welfare. While these directions are promising, they also show up the limitations of the approach, even when the choice-based approaches are stretched to their limits. Choice-based models must address the issue of choices that depart from

---

[4] There should be no presumption that, in any absolute sense, the actual behavior of humans should either be termed as a bias or a misperception. Indeed, it would be more appropriate to term the behavior of humans in neoclassical economics, whenever it is empirically refuted, as a bias or misperception relative to the actual behavior of humans that behavioral economics aims to highlight and explain.

those expected under the rational benchmark. In a leading model, one deals with this issue by trimming-away the anomalous choices. However, such trimming-away necessitates the use of either non-choice data, or the invocation of a welfare criterion for trimming the choices, which is what one is trying to construct in the first place. We also consider the extension of this framework to issues of limited attention. We revisit these issues once again in Chapter 5.

The limitations of the choice-based approach, despite commendable progress in this direction, have prompted some to focus on preferences rather than choice. We also consider the development of alternative frameworks such as the *contractarian approach*, which have been used to criticize nudges. In this approach, interventions take the form of directly providing information to individuals about their behavioral biases. But the fact that information framing is almost never neutral, and that there must be some choice architect who must decide on the framing of information, is as fatal to the contractarian approach as the one that it criticizes.

In the last section, we give readers a flavor of the rapidly developing literature in behavioral public economics. We discuss how we might formulate traditional public finance concepts such as tax incidence and the excess burden of taxes in the presence of behavioral factors, such as limited attention. We also briefly comment on reduced form approaches to behavioral welfare economics that nest a range of behavioral explanations.

None of the frameworks considered in Part II will persuade all readers of the book. This, despite scholarship of a high quality, flags up the inherent and deep difficulty of dealing with the underlying issues that straddle neoclassical economics, behavioral economics, philosophy, and ethics.

Part III of the book, which is limited to Chapter 4, offers a brief and selective introduction to the rapidly growing field of *neuroeconomics*. The treatment here is best thought of as a brief taster course in neuroeconomics. The aim of neuroeconomics is not only to identify the brain regions that are activated during economic choices, but also to uncover the underlying neural circuits, and measure neural activity, that might suggest new economic theories, and enable new predictions. The hope is that, in due course, economic models can successfully make joint predictions about choice behavior and the relevant neural circuitry. Most of the behavioral theories discussed in this book have not required neural foundations. Whether neural foundations will successfully underpin most behavioral theories in due course cannot be answered with certainty at the moment. However, impressive progress is being made in that direction.

Neuroeconomics is a relatively new field in economics and it is also one of the fastest growing. While our understanding of the neural underpinnings of behavior continues to improve, there is still much disagreement about the neural foundations of behavior. Indeed some readers may even object to the inclusion of such a chapter in a book that has the word "Foundations" in its title. However, it would be a mistake to ignore this field, yet at the same time it must be realized that many of the results are tentative and speculative at the moment. Given the rapid progress in the field, this state of affairs could change quickly.

We introduce the reader to the major brain areas that are of interest to neuroeconomists and give a brief outline of the two main kinds of methods in neuroeconomics: *Measurement techniques* and *manipulation techniques*. Measurement techniques measure some aspect of brain activity; examples are single-neuron recordings, positron emission tomography, and functional magnetic resonance imaging. Manipulation techniques can alter activity in specific areas of the brain, allowing for an observation of the associated behavioral change; examples include transcranial magnetic stimulation, transcranial direct current stimulation, and brain lesion studies. Each of the techniques has advantages and disadvantages, hence, data from several complementary techniques helps us to build a better picture of the neural correlates of behavior. Some of the most interesting results come from attempts to predict the direction of causality.

We only focus on the neural underpinnings of some aspects of human behavior outlined in the first four parts of the book: Behavioral decision theory with a focus on prospect theory; social preferences with a focus on inequity aversion, social trust, and punishment; time preferences with a focus on two alternative models, the $\beta - \delta$ model, and the planner–doer model; and strategic interaction with a focus on the neural underpinnings of equilibrium and non-equilibrium reasoning, as embodied in level-k and CH models. Finally, we briefly comment on pharmacoeconomics, which studies the change in human behavior when one interferes with the neuromodulator system, with a focus on the effects of oxytocin.

Finally, Chapter 5 gives the guide to further reading. It considers newer developments and extensions of some of the topics considered in this volume. Among topics in emotions, we consider issues of persistent temptation and the optimal timing of self control, as well as more empirical evidence on projection bias that comes from a variety of sources. Among topics in neuroeconomics we consider the neural measurement of regret and then show how this predicts well subsequent investment choices; we also examine the effects of the neuropeptide arginine vasopressin (AVP) on strategic choices.

The main focus of Chapter 5 is overwhelmingly on behavioral welfare economics; seven out of the ten sections are devoted to it. We argue for a holistic approach to behavioral public policy in which, in addition to libertarian paternalism we also allow space for the use of policy instruments typically used in hard paternalism, e.g., taxes and subsidies. We consider more evidence for the efficacy of nudges such as reminders, and evidence that reveals nudges may also have unexpected effects in crowding out other policy instruments or actions. We present two theoretical models of default options and the associated empirical evidence. The first model has a cost of overriding defaults and the second model derives the perception perfect equilibrium (see Volume 3) for choices involving the take up of a savings plan under default savings rates and various degrees of unawareness of self control problems. Continuing our discussion from Chapter 3 on behavioral public economics, we consider the deadweight loss from the taxation of sugary drinks in the presence of externalities and internalities. We also consider the intellectual merit of the dual model implicit or explicit in the modern choice based approach in behavioral welfare economics. The dual model assumes that there exist rational underlying latent preferences that accord with the textbook neoclassical economic actor and observed psychological preferences (through choices) that are consistent with the preferences of actors in a behavioral economics course. The agenda then is to purify psychological preferences to recover the underlying rational preferences on which one may base revealed preference normative analysis. We examine also the implications of this dual model for the literature on nudges. These issues lie at the very heart of the subject matter of behavioral welfare economics.

I have now come to the end of this seven-volume series on behavioral economics. I thank you, the reader, for persevering with the book and I hope that it adds to your understanding of behavioral economics, and makes you aware of the set of open questions, puzzles, and the challenges that lie ahead. I also hope that it conveys to you the excitement around new research in this area, to which if you not already a contributor, then this book may serve to invite you to be one. On a personal note, tampered with relief at the completion of this book, comes greater humility of what we as economists do not yet know. While I might know a bit more than the time that I started writing this book, my sense of ignorance is greater, as is my excitement to confront some of the challenges that lie ahead. There is no going back to how things once were. Economics has changed forever, and for the better.

Introduction to Behavioral Economics and the Book Volumes

The *neoclassical framework* in economics provides a coherent and internally consistent body of theory that offers rigorous, parsimonious, and falsifiable models of human behavior.[1] Augmented with auxiliary assumptions, it is flexible enough to analyze a wide range of phenomena. In actual practice, the neoclassical framework includes, but is not restricted exclusively to, consistent preferences, subjective expected utility, Bayes' rule to update probabilities, self-regarding preferences, emotionless deliberation, exponential discounting, unlimited cognitive abilities, unlimited attention, unlimited willpower, and frame and context independence of preferences.[2] Neoclassical economics is also typically underpinned by optimization-based solution methods and an equilibrium approach.

In principle, the neoclassical framework is capable of relaxing many of its standard assumptions. For instance, it can allow for reference dependence preferences, social preferences, frame dependent preferences, and non-exponential models of discounting. However, these extensions are rare in actual practice, and when they are made, the neoclassical framework typically does not have fundamental new insights to offer. For instance, adding reference dependent preferences generates few, if any, insights in the absence of a theory about how human behavior differs in the domains of gains and losses relative to a reference point. Similarly, adding other-regarding preferences without attempting to fit such a model to the behavior of humans, particularly to the evidence from experimental games, offers little progress. For these reasons, my use of the term *neoclassical economics* is shorthand for *the typical practice in neoclassical economics*.

The intellectual developments in neoclassical economics are impressive. However, its empirical success in predicting and explaining human behavior is modest. Indeed, an impressive, thorough and detailed body of experimental, neuroeconomic, and field evidence, based on several decades of work, raises serious concerns about the core assumptions and predictions of neoclassical models. This has been matched by impressive theoretical developments, drawing on insights from psychology, biology, anthropology, sociology, and other social sciences, that

---

[1] I avoid the loaded term *standard economics* to refer to *neoclassical economics* because this might give the latter a certain empirical sanctity.

[2] I have deliberately avoided the word 'rationality' in this description of the neoclassical framework because it would have to be precisely defined. See Dhami and al-Nowaihi (2018) for the various senses in which rationality is used in neoclassical economics.

has come to be known as *behavioral economics*. These models have had much greater empirical success relative to neoclassical models.[3]

There is a danger that one may propose definitions of behavioral economics that are either too broad and have ambiguous scope, or are too narrow with limited scope; each of these outcomes would be unfair for a newly emerging field. Any falsifiable theory that replaces/modifies any of the core features of neoclassical economics, by alternatives that have a better empirical foundation in human behavior is a potential member of the class of behavioral economic theories, if it can pass stringent empirical tests.

The aim of this book is to offer an account of formal behavioral economic theory, its applications, and a discussion of the underlying experimental and field evidence.[4] The standard toolkit in neoclassical economics is adequate for the study of behavioral economics. Most behavioral models adopt an optimization framework, are typically underpinned by axiomatic foundations, are parsimonious, rigorous, falsifiable, and internally consistent.[5]

We do not attempt to pit behavioral economics against neoclassical economics in a paradigmatic battle. As in every science, we progress by taking account of evidence that suggests a refinement and improvement of existing models. In this case, the relevant improvement appears to have the steepest gradient in the direction of constructively incorporating insights from other behavioral sciences. The book outlines a new research program that offers a constructive way forward for economics by highlighting developments in behavioral economic theory, which also uses core insights from neoclassical economics. It is likely that in due course, behavioral economics will cease to exist as a separate field within economics, and this will become the normal way in which we do economics.

A distinction is sometimes drawn between experimental economics and behavioral economics.[6] However, the activity of behavioral economists and experimental economists has turned out to be complementary and collaborative, as in the natural sciences. It is often difficult to spot the dividing line between their work. For instance, experimental economists not only test the predictions of economic models, but their results have often been critical in suggesting further developments in behavioral models. Behavioral theorists on the other hand, often suggest experiments that could test their proposed theories.

The introduction to these volumes is a condensed version of the longer introduction in Volume 1 of *The Foundations of Behavioral Economic Analysis*. Section 1 briefly traces some of the historical developments that have led to modern behavioral economics. Section 2 considers important methodological issues that lie at the heart of how economists 'do' and 'should'

---

[3] Increasing the explanatory power of neoclassical economics is very worthwhile but Thaler (2015) adds another reason for studying behavioral economics in his inimitable style: "Behavioral economics is more interesting and more fun than regular economics. It is the un-dismal science."

[4] For a non-technical treatment of behavioral economics, the reader can consult the extremely readable and witty account by Thaler (2015) that offers a much more detailed historical account of developments in behavioral economics from the 1970s onwards from a personal perspective.

[5] I use the word "rigorous" purely for its practical appeal to most neoclassical economists but I agree with the sentiments expressed by Gintis (2009, p. xviii): "The economic theorist's overvaluation of rigor is a symptom of their undervaluation of explanatory power. The truth is its own justification and needs no help from rigor."

[6] Loewenstein (1999) gives a nice discussion of the methods in each of these areas and offers the following definition (p. F25): "BEs [behavioral economists] are methodological eclectics. They define themselves, not on the basis of the research methods that they employ, but rather their application of psychological insights to economics. In recent published research, BEs are as likely to use field research as experimentation...EEs [experimental economists] on the other hand, define themselves on the basis of their endorsement and use of experimentation as a research tool."

practice their craft. Section 3 considers the importance of the experimental method in behavioral economics. Section 4 briefly explains the organization of the book. There are two appendices. Appendix A outlines the random lottery incentive mechanism that lies at the heart of the modern experimental method in economics. Appendix B asks you to think of 50 questions as a problem set, but I deliberately give you very little structure at this stage in order to enable a free-spirited approach to the answers. Rigorous answers to these questions can be found in the book.

1 Some antecedents of behavioral economics

While Adam Smith's justly celebrated book, *The Wealth of Nations*, is widely cited, his other book, *The Theory of Moral Sentiments*, has received less attention. *The Theory of Moral Sentiments* reads like an agenda for modern behavioral economics; it recognizes many behavioral phenomena such as loss aversion, altruism, emotions, willpower, and the planner–doer framework (Ashraf et al., 2005). Classical economists such as Jeremy Bentham wrote about the psychological underpinnings of utility and Francis Edgeworth wrote about social preferences (Camerer and Loewenstein, 2004). Bardsley et al. (2010) trace the beginnings of experimental economics to the classical economists such as David Hume, Stanley Jevons, and Francis Edgeworth; Jevon's marginal utility analysis derived its motivation from experimental observations about the relation between stimuli and sensations.

Two factors contributed to the gradual elimination of psychology from economics. First, around the turn of the twentieth century, there was "a distaste for the psychology of their period, as well as the hedonistic assumptions of Benthamite utility" (Camerer and Loewenstein, 2004). The second was the revealed preference approach popularized by Paul Samuelson that emphasized the observation of *choice behavior* rather than the psychological foundations for choice behavior (Bruni and Sugden, 2007). Glimcher and Fehr (2014, p. xviii) write: "It cannot be emphasized enough how much the revealed-preference view suppressed interest in the psychological nature of preferences, because clever axiomatic systems could be used to infer properties of unobservable preference from choice."

Important, and path-breaking, developments in behavioral economics took place in the 1950s and 1960s that included: violations of the independence axiom of expected utility theory (Allais, 1953); violations of subjective expected utility (Ellsberg, 1961; Markowitz, 1952); demonstration of the importance of bounded rationality (Simon, 1978; Selten, 1998);[7] and early work on quasi hyperbolic discounting (Phelps and Pollak, 1968). However, at that time, this work struggled to get the attention that it deserved.

An important catalyst for the development of behavioral economics was the decline of the behavioralist school in psychology, and the emergence of cognitive psychology. Cognitive psychology emphasized the role of mental processes in the understanding of tasks involving decision making, perception, attention, memory, and problem solving. Some cognitive psychologists naturally turned their attention to testing their models against the neoclassical framework. The two most important cognitive psychologists in this category were Daniel Kahneman and Amos Tversky, whose work in the 1970s helped kick-start modern behavioral economics. Along with Richard Thaler, who was an economist by training, and was struggling to make sense of several

---

[7] Simon (1978) refers to Herbert Simon's Nobel lecture that traces the historical development of bounded rationality through the 1950s and 1960s. Selten (1998) is an English language version of a paper that appeared initially in German in 1962.

anomalies in neoclassical economics from the mid 1970s onwards, they are some of the earliest and most significant modern behavioral economists.

The second topic is the *role of experimental evidence in economics* that I consider in Section 3. The justification for this section is the continued skepticism of many economists about experimental economics, which constitutes an important part of the evidence base for behavioral economics. The following quote attributed to the Nobel Prize winner Gary Becker from a magazine interview (Camerer, 2015, p. 250) is probably not unrepresentative: "One can get excellent suggestions from experiments, but economic theory is not about how people act in experiments, but how they act in markets. And those are very different things. That may be useful to get suggestions, but it is not a test of the theory. The theory is not about how people answer questions. It is a theory about how people actually choose in market situations."

What follows is a somewhat long introduction, but this is a somewhat long book too. In mitigation, the first one third of the introduction largely deals with background material that reflects the somewhat unsettled nature of economics. My hope is that if a second edition of this book is ever written, then there would be enough convergence of views on this material so that I can safely omit it.

2 On methodology in economics

University degrees in Economics and the natural sciences typically do not require formal courses in methodology. Yet, while all the natural sciences subscribe to the scientific method and students of natural sciences instinctively know that this means, economics has taken a very different, and pernicious, direction that has little basis in the scientific method. Consider, for instance, the following quote from Gintis (2009, p. xvi) that nicely captures the essence of the problem:

Economic theory has been particularly compromised by its neglect of the facts concerning human behavior ... I happened to be reading a popular introductory graduate text on quantum mechanics, as well as a leading graduate text in microeconomics. The physics text began with the anomaly of blackbody radiation, ... The text continued, page after page, with new anomalies ... and new, partially successful models explaining the anomalies. In about 1925, this culminated with Heisenberg's wave mechanics and Schrödinger's equation, which fully unified the field. By contrast, the microeconomics text, despite its beauty, did not contain a single fact in the whole thousand-page volume. Rather the authors built economic theory in axiomatic fashion, making assumptions on the basis of their intuitive plausibility, their incorporation of the "stylized facts" of everyday life, or their appeal to the principles of rational thought.... We will see that empirical evidence challenges some of the core assumptions in classical game theory and neoclassical economics.

The actual practice of behavioral economics is influenced, directly or indirectly, by Popperian views on methodology (Popper, 1934, 1963). Popper begins by distinguishing between science and non-science. A scientific hypothesis must be falsifiable in the sense that it must specify the conditions under which the hypothesis can be rejected. Further, one can only refute theories but never prove that they are true. For instance, the observation of a million white swans is consistent with the hypothesis that "all swans are white" but does not prove that the hypothesis is true; for the very next observation could be a non-white swan.

The best recipe for the advancement of science, in the Popperian view, is to subject scientific hypotheses to stringent testing, i.e., expose the hypotheses to tests that are most likely to reject them. In the strict Popperian view, one observation that is contrary to a hypothesis rejects it. For instance, a single observation of a black swan rejects the hypothesis that all swans are white. Science progresses by advancing a new hypothesis that explains everything that a rejected hypothesis explained, but, in addition, it explains some new phenomenon that the rejected hypothesis could not. For an application of the Popperian position to economic contexts, see Blaug (1992), Hausman (1992), and Hands (2001).

One concern with the Popperian approach is that a test of a hypothesis is a joint test of the hypothesis and several auxiliary assumptions. Thus, a rejection may arise because the hypothesis is incorrect, or the auxiliary assumptions might have been rejected, or both; this is known as the *Duhem–Quine thesis* (DQT). For instance, in an experimental test that rejects mixed strategy Nash equilibrium, one might wonder if the rejection was caused by (1) one of several confounding factors, such as an inappropriate subject pool, unclear experimental instructions, and inadequate incentives, or (2) because subjects do not follow a mixed strategy Nash equilibrium. For this reason, a single refutation of a theory is not sufficient unless well replicated to account for all the main confounding factors that might be at play.

While the Popperian position is *prescriptive* (how should we best do science?), a *descriptive* view (how is science actually done?) was offered by Kuhn (1962). Kuhn noted that knowledge in science does not accumulate in a linear manner. He highlighted, instead, the role of periodic revolutions in science, or an abrupt transformation in the existing worldview, a *paradigm shift*. He distinguishes between three phases in the development of any science. In pre-science, there is no central paradigm, but there is an attempt to focus on a set of problems. In normal science, the longest of the three phases, there is the establishment of a central paradigm, great progress is made in answering many of the questions posed during pre-science, and much success is achieved in answering new questions. In a departure from the Popperian prescriptive position, in this phase, rejections of the paradigm are robustly challenged or ignored, and belief in the paradigm is unshakable. However, as anomalies gradually begin to accumulate, and reach a tipping point, a crises takes place in the paradigm. There is a sudden paradigm shift and a new paradigm that subsumes the old paradigm takes its place.

One prescriptive response to the DQT and to Kuhn's descriptive ideas, while retaining a Popperian approach, was proposed by Lakatos (1970) under the name: *The methodology of scientific research programs* (MSRP). Lakatos distinguished between a set of non-expendable statements or assumptions, which is the *hard core of a research program*, and a set of expendable auxiliary assumptions. In a distinctly non-Popperian recommendation, but reminiscent of the normal science phase of Kuhn, the hard core is insulated from refutation; this also addresses the DQT. For instance, Newtonian physics has a hard core that comprises the three laws of dynamics and a law of gravitation. Any refutation of the research program, in this phase, is then ascribed to a failure of the auxiliary assumptions, which are modified to explain the refutation.

One potential defense of this approach is that it allows for a period of time for the development of a new research program that can take account of the emerging refutations. However, a practical downside could be that proponents of a research program might engage in defensive methodology for far too long, and resist the development of a new research program that has a different hard core. To take account of this possibility, Lakatos termed a research program as *theoretically progressive* if refinements that take place by altering auxiliary assumptions but not the hard core, lead to the explanation of existing anomalies and to novel predictions. A research program is *empirically progressive* if the novel predictions are not refuted. Adherence to a hard core is only admissible if research programs are theoretically and empirically progressive.

Eventually anomalies play the most important part in giving rise to new research programs; Lakatos noted that all theories are born into and die in a sea of anomalies.[8] The reader may find below that the actual practice in behavioral and experimental economics appears to be closer to the Lakatosian view than the Popperian view.[9] For instance, in decision theory, the hard core may be thought to comprise completeness, transitivity, and first order stochastic dominance (Bardsley et al., 2010, p. 129). Indeed, neither expected utility theory nor the main behavioral alternatives such as rank dependent utility, theory of disappointment aversion, or prospect theory, are willing to relax the assumption of well-behaved preferences. This makes it difficult for most decision theories to explain framing effects, although prospect theory is potentially able to capture framing effects through changes in the reference point.

With this minimum background, consider "normal" practice in physics; I encourage the reader not to judge natural sciences by a few well-publicized outliers. In a letter to the *London Times*, dated November 28, 1919, Albert Einstein described his *theory of relativity* in comparison to *Newtonian physics*, to a lay audience. Einstein mentioned two predictions of his theory that had been confirmed (both in domains where his theory was most likely to fail, hence, these are "stringent tests"): (1) Revolution of the ellipses of the planetary orbits round the sun, which was confirmed for the orbit of Mercury. (2) The curving of light rays by the action of gravitational fields. He then mentioned one prediction that had not yet been confirmed (displacement of the spectral lines toward the red end of the spectrum in the case of light transmitted to us from stars of considerable magnitude); indeed, at the time Einstein published the theory of relativity, it was not even clear how to test this prediction. Einstein then wrote (p. 4): "The chief attraction of the theory lies in its logical completeness. If a single one of the conclusions drawn from it proves wrong, it must be given up."

I invite the reader to pause for a moment to compare Einstein's approach with the "mainstream" views in economics that I have outlined above. Indeed, as Bardsley et al. (2010, p. 8) note: "But it is surprisingly common for economists to claim that the core theories of their subject are useful despite being disconfirmed by the evidence."

In light of this brief discussion on methodology and an illustration of best practice in the natural sciences, let us return to the "neglect of the facts concerning human behavior in economics" that Herbert Gintis highlights above. Why should such a situation have arisen? In order to understand this state of affairs, consider the following three representative views, written by some of the leaders in neoclassical economics.

Dekel and Lipman (2010, p. 264) write: "Hence the choice of a model will depend on the purpose for which the model is used, the modeler's intuition, and the modeler's subjective judgment of plausibility.... One economist may reject another's intuition, and, ultimately, the marketplace of ideas will make some judgments."

Gilboa et al. (2014, F. 516) write: "In particular, we agree that: economic models are often viewed differently than models in the other sciences; economic theory seems to value generality and simplicity at the cost of accuracy; models are expected to convey a message much more than to describe a well-defined reality; these models are often akin to observations, or to

---

[8] Closer to home, economists would remember the influential *anomalies feature* that Richard Thaler wrote for the *Journal of Economic Perspectives* from 1987 to 2006. Indeed, in the very first piece, Thaler, keenly aware of methodological issues, quoted from Thomas Kuhn.

[9] For a critique of the Lakatosian approach as applied to economics, see Hands (1991) and De Marchi and Blaug (1991).

gedankenexperiments; and the economic theorist is typically not required to clearly specify where his model might be applicable and how."

Rubinstein (2006, p. 882) writes: "As in the case of fables, models in economic theory are derived from observations of the real world, but are not meant to be testable. As in the case of fables, models have limited scope. As in the case of a good fable, a good model can have an enormous influence on the real world, not by providing advice or by predicting the future, but rather by influencing culture. Yes, I do think we are simply the tellers of fables, but is that not wonderful?"

None of these representative quotes stresses the centrality of the empirical evidence in rejecting economic models or the need to design stringent tests to refute them; in fact economic models are not even meant to be tested. They also take a relativist position (one economist may reject another's intuition, and, ultimately, the marketplace of ideas will make some judgments) and take the role of models in economics as conveying "messages" or telling "fables."

Modern economics has been heavily influenced by the *instrumental position* taken by Friedman (1953), which is partly reflected in the three quotes above. Friedman argued that we should not judge economic theories by the realism of their assumptions but rather, by the accuracy of their predictions. He writes (p. 14): "Truly important and significant hypotheses will be found to have 'assumptions' that are wildly inaccurate descriptive representations of reality, and, in general, the more significant the theory, the more unrealistic the assumptions.... To be important, therefore, a hypothesis must be descriptively false in its assumptions." And shortly thereafter (p. 15) he writes: "To put this point less paradoxically, the relevant question to ask about the 'assumptions' of a theory is not whether they are descriptively 'realistic,' for they never are, but whether they are sufficiently good approximations for the purpose in hand."

A natural progression of Friedman's position can be found in Gilboa et al. (2014, F. 514): "Why does economic theory engage in relatively heavy technical analysis, when its basic premises are so inaccurate? Given the various violations of fundamental economic assumptions in psychological experiments, what is the point in deriving elaborate and carefully proved deductions from these assumptions? Why do economists believe that they learn something useful from analyzing models that are based on wrong assumptions?" Their answer to these questions is based on an identification of economic models with *case-based reasoning* rather than *rule-based reasoning*. Rule-based reasoning requires the formulation of general rules or theories. In contrast, case-based reasoning requires one to draw inferences based on similar past cases. The purpose of economic models, in this view, is to add to the bucket list of cases and analogies that can be used to draw inferences now, or at some point in the future.

These views give a fair bit of insight into contemporary thinking in economics about how we should go about practicing our craft. I also believe that acceptance of these views is widespread in the economics profession and many economists challenged on these views are surprised and outrightly dismissive. Initial intuition about economic models, whether motivated by existing empirical evidence, or a desire to make novel predictions, must begin from somewhere. Here, the role of initial conjectures as parables, useful stories, or fables to inform one's intuition about better and more complete models is surely important. But this cannot be the justification for continued reliance on a set of models that have faced persistent refutation, or to wish to shield them from refutation by seeking a special status for them.

Indeed, and it has to be said with great regret, many of the contemporary methodological views in economics are retrogressive and a license to engage in defensive methodology to protect the status quo. Friedman's approach has been much misused in economics. Consider the following entirely reasonable description of Friedman's approach to *model building* (as distinct from evaluating theories) in Gintis (2015, p. 223) that this book concurs with: "The goal of model-building [is] to create a tractable analytical structure, analyze the behavior of this structure, and test the fruitfulness of the results by comparing them with empirical data."[10]

The tendency to ignore or to discount experimental evidence in economics, despite its growing importance and prominence, when it contradicts neoclassical models is an indictment of the methodological approach taken in economics. Another important factor is that Friedman's instrumental position has been used as a license by some to make ad hoc auxiliary assumptions, and others to genuinely believe that their assumptions are literally true in an "as if" sense. Any empirical rejection of the "as if" assumptions is often rejected on the grounds that the evidence is flawed, untrustworthy, based on dubious experimental methods, or lacks external validity. This is a form of defensive methodology that is inimical to the progress of economics, and I urge the reader to resist it.

Behavioral economics offers an easier resolution of the "as if" approach. There is now compelling evidence, which shows that some of the central tenets of neoclassical economics are neither true in an "as if" sense, nor are their predictions always satisfactory when subject to stringent tests. So even on the grounds that Friedman favoured, *predictions of the relevant theory*, some of the central elements in neoclassical economics, such as self-regarding preferences, expected utility theory, exponential discounting, Bayes' Law, Nash equilibrium and its refinements, must either be significantly modified or abandoned. This book is replete with evidence that supports such a view. In particular, it is untenable to continue teaching the entire corpus of the existing status quo in economics on any scientific or logical grounds.

Schotter (2015) offers the following critique of Friedman's position. Suppose that assumptions x, y, and z lead to some theory T. Suppose also that one or more assumptions are violated by the empirical evidence, yet T makes a successful prediction. Then there are three possibilities. (1) The violated assumptions are superfluous for the theory, at least in the context where the theory was tested. (2) The violated assumptions counteract each other perfectly, so they do not affect the prediction. (3) The successful prediction is a fluke. Conversely, if the assumptions are correct and the model is complete then we expect T to make successful predictions anyway. Thus, it is difficult to justify a theory based on patently false assumptions. Schotter (2015, p. 63) observes, correctly: "after all, the assumptions are the theory."

My colleague, Ali al-Nowaihi, likes to give the following example that applies to birds who cannot swim (e.g., gannets can swim, so they are excluded). Birds fly, so one may theorize that they behave "as if" they understand the laws of aerodynamics. This is an admissible hypothesis, but then one must test the "as if" assumption. Given that air is basically a fluid, so birds might also be assumed to know the laws of hydrodynamics. If the "as if" presumption were true in this case, then birds released under water should try to swim, but they actually try to fly, and drown. Thus, the original "as if" supposition is false. If the "as if" assumptions are not tested properly, then we can never have any degree of confidence in the models based on these assumptions.

A common view in economics (shared unfortunately by some behavioral and experimental economists, I must add) appears to be that there is something rather difficult and unique about testing economic theories, relative to the natural sciences. So, at least implicitly, the argument goes, one needs to accord a "special status" to economic theories. Consider the following representative quote from Richard Lipsey's wonderful introduction to economics

---

[10] Readers interested in pursuing this approach further can consult Godfrey-Smith (2006, 2009) and Wimsatt (2007).

(Lipsey, 1979, p. 8) cited in Bardsley et al. (2010, pp. 6–7) that, I suspect, many economists would agree with: "Experimental sciences, such as chemistry and some branches of psychology, have an advantage because it is possible to produce relevant evidence through controlled laboratory experiments. Other sciences, such as astronomy and economics, cannot do this." A similar view is expressed in another celebrated text in economics (Samuelson and Nordhaus, 1985, p. 8): "Economists (unfortunately) ... cannot perform the controlled experiments of chemists or biologists because they cannot easily control other important factors. Like astronomers or meteorologists, they generally must be content largely to observe." This mainstream view is contestable, and must be contested. There appears to be a misunderstanding about the relative difficulty of testing theories in the natural sciences and in economics.

The view that testing of theories is somehow easy or easier in the natural sciences, as compared to economics, must surely be deeply offensive and insulting to experimenters in the natural sciences. The Higgs boson or Higgs particle was proposed by British physicist Peter Higgs in the early 1960s, and it took 50 years of incredibly hard efforts to confirm the particle in 2013. Particle physicists did not seek a *special status* for this theory that could insulate it from rejection. The enormously high energies required to test for the Higgs particle required the construction of a very expensive and complex experimental facility, CERN's Large Hadron Collider, that eventually confirmed the theory. Note also that Peter Higgs was made to wait 50-odd years and given the Nobel Prize in physics only after his theory was confirmed. He was not given the Nobel on any of the following criteria: elegant and beautiful theory, useful model that helped the intuition of particle physicists, or a fable or useful story that aids in the understanding of how the universe began.

Astronomers who dealt with the question of the distance of earth from distant objects, or the chemical composition of stars that are millions of light years away, did not also seek a special status for their subject. They got on with the difficult job of seeking the relevant measurements, often using indirect evidence and clever implications of theory. They were eventually successful after several decades of work. Are economists seriously arguing that their measurement problems are more difficult than the problems in the natural sciences? Cosmic microwave background radiation was first proposed in 1948, but experimentally confirmed due to an accidental discovery in 1964. DNA was first isolated in 1869, but it took the most part of a century to find the double-helix structure of DNA, and confirm it by experimental evidence in 1953. The germ theory of disease was proposed in the mid sixteenth century, yet confirmation of the theory occurred in the seventeenth century. The pool of such examples is very large. The process of discovery, measurement, and of testing the theory, can be a long and arduous one; seeking a special status for the subject is defeatist and put bluntly, lazy.

Economists opposed to lab/field data are likely to argue that the behavior of humans is too noisy, heterogeneous, and fickle, which is not a problem in the natural sciences (e.g., atoms are, after all, not subject to mood swings). This overstates the degree of difficulty in testing economic theories, relative to those in the natural sciences on at least two grounds.

1. Experimental economics has discovered systematic human behavior in many of the most important domains in economics. A small sample includes reference dependence, loss aversion, non-linear probability weighting, conditional cooperation, intention-based reciprocity, present-biased preferences, and the importance of emotions such as regret, guilt, and disappointment. These behaviors are also underpinned by neuroeconomic evidence. Replication of standard experimental results is routine, and if similar subject pools and protocols are used, experiments produce replicable data. Examples are results from double

auction experiments, and a range of games that demonstrate human prosociality, such as the ultimatum game, the gift exchange game, the trust game, and the public goods game; these examples can be multiplied manyfold, as the results in this book attest.

2. If indeed human behavior is inherently too noisy and heterogeneous, then economic theory needs to focus more efforts in this direction. When Brownian motion was discovered in 1827 by Robert Brown, in the behavior of pollen grains, physicists did not throw up their arms in despair. Important work in the late part of the nineteenth century, and by Einstein in the early twentieth century, paved the way for describing not only the mathematics of Brownian motion, but also predicting the probability distribution of particles in Brownian motion. Perhaps, in an analogous manner, economic theories need to predict the probability distribution of economic behavior, which can then be tested in experiments.

Experimental economics in the lab, and in the field, has made enormous progress in developing new econometric techniques for small samples, and in novel experimental methods. It has also deeply enhanced our understanding of human behavior and allowed for stringent testing of economic theory. This progress is inconsistent with the view that we should grant a special status to economic theories that exempts them from careful and stringent testing. The differences in experiments in economics and the natural sciences are much smaller relative to the differences in attitudes and institutions in the two fields of study. Progress in economics will be substantially enhanced if we learn from best practice elsewhere, and give up our implicit demand for special status.

3 The experimental method in economics

Work on experiments in behavioral economics gained momentum following the seminal work of Daniel Kahneman and Amos Tversky in the 1970s. However, a number of important experiments in economics were also conducted in the late 1940s, the 1950s, and the 1960s. These include Edward H. Chamberlin's testing of general competitive equilibrium (Chamberlin, 1948); Maurice Allais's work on demonstrating violations of the independence axiom in expected utility theory (Allais, 1953); Vernon Smith's work on induced value elicitation and double auction experiments in competitive settings (Smith, 1962); and Sidney Siegel's experiments on bargaining (Siegel and Fouraker, 1960). Other prominent figures who were either involved in experimental economics, or expressed an interest in it during the 1950s and 1960s included Ward Edwards, Reinhard Selten, Martin Schubik, Herbert Simon, Charles Plott, Donald Davidson, and Pat Suppes; for a brief historical sketch, see Guala (2008) and Bardsley et al. (2010).

Experimental economics is now mainstream by most yardsticks, particularly in terms of its presence in peer-reviewed journals in economics. In his early surveys on experimental economics, Roth (1987, 1988) hoped that experimental economics would perform three kinds of functions: speaking to theorists (testing economic theory), searching for facts (generating novel empirical regularities that could be modeled by subsequent theory), and whispering in the ears of princes (offering reliable policy advice). Roth (2015) takes stock of experimental economics on these criteria and finds that it is thriving. One of his case studies, on bargaining behavior, is outlined in detail in Volume 4 of the book.

At one level, there has been a complete denial of the usefulness of experiments in economics. Friedman (1953, p. 10) views the domain of empirical testing in economics to be naturally occurring field data: "Unfortunately, we can seldom test particular predictions in the social sciences by experiments explicitly designed to eliminate what are judged to be the most important disturbing influences. Generally, we must rely on evidence cast up by the 'experiments' that happen to occur." A modern critique of the experimental method in economics is offered by Levitt and List (2007). They list several objections to experimental results that I address in subsequent sections.

(1) Participants in experiments are subjected to unprecedented experimental scrutiny. Since subjects may perceive that they are being watched over by the experimenter, they may give responses that the experimenter really desires (*experimenter demand effects*; see Zizzo, 2010) or they may not reveal their true underlying preferences. For instance, they worry that participants may engage in more prosocial behavior than they really intend to.

Whilst I reserve my detailed responses to later sections, I find it somewhat curious that if subjects are accused of being influenced by experimenter demand effects, say out of reciprocity, guilt, or shame, then they appear to exhibit social preferences (or emotions reflected in beliefs may directly enter their utility functions, as in psychological game theory), which is precisely what is being disputed by the critics.

(2) In actual practice, human decisions are context-dependent and influenced by cues, social norms, and past experiences. It is not clear that experiments can capture these factors. For instance, participants in experiments may import an inappropriate "outside context" into their responses in experiments.

(3) Actual human behavior is strongly affected by stake sizes in experiments. Experiments are typically conducted with small stakes, so they might not capture the richness of human behavior that arises from varying stakes.

(4) There could be self-selection biases caused by student volunteers who might be particularly prosocial, younger, more educated, and have a higher need for approval, as compared to the average human population. In contrast, people who self-select themselves into real market situations, might be particularly suitable to do well in real markets.

(5) Choice sets in experiments might be particularly restrictive relative to the real world. For instance, there could be more prosocial options in experiments relative to the real world.

(6) The results of lab experiments may generalize poorly to real-world behavior for all of the reasons mentioned in (1) through (5), above. This issue of *external validity* of lab experiments is the main concern raised by the authors who write (p. 170): "Perhaps the most fundamental question in experimental economics is whether findings from the lab are likely to provide reliable inferences outside of the laboratory."

This discussion briefly encapsulates the modern case against experimental economics. Let us now briefly examine these claims.

3.1 *Experiments and internal validity*

Experiments allow for unprecedented control over the economic environment, hence, they have high *internal validity*, which is critical for stringent tests of economic theories. Internal validity is reduced when there are, for instance, selection issues, confounds in treatments, and unclear experimental instructions, all of which are carefully addressed in modern experimental work. Thus, in well-conducted experiments, the complicated identification strategies of field studies can be replaced by clever and much simpler experimental design.

For instance, suppose that a researcher is interested in testing if higher wages elicit higher effort in a firm; this is known as a *gift exchange game*. A field experiment is likely to be influenced by strategic behavior and reputational concerns of the workers and firms; field experiments in general, are likely to have lower internal validity. However, in a lab experiment, these factors are easily controlled, allowing one to cleanly separate the relation between a fair-wage and effort. The high degree of experimental control in lab experiments allows for replication of lab results. For the converse reason, the results of field experiments are more difficult, and sometimes impossible to replicate when one is given access to a unique field environment.

Experiments can also test the predictions of theory in a parameter space that might be difficult to observe in the field. This is similar to extreme stress tests of aircraft frames under conditions that are not normally encountered in the actual operation of the aircraft, or the exposure of bridge designs to extreme environmental conditions. In a nutshell, all this allows for more stringent tests of economic theory. Experiments are sometimes criticized on the grounds that the sample sizes are small. Falk and Heckman (2009) term this issue as a "red herring" on the grounds that there have been important developments in small sample econometrics, and many experiments do use large subject pools.

Camerer (2015) argues that there is no evidence of experimenter demand effects, despite the suspicion that there might be such effects; see also his discussion of the alternative interpretations of experimenter demand effects in Hoffman et al. (1998). There are several reasons why experimenter demand effects may be weak or non-existent. Such demand effects require two conditions. First, subjects must know the experimenter's preferred hypothesis. Second, they should be willing to sacrifice their own experimental earnings in order to favor the experimenter's preferred hypothesis.

On a-priori grounds, arguably, it is often quite hard for subjects to know the experimenter's preferred hypothesis. This arises particularly when (i) experimental instructions are carefully worded to prevent any such inference, and (ii) the experimenter might not be sure which of the competing hypotheses actually hold. However, if subjects can somehow guess the preferred hypothesis, then stakes can be raised to levels where they are too difficult to sacrifice for the sake of pleasing the experimenter. However, in most cases, the results with high stakes are not dramatically different from those with modest stakes (Camerer and Hogarth, 1999).[11] In three preference reversal experiments, Lambdin and Shaffer (2009) find that the percentage of subjects who were successfully able to guess the preferred hypothesis of the experimenter was 7%, 32%, and 3%.

The degree of anonymity in lab experiments can be varied, so it is an ideal environment to test for the effects of variation in the degree of anonymity (Bolton et al., 1998). One's actions are often observed by others in real-world situations, and in many field situations, where controlling for such scrutiny, and varying its level, is arguably even more difficult. The criticism of lab experiments on grounds of scrutiny (by the experimenter and other participants), also applies to field experiments, insofar as field subjects realize that they are in an experiment. Such experimenter demand effects may arguably, in many cases, be even stronger in field experiments, which are typically run in collaboration with governmental and semi-governmental bodies, and NGOs.

It is indeed the case that when subjects are observed in dictator game experiments in the lab, they give higher amounts (Dana et al., 2007; Haley and Fessler, 2005). In many real-world giving

---

[11] Andersen et al. (2011) consider extremely high stakes ultimatum game experiments; the stakes vary from the equivalent of 1.6 hours of work to 1,600 hours of work. The median offer by the proposer is to give 20% of the share to the respondent, but the rejection rate falls with the increase in the stake. In real life, we rarely make decisions involving 1,600 hours of work, yet social preferences were not eliminated in the experiment.

situations, actions are also observed by others; for instance, church collections that take the form of passing along a collection plate/basket, or having to declare one's charitable contributions for tax purposes. However, the effect of being observed disappears if one introduces a minimal element of strategic interaction as, say, in an ultimatum game (Barmettler et al., 2012). A more important determinant of giving in dictator games is whether income is earned or not. Giving in dictator game experiments falls to about 4.3% of an endowment of $10, when income is earned, relative to about 15% of the endowment in the case of unearned income (Cherry et al., 2002); the figure of 4.3% is closer to the corresponding field benchmark of charitable giving in the US, which stands at about 1% of income (Camerer, 2015).

A commonly heard critique of behavioral models of social preferences is that if experimentally observed social preferences are so important, then, putting it rather starkly, why do we not observe people giving envelopes stuffed with money to others (Bardsley et al., 2010, p. 53)? When dictators in experiments give out of earned income, then the extent of giving is not too far off from the rate of charitable giving (4.3% versus 1% for the case of US; see above). In the real world, subjects give money for charitable and other good causes out of after-tax income, which is not the case in the lab. So imagine that in dictator games in the lab with earned income, the dictator was told: "Here is your endowment of $10, which you have earned. We are taking 30% off as taxes, which we will partly use for redistributive purposes to the recipient in the experiment. How much of the rest will you offer to the recipient?" It would be surprising if the 4.3% giving in lab dictator games does not get closer to the 1% figure for charitable giving in the field. Similar observations apply to proposer offers and responder rejections in lab experiments that do not include a tax redistributive component. If this is the case, then giving in experiments may also be tapping into the innate human desire to redistribute to others, that is, at least partly, codified institutionally in the social welfare state.

3.2 Subject pools used in lab experiments

It is not unusual in many quarters to dismiss experiments conducted on students, the typical lab subject pool, as having limited or no relevance to testing economic theories. There are several objections to this claim that we now outline.

Economic theory does not specify the subject pool on which its predictions are to be tested. Gilboa et al. (2014, F. 516) write "the economic theorist is typically not required to clearly specify where his model might be applicable and how." Clearly, one cannot have it both ways by not specifying a subject pool and then objecting to a particular subject pool. This view has been popularized in Vernon Smith's *blame the theory argument*. Writing in the context of incentives in experiments, Smith (2001) writes in his abstract: "The rhetoric of hypothesis testing implies that game theory is not testable if a negative result is blamed on any auxiliary hypothesis such as 'rewards are inadequate.' This is because either the theory is not falsifiable (since a larger payoff can be imagined, one can always conclude that payoffs were inadequate) or it has no predictive content (the appropriate payoff cannot be prespecified)."

One concern with the student subject population is that students might not have the necessary and relevant experience to conform to the predictions of the theory. However, one can allow lab subjects to gain experience in the lab by repeatedly making decisions; indeed, many lab experiments examine such learning effects and the effects of experience. We postpone a fuller discussion of these issues to Section 3.4, where we consider the external validity of lab experiments.

Students possess higher than average education and intelligence, which should be rather favorable to tests of neoclassical economic theory that requires economic agents to possess high levels of cognitive ability. It often comes as a surprise to the critics, but student subjects are much less prosocial relative to non-student subject pools (Falk et al., 2013; Carpenter and Seki, 2011; Anderson et al., 2013).[12] In a review of 13 studies that satisfy stringent tests of comparability, Fréchette (2015) finds that either there was very little difference between the behavior of students and professionals, or students were actually closer to the predictions of neoclassical theory. CEOs are often more trusting as compared to the student population (Fehr and List, 2004). More prosocial students do not self-select themselves as subjects in experiment (Cleave et al., 2012). Students who self-select themselves into experiments are motivated by monetary rewards (Abeler and Nosenzo, 2015), or interest in experimental lab tasks (Slonim et al., 2013). This evidence stands in contrast to the characterization of students in Levitt and List (2007) (based on two studies conducted in the 1960s) as scientific do-gooders who cooperate with experimenters to seek social approval.

3.3 *Stake sizes in experiments*

Economic theory does not specify the size of the stakes for which its predictions hold. Experimental economics is typically criticized for its low stakes. The evidence on stake size effects is mixed. However, many experimental results continue to hold, at least qualitatively, even with higher stakes (Slonim and Roth, 1998; Cameron, 1999). The most prominent effect of stakes arises when one moves from hypothetical payoffs to some strictly positive incentives. However, there is much less difference between moderate and high stakes; in particular, the main effect is a reduction in the variance of responses (Camerer and Hogarth, 1999).

There are two issues with high stakes, which are understated in many critiques of experimental economics. First, the vast majority of decisions that we make in real life are low stake decisions. How many times do we buy a car, a house, or a consumer durable such as a TV/laptop? Second, the main evidence for stake effects comes from experiments themselves. Third, as Thaler (2015) notes, the insistence on high stakes arises presumably because we are supposed to pay greater attention to economic decisions involving high stakes. But our success and expertise in making economic decisions is as much a matter of practice and learning. Since high stakes decisions are rare, we get limited opportunities to learn and make optimal decisions; the converse is true of low stakes decisions. Hence, there is no supposition that high stakes decisions should be closer to the predicted outcomes in neoclassical economics. So, he argues, correctly, that economists need to make up their minds whether they wish to insist on high stakes or low stakes as the appropriate test of their theories. Either way, experiments still offer the most natural environment to test the effect of stakes, which is an argument for more, not fewer, experiments.

3.4 *The issue of the external validity of lab findings*

Camerer (2015) distinguishes between the *policy view* and the *scientific view*. In the policy view, generalizability of lab findings to the field, or *external validity*, is essential. In the scientific view, all properly gathered evidence, including lab and field evidence, serves to enhance our understanding of human behavior. In this view, there is no hierarchical relation between lab

---

[12] However, student subjects might be more prosocial when it comes to volunteering time (Slonim et al., 2013).

and field evidence, and it is a mistake to pose the issue as if one had to make a choice between the two kinds of evidence. Camerer (2015, p. 251) explains cogently: "In this view, since the goal is to understand general principles, whether the 'lab generalizes to the field' (sometimes called 'external validity' of an experiment) is distracting, difficult to know (since there is no single 'external' target setting), and is no more useful than asking whether 'the field generalizes to the lab.'"

To understand Camerer's argument more fully, consider the following simple formalization in Falk and Heckman (2009). Suppose that we are interested in some variable Y that can be explained fully by the variables $X_1, X_2, \ldots, X_n$ and the "true" functional relation between them is given by $Y = g(X_1, X_2, \ldots, X_n)$, which is sometimes known as an *all causes model*. A researcher may be interested in examining the causal effect of X_1 on Y, holding fixed all other variables $\widehat{X} = (X_2, X_3, \ldots, X_n)$. For instance, in gift exchange experiments, Y is the level of effort of a worker and X_1 is the level of wage paid by the firm. The all causes model will typically include many factors in the vector $\widehat{X}$, such as the number of firms and workers, choice sets, payoff functions, incentives, demographic characteristics, regulatory environment, and moral and social characteristics of the parties involved.

When the relevant hypothesis is tested in the lab, the researcher estimates a model of the form $Y = f(X_1, X^L)$, rather than the all causes model $Y = f(X_1, \widehat{X})$, where $X^L \neq \widehat{X}$; X^L includes variables such as incentives given in the experiment, the endowments of subjects, the subject pool, context, and the structure of payoffs. One may also conduct field experiments in which one estimates a model of the form $Y = f(X_1, X^{F_1})$, where $X^{F_1} \neq \widehat{X}$, and typically $X^{F_1} \neq X^L$. Field experiments are conducted with a particular subject pool, such as sports card traders in List (2006).

The typical claim by critics of the experimental method is that $f(X_1, X^L)$ does not satisfy external validity, but $f(X_1, X^{F_1})$ does satisfy it. Now suppose that we are interested in examining the gift exchange relation in yet another population of subjects in the field, say, part time employees at General Motors. This gives rise to yet another estimated relation $Y = f(X_1, X^{F_2})$, where X^{F_2} reflects the set of variables and their characteristics in this field experiment. Is there any particular reason why the results based on the model $Y = f(X_1, X^{F_1})$ are more relevant, as compared to $Y = f(X_1, X^L)$, for predicting the causal effects of X_1 in the relation $Y = f(X_1, X^{F_2})$? Camerer (2015, p. 256) offers his assessment (expressed in our notation): "If the litmus test of 'external validity' is accurate extrapolation to X^{F_2}, is the lab X^L necessarily less externally valid than the field setting X^{F_1}? How should this even be judged?" Falk and Heckman (2009, p. 536) go slightly further: "The general quest for running experiments in the field to obtain more realistic data is therefore misguided. In fact, the key issue is what is the best way to isolate the effect of X_1 while holding constant $\widehat{X}$."

Since the criterion for external validity is unclear, it is best to treat lab and field evidence as complementary. Lab evidence allows for much tighter control of the variables in $\widehat{X}$. Field experiments allow for a larger variation in some aspects of $\widehat{X}$ (e.g., different subject pools with different demographic and social characteristics) while lab experiments allow for larger variation in other aspects of $\widehat{X}$ (e.g., exploration of the parameter space for values that can be hard or rare to find in the field). Lab experiments allow for greater replication because they are less costly and the economic environment in the lab can be more tightly controlled, while any specific field environment could be fairly unique.

We review the evidence for the generalizability of lab evidence to the field in many parts of this book. We end this section with the following bold claim from Camerer (2015, p. 277) made from studies where the lab and field evidence can be well matched: "There is no replicated evidence that experimental economics lab data fail to generalize to central empirical features of field data (when the lab features are deliberately closely matched to field features)." Readers interested in these issues can further consult Camerer (2015, pp. 281–5) for a list of studies that show a good association of lab behavior with field behavior in studies where it is more difficult to match the lab and the field evidence due to differences in the design or subject population.

Not everyone within the experimental economics community is willing to dismiss the importance of external validity. For instance, Kessler and Vesterlund (2015) believe that aiming for external validity is important, that qualitative experimental results have high degree of external validity, and that the concerns about external validity pertain only to quantitative experimental results. However, using a relatively large number of studies, Herbst and Mas (2015) show that peer effects on worker output in lab experiments and field studies from naturally occurring environments are quantitatively very similar. Hence, experiments appear to have external validity, even for quantitative estimates.

In light of the discussion above, the reader may perhaps appreciate better the view taken in this book that all sources of evidence, lab experiments, field experiments, and field data are equally valid and complementary in nature.

3.5 *The role of incentives in economics*

The norm in experimental economics is that all decisions made by subjects, or any elicitations of their underlying preferences in experiments, should be incentive compatible. It would currently be near impossible to get an experimental paper published in an economics journal if it did not respect incentive compatibility, preferably by using monetary rewards. In contrast, psychology does not require similar adherence to incentives. Camerer and Hogarth (1999) perform a meta-study of 74 studies, over the period 1990–8, in the leading economics journals: *American Economic Review*, *Econometrica*, *Journal of Political Economy*, and *Quarterly Journal of Economics*. Not a single experimental study in this sample was published without the use of incentives. In a meta-study over the period 1988–97, Hertwig and Ortmann (2001) found that only 26% of the articles published in a leading journal in psychology, the *Journal of Behavioral Decision Making*, used monetary task related incentives.

Economists have traditionally viewed effort as aversive and requiring scarce cognitive resources. Hence, they believe that people will exert effort only if the marginal disutility of effort is exceeded by the marginal utility of monetary incentives (*extrinsic motivation*). By contrast, psychologists have stressed the *intrinsic motivation* of subjects in experiments that does not require task related monetary incentives. Psychologists do pay subjects a show-up fee and/or course credit because it may be unethical to pay less than a minimum wage for a student's time and also because the fixed fee may elicit a reciprocal response by priming intrinsic motivation. Another difference between experiments in economics and psychology is that in the former, experimental practice is much more standardized and regulated (Hertwig and Ortmann, 2001). For instance, deception is taboo in economics experiments, but its practice is variable in psychology experiments.

Smith (1976) made an early recommendation for the use of incentives, based on his experience in double auction experiments. Employing monetary incentives in experiments is also a common recommendation by some of the pioneers in the field (Davis and Holt, 1993; Roth, 1995; Smith, 1991; Smith and Walker, 1993). The effectiveness of incentives, particularly in settings outside double auction experiments, is an empirical question. Several meta-studies of the effect of incentives are now available, which show that the effect of monetary incentives on effort and performance in experiments is quite subtle. Neither of the following two extreme positions is supported by the evidence: Incentives make no difference and incentives remove all behavioral anomalies.

However, there is a caveat to these meta-studies. Since the underlying preferences are unobserved, in experiments, task performance and incentive compatibility are measured by compliance with the predictions of the underlying theory. However, the underlying theory might itself be refuted by the evidence. One might then fall back on measuring the effect of incentives on the effort undertaken by the subjects (an input), rather than the performance in the task (the output); for a brief survey of these studies, see Bardsley et al. (2010, Chapter 6). However, in many tasks, effort might not improve performance. For instance, consider subjects in experiments engaged in non-trivial strategic interaction. In most games, it would be hard for the players to hit upon the Nash equilibrium purely by deduction, even if incentives were high.

The results reported in the careful meta-study by Camerer and Hogarth (1999) are particularly instructive. In many economic environments, such as choosing among risky gambles, market trading, and bargaining, the weight of the evidence (and the modal result) shows that increasing incentives does not change the average behavior. However, incentives often reduce the variance of outcomes. Incentives may sometimes harm the performance of subjects in experiments, for instance, subjects may choke under pressure (Ariely et al., 2009); their intrinsic motivation may be crowded out, and they may engage in too much payoff-reducing experimentation to avoid negative incentives such as punishments (Hogarth et al., 1991);[13] they may place too great a reliance on personal judgment, when relying on public information would have improved payoffs (Arkes et al., 1986); they may experience motivational crowding-out, e.g., in the presence of incentives, individuals do not feel responsible for their own behavior (Gneezy and Rustichini, 2000b); individuals might be insulted by the low level of incentives (Gneezy and Rustichini, 2000a). However, for another set of problems, mostly in judgment tasks, financial incentives affect average performance. Typically, the nature of these tasks is such that increased effort improves performance. Examples include memory retrieval tasks, tasks where recalling the play in previous rounds improves predictions, or mundane tasks such as piece-rate clerical work where one might be easily bored, e.g., counting the number of occurrences of a particular alphabet on a page of English text.

The meta-study by Bonner et al. (2000) supports the results of the Camerer–Hogarth study. They find that incentives have little effect in problem solving tasks, highest positive effects in tasks where effort improves performance (e.g., clerical tasks, pain endurance, or detecting typos on a page), and weak positive effects in judgment tasks. Hertwig and Ortmann (2001) find moderately positive effect of incentives. However, their sample size is small. Only 48 out of 186 studies (26%) that they considered used financial incentives. Of these, only ten explored the effect of monetary payments. One of their suggestions is to use different treatments that do use and do not use monetary incentives to build a better picture of the effect of incentives.

Clearly, a reduction in the variance of responses in the presence of incentives, in some experiments, is desirable on the grounds that it improves the statistical power of tests. However, economics advocates a cost–benefit approach, and research funding for experiments is a scarce resource. Hence, one has to trade off the reduced variance against performing more experiments with bigger subject pools in the absence of monetary incentives. Greater variance of responses

---

[13] For a formal model that shows the trade-off between intrinsic and extrinsic motivation, see Bénabou and Tirole (2003).

produces more outliers, but as Camerer and Hogarth (1999, p. 31) point out, there are alternative solutions: "Of course, other methods might work the same magic more cheaply. Trimmed means and robust statistical methods also reduce the influence of outliers."

So what explains the absolute adherence of experimental economists to incentives as a matter of norm? Bardsley et al. (2010, pp. 249–50) conjecture a cynical explanation: "A reason often given to psychologist's opposition to them is that incentives present an obstacle to less-experienced researchers who find it harder to secure research funding. It may be that economists are less concerned by the presence of such obstacles, or even that some actively promote the use of incentives as a barrier to entry." Many psychologists remain unconvinced of the arguments that experimenters in economics propose in favor of using incentives. For instance, Read (2005, p. 265) concludes his paper as follows: ". . . there is no basis for requiring the use of real incentives to do experimental economics."

The decision to employ incentives is a part of the experimental design. But as a practical matter, experimenters interested in publishing their work in economics journals have little choice in this matter. A second issue in the design of experiments is the level of incentives and the context. Gneezy and Rustichini (2000b) use four different levels of incentives, zero, low, medium, and high, to check for the level effect and conduct two different experiments to check for context effects. In one experiment, the IQ experiment, they find that incentives improve performance when one compares the levels low and high; but there was no difference between medium and high incentives. In the second experiment, the donations experiment, donations were highest when no incentives were given; in this case, intrinsic motivation is superior to extrinsic motivation. Using the same dataset, Rydval and Ortmann (2004) find that ability levels of individuals explained greater variation in performance relative to incentives. The assessment offered by Bardsley et al. (2010, p. 253) on the level of incentives is this: "The message seems to be that in terms of the impact on cognitive effort allocation the presence of task related incentives matters more than their level."

How can an experimental economist who has decided to run experiments using incentives ensure that the responses by the subjects are incentive compatible? Typically, incentive compatibility in experiments has been defined with respect to expected utility theory; however, the behavior of the majority of people is not consistent with expected utility theory. Hence, judging incentive compatibility is a vexed task. For instance, the leading method of ensuring incentive compatible choices, the *random lottery incentive scheme* (RLI), that we outline in Appendix A, depends crucially on the *independence axiom* of expected utility theory. However, if the decision maker does not follow expected utility but follows, say, rank dependent utility or prospect theory, then the independence axiom does not hold. Thus, choices are not guaranteed to be incentive compatible.

The evidence against expected utility is now overwhelming, as we do indeed explore in this book, and the independence axiom has been rejected in many empirical tests (e.g., *Allais paradox*). Bardsley et al. (2010) argue, however, that despite the rejection of the independence axiom, empirical evidence shows that the random lottery mechanism does not bias results. They write (p. 270): "it may simply be a happy coincidence that the RLI works, by engaging a particular mental heuristic that promotes unbiased task responses." Some readers might find this argument to be weak, and will wish to seek further clarification of the underlying mechanism that makes RLI an empirically attractive option.

Another popular incentive compatible mechanism in experiments that relies on an expected utility formulation is the *Becker–DeGroot–Marshak mechanism* (BDM) (Becker et al., 1964). This is typically employed in eliciting the willingness to pay and the willingness to accept for an object.

Subjects in their roles as sellers are asked to state their valuation, v, for an object. A random price, p, is then drawn. If $p \leq v$, then a seller is not allowed to sell but if $p > v$, then the seller must sell. Subjects who follow expected utility should report their true valuations. To see this, suppose that the seller's valuation for an object is believed to be distributed randomly over the interval $[\underline{v}, \overline{v}]$, the true valuation is v, and the price is drawn randomly from the interval $[\underline{v}, \overline{v}]$, using the distribution F. Suppose that the seller chooses to declare a low valuation, $v_L < v$. In this case, the seller chooses to forgo a profitable opportunity to sell if the price turns out to be in the interval (v_L, v) and the expected forgone profits are $\int_{v_L}^{v} (v - p)dF(p) > 0$. Thus, the seller never declares a low valuation. Now suppose that the seller declares a high valuation, $v_H > v$. In this case, the seller risks the potential expected loss $\int_{v}^{v_H} (v - p)dF(p) < 0$, so he never overstates his valuation. In short, the BDM is incentive compatible under expected utility. A direct implementation of the BDM has been found not to be incentive compatible (Bohm et al., 1997). However, suppose decision makers are presented with ascending or descending prices and must choose to trade or not at these prices. In the end, one of the trades is picked at random and paid off. There is some evidence that this version of the BDM may be incentive compatible (Braga and Starmer, 2005).

Similar calculations as employed in the BDM show that the *second price auction* (bidders bid simultaneously, and the winner pays the second highest bid) is also incentive compatible under expected utility. Bardsley et al. (2010, Chapter 6) review evidence which shows that the responses in BDM and the second price auction are sensitive to experience and, in later rounds, valuations are likely to converge to the true values. But the evidence on the incentive compatibility of variants of the *Vickery auctions* (which is a more general form of second price auctions) is mixed. They write (p. 274): "the efficacy of particular elicitation mechanisms can vary across different types of tasks. Indeed, whether an elicitation mechanism works may depend on the kind of research question that motivates its use."

To summarize, the discussion on incentive compatible elicitation mechanisms in experiments raises uncomfortable questions for the practice of experimental economics. First, predicted incentive compatibility relies on theories such as expected utility theory that have inadequate empirical support. Second, there are no universally agreed on mechanisms that will guarantee incentive compatibility in experiments and it very much comes down to a matter of judgment of the experimenter. Third, despite the firm insistence of experimental economists to use task related incentives, the theoretical response to these problems (e.g., the development of incentive compatibility under behavioral decision theories) appears to be inadequate.

3.6 Is survey data of any use?

Section 3.5 shows that there is often merit in the use of incentives, e.g., usefulness in double auction experiments, judgment tasks, effort related responses as in clerical tasks, and reduction in variation of responses. However, it is fair to say that the empirical case for the use of incentives in experiments is not as strong as is typically made out within the experimental economics community. Hence, one needs to consider other sources of data too in order to build a composite picture of human behavior. Most economists mistrust *survey data* and data based on *hypothetical questions* on the grounds that subjects are not incentivized to reveal their true preferences. This is due to the traditional belief in economics that people mainly have *extrinsic* rather than *intrinsic* motivation.

In the history of behavioral economics, the reliance on hypothetical questions and survey data often gave rise to deep insights that allowed for major advances. Two prominent examples include the work of Daniel Kahneman and Amos Tversky on prospect theory (Kahneman and Tversky,

1979) based on hypothetical questions in lab experiments, and the work of Daniel Kahneman, Richard Thaler, and Jack Knetsch on fairness motivations in humans (Kahneman et al., 1986) based on hypothetical questions posed in telephone surveys. Kahneman and Tversky (1979) is the second most cited paper in all of economics, the catalyst for the Nobel Prize to Kahneman, and the source of prospect theory, which is currently the most satisfactory decision theory under risk, uncertainty, and ambiguity.[14] Yet the paper is based on hypothetical, non-incentivized, lab experiments. Any guesses if it would have been published in an economics journal today?

Another merit of studies based on hypothetical, non-incentivized, questions is that they can complement lab experiments in certain areas. Here, we consider two examples from the work of Daniel Kahneman and Amos Tversky.

Example 0.1 *Consider the identification of loss aversion (losses bite more than equivalent gains) in Kahneman and Tversky (1979). In lab experiments, it is not always easy to induce loss aversion over "large losses" because it is considered unethical in experimental economics to leave subjects out-of-pocket. The main alternative in lab experiments is to give subjects money upfront to ensure they are never out-of-pocket. However, this may contaminate their responses by the "house money effect" (gamblers who win money in a casino are more likely to gamble with it; as they say, easy come easy go). Hence, if the intrinsic motivation of subjects to answer lab questions can be trusted, then there is no harm in presenting them with hypothetical loss scenarios.*

Example 0.2 *Consider the following hypothetical, non-incentivized, lab questions from experiments conducted in a seminal paper by Kahneman and Tversky (1984). The percentage of subjects choosing each response is given in brackets.*

Imagine that the US is preparing for the outbreak of an unusual Asian disease, which is expected to kill 600 people. Two alternative programs to combat the disease have been proposed. Assume that the exact scientific estimates of the consequences of the programs are as follows:

Positive Framing: If program A is adopted, 200 people will be saved. If program B is adopted, there is a one-third probability that 600 people will be saved and a two-thirds probability that no people will be saved. Which of the two programs would you favor? (72% chose A, 28% chose B).

Negative Framing: If program C is adopted, 400 people will die. If program D is adopted, there is a one-third probability that nobody will die and a two-thirds probability that 600 people will die. Which of the two programs would you favor? (22% chose C, 78% chose D). Relative to the status quo, positive framing presents data in terms of "lives saved," while negative framing presents the same data in terms of "lives lost." Options A and C are identical, and options B and D are also identical. Under frame-invariance, the typical assumption in neoclassical economics, if A is chosen over B then C must be chosen over D (and vice versa). However, in the domain of gains (lives saved relative to the status quo), the majority (72%) chose the safe option (A) over the risky option (B). In the domain of losses (lives lost relative to the status quo) the majority (78%) chose the risky option (D) over the safe option (C). This establishes several results. First, behavior is not frame-invariant. Second, the results are not consistent with expected utility. Third, subjects are risk averse in gains and risk seeking in losses; this is one of the important insights of prospect theory.[15]

---

[14] The source for the "second most cited paper" claim is Table 2 in Kim et al. (2006).
[15] To be more precise, there is a *fourfold classification of risk attitudes* under prospect theory that depends jointly on the shapes of the probability weighting function and the utility function; see Chapter 2 in Volume 1.

Thaler (2015, p. 47) writes on the aversion to survey data: "This disdain [for survey data] is simply unscientific. Polling data, which just comes from asking people whether they are planning to vote and for whom, when carefully used by skilled statisticians ... yield remarkably accurate predictions of elections. The most amusing aspect of this anti-survey attitude is that many important macroeconomic variables are produced by surveys! ... 'jobs' data ... come from surveys conducted by the Census Bureau. The unemployment rate, ... is also determined from a survey that asks people whether they are looking for work. Yet using published survey data is not considered a faux pas in macroeconomics. Apparently economists don't mind survey data as long as someone other than the researcher collected it."

Happiness economics, which we consider in Volume 7 is based almost entirely on survey data. Policymakers appear to take serious interest in this area and survey measures of well-being and happiness are highly correlated, which is consistent with the standard that one might expect from incentivized responses. Furthermore, firms often use information gleaned from market surveys to introduce new products about which consumers have no prior experience, and alter the characteristics of existing products; the consequences of these decisions run into billions of pounds every year.

Consider an example where incentives make the problem even worse. Using hypothetical, non-incentivized questions, Lichtenstein and Slovic (1973) asked people to choose between a less risky P-bet (high probability of winning a low prize) and a more risky \$-bet (a low probability of winning a high prize). When asked to choose directly between the two bets, most people chose the low risk option, the P-bet. Yet, most people assigned a higher certainty equivalent to the \$-bet as compared to the P-bet. Thus, we have a case of *preference reversals* that cannot be explained by any model of consistent preferences. Grether and Plott (1979) suspected that the problem was caused by hypothetical choices. However, when they re-ran the experiments using incentivized subjects, the incidence of preference reversals worsened.

In sum, there are no grounds to outrightly reject survey data. Survey data has pitfalls, for instance, poll data sometimes gives misleading results, however the benefits of survey data outstrip the potential pitfalls. But other data sources also have limitations; hence, it is important to use all sources of data, surveys, experiments, and field evidence, to build a more complete picture of human behavior.

3.7 Replications in experimental economics

Replications of existing research in economics is not a hugely active area, and certainly less active relative to psychology, which has led to a replication crises in that subject because the majority of studies could not be replicated.[16] Camerer et al. (2016) replicate 18 between-subjects lab experiments published in the two leading journals, *American Economic Review* and the *Quarterly Journal of Economics*, between 2011 and 2014. They find that for 11 out of the 18 studies (61.1%) there is a significant effect in the same direction ($P < 0.05$) as reported in the main finding of each study; three more studies are also close to being successful. The remaining studies fail the replication test on this criterion. Using another method of assessment, they constructed 95% confidence intervals of the main effect size for each paper; 12 of the 18 replications (66.7%) fall within this confidence level. How high are these successful replication rates? This is a relative

---

[16] For replications in psychology, see, for instance: Open Science Collaboration. (2015). Estimating the reproducibility of psychological science: *Science* 349(6251). For a discussion of replications in several areas of economics, see the May 2017 issue (Volume 107, No. 5) of the *American Economic Review*.

question, and we simply do not have enough studies in economics and in psychology to make a comparison. When compared with this small number of studies, the authors report that the stated replication rates in economics experiments are relatively higher, but could be improved further.

Replications are critical, but they are not the only yardstick on which we should judge research. After all, if the original research questions were uninteresting and the research design was flawed, the replication can, at best, do no better. There have been suggestions to raise the significance levels for new results (Benjamin et al., 2018). Furthermore, the dependence of preferences on context, frame, and culture is widely evidenced in behavioral economics. These findings suggest that research in behavioral economics may not always be easy to replicate unless a range of contextual, cultural, and frame-dependent factors are controlled for.

4 Approach and organization of the book

This seven-volume book is an attempt to take stock of behavioral economics and aims to serve several purposes: A course text for advanced students in economics and other social sciences, a research handbook for behavioral economists, and an invitation to economists and other social scientists of all persuasions to explore this exciting new field. In its teaching role, the book would ideally be taught in a yearlong course in behavioral economics, supplemented by readings that reflect the interests of the instructor. A good example is a typical two-semester North American-style course that has 13 weeks of teaching in each semester; students meet each week for a two-hour lecture and a one-hour problem-solving class. This book tries to standardize the material in behavioral economics so that students can see behavioral economics as a coherent and widely applicable body of theory, much as they might see any other established area in economics. It is also intended to 'nudge' many idiosyncratic course outlines, that pass for behavioral and/or experimental economics at the moment, to adopt a more balanced approach.

Given the scope of the book, one can also construct a large number of coherent and interesting single-semester courses not just in behavioral economics but also in behavioral decision theory, behavioral macroeconomics, behavioral industrial organization, behavioral contract theory, topics in behavioral economics, and the like. I believe that the book should also be essential background reading for any advanced course in microeconomics in order to address Herbert Gintis' (2009, p. xvi) concern raised in Section 2, till the time that microeconomics books respond in a satisfactory manner to his suggestion.

Despite the size of the book, it is, I believe, the "minimum" amount of material that any academic who declares behavioral economics or experimental economics as their research interest, must have deep, rather than passing, familiarity with.

As the reader may have guessed from Sections 2 and 3, my main criterion for including models in this book is their consistency with the evidence, unless there is significant merit in using a model for pedagogical or other reasons. Most of the models that I use can typically explain at least as much as neoclassical models, but can also better explain data from other domains of human behavior. It is entirely possible, of course, to append auxiliary assumptions to standard neoclassical models to explain almost any set of stylized facts. However, I try to stay away from models in which these auxiliary assumptions are ad hoc fixes.

I encourage the reader to keep an open mind about behavioral economics models and judge models by the relevant empirical evidence. Models in behavioral economics are as theoretically rigorous as models in neoclassical economics, if rigor is an important criteria for the reader.

Gilboa (2009, Section 7.1) may well be right that all models are ultimately wrong. Even if this statement were true, we must consistently strive to improve our models in the light of rejections, in order to make better predictions and improve our understanding of human behavior. The sequence of these improved models may or may not ever converge to the "true model." Yet, each time we reject a model and put in its place a new one that makes better predictions, we make progress.

The level of honesty that we need as a profession is captured in the words of the Nobel Prize-winning physicist Richard Feynman (1965, p. 158) that economists would do well to embrace: "But experimenters search most diligently, and with the greatest effort, in exactly those places where it seems most likely that we can prove our theories wrong. In other words, we are trying to prove ourselves wrong as quickly as possible, because only in that way can we find progress." The "all models is wrong critique" is unhelpful at best and, if used inappropriately, it is likely to hinder progress in the subject.

For many of the topics, the book is organized in the following general style. A neoclassical theory is outlined, followed by a review of the evidence for it. If the weight of the evidence is inconsistent with the theory, then the behavioral alternatives and the evidence for or against them is described. There is a range of applications in the book for many of the behavioral theories that the reader/instructor can choose from. In order to help readers who might not be familiar with the full range of topics in behavioral economics, I err on the side of longer introductions to most of the chapters. As a first pass, readers may wish to skim through the introductions to the various volumes and chapters, in order to get a bird's-eye view of the material. This should enable readers to draw up a priority list of topics that they would wish to read or teach in their courses. I deliberately shy away from offering such a list of topics to the reader, and like a good restaurant, prefer to fall back on offering a wide menu of tempting choices, hoping that you, the reader, will keep coming back, and spread the word.

Some readers may feel that it is presumptuous to include the word "foundations" in the title of this book. However, in justification, I believe that there is now a sufficiently rich body of lab and field evidence that is well described by models of behavioral economic theory. The richness of human behavior that we can account for with these models is unprecedented in modern economics. A few of the areas in behavioral economics, notably *neuroeconomics*, are very young and I have some hesitation in bringing this material under the rubric of a book that claims to describe the foundations of a subject. Yet, omitting this material is not an attractive option, and I have erred on the side of inclusion.

I also try to flag up material that is speculative, yet promising, or where the evidence base is not sufficiently established at this point in time. Behavioral economics continues to be work in progress and despite the huge increase in understanding attained over the last several decades, a lot needs to be done. Writing this introduction upon completion of the book, and reflecting on the material, I must confess that I have never personally felt so enriched, yet so ignorant, in my life. I hope that the serious, and just the plain curious, among you, come away with a similar sentiment after reading this book.

The book is organized into seven volumes structured into multiple chapters; there are exercises at the end of each volume. The order of the volumes reflects, at least partially, the historical development of the subject, and also bears some similarity with the organization of a typical course in microeconomics. Each volume begins with an introduction to the material in that volume, and each chapter has a separate, but more detailed, introduction.

The table of contents give a bird's eye view of what is inside the book and I will not bore you with a semi-verbatim description. I should make a few broad comments though, about my organization of the material. I focus mainly on topics that readers may find to be in an unexpected location within the book.

The book opens with Volume 1 on *behavioral decision theory* because playing a game against nature under risk, uncertainty, and ambiguity, in a static setting, is one of the simplest economic problems; this abstracts from temporal and strategic concerns. However, there is an important overlap between risk preferences and time preferences, which is split between Volume 1 and Volume 3 on time preferences. Many readers might have wished to see a more thorough treatment of ambiguity. However, most of the modern developments in ambiguity are within the confines of the neoclassical models, although an important behavioral literature on source-dependent preferences is now beginning to develop that highlights the role of prospect theory.

Microeconomics texts typically begin with a discussion of the properties of human preferences, which are regarded as the primitives of the model. Most evidence now indicates that there is a mixture of individuals with purely *self-regarding preferences*, as in neoclassical economics, and those with *other-regarding preferences*. Volume 2 considers the evidence on *human sociality* and behavioral models that take account of this evidence. There is also a discussion of the implications of social preferences for competitive general equilibrium, which typically comes much later in a microeconomics course. Two important topics that lie at the heart of human motivation in economics, *social identity* and *human virtues*, appear in a stand-alone chapter in Volume 2. The inclusion of these major topics should be less surprising than the fact that most microeconomics texts have somehow contrived to exclude them.

An explicit time dimension is not fundamental to the material in Volumes 1 and 2. In Volume 3, we consider the evidence on time preferences and *behavioral models of time discounting*. The treatment of time preferences is excessively narrow in neoclassical microeconomics texts. This is because the entire psychology of time preferences is captured by a single parameter, the discount rate, in the exponential discounted utility model—the main model of time preferences in neoclassical economics. This is not just unsatisfactory in light of the richness in observed time preferences, but exponential discounting is strongly rejected by the evidence, perhaps even more so than expected utility theory.

Volume 3 is the slimmest of the seven volumes but there is likely to be much that is new and unfamiliar to many readers. This will require investment in learning new machinery such as *subadditivity*, *attribute-based models* of time preferences, and *models of reference time preferences*. I advise the serious reader to persevere with Volume 3. It is worth telling an anecdote that the reader may wish to keep in mind when an unfamiliar topic is encountered in Volume 3. When George Loewenstein, one of the leaders in time discounting, first saw the material in Volume 3, he particularly commended me for including *subadditivity* (i.e., discounting depends on how one partitions a given interval of time). However, when another group of non-specialists read the same material as part of a group reading seminar in a leading university, they were put off by the "unusual and new" concept of subadditivity. The reason subadditivity is there in the book is because it is currently supported by the evidence; its current popularity/aesthetic appeal (or lack of it) are criteria that, for this book, are not relevant.

Volume 4, perhaps the longest of the seven volumes, is on *behavioral game theory*. Classical game theory revolutionized economics by forcing it to specify explicitly the economic environment, set of players, sequence of moves, and the mapping of histories to payoffs. Anyone comparing industrial organization theory before the advent of game theory with modern industrial organization theory will immediately notice the much greater clarity achieved by modern game theoretic models (think, e.g., of models of entry deterrence). Gintis (2009) advocates keeping game theory as the common toolkit for all social sciences despite pointing out serious shortcomings in classical game theory, for instance, the assumption of common priors and the justification for a Nash equilibrium. The approach in this book concurs with this sentiment. Despite widespread belief to the contrary, the evidence has not been too kind to classical models of game theory. This is particularly the case for observed behavior in the early rounds of a game, and for equilibrium refinements that require high cognitive requirements. In particular, it stretches the imagination to believe that players could arrive at a Nash equilibrium purely by a deductive process. For instance, the cooperation rate in many static prisoner's dilemma game experiments is about 60%; cooperation here is a dominated strategy, which in classical game theory, ought never to have been played.[17]

We consider at length the evidence for classical models of game theory and the leading behavioral alternatives. Many of the main behavioral alternatives, such as *level-k models*, the *cognitive hierarchy model*, and the *quantal response equilibrium*, relax the "equilibrium in beliefs" assumption, or the assumption that players play a best response. There are several other behavioral models of strategic interaction that are in the fray. While the empirical evidence is not always consistent with these models, the most heartening aspect of the discourse in behavioral game theory is that we are actually using empirical evidence to choose among the models. You cannot convince the leaders in this field, say, Vincent Crawford or Colin Camerer, about your proposal for a new solution concept in game theory by simply appealing to the aesthetic appeal of your proposed model, or its ability to tell a useful story, or a fable, if it is not supported by the evidence. I have decided to include the topic of *psychological game theory* in Volume 4. I anticipate that some instructors may have wished to place this topic in Volume 7 on emotions, because it also deals with *anger* and *guilt*, while other instructors may have wished to see it in Volume 2, because it also deals with intentions-based reciprocity. My relatively detailed treatment of this material reflects my preference to see this material given more prominence in modern behavioral economics.

Volume 5 considers *models of bounded rationality*, and I personally believe that it is of enormous significance for the future direction of behavioral economics. It is split into three main chapters. The chapter on *judgment heuristics*, a topic that owes its origin and importance to Tversky and Kahneman (1973, 1974), brings into sharp focus the debate about the relative suitability of the *optimization approach*, and the *heuristic-based approach* to economic models.[18] This chapter is a must-read for anyone who believes that the standard neoclassical framework is satisfactory on the grounds that its predictions match the data in an 'as if' sense. The chapter on *mental accounting* considers work that Richard Thaler almost single-handedly pioneered. It deserves to see much more development and interest among theorists working in behavioral economics. The reader may not have expected a chapter on *behavioral finance* in Volume 5 but there is no better place to illustrate bounded rationality and the inefficiency of markets in the very market that is typically held up as a model of efficiency in neoclassical economics.

Volume 6 outlines the evidence on human learning and introduces traditional and *behavioral models of learning*. It contains chapter-length treatments of *evolutionary game theory, stochastic social dynamics, and complexity/machine learning*. An appendix briefly introduces the reader to the necessary technical machinery on deterministic and stochastic dynamical systems. Some instructors have wished to see the chapter on evolutionary game theory in Volume 4. One aim

---

[17] Social preferences alone cannot explain behavior of the players in the prisoner's dilemma game; see al-Nowaihi and Dhami (2015).

[18] For a discussion of alternative views on the optimization versus heuristics debate, the reader may consult the June 2013 issue of the *Journal of Economic Literature*, Volume 51, No. 2.

of this chapter is to provide evolutionary foundations for human sociality that we covered in Volume 2, and also introduce some newer and interesting topics, such as *gene-culture coevolution* that justify the location of this chapter in a volume on learning. Volume 6 is particularly instructive in evaluating the common claim that a Nash equilibrium arises if sufficient learning opportunities are provided to the subjects. A separate chapter-length treatment on stochastic social dynamics in Volume 6 might be unexpected, even for many behavioral economists who do not typically include this topic in their courses. However, I believe that this material needs to be taken more seriously, and all students of behavioral economics should have at least a basic familiarity with it.

The final volume, Volume 7, considers three different topics: emotions, behavioral welfare economics, and neuroeconomics.

Neoclassical economics typically focuses on cold and emotionless deliberation. Part 1 in Volume 7 considers the role of emotions in explaining economic phenomena. Instructors interested in teaching a course that focuses on emotions will need to combine the material here with that from other parts of the book, such as psychological game theory (Volume 4), models of regret and disappointment aversion (Volume 1), and issues of self-control and present-biased preferences (Volume 3). We also consider the Gul–Pesendorfer model of temptation that some readers might have preferred to situate in Volume 3, where issues of present-biased preferences are discussed. I have also placed the important policy relevant topic of *happiness economics* here, insofar as happiness may be considered as a type of emotion. The evidence base in happiness economics is typically constructed using survey data that not all economists are comfortable with (see Section 3.6 above), which has hampered its acceptability within academic economists. I urge economists to take this material more seriously, particularly given the correlations between various measures of well-being and happiness. Some readers may find *models of dual selves* to be somewhat out of place in this part; I partly share this concern but it was not immediately clear where better to situate this important topic.

Part 2 in Volume 7 considers issues in *behavioral welfare economics*, which is an area that is likely to experience more development in the future. If people have behavioral biases relative to the neoclassical model, then should we respect those biases or not? The debate is not just about *libertarianism* and *paternalism*, but also about exactly what these terms mean in the presence of behavioral biases.

Part 3 in Volume 7 gives a very brief tour of *neuroeconomics* that highlights the neuroeconomic foundations of just a few selected aspects of human behavior from the first four volumes of the book. In particular, I make no attempt at completeness in the treatment of neuroeconomics; several excellent and more authoritative sources are available (e.g., Glimcher et al., 2009; Glimcher and Fehr, 2014).

There are some omissions from the book that are partly dictated by technological considerations such as the physical size of the book, the current importance of these topics in behavioral economics, and last but not least, by my own lack of competence in these areas. *Complexity theory*, *agent-based models*, and *machine learning*, missing in the 2016 book, are now considered in Volume 6. For further details on policy-based applications of complexity, see Colander and Kupers (2014); for a general introduction to complexity, see Mitchell (2009), and for several other issues in agent-based models, see Tesfatsion and Judd (2006); for a short and balanced review, see Farmer and Foley (2009). I give insufficient attention to the *epistemic foundations of equilibrium concepts* in classical and behavioral game theory; see Dekel and Siniscalchi (2015) for a recent review, and Gintis (2009) for a critique of the epistemic foundations of classical game theory.

5 Appendix A: The random lottery incentive mechanism

Consider the *random lottery incentive mechanism* (RLI) that is widely employed to pay subjects in experiments. Suppose that expected utility maximizing subjects in an experiment perform n tasks from a set of tasks $T = \{t_1, \ldots, t_n\}$. Let task t_i involve choosing from a set of lotteries, $\mathcal{L}_i$ and define $\mathcal{L} = \cup_i \mathcal{L}_i$ as the set of all lotteries considered in the n tasks. Consider a subject in the experiment whose preferences over pairs of elements in $\mathcal{L}$ are represented by $\succeq$. At the beginning of the experiment, subjects are told that one of the tasks will be picked at random once all tasks are completed, and their choice in that task will be paid to them for real. Let us abstract from issues of a possible show-up fee for the experiment that we have already commented on above.

Suppose that in any task, t_i, the most preferred lottery of the subject is L_i^*. Conditional on the incentive structure described above, should the subject choose L_i^*? An elicitation method is incentive compatible if the answer is yes. The probability that task i is chosen to be rewarded at the end of the experiment is $\frac{1}{n}$. With the complementary probability $1 - \frac{1}{n}$, any of the other $n - 1$ tasks might be chosen to be rewarded. Let the choice made by the subject on any task t_j, $j \neq i$ be L_j. Let us denote by $(L_1, p_1; \ldots; L_i^*, p_i; \ldots; L_n, p_n)$ the compound lottery in which lottery L_j is played with probability p_j. From the *independence axiom* of expected utility theory that should be familiar to most undergraduates in economics (see Volume 1 for details), we know that since $L_i^* \succeq \widehat{L}_i$ for all $\widehat{L}_i \in \mathcal{L}_i$, it follows that

$$\left(L_1, \frac{1}{n}; \ldots; L_i^*, \frac{1}{n}; \ldots; L_n, \frac{1}{n}\right) \succeq \left(L_1, \frac{1}{n}; \ldots; \widehat{L}_i, \frac{1}{n}; \ldots; L_n, \frac{1}{n}\right) \text{ for all } \widehat{L}_i \in \mathcal{L}_i. \qquad (0.1)$$

In words, the independence axiom says that if $L_i^* \succeq \widehat{L}_i$ then the decision maker prefers any mixture of lotteries that gives L_i^* over an identical mixture that contains $\widehat{L}_i$ in its place. Thus, the subject will choose L_i^* in task t_i. We can show this to be true for all tasks $t_j \in T$. Thus, RLI is incentive compatible.

6 Appendix B: In lieu of a problem set

This section poses 50 problems that you will encounter in this book and tailored to the material presented in the introduction. If you are already familiar with a particular problem, just move on to the next one. The problems range from straightforward applications of the material in the introduction to slightly more challenging ones. I deliberately avoid giving too much structure to the problems, so that you can try to solve them by writing your own models in a free-spirited manner. If you wish to use the neoclassical model to solve a problem, then think carefully about the auxiliary assumptions that you invoke. In particular, do ask yourself if the auxiliary assumptions that you use are ad hoc or not. You will encounter the solutions to these problems, and many others, as you progress through the book; this will also give you an opportunity to check your initial responses.

1. Many taxi drivers quit too early on rainy days in New York when the effective wage rate is actually very high. In other words, why is it so hard to find a taxi on a rainy day in New York?
2. Why do owners of objects, humans, or chimps, value them more than non-owners (under neoclassical economics, everyone should value objects at their opportunity cost)?

3. If people play Russian roulette, why are they likely to pay more to reduce the number of bullets from 1 to 0, as compared to from 4 to 3 (check that under expected utility these two choices should be equally valuable)?

4. From 1926 to about the mid 1980s, the annual real return on stocks has been about 7% with a standard deviation of 20%, while the annual real return on treasury bills has been less than 1%. In neoclassical economics, a coefficient of relative risk aversion of about 30 can explain these findings, but the actual coefficient is around 1. This is the *equity-premium puzzle*. How can you explain the equity-premium puzzle?

5. A decision maker has initial wealth, *w*. Suppose that at all levels of wealth, he prefers to keep his wealth rather than play the lottery L_1 : win $11 or lose $10 with equal chance, for any *w*. Then, under expected utility theory, the decision maker will prefer the lottery L_1 to the lottery L_2: lose $100 and win an infinite amount with equal probability (*Rabin's paradox*). Thus risk aversion over small stakes, under expected utility theory, implies implausible risk aversion over large stakes. Does expected utility correctly encapsulate the risk attitudes of an individual? Can you think of modifications to expected utility that will explain Rabin's paradox?

6. For an amateur tax evader, the actual probability of audit is 1–3% and the penalty for being caught is (i) return of evaded taxes, plus (ii) fine at the rate of 1–2 times evaded tax. A quick back of the envelope calculation will show that this implies a return on tax evasion of about 96–98%. If you are an expected utility maximizer and have a coefficient of relative risk aversion of about 70 or above, you will pay your taxes; but, empirically, the coefficient is about 1. Since there are very few assets with this return, why do people pay any taxes?

7. Why do people not buy insurance against very low probability events such as natural hazards, even when insurance is better than actuarially fair and the losses of insurance firms are underwritten by the government?

8. In everyday conversations about risky decisions, people speak of *optimism*, *pessimism*, *disappointment*, and *regret* (think only of pure risk in a simple game against nature). Can neoclassical decision theory under risk account for these emotions?

9. In recessions, why do firms typically prefer to lay-off workers rather than cut wages?

10. Why do most people find a cut in the nominal wage of 5% under zero inflation to be more unfair relative to a nominal wage increase of 2% under 7% inflation? What are the implications for macroeconomics?

11. In experiments on redistributive taxes, why do people often choose a smaller, more equally distributed, cake as compared to one in which they get a larger share of a very unequally distributed cake?

12. Should we generally expect any difference in outcomes relative to the neoclassical case if a minority of players have other-regarding preferences (i.e., also care about payoffs of others in addition to their own)? You may think of optimal contracts (static and finitely repeated) between a principal and two agents in a production task where both agents are essential. One of the agents has self-regarding preferences, but the other has other-regarding preferences; the principal does not know who's who.

13. Why are individuals often willing to punish third-parties for observed norm violations between other players even when their own payoffs have not been affected?

14. Why do workers often respond to higher wage offers of firms by working harder, even in 'static games', where they could take the money and run? Why, in these static problems, may firms choose to offer high wages that exceed the opportunity cost of hiring workers?

How might you distinguish the predictions of this model from the model of efficiency wages?

15. Why may firms sometimes choose to offer non-enforceable bonus contracts to workers in preference to enforceable incentive contracts, even in static problems? And why might the choice of effort by workers under bonus contracts be relatively higher as compared to that under incentive contracts?

16. Why do moral suasion, trust, and giving workers a goal/sense of purpose or a particular company identity, often outperform monetary incentives?

17. Why do people not lie maximally even when their behavior is guaranteed to remain completely anonymous? And why do we teach children not to lie, act morally rather than opportunistically, and help those who are less fortunate, rather than the neoclassical prescriptions about human behavior (maximize your payoffs/utility subject to technological constraints, but ignore any moral or ethical considerations relative to payoff maximization)?

18. Consider Akerlof and Kranton's (2005, p. 9) description of the following initiation process at the US West Point military academy. "On plebes' first day... they strip down to their underwear. Their hair is cut off. They are put in uniform. They then must address an older cadet, with the proper salute... must stand and salute and repeat, and stand and salute and repeat, until they get it exactly right, all the while being reprimanded for every tiny mistake." How would an economist brought up on the theory of incentives and organizations make sense of this initiation ceremony?

19. Why does the law make a distinction between murder and manslaughter, assigning much lower punishments for manslaughter for the same harm to the victim?

20. Most people would prefer one apple today to two apples tomorrow, but they prefer two apples in 51 days to one apple in 50 days. How can you explain this preference reversal?

21. Discounting over an entire time interval $[\underline{t}, \overline{t}]$ in one go, turns out to be smaller, relative to discounting over n successive sub-intervals $[\underline{t}, t_1], [t_1, t_2], \ldots, [t_{n-1}, \overline{t}]$; this is known as *subadditive discounting*. Under exponential discounting, the two answers should be identical. What modifications do you think are needed to the exponential discounting model to explain this empirical finding?

22. Why does the data (e.g., for the US) show a sharp drop in consumption at retirement?

23. Why do people simultaneously hold illiquid assets and credit card debt?

24. Why do people procrastinate so much?

25. Why do people often pay more for an annual gym membership when they could save money on a pay-as-you-go basis?

26. In normal form games in which a Nash equilibrium can be found with more than 2–3 steps of iterated elimination of dominated strategies, the experimental evidence often shows that the outcome is not a Nash equilibrium. Does this evidence cause you to have any reservations about equilibrium concepts in classical game theory or a desire to modify them? If so, how?

27. Why do we observe far more cooperation in a one-shot prisoner dilemma game (about 60% of the time) relative to the prediction of classical game theory that predicts no cooperation under the assumption that people have self-regarding preferences? Bear in mind that the prisoners' dilemma game is possibly the most widely used game in the social sciences as a metaphor for human cooperation (or the lack of it), so this is not an unimportant result that can be ignored.

28. Empirical evidence shows that in centipede games, the backward induction outcome (play down at the first node) is played less than 10% of the time. In six-node centipede games, in a majority of the cases, players move across to at least the fourth node. How can you explain these findings? Does your explanation have testable implications?

29. If you are unconvinced by the experimental method, can you come up with a few "stringent" non-experimental tests of classical game theory using real-world data?

30. Why do bargaining negotiations often stall with adverse consequences for both parties (union strikes, wars, family gridlocks over issues) even when issues of asymmetric information are not salient? This is particularly the case in conditions where the classical alternating offers bargaining game predicts an immediate bargaining solution without delay.

31. You live in Italy and as most folks who live there, you typically don't tip cab drivers. However, one week you go abroad, and take a taxi to a friend's house who lives in the countryside in a country where there is a norm for tipping taxi drivers. A 70-year-old meek-looking and frail taxi driver delivers you safely to your destination. Would you honour the norm of tipping him or just walk away? Suppose you answered that you would pay the tip. Is your behavior consistent with classical game theory? If not, then which feature of classical game theory could be altered to explain your tipping behavior?

32. Why are winners of common value auctions often 'cursed' in the sense that they make far less money than they anticipated?

33. Eyetracking data from a three-round, two-player bargaining game whose structure is hidden from view, but searchable by using mouse clicks, reveals the following. Most subjects search for payoffs and the size of the cake to be divided in each round, forward from the first round rather than backward from the third round. Furthermore, subjects trained in backward induction do search backwards more often. Does this in any way make you uneasy about equilibrium concepts in classical game theory, or would you simply discount this evidence?

34. Why do interrogators often conduct around-the-clock interrogation of suspects?

35. Why might many people end up marrying or proposing marriage/seeking divorce without sufficient deliberation, or buy consumer durables in haste? Can you think of any legal interventions that take such human behavior into account? Would such legal interventions be necessary for the typical individual in the neoclassical framework?

36. Why are we typically happy to buy consumer durables on installments, yet prefer to prepay for a holiday?

37. Why do smokers and alcoholics often pay money at rehab clinics to get rid of their addictions? Recall that the typical model of addiction in neoclassical economics assumes that people choose to get rationally addicted, taking account of the relevant costs and benefits now, and in the future.

38. Why do many cigarette smokers report an increase in happiness following an increase in excise duty on cigarettes (based on US and Canadian data)?

39. A town is served by two hospitals. In the larger hospital, about 45 babies are born each day, and in the smaller hospital, about 15 babies are born each day. As you know, about 50% of all babies are boys. However, the exact percentage varies from day to day. For a period of one year, each hospital recorded the days on which more than 60% of the babies born were boys. Which hospital do you think recorded more such days? 53 students in the sample said that both hospitals are equally likely to have recorded such days and 21 students each chose the larger and the smaller hospital, respectively. Are the students behaving like the

agents in neoclassical economics (sometimes known as *Econs*)? If not, what does their behavior reveal?

40. Why do sales at lotto stores that have sold a winning ticket soar in the immediate weeks following the lotto win (this positive effect on sales persists for up to 40 weeks following the lotto win)? How can you test the hypothesis that "the winning store just produced more interest among the local population to buy more lotto tickets, so that this finding is perfectly consistent with neoclassical economics"?

41. Why do so many mergers fail, yet we often observe waves of mergers from time to time?

42. Why do people find it more difficult to make a choice when the set of choices expands (people choose easily among three types of jams, but often struggle to choose among 27 types of jams)?

43. There is much cross-country variation in organ donation rates in European countries (98% in Austria, but 12% in Germany; 99.9% in France, but 17.7% in the UK; 85.9% in Sweden, but 4.25% in Denmark). It turns out that in countries with high organ donation rates, people are automatically enrolled in the organ donation program, but can opt-out if they wish. The situation is exactly the reverse in countries with low organ donation rates, where people can opt-in if they wish. Can this empirical fact be explained under neoclassical economics? If you answer yes, then be careful in stating your auxiliary assumptions and think of the evidence for these assumptions.

44. There are only two cab companies in the city, Green and Blue; 85% of the cabs are Green. There was an accident last night. A witness comes forward to testify that the cab involved in the accident was Blue. In similar conditions, the reliability of the witness is 80%, i.e., the probability that he gets it wrong is 20%. What is the probability that the actual cab involved in the accident was Blue? The median and modal response was 80%. Are the students behaving like the agents in neoclassical economics? If not, what does their behavior reveal?

45. Why do buyers of a new car often find that the particular model they drive suddenly appears more common on the roads?

46. Why do marketing people play on alternative ways of framing information that has identical information-content? Why, for instance, may swimsuit models be placed next to sports cars in advertisements, when the main role of advertisement in the neoclassical framework is to convey information to potential buyers?

47. Why do sales drop if publicly known sales taxes are displayed on price stickers rather than being added at the check-out counter?

48. Why might the financial market price skewness in asset returns?

49. Why are so many financial crises accompanied by no-news (i.e., no information related to fundamental values)?

50. Consider the probability of success that entrepreneurs assign to their startups. In one empirical study, only 5% of startup entrepreneurs believe that their odds are any worse than comparable enterprises and a third believe that their success is assured. Based on French data, 56% expect 'development' and only 6% of startup entrepreneurs expect 'difficulty'; three years on, the respective figures are 38% and 17%. Empirically, only half of all startups survive beyond three years and the high failure rate among startups is widely reported in the popular press. How can we square these figures with the supposed rationality of participants in corporate finance? How should we react to this sort of evidence?

REFERENCES FOR INTRODUCTION

Abeler, J. and Nosenzo, D. (2015). Self-selection into laboratory experiments: pro-social motives versus monetary incentives. *Experimental Economics* 18(2): 195–214.

Allais, M. (1953). La psychologie de l'homme rationnel devant le risque: critique des postulats et axiomes de l'école Américaine. *Econometrica* 21: 503–46.

al-Nowaihi, A. and Dhami, S. (2015). Evidential equilibria: heuristics and biases in static games of complete information. *Games* 6(4): 637–77.

Andersen, S., Ertaç, S., Gneezy, U., Hoffman, M., and List, J. A. (2011). Stakes matter in ultimatum games. *American Economic Review* 101(7): 3427–39.

Anderson, J., Burks, S. V., Carpenter, J. et al. (2013). Self-selection and variations in the laboratory measurement of other-regarding preferences across subject pools: evidence from one college student and two adult samples. *Experimental Economics* 16: 170–89.

Ariely, D., Bracha, A., and Meier, S. (2009). Doing good or going well? Image motivation and monetary incentives in behaving prosocially. *American Economic Review* 99(1): 544–55.

Arkes, H. R., Dawes, R. M., and Christensen, C. (1986). Factors influencing the use of a decision rule in a probabilistic task. *Organizational Behavior and Human Decision Processes* 37: 93–110.

Ashraf, N., Camerer, C. F., and Loewenstein, G. (2005). Adam Smith, behavioral economist. *Journal of Economic Perspectives* 19(3): 131–45.

Bardsley, N., Cubitt, R., Loomes, G., Moffatt, P., Starmer, C., and Sugden, R. (2010). *Experimental Economics: Rethinking the Rules*. Princeton, NJ: Princeton University Press.

Barmettler, F., Fehr, E., and Zehnder, C. (2012). Big experimenter is watching you! Anonymity and prosocial behavior in the laboratory. *Games and Economic Behavior* 75(1): 17–34.

Becker, G. M., DeGroot, M. H., and Marschak, J. (1964). Measuring utility by a single-response sequential method. *Systems Research* 9: 226–32.

Bénabou, R. and Tirole, J. (2003). Intrinsic and extrinsic motivation. *Review of Economic Studies* 70(3): 489–520.

Benjamin, D. J., Berger, J. O., Johannesson, M., Nosek, B. A., Wagenmakers, E. J., Berk, R., and Morgan, S. L. (2018). Redefine statistical significance. *Nature Human Behaviour* 2(1): 6–10.

Benjamin, D. J., Cesarini, D., Chabris, C. F. et al. (2012). The promises and pitfalls of genoeconomics. *Annual Review of Economics* 4: 627–62.

Blaug, M. (1992). *The Methodology of Economics, Or, How Economists Explain*. Cambridge and New York: Cambridge University Press.

Bohm, P., Lindén, J., and Sonnegård, J. (1997). Eliciting reservation prices: Becker-DeGroot-Marschak mechanisms vs. markets. *Economic Journal* 107: 1079–89.

Bolton, G. E., Zwick, R., and Katok, E. (1998). Dictator game giving: rules of fairness versus acts of kindness. *International Journal of Game Theory* 27(2): 269–99.

Bonner, S. E., Hastie, R., Sprinkle, G. B., and Young, S. M. (2000). A review of the effects of financial incentives on performance in laboratory tasks: implications for management accounting. *Journal of Management Accounting Research* 13: 19–64.

Braga, J. and Starmer, C. (2005). Preference anomalies, preference elicitation and the Discovered Preference Hypothesis. *Environmental and Resource Economics* 32: 55–89.

Bruni, L. and Sugden, R. (2007). The road not taken: how psychology was removed from economics, and how it might be brought back. *Economic Journal* 117: 146–73.

Camerer, C. F. (2015). The promise and success of lab-field generalizability in experimental economics: a critical reply to Levitt and List. In G. R. Fréchette and A. Schotter (eds.), *Handbook of Experimental Economic Methodology*. Oxford: Oxford University Press. pp. 249–95.

Camerer, C. F., Dreber, A., Forsell, E., Ho, T.-H., Huber, J., Johannesson, M., Kirchler, M., Almenberg, J., Altmejd, A., Chan, T., et al. (2016). Evaluating replicability of laboratory experiments in economics. *Science* 351(6280): 1433–1436.

Camerer, C. F. and Hogarth, R. M. (1999). The effects of financial incentives in experiments: a review and capital-labor-production framework. *Journal of Risk and Uncertainty* 19(1–3): 7–42.

Camerer, C. F. and Loewenstein, G. (2004). Behavioral economics: past, present, future. In C. F.

Camerer, G. Loewenstein, and M. Rabin, (eds.), *Advances in Behavioral Economics*. New York: Russell Sage, pp. 3–51.

Cameron, L. A. (1999). Raising the stakes in the ultimatum game: experimental evidence from Indonesia. *Economic Inquiry* 37(1): 47–59.

Carpenter, J. P. and Seki, E. (2011). Do social preferences increase productivity? Field experimental evidence from fishermen in Toyama Bay. *Economic Inquiry* 49(2): 612–30.

Chamberlin, E. H. (1948). An experimental imperfect market. *Journal of Political Economy* 56(2): 95–108.

Cherry, T., Frykblom, P., and Shogren, J. (2002). Hardnose the dictator. *American Economic Review* 92(4) 1218–21.

Cleave, B. L., Nikiforakis, N., and Slonim, R. (2012). Is there selection bias in laboratory experiments? The case of social and risk preferences. *Experimental Economics* 16(3): 372–82.

Colander, D. and Kupers, R. (2014). *Complexity and the Art of Public Policy: Solving Society's Problems from the Bottom Up*. Princeton, NJ: Princeton University Press.

Dana, J., Weber, R. A., and Kuang, J. X. (2007). Exploiting moral wriggle room: experiments demonstrating an illusory preference for fairness. *Economic Theory* 33: 67–80.

Davis, D. D. and Holt, C. A. (1993). *Experimental Economics*. Princeton, NJ: Princeton University Press.

De Marchi, N. and Blaug, M. (eds.) (1991). *Appraising Economic Theories: Studies in the Methodology of Research Programmes*. Cheltenham: Edward Elgar.

Dekel, E. and Lipman, B. L. (2010). How (not) to do decision theory. *Annual Review of Economics* 2: 257–82.

Dekel, E. and Siniscalchi, M. (2015). Epistemic game theory. In H. P. Young and S. Zamir (eds.), *Handbook of Game Theory with Economic Applications*, Volume 4. Amsterdam: Elsevier, pp. 619–702.

Dhami, S. and al-Nowaihi, A. (2018). Rationality in Economics: Theory and Evidence. CESifo Working Paper No. 6872. Forthcoming in *Handbook of Rationality*. Cambridge, MA: MIT Press.

Ellsberg, D. (1961). Risk, ambiguity, and the Savage axioms. *Quarterly Journal of Economics* 75(4): 643–69.

Falk, A. and Heckman, J. J. (2009). Lab experiments are a major source of knowledge in the social sciences. *Science* 326: 535–38.

Falk, A., Meier, S., and Zehnder, C. (2013). Do lab experiments misrepresent social preferences? The case of self-selected student samples. *Journal of the European Economic Association* 11(4): 839–52.

Farmer, J. D. and Foley, D. (2009). The economy needs agent-based modelling. *Nature* 460: 685–6.

Fehr, E. and List, J. A. (2004). The hidden costs and returns of incentives: trust and trustworthiness among CEOs. *Journal of the European Economic Association* 2(5): 743–71.

Feynman, R. (1965). *The Character of Physical Law*. Cambridge, MA: MIT Press.

Fréchette, G. R. (2015). Laboratory experiments: professionals versus students. In G. R. Fréchette and A. Schotter (eds.), *Handbook of Experimental Economic Methodology*. Oxford: Oxford University Press, pp. 360–90.

Friedman, M. (1953). *The Methodology of Positive Economics*. Chicago, IL: University of Chicago Press.

Gilboa, I. (2009). *Theory of Decision Under Uncertainty*. Cambridge: Cambridge University Press.

Gilboa, I., Postlewaite, A., Samuelson, L., and Schmeidler, D. (2014). Economic models as analogies, *Economic Journal* 124: F513–F533.

Gintis, H. (2009). The Bounds of Reason: *Game Theory and the Unification of the Behavioral Sciences*. Princeton, NJ: Princeton University Press.

Gintis, H. (2015). Modeling homo-socialis: a reply to critics. *Review of Behavior Economics* 2: 211–37.

Glimcher, P. W., Camerer, C. F., Fehr, E., and Poldrack, R. A. (2009). *Neuroeconomics*. Amsterdam: Academic Press, Elsevier Inc.

Glimcher, P. W. and Fehr, E. (eds.) (2014). *Neuroeconomics*. Amsterdam: Elsevier Inc.

Gneezy, U. and Rustichini, A. (2000a). A fine is a price. *Journal of Legal Studies* 29(1): 1–17.

Gneezy, U. and Rustichini, A. (2000b). Pay enough or don't pay at all. *Quarterly Journal of Economics* 115(3): 791–810.

Godfrey-Smith, P. (2006). The strategy of model-based science. *Biology and Philosophy* 21: 725–40.

Godfrey-Smith, P. (2009). Models and fictions in science. *Philosophical Studies* 143: 101–16.

Grether, D. M. and Plott, C. (1979). Economic theory of choice and the preference reversal phenomenon. *American Economic Review*. 69(4): 623–38.

Guala, F. (2008). Experimental economics, history of. In S. N. Durlauf and L. E. Blume (eds.), *The New Palgrave Dictionary of Economics*. 2nd edition. Basingstoke: Palgrave Macmillan.

Haley, K. J. and Fessler, D. M. T. (2005). Nobody's watching? Subtle cues affect generosity in an anonymous economic game. *Evolution and Human Behavior* 26(3): 245–56.

Hands, D. W. (1991). The problem of excess content: Economics, novelty, and a long Popperian tale. In M. Blaug and N. DeMarchi (eds.), *Appraising Economic Theories*. Aldershot: Edward Elgar, pp. 58–75.

Hands, D. W. (2001). *Reflections Without Rules: Economic Methodology and Contemporary Science Theory*. Cambridge: Cambridge University Press.

Hausman, D. (1992). *The Inexact and Separate Science of Economics*. Cambridge: Cambridge University Press.

Herbst, D. and Mas, A. (2015). Peer effects on worker output in the lab generalize to the field. *Science* 350: 545–9.

Hertwig, R. and Ortmann, A. (2001). Experimental practices in economics: a methodological challenge for psychologists? *Behavioral and Brain Sciences* 24(3): 383–403.

Hoffman, E., McCabe, K. A., and Smith, V. L. (1998). Behavioral foundations of reciprocity: experimental economics and evolutionary psychology. *Economic Inquiry* 36: 335–52.

Hogarth, R. M., Gibbs, B. J., McKenzie, C. R. M., and Marquis, M. A. (1991). Learning from feedback: exactingness and incentives. *Journal of Experimental Psychology: Learning, Memory and Cognition* 17: 734–52.

Kahneman, D., Knetsch, J. L., and Thaler, R. H. (1986). Fairness as a constraint on profit seeking: entitlements in the market. *American Economic Review* 76(4): 728–41.

Kahneman, D. and Tversky, A. (1979). Prospect theory: an analysis of decision under risk. *Econometrica* 47(2): 263–91.

Kahneman, D. and Tversky, A. (1984). Choices, values, and frames. *The American Psychologist* 39: 341–50.

Kessler, J. B. and Vesterlund, L. (2015). The external validity of laboratory experiments: the misleading emphasis on quantitative effects. In G. R. Fréchette and A. Schotter (eds.), *Handbook of Experimental Economic Methodology*. Oxford: Oxford University Press, pp. 391–406.

Kim, E. H., Morse, A., and Zingales, L. (2006). What has mattered to economics since 1970. *Journal of Economic Perspectives* 20, 189–202.

Kuhn, T. S. (1962). *The Structure of Scientific Revolutions*. Chicago, IL: University of Chicago Press.

Lakatos, I. (1970). Falsification and the methodology of scientific research programmes. In I. Lakatos and A. Musgrave (eds.), *Criticism and the Growth of Knowledge*. Cambridge: Cambridge University Press, pp. 91–196.

Lambdin, C. G. and Shaffer, V. A. (2009). Are within-subjects designs transparent? *Judgement and Decision Making* 4(7): 554–66.

Levitt, S. D. and List, J. A. (2007). What do laboratory experiments measuring social preferences reveal about the real world? *Journal of Economic Perspectives* 21(2): 153–74.

Lichtenstein, S. and Slovic, P. (1973). Response-induced reversals of preference in gambling: an extended replication in Las Vegas. *Journal of Experimental Psychology* 101(1): 16–20.

Lipsey, R. G. (1979). An Introduction to Positive Economics. 5th edition. London: Weidenfeld and Nicolson.

List, J. A. (2006). The behavioralist meets the market: measuring social preferences and reputation effects in actual transactions. *Journal of Political Economy* 114(1): 1–37.

Loewenstein, G. F. (1999). Experimental economics from the vantage-point of behavioural economics. *Economic Journal* 109(453): 25–34.

Markowitz, H. (1952). The utility of wealth. *Journal of Political Economy* 60(2): 151–8.

Mas-Collel, A., Whinston, M. D, and Green, J. R. (1995). *Microeconomic Theory*. New York: Oxford University Press.

Mitchell, M. (2009). *Complexity: A Guided Tour*. Oxford: Oxford University Press.

Phelps, E. and Pollak, R. A. (1968). On second best national savings and game equilibrium growth. *Review of Economic Studies* 35(2): 185–99.

Popper, K. (1934). *Logik der Forschung* (Hutchinson & Company published the translation by

Karl Popper titled The Logic of Scientific Discovery in 1959).

Popper, K. (1963). *Conjectures and Refutations: The Growth of Scientific Knowledge*. London: Routledge and Kegan Paul.

Read, D. (2005). Monetary incentives, what are they good for? *Journal of Economic Methodology* 12(2): 265–76.

Roth, A. E. (1987). Laboratory experimentation in economics. In T. Bewley (ed.), *Advances in Economic Theory*, Fifth World Congress. Cambridge: Cambridge University Press, pp. 269–99.

Roth, A. E. (1988). Laboratory experimentation in economics: a methodological overview. *Economic Journal* 98: 974–1031.

Roth, A. E. (1995). Introduction to experimental economics. In J. H. Kagel and A. E. Roth (eds.), *The Handbook of Experimental Economics*. Princeton, NJ: Princeton University Press, pp. 3–109.

Roth, A. E. (2015). Is experimental economics living up to its promise? In G. R. Fréchette and A. Schotter, (eds.), Handbook of Experimental Economic Methodology. Oxford: Oxford University Press, pp. 13–40.

Rubinstein, A. (2006). Dilemmas of an economic theorist. *Econometrica* 74(4): 865–83.

Rydval, O. and Ortmann, A. (2004). How financial incentives and cognitive abilities affect task performance in laboratory settings: an illustration. *Economics Letters* 85: 315–20.

Samuelson, P. A. and Nordhaus, W. (1985). *Economics*. New York: McGraw Hill.

Schotter, A. (2015). On the relationship between economic theory and experiments. In G. R. Fréchette and A. Schotter (eds.), *Handbook of Experimental Economic Methodology*. Oxford: Oxford University Press, pp. 58–85.

Selten, R. (1998). Features of experimentally observed bounded rationality. *European Economic Review* 42(3–5): 413–36.

Siegel, S. and Fouraker, L. E. 1960. *Bargaining and Group Decision Making*. New York: McGraw-Hill.

Simon, H. A. (1978). Rational decision-making in business organizations. Nobel Memorial Lecture, December 8, 1978.

Slonim, R. and Roth, A. E. (1998). Learning in high stakes ultimatum games: an experiment in the Slovak Republic. *Econometrica* 66(3): 569–96.

Slonim, R., Wang, C., Garbarino, E., and Merret, D. (2013). Opting-in: participation bias in economic experiments. *Journal of Economic Behavior and Organization* 90: 43–70.

Smith, V. L. (1962). An experimental study of competitive market behavior. *Journal of Political Economy* 70: 111–37.

Smith, V. L. (1976). Experimental economics: induced value theory. *American Economic Review* 66: 274–9.

Smith, V. L. (1991). Rational choice: the contrast between economics and psychology. *Journal of Political Economy* 99: 877–97.

Smith, V. L. (2001). From old issues to new directions in experimental psychology and economics. *Behavioral and Brain Sciences* 24(3): 428–9.

Smith, V. L. and Walker, J. M. (1993). Monetary rewards and decision cost in experimental economics. *Economic Inquiry* 31: 245–61.

Tesfatsion, L. and Judd, K. L. (eds.) (2006). *Handbook of Computational Economics, Volume 2: Agent-Based Computational Economics*. Amsterdam: North Holland.

Thaler, R. H. (2015). *Misbehaving: The Making of Behavioral Economics*. New York: W. W. Norton.

Tversky, A. and Kahneman, D. (1973). Availability: A heuristic for judging frequency and probability. *Cognitive Psychology* 5(2): 207–32.

Tversky, A. and Kahneman, D. (1974). Judgment under uncertainty: heuristics and biases. *Science* 185: 1124–30.

Wimsatt, C. W. (2007). *Re-Engineering Philosophy for Limited Beings*. Cambridge, MA: Harvard University Press.

Zizzo, D. J. (2010). Experimenter demand effects in economic experiments. *Experimental Economics* 13(1): 75–98.

PART I

EMOTIONS

CHAPTER 1
Emotions and Human Behavior

1.1 Introduction

In this chapter, we motivate the use of emotions to explain human behavior. In contrast to the cold, emotionless, deliberations undertaken by *Homo oeconomicus*, the introduction of emotions provides a more satisfactory explanation of many economic phenomena. A wealth of empirical evidence provides a compelling case for taking emotions more seriously in all areas of economics.

In Section 1.2, we focus on intense physiological states such as hunger, moods, thirst, and physical pain that are collectively referred to as *visceral influences* (Loewenstein, 1996). Visceral influences can induce individuals to take actions that are often contrary to their own self-interests. Yet individuals often underestimate the effect of visceral influences on their past, current, and future behavior. The usual practice in economics is to consider future emotional states arising from current decisions, as in *regret theory*, *disappointment aversion* (Volume 1) and *guilt aversion*, *shame aversion*, and *reciprocity* (Volume 4); these are *anticipated emotions*. A strong case has been made for considering the role of emotions at the time of making decisions, i.e., *anticipatory emotions*, such as anxiety and dread that we consider in this volume (Loewenstein, 2000).

The issue of the rationality of emotions is an interesting one (Damasio, 1994). Individuals who have suffered damage to the emotional centers of their brains are unable to experience emotional states associated with fear. When faced with risky situations that entail occasional large losses and overall negative expected values, these individuals make extremely risky decisions. Damasio and several others have argued that the absence of emotions is detrimental to sound cognitive decisions, hence, on net, emotions must be rational. Emotions need not always enable us to take socially optimal actions although emotions such as compassion and empathy often do lead to prosocial actions for individuals and groups. For instance, our insensitivity to many global problems such as global warming, and poverty and hunger in poor countries may be caused by a problem of insufficient emotions in these domains (Loewenstein, 2010).

In the final part of Section 1.2, we consider the role of anticipatory emotions in decision making under risk, based on the idea of *risk as feelings* (Loewenstein et al., 2001). In many risky situations, individuals do not behave in an entirely consequentialist manner (i.e., they do not pay sufficient attention to probabilities and outcomes). We consider how emotional states may influence the types of decisions made under risky environments. This gives an alternative, affective, account of decision making under risk that deserves to be taken more seriously by economists of all persuasions.

Visceral influences are often activated by external stimuli, which we refer to as *cues*. Traditional habit formation models do not consider the role of cues (Becker and Murphy, 1988). In Section 1.3, we consider the role of stochastic cues in models of habit formation (Laibson, 2001; Bernheim and Rangel, 2004). The nature of the solution under the cues and the no-cues models is very similar. If the stock of habits exceeds a threshold, then the individual optimally engages in the harmful activity, otherwise not. In traditional habit formation models, the main upshot of this feature is that once rationally addicted, individuals stay addicted. However, in the cues model, the harmful activity is dictated by the observation of a cue. In order to wean themselves off addiction, individuals may then engage in active cue-management, while self-interested firms may try to counter this by making consumption-inducing cues more salient. Models of addiction are also considered in subsequent Sections 1.6 and 1.7, and in applications of present-biased preferences in Volume 3 of the book that readers interested in a fuller treatment should consult.

We often feel anxious about an uncertain future. Will my pension contributions be sufficient for my retired life? Will early retirement turn out to be a good decision? Should I buy or sell stocks in the current economic environment? Anticipation of a stressful event can create anxiety that in some cases is worse than the event itself, e.g., an impending visit to a dentist. Such feelings of anxiety are caused by *anticipation* of future events, and they are *aversive*. Future events need not, however, always be unpleasant. We might savor a pleasurable experience such as waiting for a dessert at the end of a meal. Or, we might be excited about a forthcoming pleasurable vacation.

For both pleasant and unpleasant events, individuals often exhibit a negative discount rate. This typically takes the form of postponing a pleasant experience (dessert at the end of a meal) and preponing an unpleasant one (taking out an aching and doomed tooth sooner rather than later). This evidence is contrary to the predictions of the discounted utility model, which does not take account of anticipal utility and anticipal disutility from future events. Section 1.4 shows how such anticipal feelings can be incorporated into a formal model (Loewenstein, 1987).

It is natural to suppose that anxiety about future events may be associated with uncertainty about the future. In Section 1.5, we consider a utility representation of preferences under anxiety (Caplin and Leahy, 2001). We use this preference representation to derive equilibrium prices of assets whose returns are ex-ante random. The randomness of returns creates feelings of anxiety. When investors exhibit anxiety, risky stocks are priced even higher relative to the case of no-anxiety. This provides one possible explanation for the *equity premium puzzle* that does not rely on loss-aversion. Furthermore, the price of riskless assets in the presence of anxiety is relatively higher because they provide a "peace of mind function" for the investor that stocks with fluctuating returns cannot.

In the absence of any random shocks, the typical assumption in economics is that individuals are fully aware of their future tastes. When the predictions of future tastes differ from their actual realization, despite no inherent randomness in the model, then the individual is said to make a *projection bias*. Section 1.6 considers issues of projection bias (Loewenstein et al., 2003). For instance, among patients who await kidney transplants, those who are successful (unsuccessful) in getting a transplant overestimate (underestimate) their future quality of life (Smith et al., 2008). A distinguishing feature of projection bias is that individuals use their current state disproportionately to predict their future states. Hungry shoppers choose far more groceries for future consumption, relative to satiated shoppers, even when they have the same future needs (Read and van Leeuwen, 1998).

Individuals who have projection bias make *time inconsistent choices*, without being aware of it. Under the influence of projection bias, in a *hot state*, individuals might, for instance,

(i) end up buying goods that they regret later, and (ii) end up marrying/divorcing without sufficient deliberation. In response to these concerns, (i) consumer regulation provides a 21-day cooling-off period during which goods can be returned, provided they are in a satisfactory state, and (ii) the law typically requires a cooling-off period before which applications for marriage and divorce cannot be filed. Projection bias also provides an alternative explanation for why individuals may get addicted. First, they might underestimate the (negative) effect of current consumption on future utility. Second, they might under-appreciate the formation of habit, i.e., addiction to the harmful product. We give two formal applications of projection bias; a two-period model of habit formation, and the purchase of consumer durables.

What does it mean to say that one alternative is more tempting relative to another? Can one provide an axiomatization of preferences that incorporates some plausible notion of *temptation*? Consider a two-period model. In the first period, the individual chooses between a set of *menus*. In the second period, the individual chooses an element from the menu that was chosen in the first period. Preferences exhibit *temptation* if the individual prefers to exclude certain menus from first period choice. By contrast, under the typical preferences specified in neoclassical economics, more options never hurt. If exclusion of the temptation is not possible, then the individual may either be able to exercise self-control in the second period or succumb to the temptation. We give a utility representation of temptation preferences in Section 1.7 (Gul and Pesendorfer, 2001; Dekel et al., 2001). We also show that temptation preferences can also arise in a model of competing dual selves, when there is some uncertainty about the eventual winner in a contest between them (Bénabou and Pycia, 2002).

When individuals have self-control problems, such as those arising from temptations, the standard prescription in a range of models is to commit to eliminate options that lead to such temptations. Section 1.8 considers an important trade-off associated with the removal of temptations in a model of multiple selves (Amador et al., 2006). Eliminating a subset of the options has the benefit of reducing/eliminating temptations, but at the cost of reduced flexibility, especially when new information is likely to arrive in the future. For instance, in the context of intertemporal choice, a reduction in temptations might improve the savings rate of an individual. However, if the future marginal utility turns out to be unexpectedly low, then the improvement in savings might not have been as worthwhile. In the context of this framework, we derive the justification for a minimum savings rule when current selves have asymmetric information about the subsequent selves. Within the two type case, we also derive conditions under which the first best can be implemented.

Modern economics typically relies on the notion of *decision utility*—the utility experienced at the time of the decision. An older tradition in economics emphasizes *experienced utility*—the hedonic experience associated with an outcome (Bentham, 1798). The modern approach is based on checking if preferences are consistent with the axioms of rational choice—this is encapsulated in the revealed preference approach. However, in many cases, the well-being of individuals is influenced by outcomes that they cannot directly choose. Examples include inflation, unemployment, income inequality, environmental degradation, crime, health shocks, accidents, and exogenous income shocks. In these cases, revealed preference arguments cannot be used to infer the well-being of individuals. If one is willing to take experienced utility seriously, then it is hard to justify exclusive reliance on the revealed preference approach in economics.

Section 1.9 considers an alternative approach to well-being, based on *experienced utility*. In this approach, individuals are asked directly to report their well-being, life satisfaction, and health status. Clearly, self-reported survey questions that report experienced utility are subjected to biases, such as *duration neglect*, and *peak-end evaluation* (Kahneman et al., 1997). However, subjective measures of well-being are consistent with the actual choices for the vast majority of subjects and these measures are the best predictors of choices (Benjamin et al., 2012). Such subjective measures successfully predict a range of phenomena such as job quits, probability of suicides, productivity, and the probability of a divorce. Despite the drawbacks of self-reported measures of well-being, it may still be preferable to use them rather than have experts guess the well-being of individuals. Furthermore, survey questions may catch people in a deliberative mood rather than an emotional state, hence, self-reported measures may have normative value (Benjamin et al., 2014).

Evidence from many countries showed that at any point in time, richer individuals are happier. However, over time, while GDP growth takes place, mean self-reported happiness stays almost unchanged. This has come to be known as the *Easterlin paradox* (Easterlin, 1974). The main explanation offered for the paradox is that individuals adapt to the higher level of income, and simply raise their aspiration levels. In this view, self-reported happiness is a measure of the difference between actual incomes and aspiration incomes (Easterlin 1974, 1995).

This evidence has been contested in recent years in a series of papers, which argue that mean happiness is increasing in the levels of income over time, hence, there is no Easterlin paradox (Deaton, 2008; Stevenson and Wolfers, 2008, 2013). The main reasons for the difference in conclusions is newer datasets (Gallup World Poll rather than the World Values Survey, which formed the basis of earlier results) that provide data on a more inclusive set of poorer countries, and use a more representative sample. Easterlin has responded with the argument that while the paradox might not hold in the short run, it does hold in the long run (Easterlin et al., 2010). We end Section 1.9 with a brief note on the correlates of self-reported well-being, such as inflation, unemployment, health, income inequality, and democracy.

1.2 Visceral influences and the rationality of emotions

1.2.1 *Visceral influences*

One manifestation of emotions that has an important influence on human decision making is intense physiological states that are lumped under the term *visceral factors/influences*. Examples include hunger, thirst, moods, physical pain, and craving for a drug. So, for instance, consider the visceral factor of sleep deprivation in its extreme form. Individuals do not make a rational decision to fall asleep behind the wheel of their car, but some people do go off to sleep, with disastrous consequences. Overeating, compulsive shopping, and drug addiction are other examples where strong visceral influences can lead to suboptimal behavior.

Loewenstein (1996) has drawn attention to the role of visceral influences in influencing choices. Two important features of visceral influences are the following.

1. *Current visceral factors can have a "disproportionate" influence on current behavior*: When visceral influences are weak, individuals can control them better. However, when they are "intense," the individual gives almost exclusive attention to these influences at the expense of other objectives. Under extreme visceral influences, the individual may behave as if the discount factor were zero. Hence, such factors might drive a wedge between the optimum emotions-free decisions of an individual and actual behavior.

   Under the influence of visceral factors, individuals can often be aware of the wedge between their actions and best interests. However, they nevertheless persist in taking actions that are contrary to their self-interest. For instance, in a visceral state of anger, an individual, in the heat of the moment, could say something that is deeply regretted later, and lead to a poor outcome. Indeed, some individuals may be aware of their propensity to engage in such behavior.

An extreme example of visceral influences is the behavior of individuals who have various *phobias* that they fully know are non-threatening but are still unable to use rational judgment to counter them. Police and military interrogators use extreme visceral influences such as pain, hunger, or sleep deprivation to elicit confessions. Or, as a strike deadline approaches, labor negotiations often go "round the clock," evoking the extreme visceral influence of sleep deprivation that is more likely to elicit concessions. Both sides, perhaps due to mutual awareness of a potential bargaining impasse, agree to this bargaining structure.

In conclusion, unlike the assumptions of neoclassical economic theory, on many occasions individuals do not operate at the *cool end* of the spectrum of human emotions. Despite a degree of self-awareness of the problem, they can at times operate at the *hot end* of the spectrum, with detrimental consequences to their self-interest.

2. *Individuals typically underestimate the importance of visceral factors in determining their past, current, and future behavior*: Loewenstein (1996) reports the following empirical result. Prior to the onset of labor, pregnant women were asked to make a non-binding decision on whether they will require an anaesthetic during labor. A majority were optimistic that they would not need an anaesthetic. However, acute pain is often an extreme visceral influence. Once labor set in, a high proportion of the women reversed their earlier decision. Hence, individuals can underestimate the effect of visceral influences on future behavior.

The "endowment effect" can also be thought of as evoking the visceral factor of attachment. Individuals underpredict future endowment effects. Individuals also often forget or underreport the visceral influence of pain in the past; memories of pain seem qualitatively different from other sorts of memories.

These concerns are contrary to the behavior of individuals in models where they *rationally decide* to be addicts, in full knowledge of all future consequences, as in Becker and Murphy (1988). By contrast, visceral influences explain drug addiction by a serious error of judgment on the part of individuals, who underestimate the pain of withdrawal and craving for the drug, caused by the visceral activity of addiction.

Visceral factors are not *tastes* or *preferences*, as understood in conventional economic theory. Visceral influences arise from external stimulation or deprivation, hence, they may be more volatile than tastes. As Loewenstein (1996, p. 273) puts it: "In contrast, changes in preferences are caused by slow experience and reflection, are typically not anticipated, and do not imply a permanent change in behavior." Furthermore, Loewenstein cites evidence to show that tastes and visceral factors draw on different neurophysiological mechanisms. Visceral factors are likely to have a common neurophysiological mechanism. Evidence for this assertion comes from the observation that behavior contrary to one's self-interest, arising from a range of visceral influences, can be mitigated by using a single drug, Fluoxetine.

The origin of visceral factors are most likely evolutionary. For instance, the fitness of animals who respond to hunger by focusing exclusively on the search for food, might have been higher. However, such behavior could also be a double edged sword. For instance, moderate fear may lead to actions that are conducive for survival, but extreme fear can petrify an individual and hinder rational action.

Under the influence of visceral factors, individuals focus more on their needs and less on others. Interrogators have long known that under appropriate visceral influences, e.g., extreme torture, otherwise sincere individuals are likely to betray collaborators, friends, and family.

1.2.2 *Rationality and emotions*

Is it rational to have emotions? One possibility is that our judgment may be clouded in the presence of emotions, hence, we may make suboptimal decisions (Baumeister et al., 1994; Baumeister et al., 2007; Frijda and Mesquita, 1994). For instance, one may make a reckless purchase in a hot state of mind and regret it later, once the initial emotion subsides. The presence of cooling-off periods, enshrined in law in many countries, appears to be a regulatory response to this possibility.

On the other hand, using data from neurobiological studies, Damasio (1994) argues that emotions aid us in taking better decisions. For supporting findings and the evidence, see Bechara et al. (1994, 1996, 1997, 1999) and Damasio (1996). Using data from individuals who had suffered damage to the emotional regions of their brains, e.g., damage to the ventromedial prefrontal region,[1] Damasio draws several conclusions from the behavior of individuals who suffer such kind of brain damage; we summarize some of these conclusions, below.

1. They are less likely to conform to social norms, which might lead them to suffer social sanctions.
2. They may procrastinate more in social situations because they are less likely to suffer from the guilt and embarrassment of letting others down.
3. They may do worse in decision tasks. For instance, in one experiment, individuals had to choose from four possible decks of cards, A, B, C, and D. Decks A and B contained high payments and occasional large losses, so that the expected temporal payoffs were negative. Decks C and D contained low payments but positive expected temporal payoffs. Observing the data over time, it was possible to learn that it is a dominated strategy to choose decks A and B. Yet, those with damage to the emotional regions of the brain continued to choose decks A and B, while those who did not suffer from the damage learned to pick decks C and D. A possible interpretation of these findings is that individuals with brain damage did know that decks A and B are associated with occasional large losses, but they lack a fear response that would have led to the avoidance of decks A and B. Indeed, over time, such individuals could go bankrupt. Similar results are expected from psychopathic criminals, who are insensitive to the future consequences of their actions.

   These results, however, cut both ways. For instance, one could design an experiment such that, while decks A and B have large occasional losses, the expected temporal value of choosing these decks is higher as compared to choosing decks C and D. In this case, those with a damaged ventromedial prefrontal region may earn a higher long-run return.

   Smith and Dickhaut (2005) find that they can make better predictions of prices in English and Dutch auctions when they take account of the heart rates of participants, just prior to making choices. An interesting finding is that emotions play a role in price determination in Dutch auctions but not in English auctions. Hence, there might be important

---

[1] This region of the brain is found to be active when individuals make choices; see Glimcher et al. (2009). Individuals with damage to the ventromedial prefrontal region otherwise appear to be normal in respect of memory, intellegence, and language comprehension.

complementarities between emotions and the determination of economic outcomes under some institutions, but not others.

When choices are cognitively challenging, individuals may often make choices based on physiological signals, or emotional states, associated with outcomes. This is also sometimes known as the *somatic markers* hypothesis. For instance, a coiled object on the side of the street may initiate immediate fear, and the fight-or-flight response, bypassing the cognitive system. Avoidance of decks A and B after a period of learning may also be based on the fear of losing a large amount, while patients with ventromedial prefrontal damage exhibit no such fear.

The debate on the rationality of emotions, despite the influential work of Damasio and his colleagues, is not a settled one. For instance, anger may be a suitable emotion to get a larger share of the cake when aggression is required to determine the division of the cake. However, more irascible individuals may be shunned by others in subsequent divisions of the cake and may lose out in the long run. The economic models that we consider in subsequent sections allow for a more explicit consideration of these opposing forces.

Are emotional states induced voluntarily or involuntarily? The somatic markers hypothesis is based on the assumption that emotional states are induced involuntarily. Sinaceur and Tiedens (2006) provide evidence to show that individuals may also make use of emotional states in a strategic manner to gain advantage in bargaining situations. Meshulam et al. (2012) provide evidence that suggests many individuals can induce emotional states at will. In their experiments, players play a modified dictator game in which they play the role of recipients who receive low, medium, and high offers. Their emotional response, in terms of skin conductance response (SCR) and heart rates, is measured, while they receive the different offers. These measurements can determine if their emotional state is angry, calm, or happy.

Subjects are given incentives to exhibit various emotional states, depending on the offers received. For instance, when they receive a low offer, they are given a bonus if their emotional response is angry. Likewise they are given a bonus to demonstrate a happy state in the case of a high offer. In addition, at the end of the experiment, subjects fill in a questionnaire in which they are given two vignettes in which an individual suffers harm from another's negligence. Subjects were then asked to rate their punitiveness towards the negligent individual on a 1–7 scale. This is used to classify individuals into those who are naturally angry, calm, and happy.

Figure 1.1 shows the main results. More angry subjects (as measured by scores on the 1–7 response to the two vignettes) are also angrier when they receive low offers (as measured by SCR and the heart rate). Since individuals are responding to the incentive effect of bonuses, if they demonstrate the required emotional state, the authors conclude that emotions are voluntary and rational. There is an asymmetry between angry and happy individuals; the latter are not able to fully muster the necessary emotions to take advantage of the bonus on offer. This finding could be a useful candidate for further exploration; the authors speculate that prospect theory may be a possible explanation.

Formal theoretical models of the rationality of emotions are in their infancy. Winter et al. (2014) propose that players choose their strategies and their mental states simultaneously. They define the notion of a *mental equilibrium* in which roughly, (i) the chosen strategies of the players are a Nash equilibrium for a given mental state, and (ii) the mental state of each player is a best response to the mental states of other players. The epistemic foundations of a Nash equilibrium show just how strong the underlying conditions are and the outcomes of many games are not consistent with equilibrium concepts (see Volume 4). The cognitive requirements

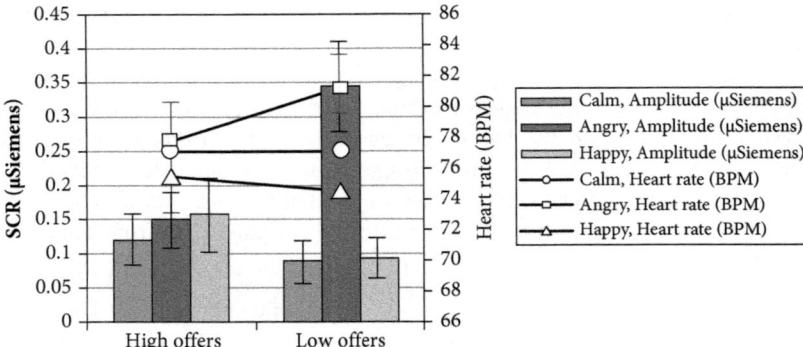

Figure 1.1 Skin conductance response (SCR) amplitude and heart rate (HR), 0–12 s after offer presentation onset. Bars represent mean amplitude of SCR for high and low offers of participants in each condition. Lines represent mean HR during the presentation of high and low offers. Error bars: plus/minus SEM.

Source: "Rational emotions," Meir Meshulam, Eyal Winter, Gershon Ben-Shakhar, and Itzhak Aharon, *Social Neuroscience*, 7(1), (2012). Reprinted by permission of Taylor & Francis Ltd.

for a mental equilibrium are likely to be even stronger. Ultimately, the usefulness of this line of research, particularly for experimental results, is an open question. Perhaps the framework of a mental equilibrium may have greater usefulness in understanding the development of emotions in certain contexts over a longer, evolutionary, time period. Winter (2014) makes a case for the rationality of emotions that follows in large part from the notion of a mental equilibrium. In the mental equilibrium framework, being angry is necessarily a rational response that is codified as a part of the equilibrium. For an alternative approach that is able to distinguish between anger caused by the intentionality (or lack of it) of the behavior of others using a psychological game theory approach, see the interesting paper by Battigalli et al. (2015).

Loewenstein (2010) proposes that many global problems may be caused by the problem of insufficient emotion. For instance, we may not feel sufficiently emotionally distressed about global warming, or hunger, poverty, and disease in the poorer countries, hence, we react inadequately. Even during wars and genocides, humans appear to feel inadequate emotions for the victims who are often dehumanized through propaganda that paints them as outsiders or dangerous to one's own world view. Statistics of lives lost through wars and genocides often move us insufficiently. Insufficient emotions could be an evolutionary adaptation. For instance, they prevent us from being immobilized by the large number of emotionally disturbing events around us. Perhaps for this reason, we are emotionally more sensitive to next of kin or close members of our own social group, a phenomenon known as *parochial altruism*.

Vividness of events plays an important role in our emotional arousal. For instance, we are less moved by statistics of accidents, poverty, child labor, and disease, but more moved by graphic stories of individuals who have suffered, particularly women and children. Good storytellers often weave personal, individual narratives within complex social situations, for greater effect. For similar reasons, simple cost–benefit analyses, say, associated with global warming, or the cost of saving a life in a poor country, can sometimes be an inadequate impetus for many of us to be proactive.

There is a contrast between the work of economists and psychologists in terms of the role played by emotions in guiding human behavior. Economists have traditionally incorporated *anticipated emotions*, such as regret and disappointment (see Volume 1 of the book). These are emotions that are not experienced at the time of making decisions, but are experienced in the future when the outcomes of current decisions materialize. By contrast, psychologists have stressed the role of *anticipatory emotions*. These are emotions such as fear, dread, and anxiety that are experienced at the time of decision making. Loewenstein (2000) and Loewenstein et al. (2001) make a compelling case for incorporating anticipatory emotions into economics. While the ideas apply quite generally, the thrust of our discussion below is to consider the effects on decisions under risk.

We now outline some of the main ideas from the seminal work of Loewenstein et al. (2001). Each of the assertions below are backed by good evidence; the interested reader should consult Loewenstein et al. (2001) for an exhaustive list of about 200 references that we omit.

Classical decision theories such as expected utility, rank dependent utility, and prospect theory are *consequentialist* in the sense that decision makers are assumed to be solely influenced by the probabilities and outcomes. In a series of papers, Paul Slovic and co-authors (see, e.g., Slovic et al., 2002) have highlighted anticipatory emotions such as dread and risk of the unknown in determining the outcomes of decisions under risk. By contrast, consequentialist factors such as probabilities and outcomes play little role in the decisions. For instance, some individuals may experience dread and anxiety at the mere thought of air travel, while being perfectly comfortable with travel by car. However, the probability of car accidents, per mile traveled, is much higher. Phobias are an extreme form of these kinds of anxieties. High-risk activities, even if associated with a high positive expected value, may be associated with negative emotions, hence, they may be avoided, which is consistent with the somatic markers hypothesis.

Empirical evidence suggests that jurors often make decisions based on their gut feelings. The difficulty in making decisions can evoke negative emotions even when all possible consequences are positive. People in good moods often make optimistic choices, while people in bad moods make pessimistic choices. When people are exposed to "sad" newspaper articles, their estimates of risk for a range of potential causes of death are higher, relative to people who read "happy" newspaper articles. Under induced anxiety, people choose low risk and low reward options.

The emotional and cognitive pathways in the brain are different, hence, it is not surprising that decisions made in the presence of emotional factors are different from the decisions made under purely cognitive considerations. Loewenstein et al. (2001) highlight the transmission channels behind these differences as well as the differences in outcomes under the two. Their approach to decision making under risk, which they term as *risk as feelings theory*, is a mixture of consequentialist and non-consequentialist reasoning. The outcomes under this theory can differ substantially from the predictions of standard decision theory in economics, particularly when anticipatory emotional reactions are strong, relative to the cognitive evaluations.

A schematic outline of the risk as feelings thesis is shown in Figure 1.2. Following the bottom row of arrows from left to right in the figure, behavior under risk can manifest independently of the associated probabilities and outcomes. Indeed, the top two channels in the figure show that behavior can arise under a combination of outcomes and emotions (ignoring probabilities) or probabilities and emotions (ignoring outcomes). Each of these channels makes a prediction that cannot be made under traditional models of risk in economics.

The ability of individuals to form vivid images associated with risky outcomes, an ability that differs among individuals, can affect risky choices. For instance, individuals could underinsure themselves from risks that cannot be vividly imagined. Vividness may be enhanced by knowing someone who has suffered from the negative consequences of a risky situation. Thus, as noted above, individuals are less affected by statistics associated with risk and more affected by personal

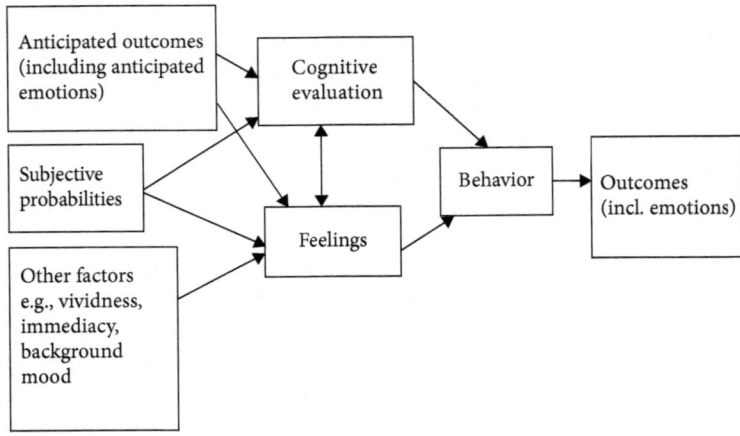

Figure 1.2 Schematic description of the "risk as feelings" thesis.

Source: Copyright © 2001 by the American Psychological Association. Reproduced with permission. "Risk as feelings." Loewenstein, George F., Weber, Eike U., Hsee, Christopher K., and Welch, Ned. *Psychological Bulletin* 127(2), Mar. 2001, 267–86. The use of APA information does not imply endorsement by APA.

human stories of suffering that evoke greater emotion. However, inducing too much anxiety by, say, public information, may lead to avoidance of the relevant public information, forgoing the necessary risk mitigation activities, by some individuals. For instance, public information on the importance of self-examination to allow for early detection of breast cancer has led many women to avoid the necessary self-examination, on account of the presence of anticipatory anxiety. Many empirical studies show that women are more risk averse than men. Women are also known to engage in better and more vivid imagery as compared to men. Perhaps women can feel more negative emotions associated with losses, hence, they appear to be relatively more risk averse.

Decision makers are often not very sensitive to variations in probabilities within a broad set of values. Hence, contrary to consequentialist models of risk, they typically do not react as much to changes in probability from, say, 1 in 100,000, to 1 in 1,000,000. In a large number of experiments in psychology, the probability of receiving an impending shock had little effect on anticipatory anxiety. For vivid outcomes, say, a brief and painful electric shock, the sensitivity to probabilities is low. By contrast, in the presence of pallid outcomes (i.e., low emotions and vividness), say, losing $20, the degree of sensitivity to probabilities is relatively higher. These sorts of considerations might explain why the *probability weighting function* (see Volume 1 of the book) is relatively flat for mid-range probabilities and why the degree of flatness may depend on anticipatory anxiety.

One explanation for the high take-up rates of expensive warranties is that people do not pay adequate attention to the probability of breakdowns. They appear to think immediately of the "peace of mind" associated with the warranty, which is an anticipatory emotion. Indeed, salesmen rarely highlight probabilities of breakdown, and emphasize the convenience and peace of mind aspects of owning the warranty. Lottery sellers similarly appeal to anticipatory emotions when they use slogans such as "buy a dream" and many people ignore the odds of winning the lottery. We did not consider any of these issues in Volume 1, and neither has the economics profession given adequate attention to this line of research; clearly, it deserves more attention and respect.

1.3 Cue-conditioned behavior and habit formation

Visceral influences are typically activated by external stimuli or *cues* that heighten certain desires. The desire for consumption, in particular, can be enhanced by a number of cues; we will refer to this as *cue-conditioned consumption*. For instance, the smell of freshly made cookies might create a craving for them. Cue-conditioned consumption, like visceral influences, is not specific to humans. In a famous experiment, conducted more than a century ago, Pavlov (1904) found that if bells are rung at the same time as food is given to a dog, after some period of conditioning, the ringing of bells alone is sufficient to produce salivation in the dog.

Cues can be individual-specific, for instance, the desire for a particular food might be conditioned on the cue being a rainy day. But some cues apply to most of us, perhaps because these have been acquired through a common evolutionary history. For instance, the desire for immediate consumption is heightened by the smell and sight of food. This *current-bias* for consumption does not arise through time discounting (e.g., hyperbolic discounting) but through the proximity of a cue that acts as an external stimulus.

Furthermore, cues often increase the marginal utility from consumption. So, for instance, the smell of baking cookies whets the appetite for them. Cues might also trigger physiological compensatory mechanisms in the body. So, for instance, cues might offset the harmful effects of a drug. For that reason, addicts often need increasingly larger amounts of a drug to get the same "kick."

Laibson (2001) formalizes the effect of cues on habit forming behavior. This model is also useful to illustrate the rational addiction model of Becker and Murphy (1988, 1993). Laibson describes the central premise of his theory as follows. "The cues model in the current paper captures these patterns by assuming that habit formation effects are turned on and off by the presence of cues (i.e. sensory inputs) that have been associated with past consumption of habit-forming goods." Unlike the second premise of the visceral influences model in Section 1.2.1, it is assumed here (as also in Becker and Murphy, 1988) that individuals make a rational decision to be addicted to, or abstain from, a particular habit forming activity. Thus, the cues model can be thought of as one formalization of the first premise of the visceral influences model in Section 1.2.1, i.e., current visceral factors can have a disproportionate influence on current behavior.

Suppose that time is discrete, so $t = 0, 1, 2, \ldots$ The individual lives infinitely and uses exponential discounting. In each period, the individual chooses one of two possible activities. A *habit-forming activity*, or activity 1, that is potentially habit forming, and a *secondary activity*, or activity 0, that is not habit forming; the activity set is denoted by $a = \{0, 1\}$.

Before choosing the activity, the individual observes a *cue* that has no economic significance; i.e., the cue is neutral. Ex-ante, the cue is random and takes on one of two discrete values, Red (R) or Green (G), indexed by j. The probability distribution of the cues is given by:

$$\Pr(R) = \mu^R \geq 0, \ \Pr(G) = \mu^G \geq 0, \text{ and } \mu^G + \mu^R = 1. \tag{1.1}$$

In any period t, the individual observes the cue and then makes a choice from the set a. Denote the cue-conditioned choice by $a_t^j = \{0, 1\}$ when the individual observes the cue $j = R, G$. So, for instance, the pair of choices $\left(a_t^R = 1, a_t^G = 0\right)$ means that in period t, the individual undertakes the habit-forming activity only when the cue is R. We wish to determine the optimal temporal sequence of actions $\left(a_0^R, a_0^G\right), \left(a_1^R, a_1^G\right), \left(a_2^R, a_2^G\right), \ldots$

The utility function is influenced by two *stock variables*, or *compensatory processes*, each activated in any given period by the realization of the cue. Denote these compensatory processes in period t by x_t^R, x_t^G; these variables are of the nature of stocks. The Red cue only activates the x_t^R process, while the green cue only activates the x_t^G process. An inactivated process, in any period, experiences no change in value. In particular, the evolution of the two processes is given by the following two equations:

$$\begin{cases} x_{t+1}^R = \theta x_t^R + (1-\theta)\, a_t^R;\ x_{t+1}^G = x_t^G, & \text{if time } t \text{ cue is } j = R \\ x_{t+1}^G = \theta x_t^G + (1-\theta)\, a_t^G;\ x_{t+1}^R = x_t^R, & \text{if time } t \text{ cue is } j = G \end{cases}, \quad 0 < \theta < 1. \qquad (1.2)$$

Hence, the activated process at time $t+1$ is a convex combination of the time t stock and the decision. The initial values of the stock variables are denoted by $x_0^R \in [0,1], x_0^G \in [0,1]$, and are given exogenously. Since $a_t^j = \{0,1\}$, $x_{t+1}^j \in [0,1]$ for all t.

Like the stock variables, the instantaneous utility is also cue-contingent. The utility of the secondary activity, activity 0, is normalized at $\bar{u}$. The stochastic cues trigger a change in preferences. The instantaneous utility in period t, following the two cues is given by

$$U_t(a_t^j, x_t^j) = u\left(a_t^j - \gamma x_t^j\right) + \left(1 - a_t^j\right)\bar{u};\ j = R, G,\ 0 < \gamma < 1. \qquad (1.3)$$

Since $a_t^j = \{0,1\}$, the utility from the secondary activity, $\bar{u}$, kicks in only when the individual chooses the secondary activity, i.e., $a_t^j = 0$. The function $u\left(a_t^j - \gamma x_t^j\right)$ is twice continuously differentiable and it reflects the instantaneous utility from the current decision, a_t^j, and from the stock of the habit-forming activity, x_t^j. It is increasing, $u' > 0$, and strictly concave, $u'' < 0$.

To understand the nature of instantaneous utility at time t, and for $j = R, G$, suppose that the habit-forming activity is drug addiction.

1. The decision to consume drugs in the current period, $a_t^j = 1$, increases current utility, but at an opportunity cost of $\bar{u}$. If the individual has been consuming high levels of drugs in the past, then the stock variable x_t^j is high. Thus, current utility from consuming drugs is low, i.e.,

$$\frac{d}{dx_t^j} u\left(a_t^j - \gamma x_t^j\right) = -\gamma u' < 0. \qquad (1.4)$$

2. Higher drug consumption in the past, reflected in an increase in the stock variable, x_t^j, increases the current marginal utility of consumption, i.e.,

$$\frac{d^2}{dx_t^j da_t^j} u\left(a_t^j - \gamma x_t^j\right) = -\gamma u'' > 0. \qquad (1.5)$$

These features are standard in habit formation models. The individual chooses the time path of actions $\left(a_0^R, a_0^G\right), \left(a_1^R, a_1^G\right), \left(a_2^R, a_2^G\right), \ldots,$ where $a_t^j \in \{0,1\}$, to maximize present discounted value of expected utility,

$$\sum_{t=0}^{\infty} \delta^t \left[\mu^R \left[u\left(a_t^R - \gamma x_t^R \right) + \left(1 - a_t^R \right) \overline{u} \right] + \mu^G \left[u\left(a_t^G - \gamma x_t^G \right) + \left(1 - a_t^G \right) \overline{u} \right] \right],$$

subject to the evolution of the stock variables in (1.2); $\delta \in (0,1]$ is the discount factor.

An early discussion of habit formation can be found in Duesenberry (1949) and a formalization is given in Pollack (1970). Becker and Murphy (1988) provided an additional impetus to this class of models. A discrete time version of the Becker–Murphy model can be recovered from the cues model in which the cue takes only one possible value, i.e., one of μ^R, μ^G is zero. This *no-cues model*, and its solution, also helps gain insights into the solution to the cues model. For this reason, we turn to the no-cues model, next.

1.3.1 *Solution to the no-cues model*

Suppose that the cue takes only one possible value. Thus, we can omit the superscript $j = R, G$ that we used to distinguish between different values of the cues. The problem for an individual in the no-cues model is to choose the time path of cue-independent actions $(a_1, a_2, \ldots)$, where $a_i \in \{0,1\}$, in order to maximize

$$\sum_{t=0}^{\infty} \delta^t \left[u\left(a_t - \gamma x_t \right) + \left(1 - a_t \right) \overline{u} \right], \tag{1.6}$$

subject to the constraint

$$x_{t+1} = \theta x_t + (1 - \theta) a_t.$$

This is a standard problem in dynamic programming. The Bellman equation is written as

$$V(x \mid \delta) = \underset{a \in \{0,1\}}{Max} \left[u\left(a - \gamma x \right) + \left(1 - a \right) \overline{u} + \delta V\left(\theta x + \left(1 - \theta \right) a \right) \mid \delta \right]. \tag{1.7}$$

Let us motivate the solution through the following intuition. As the stock of habits increases, it has two opposing effects. (i) From (1.4), it reduces current and future utility. (ii) From (1.5), the marginal utility from undertaking the habit-forming activity increases. The first effect reduces the incentive to undertake the habit-forming activity, and the second effect increases it. It follows intuitively that if the stock of habits is large enough, say, greater than some threshold value $\tilde{x}$, the second effect dominates, so it is optimal to choose the habit-forming activity $a = 1$. Otherwise, the secondary activity is chosen, $a = 0$. We summarize this result in Proposition 1.1, below. The proof is not difficult but it is lengthy; an exercise asks for a proof of the problem and gives hints to solve it.

Proposition 1.1 *(Laibson; 2001): In the no-cues problem, there exists some threshold value of the stock variable, $\tilde{x}$, such that the optimal decision rule of the individual is*

$$a = \begin{cases} 1 & \text{if } x > \tilde{x} \\ 0 & \text{if } x < \tilde{x} \end{cases}.$$

When $x = \tilde{x}$, some sort of tie breaking rule can be used. Several comparative static results can be derived. The threshold value, $\tilde{x}$, is increasing in $\overline{u}$ and δ. An increase in the habit-forming activity increases the future stock of habits, hence, it reduces future utility. An increase in δ makes this reduction of future utility more salient. Hence, the threshold $\tilde{x}$ must be larger for the habit-forming activity to be undertaken. A higher value of $\bar{u}$ increases the relative utility of the secondary activity, hence, the marginal utility of the habit-forming activity must be correspondingly higher. From (1.5) this occurs if the stock of habits is higher, hence, we need a higher threshold, $\tilde{x}$.

Example 1.1 *(The dynamic programming solution in a two-period model): Given the importance of the no-cues model for forming intuition about the solution of the cues model, consider a two-period example. Using (1.6), the individual wishes to maximize the intertemporal utility* $U_1(a_1,x_1) + \delta U_2(a_2,x_2)$, *or*

$$[u(a_1 - \gamma x_1) + (1 - a_1)\bar{u}] + \delta[u(a_2 - \gamma x_2) + (1 - a_2)\bar{u}] \tag{1.8}$$

subject to the constraint

$$x_2 = \theta x_1 + (1 - \theta)a_1, \text{ and } x_1 \text{ given.} \tag{1.9}$$

The problem of the decision maker is to choose $a_1 \in \{0,1\}$ *and* $a_2 \in \{0,1\}$. *Let the utility function take the CARA form, so* $u(c) = \frac{-b}{\alpha}e^{-\alpha c}$, $\alpha, b > 0$; *since we are not fundamentally interested in the degree of curvature of the utility function, suppose* $\alpha = 1$. *Check that* $u' > 0$ *and* $u'' < 0$ *are satisfied. For pedagogical simplicity, let* $\delta = 1$ *so the individual does not discount future utility. Denote the optimal value of the action in any period by* a_t^*, $t = 1,2$. *In the second period, the decision maker chooses* a_2, *given* x_2. *It is optimal to choose* $a_2^* = 1$ *if*

$$-be^{-(1-\gamma x_2)} > -be^{\gamma x_2} + \bar{u}$$

or

$$x_2 > \tilde{x} = \frac{1}{\gamma}\ln\left(\frac{\bar{u}/b}{1 - e^{-1}}\right). \tag{1.10}$$

If the inequality in (1.10) is reversed, then $a_2^* = 0$. *The threshold value* $\tilde{x}$ *is increasing in the outside option,* $\bar{u}$, *as claimed earlier. Suppose that the parameter values are*

$$\gamma = 0.7, \bar{u} = 1, b = 1.25, \text{ and } \theta = 0.5. \tag{1.11}$$

Then (to three decimal places) $\tilde{x} = 0.423$, *which gives the decision rule*

$$a_2^* = \begin{cases} 1 & \text{if } x_2 > 0.423 \\ 0 & \text{if } x_2 < 0.423 \end{cases}. \tag{1.12}$$

The second period utility is $U_2(a_2^*, x_2) = -be^{-(a_2^* - \gamma x_2)} + (1 - a_2^*)\bar{u}$. *Substituting* x_2 *from (1.9) in* U_2 *we get*

$$U_2(a_2^*, \theta x_1 + (1 - \theta)a_1) = \begin{cases} -be^{-(1 - \gamma(\theta x_1 + (1-\theta)a_1))} & \text{if } x_2 > 0.423 \\ -be^{\gamma(\theta x_1 + (1-\theta)a_1)} + \bar{u} & \text{if } x_2 < 0.423 \end{cases}. \tag{1.13}$$

The unconstrained first period optimization problem of the individual is

$$a_1^* \in \arg\max_{a_1 \in \{0,1\}} -be^{-(a_1 - \gamma x_1)} + (1 - a_1)\bar{u} + U_2(a_2^*, \theta x_1 + (1 - \theta)a_1), \tag{1.14}$$

where x_1 is given exogenously, U_2 is given in (1.13), and the parameter values are given in (1.11).

I. The simplest case arises when the initial stock of habits is $x_1 = 0$. Using (1.9),

$$x_2 = \begin{cases} 0.5 & \text{if } a_1 = 1 \\ 0 & \text{if } a_1 = 0 \end{cases}. \tag{1.15}$$

From (1.12) and (1.15), if the individual chooses $a_1 = 1$, then it is optimal to choose $a_2^* = 1$, otherwise if $a_1 = 0$, then the optimal second period choice is $a_2^* = 0$.

If the individual chooses $a_1 = 1$, then, using the parameter values in (1.11), his utility is $-(1.25)e^{-1} - (1.25)e^{-(1-0.7(0.5))} = -1.1124$. If he chooses $a_1 = 0$, his utility is $-(1.25)e^{-0} + 1 - (1.25)e^{0} + 1 = -0.5$. Hence, $a_1^* = 0$. In summary, when $x_1 = 0$ and given the parameters values in (1.11), the optimal dynamic programming solution is $(a_1^*, a_2^*) = (0,0)$.

II. Suppose at the other extreme that the initial stock of habits is high, $x_1 = 1$. In this case, for any of the two choices, $a_1 \in \{0,1\}$, we have $x_2 \geq 0.5$, so, from (1.12), $a_2^* = 1$. Thus, irrespective of the first period choice of the individual, the second period action is identical. By choosing $a_1 = 1$, the decision maker's utility is

$$- (1.25)e^{-(1-0.7)} - (1.25)e^{-(1-0.7)} = -1.852, \tag{1.16}$$

and if $a_1 = 0$, the utility is

$$- (1.25)e^{-(-0.7)} + 1 - (1.25)e^{-(1-0.7(0.5))} = -2.1697. \tag{1.17}$$

Hence, $a_1^* = 1$.

Thus, starting from a high enough stock of habits, the individual is more likely to undertake the action, say, drug consumption, in each period. However, starting from a low stock of habits, the individual is likely to refrain from drug consumption. In the case of smoking, the initial stock of drugs may well be determined by factors such as smoking in the peer group, or exposure to passive smoking at home. Hence, addiction to smoking may become an accident of history rather than a rational choice. ■

1.3.2 Solution to the cues model

The solutions to the model with and without cues are very similar because a given cue only activates one of the two compensatory processes or stock variables. The Bellman equation for the cues model is given by

$$W\left(x^R, x^G\right) = \frac{\mu^R}{1 - \delta\mu^G} V\left(x^R \mid \widetilde{\delta} = \frac{\delta\mu^R}{1 - \delta\mu^G}\right) + \frac{\mu^G}{1 - \delta\mu^R} V\left(x^G \mid \widetilde{\delta} = \frac{\delta\mu^G}{1 - \delta\mu^R}\right),$$

where $V\left(x \mid \widetilde{\delta} = z\right)$ is the solution to the no-cues Bellman equation when the discount factor $\widetilde{\delta}$ takes the value z and μ^R, μ^G are defined in (1.1). The solution in the presence of cues turns out to be a simple generalization of Proposition 1.1. We state this result in Proposition 1.2.

Proposition 1.2 *(Laibson, 2001): In the presence of cues, there exist threshold values $\tilde{x}^R$ and $\tilde{x}^G$ such that the optimal decision of the individual is given by*

$$a^R = \begin{cases} 1 & \text{if } x^R > \tilde{x}^R \\ 0 & \text{if } x^R < \tilde{x}^R \end{cases}.$$

$$a^G = \begin{cases} 1 & \text{if } x^G > \tilde{x}^G \\ 0 & \text{if } x^G < \tilde{x}^G \end{cases}.$$

As in Proposition 1.1, when $x^R = \tilde{x}^R$ or $x^G = \tilde{x}^G$, then some tie breaking rule can be used to determine the optimal action. From Proposition 1.2, if (i) the cue is Red and the stock $x^R > \tilde{x}^R$, then the individual undertakes the habit-forming activity, and (ii) if the cue is Green and the stock $x^G > \tilde{x}^G$, then the individual also undertakes the habit-forming activity. In the complementary cases, the individual undertakes the secondary activity. As in the no-cues model, the threshold values are increasing in δ and $\bar{u}$. Figure 1.3, drawn in (x^R, x^G) space, shows the direction of evolution of the state variables for each possible value of the states.[2] The figure shows the threshold values $\tilde{x}^R, \tilde{x}^G$ that partition the diagram into four quadrants, labeled I–IV; arrows indicate the direction of motion in each quadrant. We also show the four steady states of the model, $(0,0)$, $(1,1)$, $(0,1)$, $(1,0)$, and one trajectory in each quadrant that converges to a steady state. The adjustment processes in (1.2) imply a gradual adjustment path, unless θ is close to its extreme values of zero or one.

The steady states $(0,0)$ and $(1,1)$ can be used to illustrate the dynamics in the no-cues Becker–Murphy model. At the steady state $(0,0)$, the individual always undertakes the secondary activity ($a = 0$, no-addiction) because $x^R < \tilde{x}^R$ and $x^G < \tilde{x}^G$. At the steady state $(1,1)$, the individual always undertakes the habit-forming activity ($a = 1$, addiction), irrespective of the realization of the cue. These are the cue-independent history-dependent states, as shown in Example 1.1.

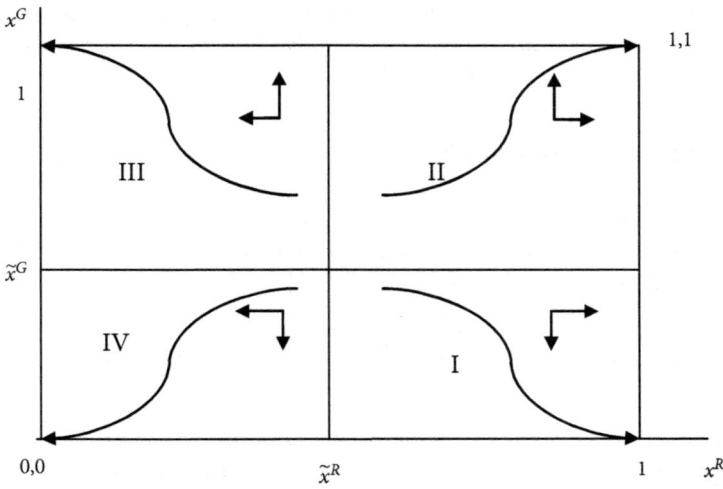

Figure 1.3 Dynamics in the cue-dependent model.

[2] Despite the presence of discrete time, we have shown continuously differentiable phaselines for a clearer diagram.

The other two steady states, $(0,1),(1,0)$, are the cue-dependent states and illustrate the additional steady states that can arise once we allow for the introduction of cues. Consider quadrant I where $x^G < \tilde{x}^G$ and $x^R > \tilde{x}^R$; here the individual chooses the secondary activity ($a = 0$, no-addiction) if the cue is Green, and the habit-forming activity ($a = 1$, addiction) when the cue is Red (see Proposition 1.2). The intuition follows from Example 1.1. If the stock of the habit-forming activity is high enough, then the marginal utility from the habit-forming activity is greater than from the secondary activity, so the habit-forming activity is preferred. At the steady state $(0,1)$ the individual's action is also cue-dependent; choose the secondary activity if the cue is Red and the habit-forming activity when the cue is Green.

The cues, however, are completely neutral and have no economic significance in the model. The theory, therefore, explains how neutral cues can come to form the basis of behavior, provided that the individual believes in them in the sense that they directly enter into the utility function, (1.3). One prediction of the model is that since the stochastic cues trigger a change in preferences (see (1.3)) individuals may check themselves into rehab centers in order to avoid the cravings associated with the cues. For this, one needs to invoke models of multiple selves or planner-doer models, in which the current self is more patient about future choices relative to the future selves.

In the Becker–Murphy model, once addicted, the individual rationally stays addicted forever. However, in the model with cues, the individual's consumption of a harmful good depends on the observed cues. In actual practice, we do observe that people engage in cue-management that sometimes successfully controls consumption of the harmful good. At the same time, firms may wish to sell more by highlighting the salience of certain cues that induce individuals to consume their products, even if they are harmful.

Laibson (2001, pp. 107–8) gives examples of *cue-management behaviors* that include: hiding cigarettes, avoiding parties where alcohol will be served, and using the candy-free checkout lane. However, counter practices by firms include: installing hotel minibars in which snacks and alcohol are visible, even if the minibar has not been opened; generating artificial appetite-arousing food smells in supermarkets; packaging snack food in see-through containers; visually displaying dessert options in restaurants; and placing candy and gum in all checkout lanes to take advantage of impulse buying. Thus, an emotions-augmented account of the Becker–Murphy model gives a better explanation of several important aspects of human behavior.

This is not the only place in the book where we treat issues of addiction. Addiction can be explained through several channels. We explain it using present-biased preferences in Volume 3 of the book (e.g., Gruber and Köszegi, 2001); using projection bias in Section 1.6; and using models of temptation utility in Section 1.7. Other than models of projection bias, individuals do not make mistakes; they simply make rational choices at each instant in time.

The possibility of mistakes in the presence of stochastic cues is considered by Bernheim and Rangel (2004). Stochastic cues are also a feature of the Laibson model, but the possibility of mistakes is not. An important difference in predictions between the Bernheim–Rangel model and the Laibson model is that in the former, individuals who wish to check into rehab centers fully appreciate that they will experience cravings for harmful goods. However, they hope that by checking into the rehab centers they will be able to control their actions in response to the cravings. In the Laibson model, individuals check in because they think they will be able to control their cravings by, say, avoiding the cues that give rise to the cravings.

None of the other models of addiction that we consider in this book, except for projection bias, allow for mistakes. In the presence of a projection bias, individuals might currently under-appreciate the difficulty of kicking a future habit. Indeed, models of present-biased preferences and temptation utility assign no role to the empirically important phenomenon of cues either. Present-biased preferences, in addition, do not differentiate between addictive and non-addictive goods.

1.4 Anticipation and delay under certainty

The idea that anticipation about future outcomes gives rise to current utility, or *anticipal utility*, is not new in economics. It goes back to Bentham (1789) who placed anticipation of consumption on a footing similar to physical consumption in that they potentially impart pleasure and pain. These Benthamite ideas were applied further by Jevons (1905) who gave particular emphasis to the "memory of past events" and "anticipations of future events" in causing pleasure and pain. Anticipations may take the form of *anticipal pleasure* and *anticipal pain*, depending on whether the events cause *savoring* or *dread*. Anticipations may lead us to postpone consumption, as for instance, a dessert at the end of a meal. Indeed, we may exhibit negative discount rates for such cases.

Loewenstein (1987) provides a theoretical framework for anticipal utility under certainty that we now outline. Issues arising from uncertainty are considered in Section 1.5 below. Loewenstein reports the following experiment. Among other options (not reported here) students were asked how much they would pay now to (1) obtain a kiss from a movie star of their choice, and (2) avoid receiving a non-lethal 110 volt shock. These events occurred at various time delays: 0, 3 hours, 24 hours, 3 days, 1 year, and 10 years. The results are shown in Figure 1.4.

The outcomes in Figure 1.4 are at odds with the prediction of the discounted utility (DU) model. Under positive discounting, the DU model predicts that the immediate occurrence of the pleasant event (kiss) would be most valued because the discounted value of the event occurring in the future is lower. However, subjects were willing to pay the most for the kiss to be delayed

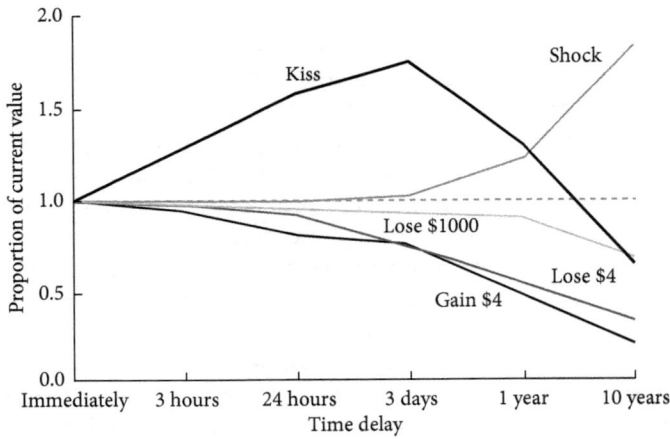

Figure 1.4 Maximum payment as a proportion of current value to obtain/avoid outcomes at selected time delays.

Source: Loewenstein, G. (1987), "Anticipation and the valuation of delayed consumption," *Economic Journal* 97, 666–84. © 1987 Royal Economic Society.

by three days, in line with the prediction of anticipal utility. Anticipal utility for a kiss exhibits a hump shaped pattern, peaking at three days.

Similarly, DU predicts that an unpleasant event (shock) should be delayed because the discounted value of a negative event is lower. In contrast, subjects found the unpleasant event more painful the longer the delay, hence, they were willing to pay more now to avoid shocks the later they were supposed to occur. The analogy is with the common preference of getting an aching tooth out earlier rather than later. Hence, individuals appear to prefer the unpleasant event to occur immediately to avoid the anticipal pain of the event.

We now incorporate Jevon's *anticipal pleasure* and *anticipal pain* in a standard DU model. Consider an individual who, at some initial time t_0, must decide to engage in a single act of consumption of one unit of a good at time $T > 0$. There are two kinds of utilities. The act of consumption at time T confers a utility v per period over periods $[T, T + L]$, $L > 0$, which occurs, for instance, for consumer durables. Thus, denoting the consumption utility experienced at time t by u_t^c we have

$$u_t^c = \begin{cases} v & T \leq t \leq T + L \\ 0 & otherwise \end{cases}. \tag{1.18}$$

We consider here the case of *anticipal pleasure* and indicate later the implications arising from *anticipal pain*. The consumer derives anticipation utility, u_t^a, at time $t \in [t_0, T]$ from the *entire stream of consumption between time periods $T \leq t \leq T + L$*. Anticipation utility arises prior to the act of consumption, while consumption utility arises during the act of consumption. Hence, for times $T \leq t \leq T + L$ when the individual derives consumption utility, anticipal utility is zero. Conversely, during times $t_0 \leq t \leq T$ the individual derives anticipal utility but no consumption utility. Let $\alpha > 0$ be a measure of the anticipation or vividness of the consumption experience to follow. Let σ be the discount rate applicable to anticipated consumption; it need not equal the traditional discount rate r that applies to actual consumption (see (1.20)), then

$$u_t^a = \alpha \int_T^{T+L} e^{-\sigma(\tau - t)} v d\tau, \, t_0 \leq t \leq T,$$

$$= \frac{\alpha v}{\delta} e^{-\sigma(T-t)} \left(1 - e^{-\sigma L}\right). \tag{1.19}$$

From (1.19), we can make the following inferences that were noted by Jevons (1905).

$$\frac{\partial u_t^a}{\partial L} > 0, \frac{\partial u_t^a}{\partial v} > 0, \frac{\partial u_t^a}{\partial t} > 0, \frac{\partial^2 u_t^a}{\partial t^2} > 0; 0 \leq t \leq T.$$

Hence, instantaneous anticipal utility over $t \in [t_0, T]$ increases as one approaches the date of actual consumption. Moreover, it increases at an increasing rate. Think, for instance, about the approaching date of a long anticipated holiday. The future per-period enjoyment from the holiday, v, and the length of the holiday, L, also increase anticipal utility.

We can now combine the instantaneous consumption and anticipal utilities over the time interval $[t_0, T + L]$ into total intertemporal utility from the one-off consumption decision:

$$U = \int_{t_0}^T u_t^a e^{-rt} dt + \int_T^{T+L} u_t^c e^{-rt} dt, \tag{1.20}$$

where $r > 0$ is the conventional discount rate used in exponential discounting functions. Substituting (1.18) and (1.19) in (1.20) we get

$$U = \int_{t_0}^{T} \frac{\alpha v}{\delta} e^{-\sigma(T-t)} \left(1 - e^{-\sigma L}\right) e^{-rt} dt + \int_{T}^{T+L} v e^{-rt} dt. \tag{1.21}$$

Simplifying (1.21), we get

$$U = v \left[\frac{\alpha}{\sigma(\sigma - r)} \left(e^{-rT} - e^{-\sigma T} \right) \left(1 - e^{-\sigma L} \right) + \frac{1}{r} e^{-rT} \left(1 - e^{-rL} \right) \right]. \tag{1.22}$$

Will the consumer ever want to delay consumption, i.e., is the optimal starting date of consumption, T^*, greater than t_0? To answer this question, differentiate (1.22) with respect to T

$$\frac{\partial U}{\partial T} = v \left[\frac{\alpha \left(1 - e^{-\sigma L}\right)}{\sigma(\sigma - r)} \left(\sigma e^{-\sigma T} - r e^{-rT} \right) - \left(1 - e^{-rL} \right) e^{-rT} \right]. \tag{1.23}$$

The first term in (1.23) gives the marginal benefit of anticipal utility (or savoring), while the second term captures the delay costs. In the absence of the first term, we get the classical outcome under discounted utility, namely, that the individual should engage in immediate consumption of goods that give anticipal pleasure.

Suppose that $t_0 = 0$. If $\frac{\partial U}{\partial T}\big|_{T=0} > 0$, then the individual will like to defer consumption from the present date. Using (1.23), we have

$$\frac{\partial U}{\partial T}\bigg|_{T=0} = v \left[\frac{\alpha}{\sigma} \left(1 - e^{-\sigma L} \right) - \left(1 - e^{-rL} \right) \right],$$

thus,

$$\frac{\partial U}{\partial T}\bigg|_{T=0} > 0 \Leftrightarrow \frac{\alpha}{\sigma} \left(1 - e^{-\sigma L} \right) > \left(1 - e^{-rL} \right). \tag{1.24}$$

From (1.24), factors conducive to delaying are: high α (greater salience of anticipal utility), and low σ (lower discounting of future anticipated outcomes). U is a twice continuously differentiable function on the compact set $[0, L]$. Hence, if condition (1.24) is met, then there is at least one optimal time for consumption $T^* > 0$ that maximizes the individual's utility. The outcome $T^* > 0$ immediately contradicts the predictions of the discounted utility model without anticipal considerations.

We leave the reader to derive the corresponding conditions in the case of unpleasant outcomes. Discounted utility theory predicts delayed consumption in this case, while the incorporation of anticipal utility opens up the possibility that the individual would like to speed up consumption.

1.5 Fear and anxiety under uncertainty

In Volume 1, we considered ex-post disappointment in static models (Bell, 1985; Loomes and Sugden, 1986). Ex-post disappointment presupposes, however, that there must have been ex-ante hopefulness or anxiety about an event. Hence, the appropriate scope of such models would appear to be dynamic. The model in Section 1.4 considered feelings of anxiety under certainty. However, since anxiety is often caused by uncertainty about future events, we need a model that considers uncertainty explicitly. Caplin and Leahy (2001) provide one such model, within an expected utility framework, which they call *psychological expected utility*.

1.5.1 *An outline of the framework*

Consider a two-period model. We first present a brief outline of Caplin and Leahy's general framework and then deal with a concrete life-cycle example. Suppose that the set of psychological states in the two periods are vectors of real numbers $X_t \subseteq R^{n_t}$, $t = 1, 2$. Let $X = X_1 \times X_2$ be the Cartesian product of the set of possible psychological states in the two periods, and let $P(X)$ be the space of all probability distributions over X.

> **Example 1.2** *Suppose that the emotional states are happiness, elation, and disappointment, denoted respectively by h, e, d. Let $X_1 = \{h\}$ and $X_2 = \{e, d\}$. The model requires us to put numerical values on these psychological states that are real numbers, for instance, $h = 1, e = 2, d = 3$. Then we have $X = X_1 \times X_2 = \{(h, e), (h, d)\} = \{(1, 2), (1, 3)\}$. Consider two illustrative probability distributions over X, $p, q \in P(X)$ such that $p = (p_1, p_2) = (0.3, 0.7)$ and $q = (q_1, q_2) = (0.5, 0.5)$.*

> **Definition 1.1** *We assume that $P(X)$ is a mixture space. Thus, for any $\lambda \in [0, 1]$ and any $p, q \in P(X)$ there exists an element $p\lambda q \in P(X)$ such that for any $x \in X$ we have $p\lambda q(x) = \lambda p(x) + (1 - \lambda)q(x)$.*

The individual has preferences $\succeq$ that are defined directly over $P(X)$. We make the following standard assumptions on preferences that readers familiar with expected utility theory will easily relate to.

A1: $\succeq$ is complete and transitive.

A2: (Substitution axiom) For all $p, q, r \in P(X)$ and $\lambda \in [0, 1]$, $p \succeq q$ implies $p\lambda r \succeq q\lambda r$.

A3: Let $p, q, r \in P(X)$ such that $p \succeq q$ and $q \succeq r$. Then there exists numbers $\lambda_1, \lambda_2 \in [0, 1]$ such that $p\lambda_1 r \succeq q$ and $q \succeq p\lambda_2 r$.

A4: (Indifference) Let $p, q \in P(X)$ such that for any $x = (x_1, x_2)$, $p(x) = (p_1(x_1), p_2(x_1))$, and $q(x) = (q_1(x_1), q_2(x_1))$, where $p_t(x_t)$ and $q_t(x_t)$ are respective probabilities of the vector of psychological state x at time t (see Example 1.2). If $(p_1(x_1), p_2(x_1)) = (q_1(x_1), q_2(x_1))$ then $p \sim q$.

A5: (Continuity) Let $\lambda \in [0, 1]$ and $p, q \in P(X)$. Then, the sets $\{z : p\lambda q \succeq z\}$ and $\{z : z \succeq p\lambda q\}$ are closed.

Since preferences are defined directly on probability distributions over X, assumption A1 alone ensures that a utility representation exists.

> **Proposition 1.3** *(Expected utility representation) Suppose that only assumption A1 holds. Then there exists a utility function $U: X \to R$ such that for any $p, q \in P(X)$, if $p \succeq q$, then $E_p U \geq E_q U$, where $E_r U$ is the expected utility under the probability density $r \in P(X)$.*

> **Example 1.3** *In Example 1.2 suppose that $p \succeq q$. Then Proposition 1.3 implies that*

$$E_p U \geq E_q U \Leftrightarrow 0.3u(h, e) + 0.7u(h, d) \geq 0.5u(h, e) + 0.5u(h, d). \qquad (1.25)$$

> **Proposition 1.4** *(Additive separability of the representation; Caplin and Leahy, 2001) Suppose that assumptions A1–A5 hold. Let $p, q \in P(X)$. Then the utility function in Proposition 1.3, U, takes an additive form, such that $U(x) = u_1(x_1) + u_2(x_2)$, where $u_t: X_t \to R$ for $t = 1, 2$.*

Example 1.4 *Continuing with Example 1.3, the function u in (1.25) can be specialized to the form, $u(h, e) = u_1(h) + u_2(e)$, and $u(h, d) = u_1(h) + u_2(d)$.*

The set of possible consumption levels (or prizes) in the two periods are monetary and given by $Z_t \subseteq R^{n_t}$, $t = 1, 2$. In any period $t = 1, 2$ the psychological state X_t is realized immediately after a choice is made from the consumption set Z_t. Hence, there is no within-period anticipal utility. Anxiety is caused by anticipation of future events, hence, there is no anxiety in the second period of a two-period model. To simplify the exposition, let the psychological and physical states coincide in period 2, i.e., $Z_2 = X_2$. However, in the first period, the realization of the psychological state $x_1 \in X_1$ depends on two factors.

1. The draw from the consumption set $z_1 \in Z_1$.
2. Uncertainty about the outcomes in the second period, Z_2. In order to formalize the second effect, let l_2 be a probability distribution over Z_2.

We can now use the framework of Kreps and Porteus (1978) to deal with *evolving uncertainty* that is implicit in this formulation. Let $Y_1 = Z_1 \times l_2$ and denote a typical element of Y_1 by $y_1 = (z_1, l_2)$. Let l_1 be the space of all probability distributions over Y_1. Following Kreps–Porteus, elements of l_1 are called *temporal lotteries*. Define a function $\phi : Y_1 \to Z_1 \times X_1$ that specifies how elements of the set Y_1 translate into first period consumption levels and psychological states at time $t = 1$.

Recalling that $Z_2 = X_2$, Caplin and Leahy then define the following utility function over temporal lotteries

$$V(y_1) = u_1\left[\phi(y_1)\right] + E_{l_2} u_2\left[x_2\right], y_1 \in Y_1, x_2 \in X_2. \tag{1.26}$$

Equation (1.26) looks like the standard time separable functional form. However, the innovation here is that the distribution, l_2, over second period outcomes is included in the first period utility function. Hence, the anxiety created by anticipation of future uncertainty affects current utility. We now look at a specific example using (1.26).

1.5.2 *Life-cycle consumption, portfolio choice, and asset prices under anxiety*

As an application of the Caplin–Leahy framework, we now consider a two-period model of consumption-portfolio choice. In the first period, a representative consumer is endowed with e_1 units of a non-storable consumption good, and 1 unit each of N productive assets. A unit of each asset yields a random output equal to $s_i \in S_i$, $i = 1, \ldots, N$ in terms of the second period consumption good. There are competitive markets and the competitively determined price of the ith asset in period 1, in terms of the consumption good, is p_i. The representative-agent nature of the model implies that the aggregate supply of each asset in the economy is unity as well.

The portfolio allocation problem in the first period is to choose the amount θ_i of the ith asset to buy, $i = 1, \ldots, N$. The consumer's first period budget constraint is given by

$$c_1 + \sum_{i=1}^{N} \theta_i p_i = e_1 + \sum_{i=1}^{N} p_i. \tag{1.27}$$

The RHS of (1.27) is the representative consumer's first period income. It is the sum of income from the non-storable consumption good and income from ownership of the assets. The LHS is the total expenditure, which can be split into first period consumption c_1 and investment in a portfolio of N assets. Given the definition of p_i, the units on both sides of (1.27) are in terms of the first period consumption good.

Second period income is the sum of incomes from investments in each of the N assets made in period 1. Income from the ith asset in the second period is $\theta_i s_i$, which is a random variable because s_i is random. Hence, second period consumption, c_2, is bounded above by the random second period income $\sum_{i=1}^{N} \theta_i s_i$.

In terms of the notation in Section 1.5.1, we proceed as follows. Define the physical prizes in each period to be identical to the consumption in that period, so $Z_1, Z_2 \subseteq R$ and $c_t \in Z_t$, $t = 1, 2$. Thus, a typical element of Z_2, depending on the realization of the random terms $s_i \in S_i$, is given by

$$c_2 \equiv z_2 = \sum_{i=1}^{N} \theta_i s_i. \tag{1.28}$$

On account of the randomness in returns, s_i, from the perspective of period 1, c_2 is random. Furthermore, each portfolio choice, $\theta = (\theta_1, \theta_2, \ldots, \theta_N)$, assumed to belong to a compact set, Θ, alters the moments of this random variable. Insofar as uncertainty about the second period creates anxiety in the first, each portfolio choice is associated with a possibly different level of anxiety.

Define l_2 as the probability distribution over Z_2. From (1.28), second period outcomes depend on θ, so it is more illustrative to write $l_2 = l_2(\theta)$. The space of *temporal lotteries* is the set of pairs $y_1 = (c_1, l_2)$. The psychological state in period 1 can now be found by using the function $\phi : Y_1 \rightarrow Z_1 \times X_1$. Let us assume a particular function, $\phi(y_1) = (c_1, a(l_2))$, where $a(l_2)$ is assumed to be a differentiable function of l_2 that captures the anxiety associated with the distribution l_2 over second period outcomes, and $c_1 \in Z_1$. Noting the dependence of l_2 on θ we may write $\widetilde{a}(\theta) = a(l_2(\theta))$. The temporal expected utility in (1.26) now takes the form

$$V(c_1, l_2) = u_1(c_1, \widetilde{a}(\theta)) + \beta E_{l_2} u_2(c_2). \tag{1.29}$$

Substituting (1.27), (1.28) in (1.29), the unconstrained problem of the consumer is

$$\theta^* \in \arg\max_{\theta \in \Theta} u_1 \left(e_1 + \sum_{i=1}^{N} p_i - \sum_{i=1}^{N} \theta_i p_i, \widetilde{a}(\theta) \right) + \beta E_{l_2} u_2 \left(\sum_{i=1}^{N} \theta_i s_i \right). \tag{1.30}$$

The first order condition for an interior solution is

$$-p_i \frac{\partial u_1}{\partial c_1} + \frac{\partial u_1}{\partial \widetilde{a}} \frac{\partial \widetilde{a}}{\partial \theta_i} + \beta E_{l_2} s_i \frac{\partial u_2}{\partial c_2} = 0; i = 1, 2, \ldots, N. \tag{1.31}$$

The condition (1.31) is a standard Euler equation with the addition of an extra term (the second term) to account for anxiety. This is an arbitrage condition that illustrates the trade-off from reducing first period consumption by a unit (first term) and purchasing an extra unit of the ith asset that gives a random return s_i in the second period (third term). The second term captures the marginal effect of anxiety on first period utility that arises from the purchase of an extra unit of the ith asset.

Each asset is in fixed supply of one unit. Competitive market clearing ensures that the price of the ith asset, p_i, adjusts so as to clear the market for the asset. Given that we have a representative agent model, market clearing of the one unit implies

$$\theta_i^* = 1, i = 1, 2, \ldots, N, \tag{1.32}$$

or $\theta^* = \mathbf{1}$, where $\mathbf{1}$ is a vector of ones, so $\tilde{a}(\theta^*) = \tilde{a}(\mathbf{1})$. Substituting $\theta_i^* = 1$ in (1.27) we get the optimal consumption as

$$c_1^* = e_1. \tag{1.33}$$

Substituting $\theta_i^* = 1$ in (1.28), we get

$$c_2 = \sum_{i=1}^{N} s_i. \tag{1.34}$$

Substituting (1.32), (1.33), (1.34) in (1.31), the price of the ith asset can be solved out as

$$p_i^* = \frac{1}{\frac{\partial u_1(e_1, \tilde{a}(\mathbf{1}))}{\partial c_1}} \left[\frac{\partial u_1(e_1, \tilde{a}(\mathbf{1}))}{\partial \tilde{a}} \frac{\partial \tilde{a}(\mathbf{1})}{\partial \theta_i} + \beta E_{I_2} s_i \frac{\partial u_2\left(\sum_{i=1}^{N} s_i\right)}{\partial c_2} \right]. \tag{1.35}$$

Anxiety is *aversive*, so $\frac{\partial u_1(e_1, \tilde{a}(\mathbf{1}))}{\partial \tilde{a}} < 0$. Note that in the absence of anxiety we get $\frac{\partial u_1(e_1, \tilde{a}(\mathbf{1}))}{\partial \tilde{a}} = 0$. Since $\frac{\partial u_1}{\partial c_1} > 0$, we immediately get our first result.

Proposition 1.5 *Anxiety alters the price of assets. If (i) $\frac{\partial \tilde{a}(\mathbf{1})}{\partial \theta_i} > 0$, then the price of the asset is relatively lower as compared to the no-anxiety case and the expected rate of return is higher, and if (ii) $\frac{\partial \tilde{a}(\mathbf{1})}{\partial \theta_i} < 0$, then the price of the asset is relatively higher as compared to the no-anxiety case and the expected rate of return is lower.*

The formula in (1.35) depends on $\frac{\partial \tilde{a}(\mathbf{1})}{\partial \theta_i}$. Consider the following mean-variance functional form for anxiety,

$$a(I_2) = -\alpha E_{I_2} c_2 + \gamma Var_{I_2}(c_2), \alpha > 0, \gamma > 0. \tag{1.36}$$

Hence, anxiety from investment in any vector of assets is increasing in the variance of second period consumption and decreasing in the average level of second period consumption. Using (1.28) we get

$$Var_{I_2}(c_2) = \sum_{i=1}^{N} \theta_i^2 Var(s_i) + \sum_{i=1}^{N} \sum_{j=1, j \neq i}^{N} \theta_i \theta_j Cov(s_i, s_j). \tag{1.37}$$

$$E_{I_2}(c_2) = \sum_{i=1}^{N} \theta_i E_{I_2}(s_i).$$

Hence, it follows that

$$\frac{\partial Var_{I_2}(c_2)}{\partial \theta_i} = 2\left(\theta_i Var(s_i) + \sum_{j=1, j \neq i}^{N} \theta_j Cov(s_i, s_j)\right) = 2Cov(c_2, s_i). \tag{1.38}$$

$$\frac{\partial E_{I_2}(c_2)}{\partial \theta_i} = E_{I_2}(s_i). \tag{1.39}$$

Using (1.36), (1.38), (1.39) we get

$$\frac{\partial \tilde{a}(\mathbf{1})}{\partial \theta_i} = -\alpha E_{I_2}(s_i) + 2\gamma Cov(c_2, s_i). \tag{1.40}$$

Substituting (1.40) in (1.35), we can now derive the prices of the N assets in terms of the fundamentals. For $i = 1, \ldots, N$, the optimal asset price is

$$p_i^* = \frac{1}{\frac{\partial u_1(e_1, \tilde{a}(1))}{\partial c_1}} \left[\frac{\partial u_1(e_1, \tilde{a}(1))}{\partial \tilde{a}} \left[-\alpha E_{l_2}(s_i) + 2\gamma \, Cov(c_2, s_i) \right] + \beta E_{l_2} s_i \frac{\partial u_2\left(\sum_{i=1}^N s_i \right)}{\partial c_2} \right]. \quad (1.41)$$

Suppose that the ith asset is riskless, so $Cov(c_2, s_i) = 0$, hence, $\frac{\partial \tilde{a}(1)}{\partial \theta_i} = -\alpha E_{l_2}(s_i) < 0$ because a riskless asset would be held in the portfolio only if its expected return, $E_{l_2}(s_i)$, is positive. The next proposition directly follows from Proposition 1.5.

Proposition 1.6 *For a riskless asset, the price of the asset under anxiety is relatively higher and so the expected rate of return is relatively lower.*

In the presence of anxiety, by investing in a riskless asset, the investor is purchasing "peace of mind" so he is prepared to pay a relatively higher price as compared to the no-anxiety case. On the other hand, stocks are risky and the fluctuation in their returns causes anxiety. So their purchase is likely to (i) increase the expected value, which is anxiety reducing, and (ii) increase the variance of second period consumption, which is anxiety enhancing. From (1.40), the trade-off between risk and return on the level of anxiety depends on the relative magnitudes of α and γ and the underlying probabilistic structure. The next result directly follows from these observations and Proposition 1.5.

Proposition 1.7 *Suppose that γ is "sufficiently large" as compared to α in the sense that $\frac{\gamma}{\alpha} > \frac{E_{l_2}(s_i)}{2|Cov(c_2, s_i)|}$.*

    (i) *If $Cov(c_2, s_i) < 0$, then $\frac{\partial \tilde{a}(1)}{\partial \theta_i} < 0$, so the price of the asset under anxiety is relatively higher and the expected rate of return is lower.*

    (ii) *If $Cov(c_2, s_i) > 0$, then $\frac{\partial \tilde{a}(1)}{\partial \theta_i} > 0$. In this case, the price of the risky asset under anxiety is relatively lower and so the expected rate of return is relatively higher.*

Proposition 1.7(ii), which is the psychologically more interesting case, shows that the ownership of a risky stock creates anxiety, which reduces its price and increases its return relative to the no-anxiety case. This provides one possible explanation for the *equity premium puzzle* that we consider in more detail in Volumes 1 and 5 of the book. The equity premium puzzle refers to the gap between returns on equities and bonds that cannot be explained by differences in the risk characteristics of the two financial assets.

One may distinguish between anxiety and risk aversion. Anxiety is an anticipatory feeling that arises before the resolution of an event, while under expected utility, risk aversion is a property of the curvature of the utility function. By considering risk aversion in the absence of anxiety, traditional measures of risk aversion might be partially capturing anxiety.

There are several other applications of the Caplin–Leahy framework. For an application to the revelation of information by a concerned party to an uninformed party, see Caplin and Leahy (2004). An example of this setting is a doctor who considers revealing information about a life threatening condition to two kinds of patients. An information-avoiding patient who avoids anxiety by shunning new information and an information-seeking patient who seeks information to lower anxiety (e.g., to rule out potentially worse possibilities). The natural vehicle of analysis for such a model is psychological game theory that we develop in Volume 4 of the book. Caplin and Eliaz (2003) consider the possibility that individuals may be put off by the anxiety of a positive test result and, therefore, avoid AIDS testing. They embed the Kreps–Porteus preferences used above, into a mechanism design approach to propose an optimal mechanism that encourages testing and reducing the incidence of the disease.

1.6 Projection bias

Projection bias arises when individuals make predictions of their future tastes that are disproportionately influenced by their current tastes; ex-post these predictions typically turn out to be false. Consider the following examples.

Example 1.5 *Smith et al. (2008) asked patients awaiting a kidney transplant to predict their quality of life in a year's time if they did or did not receive the transplant. The subjects were then followed up a year later and asked to report on their actual quality of life. The predictions failed systematically. The quality of life predicted by patients who received (did not receive) the transplant was lower (higher) relative to the actual quality of life.*

Example 1.6 *When ordering food at the beginning of a meal, in a hungry state, we need to predict how hungry we will be at the end of the meal. We often overestimate our future hunger and order more than we can eat. Furthermore, shopping on an empty stomach leads people to buy more (Gilbert et al., 2002). When making the decision to smoke, an individual needs to predict how the future desire for smoking will be affected. An underappreciation of the effect on the future desire to smoke often leads to greater current overconsumption.*

Example 1.7 *Read and van Leeuwen (1998) asked office workers to choose among healthy and unhealthy snacks to be received in a week's time. When asked to make this decision, office workers were in one of two possible states. In the hungry state, the question was posed just before lunchtime, and subjects were more likely to choose the unhealthy snack. However, in the satiated state, the question was posed just after lunchtime, and subjects were more likely to choose the healthy snack. The authors conclude that subjects in a currently hungry state overestimate their future hunger; in contrast, satiated subjects underestimate future hunger. In other words, people project their current tastes onto future tastes.*

What accounts for projection bias? Loewenstein et al. (2003) argue that the reason is two-fold. First, the ability of humans to adapt to changes is remarkably good. Second, individuals underestimate the extent of their adaptation. The two main stylized facts about projection bias that we need for the moment are:

1. Individuals are able to predict the *direction* of taste changes.
2. Individuals under-appreciate the true *magnitude* (or absolute value) of the change.

Suppose that we measure the current hunger-state of an individual on a scale of 1 (very satiated) to 10 (very hungry). Assume that normally the individual experiences a hunger-state of about 5. Suppose that we consider individuals who are currently at the two extremes, 1 and 10, and ask them to predict their hunger-state in the future. The first stylized fact implies that both individuals will report future hunger-states in the direction of 5. However, the second stylized fact implies that they will underappreciate the full extent of the movement to 5. For instance, the very satiated individual may predict a future hunger-state of 3, while the very hungry individual may predict a hunger-state of 7.

The two stylized facts also provide a plausible explanation of the endowment effect. Before obtaining a mug, individuals are not adapted to owning the mug and underappreciate the satisfaction derived from its ownership, hence, they undervalue it. After obtaining the mug, individuals adapt to ownership but underappreciate how well they will adapt if they were to be deprived of it, hence, they overvalue it.

1.6.1 Preferences under projection bias

Suppose that an individual lives for T periods, $t = 1, 2, \ldots, T$. The instantaneous utility in period t is given by $u(c_t, s_t)$, where c_t is consumption at time t and s_t is the state of the world at time t that reflects tastes of the individual. The set of possible states is $S \subset \mathbb{R}^n$. Given the current state, s_t, the individual's prediction of utility from consumption c and state $s_{t'} \in S$ is given by $\widetilde{u}(c, s_{t'} \mid s_t)$.

We now give a definition of projection bias that incorporates stylized facts 1 and 2.

Definition 1.2   (Loewenstein et al., 2003): An individual exhibits projection bias if for all c, s_t and $s_{t'}$ there exists $\alpha \in [0,1]$ such that

$$\widetilde{u}(c, s_{t'} \mid s_t) = \alpha u(c, s_t) + (1 - \alpha) u(c, s_{t'}); \; \alpha \in [0,1]. \tag{1.42}$$

In Definition 1.2, the prediction of future utility is a linear combination of the current instantaneous utility and the actual instantaneous utility in the relevant state. The central feature is that current tastes, as reflected in s_t, affect one's prediction of future tastes. If $\alpha = 0$, then we have the classical case of no projection bias. When $\alpha = 1$, the individual has extreme projection bias and equates current tastes fully with future tastes. Intermediate values of α capture varying degrees of projection bias. In particular, for $0 < \alpha < 1$, the individual accurately predicts the direction of change in tastes but underpredicts their magnitude.

Example 1.8   Consider two states of the world, hungry (state h), and not hungry (state n). Suppose that we have only one consumption good c and an identical consumption level in each period. Then we have the following four cases.

$$\widetilde{u}(c, h \mid h) = \alpha u(c, h) + (1 - \alpha) u(c, h) = u(c, h). \tag{1.43}$$

$$\widetilde{u}(c, n \mid h) = \alpha u(c, h) + (1 - \alpha) u(c, n). \tag{1.44}$$

$$\widetilde{u}(c, n \mid n) = \alpha u(c, n) + (1 - \alpha) u(c, n) = u(c, n). \tag{1.45}$$

$$\widetilde{u}(c, h \mid n) = \alpha u(c, n) + (1 - \alpha) u(c, h). \tag{1.46}$$

From (1.43), (1.45), there is no projection bias if the future and current states are identical. But from (1.44), (1.46) projection bias exists if $\alpha \neq 0$ and the two states differ. Suppose that

$$u(c, h) = 20, \; u(c, n) = 10, \; \alpha = 0.5,$$

then we have $\widetilde{u}(c, n \mid h) = \widetilde{u}(c, h \mid n) = 15$. If the current state is n and the future state is h, then the change in predicted utility is 5. Reversing the states, the change in predicted utility is -5. In each case, the direction of change is correct (stylized fact 1), but the absolute value of the change is $5 < 10$. However, in the absence of projection bias, the absolute value of the change is 10. Hence, in each case, the magnitude of the change is underappreciated (stylized fact 2).

In writing down the individual's intertemporal preferences in the presence of projection bias, there are two polar cases to consider.

1. The individual has complete foresight about the entire future temporal path of states $s_1, s_2, \ldots, s_T$: In this case, the intertemporal utility at date $t = 1$ is given by

$$U(c_1, c_2, \ldots, c_T \mid s_1) = u(c_1, s_1) + \sum_{\tau=2}^{\tau=T} \delta^{\tau-1} \tilde{u}(c_\tau, s_\tau \mid s_1), \qquad (1.47)$$

where δ is the discount factor and $\tilde{u}$ is defined in (1.42).

2. There is uncertainty over the future states: Denote by E_1, the expectation operator taken at date 1, over the relevant probability distribution over future states. Then, the expected intertemporal utility is given by

$$E_1 U(c_1, c_2, \ldots, c_T \mid s_1) = u(c_1, s_1) + E_1 \sum_{\tau=2}^{\tau=T} \delta^{\tau-1} \tilde{u}(c_\tau, s_\tau \mid s_1). \qquad (1.48)$$

Time inconsistency problems can arise when individuals have projection bias because the prediction of individuals about their future tastes will often not be realized. For instance, in (1.44), (1.46), if $\alpha \neq 0$, then $\tilde{u}(c, n \mid h) \neq u(c, n)$ and $\tilde{u}(c, h \mid n) \neq u(c, h)$. Since the projection bias arises from an inaccurate prediction, individuals would not know it (for otherwise they could easily correct it by setting $\alpha = 0$). Hence, individuals perceive preferences to be time consistent but they are not. The model does not address possible learning by individuals when predictions do not come out to be true. In other words, individuals are unaware that they might be making systematic forecasting errors. This does typically arise when humans are hardwired to engage in certain behaviors; considerable cognitive effort and practice are needed to shed such behaviors. The reasonableness of this assertion is not a matter of theoretical plausibility, but of the empirical evidence.

1.6.2 *Habit formation, life-cycle consumption, and projection bias*

Consider a consumer with projection bias who, at time $t = 1$, allocates a given initial income Y over T periods. For pedagogical simplicity, there is no uncertainty, the discount factor $\delta = 1$, the interest rate is zero, and there is a single consumption good. The actual instantaneous utility of the consumer at time t is given by $u(c_t, s_t)$, where $c_t \geq 0$ is consumption and $s_t \geq 0$ is the state of the world at time t. Preferences are of the habit formation type, i.e.,

$$u(c_t, s_t) = v(c_t - s_t), \, v' > 0, v'' < 0. \qquad (1.49)$$

s_t is to be interpreted as the stock of habits that evolves in the following manner

$$s_{t+1} = (1 - \lambda) s_t + \lambda c_t; \, \lambda \in (0, 1]. \qquad (1.50)$$

Current consumption adds to the habit stock, and the initial habit stock, $s_1 > 0$, is given.
Solving (1.50) recursively, we get

$$s_{t+1} = (1 - \lambda)^t s_1 + \lambda c_t + \lambda(1 - \lambda)^1 c_{t-1} + \lambda(1 - \lambda)^2 c_{t-2} + \ldots + \lambda(1 - \lambda)^{t-1} c_1. \qquad (1.51)$$

This setup satisfies the following two standard features of the habit formation model.

1. Current consumption, by adding to the stock of habit, directly reduces utility in all future time periods. Using (1.49), (1.51) we get

$$\frac{\partial u(c_t, s_t)}{\partial c_{t-k}} = -\lambda (1 - \lambda)^{k-1} v'(c_t - s_t) < 0; \; k = 1, 2, \ldots, t-1. \tag{1.52}$$

Hence, one needs to consume ever greater amounts to get the same "kick" from a habit.

2. The marginal utility from current consumption is increasing in the current stock of habits because

$$\frac{\partial}{\partial s_t} \left(\frac{\partial u(c_t, s_t)}{\partial c_t} \right) = -v''(c_t - s_t) > 0. \tag{1.53}$$

Given (1.42), (1.47), (1.49), and $\delta = 1$, the consumer's optimization problem at time $t = 1$ is to choose $c_1, c_2, \ldots, c_T$ in order to maximize

$$U(c_1, c_2, \ldots, c_T \mid s_1) = v(c_1 - s_1) + \sum_{\tau=2}^{\tau=T} [\alpha v(c_\tau - s_1) + (1 - \alpha) v(c_\tau - s_\tau)], \tag{1.54}$$

subject to the equation of motion for the stock variable (1.50), which we rewrite as

$$s_{t+1} - s_t = \lambda (c_t - s_t); \text{ given } s_1 > 0, \tag{1.55}$$

and the intertemporal budget constraint, under the assumption of zero interest rate, is

$$\sum_{\tau=1}^{\tau=T} c_\tau = Y. \tag{1.56}$$

Denote the solution under no-projection bias ($\alpha = 0$), or the unbiased solution, by $c_1^u, c_2^u, \ldots, c_T^u$, and the solution under projection bias ($\alpha > 0$), or the biased solution, by $c_1^b, c_2^b, \ldots, c_T^b$. The qualitative features of the solution for the general case can by found in Loewenstein et al. (2003).[3]

We derive below the closed-form solution for an illustrative two-period model, $T = 2$, and assuming log preferences

$$v(c_t - s_t) = \ln(\theta + c_t - s_t); \; \theta \geq 0.$$

Assume that, for all t, $\theta + c_t - s_t > 0$, so we have a well-defined utility function with $v' > 0$, $v'' < 0$.

For $T = 2$, substituting s_2 from (1.55) and c_2 from (1.56) into (1.54), the consumer chooses c_1 to maximize the following concave utility function

$$U(c_1, c_2 \mid s_1) = \ln(\theta + c_1 - s_1) + \alpha \ln[\theta + Y - c_1 - s_1]$$
$$+ (1 - \alpha) \ln[\theta + Y - (1 + \lambda) c_1 - (1 - \lambda) s_1],$$

---

[3] The solution to the general case cannot be obtained by the usual optimal control methods. The reason is that the presence of a habit stock variable does not allow one to reduce the system to a system of first order difference equations. What one would get, for instance, by eliminating the shadow prices, at any point t, is a system of two $t - 1$ order difference equations in c, s. Hence, the qualitative features of the solution can only be derived by using the method of induction.

given the initial state variable s_1. We assume an interior solution throughout. The first order condition with respect to c_1 is

$$\frac{1}{\theta + c_1 - s_1} - \frac{\alpha}{\theta + Y - c_1 - s_1} - \frac{(1-\alpha)(1+\lambda)}{\theta + Y - (1+\lambda)c_1 - (1-\lambda)s_1} = 0. \tag{1.57}$$

Consider first, the absence of projection bias, so $\alpha = 0$. Evaluating (1.57) at $\alpha = 0$, the unbiased solution, c_1^u, is given by

$$c_1^u = \frac{1}{1+\lambda}\left(\frac{\widetilde{Y}}{2} + \lambda s_1\right), \tag{1.58}$$

where

$$\widetilde{Y} = Y - \lambda\theta.$$

We can rewrite (1.58) as $c_1^u = \frac{1}{1+\lambda}\left(\frac{\widetilde{Y}}{2} - s_1\right) + s_1$, so a sufficient condition for $c_1^u > s_1$ is that $\frac{\widetilde{Y}}{2} > s_1$. We next show that when an individual consumes more than her stock of habits, then she consumes an increasing profile of consumption. This outcome occurs if the initial stock of habits is sufficiently small.

Proposition 1.8 *Suppose that there is no projection bias. If $\frac{\widetilde{Y}}{2} > s_1$ (or $c_1^u > s_1$), then $c_1^u < c_2^u$.*

Proof: (a) Substituting (1.58) in (1.56). Then, for $T = 2$, the optimal solution for c_2^u is

$$c_2^u = c_1^u + \left(\frac{2\lambda}{1+\lambda}\right)\left(\widetilde{Y} - 2s_1\right) + \lambda\theta. \tag{1.59}$$

From (1.58) we get

$$c_1^u - s_1 = \frac{1}{1+\lambda}\left(\frac{\widetilde{Y}}{2} - s_1\right). \tag{1.60}$$

From (1.60), $c_1^u > s_1 \Leftrightarrow \frac{\widetilde{Y}}{2} > s_1$, which implies, from (1.59), that $c_2^u > c_1^u$. ∎

The analogous result when there are T time periods is given below.

Proposition 1.9 *(Loewenstein et al., 2003): If $c_t^u > s_t$ for some t, then $c_t^u < c_{t+1}^u < c_{t+2}^u < \ldots < c_T^u$.*

From Proposition 1.8, we get the standard result in habit formation models that $s_1 = 0$ is a sufficient condition for an increasing profile of optimal consumption. By frontloading consumption, in this case, the stock of habits is raised early on, reducing the marginal utility of consumption in the subsequent periods. Hence, planning an increasing profile of consumption, is optimal.

Let us now introduce the possibility of projection bias. The next proposition states the main result.

Proposition 1.10 *Suppose $T = 2$ and there is projection bias ($\alpha > 0$). If $\frac{\widetilde{Y}}{2} > s_1$ (so $c_1^u > s_1$), then $c_1^u < c_1^b$.*

Proof: Implicitly differentiate (1.57) with respect to α

$$\frac{\partial c_1}{\partial \alpha} = \left(-\frac{\partial^2 U}{\partial c_1^2}\right)^{-1} \left(\frac{(1+\lambda)}{\theta + Y - (1+\lambda)c_1 - (1-\lambda)s_1} - \frac{1}{\theta + Y - c_1 - s_1}\right). \tag{1.61}$$

For $\frac{\partial c_1}{\partial \alpha} > 0$, we require that $\frac{(1+\lambda)}{\theta+Y-(1+\lambda)c_1-(1-\lambda)s_1} > \frac{1}{\theta+Y-c_1-s_1} \Leftrightarrow Y > 2s_1 - \theta$. But we know from Proposition 1.8 that the condition $\frac{\tilde{Y}}{2} > s_1$ ensures that $c_1^u > s_1$, and $\frac{\tilde{Y}}{2} > s_1 \Leftrightarrow Y > 2s_1 - \theta$. Hence, if $\frac{\tilde{Y}}{2} > s_1$ (so $c_1^u > s_1$), then $\frac{\partial c_1}{\partial \alpha} > 0$. Since c_1^u corresponds to the optimal solution when $\alpha = 0$ and c_1^b corresponds to the optimal solution when $\alpha > 0$ it follows that $c_1^u < c_1^b$, as claimed. ■

The analogous result when there are T time periods is given in Proposition 1.11 below.

Proposition 1.11 *(Loewenstein et al., 2003): If $c_1^u > s_1$ and $\alpha > 0$, then $\sum_{\tau=1}^{t} c_\tau^u < \sum_{\tau=1}^{t} c_\tau^b$ for $t < T$.*

The intuition behind Proposition 1.10 is as follows. Projection bias implies an underappreciation of the magnitude of change. Here, the consumer underappreciates the effect of habit formation as well as the negative effect of the current stock on all future instantaneous utilities. Hence, relative to the unbiased case, the consumer with projection bias consumes too much. Therefore, a person with projection bias will consume her income "too quickly" relative to the optimal unbiased consumption profile. An important implication of this idea is that consumers might not save enough. This provides an alternative explanation of the savings inadequacy problem that does not rely on arguments of present-biased preferences (see Volume 3 of the book).

1.6.3 *An application to consumer durables*

Suppose that a consumer can purchase one unit of a consumer durable at time $t = 1$ at some price P that provides a stream of utility $d_1, d_2, \ldots, d_T$. The consumer's "state" in any period is the utility in that period, i.e., $s_t = d_t$, $t = 1, \ldots, T$. There is no discounting, so the discount factor $\delta = 1$. Suppose that the consumer buys the good in period 1. Then her true or unbiased utility (corresponding to $\alpha = 0$), U^u, is given by

$$U^u = \sum_{\tau=1}^{\tau=T} d_\tau - P = T\bar{d} - P, \tag{1.62}$$

where $\bar{d} = \frac{1}{T} \sum_{\tau=1}^{\tau=T} d_\tau$ is the mean, across time, of instantaneous utility.

The intertemporal utility of a consumer who has projection bias, U^b, at time $t = 1$, is given by

$$U^b = \sum_{\tau=1}^{\tau=T} [\alpha d_1 + (1-\alpha)d_\tau] - P = T\bar{d} + \alpha T\left(d_1 - \bar{d}\right) - P. \tag{1.63}$$

Using (1.62), (1.63) it follows that

$$U^b \gtrless U^u \text{ if } d_1 \gtrless \bar{d}. \tag{1.64}$$

From (1.64), if $d_1 > \bar{d}$, then a consumer with projection bias may buy the consumer durable even if in the absence of projection bias he does not buy (e.g., if $T\bar{d} - P < 0$ and $T\bar{d} - P + \alpha T\left(d_1 - \bar{d}\right) > 0$). Hence, a person with projection bias may be too sensitive to her valuation at the time of purchase. Insofar as the valuation may be influenced by an emotional *hot state*, it plays a disproportionate role in the presence of projection bias.

Businesses might wish to exploit the tendency of consumers to buy in a *hot state*. They may induce such a state through sales hype, attractive displays, in-store music, and one-click shopping on the Internet. Often salesmen will offer a discount, conditional on buying today, but the discount is not available if the purchase is delayed. Sellers might also try to turn non-durable goods into durable goods. So, for instance, they might sell an annual or bi-annual membership to a health club rather than a daily one.

DellaVigna and Malmendier (2002) provide evidence that people overpay for health club membership, by buying on an annual basis, relative to a "pay as you use" basis. One possible explanation is that people have self-control problems; once people sign up to a health club membership, they procrastinate and do not fully use it (see Volume 3 of the book). However, the explanation based on projection bias suggests that people overestimate their use of the membership because at the time of signing, they are in a hot state. In the future, they cool down as their enthusiasm wanes, and they underuse their membership. However, due to projection bias, individuals underpredict the extent to which they will cool down.

This has interesting implications for government policy. In the US and UK, for instance, "cooling-off" laws allow consumers to cancel their purchase within a certain number of days subsequent to the purchase. One interpretation of these laws is that they are designed to counter the effect of projection bias. Such laws can also alter the incentives of salespersons to mis-sell because they too wish to reduce costly returns of their products. Thus, salespersons are more likely to highlight longer-run implications of a purchase decision to the consumer that are more consistent with the cooler rather than the hotter end of the spectrum of human emotions.

1.6.4 *Other applications of projection bias*

Habit formation is a plausible hypothesis that is based on the psychological foundations of adaptation. However, evidence of habit formation is not readily available; but see Dynan (2000) for some experimental evidence. Projection bias suggests one explanation for why it might be hard to find evidence of such behavior, even if individuals exhibit it. Projection bias might lead people to underreact to habit formation. For instance, using (1.57), if the individual has extreme projection bias, say, $\alpha = 1$, then the individual's optimal consumption profile is $c_1 = Y/2, c_2 = Y/2$ whether habit formation is present or absent. Hence, projection bias might mask the presence of habit formation even if it exists.

Projection bias might also explain why many pledges of charitable support are not eventually honored. This happens particularly when a major disaster occurs that elicits a widespread feeling of empathy. If individuals make their pledges in a hot state, they overestimate their charitable urges in the future. One's own future-selves might not honor the earlier pledge because they make decisions in a cooler state, once the immediate shock of the disaster lessens.

Habit formation models often find it difficult to explain why people develop harmful habits such as addiction in the first place.[4] Projection bias provides two potential explanations. First,

---

[4] See, however, Bernheim and Rangel (2004), above, who explain addiction as a mistake.

people underestimate the (negative) effect of current consumption on future utility. Second, individuals might under-appreciate the formation of the addictive habit.

The making of decisions in hot states that characterizes individuals with projection bias might also explain why some people get married without sufficient deliberation. Or why costly proposals to get married are sometimes reversed. Or why people undertake costly actions/ commitments in moments of rage or extreme generosity. The existence of cooling-off periods could be one way of mitigating the harmful consequences of such actions. For instance, there are mandatory time intervals between filing for marriage or divorce.

Such decisions are, of course, irreversible for suicides. If individuals in a currently depressed state predict, on account of projection bias, that their future states are also likely to be similar, then their predicted lifetime discounted value of life is relatively lower. Hence, some individuals might, on the spur of the moment, make a disastrous and irreversible decision to end their life. Such individuals, if they are known to the social services, are typically closely monitored for the existence of such hot states.

1.7 Temptation preferences: a revealed preference approach

Models of dual selves and models that consider the interaction between the emotional and the cognitive system in the brain rely on the premise that human behavior is the outcome of *brain modularity*. The primitives in such a model are the relevant modules in the brain and their interaction.

The neoclassical approach takes preferences as the relevant primitives and uses the revealed preference approach to recover the underlying preferences. In this approach, individuals face temptations but may either make *commitments* to eliminate them, or they might not be able to eliminate the temptations. There are two possibilities—individuals may either exercise *self-control*, or they may succumb to the temptations. This section considers these issues.

Consider two time periods. In the first period, the individual chooses from a set of *menus* and has preferences over menus given by $\succsim_1$. The items in the menu can be outcomes or, more generally, probability distributions over outcomes. In the second period, conditional on the chosen menu in the first period, the individual chooses items in the menu, based on second period preferences, $\succsim_2$. The underlying framework was introduced by Kreps and Porteus (1978).

> **Example 1.9** *Consider two periods and two possible restaurants: A vegetarian restaurant, V, that sells healthy but bland food and a fast food restaurant, F, that sells unhealthy, but tempting food. In the first period, the individual needs to choose over three possible "menus": {V}, {F} and {V, F}. Menus are defined more formally below. For the moment, if menu {V} (respectively {F}) is chosen in the first period, then, in the second period, the individual can only visit restaurant V (respectively restaurant F). If menu {V, F} is chosen, then the individual can choose any of the two restaurants V or F in the second period. The first period preferences over menus are denoted by $\succsim_1$. In the second period, the individual can visit any of the restaurants in the chosen menu (if there is a single option on the menu, then the second period choice is trivial). Second period preferences over restaurants in the chosen menu are given by $\succsim_2$.*
> *Option F is said to be a temptation if {V} $\succsim_1$ {V, F}. In this case, in the first period, the individual would like to commit to just choose option V rather than having to choose among options V and F in the second period. Conditional on the first period preferences*

$\{V\} \succsim_1 \{V,F\}$, *suppose that the individual cannot commit to choosing* $\{V\}$. *In this case, in the second period, the individual faces a choice from the menu* $\{V,F\}$. *If the individual chooses F, he gives in to temptation, and if he chooses V, he is said to exercise self-control.*

The seminal theoretical models that explore these issues are Gul and Pesendorfer (2001, 2004, 2005, 2007) and Dekel et al. (2001). In Example 1.9, temptation arises on account of second period preferences, $\succsim_2$. First period preferences may dictate a preference for commitment. Noor (2011) introduces the possibility that individuals might also be tempted by menus in the first period. For instance, the very fact that F is a tastier, although unhealthy, option may create a preference for the menu $\{V,F\}$ over the menu $\{V\}$. The subsequent discussion relies on Gul and Pesendorfer (2001), henceforth, GP.

1.7.1 *The formal model*

Consider a two-period model. Suppose that $C = \{c_1, c_2, \ldots, c_n\}$ are the possible levels of consumption in period 2. Let ΔC be the set of probability distributions over C; we denote typical elements of ΔC by lowercase alphabets such as p, q, r. Thus, a typical element p in ΔC takes the form $p = (p_1, \ldots, p_n)$, such that $\sum_{i=1}^{n} p_i = 1$, and $p_i \geq 0$ for all $i = 1, \ldots, n$; the interpretation of p_i is the probability of consumption c_i.

Let Z be the set of all non-empty compact subsets of ΔC. The set Z comprises all possible menu of choices that, in period 1, the individual can choose from. We will typically denote elements of Z, or *menus*, as M_i, M_j, M_k, and so on. Denote the preferences of the individual over elements in the set Z, or his first period preferences, by $\succsim_1$. For instance, $M_i \succsim_1 M_j$ means that menu M_i is "at least as good as" M_j. The corresponding strict preference and indifference relations are given, respectively, by $\succ_1$ and $\sim_1$.

Suppose that the menu chosen in the first period is M_i. In the second period, the individual makes an optimal choice from M_i. An element $m_i \in M_i$ induces a second period lottery of the form $(c_1, p_1; \ldots c_n, p_n)$. Second stage preferences, $\succsim_2$, are defined over ΔC.

Define the following mixture operation over elements of the set Z. For any $M_i, M_j \in Z$ and $0 < \lambda < 1$, we have

$$\lambda M_i + (1 - \lambda) M_j = \{\lambda q + (1 - \lambda) p, \text{ where } q \in M_i, p \in M_j\}.$$

The binary preference relations $\succsim_1$ and $\succsim_2$ are the primitives of the model and they satisfy the following conditions for $M_i, M_j, M_k \in Z$.

A1: (Preference relations) $\succsim_1$ and $\succsim_2$ are complete and transitive.

A2: (Strong continuity) The sets $\{M_i \in Z : M_i \succsim_1 M_j\}$, $\{M_i \in Z : M_j \succsim_1 M_i\}$, and the set $\{p \in \Delta C : p \succsim_2 q\}$ are closed.

A3: (Independence) If $M_i \succ_1 M_j$, then for all $0 < \lambda < 1$,

$$\lambda M_i + (1 - \lambda) M_k \succ_1 \lambda M_j + (1 - \lambda) M_k.$$

A4: (Set betweenness) $M_i \succsim_1 M_j \Rightarrow M_i \succsim_1 M_i \cup M_j \succsim_1 M_j$.

Axioms A1–A3 are standard in economics and are used, for instance, in the axiomatic derivation of the expected utility formula. However, Fudenberg and Levine (2006) and Fudenberg (2006) argue that the independence axiom is less plausible when economic agents have self-control problems. They argue that the evidence that self-control is a scarce resource, which gets depleted with cognitive load is not consistent with the independence axiom.

The new axiom is *set betweenness* that we now explain in more detail by considering the following cases.

1. $M_i \sim_1 M_i \cup M_j \succ_1 M_j$: The preference $M_i \sim_1 M_i \cup M_j$ indicates that the preferred choice belongs to the set M_i. In this case, adding the option M_j to M_i is irrelevant. Hence, M_j is not a temptation.

2. $M_i \succ_1 M_i \cup M_j \sim_1 M_j$: From the first preference, the individual prefers M_i to the case where both M_i and M_j are available. Such an alternative, M_j, is termed as a *temptation*. From the second preference, when faced with a choice between elements of the sets $M_i \cup M_j$ and M_j the individual chooses an element from the set M_j. Hence, ex-ante the individual prefers to exclude the set M_j altogether from the available options. But, from the preference $M_i \cup M_j \sim_1 M_j$, if the option M_j is available, then the individual succumbs to the temptation.

3. $M_i \succ_1 M_i \cup M_j \succ_1 M_j$: The preference $M_i \succ_1 M_i \cup M_j$ reveals that M_j is a temptation. However, the preference $M_i \cup M_j \succ_1 M_j$ differentiates this from the previous case. In this case, even when the option M_i and the temptation M_j are jointly available at the time of making the choice, the individual successfully resists the temptation, possibly by using some form of costly *self-control*.

To summarize, there are three possibilities. Either there is no temptation (case 1) or there is a temptation that cannot be resisted (case 2) or there is a temptation that can be successfully resisted (case 3).

We have made sufficient assumptions to ensure that utility functions exist that represent the preferences, $\succsim_1$ and $\succsim_2$.

> **Definition 1.3** *(i) A utility function $U \colon Z \to \mathbb{R}$ represents the first period preferences $\succsim_1$ if for $M_i, M_j \in Z$, $M_i \succsim_1 M_j \Leftrightarrow U(M_i) \geq U(M_j)$.*
>
> *(ii) A utility function $u \colon \Delta C \to \mathbb{R}$, sometimes called lottery utility, represents the second period preferences $\succsim_2$ if for $p, q \in \Delta C$, $p \succsim_2 q \Leftrightarrow u(p) \geq u(q)$. Furthermore, u is said to be linear if*
>
> $$u(\lambda p + (1 - \lambda)q) = \lambda u(p) + (1 - \lambda)u(q). \tag{1.65}$$

There is no difference between first stage and second stage preferences when the role of temptation preferences is ignored. In this case, the individual evaluates each menu $M_i \in Z$ by computing the expected utility, as in (1.65), for each element, $m_i \in M_i$ and then picking the element with the highest expected utility. This motivates the next definition.

> **Definition 1.4** *(Classical preferences): Suppose that an individual satisfies the conditions on the utility function in Definition 1.3(ii). The individual has classical preferences if he proceeds as follows. (i) For each menu $M_j \in Z$, let $p_j^* \in \arg\max_{p \in M_j} u(p)$. (ii) Pick the menu, $M_k \in \arg\max_{M_j \in Z} u(p_j^*)$. In this case, the pair of preferences $(\succsim_1, \succsim_2)$ are called classical preferences.*

It is obvious from Definition 1.4 that an individual who has classical preferences cannot be worse off by expanding the size of the menu. The reason is that at worst, the expected utility of all new items added to the menu will have an expected utility lower than the maximal element in the old menu. But then, the decision maker will simply not chose from any of the new elements in the menu. So, for classical preferences, we have the following condition

$$M_i \succ_1 M_j \Rightarrow M_i \cup M_j \sim_1 M_i. \tag{1.66}$$

We now introduce an axiom that connects first and second period preferences.

A5: If $M_i \cup \{p\} \succ_1 M_i$, then $p \succsim_2 q$ for all $q \in M_i$.

Axiom A5, sometimes known as the *sophistication axiom* (see Lipman and Pesendorfer, 2013), requires that if the individual prefers to add an option p to a menu in M_i, then that option must be chosen over all others in M_i in period 2. Axiom A5 is not always innocuous. For instance, firms may offer new contracts to existing customers (adding to their menus) in order to make existing contracts look more attractive, even when they know that such contracts will not be chosen.

We now state the main result in the absence of temptation preferences.

> **Proposition 1.12** *(Classical preferences; Kreps, 1979; Gul and Pesendorfer, 2001): Suppose that the following conditions hold. (i) For all $M_i, M_j \in Z$, condition (1.66) holds. (ii) Axioms 1–5 hold. Then $(\succsim_1, \succsim_2)$ are classical preferences. Furthermore, if $(\succsim_1, \succsim_2)$ are classical preferences, then conditions (i) and (ii) hold.*

Once we depart from classical preferences and introduce the role of temptation, then the condition in (1.66) need not hold any longer. Indeed, we may have $M_i \succ_1 M_i \cup M_j$ so that individuals prefer to have a smaller set of choices in their menus in order to avoid temptation. The main result of GP can be stated in the following theorem.

> **Proposition 1.13** *(Self-control preferences; Gul and Pesendorfer, 2001): The preference relation $\succsim_1$ satisfies Axioms A1–A4, if and only if, there exists a utility function U satisfying Definition 1.3(i), and utility functions u and v satisfying Definition 1.3(ii) such that*
>
> $$U(M) = \max_{p \in M} \left[u(p) + v(p) \right] - \max_{p \in M} v(p), \, M \in Z. \tag{1.67}$$
>
> *We may call such preferences self-control preferences.*

If preferences can be represented as in (1.67), we say that they have a (u, v) representation. Given below in Section 1.7.2 is a proof of Proposition 1.13, using the planner–doer framework in Bénabou and Pycia (2002). While the planner–doer framework is not in the tradition of the revealed preference framework, the proof shows nicely the potential relation between the two frameworks.

One of the problems at the end of the chapter asks you to show that the following proposition is true.

> **Proposition 1.14** *Classical preferences (Definition 1.4) are a special case of self-control preferences (see Proposition 1.13) if either (i) v is an affine transformation of u, i.e., $v = \alpha u + \beta$ for some $\alpha \geq 0$ and $\beta \in \mathbb{R}$, or (ii) u is a constant function. Furthermore, when v is a non-affine transformation of u, i.e., $v = \alpha u + \beta$ but $\alpha < 0$ and $\beta \in \mathbb{R}$, then the individual has a sole desire for commitment.*

Three main features underlie the GP framework.

B1: Suppose that the individual chooses the menu $M \in Z$ in period 1. The individual's preferences in the second period depend on tuples of the form (M, p), where $p \in M$.

In the second period, the individual's optimization problem is

$$\max_{p \in M} \left(u(p) + v(p) \right). \tag{1.68}$$

B2: Conditional on the chosen menu $M \in Z$ in period 1, suppose that the individual chooses some element $p^* \in M$ in the second period; this is the solution to (1.68). Then the first period utility of the individual is given by

$$U = u(p^*) + v(p^*) - \max_{p \in M} v(p). \tag{1.69}$$

From (1.68), the last term $\max_{p \in M} v(p)$ in (1.69) does not affect the actual choice made in the second period. It does, however, affect the individual's level of welfare. Temptation lowers the individual's utility. The second period preferences directly induce first period preferences over menus given in (1.67). In other words, in the first period, for each menu, $M \in Z$, the individual computes (1.69), and assigns a level of utility to it.

B3: In period 1, $M_i \succsim_1 M_j$ if and only if $U(M_i) \geq U(M_j)$.

Suppose that the individual chooses the menu $M \in Z$ in period 1. Denote by $p^* \in M$, the solution to the problem stated in (1.68). Suppose that p^* is unique and suppose that the individual could commit to a singleton menu $\{p^*\}$ in the first period. Using (1.69)

$$U(p^*) = u(p^*) + v(p^*) - v(p^*) = u(p^*). \tag{1.70}$$

For this reason, GP refer to u as the *commitment ordering over outcomes*. It represents the utility from singleton menus.

Now suppose that the individual were to choose a larger (non-singleton) set M of alternatives in period 1 that contains p^*. Suppose also that the individual is able to resist any potential temptations so that the chosen alternative is still p^* in the second period. Then, using (1.68), (1.69), (1.70), welfare loss to the individual is given by

$$U(p^*) - U(M) = u(p^*) - \left(u(p^*) + v(p^*) - \max_{p \in M} v(p) \right) = \max_{p \in M} v(p) - v(p^*). \tag{1.71}$$

Hence, the term $\max_{p \in M} v(p) - v(p^*)$ has the interpretation of *cost of self-control*. The more tempting the alternatives in the larger set M, the greater is the cost of self-control. For this reason GP, refer to $v(p)$ as the individual's *temptation ordering*.

Example 1.10   *Consider two possible menus, $M_1 = \{p\}$ and $M_2 = \{p, q\}$. Suppose that*

$$u(p) > u(q) \text{ and } v(q) > v(p). \tag{1.72}$$

We now show that the individual responds to temptation by choosing the smaller menu, M_1, if commitment is possible. If commitment is not possible, and menu M_2 is chosen, then the individual must choose, in period 2, whether to give in to temptation or to exercise self-control. Using (1.70), we have $U(M_1) = u(p)$, while using (1.67), (1.72),

$$U(M_2) = \max \left\{ u(p) + v(p), u(q) + v(q) \right\} - v(q).$$

Consider now the following two cases.

I. Let $\max\{u(p) + v(p), u(q) + v(q)\} = u(p) + v(p)$. *In this case,*

$$U(M_2) = u(p) - (v(q) - v(p)) < u(p) = U(M_1). \qquad (1.73)$$

II. Let $\max\{u(p) + v(p), u(q) + v(q)\} = u(q) + v(q)$. *In this case,*

$$U(M_2) = u(q) < u(p) = U(M_1). \qquad (1.74)$$

Using (1.73), (1.74) we get $\{p\} \succ_1 \{p,q\}$, *hence, q is a temptation. In (1.73), the individual can exercise self-control in period 2 and does not succumb to temptation. However, there is a cost of self-control, given by the term* $v(q) - v(p)$. *In (1.74), the individual succumbs to temptation. Indeed when preferences,* $\succ_1$, *have a* (u,v) *representation it can be shown that q tempts p in the sense* $\{p\} \succ_1 \{p,q\}$ *if and only if (1.72) holds.*

Suppose that, in addition, a third menu $M_3 = \{q\}$ *is available. In this case,*

$$U(M_3) = u(q) < u(p) = U(M_1). \qquad (1.75)$$

Of the two cases, I and II, considered above, let us focus only on case I: Using (1.73) we have

$$U(M_2) \gtreqqless U(M_3) \Leftrightarrow u(p) - u(q) \gtreqqless v(q) - v(p).$$

The interesting case is the one where $u(p) - u(q) > v(q) - v(p)$, *so that* $U(M_2) > U(M_3)$. *Hence, the overall picture in this case is*

$$\{p\} \succ_1 \{p,q\} \succ_1 \{q\}. \qquad (1.76)$$

Thus, q is a temptation and the individual successfully exercises self-control if presented with the menu M_2. *From (1.76), we get the main empirical prediction of this class of models. Namely, that an individual prefers to commit even when the individual will not engage in choice reversals. However, Lipman and Pesendorfer (2013) write: "We are unaware of any experimental or empirical study that seeks to document self-control." Clearly this is an area that is in urgent need for empirical testing.*

We now consider the invariance of GP preferences to affine transformations of commitment utility, u, and temptation utility, v.

Proposition 1.15 *(Gul and Pesendorfer, 2001): Suppose that preferences,* $\succ_1$, *have a* (u,v) *representation (see Proposition 1.13). Suppose also that* u, v *are non-constant and v is not an affine transformation of u (see Proposition 1.14). Then* $(\widehat{u}, \widehat{v})$ *also represent the preferences* $\succ_1$ *if and only if there exist* $\alpha > 0$ *and* $\beta_u, \beta_v \in \mathbb{R}$ *such that* $\widehat{u} = \alpha u + \beta_u$ *and* $\widehat{v} = \alpha v + \beta_v$.

A special case of temptation preferences arises in the context of time inconsistency (Strotz, 1955). These preferences, known as Strotz preferences, ensure that the long-run plans of the individual are time consistent. In a two-period model, the preferences prescribe the following lexicographic ordering. Begin with period 2, where some menu $M \in Z$ has already been chosen. The individual then maximizes temptation utility, v, over all elements in the menu M; suppose that the maximal element is $p \in M$. Rolling back to the first period, the individual then assigns to the menu M, the number $u(p)$, where u is commitment utility. Finally, the individual chooses the menu with the maximal commitment utility. This is stated in the next definition.

Definition 1.5 *(Strotz, 1955): Suppose that a preference pair* $(\succsim_1, \succsim_2)$ *can be represented by the following utility function:*

1. *For any first stage choice of $M \in Z$, and $p, q \in M$, $p \succsim_2 q$ if and only if the following lexicographic ordering holds*

$$v(p) > v(q), \text{ or } v(p) = v(q) \text{ and } u(p) > u(q). \tag{1.77}$$

2. *Looking ahead at the second period choice from any menu $M \in Z$, as given in (1.77), first period preferences $\succsim_1$, satisfy*

$$U(M) := \max_{p \in M} u(p) \text{ such that } v(p) \geq v(q) \text{ for all } q \in M.$$

The preference pair $(\succsim_1, \succsim_2)$ so defined is said to be a Strotz pair or that $\succsim_1$ can be represented by a Strotz utility function.

Proposition 1.13 also holds for Strotz preferences. Thus, the binary relation $\succsim_1$ satisfies Axioms 1–4 if and only if it is a Strotz preference. Furthermore, a modified form of Proposition 1.15 also holds for Strotz preferences.[5]

Example 1.11 *(Lipman and Pesendorfer, 2013): Consider the following example of time inconsistent choices that is explained using quasi-hyperbolic discounting, or (β, δ) preferences, in Strotz (1955), Phelps and Pollak (1968), and Laibson (1997).[6] Suppose that there are two time periods and $C = \{(c_1, c_2) \in [0, \bar{c}]^2\}$ where $\bar{c}$ is an upper bound on consumption in each period. Consider the following Strotz preferences (Definition 1.5):*

$$\begin{cases} u(c_1, c_2) = w(c_1) + \delta w(c_2) \\ v(c_1, c_2) = w(c_1) + \beta \delta w(c_2) \end{cases}, \quad 0 < \beta < 1,$$

where u is commitment utility that applies to ex-ante choices in period 1, and v is temptation utility that applies to choices in period 2. Hence, in period 2, the individual will choose the consumption pair $(0, l)$ over $(s, 0)$ if $\beta \delta w(l) > w(s)$. In period 1, the individual must choose the optimal menu using commitment utility, u. He chooses the menu $M_1 = \{(0, l)\}$ over the menu $M_2 = \{(s, 0)\}$ if $\delta w(l) > w(s)$. Choice reversals occur if

$$\delta w(l) > w(s) > \beta \delta w(l).$$

Here commitment utility chooses $(0, l)$ over $(s, 0)$, and temptation utility chooses $(s, 0)$ over $(0, l)$, if presented with the menu $M_3 = \{(s, 0), (0, l)\}$. Faced with this possibility, in period 1 the individual might exercise self-control if it is not too costly, by choosing only the menu M_1.

We refer the reader to the excellent survey by Lipman and Pesendorfer (2013) to pursue other developments in this literature. These include the idea that temptations might take the form of deliberate distortion in beliefs; see Epstein (2006), Epstein and Kopylov (2007), and Epstein et al. (2008). For instance, individuals might have a temptation to believe that a flood in the neighboring county will not cause them any flood risk, so that they can avoid buying insurance. Relative to the Bayesian benchmark, this model can lead to overreaction and underreaction to new information. For extensions to multiple periods, see Gul and Pesendorfer (2004) and Krussel et al. (2010).

---

[5] The only difference is that we need separate values of α, say, $\alpha_u, \alpha_v > 0$ for, respectively, the utility functions $\widehat{u}$ and $\widehat{v}$; see Lipman and Pesendorfer (2013).

[6] This case is discussed at length in Volume 3 of the book.

1.7.2 *Interpreting temptation preferences in a planner–doer framework*

It is possible to derive GP preferences in the planner–doer framework in the tradition of Thaler and Shefrin (1981). This can help to provide a useful reinterpretation of the GP model. Bénabou and Pycia (2002) pursue this approach that we describe below.

Let the set of outcomes be C, let ΔC be the set of probability distributions over C, and let Z be the set of nonempty compact subsets of ΔC. Suppose there are two time periods and there is a long-lived planner (say, the cognitive system) and a short-lived myopic doer (say, the emotional system) in each period. The doer only cares about temptation utility, $v : \Delta C \to \mathbb{R}$, while the planner cares about the sum of commitment utility, $u : \Delta C \to \mathbb{R}$, and temptation utility, i.e., $u + v$. As in the GP model, the individual chooses menus, M, from the set $Z \subset \Delta C$. Once a menu is chosen in period 1, there are two possibilities for the second period choice of an outcome in M, given by

$$
\begin{cases}
x \in \arg\max_{x' \in M} \{u(x') + v(x')\} & \text{if choice is made by planner.} \\
y \in \arg\max_{y' \in M} v(y') & \text{if choice is made by doer.}
\end{cases}
\tag{1.78}
$$

As in the Loewenstein and O'Donoghue (2004, 2007) model (see Section 2.2.2 below), we assume that the cognitive and the emotional systems simultaneously incur respective costs $r_c > 0$ and $r_e > 0$ to probabilistically influence the final outcome. The authors write (p. 423): "One can also think of the two subselves as lobbying the brain's motor control areas in the same way as interest groups lobby the government." The respective probabilities, p_c, p_e, that either of the cognitive and the emotional systems is decisive in making the final choice, are directly proportional to the resources expended, in the following manner.

$$
p_c = \frac{r_c}{r_e + r_c}; \; p_e = \frac{r_e}{r_c + r_e}, \text{ and } p_c + p_e = 1.
\tag{1.79}
$$

We suppose that the costs r_c, r_e are drawn, respectively, from some compact sets $S_c \subseteq R_+$ and $S_e \subseteq R_+$. We are interested in a static Nash equilibrium in the actions of the emotional and cognitive systems, (r_c^*, r_e^*). In light of (1.78), (1.79), the respective objective functions of the emotional and the cognitive system are given by

$$
U^e = p_c(r_c, r_e) v(x) + p_e(r_c, r_e) v(y) - r_e.
\tag{1.80}
$$

$$
U^c = p_c(r_c, r_e)(u(x) + v(x)) + p_e(r_c, r_e)(u(y) + v(y)) - r_c.
\tag{1.81}
$$

Solving the two first order conditions $\frac{\partial U^e}{\partial r_e} = 0$ and $\frac{\partial U^c}{\partial r_c} = 0$, simultaneously, for an interior solution, we get the unique optimal solution

$$
r_e^* = \frac{(r_e + r_c)^2}{(u(x) + v(x)) - (u(y) + v(y))}; \; r_c^* = \frac{(r_e + r_c)^2}{v(y) - v(x)}.
\tag{1.82}
$$

Substituting (1.82), in (1.79), the unique respective probabilities are

$$
p_e = \frac{v(y) - v(x)}{u(x) - u(y)}; \; p_c = \frac{u(x) + v(x) - u(y) - v(y)}{u(x) - u(y)}.
\tag{1.83}
$$

Having determined period 2 choices, let us now revert back to period 1. Suppose that in period 1, the individual evaluates date 2 lotteries using expected utility, and individual outcomes using her *commitment preferences u*. Then, ex-ante, the choice set M gives a level of expected utility

$$EU(M) = p_c u(x) + p_e u(y). \tag{1.84}$$

Substituting (1.83), in (1.84) we get

$$EU(M) = u(x) + v(x) - v(y). \tag{1.85}$$

Using (1.78), we can rewrite (1.85) as

$$EU(M) = \max_{x' \in M} \{u(x') + v(x')\} - \max_{y' \in M} v(y'). \tag{1.86}$$

Equations (1.67) and (1.86) are identical, as claimed. Thus, the planner–doer model in which emotions or cognition are probabilistically decisive in the second period, generates the same first period preferences as in GP.

1.8 Temptation and conflicts between commitment and flexibility

When individuals have self-control problems, say, arising through temptation, the standard prescription, in a range of models, is to commit to eliminate options that lead to such temptations. Amador et al. (2006) point out an important trade-off in this context. Eliminating a subset of the options has the benefit of reducing/eliminating temptations, but at the cost of reduced flexibility, especially when new information is likely to arrive in the future. For instance, in the context of intertemporal choice, a reduction in temptations might improve the savings rate of an individual; however, if the future marginal utility turns out to be too low, then the improvement in savings might not have been as worthwhile.

Consider a simple two-period example. In the first period, the individual can choose to buy one of two prepaid skiing holiday in the Alps: a nonrefundable holiday and a refundable holiday. The nonrefundable holiday is relatively cheaper. The individual can commit to eliminating temptations in the first period that lead him to buy the nonrefundable option. However, in the second period, due to an unfortunate accident, the individual is unable to enjoy the fruits of his first period efforts. Ex-post, he would have been better off buying the more expensive, but refundable option. If the individual had foreseen the possibility of such an event, his decision would have been the outcome of a *preference for commitment*, as well as a *preference for flexibility*.

We explore these considerations in the model of Amador et al. (2006) below, using a *multiple-selves* framework. This class of models is considered in more detail in Volume 3 of the book. Here we simply note that the individual has multiple selves, one for each time period. Each of the multiple selves has its own objective function and none of the selves can directly control the other, although indirect control is possible.

Consider a three-period model of a single, representative, individual. Time periods are subscripted by $t = 0, 1, 2$. The individual has initial endowment y at time $t = 0$. There is no consumption in period 0 ($t = 0$) and consumption in period 1 ($t = 1$) is given by $c_1 = c$.

The individual saves an amount k at time $t = 1$, to be carried into the second period ($t = 2$). There is no other source of income, and the interest rate on savings is normalized to zero, so $c_2 \equiv k$. Thus, the budget set of the individual in period 1 is given by

$$B = \left\{ (c,k) \in \mathbb{R}_+^2 : c + k \leq y \right\}. \tag{1.87}$$

The individual has multiple selves and we shall refer to the self in period t as self-t. Self-2 has no important economic decisions to make, so we ignore it for the moment. Self-0 is the *principal*, while self-1 is the *agent*. The descriptions of the problems for self-0 and self-1 are given below.

1. In period 1, the preferences of self-1 are defined over first period consumption, c, and second period consumption, k. These preferences are given by

$$\theta u(c) + \beta v(k), \tag{1.88}$$

   where $\theta > 0$, $0 < \beta \leq 1$ are taste parameters, and u, v are increasing, concave and twice continuously differentiable functions. The parameter θ is private information to self-1, but self-0 knows that it takes on two possible values, θ_L, θ_H, with respective probabilities $p, 1 - p$, and $0 < \theta_L < \theta_H$.

2. Self-0 does not know the value of θ but knows its distribution. The preferences of self-0 are given by

$$E[\theta u(c) + v(k)], \tag{1.89}$$

   where E denotes the expectation operator with respect to θ. Notice that self-1 has a bias toward first period consumption ($\because 0 < \beta \leq 1$) but self-0 has no such bias. The *strength of the bias towards current consumption* is given by the term $1 - \beta$, so the greater is β, the lower is the bias towards current consumption.

1.8.1 *First best outcome*

Suppose that the principal (self-0) has full information on θ. The first best solution maximizes the utility of the principal, given in (1.89), subject to the budget constraint, given in (1.87). Thus, under the first best, there is no bias towards current consumption. Denoting the solution by $(c^*(\theta), k^*(\theta))$, $\theta = \theta_L, \theta_H$, we have

$$c^*(\theta) \in \arg \max_{c \in [0,y]} \left[\theta u(c) + v(y - c) \right].$$

The first order condition is given by

$$\theta u'(c^*(\theta)) = v'(y - c^*(\theta)). \tag{1.90}$$

Substituting $c^*(\theta)$ from (1.90) into (1.87) we get $k^*(\theta) = y - c^*(\theta)$. Since u, v are strictly concave, so the first best is unique. Implicitly differentiating (1.90)

$$\frac{dc^*(\theta)}{d\theta} = \frac{-u'}{\theta u'' + v''} > 0. \tag{1.91}$$

Using (1.87), (1.91), we get the following monotonicity condition.

Lemma 1.1 *At the first best allocation $c^*(\theta_H) > c^*(\theta_L)$ and $k^*(\theta_H) < k^*(\theta_L)$.*

Thus, under full information, consumption is higher when the marginal utility of consumption at $t = 1$ is higher. We shall sometimes denote $c^*(\theta_i)$ and $k^*(\theta_i)$ by, respectively, c_i^* and k_i^*, $i = H, L$.

1.8.2 The optimal commitment solution under asymmetric information

Now suppose that self-0 does not know θ. Self-1 cannot control (even by exercising costly control) the temptation toward current consumption arising from $0 < \beta \leq 1$. Self-0 now optimally chooses an appropriate budget set $B = \bar{B}$ in the full knowledge that self-1 is decisive in making the consumption–savings choice. The main trade-off in the model is to tailor consumption to the taste shock θ that is unobserved at $t = 0$ (flexibility) and restrict consumption opportunities for self-1 due to present-biased preferences (commitment).

Hence, the problem of self-0 is to choose $\bar{B}$ in order to maximize (1.89), subject to the constraint that the choice of self-1, $\bar{c}(\theta), \bar{k}(\theta)$, will be made according to

$$\left(\bar{c}(\theta), \bar{k}(\theta) \right) \in \underset{c,k \in \bar{B}}{\arg\max} \, \theta u(c) + \beta v(k).$$

This problem is equivalent to the following problem in which self-0 directly chooses the allocations $(c_i, k_i) = (c(\theta_i), k(\theta_i))$, $i = L, H$ in order to maximize her objective

$$Z = \left(1 - p\right) [\theta_H u(c_H) + v(k_H)] + p [\theta_L u(c_L) + v(k_L)], \tag{1.92}$$

subject to the following constraints.

$$IC_H : \theta_H u(c_H) + \beta v(k_H) \geq \theta_H u(c_L) + \beta v(k_L). \tag{1.93}$$

$$IC_L : \theta_L u(c_L) + \beta v(k_L) \geq \theta_L u(c_H) + \beta v(k_H). \tag{1.94}$$

$$c_H + k_H \leq y; \quad c_L + k_L \leq y. \tag{1.95}$$

Effectively, we have that $\bar{B} = \{(c_H, k_H), (c_L, k_L): (1.95) \text{ holds}\}$, so one allocation is chosen for each type. (1.92) is just a restatement of (1.89) to take account of the uncertainty of self-0 about the values of θ, while (1.93), (1.94) are, respectively, the incentive compatibility conditions for types θ_H and θ_L; we denote these, respectively, by IC_H and IC_L. The incentive compatibility constraint ensures that each type prefers its intended allocation. There are no participation constraints because it is not clear what an outside option might be in a model of multiple selves. Finally, condition (1.95) requires that the type-contingent budget constraint must be respected.

We first show that if the *strength of bias towards current consumption* is low enough (or β is high enough), then there is no problem in implementing the first best allocation; this result does not hold for a continuum of types.

Proposition 1.16 *There exists some $\bar{\beta} \in \left(\frac{\theta_L}{\theta_H}, 1 \right)$ such that for all $\beta \in \left[\bar{\beta}, 1 \right]$, the first best allocation $\left(c_L^*, k_L^* \right), \left(c_H^*, k_H^* \right)$ can be implemented under asymmetric information.*

Proof: Suppose that we evaluate IC_L at the first best allocation (c_i^*, k_i^*) when $\beta = 1$. By definition, IC_L is satisfied, so

$$\theta_L u(c_L^*) + v(k_L^*) > \theta_L u(c_H^*) + v(k_H^*) \Leftrightarrow v(k_L^*) - v(k_H^*) > \theta_L \left[u(c_H^*) - u(c_L^*) \right]. \qquad (1.96)$$

The strict inequality in (1.96) arises because the first best is unique. From (1.96), it follows that there exists some $\overline{\beta} < 1$ such that

$$\overline{\beta} \left[v(k_L^*) - v(k_H^*) \right] = \theta_L \left[u(c_H^*) - u(c_L^*) \right]. \qquad (1.97)$$

$$\Rightarrow \overline{\beta} = \frac{\theta_L \left[u(c_H^*) - u(c_L^*) \right]}{\left[v(k_L^*) - v(k_H^*) \right]}. \qquad (1.98)$$

$$\Rightarrow \overline{\beta} \geq \theta_L \frac{u'(c_H^*)}{v'(k_H^*)}. \qquad (1.99)$$

$$\Rightarrow \overline{\beta} \geq \frac{\theta_L}{\theta_H}. \qquad (1.100)$$

Expression (1.99) follows from the property that for an increasing and concave function, w, $w'(c_H^*) \leq \frac{w(c_H^*) - w(c_L^*)}{c_H^* - c_L^*}$ and $k_L^* - k_H^* = c_H^* - c_L^*$, while (1.100) follows from (1.99) by using the first order condition under full information, (1.90). From (1.97), IC_L evaluated at the first best allocation holds for all $\beta \geq \overline{\beta}$. Analogously, evaluating IC_H at the first best allocation, a simple calculation shows that it holds if

$$\beta \leq \frac{\theta_H \left[u(c_H^*) - u(c_L^*) \right]}{\left[v(k_L^*) - v(k_H^*) \right]}.$$

Using (1.98) this implies that

$$\beta \leq \frac{\theta_H}{\theta_L} \overline{\beta}.$$

Using (1.100), $\frac{\theta_H}{\theta_L} \overline{\beta} > 1$, so IC_H, evaluated at the first best allocation, holds for all $\beta \leq 1$.

Thus, for all $\beta \in \left[\overline{\beta}, 1 \right]$, IC_L, IC_H hold at the first best allocation, which is therefore, implementable. ∎

Denote the asymmetric equilibrium solution by $\left(\overline{c}_H, \overline{k}_H \right)$, $\left(\overline{c}_L, \overline{k}_L \right)$. We now show that for high enough temptation $(1 - \beta)$, it is optimal to bunch the types, while for intermediate levels of temptation, it is optimal to separate the types. Bunching shares a common feature with *minimum savings rules* in other models, namely, that types above some threshold have the same consumption and saving bundle.

Proposition 1.17 *(Amador et al., 2006)*

(a) *If $\beta > \frac{\theta_L}{\theta_H}$, then a separating equilibrium exists such that $\overline{c}_H > \overline{c}_L$ and $\overline{k}_H < \overline{k}_L$. Both inequalities in (1.95) bind at the optimal solution.*

(b) *If $\beta \leq \frac{\theta_L}{\theta_H}$, then bunching is optimal, i.e., $\overline{c}_H = \overline{c}_L$ and $\overline{k}_H = \overline{k}_L$. Both inequalities in (1.95) bind at the optimal solution.*

In Volume 3 we considered evidence that individuals do not save enough towards their retirement. Suppose that the government imposed a minimum savings requirement on all individuals, independent of their types. Is there a justification for such a *minimum savings rule* in a model of multiple selves where selves have asymmetric information about the subsequent selves? From Proposition 1.17(b), the answer is in the affirmative. A second contribution of the analysis in this section is to show that the removal of all tempting options, is suboptimal. Rather, individual allocations, tailored to the flexible needs of different types (see Proposition 1.17(a)) are optimal. Only when β is low enough as in Proposition 1.17(b) (self-control problems of self-1 are high enough), does self-0 remove the flexibility associated with a separating equilibrium and forces each type to save the same amount (commitment).

1.8.3 *Some empirical evidence on self-control*

There is surprisingly little formal evidence on the direct measurement of self-control, although one observes potential implications of self-control problems such as inadequate savings for retirement. There is now a fair bit of evidence on hyperbolic discounting that leads to self-control problems; see Volume 3 of the book for details that we omit here.

Ameriks et al. (2007) is a relatively unusual study that tries to directly measure self-control problems. The authors assume that individuals correctly predict their future self-control problems, while anecdotal evidence suggests that individuals may be imperfectly aware of these problems. Survey data is used to pose hypothetical choices, so there is no guarantee that their procedure is incentive compatible; this would be more of a concern for experimental economists, although the view taken in this book is that all forms of evidence, including survey data, is admissible.

The study proceeds as follows. Individuals are told that they have won ten certificates and each certificate entitles them to eat one free meal at a good restaurant. The certificates must be used entirely within the first two years, otherwise they are not valid. One measure of the contribution of self-control problems is the self-reported expected-ideal (EI) gap. This is the gap between the stated *expected* number of gift certificates that people use and the *ideal* number of gift certificates they would like to use in year 1 as compared to year 2. For 60% of the sample, the ideal split of the certificates over the two years is 50–50. Of the remaining sample, 15% wished to use all their certificates in the first year.

The EI gap is found to be quite small, suggesting low self-control problems. For 95% of the sample, the EI gap belongs to the set $\{-2, -1, 0, 1, 2\}$. Approximately two-thirds of the subjects choose the modal value of the EI gap, which is 0. In a regression analysis, individuals with higher self-reported value of the degree of conscientiousness exhibit smaller absolute values of the EI gap. Older individuals exhibit a smaller absolute value of the EI gap, suggesting that temptations fall with age. This may be helpful in understanding why we typically do not observe consumption splurges from lump-sum liquid retirement incomes.

In order to further explore self-control problems, subjects in the sample were given a choice to precommit to the number of certificates that they could use in the first year. This gives rise to another measure, the revealed preference (RP) gap. This is the difference between the expected number of certificates that subjects hope to consume in the first year and the number they would like to commit to. The RP gap turns out to be quite low and is indicative of low self-control problems. Only 10% of the subjects have a desire to impose strictly binding constraints on themselves. Perhaps, as in the work of Amador et al. (2006), they have a preference for flexibility.

1.9 Happiness economics

The dominant practice in economics is to infer the utility function of individuals from their actual choices and to use the utility function to predict the choices that people make. We may refer to such utility as *decision utility* or *wantability*. Bentham (1789) had in mind a different concept, namely, *experienced utility*, which is not normally considered in modern economics. Experienced utility is the hedonic experience associated with an outcome. As such, one may obtain it by integrating the instantaneous experienced utilities associated with an outcome.

1.9.1 *Why should we be interested in subjective well-being?*

Kahneman and Thaler (2006, p. 222) write: "In the older interpretation of utility, the question of whether choices maximize utility has a simple meaning: do people choose the options that they will most enjoy? In modern decision theory, which ignores the distinction, the question is quite different: are preferences consistent and do they satisfy the axioms of rational choice?" Insofar as the stream of instantaneous utilities has accrued in the past, the individual has to contend with issues of imperfect memory; in this case, experienced utility is sometimes known as *remembered utility*. If instantaneous utilities accrue in the future (say, a purchase of a consumer durable), the individual might be subjected to projection bias (see Section 1.6 above). In this case, (the yet to be) experienced utility is sometimes known as *predicted utility*. Hence, an important issue is whether experienced utility can be successfully measured.

Kahneman et al. (1997) review the evidence on remembered utility, drawing on Varey and Kahneman (1992), Fredrickson and Kahneman (1993), Kahneman et al. (1993), and Redelmeier and Kahneman (1996). The typical procedure in these studies is to measure the discomfort of the subjects, say, during a colonoscopy, every 60 seconds (instantaneous utilities) and then ask them to report the disutility of the entire procedure at the end (remembered utility). The remembered utility can then be compared to the reports of instantaneous utilities. For a preference representation that takes account of these features, see Kahneman et al. (1997). The two main findings are as follows.

1. *Peak-end evaluation.* Peak-end utility is measured as a combination of the (i) average of the remembered peaks of past instantaneous utilities, and (ii) the instant utility towards the end of the experience. Peak-end evaluation has the following two implications. (a) *Duration neglect*: The duration of the experience has little effect if the average of the remembered peaks does not change much. (b) *Violations of temporal monotonicity*: Since peak-end evaluation weights the latest episode of utility, if there is a particularly low (respectively, high) recent instantaneous utility experience, overall remembered utility can be reduced (respectively, increased).
2. *Decisions by remembered utility*: When comparing two streams of past utilities and evaluating them by peak-end evaluation, the decision maker chooses the one with the highest remembered utility.

Subjective well-being relies on *expressed preferences* rather than on *revealed choice*. Revealed preference cannot be relied upon to judge the utility implications for individuals in cases where they have little or no effect on the outcome. Examples include environmental degradation, income inequality, fairness of the tax system, social capital, quality of governance, inflation, and unemployment. Indeed, in these cases, self-reported measures of *life satisfaction*, *well-being*, or *happiness* (the literature often uses these terms interchangeably), may provide an insight into the utility effects on individuals.

Utility is ordinal in the revealed preference approach. If a utility function, u, represents preferences, so does the function $\phi(u)$, where ϕ is any monotonically increasing transformation of u. Hence, based on actual choices made by individuals, we cannot know which utility function in the class of all monotonically increasing transformations of u we have actually measured. Yet, we routinely hear individuals making statements of the form: Peter is happier than John. The ability to make interpersonal comparisons of utility suggests that individuals may have some underlying cardinal measure of preferences.

Many of the measures of well-being are non-pecuniary. Economic policy that focuses purely on pecuniary measures of well-being will, therefore, not optimize overall well-being. *Subjective well-being* encompasses both *experienced utility* and *procedural utility* (Frey and Stutzer, 2002). Procedural utility refers to the actual procedure that leads to an outcome; see, for instance, Volume 2 for a discussion of procedural fairness.

Can subjective well-being be measured? Traditionally the economics profession has been suspicious of self-reported measures of well-being that are based on hypothetical questions and the absence of incentives. Furthermore, the memories of subjects could be imperfect, they may be subject to projection bias, to framing, and to emotional and contextual effects. However, the implications of these potential errors depend on the intended usage of the data. Senik (2014) offers the following interesting quote attributed to Alan Blinder: "If molecules could talk, would physicists refuse to listen?"

The self-reported on subjective well-being data are typically intended to provide an ordinal measure of well-being, and identify the determinants of well-being and happiness. For instance, we might be interested to see if reported subjective well-being is higher or lower when the quality of governance increases. The numerical increase in the reported subjective well-being is of lesser importance for this question. There is typically a high degree of consistency in this data, both in time series and cross-sectional data. Reassuringly, there is a high correlation between various measures of self-reported happiness. These considerations lead many to believe that individuals are perfectly capable of answering questions about subjective well-being in a consistent manner; see Frey and Stutzer (2002, Section 2.3) for the supporting evidence and the details.

Benjamin et al. (2012) evaluate the claim that *subjective well-being* (SWB) is a good proxy for utility in the sense that individuals make choices that would maximize their subjective well-being. Using three different samples, they give subjects a series of hypothetical choices in a variety of scenarios. Consider one of the scenarios, Scenario 1, in which individuals are asked to consider the trade-off between sleep and income.

"Say you have to decide between two new jobs. The jobs are exactly the same in almost every way but have different work hours and pay different amounts.

Option 1: A job paying $80,000 per year. The hours for this job are reasonable, and you would be able to get about 7.5 hours of sleep on the average work night.

Option 2: A job paying $140,000 per year. However, this job requires you to go to work at unusual hours, and you would only be able to sleep around 6 hours on the average work night.

Between these two options, taking all things together, which do you think would give you a happier life as a whole?"

At this point, subjects indicate a preference for one of the options and also indicate the intensity of the choice, based on a three point scale. Having answered this subjective well-being question, subjects are asked the following *choice question.*

"If you were limited to these two options, which do you think you would choose?"

For the choice question as well, subjects make one of the choices and indicate the intensity of the preference on a three point scale.

A total of 13 different scenarios were used across the subject pool. Subjects are given choices for jobs or housing options that trade-off financial rewards versus more sleep (Scenario 1), a shorter commute (Scenario 12), being around friends (Scenario 13), making more money relative to others (Scenario 3), and so on. In other scenarios, subjective well-being is not the only consideration. For instance, in Scenario 4, subjects choose between two career paths. One involves an easier life with fewer sacrifices, while another promises posthumous impact and fame. Scenario 2 involved an ethical choice: A more convenient option versus one that is the "right thing to do."

The main results are as follows. Across all samples, the *SWB ranking* of the two options and the *actual choices* match for 83% of all respondents. For one sample, the Denver sample, only 13% of the rankings do not match, and for another, the Cornell sample, only 24% of the rankings do not match. Thus, subjective well-being is a good predictor of actual choices. However, for both samples, a test of proportions rejects the null hypothesis that the proportion of subjects making choice 1 is the same in the subjective well-being question and the choice question. When one of the options involves more money, respondents are more likely to choose the option with more money in the choice question, relative to predicting that this option will yield greater subjective well-being.

In order to explain the difference between the two sets of questions, the authors introduce several new explanatory variables for the Cornell sample. These include the following variables, each measured on a seven point scale: Your family's happiness, social life, control over life, level of spirituality, social status, and sense of purpose. When actual choices are regressed on subjective well-being and 11 other variables, it turns out that subjective well-being predicts choices better than all the other variables combined. Further, on average, the increase in explanatory power that is achieved by adding the 11 extra variables is modest, although in some scenarios the increase is substantial.

These results establish the importance of measures of social well-being as well as offer caveats about its use. The evidence requires us to take more seriously this line of research. The evidence supports plausible links of self-reported measures of well-being with meaningful economic variables. These include, for instance, the ability of these measures to predict job quits (Clark, 2001), probability of suicides (Helliwell, 2007), productivity (Oswald et al., 2015), and probability of a future divorce among couples (Guven et al., 2012).

A dominant tradition in the literature, as we shall see below, equates subjective well-being with self-reported measures of happiness, health, and life satisfaction; this is the approach that we shall take in this section. Indeed, in this approach, these self-reported measures of well-being are taken to directly reflect utility. But what constitutes subjective well-being? Benjamin et al. (2014) explore this issue. In addition to happiness, their list includes goals, achievements, freedom, morality, and relationships. They find that happiness, health, and life satisfaction do indeed play a major role in well-being, but so do many other variables such as the quality of relationships, financial and physical security, morality, and freedom of choice.

We have considered the importance of character virtues, typically suppressed in neoclassical economics, in Volume 2 of the book. The empirical results in Benjamin et al. confirm the importance of character virtues for well-being. Indeed, many of the variables that they find important for well-being correspond to the use in Sen (1985, 1992) of *functionings* and *capabilities*; the former refers to material standards of living and the latter to opportunities to achieve the relevant functionings, and to individual freedoms.[7]

There is a recognition in the literature that self-reported measures of well-being may not always give an accurate picture of utility, due to some of the reasons considered above. Yet, there is merit in considering these measures on two counts. First, as Benjamin et al. (2014, p. 2703) write: "Nonetheless, we believe it is more attractive to rely on what people's own stated preferences suggest about what they themselves care about than to paternalistically rely on the opinions and introspections of 'experts' (such as researchers and policymakers) regarding which aspects to track and how to weight them." Second, there might be a normative use of self-reported measures of well-being. These measures may embody deliberative responses to a greater extent (as compared to emotional responses) that are more reflective of the actual welfare of the individuals.

Carter and McBride (2013) provide evidence that the shape of experienced utility is similar to the S-shaped utility function under prospect theory. Furthermore, they also report some evidence for loss aversion. The similarity between decision utility and experienced utility at a fundamental level, despite individual-level heterogeneity, is clearly an important development that needs to be replicated and refined.

1.9.2 *The relation between life-satisfaction/happiness and GDP*

The relation between self-reported measures of life-satisfaction/happiness and GDP lies at the heart of the subject of subjective well-being. Many surveys prefer the word *life satisfaction* to *happiness* as it may be considered to invoke lesser emotional feelings. Recent research has thrown the conventional wisdom in the area into a state of flux. In this section, we shall primarily be interested in the relation between happiness and income. However, there might also be a relation between happiness and wealth; for the emerging evidence, see Senik (2014).

Early work in this area is associated with the contribution of Easterlin (1974). Van Praag (1968, 1971) had already started analyzing issues of subjective well-being using survey questionnaire techniques, a few years earlier. The results can be illustrated using a more updated dataset for the US, shown in Figures 1.5 and 1.6. The data are from the United States General Social Survey. The self-reported measure of happiness takes the form of the following question: "Taken all together, how would you say things are these days—would you say that you are (3) very happy, (2) pretty happy, or (1) not too happy?"

Figure 1.5 shows that for the cross-sectional data from 1994, average US happiness increases with per capita real household income. So the richer appear to be happier. Furthermore, the curve shows diminishing marginal utility of income if we accept that happiness reflects utility. From this, we might expect that, since per capita real GDP has an upward trend, average happiness should increase over time. However, from Figure 1.6, we see that, while GDP per capita increases over time, average happiness is flat. This has come to be termed as the *Easterlin paradox*.

When Figure 1.5 is drawn for a cross section of countries, using the *World Values Survey*, the relationship between life satisfaction and GDP is relatively flat for incomes above $10,000. Hence, further increases in income do not lead to appreciable increases in well-being; see for

---

[7] For the social welfare foundations of economics in the presence of these measures of well-being, see Fleurbaey (2009) and Fleurbaey and Blanchet (2013).

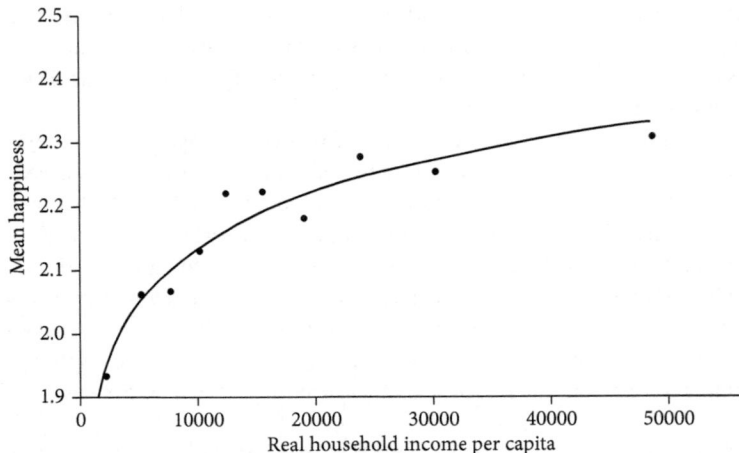

Figure 1.5 Mean happiness and real household income for a cross section of Americans in 1994.
Source: Di Tella and MacCulloch (2006) with permission from the American Economic Association.

Figure 1.6 Relation between mean happiness and real per capita GDP for the US between 1975 and 1997.
Source: Di Tella and MacCulloch (2006) with permission from the American Economic Association.

instance Figure 4 in Frey and Stutzer (2002) and see also Figure 1.11 below. The idea is that income adds to happiness until basic needs are met, but not beyond that point (Veenhoven, 1991). Deaton (2008) presents the alternative idea, namely, that only after basic needs have been met can individuals derive happiness for cultural and intellectual pursuits. This view will have a bearing for the emerging results that we review below.

For a replication of the results in Figure 1.6 to other developed countries such as Japan, France, Germany, United Kingdom, Switzerland, see Easterlin (1995), Frey and Stutzer (2000), Blanchflower and Oswald (2004), Myers (2000), and Di Tella et al. (2001).[8] Regressions of life

---

[8] For a book length treatment of this evidence, see Layard (2005).

satisfaction on lagged incomes show that individuals adapt to changes in income over a relatively short span of a few years. Based on German micro-level data, Di Tella et al. (2010) find complete adaptation within four years of the unification of Germany.

As an illustrative example, consider the results from Japan, over the period 1958–91, in Figure 1.7. The data is drawn from Penn World Tables and the World Database of Happiness. Self-reported happiness was measured on a four point scale; average happiness was 2.7 in 1958, and despite spectacular growth in per capita real GDP, it was 2.7 in 1991 as well. These results are very similar to those in Figure 1.6 and reinforce the Easterlin paradox.

The cross-sectional findings that we report above, only establish a correlation between happiness and income but do not establish any causal direction. One may expect that higher income makes people happier. However, there could also be reverse causation in which happier people earn more, perhaps because they are more productive or are able to deal with job stress better (Kenny, 1999; Graham et al., 2004).

One natural experiment to establish the direction of causality is to examine the before and after happiness of people who unexpectedly win the lottery. Gardner and Oswald (2007) use the British Household Panel Survey (BHPS) to examine this question. The survey contains a mental well-being measure based on 12 questions. For each question, the lowest well-being score is 3 and the highest is 0. Thus, the aggregate worst well-being score is 36 and best is 0. A simple sum of these scores across the 12 questions for each subject gives the General Health Questionnaire score (GHQ) for the subject. Using data over 1998–2001, the authors cull out individuals who have won differing amounts of money in the lottery. There are 4,822 observations for individuals who have won a small amount (less than £999) and 137 observations on medium-sized wins (greater than £1000).

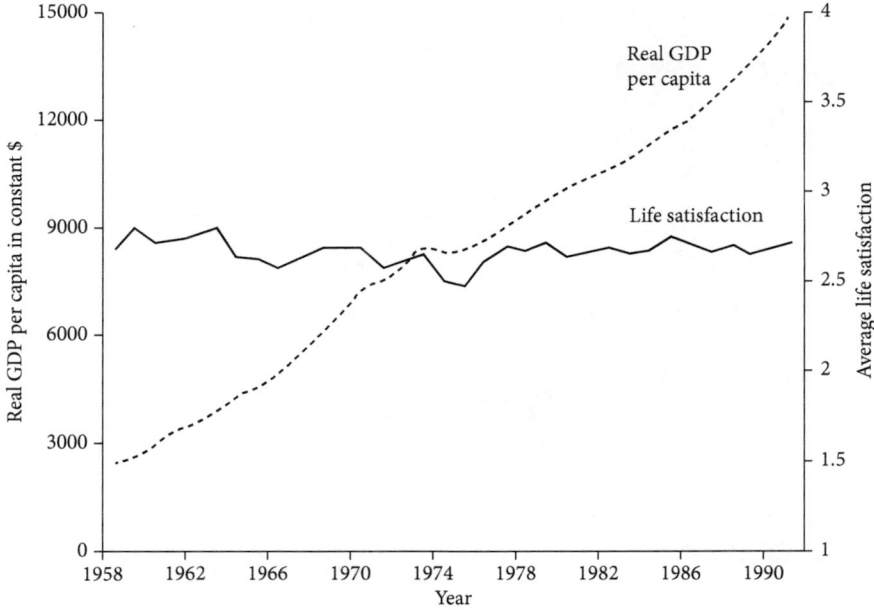

Figure 1.7 The Easterlin paradox for Japan, over the period 1958–1991.

Source: Frey and Stutzer (2002) with permission from the American Economic Association.

The results are shown in Figure 1.8 for the three groups titled: No win (the control group), small-sized wins (£1–£999), and medium-sized wins (£1000 and above). The mean change in GHQ scores is reported for each group and for various time intervals, assuming that the lottery win takes place in period T. The standard errors are reported in the corresponding figures on the right.

In the first row in Figure 1.8, labeled (a), there is an increase in mental stress in the year of the win, particularly for medium-sized wins. In the second row, labeled (b), there is no difference in the GHQ score changes for non-winners and winners of small amounts in the year immediately after the win. However, there is an increase in mental well-being (fall in GHQ score) for individuals who have medium-sized wins. This is even more pronounced if one considers the two-year interval on either side of the win. The standard errors allow one to reject the null hypothesis at 5% that there is no change in the GHQ score for medium-sized winners. In a nutshell, small wins do not matter but larger wins raise happiness. In this case, the causality runs from income to happiness. For related findings see also Brickman et al. (1978).

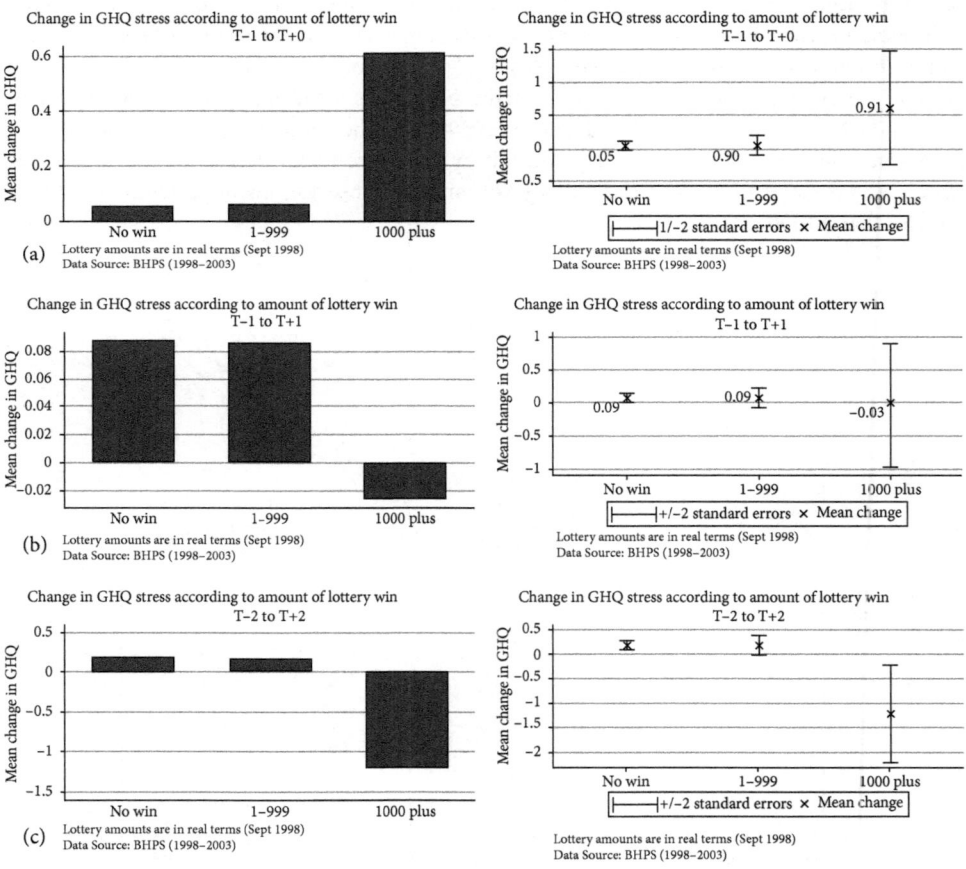

Figure 1.8 Before-win and after-win happiness of people who win the lottery.

Another exogenous variation in income is explored by Frijters et al. (2004). They find that after the fall of the Berlin Wall, the resulting increase in income in East Germany had a positive causal effect on reported happiness.

What accounts for the Easterlin paradox? Drawing on the work of Veblen ([1899] 1973) and Duesenberry (1949), Easterlin (1974, 1995, 2001) gives an explanation in terms of *relative income concerns* and *shifting aspiration levels*. Put simply, people feel happier with higher incomes but if everyone's income increases, then, given sufficient time, happiness does not increase. Aspiration adaptation theories postulate that the happiness of individuals depends on the gap between the actual realization of their income and their aspiration level; the higher the gap, the greater is the happiness. Furthermore, increases in income give temporary increases in happiness as the aspiration level adjusts upwards, eventually swamping the increase in happiness; this is sometimes known as the *hedonic treadmill* (Brickman and Campbell, 1971; Diener et al., 2006).

These adaptation features are similar to models of habit formation that we have studied in this chapter. Another explanation is based on the *set point theory of happiness*. In this theory, individuals have some inherent level of happiness; temporary shocks can lead to short-term departures in happiness but happiness eventually returns to its inherent level (Easterlin, 2003). The finding that approximately 33% of the variation in life satisfaction is on account of genetic factors is consistent with this explanation (De Neve et al., 2012). Furthermore, there have been attempts to isolate a gene for happiness (De Neve, 2011).

We have considered utility functions that depend on relative incomes in Volume 2; see, for instance, the model of Bolton and Ockenfels (2000). Clark and Oswald (1996) provide evidence that British workers form an income reference group with other workers who have shared labor market characteristics. Knight et al. (2009) use Chinese household data to show that the main reference group is other households in the same village. For empirical evidence that shows the dependence of well-being on the difference between actual income and income aspirations, see, for instance, Stutzer (2004) and Knight and Guanatilaka (2012). Luttmer (2005) shows that controlling for an individual's income, higher incomes of neighbors reduce self-reported happiness.

Kuhn et al. (2011) exploit the exogenous variation in income caused by the Dutch postcode lottery in which the set of winners is all the buyers of the lottery tickets in a particular postcode. Each winner wins 12,500 euros per ticket and one of the postcode winners is chosen to additionally receive a brand new BMW. The data allow for tracking the consumption patterns of the winners and their neighbors. The neighbors of winners who receive a BMW, are also more likely to buy a BMW. Angelucci et al. (2009) also find positive social spillover externalities of bimonthly conditional grants to rural communities in Mexico, designed to improve their education, health, and nutrition.

The issue of reference groups is of great interest in many different literatures in behavioral economics. In this regard, the work of Clark and Senik (2010) is particularly important. They use data from 18 European countries in Wave 3 of the European Social Survey in which income comparison questions were asked for the year 2006–7; they restricted the sample to the working age population, 16–65. We now briefly describe their methods and results.

The two relevant questions asked in the Survey were the following. (1) "How important is it for you to compare your income with other people's income?" The answers could be chosen on a discrete scale of 0 (not at all important) to 6 (very important). (2) "Whose income would you be most likely to compare with your own? Please choose one of the groups on this card: Work colleagues/ Family members/ Friends/ Others/ Don't compare/ Not applicable/ Don't know." The first question about the *intensity of comparison* was answered by 19,053 respondents; 25% choose 0 (comparisons not important). However, for the remaining 75% of the subjects, income comparisons are important. Each of the numbers 1–4 is chosen by approximately 15% of the subjects; the numbers 5 and 6 are chosen by approximately 10% and 5% of the subjects, respectively.

The responses to the second question are shown in Table 1.1. Here, 35.9% of the 18,936 respondents claim that they do not compare their incomes. In Q1, this percentage was 25, so there is a degree of time inconsistency of choices for some respondents. However, 73% of those who chose 0 in Q1, choose Don't compare in Q2, so they are consistent. Of those who compare, the vast majority compares their income with work colleagues and the next most significant group is friends.

An important finding is that there is a negative correlation between intensity of comparison (higher numbers chosen on Q1) and real per capita GDP across countries as well as within countries; see Figure 1.9. A regression analysis shows that poorer households compare their incomes more to others. Self-employed compare less, singles compare more, and there are no noticeable gender effects. There are differences in cross-country effects of the intensity of comparison; Eastern European countries compare more relative to Western European countries.

Regarding Q2, self-employed subjects who compare are more likely to compare with family members and friends. The self-employed, on average, also appear happier as compared to the employed, possibly due to the greater job autonomy that they have; see Frey and Benz (2008) for the evidence. The employed are more likely to compare with colleagues. Women are more likely to compare with family members and income comparisons increase among the 25+ age group. Eastern Europeans are less likely to compare to other family members; such a comparison is more likely in Spain, Poland, Finland, and Ireland. Countries in central continental Europe compare more with colleagues.

Those who compare more are less happy. The correlation coefficient between the intensity of income comparison and subjective happiness is negative and significant. The well-being correlation with income comparisons is smaller for richer as compared to the poorer individuals. The correlation of income comparisons with well-being depends on the reference group. Individuals who compare with colleagues are significantly happier than others who compare with friends. One possibility is that comparison with colleagues signals to individuals that their future incomes might be higher, but that is not true in a comparison with friends. Finally, those who compare more are also more likely to favor greater income redistribution.

Table 1.1 Responses to the income comparison question.

	Observations	%
Work colleagues	6874	36.3
Family members	1103	5.8
Friends	2825	14.9
Others	1344	7.1
Don't compare	6789	35.9
Total	18936	100.0

Source: Clark and Senik (2010).

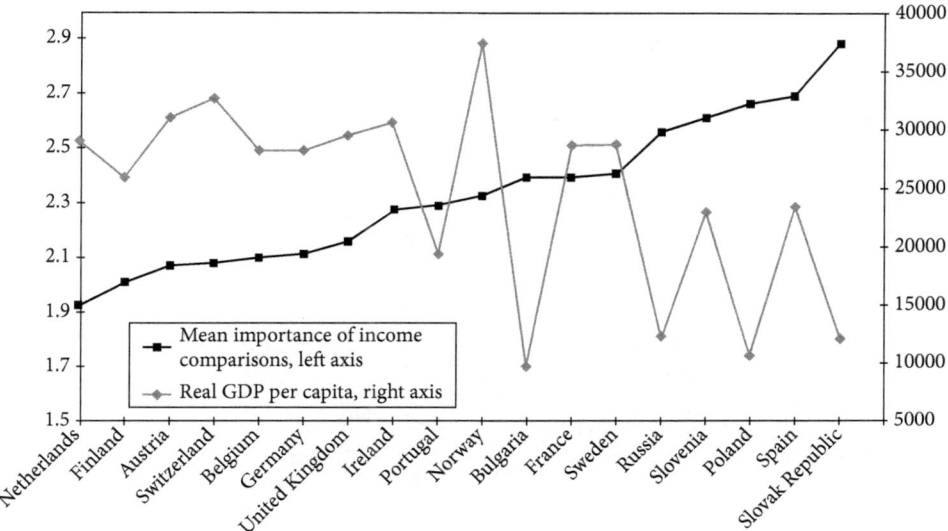

Figure 1.9 Comparisons of own incomes with the incomes of others in a cross section of countries with different income levels.

Source: Reprinted from Clark, A. E. and Senik, C. (2010), "Who compares to whom? The anatomy of income comparisons in Europe." *The Economic Journal* 120: 573–94. © Clarke, A. E. and Senik, C. Journal compilation © Royal Economic Society 2010.

Recent years have, however, seen a re-evaluation of some of the evidence considered above. This re-evaluation is based on alternative sources of information, such as the Gallup World Poll in 2006, and a consideration of the results based on a fuller set of countries and time periods. The results from the Gallup World Poll have a much fuller list of poorer countries as compared to the World Values Survey. These results, as we show below, question the very existence of an Easterlin paradox.

The Gallup World Poll asks questions about *life satisfaction* on an 11-point scale, while the World Values Survey asked questions about *happiness* on a 3-point scale. It is common practice in much of the literature to treat life satisfaction and happiness as synonymous; see Van Praag et al. (2011) for supporting arguments. However, Deaton (2008) distinguishes between the two. He argues that life satisfaction involves making an overall evaluation of one's life, while happiness reflects an effect that can be gauged from *experiential questions* such as asking the individual if they have been smiling a lot, or if they have been depressed?

Figure 1.10 shows the relation between mean life satisfaction from the Gallup World Poll and the log of per capita GDP for 2003 (x-axis). Three curves are shown. The two outer curves are for two different age groups (the upper curve is for ages 15–25 and the lower for 60 plus) and the middle curve is the average across all age groups. The sizes of the circles represent the associated country sizes. The relation between log of per capita income and mean life satisfaction is approximately linear. When the absolute level of per capita GDP is used, the relationship between life satisfaction and income is increasing and concave. This is shown in Figure 1.11 in which the data from the World Values Survey (10-point scale) is shown as the shaded circles and the Gallup World Poll data (11-point scale) is shown as hollow circles.

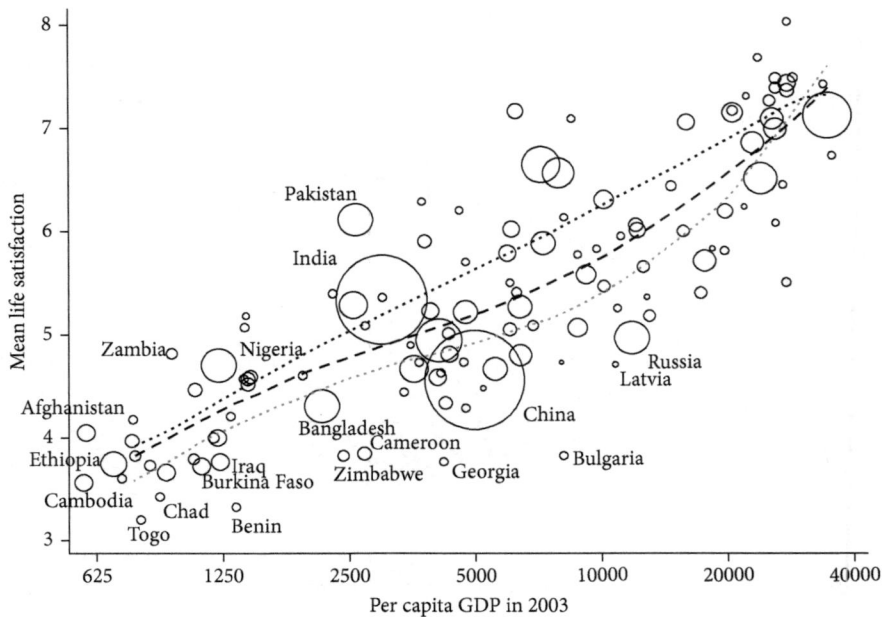

Figure 1.10 The relationship between life satisfaction and income.

Source: Deaton (2008) with permission from the American Economic Association.

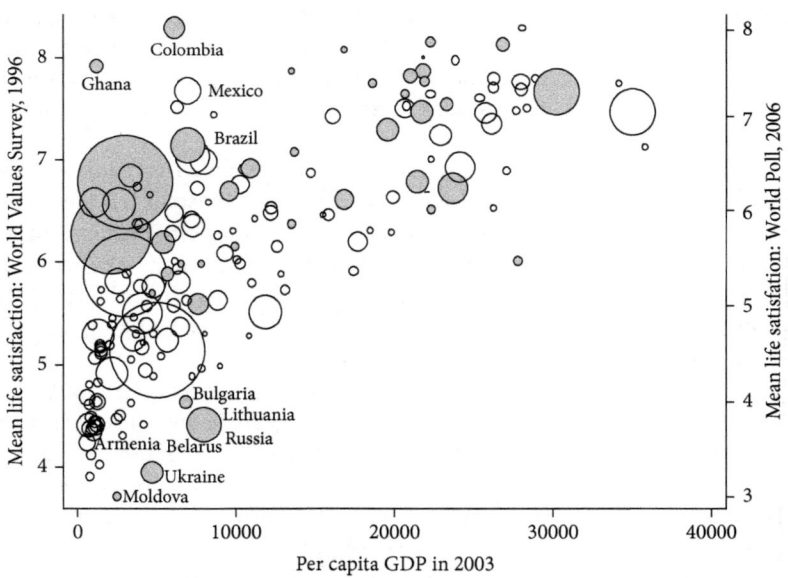

Figure 1.11 The relationship between life satisfaction and income.

Source: Deaton (2008) with permission from the American Economic Association.

Deaton (2008) draws the following conclusions from Figures 1.10 and 1.11.

1. From Figure 1.11, individuals in richer countries in North America, Japan, Australasia, and Western Europe have higher mean life satisfaction (7.5–8.5 on an 11-point scale) relative to those in poorer countries in sub-Saharan Africa, Haiti, and Cambodia (3.1–4.5). In general the relation between life satisfaction and income is upward sloping.

2. Earlier research based on World Values Survey identified a cutoff income of about $10,000 (Layard, 2003) or $20,000 (Layard, 2005) beyond which income is unrelated to happiness. This assertion was widely made; see, for instance, Diener and Seligman (2004), Di Tella et al. (2003), and Frey and Stutzer (2002). Figure 1.10 paints a contrary picture. Indeed there is an almost linear relation between life satisfaction and log of income at all income levels. If anything, the relationship is the steepest for very high income levels. This is supported by the regression results in Deaton (2008).

3. The main reasons for the difference in results between the World Values Survey and the Gallup World Poll are as follows. First, the relative coverage of poor countries in the Gallup Poll is much richer, as reflected in Figure 1.11; there are hardly any filled-in circles for very low levels of income. Second, there is a disproportionate share of Eastern European countries in the World Values Survey who had middling incomes as well as great dissatisfaction following the events of the breakdown of the former Soviet Union. Third, the World Values Survey in relatively poor countries of that time (Ghana, Nigeria, India, China) sampled the relatively better-off individuals in the poorer countries, in order to ensure comparability with the individuals in the richer countries. Presumably these individuals had much higher levels of happiness relative to the representative individuals in these countries. But this led to a much flatter relation between income and happiness.

4. Life satisfaction is age-dependent. The life satisfaction for the 15–25-year-olds is highest, while that of individuals aged 60 or above is the lowest. Life satisfaction declines with age for most countries in the world except for the highest income countries such as the US, Canada, the UK, Australia, and New Zealand, where it is U-shaped; see Deaton (2008) for details.

Stevenson and Wolfers (2008, 2013) and Sacks et al. (2013) also provide evidence that supports the analysis of Deaton (2008). Figure 1.12 gives more recent data based on a sample of 155 countries from the first five waves of the Gallup World Poll over the period 2008–12; it captures 95% of the world's population.

The simple correlation between life satisfaction and log of per capita GDP is 0.79; the regression coefficient in a simple OLS regression is 0.335 with a standard error of 0.018. The regression line is shown as the unbroken line in Figure 1.12, while the dashed line is a non-parametric line. The two lines are closely aligned. In particular, the non-parametric line does not flatten out beyond some income threshold. Choosing a threshold level, say, $15,000, and fitting separate linear regressions for countries below and above the threshold, the authors are unable to reject the null hypothesis that the regression coefficients are identical. Indeed, the relationship between life satisfaction and income appears quite steep when life satisfaction is plotted against income for the 25 largest countries; see Figure 1.13.

These results are supported by Inglehart et al. (2008), Diener et al. (2013), and Veenhoven and Vergunst (2013). The response by Easterlin et al. (2010) and Easterlin (2013) is that the positive relation between income and happiness is a short-term one and in the long term (ten years or more) there is no relation between the two. For instance, Easterlin et al. (2010) write in

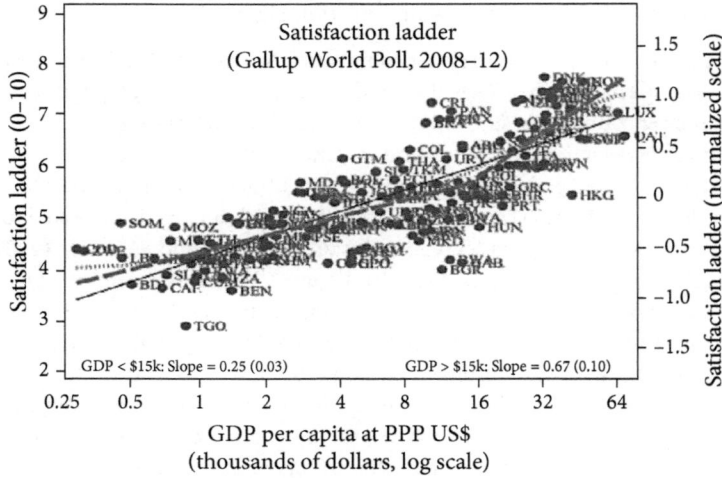

Figure 1.12 The relationship between life satisfaction and per capita GDP for 95% of the world's population.
Source: Stevenson and Wolfers (2013) with permission from the American Economic Association.

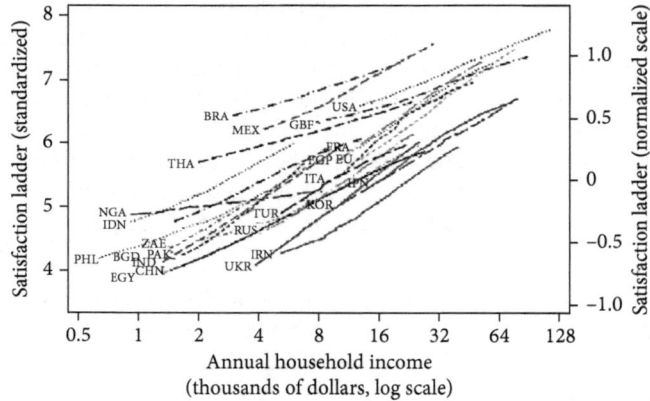

Figure 1.13 Relation between life satisfaction and income for the 25 largest countries.
Source: Stevenson and Wolfers (2013) with permission from the American Economic Association.

their abstract: "Recent critiques of the paradox, claiming the time series relationship between happiness and income is positive, are the result either of a statistical artifact or a confusion of the short-term relationship with the long-term one." However, this conclusion has been contested by the proponents of a positive relation between happiness and per capita GDP. Beja (2014) proposes a compromise. He uses very long time series data (1973 to 2012) for a cross section of European countries and finds that, while the relation between happiness and income is a positive one, it is weak and economically not significant enough.

In light of these disparate results, the Easterlin paradox no longer enjoys undisputed acceptance in the profession, which it did a decade ago.

1.9.3 *Other important economic correlates of well-being*

We consider a range of correlates of well-being in this section. These include, unemployment, inflation, income inequality, social capital, health, and democratic institutions. An alternative approach is to consider *domain satisfaction*. This refers to a more disaggregated measure of satisfaction that studies the determinants of satisfaction in individual domains such as job satisfaction, and financial satisfaction (we have considered health satisfaction above). For a further discussion of these issues and the relevant empirical evidence, we refer the reader to the survey by Van Praag and Carbonell (2011).

UNEMPLOYMENT AND INFLATION

Di Tella et al. (2001) explore the foundations of the standard social welfare function in macro-economics that typically proposes quadratic losses in unemployment and inflation. They regress measures of happiness on inflation and unemployment, using a very large cross-country dataset from 12 European countries and the US; as is typical in these studies, they allow for country fixed effects and time trends.[9]

Both unemployment and inflation are found to reduce happiness. A one percentage point increase in unemployment from 9% (the mean unemployment rate at the time of the empirical study) to 10% reduces life satisfaction by 0.028 when happiness is measured on a scale of 1 to 4. On the same scale, a one percentage increase in inflation from the sample mean rate of 8% to 9%, reduces happiness by 0.01. Both effects are substantial. However, unemployment is relatively more deleterious for happiness. On average, individuals are willing to trade a 1 percentage point increase in unemployment against a 1.7 percentage point increase in the inflation rate.

These results have been replicated. Using data from 16 European countries, Wolfers (2003) finds that a one percentage point increase in unemployment causes 4.7 times as much unhappiness as a one percentage point increase in the inflation rate. Reference point effects have been identified in the observed aversion of unemployment. The happiness reducing effect of unemployment is smaller if the fraction of other people in the region who are unemployed is larger, or a partner is unemployed; presumably this reduces the stigma attached with being unemployed (Clark, 2003).

Unemployment is possibly more aversive to happiness than any other single characteristic, even more aversive than divorce or separation, and relatively more aversive for the more educated (Clark and Oswald, 1994). The causality runs from unemployment to unhappiness, rather than the other way around (Winkelmann and Winkelmann, 1998). It appears that the unhappiness of the unemployed cannot be accounted for, purely by their lower income. Thus, there are psychic costs of unemployment.

Psychic costs arising through anxiety, depression, loss of self-esteem, resort to alcoholism, stigma costs, scarring costs of unemployment, and strained relationships all appear to play a role in greater unhappiness.[10] Luechinger et al. (2010) test for anticipatory anxiety among

---

[9] The European data is taken from the Euro-Barometer Survey Series, the US data is taken from the United States General Social Survey, and the data on unemployment and inflation is taken from OECD statistics. The dataset used in the study contains about a quarter of a million individuals.

[10] For the importance of non-pecuniary costs of unemployment, see Kassenboehmer and Haisken-DeNew (2009). For the relation of non-pecuniary costs with social work norms, see Clark (2003) and Stutzer and Lalive (2004). For limited adaptation to unemployment and its scarring role, see Clark et al. (2001), Clark (2006), and Knabe and Rätzel (2011).

the unemployed by comparing private and public sector employees in Germany. Public sector employees have greater job security. For this reason, private sector workers exhibit relatively greater anxiety towards general economic shocks. For state-level panel data, Ruhm (2000) finds that there is a positive correlation between unemployment and the number of suicides in a state.

The picture emerging from this analysis shows up the inadequacy of macroeconomic explanations, in the tradition of real business cycle models, that solely use the transmission channel of voluntary unemployment as an explanation of unemployment. If people were voluntarily unemployed, it would be difficult to account for their pronounced unhappiness and low self-reported measures of well-being. This not only illustrates the usefulness of happiness economics, but also raises uncomfortable questions about the dominant practice in macroeconomics for so long.

INCOME INEQUALITY AND HAPPINESS

While the relation between happiness and income is well documented, there is comparatively less work on the relation between inequality and happiness. Alesina et al. (2004) find that inequality reduces happiness. However, while the relation is strong and statistically significant in the case of Europe, it is far weaker in magnitude for the US. The authors conjecture that upward income mobility is greater in the US relative to Europe. So individuals who are poorer do not see inequality as unduly limiting their future prospects in the US; hence, inequality has a lesser impact on their happiness.

HEALTH SATISFACTION AND HAPPINESS

Figure 1.14 shows the relation between health satisfaction and per capita GDP. The non-parametric regression curves are upward sloping, indicating that higher income is associated with greater health satisfaction. Health satisfaction falls with age. For the richest countries, the 50–59 age group has a lower health satisfaction relative to the two older groups.

Countries from the former Soviet Union exhibit extremely low health satisfaction. Other countries in the low health satisfaction group include Haiti, Rwanda, Burundi, Uganda, Cambodia, and Benin. Deaton (2008) reports that a fall in life expectancy due to HIV/AIDS cannot fully explain the poor levels of health satisfaction in sub-Saharan Africa.

Causality need not just run from good health to happiness. Indeed, happier people are likely to be healthier (Diener and Chan, 2011). Other variables may be correlated with both; hence, the relationship between health and happiness may reflect these other factors, particularly genetic factors (De Neve et al., 2012). There is also significant adaptation to health disabilities. Oswald and Powdthavee (2008) report that within three years, individuals adjust to 30% of the effect of severe disability and 50% of the effect of moderate disability.

Oswald and Wu (2011) use state-level data for the US that is based on telephone surveys of the mental health of the respondents and questions about their life satisfaction and incomes in the previous month. They find a high degree of heterogeneity among the US states. Particularly interesting is the result that the high GDP states in the sample are less happy; Louisiana is one of the happier states, while California is not happier than the other states. The authors' preferred explanation is based on Adam Smith's idea of compensating wage differential. States with lower life satisfaction have to offer a compensating income differential. However, there is no correlation between mental health and per capita state GDP.

SOCIAL CAPITAL AND HAPPINESS

Social capital refers to the effects of social networks, including the associated norms of trust and reciprocity, on production efficiency and well-being (Coleman, 1993; OECD, 2001). Helliwell and Putnam (2004, p. 1436) write: "Social capital can be embodied in bonds among family, friends and neighbors, in the workplace, at church, in civic associations, perhaps even in Internet based 'virtual communities'." They use cross-sectional data from the World Values Survey, the European Values Study, and the Canadian Benchmark Survey comprising 29,000 observations. A range of variables is considered at the national/community level and at the individual level, such as average trust, trust in neighbors and police, membership in associations, governance, the importance of God/religion, and marital status.

The authors report a range of findings that are consistent with the importance of social capital for well-being. Being married improves happiness and life satisfaction, particularly in comparison with those who are divorced or separated; this reflects the effect of family level social capital. Church attendance reflects community level social capital. Those who attend Church and have a strong belief in God, trust others more. Frequent interactions with friends and neighbors are associated with higher well-being. Those who report that they live in a high trust neighborhood report higher life satisfaction and happiness as well as better health.

This literature continues to expand. For the effects of social capital on long-term trends in subjective well-being, see Sarracino (2010); for the positive effects of volunteer work on well-being, see Meier and Stutzer (2008); and for the public goods nature of social capital, see Becchetti et al. (2008).

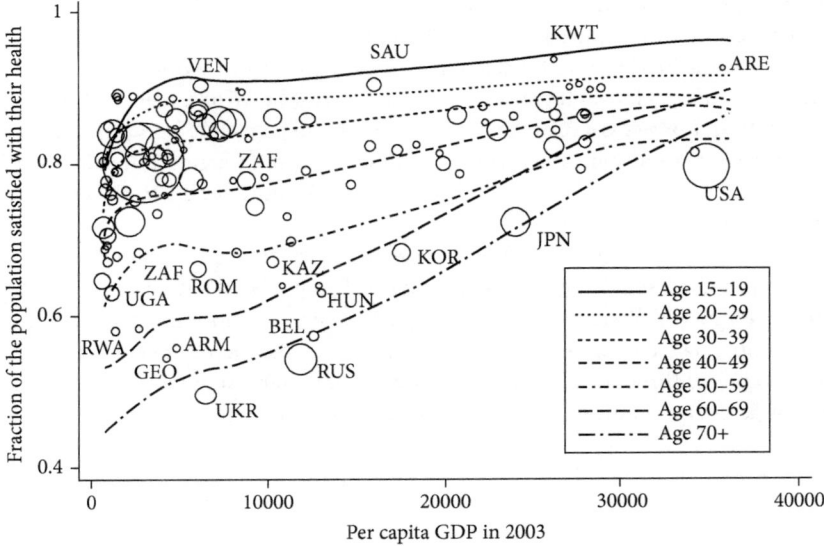

Figure 1.14 Non-parametric regressions of average health satisfaction against per capita GDP for seven age groups. GDP is measured in purchasing power parity chained dollars at 2000 prices.
Source: Deaton (2008) with permission from the American Economic Association.

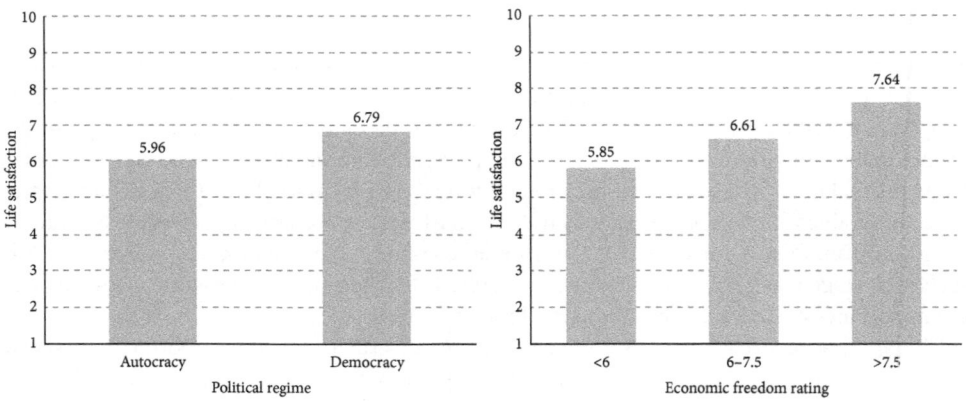

Figure 1.15 The relationship between economic freedom, democracy, and well-being and happiness.

Source: Rode, M., Knoll, B., and Pitlik, H. (2013). "Economic freedom, democracy, and life satisfaction," in James Gwartney, Robert Lawson, and Joshua Hall (eds.), *Economic Freedom of the World: 2013 Annual Report* (Fraser Institute): 215–33. www.freetheworld.com. Reprinted with kind permission of The Fraser Institute.

DEMOCRACY, FREEDOM, AND LIFE SATISFACTION

Economic freedom and democracy might also directly contribute to well-being and happiness. This is illustrated directly in Figure 1.15; the left panel shows life satisfaction in autocracies and democracies, and the right panel shows life satisfaction under different economic freedom ratings (higher rating shows higher freedom).

Economic freedom is measured by the EFW index published in *Economic Freedom of the World: 2012 Annual Report*. Life satisfaction is measured by the World Values Survey. The classification of countries into autocracies and democracies is based on Cheibub et al. (2010). In a regression analysis, Rode et al. (2013) show that the effects of economic freedom and democracy on life satisfaction are significant at 1%. One possible transmission channel is that in a democracy, politicians respect the choices of people, giving the latter a feeling of well-being (Frey and Stutzer, 2002).

Veenhoven (2000) shows that for 38 developed countries, indices of political freedom, economic freedom, and personal freedom have a statistically significant correlation with happiness. Furthermore, economic freedom enhances happiness relatively more in poorer countries and political freedom relatively more in richer countries. Direct democracy refers to the exercise of direct citizen choices through referenda. Frey and Stutzer (2000) show that Swiss cantons with higher direct democracy indices are also associated with higher self-reported happiness.

CHAPTER 2

Interactions between Emotions and Cognition

2.1 Introduction

Observed human behavior is the outcome of interactions between a *cognitive* and an *emotional* module/system in the brain. The emotional system is thought to be quick, reactive, and automatic; it is typically modeled as operating at the hot end of the spectrum of human emotions. The cognitive system is slow, deliberative, focuses on the larger goals, and operates at the cold end of the spectrum of human emotions. The human emotional system is shared in common with many other mammals, but the cognitive system is unique to humans, although some elementary functions are shared with close primate relatives such as chimps. The cognitive system, developed about 150,000 years ago, and was superimposed on top of the existing emotional system. The objectives of the two modules can be in harmony or, in the more interesting case, in conflict (Tooby and Cosmides, 1992; Wilson, 2012). In this chapter, we consider the economic implications of competition and cooperation between emotions and cognition.

Section 2.2 introduces the reader to models of *dual brain modules*, or simply dual process models. In Section 2.2.1, we introduce the main premise of these models. In Section 2.2.2, we describe a general blueprint for the interaction between the emotional and the cognitive processes (Loewenstein and O'Donoghue, 2004, 2007). The blueprint is speculative in several respects, does sometimes make heroic assumptions, and one cannot always disentangle the source of observed behavior as cognitive or emotional. However, the model is an important first pass, relies on plausible ideas, is very general, and is suitable for serving as a template for the development of further ideas. It has the potential to derive simple relations and concepts in behavioral economics, endogenously, and in a simple manner, playing a role similar to that of IS-LM analysis in macroeconomic analysis. We show that the model can give important insights into behavioral models of risk, time preference, and social preferences.

In Section 2.3, we model the interaction between a patient long-run self and a myopic short-run self in a simple consumption–savings problem (Fudenberg and Levine, 2006). In the absence of a commitment technology, the long-run self can control the consumption splurges of the short-run self through the exercise of costly willpower. We examine the dependence of optimal consumption plans on willpower costs. In a richer model, we then consider the presence of a commitment technology. Here, we show that for small windfalls in income, an increase in unanticipated income is fully consumed, while large windfalls are saved. In the absence of any costs of control, the individual never fully splurges on consumption.

It is possible that parts of the brain could have access to private information that other brain areas might not possess (Berns et al., 1997). In other contexts, it is possible that individuals might have restricted access to their own motives and beliefs (Brocas and Carrillo, 2008). People might infer their own emotions or abilities from their actual behavior. They could also take their donation of money as evidence of their altruism, or their ability to jog in extreme heat as evidence of their willpower (Bodner and Prelec, 2003).

In Section 2.4, we consider a somewhat speculative two-period model of interaction between a principal (cognitive system) and an agent (emotional system) when the agent has asymmetric information about its preferences (Bodner and Prelec, 2003; Brocas and Carillo, 2008). We contrast the allocation of consumption and effort under full information with the case of asymmetric information. It turns out that an endogenous rate of time preference develops, despite the fact that the cognitive system undertakes no time discounting. The model does leave open several questions that are not answered in a fully satisfactory manner. For instance, how are contracts between competing brain modules enforced? How should one treat the participation constraint of a brain module? What does renegotiation of contracts mean in this case?

When a current self interacts with her future selves, the decision to acquire information has considerable strategic importance. By acquiring information, one makes all of one's own future selves aware of that information. If there is a possibility that the future selves will use this information to the detriment of the current self, then the current self might choose to be strategically uninformed. For instance, individuals vastly overestimate the effect of smoking on lung cancer (Viscusi, 1990; Lundborg and Lindgren, 2004). However, such information is freely and easily available. Why then do individuals choose not to acquire such information? One possibility, that we consider in Volume 3, is that individuals procrastinate to acquire the relevant information (O'Donoghue and Rabin, 1999).

But in this chapter we consider alternative explanations. Section 2.5 considers formal models that address these issues within the framework of models of multiple selves. We first consider, in Section 2.5.1, a simple three-period model of strategic information transmission (Carrillo and Mariotti, 2000). The current self has to decide whether to learn something of strategic importance that determines the consumption behavior of future selves. We derive the conditions under which such learning is justified, relative to being strategically uninformed.

In models of asymmetric information in economics, information asymmetry typically pertains to the types of other players. Psychological evidence, however, suggests that individuals often have doubts about who they really are. Individuals often engage in introspection and reflection in an attempt to figure out the motivation, justification, and the implications of their current and past actions. Individuals often question their ability to successfully undertake a task, and sometimes struggle to discover their true underlying preferences.

Actions taken by individuals, who have asymmetric information about some relevant characteristics of their own self, are sometimes characterized by self-deception and at other times by repentance. Another relevant feature is the presence of *imperfect willpower* in humans; for instance people might lack the willpower to reduce or to give up smoking, or keep to a deadline. Finally, people might have *imperfect recall* and *motivated cognition*, i.e., they actively seek ways of managing the awareness about the degree to which subsequent selves can recall past events. In Section 2.5.2, we formally consider these issues in a model where individuals have asymmetric information about their own abilities, motivation, or self-confidence and they attempt to strategically manage the information available to their future selves (Bénabou and Tirole, 2002, 2004). Among other predictions, this model has the potential to explain the roles of strategic ignorance, selective memory transmission, and self-handicapping.

2.2 Emotions and a two-modules view of the brain

In this section, we explore the implications for human behavior when the brain is viewed as comprising of two modules: an emotional module and a cognitive module. While our focus will be on economic models of more recent vintage, there is also an older literature on these models in psychology (Schneider and Shiffrin, 1977a, 1977b).

2.2.1 *An introduction to the two-modules view*

One may imagine the brain as a group of modules, or a *confederation of mechanisms* in the language of Cohen (2005), that jointly determine human behavior. These modules could have different objectives. The desired behavioral outcomes of the competing modules may sometimes be in agreement, while at other times, these could be in conflict. The premise in these models is that observed human behavior is the outcome of competition among these modules.

A useful abstraction, that has a long history in many diverse literatures, is to consider the brain as having just two main modules. One controls emotions, while the other has a cognitive function; see Loewenstein and O'Donoghue (2004, 2007) for a lucid and informative review that we draw on here. Adam Smith used the terms *passions* versus *impartial spectator* to capture the emotions versus cognitive contrast. *Passions* describe motivational forces and other visceral states such as anger, hunger, and thirst. The *impartial spectator* refers to an ability to stand back, or be emotionally neutral in some sense, and take an impartial view of one's emotional motivations. Freud (1924) referred to a similar conflict between the *id* and the *ego*. Such dual process models are also common in modern psychology; see for instance Chaiken and Trope (1999).

In common usage, we often speak of the *feeling of being in two minds*, or *the conflict between the heart and the mind*; these phrases appear to illustrate the conflict between emotions and cognition. The conflict between emotions and cognition is likely to have an evolutionary explanation (Dawkins, 2006; Tooby and Cosmides, 1992; Massey, 2002; Wilson, 2012). When humans departed from their primate relatives in their evolutionary history, about 6 million years ago, the human brain was not redesigned from scratch. Cognitive abilities, the ability to think about broader goals, and the broader implications of one's actions, were developed by adding brain structures on top of the existing brain structures. The most notable new brain structure in this regard is the prefrontal cortex, which has developed significantly in relatively recent evolutionary history.

Emotionality clearly preceded rationality in the evolutionary sequence. Define emotions for the moment, as in Cohen (2005), as low level automatic psychological processes that are engaged by stimuli (or memories) and are associated with strong positive and negative psychic utility. For instance, witness the emotion of fear that is triggered by observing a coiled object on a dark street.

As rationality developed, it did not replace emotionality as the basis of human interaction. Rather, rational abilities were gradually added to the existing, and simultaneously developing, emotional capacities. Indeed, the neural anatomy essential for full rationality, the *prefrontal cortex*, is a recent evolutionary innovation. It only emerged in the last 150,000 years of a 6-million-year existence, representing only about 2.5% of humanity's total time on earth.

Three features of evolution, namely, that it is *efficient, opportunistic,* and *conservative,* are important in this regard; see for instance Cohen (2005). Evolution is *efficient* in the sense that, conditional on the environment, it optimally meets the needs of the organism. It is *opportunistic* in the sense that it produces solutions that are closely tailored to the environment.[1] Finally, it is *conservative* in the sense that it is reluctant to discard older solutions (e.g., existing brain structures) as new environmental situations arise, even if the older solutions are not well adapted to the new environment. Evolution may also develop additional solutions/structures to deal with long-lasting changes in the environment.

Metcalfe and Mischel (1999) also make a distinction between a hot emotional module or process, and a cool cognitive module. The emotional response is rapid, automatic, simple, relatively inflexible, and attuned to particular stimuli. The cognitive response is just the opposite, i.e., it is reflective, deliberate, slower, and more flexible. The former is limited to a small number of goals, while the latter can generate behavior that is consistent with a large number of broader goals. Cohen (2005) describes this as the familiar trade-off between speed and specialization that is faced by engineers in the design of computers.

2.2.2 An illustrative framework

We now consider a general framework for the interaction between the emotional and the cognitive system, following the work of Loewenstein and O'Donoghue (2004, 2007). We begin by noting the drawbacks of this approach. Many of the assumptions in the illustrative applications may appear arbitrary, yet they are plausible. Nor can one always cleanly separate observed behavior based on the source, cognitive or emotional, that gives rise to it. This framework cannot be used to fully justify the importance of the dual process model for explaining behavioral phenomena, nor make watertight predictions. Yet, it does take an important first step in this direction and has the potential to serve as the basis of further models that can lead to much needed theoretical developments in the area.

The emotional and cognitive processes/systems are also respectively termed as the *affective* and the *deliberative* processes/systems. The emotional system, because it is automatic and quick, initially comes into play when an individual faces some stimulus (Baumeister and Vohs, 2003). The stimulus could be external (coiled object on a dark street) or internal (drop in blood glucose levels).

The cognitive system, because it is reflective and considers broader goals, can influence the emotional system by the exercise of costly *willpower*. Willpower has three relevant features for our purpose. First, it is a limited resource and can get depleted. Second, cognitive load reduces the ability to exert willpower. Third, willpower can be depleted by stress; for instance, Shiffman and Waters (2004) find that relapse among cigarette smokers was often preceded by a stressful event.[2]

---

[1] For a more detailed discussion of these issues, see Volume 6 of the book where we distinguish between changes in the environment that occur with different speeds. Long-run changes induce changes in the structure of the DNA. But for short-run and medium-run changes, other responses, such as gene-culture coevolution, are more efficient.

[2] For a model of the effect of stress on reducing well-being that works through a cognitive load channel, see Wälde (2015).

The second feature of willpower is suggested by the experiments of Shiv and Fedorikhin (1999) who employed two groups of subjects. The first group was subjected to a high cognitive load and was asked to memorize a 7-digit number. The second group was subjected to a low cognitive load and asked to memorize a 2-digit number. The subjects were then required to walk to another part of the building to report their memorized number. On the way, they were presented with a high calorie cake and a fruit salad. A larger fraction of subjects who were subjected to a high cognitive load (63%) chose the cake, relative to the those who were subject to a low cognitive load (42%). There was only a slight difference between the two conditions when the same objects were presented symbolically in the form of photographs.

The cognitive system operates at the cool end of the spectrum and deliberates about broader goals. Thus, as a first pass, assume that it has the same objectives as the rational agent in neoclassical economic models. So, for instance, when the cognitive system faces a risky lottery, it uses expected utility theory to evaluate the lottery, and when it faces an intertemporal stream of consumption, it uses exponential discounting to evaluate the consumption stream.

The emotional system operates at the hot end of the spectrum and focuses on immediate goals. As a first pass, assume that it behaves in a manner that is consistent with the recent evidence in behavioral economics. So it uses loss aversion when presented with gains and losses and uses hyperbolic discounting when evaluating an intertemporal stream of consumption.

The cognitive system cares about the moral and ethical dimensions of a situation, while the emotional system is driven between the two extremes of purely self-regarding and purely altruistic behavior. Which of these extremes is activated depends perhaps on a set of cues which activate such emotions. In related literature, Bernheim and Rangel (2004) also assume that the brain operates in one of two states, a cold state or a hot state. The state depends stochastically on the environmental conditions (which in turn could depend on actions taken in the past). However, their primary focus is on the cold state, which maximizes expected discounted utility, while the hot state is assumed to follow a simple rule. They take as their welfare measure, the preferences of the cold state.[3]

The schematic outline of the dual process model is shown in Figure 2.1. A stimulus, s, which belongs to a set S, activates the emotional and the cognitive systems. In particular, it activates an emotional/motivational state $m(s)$, and a cognitive state $c(s)$; the set of emotional and cognitive states could themselves be subsets of S. The problem is to choose the optimal behavior x from a set $X \subseteq \mathbb{R}$, given that the two systems have different objective functions and none fully dominates the other.

In particular, the objective function of the emotional system is given by $U^e(x, m(s))$ and it does not depend on the cognitive state, $c(s)$. The cognitive system has the objective function $U^c(x, m(s), c(s))$. Since the cognitive system cares about broader goals, it takes account of the emotional state induced by the stimulus, $m(s)$, as well as the cognitive state, $c(s)$. We assume that U^e and U^c are strictly concave in x and twice continuously differentiable in all arguments. The set X is compact, so that the respective maximizers x^e, x^c are unique, and are continuous functions of the parameters. Assume that $\frac{\partial}{\partial m} \left(\frac{\partial U^e}{\partial x} \right) > 0$, i.e., an increase in the motivational state increases the marginal utility of the emotional system from increasing behavior, x. We also assume that $\frac{\partial}{\partial c} \left(\frac{\partial U^c}{\partial x} \right) > 0$.

---

[3] In Benhabib and Bisin (2005), individuals can either invoke an automatic emotional system that is susceptible to temptation or a costly cognitive system that does not succumb to temptation. They explore an internal control mechanism that takes the form of a simple cutoff rule in a consumption–savings problem. Models of multiple selves (see Volume 3 of the book) do not allow for this internal control mechanism.

Finally, observed behavior is the outcome of the interaction between the emotional and the cognitive systems. For instance, the proximity of tempting foods could create an emotional state of hunger. Faced with such a stimulus at lunchtime, the objectives of the cognitive and emotional systems are likely to be in agreement with each other. However, faced with such a tempting stimulus between lunch and dinner, the cognitive system of an individual on a diet is likely to recommend the opposite course of action to the emotional system. It is this latter situation where the desired actions of the two systems are potentially in conflict, that is the most interesting for our purposes.

What determines the relative strength of activation of the emotional and the cognitive systems, when faced with a cue? Several factors play an important role. These include the following. (i) Physical proximity of the stimulus (Mischel et al., 2003). Food is more tempting if it is placed nearby, or if its consumption by others is observed. (ii) *Changes* versus *levels* of stimuli (Frederick and Loewenstein, 1999). The emotional system is more likely to respond to changes than to levels. (iii) Vividness of stimuli (Loewenstein et al., 2001). We are often more deterred from speeding if we directly observe an accident in graphic detail relative to reading about the annual road fatality statistics.

To economize on notation, we suppress the state, s, in the objective functions of the two systems by assuming a fixed state. We assume that the individual has sufficient time to choose actual behavior so that the eventual choice is made by the cognitive system. Using the standard terminology in economics, one may think of the cognitive system as a *benevolent principal* and the emotional system as the *agent*.

We shall primarily be interested in a static model. However, we first make a few observations on willpower in a dynamic model; index discrete time by t.[4] Willpower costs exerted by the cognitive system are directly proportional to the extent to which the emotional system is moved

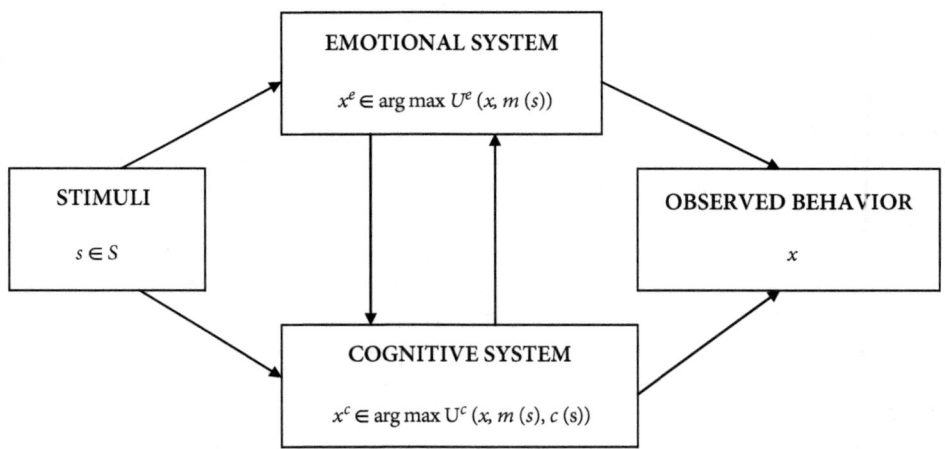

Figure 2.1 Schematic representation of the dual process model.

---

[4] An exercise at the end of the chapter, based on Ozdenoren et al. (2012), provides a more rigorous, but also more specialized, framework of analysis.

from its most preferred behavior at time t, x_t^e, to some $x \neq x_t^e$ that might be in the individual's longer-term interest. Thus, the willpower, w_t, exerted by the cognitive system at time t is given by

$$w_t(x_t) = U_t^e(x_t^e, m) - U_t^e(x_t, m). \tag{2.1}$$

Let W_t be the stock of willpower at time t. The stock of willpower carried forward from time t to $t+1$ is given by $W_{t+1} = f(w_t, W_t)$, such that $f_1 < 0$ and $f_2 > 0$. Thus, exertion of willpower effort in any period depletes the stock of willpower carried over to the next period ($f_1 < 0$). For instance, depletion of willpower can lead to a greater incidence of impulse buying (Vohs and Faber, 2007). Furthermore, *ceteris paribus*, a greater current stock of willpower transforms into a greater stock of willpower next period ($f_2 > 0$). These ideas are fundamental to an understanding of the role of willpower in a dynamic analysis (Baumeister and Vohs, 2003).

We shall only focus on the static case below. Omitting time subscripts, (2.1) can be written as

$$w(x) = U^e(x^e, m) - U^e(x, m). \tag{2.2}$$

The objective of the principal, or the cognitive system, is to choose $x \in X$ to maximize

$$V^c(x) = U^c(x, m, c) - \phi(W, \sigma) w(x), \tag{2.3}$$

where $\phi(W, \sigma) \geq 0$ represents per unit willpower cost, and σ is cognitive load/stress. Consistent with the evidence reviewed above, $\phi_1 < 0$ and $\phi_2 > 0$. Thus, per unit willpower costs are decreasing in the stock of willpower but increasing in the cognitive load/stress facing the individual. Substituting (2.2) in (2.3) and noting that x^e is fixed for a given stimulus, hence, omitting the term $U^e(x^e, m)$, we can write the maximization problem of the cognitive system as

$$x^* \in \arg\max_{x \in X} V^c(x) = U^c(x, m, c) + \phi(W, \sigma) U^e(x, m), \phi \geq 0. \tag{2.4}$$

As $\phi(W, \sigma) \to 0$, $x^* \to x^c$ and as $\phi(W, \sigma) \to \infty$, $x^* \to x^e$. The cognitive system makes the eventual decision, so it is like a chief executive of the brain. However, the objective function in (2.4) also bears another interpretation if we recognize that for a fixed state, $U^c(x^c, m, c)$ and $U^e(x^e, m)$ are fixed numbers. Choosing x to maximize (2.4) is equivalent to minimizing the following.

$$x \in \arg\min \left[U^c(x^c, m, c) - U^c(x, m, c) \right] + \phi(W, \sigma) \left[U^e(x^e, m) - U^e(x, m) \right]. \tag{2.5}$$

The interpretation of (2.5) is that actual behavior is chosen in order to minimize the weighted sum of two costs. Namely, the cost of moving the emotional and the cognitive systems from their most preferred behaviors; the relative weight placed on the cost faced by the emotional system is $\phi(W, \sigma)$.

Our framework of analysis is based on the following three premises.

A1: The cognitive system behaves like the textbook economic agent that operates in a world of emotionless deliberation.

A2: Evidence from the behavior of animals who lack the prefrontal cortex and who share their primitive mammalian brain with us is used to infer the preferences of the emotional system.

A3: When the required evidence in A2 is not available, then the actual behavior of humans is used to recover the preferences of the emotional self.

We now apply this framework to three different domains: Intertemporal choice, behavior under risk, and social preferences. This gives rise to a range of applications. A partial list includes: the effectiveness of advertising even when it conveys no useful information, breakdown of bargaining when there are mutual gains to be shared, unpleasant divorces, and behavior in financial markets.

INTERTEMPORAL CHOICE

Assume that the cognitive system is driven by long-term payoffs and it uses exponential discounting. Evidence from animal studies suggests extreme myopia in pigeons. There is also evidence of myopia in monkeys (Tobin et al., 1996; Stevens et al., 2005). So the objective of the emotional system is also assumed to be myopic.

Formally, suppose that an individual faces a stream of dated consumption levels, $x_1, x_2, \ldots, x_T$. In line with premise A1, the utility of the cognitive system is $U^c = \sum_{j=1}^{T} \delta^{j-1} x_j$, where δ is the discount factor. Using premise A2 and the evidence from animal behavior, the emotional system is myopic and disregards future consumption levels, so its utility is given by $U^e = \lambda x_1$, where $\lambda > 0$. Substituting these expressions in (2.4) we get

$$V^c = \sum_{j=1}^{T} \delta^{j-1} x_j + \phi(W, \sigma) \lambda x_1. \tag{2.6}$$

Maximizing (2.6) is equivalent to maximizing

$$\widetilde{V}^c = x_1 + \beta \sum_{j=2}^{T} \delta^{j-1} x_j, \text{ where } 0 \leq \beta = \frac{1}{1 + \lambda \phi(W, \sigma)} < 1. \tag{2.7}$$

The preferences expressed in (2.7) are the (β, δ) preferences of *quasi-hyperbolic discounting* (see Volume 3 of the book). Depletion of willpower (reduction in W) or an increase in the cognitive load (increase in σ) increases $\phi(W, \sigma)$. Equivalently, the testable prediction of the model is that these changes (reduction in W and increase in σ) decrease β, resulting in more myopic behavior. The Shiv and Fedorikhin (1999) results mentioned above are consistent with this prediction. Vohs and Heatherton (2000) find that willpower depletion among dieters leads them to buy more ice cream. Benjamin et al. (2013) give problems to Chilean high school students with short-term and long-term trade-offs. Cognitive load leads to a reduction in short-term patience. Another prediction of the model that can be derived from its interpretation in (2.5) is that an increase in $\phi(W, \sigma)$ puts greater weight on the relative cost of moving the emotional system away from its most preferred outcome. So factors that enhance the emotional desire such as proximity to stimuli are predicted to lead to greater myopia. The results of Mischel et al. (2003) mentioned above are supportive of this prediction.

BEHAVIOR UNDER RISK

Suppose that an individual faces the lottery

$$L = (x_1, p_1; x_2, p_2; \ldots; x_n, p_n),$$

where $x_i \in \mathbb{R}$ is the ith outcome, $p_i \geq 0$ the associated probability, and $p_1 + \ldots + p_n = 1$. Given premise A1, we assume that the cognitive system uses expected utility theory. We assume the special case of expected value maximization, so

$$U^c = \sum_{j=1}^{n} x_i p_i. \tag{2.8}$$

What preferences should we assign to the emotional system? These issues were considered in more detail in Section 1.2.2 (Loewenstein, 2001). In studies that measure physiological response to unexpected events, the intensity of the shock rather than the likelihood of receiving it, is the key. Other studies show that mental images of outcomes are the key to eliciting emotional responses, and that such responses are invariant to probabilities of outcomes (Loewenstein and O'Donoghue, 2007). For the evidence that individuals often ignore information on probabilities when purchasing house insurance, see Kunreuther et al. (1978).

Ditto et al. (2006) gave 80 undergraduates the option to undertake or avoid the following risky task: Work on a boring task in the lab for an extra 30 minutes with a probability that could be high (more risky) or low (less risky). The prize was chocolate chip cookies. Participants who could see and smell the cookies while they made their decision were less sensitive to risk information. In this case, under high risk and low risk, respectively, 80% and 85% of the players opted to undertake the task. In contrast, when the cookies were merely described (but not seen or smelt), participants were much more sensitive to the level of risk; 45% played the game under high risk and 95% under low risk. Insofar as the sight and smell of the cookies engages the emotional system, this evidence lends further support to the view that information on probabilities is relatively less salient for the emotional system.

In light of this evidence, suppose that the utility function of the emotional system is $U^e = \sum_{j=1}^{n} x_i / n = \bar{x}$, i.e., it cares only for the unweighted average of the outcomes, ignoring probabilities. Substituting U^c, U^e in (2.4) we get

$$V^c = \sum_{j=1}^{n} x_i p_i + \phi(W, \sigma) \bar{x}. \tag{2.9}$$

Maximizing (2.9) is equivalent to maximizing

$$\hat{V}^c = \sum_{j=1}^{n} \pi_i x_i, \text{ where } \pi_i = \frac{p_i + \phi/n}{1 + n\phi}. \tag{2.10}$$

It is evident from (2.10) that

$$p_i \gtrless \pi_i \text{ as } p_i \gtrless \frac{1}{n^2} = \hat{p}. \tag{2.11}$$

Hence, when the probability of an event is low enough ($p_i < \hat{p}$), then the decision weight is higher than the probability; the converse is true for high probability events ($p_i > \hat{p}$). This is consistent with an *inverse S-shaped* π. From Volume 1 we know that the probability weighting function is inverse S-shaped. Thus, $\hat{V}^c$ is similar to the objective function of a prospect theory maximizer, as in the original 1979 version of prospect theory (see Volume 1), but not with rank dependent utility or with the cumulative probability version of prospect theory in Tversky and Kahneman (1992). Noting that $\partial \pi_i / \partial \phi > 0$ and $\phi_1 < 0$, $\phi_2 > 0$ we can predict when π becomes more or less S-shaped. If an individual's willpower is depleted or there is a greater cognitive load, then the decision weights should become more S-shaped.

A pervasive experimental finding when there are both positive and negative outcomes in a lottery, *L*, is *loss aversion*. Loss aversion implies that losses are more salient than equivalent gains, i.e., the absolute value of disutility from losses is greater than the utility from gains that are of the same magnitude. There is evidence that close primate relatives such as capuchin monkeys also exhibit loss aversion (Chen et al., 2006; see Volume 1 for details). Using premises A2, A3, we postulate that the emotional system exhibits loss aversion according to the following utility function.

$$U^e = \begin{cases} x_i & if & x_i \geq 0 \\ \lambda x_i & if & x_i < 0 \end{cases}, \tag{2.12}$$

where $\lambda > 1$ is the parameter of loss aversion. Substituting (2.8), (2.12) in (2.4) we get that maximizing V^c is equivalent to maximizing

$$\overline{V}^c = \sum_{j=1}^{n} v(x_i), \tag{2.13}$$

where

$$v(x_i) = \begin{cases} x_i & if & x_i \geq 0 \\ \hat{\lambda} x_i & if & x_i < 0 \end{cases}, \text{ and } \hat{\lambda} = \frac{p_i + \lambda\phi}{p_i + \phi} > 1.$$

Hence, a loss averse emotional system induces loss aversion in the cognitive system. Furthermore, $\hat{\lambda} < \lambda$ so the cognitive system is less loss averse relative to the emotional system. Noting that $\partial\hat{\lambda}_i/\partial\phi > 0$ and $\phi_1 < 0$, $\phi_2 > 0$, willpower depletion and an increase in the cognitive load lead to an increase in the loss aversion of the cognitive system, $\hat{\lambda}$. Also, factors such as proximity of the stimuli that enhance the role of the emotional system (increase in ϕ) increase $\hat{\lambda}$. Benjamin et al. (2013) provide some evidence that is consistent with the first prediction. See Loewenstein and O'Donoghue (2007) for evidence supporting the second prediction.

SOCIAL PREFERENCES

Consider two individuals, labeled 1 and 2, who have respective material payoffs of x_1 and x_2. There is evidence that the cognitive system takes account of the payoffs of others, consistent with some notion of an equitable or ethical payoff (Loewenstein and O'Donoghue, 2007). Thus, the utility of the cognitive system for individual $i = 1, 2$, is assumed to be given by $U_i^c = x_i + w_i^c x_j$, $j = 1, 2$ and $j \neq i$; $w_i^c > 0$ is the weight put by the cognitive system on the payoff of the other player, x_j.

Animals as well as humans often demonstrate empathy and sympathy towards others. Loewenstein and O'Donoghue (2007) review some relevant evidence; they write (p. 41) "rats who view a distressed fellow rat suspended in air by a harness will press a bar to lower the rat back to safe ground." In another experiment, as one rat is subjected to electric shocks, another rat, who is watching, retreats to a corner, motionless. In yet another experiment, monkeys could pull one of two chains to receive food with one of the chains delivering twice the amount but also an electric shock to another monkey in sight. Two thirds of the monkeys preferred the "less food" chain; one monkey refused to pull either chain for 5 days and another refused for 12 days.[5] In general, it appears that the emotional system can demonstrate extreme empathy or antipathy

---

[5] For a review of these studies, see Preston and de Waal (2002).

towards others. We assume that the preferences of the emotional system of individual $i = 1, 2$, are given by $U_i^e = x_i + w_i^e x_j$, $j = 1, 2$ and $j \neq i$, and $w_i^e \gtrless 0$; a positive weight captures altruism and a negative weight captures envy.

Substituting U_i^c, U_i^e in (2.4) we get

$$V^c = x_i + w_i^c x_j + \phi(W, \sigma) \left[x_i + w_i^e x_j \right]. \tag{2.14}$$

The cognitive system chooses x_i, x_j to maximize V^c in (2.14); equivalently, it maximizes

$$V^{c*} = x_i + \omega_i x_j, \text{ where } \omega_i = \frac{(w_i^c + \phi w_i^e)}{1 + \phi}.$$

It is clear that

$$\omega_i \gtrless w_i^c \Leftrightarrow w_i^e \gtrless w_i^c.$$

Hence, the emotional system might induce the cognitive system to assign a lower weight to the payoff of the other player when $w_i^e < w_i^c$. Indeed, if $w_i^e < 0$ and $\frac{w_i^c}{\phi} < |w_i^e|$, then the cognitive system, which is inherently altruistic ($w_i^c > 0$), becomes envious, $\omega_i < 0$, and derives utility by lowering the payoff of the other individual. If, on the other hand, $w_i^e > w_i^c$, then the emotional system amplifies the altruism of the cognitive system. Furthermore, ω_i is increasing (decreasing) in per unit costs of willpower, ϕ, if $w_i^e - w_i^c$ is positive (negative). Hence, depending on the relative empathy triggered in the emotional system, it is possible that a decrease in willpower or an increase in cognitive load/stress (which increase ϕ) can either increase or decrease a concern for the payoff of others.

A NOTE ON WELFARE COMPARISON

Neoclassical economics typically uses revealed preference arguments to make welfare comparisons. An individual's actual choices are used to make inferences about preferences. These preferences can be used to make statements about the well-being of the individual when the environment changes. Central to this exercise is the view that individuals choose options that maximize their well-being.

Behavioral economics, on the other hand, shows that individuals might not always behave in their best interest. Should a social planner stand back and respect individual preferences? In the context of the dual process models, two main candidate functions for behavioral welfare economics are U^c and V^c (see (2.3) for the relation between the two); as a first pass we rule out U^e as it may be too unstable with respect to the stimulus. However, there are interesting arguments associated with each of them.

The main argument in favor of U^c is that it captures the behavior of the cognitive system from a detached perspective. But there are two important drawbacks of using U^c. First, the set of emotional states is an argument of U^c and so imparts to it a degree of instability. Second, most people would agree that, fixing outcomes, a policy that reduced the need to exercise willpower and so reduced per unit willpower costs, ϕ, would be an improvement. This is not guaranteed by U^c. While the second of these criticisms can be avoided by considering V^c as the appropriate criterion, however, the presence of emotional states as an argument in V^c does not eliminate the first criticism. Thus, advertising by firms might appeal to the emotional system of an individual, so it also has an affect on V^c, yet the advertisements might not always promote the best long-term interests of the individual. For instance, for a long time, advertisements associated cigarette smoking with a macho image, yet the advertised product was known to the cigarette companies to be harmful to the consumers.

2.3 A dual selves model with costly commitment

One possible framework to model emotions is to consider each individual as comprising of a patient long-run (LR) self and a myopic short-run (SR) self. These are models of *dual selves*. An example is the Shefrin and Thaler (1988) model that we considered in Volume 3 of the book. Here, we consider another model in this tradition, due to Fudenberg and Levine (2006).

A model that is related to the dual selves model is the model of *multiple selves* (see Volume 3 of the book). Fudenberg–Levine claim that dual selves models are better grounded in psychological evidence, and are analytically simpler. Furthermore, these models typically have a unique equilibrium, while models of multiple selves often have multiple equilibria. We use a simple consumption–savings model to illustrate the dual selves model.

2.3.1 *The model without commitment*

Consider an infinitely lived consumer who makes a consumption–savings decision in each time period $t \in T = \{1, 2, \ldots\}$. In any period, the consumer has wealth y_t, which can either be consumed, c_t, or saved, s_t. There is no other source of income. There is an exogenous and time-invariant gross return of $R = 1 + r$ on each unit of savings carried over to the next period, hence, $y_{t+1} = Rs_t$. Initial wealth y_1 is given exogenously. Suppose that the marginal propensity to save is α_t in period $t \in T$ so that $s_t = \alpha_t y_t$ and $c_t = (1 - \alpha_t) y_t$. The resource constraint at time $t + 1$ is given by

$$y_{t+1} = R\alpha_t y_t, \, t \in T. \tag{2.15}$$

The objective of the SR self is to myopically maximize current utility. Thus, the SR self chooses α_t to maximize

$$u(y_t, \alpha_t) = \log(1 - \alpha_t) y_t = \log c_t, \, t \in T. \tag{2.16}$$

In the absence of any control exerted by the LR self, the optimal choice of the SR self, from (2.16), is to choose $\alpha_t = 0$, i.e., consume the entire current income.

The LR self can induce the SR self to choose some non-zero marginal propensity to save, $\alpha_t > 0$, by expending some self-control or willpower costs, $C(y_t, \alpha_t)$. Assuming that these costs are linear and proportional to the amount saved, we get

$$C(y_t, \alpha_t) = \gamma \left[\log(1 - 0) y_t - \log(1 - \alpha_t) y_t \right] = -\gamma \log(1 - \alpha_t), \, t \in T. \tag{2.17}$$

In (2.17), $\gamma > 0$ is the marginal cost of inducing the SR self to save extra. Furthermore, C is increasing and convex in α_t.

The LR self uses exponential discounting to maximize the present discounted value of lifetime consumption, subject to the resource constraint in (2.15). Hence, the utility of the LR self is given by

$$U = \sum_{t=1}^{\infty} \delta^{t-1} \left[u(y_t, \alpha_t) - C(y_t, \alpha_t) \right], \tag{2.18}$$

where $0 < \delta < 1$ is the discount factor, $u(y_t, \alpha_t)$ is defined in (2.16), and $C(y_t, \alpha_t)$ is defined in (2.17). Comparing (2.16), (2.18), the instantaneous utility functions of the LR self and the SR self are identical, except for the costs of self-control. Substitute (2.16), (2.17) in (2.18) and add and subtract $\gamma \log(1 - \alpha_t) y_t$ from the instantaneous utility function to get

$$U = \sum_{t=1}^{\infty} \delta^{t-1} \left[(1 + \gamma) \log(1 - \alpha_t) y_t - \gamma \log y_t \right]. \tag{2.19}$$

The problem of the LR self is to choose the sequence of marginal propensities to save, $\{\alpha_t\}_1^{\infty}$, in order to maximize (2.19) subject to the constraint (2.15). Fudenberg and Levine (2006) show that the unique solution is a constant, time-invariant, savings rate, α, that lies between zero and one.[6] When $\alpha_t = \alpha$ for all t, then (2.15) can be solved recursively to give

$$y_t = (R\alpha)^{t-1} y_1, \tag{2.20}$$

where y_1 is the initial level of wealth. Substitute (2.20) in (2.19) we get

$$U = \frac{(1 + \gamma)}{1 - \delta} \left[\log(1 - \alpha) + \log y_1 \right] + \frac{\delta}{(1 - \delta)^2} \log R\alpha. \tag{2.21}$$

Since we have an interior and unique solution, using $\frac{\partial U}{\partial \alpha} = 0$, we get the optimal value of α,

$$\alpha = \frac{\delta}{1 + \gamma(1 - \delta)}. \tag{2.22}$$

As γ, the per unit cost of inducing the SR self to save an extra unit increases, it becomes optimal to reduce α, the marginal propensity to save. Furthermore, $\frac{\partial}{\partial \delta} \left(\frac{\partial \alpha}{\partial \gamma} \right) > 0$, thus, as the degree of patience (as reflected in the magnitude of δ) increases, the marginal impact of self-control costs on the savings rate increases.

In the special case of no self-control costs, we have $\gamma = 0$; in this case, using (2.22), the optimal savings rate, denoted by α^*, is

$$\alpha^* = \delta. \tag{2.23}$$

Hence, optimal consumption in the absence of self-control costs is

$$c_t^* = (1 - \delta) y_t, \ t \in T. \tag{2.24}$$

Substitute (2.23) in (2.21) to get

$$U = \frac{1}{1 - \delta} \left[\log(1 - \delta) + \log y_1 \right] + \frac{\delta}{(1 - \delta)^2} \log R\delta. \tag{2.25}$$

---

[6] The proof is available in the supplementary section of an earlier version of the paper by Fudenberg and Levine (2006) and applies to any CRRA utility function of which log utility is a special case.

In the absence of self-control costs, (2.25) expresses lifetime utility of the LR self as a function of initial wealth, y_1, the discount factor, δ, and the rate of return on savings, R.

2.3.2 *Commitment via a cash-in-advance constraint*

So far we have assumed that the LR self does not have access to a commitment technology. For that reason, the LR self can only control the SR self through the costly exercise of willpower. We now allow for the possibility that such a technology is available; essentially we wish to give the LR self the power to remove the source of temptation for the SR self. Each period is now divided into two sequential subperiods: the *bank subperiod* and the *nightclub subperiod*.

At any time t, in the first subperiod, the bank subperiod, there is no consumption temptation. The LR self chooses, in this period, to save some amount $s_t = \alpha_t y_t$. This amount is kept in the bank and available only in the next period at time $t + 1$. The rest, $x_t = (1 - \alpha_t)y_t$, is passed on to the second subperiod in time t, as cash. In the nightclub subperiod, the SR self has access to the cash amount, x_t, and it consumes an amount, c_t, such that $0 \leq c_t \leq x_t$; consumption always takes place only in the nightclub subperiod. The discount factor between two successive nightclub subperiods is δ.

Any cash leftover from the nightclub subperiod of period t, i.e., $x_t - c_t \geq 0$, is deposited into the bank and carried over to period $t + 1$, along with the savings, s_t, made in the bank subperiod of period t. There is a time-invariant gross return R on savings, hence, the individual's wealth at the beginning of period $t + 1$ is

$$y_{t+1} = R(s_t + x_t - c_t). \tag{2.26}$$

We look at two possible subcases.

I. *Savings is the only source of income*

The LR self can costlessly impose any savings rate in any period by controlling the amount of cash available to the SR self to spend; this is the commitment technology. From (2.23), we know that in the absence of self-control costs, $\alpha^* = \delta$. This savings rate can be readily implemented by choosing to pass on the cash

$$x_t = (1 - \delta)y_t, \tag{2.27}$$

to the SR self in the nightclub period. Since the SR self is completely myopic, it will immediately consume all the cash received.

II. *Stochastic income augments savings income*

At $t = 1$, the cash available for the SR self in the nightclub period is x_1. Now suppose that in the first, and only the first, nightclub subperiod, the SR self faces additive income uncertainty of the following form: Income is $x_1 + \tilde{z}_1$, where $\tilde{z}_1$ is a random variable with density f. The interpretation is that the income of the SR self is $x_1 + z_1$ with probability $f(z_1)$ for any z_1 in the support of f. Then the budget constraint for the SR self, for a particular realization z_1, in the first nightclub period is given by

$$c_1 \leq x_1 + z_1. \tag{2.28}$$

We need to study the individual's optimization problem for each possible realization, z_1. Second period wealth is given by

$$y_2 = R(s_1 + x_1 + z_1 - c_1) \equiv R(y_1 + z_1 - c_1), \tag{2.29}$$

where $s_1 + x_1 \equiv y_1$ and $y_1 + z_1$ gives the actual income in period 1. Net of first period consumption, c_1, the savings are invested at a gross rate R to give y_2.

The random income is available only in the first nightclub subperiod, leading to a potential violation of the cash-in-advance constraint for the SR self. Hence, the first best outcome is no longer guaranteed. The SR self in the first nightclub subperiod could have extra cash, z_1, to play around with, hence, the LR self, in the first period, might wish to exert costly willpower effort. The cost of this effort is as given in (2.17),

$$C = \gamma \left[\log(x_1 + z_1) - \log c_1 \right].$$

The first period utility of the LR self is $\log c_1 - \gamma \left[\log(x_1 + z_1) - \log c_1 \right]$, which can be written as

$$(1 + \gamma) \log c_1 - \gamma \log(x_1 + z_1). \tag{2.30}$$

From the second period onwards, however, there is no need to exert costly willpower because the SR self faces no subsequent income uncertainty and, so, the cash-in-advance constraint is never violated. Hence, the lifetime utility of the LR self starting from period 2 is found by substituting $y_2 = y_1 \equiv s_1 + x_1$ in (2.25) (taking account that we are summing from period 2 onwards) to give

$$\frac{\delta}{1 - \delta} \left[\log(1 - \delta) + \log y_2 \right] + \frac{\delta^2}{(1 - \delta)^2} \log R\delta. \tag{2.31}$$

Putting together (2.30), (2.31), the LR self maximizes

$$(1 + \gamma) \log c_1 - \gamma \log(x_1 + z_1) + \frac{\delta}{1 - \delta} \left[\log(1 - \delta) + \log y_2 \right] + \frac{\delta^2}{(1 - \delta)^2} \log R\delta, \tag{2.32}$$

subject to (2.29). We ignore the constraint (2.28) for the time being. The first order condition with respect to c_1 gives the optimal value of first period consumption

$$c_1^* = (1 - \theta) \left(y_1 + z_1 \right), \text{ where } \theta = \frac{\delta}{\delta + (1 + \gamma) (1 - \delta)} < 1. \tag{2.33}$$

From (2.23), (2.24) in the absence of self-control problems, optimal consumption is $(1 - \delta) y_1$. One gets a similar result from (2.33) when willpower costs per unit $\gamma = 0$; here one gets $c_1^* = (1 - \delta) \left(y_1 + z_1 \right)$.

Whether the individual gets to consume the optimal amount c_1^*, given in (2.33), depends on whether the ignored constraint (2.28) holds. If $c_1^* \leq x_1 + z_1$, then c_1^* is implemented. If $c_1^* > x_1 + z_1$, then the first period consumption is constrained by the upper bound $x_1 + z_1$, so all pocket cash is consumed by the SR self in the first nightclub subperiod.

Suppose $c_1^* \leq x_1 + z_1$. Since x_1 is the solution to $\gamma = 0$ we know from (2.27), that $x_1 = (1 - \delta) y_1$. Substituting this in (2.28), if

$$c_1^* \leq (1 - \delta) y_1 + z_1 \qquad\qquad (2.34)$$

then the optimal consumption plan is implemented. Define by z_1^* the value of z_1 such that (2.34) just binds, i.e.,

$$\left(1 - \frac{\delta}{\delta + (1 + \gamma)(1 - \delta)}\right)(y_1 + z_1^*) = (1 - \delta) y_1 + z_1^*,$$

which gives $z_1^* = \gamma (1 - \delta) y_1$.

Figure 2.2 plots the two terms on the left- and the right-hand sides of (2.34). c_1^* is plotted for two values of $\gamma = 0$ and $\gamma > 0$. When $\gamma = z_1 = 0$, then $c_1^* \mid_{\gamma=0, z_1=0} = (1 - \delta) y_1$; the slope of $c_1^* \mid_{\gamma=0}$ is $1 - \delta$. An increase in γ reduces the value of θ in (2.33), hence, increasing the intercept and slope of the curve $c_1^* \mid_{\gamma>0}$ relative to that of $c_1^* \mid_{\gamma=0}$. The intersection of the curves $c_1^* \mid_{\gamma>0}$ and $(1 - \delta) y_1 + z_1$ in (z_1, c_1) space corresponds to $z_1 = z_1^*$.

For all $z_1 < z_1^*$, $c_1^* > (1 - \delta) y_1 + z_1$, hence, consumption is bounded above by $(1 - \delta) y_1 + z_1$ and the SR self does not deposit any cash in the bank to be carried forward to the next period. For all $z_1 > z_1^*$, $c_1^* < (1 - \delta) y_1 + z_1$, hence, the SR self deposits surplus cash into the bank for the next period. In the absence of self-control problems ($\gamma = 0$) we have $z_1^* = 0$, hence, the SR self does not spend all the increment in income, for any level of $z_1 > 0$.

Consider the case $\gamma > 0$. It follows that in the range of small windfalls, $z_1 < z_1^*$, an increase in unanticipated income is fully consumed (because $c_1^* > (1 - \delta) y_1 + z_1$). On the other hand, in the range of large windfalls, $z_1 > z_1^*$, an increase in unanticipated income is not fully consumed (because $c_1^* < (1 - \delta) y_1 + z_1$).

A final implication is that in an appropriately modified model where the windfall gains are deposited in a bank, the marginal propensity to consume out of these gains would be lower. The reason is that the LR self cares about future time periods and, hence, would desire to smooth out consumption.

Fudenberg–Levine show that by assuming a convex cost of delay in the model above, they can explain other behavioral findings. These include the Allais paradox and the positive relation

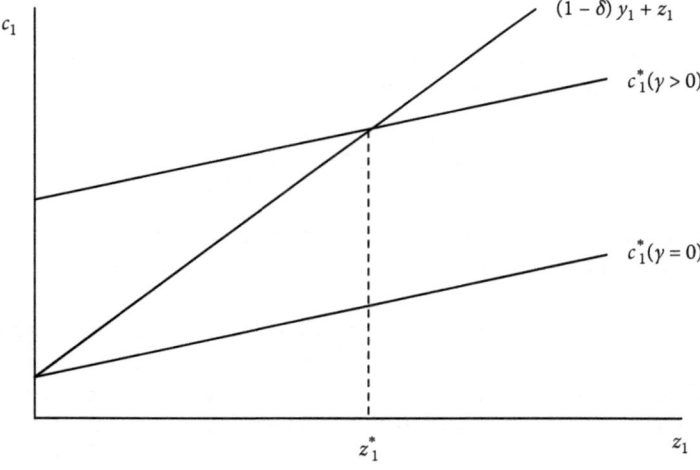

Figure 2.2 Willpower costs and optimal consumption.

between cognitive load and risk aversion. Benjamin et al. (2013) give empirical evidence to show that as cognitive load increases, people become more risk averse. Cognitive load was induced by asking the subjects to remember a seven-digit number when they play lotteries in Allais-type paradoxes. This can also provide an explanation for the Allais paradox. However, this does not explain why the Allais paradox should arise in the absence of cognitive load (see Volume 1 of the book).

Fudenberg–Levine also fit their model to estimated macroeconomic parameters such as the interest rate and the coefficient of relative risk aversion. However, some of the results are quite sensitive to the parameters used. It is also not clear how this model would explain a range of other behavioral regularities that rely on reference dependence, loss aversion, and non-linear probability weighting (see Volume 1 of the book for details).

2.4 Information asymmetries between emotions and cognition

In this section, we consider a somewhat speculative framework that models the interaction between a myopic emotional system/module and a farsighted cognitive system/module in the presence of information asymmetries between the two (Brocas and Carillo, 2008).[7] To borrow an analogy from principal–agent models, the cognitive module is the principal and the emotional module is the agent.

Suppose that there are only two time periods, $t = 1, 2$. In each period, the individual's consumption and labor are denoted, respectively, by

$$c_t \geq 0, \quad l_t \in [0, L], \tag{2.35}$$

where L is, say, an upper limit on available labor time. The emotional system is self-regarding and myopic, so it cares only about instantaneous utility, which takes the quasilinear form

$$U_t(c_t, l_t; \theta_t) = \theta_t u(c_t) - l_t; \theta_t > 0. \tag{2.36}$$

θ_t is a parameter of preferences that enhances the marginal utility of consumption. We assume that θ_t is *iid* over time and takes two possible values, θ_L, θ_H, with associated probabilities $p, 1 - p$, and $0 < \theta_L < \theta_H$.[8] Furthermore, u is twice continuously differentiable and $u' > 0, u'' < 0$.

In contrast to the emotional system, the cognitive system is utilitarian and farsighted, with preferences given by $U_1 + U_2$. The cognitive system is treated as the *principal* and the emotional system in period $t = 1, 2$ is the *agent* in that period.

The individual can transform one unit of labor into one unit of income, so the wage rate is 1. Saving, s, made in period 1, earns a risk-free per unit rate of return, $r > 0$. The budget constraints in the two periods are respectively

$$c_1 + s \leq l_1 \text{ and } c_2 \leq l_2 + (1 + r)s. \tag{2.37}$$

---

[7] For a brief survey of these models that also considers a wider range of issues such as a better understanding of memory and multitasking, see Brocas and Carillio (2014).

[8] Brocas and Carillo (2008) consider a continuous distribution of θ. However, our two types case is able to illustrate the main points.

Second period consumption can be increased not just by working hard in period 2 but also by working hard and saving more in the first period. This feature will be important in the model. Since the marginal utility of consumption is always positive, the budget constraints hold with equality. Eliminating s from the two budget constraints, we get the intertemporal budget constraint

$$c_1 + \frac{c_2}{(1+r)} = l_1 + \frac{l_2}{(1+r)}. \tag{2.38}$$

2.4.1 *The full information equilibrium*

Under full information, the principal (the cognitive system) knows the values of θ_1, θ_2. This enables it to design contracts $\{c_1(\theta_1), l_1(\theta_1)\}$, $\{c_2(\theta_2), l_2(\theta_2)\}$, respectively, for the two agents, namely, the emotional systems at dates $t = 1$ and $t = 2$.[9] The principal chooses c_1, l_1, c_2, l_2 in order to maximize the following objective function

$$(\theta_1 u(c_1) - l_1) + (\theta_2 u(c_2) - l_2), \tag{2.39}$$

subject to the feasibility constraints in (2.35) and the intertemporal budget constraint in (2.38). Ignoring (2.35) for the time being, the Lagrangian is

$$Z = (\theta_1 u(c_1) - l_1) + (\theta_2 u(c_2) - l_2) + \lambda \left[l_1 + \frac{l_2}{(1+r)} - c_1 - \frac{c_2}{(1+r)} \right],$$

where λ is the Lagrangian multiplier on the intertemporal budget constraint. The first order conditions for an interior solution to c_1, c_2 are

$$\frac{\partial Z}{\partial c_1} = 0 \Leftrightarrow \theta_1 u'(c_1) = \lambda. \tag{2.40}$$

$$\frac{\partial Z}{\partial c_2} = 0 \Leftrightarrow \theta_2 u'(c_2) = \frac{\lambda}{1+r}. \tag{2.41}$$

The partial derivatives of the Lagrangian with respect to l_1, l_2 are,

$$\frac{\partial Z}{\partial l_1} = -1 + \lambda, \tag{2.42}$$

$$\frac{\partial Z}{\partial l_2} = -1 + \frac{\lambda}{1+r}. \tag{2.43}$$

It can be shown that there is no interior solution to the labor supply in both periods. Suppose to the contrary that $l_1, l_2 \in (0, L)$. Then (2.42), (2.43) hold with equality. But this implies that $r = 0$, a contradiction. There is a boundary solution $l_1 = L$ at which $\frac{\partial Z}{\partial l_1} > 0$. The intuition is that one unit of labor in period 1 generates one unit of income (and one unit of disutility). This can be converted to $1 + r$ units of second period consumption. Since there is no discounting between

---

[9] This is clearly a massively reduced-form and fairly strong assumption, the microfoundations of which are not entirely established.

the two periods, and $r > 0$, it is optimal that the full information solution to first period labor supply attains its upper bound, $l_1^F = L$ and the solution to l_2 is an interior one, so $\lambda = 1 + r$.

Substituting λ in (2.40), (2.41) gives the solution for c_1 and c_2. Given $l_1^F = L$, l_2 can then be recovered from (2.38). Thus, the solution under full information is given by

$$\theta_1 u' \left(c_1^F \right) = 1 + r. \tag{2.44}$$

$$\theta_2 u' \left(c_2^F \right) = 1. \tag{2.45}$$

$$l_1^F = L, l_2^F = c_1^F (1 + r) + c_2^F - L(1 + r). \tag{2.46}$$

The conditions (2.44), (2.45) equate the marginal utility of consumption in periods 1 and 2, respectively, with the opportunity cost. Each unit of consumption in period 1 leads to $1 + r$ units of forgone second period consumption, while the opportunity cost of an extra unit of consumption in period 2 is one unit of forgone leisure. From (2.46), we can check if the solution to l_2 is an interior one.

2.4.2 The asymmetric information equilibrium

Now suppose that only the emotional system knows the true value of θ_t, $t = 1, 2$. Using backward induction, we first solve the period 2 problem. In period 2, the preferences of the emotional system and the cognitive system coincide because there is no future to worry about. The second period optimization problem is to choose c_2, l_2 to maximize

$$\theta_2 u (c_2) - l_2,$$

subject to the budget constraint

$$c_2 \leq l_2 + (1 + r)(l_1 - c_1),$$

where we have used $s = (l_1 - c_1)$. Since $u' > 0$, the budget constraint binds. We can substitute l_2 from the binding budget constraint into the objective function to get an unconstrained optimization problem in c_2. The optimal solution, $c_2^*(\theta_2)$, can be found from the first order condition

$$\theta_2 u' \left(c_2^* \right) = 1, \tag{2.47}$$

i.e., marginal utility from consumption equals its opportunity cost. The optimal second period labor supply, $l_2 = l_2^*$, can now be found from the budget constraint

$$l_2^*(\theta_2) = c_2^*(\theta_2) + (l_1 - c_1)(1 + r). \tag{2.48}$$

In the first period, the preferences of the two systems are in conflict. Hence, the full information contracts are not incentive compatible under asymmetric information. Under full information, $\theta_1 u' \left(c_1^F \right) = 1 + r$ and $l_1(\theta_L) = l_1(\theta_H) = L$. Since $0 < \theta_L < \theta_H$ it follows that $c_1^F(\theta_L) < c_1^F(\theta_H)$. Type θ_L will then benefit by misstating type to be θ_H in order to receive extra consumption without working harder. Hence, the principal (cognitive system) needs to design incentive compatible contracts.

Denote the contracts under asymmetric information by $\{c_1(\theta_L), l_1(\theta_L)\}$ and $\{c_1(\theta_H), l_1(\theta_H)\}$. While private contracts are enforceable by law or by the oversight of third parties, what prevents the cognitive system from reneging on the promised consumption, once the contractual amount of labor has been put in? There are no clear cut answers to these difficult questions. Brocas and Carillo (2008) conjecture that other areas of the brain might be involved in such enforcement and claim supporting evidence from neuroscientific studies.

We can use the revelation principle to find the first period optimal contracts $\{c_1(\theta_L), l_1(\theta_L)\}$ and $\{c_1(\theta_H), l_1(\theta_H)\}$ as the solution to the following problem.

$$\underset{\{c_1(\theta_1), l_1(\theta_1)\}}{Max} E_{\theta_1}\left[\theta_1 u(c_1(\theta_1)) - l_1(\theta_1)\right] + E_{\theta_2}\left[\theta_2 u\left(c_2^*(\theta_2)\right) - l_2^*(\theta_2)\right]. \tag{2.49}$$

Subject to (2.35), (2.47), (2.48), and the two incentive compatibility constraints for types θ_L, θ_H, respectively,

$$IC_L : \theta_L u(c_1(\theta_L)) - l_1(\theta_L) \geq \theta_L u(c_1(\theta_H)) - l_1(\theta_H). \tag{2.50}$$

$$IC_H : \theta_H u(c_1(\theta_H)) - l_1(\theta_H) \geq \theta_H u(c_1(\theta_L)) - l_1(\theta_L). \tag{2.51}$$

The objective function in (2.49) reflects uncertainty arising from the two periods. The operators E_{θ_1} and E_{θ_2} denote, respectively, expectations with respect to θ_1 and θ_2; each variable takes the value θ_L with probability p and θ_H with probability $1 - p$. The IC_L constraint requires that type θ_L cannot do better by mimicking type θ_H, while the IC_H constraint rules out similar mimicking by type θ_H. A notable difference from standard mechanism design problems is the absence of participation constraints, as it is not clear what they would imply in the current context.

The most important insight of the model can be obtained directly from the two incentive compatibility constraints. As in standard mechanism design models, IC_H binds.[10] From the binding IC_H constraint we get

$$l_1(\theta_H) = \theta_H\left[u(c_1(\theta_H)) - u(c_1(\theta_L))\right] + l_1(\theta_L). \tag{2.52}$$

Substituting (2.52) in IC_L we get that $u(c_1(\theta_H)) \geq u(c_1(\theta_L))$, or $c_1(\theta_H) \geq c_1(\theta_L)$, so the level of consumption is monotonic in the type. From IC_L, we also get that

$$\theta_L\left[u(c_1(\theta_H)) - u(c_1(\theta_L))\right] + \left[l_1(\theta_L) - l_1(\theta_H)\right] \leq 0. \tag{2.53}$$

Since $u(c_1(\theta_H)) \geq u(c_1(\theta_L))$, a necessary condition for (2.53) to hold is that

$$l_1(\theta_L) \leq l_1(\theta_H). \tag{2.54}$$

This brings us to the crux of the solution. Type θ_L would like to claim to be type θ_H if it cared about consumption alone (because $c_1(\theta_H) \geq c_1(\theta_L)$). Anticipating this incentive, the principal cleverly designs the contracts in such a way that (2.54) holds, so if type θ_L wants to consume more, then it must also work more. Since more work entails greater disutility, if $l_1(\theta_H)$ is sufficiently high, then type θ_L no longer has an incentive to misrepresent its type. The authors interpret this finding as explaining behaviors such as: "I will spend the weekend in Palm Springs only if I finish

---

[10] Brocas and Carillo (2008) demonstrate this property when θ has a continuous distribution.

the paper by Friday" or "If I decide to watch the soccer game today, then I must first complete the referee report today."

These insights motivate the following general result for the case of continuous distributions.

> **Proposition 2.1** *(Brocas and Carillo, 2008): Suppose that θ_1 and θ_2 are distributed continuously over the interval $[\underline{\theta}, \overline{\theta}]$. The density of θ_1 is $f(\theta_1)$ and the distribution function is $F(\theta_1)$. Under asymmetric information, the optimal contracts are as follows.*
>
> *(i) At time $t = 1$: There exists a cutoff point $\theta_c < \overline{\theta}$ such that the optimal contracts for all types $\underline{\theta} \le \theta_1 < \theta_c$, denoted by $\left\{c_1^*(\theta_1), l_1^*(\theta_1)\right\}_{\underline{\theta}}^{\theta_c}$, are given by*
>
> $$\left[\theta_1 + r\left(\theta_1 + \frac{F(\theta_1)}{f(\theta_1)}\right)\right] u'\left(c_1^*(\theta_1)\right) = 1 + r, \tag{2.55}$$
>
> *while the optimal amount of labor elicited in the first period is*
>
> $$l_1^*(\theta_1) = L - \left[\overline{\theta} u\left(c_1^*(\overline{\theta})\right) - \theta_1 u\left(c_1^*(\theta_1)\right) - \int_{\theta_1}^{\overline{\theta}} u\left(c_1^*(x)\right) dx\right] < L. \tag{2.56}$$
>
> *For all $\theta_c \le \theta_1 \le \overline{\theta}$ there is pooling of contracts. Each of these types is given the contract $\left\{c_1^*(\theta_c), L\right\}$, where $c_1^*(\theta_c)$ is the optimal consumption given in (2.55), and evaluated at $\theta_1 = \theta_c$.*
>
> *(ii) At time $t = 2$: The principal allows the time 2 agent to choose any consumption–labour pair that satisfies the intertemporal constraint (2.38). The agent then, voluntarily, chooses*
>
> $$u'\left(c_2^*(\theta_2)\right) = \frac{1}{\theta_2} \text{ and } l_2^*(\theta_2) = (1 + r)\left(c_1^*(\theta_1) - l_1^*(\theta_1)\right) + c_2^*(\theta_2); \theta_2 \in [\underline{\theta}, \overline{\theta}].$$

Since $\theta_1 + r\left(\theta_1 + \frac{F(\theta_1)}{f(\theta_1)}\right) > \theta_1$, it follows by comparing (2.44) with (2.55) that $c_1^*(\theta_1) > c_1^F(\theta_1)$, hence, consumption in the first period under asymmetric information is larger than that under full information. This reflects the information rents derived by the better informed agent in period 1. From (2.46), (2.56), under asymmetric information, the first period emotional system is asked for a lower amount of labor relative to that under full information. Hence, relative to full information, first period consumption is larger and first period labor supply is smaller. Thus, it is as if an endogenous rate of time preference develops under asymmetric information despite the fact that the cognitive self undertakes no time discounting.

2.5 Strategic ignorance, confidence, and self-esteem

In this section we consider models of multiple-selves in which individuals may have asymmetric information about some aspects of their own characteristics; for instance, about their willpower, ability, or motivations. Individuals might engage in introspection to discover themselves, or use their performance in a task to discover their underlying motivations or abilities. In this scenario, individuals might decide to strategically transmit or hide information to their own future selves, or even manage their degree of awareness of personal qualities. Among the set of phenomena explained by this model are the roles of strategic ignorance, selective memory transmission, and self-handicapping.

2.5.1 *Strategic ignorance*

Consider a three period version of the multiple selves model in Carrillo and Mariotti (2000), where time $t = 1,2,3$; the self in period t is denoted by self t. Each self, in each period, is risk neutral and makes a simple binary consumption choice $x_t \in \{0,1\}$; 0 denotes abstinence and 1 denotes consumption of a free good (introducing a cost of acquiring the good does not alter the qualitative predictions). To simplify further, we assume that self 3 chooses $x_3 = 0$. Current consumption increases instantaneous utility of self t but it reduces the utility of self $t + 1$ by $e > 1$ units (negative externality) with some probability $\theta \geq 0$; e.g., the good could be some unhealthy food/lifestyle.[11] θ is distributed uniformly over $[0,1]$ with cumulative density F; all selves are aware of the relevant distribution. In addition to the consumption decision, self 1 has to decide whether to costlessly learn the true value of θ.

The instantaneous utility of self t is given by

$$u_t = x_t - y_t, \tag{2.57}$$

where y_t is the externality caused by the consumption decision of self $t - 1$, so

$$y_t = \begin{cases} 0 & if \quad x_{t-1} = 0 \\ \theta e & if \quad x_{t-1} = 1 \end{cases}, \tag{2.58}$$

with the assumption that $x_3 = 0$. Preferences take the special *quasi-hyperbolic* $(\beta, 1)$ *form*, $0 < \beta < 1$ (see Volume 3 of the book), so the utility of self t is

$$U_t = \begin{cases} u_1 + \beta (u_2 + u_3) & if \quad t = 1 \\ u_2 + \beta u_3 & if \quad t = 2 \\ u_3 & if \quad t = 3 \end{cases}. \tag{2.59}$$

From (2.57), (2.58), (2.59) and the assumption that $x_3 = 0$, we can recursively solve backwards to work out the intertemporal utility of the successive selves.

$$U_3 = -\theta e x_2; \; x_2 \in \{0,1\}. \tag{2.60}$$

$$U_2 = (x_2 - \theta e x_1) + \beta (-\theta e x_2) = x_2 (1 - \beta \theta e) - \theta e x_1; \; x_1, x_2 \in \{0,1\}. \tag{2.61}$$

$$U_1 = x_1 + \beta (x_2 - \theta e x_1) + \beta (-\theta e x_2) = x_1 (1 - \beta \theta e) + x_2 \beta (1 - \theta e); \; x_1, x_2 \in \{0,1\}. \tag{2.62}$$

Assume that $\frac{1}{\beta e} < 1$. We also make the tie-breaking assumption that when self t is indifferent between consuming and not consuming, he chooses to consume.

Using (2.62), the following three cases arise for self 1.

1. $0 \leq \theta \leq 1/e$: If $0 \leq \theta \leq 1/e$, then $1 - \beta \theta e > 0$ and $1 - \theta e \geq 0$. Thus, self 1 would like to consume in period 1 ($x_1 = 1$) and would also like self 2 to consume ($x_2 = 1$).
2. $\frac{1}{e} < \theta \leq \frac{1}{\beta e}$: If $\frac{1}{e} < \theta \leq \frac{1}{\beta e}$, then $1 - \beta \theta e \geq 0$ and $1 - \theta e < 0$. Thus, self 1 prefers to consume ($x_1 = 1$), and prefers self 2 to abstain from consumption ($x_2 = 0$).
3. $\frac{1}{\beta e} < \theta \leq 1$: In this case, self 1 prefers to abstain in both periods ($x_1 = x_2 = 0$).

---

[11] Carrillo and Mariotti (2008) also consider the more general case when current consumption creates a negative externality for all future selves.

With the present bias implied by $(\beta, 1)$ preferences, the preferences of self 2 are different from the preferences of self 1. Furthermore, self 1 cannot bind the choices of self 2.

4. From (2.61), it is apparent that self 2 will consume ($x_2 = 1$) if $1 - \beta\theta e \geq 0$, or $0 < \theta \leq \frac{1}{\beta e}$. Otherwise, if $\frac{1}{\beta e} < \theta \leq 1$, then self 2 abstains, $x_2 = 0$.

For self 1, if θ is high enough (as in cases 2 and 3 above), so that x_2 causes a large enough negative externality in period 3, then self 1 prefers $x_2 = 0$. However, self 2 is relatively biased towards x_2 on account of his current bias and so always prefers $x_2 = 1$ unless $\frac{1}{\beta e} < \theta \leq 1$. We summarize these results in the following proposition.

Proposition 2.2 *Consider the split of the domain of θ into three regions.*

(i) *If $\theta \in \left[0, \frac{1}{e}\right]$, then there is no conflict between the choices of selves 1 and 2 and both choose $x_1 = x_2 = 1$.*

(ii) *If $\frac{1}{e} < \theta \leq \frac{1}{\beta e}$, then there is strategic conflict between the two selves; self 1 prefers $x_2 = 0$, while self 2 prefers $x_2 = 1$.*

(iii) *If $\frac{1}{\beta e} < \theta \leq 1$, then there is no conflict and selves 1 and 2 prefer $x_2 = 0$.*

Suppose that self 1 can learn the true value of θ. As soon as the value of θ is learnt, self 2 is also privy to it. If the value is not learnt then self 2 can, at best, rely on the knowledge of the underlying distribution, F. For now, we assume that memory cannot be manipulated, although we relax this assumption in Section 2.5.2 below. Self 1 then knows that if $\theta \leq \frac{1}{e}$ or $\frac{1}{\beta e} < \theta$ then there is no conflict with self 2, but for intermediate ranges of θ, $\frac{1}{e} < \theta \leq \frac{1}{\beta e}$, there is conflict.

Proposition 2.3 *(No learning): Suppose that self 1 decides not to learn the true value of θ. If $E[\theta] \in \left[0, \frac{1}{\beta e}\right]$, then $x_1 = x_2 = 1$. However, if $\frac{1}{\beta e} < E[\theta]$, then $x_1 = x_2 = 0$.*

Proof: Since all selves are risk neutral and utility is linear in θ, from (2.61), we have

$$EU_2 = x_2 \left(1 - \beta e E[\theta]\right) - e x_1 E[\theta].$$

Thus, self 1 believes that self 2 will choose $x_2 = 1$ if $E[\theta] \in \left[0, \frac{1}{\beta e}\right]$, otherwise $x_2 = 0$. From (2.62), we have

$$EU_1 = x_1 \left(1 - \beta e E[\theta]\right) + x_2 \beta \left(1 - e E[\theta]\right).$$

So self 1 chooses $x_1 = 1$ if $E[\theta] \in \left[0, \frac{1}{\beta e}\right]$, otherwise $x_1 = 0$. ∎

Let us now compute the utility of self 1 from the learning and the no learning options.

1. *Learning*: Denote the expected utility of self 1 from learning the true value of θ by U_1^L. Note that U_1^L is the utility under the learning option, but before the value of θ has been learned. Then,

$$U_1^L = F\left(\frac{1}{\beta e}\right)\left[1 + \beta - 2\beta e E\left[\theta \mid \theta \leq \frac{1}{\beta e}\right]\right], \tag{2.63}$$

where $F\left(\frac{1}{\beta e}\right)$ is the cumulative probability that θ is at most equal to $\frac{1}{\beta e}$. In this case, selves 1 and 2 prefer to consume in their respective periods. The term in the square braces follows from risk neutrality, when (2.62) is evaluated at $x_1 = x_2 = 1$. With the complementary probability $1 - F\left(\frac{1}{\beta e}\right)$, none of the selves wants to consume and there is no externality caused to any self.

2. *No learning*: Denote the expected utility of self 1 if she chooses not to learn the true value of θ by U_1^N; in this case self 2 only knows the distribution F of θ. Then, using Proposition 2.3 we get

$$U_1^N = \begin{cases} 1 + \beta - 2\beta E[\theta] e & \text{if} \quad E[\theta] \leq \frac{1}{\beta e} \\ 0 & \text{if} \quad E[\theta] > \frac{1}{\beta e} \end{cases}. \tag{2.64}$$

We get the following main result.

Proposition 2.4

(a) If $E[\theta] \leq \frac{1}{\beta e}$, then $U_1^N < U_1^L$, so the individual prefers to be strategically informed about θ.

(b) If $E[\theta] > \frac{1}{\beta e}$, then $U_1^N > U_1^L$ if $E\left[\theta \mid \theta \leq \frac{1}{\beta e}\right] > \frac{1+\beta}{2\beta e}$.

Proof: Since θ is distributed uniformly over $[0, 1]$, it follows that

$$E[\theta] = \frac{1}{2}, \quad E\left[\theta \mid \theta \leq \frac{1}{\beta e}\right] = \frac{1}{2\beta e}, \quad F\left(\frac{1}{\beta e}\right) = \frac{1}{\beta e}. \tag{2.65}$$

(a) Suppose that $E[\theta] \leq \frac{1}{\beta e}$. Substituting (2.65) in (2.63), (2.64) it follows that

$$U_1^N < U_1^L \Leftrightarrow 0 < (e - 1)\left(\beta - \frac{1}{e}\right),$$

which is true because of the assumptions (i) $\frac{1}{\beta e} < 1$ so $\beta e > 1$, and (ii) $e > 1$.

(b) Suppose that $E[\theta] > \frac{1}{\beta e}$. In this case $U_1^N = 0$, so the condition $U_1^N > U_1^L$ reduces to $U_1^L < 0$. The stated result now follows directly from (2.63). ∎

The intuition for Proposition 2.4 arises from the interval $\theta \in \left(\frac{1}{e}, \frac{1}{\beta e}\right]$ in which self 1 prefers $x_2 = 0$ but self 2 prefers $x_2 = 1$. Self 1 prefers to be strategically uninformed if this leads to self 2 abstaining from consumption. This occurs when $E[\theta] > \frac{1}{\beta e}$. However, this is only a necessary condition because ignorance chosen by self 1 also entails costs. For instance, it might be that $\theta > \frac{1}{\beta e}$, in which case selves 1 and 2 both prefer $x_2 = 0$. The condition $E\left[\theta \mid \theta \leq \frac{1}{\beta e}\right] > \frac{1+\beta}{2\beta e}$ in Proposition 2.4 ensures that conditional on $E[\theta] > \frac{1}{\beta e}$, θ is closer to $\frac{1}{\beta e}$ rather than to 0. The finding by Lundborg and Lindgren (2004) that individuals with higher perceived risks are less likely to be smokers offers some partial support for this theory.

2.5.2 Confidence, motivation, and self-esteem

Bénabou and Tirole (2002, 2003) consider situations where the subsequent selves of an individual might have some asymmetric information (*imperfect self-knowledge*) about the current self; we distinguish between *good* and *bad* types. A good type has *high levels of willpower*. Depending on the context, a good type might keep to deadlines, or see tasks through to completion once they have been initiated, or undertake a high level of productive effort. By contrast, a *bad type* has *inadequate willpower*. The current self might wish to undertake costly actions to convince subsequent selves of being a good type. However, the actions by a current self to convince subsequent selves of his type must be incentive compatible.

There are at least three main building blocks of the work by Bénabou and Tirole in this regard. The first two, *imperfect self-knowledge* and *imperfect willpower*, have been mentioned above in the other models in this chapter. The third building block is *imperfect recall and motivated cognition*. Imperfect recall implies, roughly, that an individual might manage, wilfully or otherwise, how past actions are remembered. The thrust of the argument is not that memory can simply be wilfully suppressed, but rather that the awareness of events in the past can be manipulated.

Consider for instance the following examples. (i) Our memory of past actions can often be self-serving. We tend to remember our successes more than our failures. We might, wrongly, ascribe our lack of success to external factors, or blame others for it. (ii) The intensity of past visceral states in our memories might diminish gradually with time. (iii) By taking down written records of an event, sharing them with friends and rehearsing the records, offers at least partial protection from memory loss. But in many cases, we choose not to. (iv) We can control the vividness of the memory of an event by choosing the degree of attention we give to it. We sometimes pay insufficient attention to events that are unpleasant. At the extreme, we can sometimes get drunk to try to forget unpleasant events. Memory also decays naturally with time, especially if not consciously rehearsed; the latter is of course an endogenous decision.

We operationalize this as follows. At any instant of time, the current self chooses some action and the probability with which the subsequent selves can recall this action. It is possible that the current self chooses to engage in wilful self-deception. Subsequent selves are aware of the incentive for self-deception, hence, good news might get discounted in equilibrium, especially if it is likely to arise from too much self-deception. However, some self-deception might actually help. For instance, if the decision of the future selves to undertake an activity depends on the belief in their abilities, or in their "self-confidence," then the current self might undertake actions that strengthen this belief.

There are at least three main reasons why individuals might wish to have a more optimistic and confident view of themselves, relative to a more realistic one. First, confidence in one's abilities might directly enhance utility. Second, it might have a signaling value; self-belief might be a signal to others of one's abilities. Third, it might have a motivational value for one's future selves.

We now examine the motivational value of self-confidence in the context of the three period model of Bénabou and Tirole (2002). Consider a risk-neutral individual with an economic lifespan of three periods $t = 1, 2, 3$. There are multiple selves, so there is a distinct self of the individual in each period. Each self uses hyperbolic discounting and has $(\beta, 1)$ preferences, $0 < \beta < 1$. The decisions faced by the different selves are as follows.

1. Self 1 chooses an action that affects her flow payoff u_1 and the date 2 information structure. Denote by $\theta \in [0, 1]$, a random variable, such as self-confidence or ability, over which the beliefs of self 1 are given by the distribution function $F_1(\theta)$. Self 1 can alter the date 2 information structure by engaging in costly self-deception that lowers current payoff u_1, but generates a more optimistic belief in abilities for subsequent selves, in particular, for self 2.

2. Self 2 can undertake some action or project that has current costs $c \in [0, 1]$ in terms of effort or resources at date 2. The project is successful with probability θ. If successful, the

project yields a payoff of 1 unit that is obtained at date 3. The beliefs of self 2 are given by the distribution function $F_2(\theta)$.

Define the mean of θ with respect to the distribution function $F_i(\theta)$ by $\overline{\theta}_i = \int_0^1 \theta dF_i(\theta)$. Individuals are risk neutral and payoff functions are linear in θ, so the mean, $\overline{\theta}_i$, encompasses everything that the individual needs to know about the randomness in the model. In other words, $\overline{\theta}_i$ is a sufficient statistic for $F_i(\theta)$.

The expected payoff of self 2, $E_2[U]$, is given by

$$E_2[U] = \begin{cases} -c + \beta E_2\theta = -c + \beta\overline{\theta}_2 & \text{if activity is undertaken} \\ 0 & \text{if activity is not undertaken} \end{cases}, \beta \in (0,1), \qquad (2.66)$$

where E_2 is the expectation operator with respect to the distribution $F_2(\theta)$. (2.66) shows that the cost of the activity is borne in the current period but the reward is received in the next period. Self 2 undertakes the activity if $-c + \beta\overline{\theta}_2 > 0$, or[12]

$$\overline{\theta}_2 > \frac{c}{\beta} > c. \qquad (2.67)$$

If self 2 knew the true value of θ, then she would undertake the action only if

$$\theta > \frac{c}{\beta} > c. \qquad (2.68)$$

The expected payoff of self 1, $E_1[U]$, depends on the choice made by self 2 and is given by

$$E_1[U] = \begin{cases} u_1 + \beta(-c + \overline{\theta}_2) & \text{if self 2 undertakes the activity} \\ u_1 & \text{if self 2 does not undertake the activity} \end{cases}. \qquad (2.69)$$

Self 1 prefers self 2 to undertake the activity if $u_1 + \beta(-c + \overline{\theta}_2) > u_1$, or

$$\overline{\theta}_2 > c. \qquad (2.70)$$

If self 1 knew θ, then she would want the action to the undertaken if $\theta > c$. Comparing (2.67), (2.70) the crucial interval of disagreement between selves 1 and 2 is $c < \overline{\theta}_2 \leq \frac{c}{\beta}$. We summarize the main result from the discussion so far.

Lemma 2.1 *If θ is unknown to both selves, then the following hold. (1) If $c < \overline{\theta}_2 \leq \frac{c}{\beta}$, self 2 will not undertake the activity, but self 1 would like the activity to be undertaken. (2) If $\overline{\theta}_2 < c$, then none of the selves want the activity to be undertaken. (3) If $\overline{\theta}_2 > \frac{c}{\beta}$, then both selves would like the activity to be undertaken.*

MAINTAINING THE OPTIMAL DEGREE OF CONFIDENCE

Suppose that self 1 were to learn about the true value of θ. Should self 1 choose to transmit this information to self 2? The answer depends on the value of θ as well as on the credibility of

---

[12] We do not consider the case when a self is indifferent between two choices but this can be readily incorporated by assuming some tie breaking rule.

information transmission. Suppose that information is completely credibly transmitted, hence, immediately believed by self 2. Thus, if self 1 chooses to reveal information, he cannot lie about the state, θ. We distinguish between two main cases.

Case I ($\overline{\theta}_2 > \frac{c}{\beta}$): From (2.67), self 2 will undertake the activity in the absence of any information from self 1. Using (2.69), the expected utility of self 1 from not passing on any information to self 2 is given by

$$E_1[U] = u_1 + \beta(-c + \overline{\theta}_1), \tag{2.71}$$

where we have used the fact that in the absence of any transmitted information, $\overline{\theta}_1 = \overline{\theta}_2$.

On the other hand, if information is passed on to self 2, then, using (2.68), self 2 will only take the action when $\theta > \frac{c}{\beta}$. Hence, from an ex-ante perspective, before self 1 makes the decision to know θ, the expected utility of self 1 from the decision to pass on the information is

$$E_1[U] = u_1 + \beta \int_{c/\beta}^{1} (-c + \theta)dF_1(\theta). \tag{2.72}$$

Subtracting (2.71) from (2.72), the *information disclosure value* to self 1, denoted by D, can be written as

$$D = \beta \left[\int_0^c (c - \theta)dF_1(\theta) - \int_c^{c/\beta} (\theta - c)dF_1(\theta) \right] = \beta[G - L], \tag{2.73}$$

where

$$G = \int_0^c (c - \theta)dF_1(\theta) \text{ and } L = \int_c^{c/\beta} (\theta - c)dF_1(\theta)$$

denote, respectively, the gain and loss to self 1 from information disclosure; we explain in more detail below.

1. Suppose that self 1 learns $\theta < c$. Because $\overline{\theta}_2 > \frac{c}{\beta}$, self 2 will undertake the action in the absence of the information (overconfidence), but not if the information were to be revealed. Both selves do not wish the project to be undertaken if $\theta < c$, so self 1 reveals the information. By doing so, self 1 covers for the *risk of overconfidence* on the part of self 2. This corresponds to the term G in (2.73).

2. Suppose that self 1 learns $c < \theta < \frac{c}{\beta}$. In this case, self 1 would like the action to be undertaken, but because $\overline{\theta}_2 > \frac{c}{\beta}$, self 2 will undertake the action anyway, even in the absence of the information. Providing self 2 more information, i.e., that $c < \theta < \frac{c}{\beta}$ would prevent it from undertaking the action. Hence, there is a loss to self 1 from having an informed self 2, thus, self 1 prefers to *maintain the confidence* of self 2. This corresponds to the term L in (2.73).

3. Finally, if $\theta > \frac{c}{\beta}$, then self 1 is indifferent to revealing or not revealing the information because self 1 wishes the project to be undertaken and self 2 would undertake it anyway because $\overline{\theta}_2 > \frac{c}{\beta}$.

If the "risk of overconfidence motive" is stronger, then self 1 transmits information. If, however, the "confidence maintenance motive" is relatively stronger, then self 1 does not transmit information. Note that when $\beta = 1$, so the individual uses exponential discounting, then $D = G > 0$, so self 1 always transmits information; in this case the objectives of selves 1 and 2 are fully aligned. As β decreases and the present bias of self 2 increases, L increases and D falls. Thus, if the present bias of self 2 is higher, then the confidence maintenance motive dominates and so information is less likely to be transmitted.

Case II ($\overline{\theta}_2 < \frac{c}{\beta}$): Using (2.67), self 2 will not undertake the activity in the absence of additional information. In this case, self 2 will undertake the activity only if self 1 reveals $\theta > \frac{c}{\beta}$. Hence, the expected gain to self 1 from providing information to self 2 is given by

$$D = \beta \int\limits_{c/\beta}^{1} (\theta - c) dF_1(\theta) > 0.$$

Since $D > 0$, so information is always transmitted. In this case, the individual always looks for feedback on his ability.

DEGREES OF SELF-CONFIDENCE

Suppose that we have two individuals with different degrees of initial self-confidence. Which one is more eager to transmit information to its future selves? Consider two individuals whose initial beliefs about the distribution of θ are given, respectively, by the distribution functions $F(\theta)$ and $G(\theta)$; the associated density functions are $f(\theta)$ and $g(\theta)$. The domain of θ is $[0, 1]$.

> **Definition 2.1** (*Confidence*): *The individual with the distribution function $F(\theta)$ is said to be relatively more confident as compared to the individual with the distribution function $G(\theta)$ if the monotone likelihood ratio property is satisfied*
>
> $$\frac{f(\theta_L)}{g(\theta_L)} < \frac{f(\theta_H)}{g(\theta_H)} \ \forall \ \theta_L < \theta_H \ in \ [0, 1]. \tag{2.74}$$

Definition 2.1 requires that the more confident individual places a relatively higher probability on the higher value of θ. A straightforward implication of (2.74) is

$$F(\theta) < G(\theta) \ \forall \ \theta \in [0, 1], \tag{2.75}$$

i.e., the distribution function of a more confident individual, first order stochastically dominates the distribution function of a less confident individual. Let $\overline{\theta}_1^F, \overline{\theta}_1^G$ denote, respectively, the expected values taken with respect to F and G. We assume that

$$\overline{\theta}_1^F > \overline{\theta}_1^G > c/\beta. \tag{2.76}$$

From (2.76), in the absence of additional information (so $\overline{\theta}_1^F = \overline{\theta}_2^F$ and $\overline{\theta}_1^G = \overline{\theta}_2^G$), self 2 will, undertake the activity, irrespective of the degree of initial confidence.

From (2.73), $D \geq 0$ if and only if

$$\int\limits_0^c (c - \theta) dF_1(\theta) \geq \int\limits_c^{c/\beta} (\theta - c) dF_1(\theta) \Leftrightarrow \int\limits_0^{c/\beta} (\theta - c) dF_1(\theta) \leq 0.$$

Integrating by parts we get

$$|(\theta - c)F_1(\theta)|_0^{c/\beta} - \int_0^{c/\beta} F_1 d(\theta) \leq 0,$$

or

$$\int_0^{c/\beta} \frac{F_1(\theta)}{F_1(c/\beta)} d\theta \geq \left(\frac{1-\beta}{\beta}\right)c. \tag{2.77}$$

A similar expression applies for the individual who holds beliefs given by the distribution function G_1. Using (2.74), we have

$$\frac{F_1(\theta)}{F_1(c/\beta)} < \frac{G_1(\theta)}{G_1(c/\beta)} \ \forall \theta \leq c/\beta. \tag{2.78}$$

From (2.77), (2.78) it follows that (2.77) is more likely to hold for the less confident individual who has the initial distribution function G_1. Hence, and equivalently, D is more likely to be positive for the less confident individual, i.e., she is more likely to transmit information. A more confident individual has more to lose by transmitting information.

SELF-HANDICAPPING AND SELF-ESTEEM

A puzzling aspect of behavior is that individuals sometimes take actions that are not conducive to good performance. Examples include, anxiety before an exam, witholding of effort, inadequate preparation, and setting of tasks for oneself where one is almost sure to fail. Such self-handicapping has been suggested by psychologists as a deliberate strategy to maintain self-esteem.

Suppose that $\overline{\theta}_2 > \frac{c}{\beta}$ so that in the absence of any information, self 2 will undertake the action. Suppose also that the efficient action is for self 1 to transmit information to self 2. Not transmitting any information (self-handicapping) is the alternative strategy for self 1. Suppose that the cost of such self-handicapping is zero. From (2.77), self-handicapping is the better alternative if

$$\int_0^{c/\beta} \frac{F_1(\theta)}{F_1(c/\beta)} d\theta < \left(\frac{1-\beta}{\beta}\right)c. \tag{2.79}$$

Using (2.78), it is more likely that (2.79) will hold for the more confident individual (who uses F_1 rather than G_1). Thus, more confident individuals are more likely to self-handicap; because they are more confident they have more to lose from learning the true value of their ability. This conclusion is not robust, however, to inclusion of costs of self-handicapping. More confident individuals are also less likely to receive bad signals, increasing the returns from self-handicapping; for a fuller analysis along these lines, see Bénabou and Tirole (2002).

AWARENESS MANAGEMENT

Suppose, for reasons mentioned above, one desires to have a positive self-assessment. How can this be achieved? One possibility is that we may be hardwired, on account of evolutionary reasons, to have positive self-assessment. However, many individuals suffer from a poor self-image, while others have to work for it, hence, this explanation is not entirely satisfactory. We focus instead on a simple strategic game between successive selves that stresses the roles of *motivation* and *cognition*.

Self 1 can, to an extent, influence the probability that self 2 remembers a piece of information. Hence, the *motivation* of self 1 might be to create greater memory awareness about signals that are more consistent with the long-term goals. In the absence of this greater awareness, the future selves who have "current biased preferences" may jeopardize these long-term goals. However, each self is rational and aware of the possibilities of self-deception by other selves. Thus, self 2 is *cognizant* of the incentives of self 1 to promote recall of events conducive to long-term goals.

Let $\lambda \in [0,1]$ be the probability that an event, which occurs at time $t = 1$ can be remembered by self 2 at time $t = 2$. We look only at the case where the manipulation of memory by self 1 is costless.[13] Evidence suggests that only a part of the total stock of information in one's memory can be retrieved for conscious processing at the time of decision making. There are several possible mechanisms that self 1 can make use of. Rehearsed information is more readily available, as is information that one has direct behavioral experience of. Self 1 can also avoid situations that are directly reminiscent of unpleasant and forgettable events; for instance, by tearing up pictures of a cheating spouse, or in extreme cases taking recourse to drugs and alcohol. The information content of unpleasant news can also be questioned; for instance, on getting a low grade, a student could question if the marker has adequately understood her work. Hence, we are interested in the management of awareness of memories.

Self 2 is aware of the incentives of self 1 to manipulate memory. Such skepticism on the part of self 2 is reflected in the use of Bayes' rule to update information.[14] The technology of self-deception is as follows.

At $t = 1$, self 1 receives a binary signal σ about her ability, θ. With probability q the signal is uninformative, i.e., $\sigma = \phi$ and with probability $1 - q$, the signal is "bad news," i.e., $\sigma = L$. Hence, "good news" is defined as no news. Define

$$\theta_L \equiv E[\theta \mid \sigma = L] < E[\theta \mid \sigma = \phi] \equiv \theta_H. \tag{2.80}$$

Denote the signal recollected by self 2 as $\hat{\sigma} = \{\phi, L\}$. Memories cannot be manufactured, so $\sigma = \phi \Rightarrow \hat{\sigma} = \phi$ (if the signal is uninformative, then the recollected signal is also uninformative). However, if $\sigma = L$, then this signal is remembered only with an endogenous probability λ,

$$\lambda = \Pr[\hat{\sigma} = L \mid \sigma = L]. \tag{2.81}$$

Hence, $1 - \lambda$ is the probability with which bad news is hidden from self 2.

Self 2 solves a Bayesian inference problem on observing the signal sent by self 1. She assesses the *reliability* of a *no news* message, r, by Bayes' rule:

$$r \equiv \Pr[\hat{\sigma} = \phi \mid \sigma = \phi] = \frac{q}{q + (1 - q)(1 - \lambda)}. \tag{2.82}$$

---

[13] See Bénabou and Tirole (2002) for the case where such manipulation is costly.
[14] Evidence is not consistent with individuals using Bayes' rule (see Volume 5). However, here this is not important for the qualitative results, as we show below.

The numerator of (2.82) is the prior probability of the signal ϕ and the denominator is the total probability with which the signal ϕ arises. If $\lambda = 1$, then a no news signal is completely reliable, i.e., $r = 1$. The individual's *degree of self-confidence*, $\theta(r)$, is defined as

$$\theta(r) = r\theta_H + (1 - r)\theta_L. \tag{2.83}$$

So far, we have assumed that the cost of effort c of self 1, is deterministic. We now relax this assumption; let the cost of the project, c, be a random variable drawn from $[\underline{c}, \overline{c}]$ with distribution $H(c)$ and density $h(c) > 0$. We assume that

$$\frac{\underline{c}}{\beta} < \theta_L, \quad \theta_H < \frac{\overline{c}}{\beta}. \tag{2.84}$$

Analogous to (2.67), self 2 undertakes the activity if

$$E[\theta \mid \hat{\sigma}] > \frac{c}{\beta} \Leftrightarrow c < \beta E[\theta \mid \hat{\sigma}]. \tag{2.85}$$

Hence, the expected payoff of self 1 is

$$E_1[U] = u_1 + \beta \int_0^{\beta E[\theta \mid \hat{\sigma}]} (-c + E[\theta \mid \sigma]) dH(c). \tag{2.86}$$

Suppose that self 2 was naive, and trusted the signal of self 1 without engaging in rational Bayesian updating. What expectation $E[\theta \mid \hat{\sigma}]$ would self 1 like self 2 to have? Analogous to (2.70), self 1 would like self 2 to undertake the activity when

$$E[\theta \mid \sigma] > c. \tag{2.87}$$

By manipulating the naive expectations of self 2 to be $E[\theta \mid \hat{\sigma}] = E[\theta \mid \sigma]/\beta$, the upper limit of integration in (2.86) becomes $E[\theta \mid \sigma]$. Thus, the expected payoff of self 1 is maximized (it is as if self 1 can induce self 2 to only undertake the action when it is in the former's self-interest). However, if self 2 is not naive this will not work.

Denote by $U_R(\theta_L)$ the expected utility of self 1 when the adverse information (signal L) is *concealed* and denote it by $U_C(\theta_L)$ when the signal is *revealed*. We are interested in the perfect Bayesian equilibria (PBE) of a signaling game between selves 1 and 2 in which they respectively choose λ and r (the optimal values are denoted by λ^*, r^*).

We begin by giving some intuition about the decisions of the two selves. If the bad news is hidden from self 2, it raises self-confidence from θ_L to $\theta(r^*)$ (recall that from (2.80), these are expected values). From (2.85), this additional self-confidence induces self 2 to work in the additional states of the world (a state corresponds to a cost, c) where

$$\beta\theta_L < c < \beta\theta(r^*). \tag{2.88}$$

However, the enhancement of self-confidence in this manner has a cost and a benefit. Analogous to (2.73), the net gain/loss from concealing information about the bad state is given by

$$U_C(\theta_L) - U_R(\theta_L) = \beta \left[\int_{\beta\theta_L}^{\theta_L} (\theta_L - c)\,dH(c) - \int_{\theta_L}^{\beta\theta(r^*)} (c - \theta_L)\,dH(c) \right]. \tag{2.89}$$

The first term in (2.89) is the *gain from confidence building* because over the range $\beta\theta_L < c < \theta_L$ self 1 would like self 2 to undertake effort but the latter does not wish to. The second term is the *loss from overconfidence*; over these states of the world, self 2 would like to undertake effort but self 1 does not wish self 2 to do so. The overconfidence cost is higher, the more reliability (higher r^*) self 2 places on the signal from self 1 because from (2.83), $\theta(r^*)$ is increasing in r^*.

Suppose that self 1 gets bad news, $\sigma = L$. The problem of self 1 is to choose the recall probability λ in order to maximize

$$\lambda U_R(\theta_L) + (1 - \lambda) U_C(\theta_L). \tag{2.90}$$

given the reliability, r^*, induced by his action.

Definition 2.2 *A Perfect Bayesian Equilibrium is a pair of strategies (λ^*, r^*) where $\lambda^* \in [0, 1]$, $r^* \in [q, 1]$ such that:*

(a) *Self 1 chooses the recall probability, λ^*, optimally to maximize (2.90), given the assessment reliability of self 2, r^*.*
(b) *Self 2's choice of r^* is consistent with Bayes' rule, (2.82), given the optimal choice of self 1.*

Using (2.90), the first order condition to self 1's problem is

$$U_R(\theta_L) - U_C(\theta_L) = 0. \tag{2.91}$$

Using (2.83), (2.89) in (2.91), we get

$$\beta \int_{\beta\theta_L}^{\beta(r\theta_H + (1-r)\theta_L)} (\theta_L - c)\,dH(c) = 0. \tag{2.92}$$

The main implications of (2.92) are given in Proposition 2.5 below.

Proposition 2.5 *(Bénabou and Tirole, 2002): There exist values of $\beta : \beta_L, \beta_H \in (0, 1)$ and $\beta_L < \beta_H$ such that the following hold.*

(a) *For $\beta > \beta_H$, the unique equilibrium is $\lambda^* = 1$, i.e., no news is hidden from self 2.*
(b) *For $\beta < \beta_L$ the unique equilibrium is $\lambda^* = 0$, i.e., all (bad) news is hidden from self 2.*
(c) *For $\beta \in [\beta_L, \beta_H]$ there are three possible equilibria, $\lambda^* \in \{0, \Gamma(\beta), 1\}$ where $\Gamma(\beta)$ is a decreasing function from 1 to 0 as β rises from β_L to β_H.*

The intuition behind Proposition 2.5 is straightforward. When β is very high, overconfidence is the main concern, thus, bad news is transmitted to self 2 to dampen her overconfidence. On the other hand, when β is low, the confidence of self 2 needs to be built up, so $\lambda^* = 0$. For intermediate values of β, a range of values $\lambda^* \in (0, 1)$ is optimal, so one gets multiple equilibria; see Figure 2.3.

The multiple equilibria can be explained as follows. Suppose that self 1 is very concealing of information (low λ^*). This makes self 2 discount such information even more and so

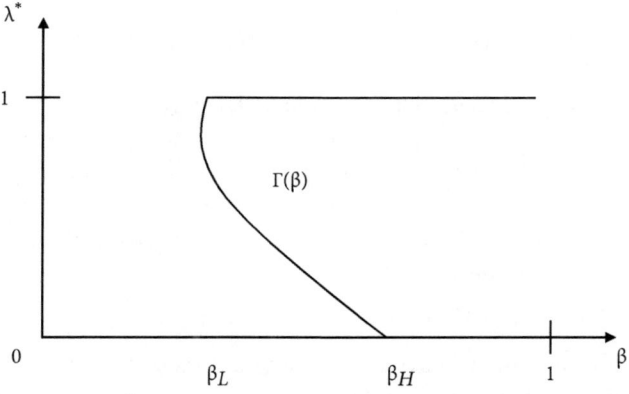

Figure 2.3 The optimal recall probability as β varies.

the risk that self 2 is overconfident increases. This makes self 1 even more keen to conceal information. On the other hand if self 1 truthfully reveals most information (high λ^*) self 2 considers it very reliable (using Bayes' rule). This gives an incentive for self 1 to be even more truthful.

In the fully censored equilibrium, $\lambda^* = 0$, no information is transmitted. In this "babbling equilibrium," the incentive for information suppression is different from Carillo and Mariotti (2000) in that self 1 does not want to suppress good news. But in trying to suppress only the bad news, she invariably ends up suppressing the good news (which, in this case, is no news). This might do more harm than good. To see this, the payoff to self 1 upon receiving good news is

$$U_R(\theta_H) = \beta \int_0^{\beta\theta(r^*)} (\theta_H - c)\, dH(c), \tag{2.93}$$

where r^* is the "reliability" inferred by self 2. Note that

$$\beta \int_0^{\beta\theta(r^*)} (\theta_H - c)\, dH(c) < \beta \int_0^{\beta\theta_H} (\theta_H - c)\, dH(c), \tag{2.94}$$

when all information is truthfully revealed to self 2. Thus, a child who is praised by her parents in most circumstances will never be sure if she really did well, even when she actually does well. Using (2.90), (2.93) the expected payoff of self 1, before receiving the ability signal is

$$W\left(\lambda^*, r^*\right) = qU_R(\theta_H) + \left(1 - q\right)\left[\lambda U_R(\theta_L) + (1 - \lambda) U_C(\theta_L)\right].$$

Thus, if the strategy is to truthfully reveal all information to self 2, the payoff of self 1 is $W(1,1)$. It is possible that $W(\lambda^*, r^*) < W(1,1)$.

Example 2.1 *Let $q = 1/2$, $\theta_L = 0$, $\theta_H = 1$, and $\bar{c} < 1$. Suppose $\lambda^* = 0$, so by Bayes' rule $r^* = q$. Note that*

$$W\left(\lambda^{*},r^{*}\right) - W\left(1,1\right) = \left(1-q\right) \int_{\beta\theta_{L}}^{\beta\theta(r^{*})} \left(\theta_{L} - c\right) dH(c) - q \int_{\beta\theta(r^{*})}^{\beta\theta_{H}} \left(\theta_{H} - c\right) dH(c). \quad (2.95)$$

Substituting $r^{*} = q = 1/2$, $\theta_{L} = 0$, $\theta_{H} = 1$ *in (2.95) we get:*

$$W\left(\lambda^{*},r^{*}\right) - W\left(1,1\right) = -\frac{1}{2}\left[\int_{0}^{\beta/2} c\,dH(c) + \int_{\beta/2}^{\beta} \left(1-c\right)dH(c)\right]. \quad (2.96)$$

Since $\bar{c} < 1$ *we get* $W\left(\lambda^{*},r^{*}\right) < W\left(1,1\right)$, *hence, the individual will not benefit from hiding information from subsequent selves.*

PERSONAL EVALUATION BIASES AND BAYES' RULE

In experimental evidence, most individuals overestimate their abilities in absolute terms and their abilities relative to others. Bénabou and Tirole (2002) cite survey evidence that shows 94% of college professors thought they were better than their average colleague. We now turn to the question of the rationality of such beliefs.[15]

Consider a large population that, using the law of large numbers, allows us to identify q, $1 - q$ as the proportions of the population that, respectively, receives the good ($\sigma = \phi$) and the bad ($\sigma = L$) signals. Suppose that less than half the population receives the good news, i.e., $q < 1/2$.

Selves 1 belonging to the proportion q can only signal good news to Selves 2. Suppose that the proportion $1 - q$, which receives the bad news, uses an identical optimal recall probability $\lambda^{*} \in (0,1)$; a symmetry argument or a unique equilibrium outcome can be used to justify this. Denote by r^{*}, the corresponding reliability placed by self 2 on the signal transmitted by self 1.

A fraction $1 - \lambda^{*}$ of Selves 2 of individuals who had bad news in period 1 forget about the bad news. Thus, the proportion of Selves 2 who overestimate their ability to be high, but actually have low ability, is $\left(1 - q\right)\left(1 - \lambda^{*}\right)$. The overestimation of their ability is $\theta\left(r^{*}\right) - \theta_{L}$; using (2.83) this is given by $r^{*}\left(\theta_{H} - \theta_{L}\right)$. Hence, the total proportion of period 2 selves who think that they have high ability is given by

$$q + \left(1-q\right)\left(1-\lambda^{*}\right).$$

If $\lambda^{*} < 1$, then this proportion is greater than the initial proportion ($q < 1/2$) that thinks that its ability is high. In fact if λ^{*} is not too high in the sense that $\lambda^{*} < \frac{1}{2(1-q)}$, then a majority of the population now, rationally, thinks that it has high ability and an ability greater than the average.

We have seen elsewhere in this book that Bayes' rule is not an accurate description of the human inference process; for instance it neglects the base rate (see Volume 5). In an earlier paper Bénabou and Tirole (1999) use a modified, less sophisticated form of the Bayes' rule as compared to (2.82); in particular, they use

$$r \equiv \Pr\left[\hat{\sigma} = \phi \mid \sigma = \phi\right] = \frac{q}{q + \pi\left(1-q\right)\left(1-\lambda\right)}, \quad (2.97)$$

where $\pi \in [0,1]$ is a measure of the individual's cognitive sophistication. So, if $\pi = 0$, then $\Pr\left[\hat{\sigma} = \phi \mid \sigma = \phi\right] = 1$, i.e., self 2 naively trusts the signal transmitted by self 1. At the other extreme, if $\pi = 1$, then the decision maker is a fully rational Bayesian decision maker.

---

[15] For an alternative account, see the Guide to Further Reading in Volume 5.

Intermediate values of π allows for more limited cognitive sophistication. The unattractiveness of $\pi = 0$ has already been alluded to before; the assumption of a complete lack of introspection is clearly a strong one. Bénabou and Tirole show that the qualitative results carry through for intermediate values of π. Hence, there does not seem to be a gain from using the alternative version of Bayes' rule in (2.97) in this case.

WILLPOWER AND PERSONAL RULES

Bénabou and Tirole (2004) look at the related issue of signaling one's willpower to their future selves. Each self now lives over two subperiods; making the decision to undertake an activity in the first and the decision to quit or continue the activity in the second. In subperiod 1, self 1 could undertake an activity that has some limited current benefits, for instance, abstinence from smoking or starting a paper. In the second subperiod, continuation of the activity becomes much more onerous. For instance, the craving created by abstinence from smoking since the morning must have worsened, or in the case of writing the paper, fatigue could have set in. In the absence of any consideration for the future, the individual would perhaps give up on the activity and not realize the full fruits of the task started in subperiod 1. However, doing so might signal to self 2 that one's willpower is low. This has potentially negative consequences for the decision that self 2 makes in undertaking the task in her first subperiod. If self 1 is aware of these long-term consequences of her decision she might continue with the activity in subperiod 2. Such models can account for personal rules such as I will quit smoking from now on.

2.6 Exercises for Part I

1. (Laibson, 2001) Consider the model in Section 1.3. Prove Proposition 1.1, i.e., show in the context of the no-cues model that the optimal decision rule of the individual is

$$a = \begin{cases} 1 & if \quad x > \tilde{x} \\ 0 & if \quad x < \tilde{x} \end{cases}.$$

Also show that the threshold value $\tilde{x}$ is increasing in the outside option, $\bar{u}$, the discount factor, δ, and the compensatory process weighting factor, θ.

2. (Caplin and Leahy, 2001) Consider the *psychological expected utility model* in Section 1.5.
(a) (Possibility and probability) There is evidence that economic agents might be influenced by *possibility* rather than *probability*; for instance, Monat et al. (1972), Bankhart and Elliot (1974), Loewenstein et al. (2001). Suppose that there is an announcement that the Federal Reserve is concerned about inflation. Why might this alter the investment behavior of economic agents independent of the probability of an interest rate increase?
(b) (Time course of anxiety) The time path of anxiety tends to be U shaped; see for instance, Breznitz (1984). Fear is greatest when individuals are first informed of an aversive event. It then diminishes for some time before increasing sharply in anticipation of the event. In light of this evidence what do you expect to be the effect on price of those assets whose risks have only been recently revealed relative to those whose risks have been known for some time?
(c) Suppose that the Federal Reserve comes across some bad piece of news such as the possible shutdown of a major bank. Assume that economic agents suffer from anxiety. Show why it might now be optimal to hide the bad news for longer relative to the standard case without anxiety.

3. (Caplin and Leahy, 2004)[16] Hopefulness, suspense, and anxiety are feelings related to uncertainty about the future. An anticipatory feeling is a feeling that anticipates the outcome of an event. These feelings are embedded here in an otherwise standard two-period consumption and saving problem. Consider an individual who is young and works in period t and is retired in period $t+1$; labor income is the only source of income and there are no inheritances or bequests. The budget constraint when young (period t) is given by

$$c_t + s_t = w_t,$$

where w_t is the wage, c_t is consumption and s_t is savings in period t. The budget constraint when old (period $t+1$) is given by

$$c_{t+1} = (1 + r_{t+1}) s_t,$$

where the return r_{t+1} on savings is the only source of uncertainty in the model. Let $\mu \equiv E_t [1 + r_{t+1}], \sigma^2 \equiv Var_t [1 + r_{t+1}]$; E_t and Var_t are, respectively, the expectation and variance operators, conditional on the information set at time t. Preferences of the individual are given by

$$U_t = E_t [\gamma [-\phi \ln a_t + \ln c_t] + (1 - \gamma) \ln c_{t+1}],$$

where a_t captures the utility-reducing anticipatory feeling in period t, and $\gamma, \phi \in [0, 1]$ are preference parameters. Following Caplin and Leahy (2004), we model anticipatory feelings as a reduction in mean and an increase in the variance of uncertain consumption c_{t+1}. In order to allow for positive and negative values of anxiety, we write anxiety as

$$\ln a_t = \zeta Var_t c_{t+1} - (1 - \zeta) E_t c_{t+1}, 0 \leq \zeta \leq 1. \tag{2.98}$$

   (a) Compute the first order condition and interpret it in the two polar cases, $\mu = 0$ and $\sigma^2 = 0$.
   (b) Consider a more general version of the objective function

$$U_t = E_t [\gamma u (a_t, c_t) + (1 - \gamma) u (c_{t+1})].$$

   Compute the first order condition for the optimal saving decision and provide an economic interpretation.
4. (Loewenstein et al., 2003) Extend the two-period model in Section 1.6.2 to three periods, $T = 3$. Recall that (c_1^b, c_2^b, c_3^b) is the optimal profile of consumption in time period $t = 1$ when the individual suffers from projection-bias ($\alpha > 0$). As time passes by, the individual's tastes change in a way that she did not predict. The individual has a chance to reoptimize in period 2. Denote by (c_2^{bb}, c_3^{bb}) the optimal consumption profile when the individual reoptimizes in time period $t = 2$ and suffers from projection bias. Show that if $c_1^b > s_1$, then we get the following result. The sign of v''' determines completely the

---

[16] I am grateful to Klaus Wälde for suggesting this problem.

sign of $c_2^{bb} - c_2^b$. In particular, if $v''' > 0$ (which holds for CARA and CRRA preferences) projection bias will repeatedly lead people to adjust their consumption plans upwards ($c_2^{bb} > c_2^b$). If $v''' < 0$, then $c_2^{bb} < c_2^b$ and if $v''' = 0$, then $c_2^{bb} = c_2^b$. Does this result provide an explanation for why individuals engage in inadequate savings?

5. (Fudenberg and Levine, 2006) Consider the four-period problem in O'Donoghue and Rabin (1999) with (β, δ) preferences, adapted to the case of a dual-self model. An agent has 4 periods to do a report. In the original problem, the pecuniary cost in successive periods of completing the report is 3, 5, 8, 13, and the benefit from doing the report is v (see Volume 3 for this problem). Assume now that the total cost of doing the report in any period is $1 + \gamma$ times the pecuniary cost, where $\gamma > 0$ is the self-control cost per unit. In any period, the decision to act is taken by the short-run self. Show the following.
   (a) If $\gamma < 10/3$, the agent acts to write the report in the first period. If prevented from writing the report in period 1, then any of the subsequent short-run selves are willing to write the report.
   (b) If $\gamma > 10/3$, then the agent never finds it optimal to act.
   (c) The knife edge case, $\gamma = 10/3$, is the only case where the agent is willing to act in intermediate periods. [Hint: Solve the game backwards starting in period 4, being careful to include the self-control costs.]

6. (Lipman and Pesendorfer, 2013) Show that classical preferences (Definition 1.4) are a special case of self-control preferences (see Proposition 1.13) if either (i) v is an affine transformation of u, i.e., $v = \alpha u + \beta$ for some $\alpha \geq 0$ and $\beta \in \mathbb{R}$, or (ii) u is a constant function. Show also that when $\alpha < 0$, $\beta \in \mathbb{R}$, and $v = \alpha u + \beta$, the individual has a sole desire for commitment.

7. (Lipman and Pesendorfer, 2013) Consider the setup of Example 1.11 for (β, δ) preferences. Benhabib et al. (2010) propose an alternative to (β, δ) preferences by introducing a fixed cost of delay. Thus, in period 1, the consumption pair $(0, l)$ is preferred over $(s, 0)$ if $\delta w(l) - f > w(s)$, where f is a fixed cost of delay associated with the later outcome, l, and $\delta > 0$ is the discount factor. What functional forms for commitment utility and temptation utility can be used to represent these preferences?

8. (Lipman and Pesendorfer, 2013) Consider the experimental results of Dana et al. (2006) for dictator games that we considered in Volume 2 of the book. The dictator splits $10 between himself and a passive recipient. Many dictators prefer to take $9 and not play the game; in this case, the recipient is given no information about the experimenter's interaction with the dictator. How can you transform this into a problem with Gul–Pesendorfer temptation preferences?

9. (Lipman and Pesendorfer, 2013; Dekel et al., 2009) Consider the model of temptation preferences in Section 1.7.
   (a) Let b denote broccoli, c denote chocolate, and p denote potato chips; c and p are the two snacks. Suppose that we have $C = \{b, c, p\}$. A dieting individual expresses the following first period preferences: $\{b\} \succ_1 \{b, c\} \succ_1 \{b, p\} \succ_1 \{b, c, p\}$ (the middle two preferences can be reversed without altering the conclusion). The preferences imply that the individual prefers to have no snacks to having at least one snack and finds having both snacks on the menu to be the worst option. These preferences appear to be plausible. Show that these expressed preferences are not consistent with the Gul–Pesendorfer and the Strotz preferences.
   (b) Let h be a healthy dish; d a small dessert; and D a large dessert. Let $C = \{h, d, D\}$. A dieting individual expresses the following first period preferences: $\{h, d\} \succ_1 \{d\}$ and

$\{h, d, D\} \succ_1 \{h, D\}$. The first preference says that the individual would like to have the option of keeping to his diet. The second preference says that the individual may wish to keep d as a compromise option on the menu. These preferences also appear plausible. However, show that they are not consistent with the Gul–Pesendorfer (u, v) preferences. (c) How would you incorporate the plausible preferences expressed in (a) and (b) into a theory of temptation preferences? [Hint: One possibility is that preferences violate WARP. A second possibility, explored formally in Dekel and Lipman (2012), is that unlike in the Gul–Pesendorfer model, there might be uncertainty. For instance, the preference $\{b, p\} \succ_1 \{b, c, p\}$ in (a) might arise because the individual is uncertain whether he will succumb to temptation. Having two tempting snacks, c and p, increases the probability that he will succumb to temptation, so he prefers it the least.]

10. (Ozdenoren et al., 2012) Consider a cake eating problem in continuous time $[0, T]$ in which a consumer maximizes utility by choosing an optimal path of consumption and consumption at time t is denoted by $c(t)$. The instantaneous utility function at time t is given by a differentiable function $U(c(t))$ with $U(0) = 0$, $U_c > 0$, and $U_{cc} < 0$. We do not consider addictive behaviors so U does not depend on past consumption. The size of the cake remaining at time t is given by $R(t)$. The initial size of the cake, $R(0)$, is given. The main difference from the standard cake eating problem in economics comes from the assumption that the consumer is endowed with a given *stock of willpower* $W(0)$. It is possible to restrain consumption but at the cost of a depletion in willpower. The rate of willpower depletion is given by $f(W(t), c(t))$ with $f_W \leq 0$, and $f_c < 0, f_{cc} > 0$ for $c \in [0, \bar{c})$. The convexity in c indicates that the more the individual restrains his consumption, the faster does willpower deplete. f is also assumed to be twice differentiable everywhere except at $\bar{c}$, continuous at $\bar{c}$, and $f_{cW} \geq 0$. Finally, $f > 0$ for $c \in [0, \bar{c})$, and $f = 0$ for $c \in [\bar{c}, \infty)$ for some $\bar{c} > 0$. Any willpower, $W(t')$, left over after the individual has finished the cake is devoted to an alternative activity that generates utility $m(W(t'))$; m is a constant function, and

$$t' = \sup\{t \in [0, T] : R(t) > 0\}.$$

Based on the description above, the optimization problem of the individual (Problem P-1) can, thus, be written as follows. The individual chooses $c(t)$ to maximize

$$V(0) = \int_0^T e^{-\rho t} U(c(t)) dt + e^{-\rho t'} m(W(t')) \tag{P-1}$$

subject to

$$\dot{R}(t) = -c(t)$$

$$\dot{W}(t) = \begin{cases} -f(W(t), c(t)) & \text{if } R(t) > 0 \\ 0 & \text{otherwise} \end{cases}$$

$$R(T) \geq 0; W(T) \geq 0; R(0) = \bar{R} \geq 0; W(0) = \overline{W} \geq 0.$$

ρ is the subjective rate of discount, and $\overline{W}$ is the initial level of willpower. (a) Derive the solution to Problem P-1 by forming the appropriate Hamiltonian. Show that the first order condition for consumption at time t can be written as

$$e^{-\rho t} U'(c(t)) + \lambda(t)\left(-f_c\right) = \alpha(t),$$

where $\lambda(t)$ is the Lagrangian multiplier on the $\dot{W}(t)$ constraint and $\alpha(t)$ is the Lagrangian multiplier on the $\dot{R}(t)$ constraint. Interpret the first order condition, in particular, the second term on the LHS that sets this condition apart from the standard conditions that ignore issues of willpower.

(b) Suppose that there is no discounting, i.e., $\rho = 0$. If $c(t) > 0$ for $t \le s \in [0, T]$, show that

$$\dot{c}(t) = \lambda(t) \frac{f w f_c - f_c w f}{U'' - \lambda(t) f_{cc}}. \tag{2.99}$$

When $\lambda = 0$, we get the classical conclusion that so long as $c(t) > 0$, $\dot{c}(t) = 0$. However, when $\lambda > 0$, whether we have an increasing or decreasing profile of consumption depends on the sign of the numerator in (2.99).

(c) This part demonstrates the importance of the initial level of willpower. Denote by W_H the minimum level of $W(0)$ such that $c(t) = \overline{R}/T$ is feasible for all $t \in [0, T]$. Denote the optimal consumption path by $c^*(t)$. Show the following. (i) If $\overline{W} \ge W_H$, then the cake is exhausted and $c^*(t) = \overline{R}/T$ for all $t \in [0, T]$. (b) If $\overline{W} < W_H$, then the cake and willpower are exhausted ($R(s) = 0$, $W(s) = 0$ for some $s \in [0, T]$) and when $c(t) > 0$, whether we have an increasing or decreasing profile of consumption depends on the sign of the numerator in (2.99).

11. (Krussel et al., 2010) Consider a representative agent two-period model with time $t = 1, 2$. Consumption in period t is denoted by c_t. The commitment ordering over outcomes is given by $\widetilde{u}(c_1, c_2) = u(c_1) + \delta u(c_2)$ where $\delta > 0$ is the discount factor and the temptation ordering is given by $\widetilde{v}(c_1, c_2) = \gamma\left(v(c_1) + \beta\delta v(c_2)\right)$ where $\beta \in (0, 1]$. Hence, while the commitment ordering takes the standard exponential discounting form, the temptation ordering takes the hyperbolic discounting form. Preferences are represented as in the Gul–Pesendorfer model, i.e.,

$$\max_{c_1, c_2} \{\widetilde{u}(c_1, c_2) + \widetilde{v}(c_1, c_2)\} - \max_{c_1, c_2} \widetilde{v}(c_1, c_2). \tag{2.100}$$

Each individual is endowed with one unit of labor in each period and an endowment of capital equal to $k_1 > 0$ at the beginning of period 1. The factors of production, labor and capital, are used by perfectly competitive firms to produce output. The production function of firms in period $t = 1, 2$ is given by $f(\overline{k}_t)$ where $\overline{k}_t$ is the aggregate per capita capital stock. Hence, in any period, the factor incomes to labor and capital are given respectively by $w(\overline{k}_t)$ and $r(\overline{k}_t)$. Let $R(\overline{k}_t) = 1 + r(\overline{k}_t)$ denote the gross return on capital. The budget constraint of the representative agent is given by

$$B(k_1, \overline{k}_1, \overline{k}_2)\left\{(c_1, c_2) : c_1 = R(\overline{k}_1)k_1 + w(\overline{k}_1) - k_2, \; c_2 = R(\overline{k}_2)k_2 + w(\overline{k}_2)\right\}. \tag{2.101}$$

(a) Show that the consumer saves the least if second period preferences were simply $\widetilde{v}(c_1, c_2)$, saves the most if second period preferences were $\widetilde{u}(c_1, c_2)$, and saves an intermediate amount when preferences are given by $\widetilde{u}(c_1, c_2) + \widetilde{v}(c_1, c_2)$.

(b) Now consider autarky in which the individual uses his own backyard technology, which we assume is given by $f(\bar{k}_t)$ and there is no recourse to private markets. Show that the same allocation is achieved as under (a). However, utility is higher under autarky. [Hint: The agent cannot trade along the market line under autarky and is limited to the opportunity set which lies under the market line. Hence, there is lower temptation under autarky].

(c) Suppose now that the government undertakes a balanced budget fiscal policy. It levies a tax τ_y on total income and a tax τ_i on first period investment. This gives the modified budget constraint

$$B(k_1, \bar{k}_1, \bar{k}_2) = \left\{ (c_1, c_2) : c_1 = \left[R(\bar{k}_1)k_1 + w(\bar{k}_1) \right](1 - \tau_y) - (1 + \tau_i)k_2, c_2 \right.$$
$$\left. = R(\bar{k}_2)k_2 + w(\bar{k}_2) \right\}$$

and the balanced budget constraint of the government is $\tau_y \left[R(\bar{k}_1)k_1 + w(\bar{k}_1) \right] = -\tau_i \bar{k}_2$. Suppose that the government is a benevolent central planner who wishes to maximize the agent's indirect utility by optimally choosing τ_y, τ_i. Derive the optimal tax rates and show that it is optimal for the government to impose an investment subsidy (i.e. $\tau_i < 0$). [The intuition is that an investment subsidy increases the cost of first period temptation that would arise from the possibility of reducing savings.]

12. (Amador et al., 2006) Consider the following three-period economy, where the time index $t = 0, 1, 2$. Society moves in period $t = 0$ to choose an appropriate constitution, while the government moves in period $t = 1$ to choose some level of public spending. Society's welfare is given by $\theta U(g) + W(c)$, where g is the level of government spending and c is private consumption. The government wants to maximize instead $\theta U(g) + \beta W(c)$, where $0 < \beta \le 1$ and $1 - \beta$ is a measure of the strength of temptation towards government spending. The resource constraint is given by $B = \{(c, g) \in \mathbb{R}_+^2 : c + g \le y\}$. A fiscal constitution is a subset $C \subset B$ that constrains the government to choose $(c, g) \in C$. The government has private information on θ. Restrict attention to pure commitment mechanisms with no transfers across types. An optimal constitution is some subset of C which maximizes the welfare of society, given the subsequent bias of the government towards g. Show that it is always optimal to limit government spending. How does the optimal solution trade off commitment versus flexibility?

REFERENCES FOR PART I

Alesina, A., Di Tella, R., and MacCulloch, R. (2004). Inequality and happiness: are Europeans and Americans different? *Journal of Public Economics* 88: 2009–42.

Amador, M., Werning, I., and G. M. Angeletos (2006). "Commitment vs. flexibility. *Econometrica* 74(2): 365–96.

Ameriks, J., Caplin, A., Leahy, J., and Tyler, T. (2007). Measuring self-control problems. *American Economic Review* 97: 966–72.

Angelucci, M. and De Giorgi, G. (2009). Indirect effects of an aid program: how do cash transfers affect ineligibles' consumption? *American Economic Review* 99(1): 486–508.

Bankhart, C. and Elliot, R. (1974). Heart rate and skin conductance in anticipation of shocks with varying probability of occurrence. *Psychophysiology* 11: 160–74.

Battigalli, P., Dufwenberg, M., and Smith, A. (2015). Frustration and anger in games. Working Paper No. 539. IGIER – Università Bocconi.

Baumeister, R. F., De Wall, C. N., and Zhang, L. (2007). Do emotions improve or hinder the decision making process? In K. D. Vohs, R. F. Baumeister, and G. Loewenstein (eds.), *Do Emotions Help Or Hurt Decision Making? A Hedgefoxian Perspective*. New York: Russell Sage Foundation Press.

Baumeister, R. F., Heatherton, T. F., and Tice, D. M. (1994). *Losing Control: How and Why People Fail at Self-Regulation*. San Diego, CA: Academic Press.

Baumeister, R. F. and Vohs, K. D. (2003). Willpower, choice, and self-control, in G. Loewenstein, D. Read, and R. F. Baumeister (eds.), *Time and Decision: Economic and Psychological Perspectives on Intertemporal Choice*. New York: Russell Sage Foundation, 201–16.

Becchetti L., Pelloni, A., and Rossetti, F. (2008). Relational goods, sociability, and happiness. *Kyklos* 61(3): 343–63.

Bechara, A., Damasio, A. R., Damasio, H., and Anderson, S. W. (1994). Insensitivity to future consequences following damage to human prefrontal cortex. *Cognition* 50(1–3): 7–15.

Bechara, A., Damasio, H., Damasio, A. R., and Lee, G. P. (1999). Different contributions of the human amygdala and ventromedial prefrontal cortex to decision-making. *Journal of Neuroscience* 19: 5473–81.

Bechara, A., Damasio, H., Tranel, D., and Damasio, A. R. (1997). Deciding advantageously before knowing the advantageous strategy. *Science* 275(5304), 1293–5.

Bechara, A., Tranel, D., Damasio, H., and Damasio, A. R. (1996). Failure to respond autonomically to anticipated future outcomes following damage to prefrontal cortex. *Cerebral Cortex* 6: 215–25.

Becker, G. S. (1996). *Accounting for Tastes*. Cambridge, MA: Harvard University Press.

Becker, G. S. and Murphy, K. M. (1988). A theory of rational addiction. *Journal of Political Economy* 96(4): 675–701.

Becker, G. S. and Murphy, K. M. (1993). A simple theory of advertising as a good or a bad. *Quarterly Journal of Economics* 153: 941–64.

Beja E. Jr. (2014). Income growth and happiness: reassessment of the Easterlin Paradox, Munich Personal RePEc Archive Paper No. 53360.

Bell, D., (1985). Disappointment in decision making under uncertainty. *Operations Research* 33: 1–27.

Bénabou, R. and Pycia, M. (2002). Dynamic inconsistency and self-control. *Economics Letters* 77(3): 419–24.

Bénabou, R. and Tirole, J. (1999). Self-confidence: intrapersonal strategies. IDEI mimeo.

Bénabou, R. and Tirole, J. (2002). Self-confidence and personal motivation. *Quarterly Journal of Economics* 117: 871–915.

Bénabou, R. and Tirole, J. (2003). Intrinsic and extrinsic motivation. *Review of Economic Studies* 67: 529–44.

Bénabou, R. and Tirole, J. (2004). Willpower and personal rules. *Journal of Political Economy* 112: 848–87.

Benhabib, J. and Bisin, A. (2005). Modeling internal commitment mechanisms and self-control: a neuroeconomics approach to consumption-saving decisions. *Games and Economic Behavior* 52(2): 460–92.

Benhabib, J., Bisin, A., and Schotter, A. (2010). Present-bias, quasi-hyperbolic discounting, and xed costs. *Games and Economic Behavior* 69(2): 205–23.

Benjamin, D. J., Brown, S. A., and Shapiro, J. M. (2013). Who is "Behavioral"? Cognitive ability and anomalous preferences. *Journal of the European Economic Association* 11(6): 1231–55.

Benjamin, D. J., Heffetz, O., Kimball, M. S., and Rees-Jones, A. (2012). What do you think would make you happier? What do you think you would choose? *American Economic Review* 102(5): 2083–110.

Benjamin, D. J., Heffetz, O., Kimball, M. S., and Szembrot, N. (2014). Beyond happiness and satisfaction: toward well-being indices based on stated preference. *American Economic Review* 104(9): 2698–735.

Bentham, J. (1789). *An Introduction to the Principle of Morals and Legislations* (reprinted Oxford: Blackwell 1948).

Bernheim, B. D. and Rangel, A. (2004). Addiction and cue-triggered decision processes. *American Economic Review* 94(5): 1558–90.

Berns, G., Cohen, D., and Mintun, M. (1997). Brain regions responsive to novelty in the absence of awareness. *Science*, 276: 1272–5.

Blanchflower, D. G. and Oswald, A. (2004). Well-being over time in Britain and the USA. *Journal of Public Economics* 88(7–8): 1359–86.

Bodner, R. and Prelec, D. (2003). The diagnostic value of actions in a self-signaling model, in I. Brocas and J. Carrillo (eds.), *The Psychology of Economic Decisions, Volume 1*. Oxford: Oxford University Press.

Bolton, G. E. and Ockenfels, A. (2000). ERC – a theory of equity, reciprocity, and competition. *American Economic Review* 90(1): 166–93.

Breznitz, S., (1984) *Cry Wolf*. Hillsdale, NJ: Lawrence Erlbaum Associates.

Brickman, P. and Campbell, D. T. (1971). Hedonic relativism and planning the good society. In M. H. Appley (ed.), *Adaptation Level Theory*. New York: Academic Press, pp. 287–302.

Brickman, P., Coates, D., and Janoff-Bulman, R. (1978). Lottery winners and accident victims: is happiness relative? *Journal of Personality and Social Psychology* 36: 917–27.

Brocas, I. and Carrillo, J. (2008). The brain as a hierarchical organization. *American Economic Review* 98(4): 1312–46.

Brocas, I. and Carrillo, J. (2014). Dual-process theories of decision making: a selective survey. *Journal of Economic Psychology* 41: 45–54.

Caplin, A. and Eliaz, K. (2003). AIDS policy and psychology: a mechanism-design approach. *The RAND Journal of Economics* 34(4): 631–46.

Caplin, A. and Leahy, J. (2001). Psychological expected utility and anticipatory feelings. *Quarterly Journal of Economics* 116: 55–79.

Caplin, A. and Leahy, J. (2004). The supply of information by a concerned expert. *Economic Journal* 114(497): 487–505.

Carillo, J. D. and Mariotti, T. (2000). Strategic ignorance as a self-disciplining device. *Review of Economic Studies* 67: 529–44.

Carter, S. and McBride, M. (2013). Experienced utility versus decision utility: putting the "S" in satisfaction. *Journal of Socio-Economics* 42: 13–23.

Chaiken, S. and Trope, Y. (eds.) (1999). *Dual-Process Theories in Social Psychology*. New York: Guilford Press.

Cheibub, J. A., Gandhi, J., and Vreeland, J. R. (2010). Democracy and dictatorship revisited. *Public Choice* 143: 67–101.

Chen, M. K., Lakshminarayanan, V., and Santos, L. R. (2006). How basic are behavioral biases? Evidence from capuchin monkey trading behavior. *Journal of Political Economy* 114(3): 517–37.

Clark, A. E. (2001). What really matters in a job? Hedonic measurement using quit data. *Labour Economics* 8: 223–42.

Clark, A. E. (2003). Unemployment as a social norm: psychological evidence from panel data. *Journal of Labor Economics* 21: 323–51.

Clark, A. E. (2006). A note on unhappiness and unemployment duration. *Applied Economics Quarterly* 52(4): 291–308.

Clark, A. E., Georgellis, Y., and Sanfey, P. (2001). Scarring: the psychological impact of past unemployment. *Economica* 68(270): 221–41.

Clark, A. E. and Oswald, A. J. (1994). Unhappiness and unemployment, *Economic Journal* 104: 648–59.

Clark A. E. and Oswald A. (1996). Satisfaction and comparison income. *Journal of Public Economics* 61: 359–81.

Clark, A. E. and Senik, C. (2010). Who compares to whom? The anatomy of income comparisons in Europe. *The Economic Journal* 120: 573–94.

Cohen, J. D. (2005). The vulcanization of the human brain: a neural perspective on interactions between cognition and emotion. *Journal of Economic Perspectives* 19(4): 3–24.

Coleman, J. S. (1993). Social capital in the creation of human capital. *American Journal of Sociology* 94: 95–120.

Damasio, A. R. (1994). *Descartes' Error: Emotion, Reason, and the Human Brain*. New York: G.P. Putman.

Damasio, A. R. (1996). The somatic marker hypothesis and the possible functions of the pre-frontal cortex. *Philosophical Transactions of the Royal Society London Series B: Biological Sciences* 351: 1413–20.

Dana, J. D., Dalian, M., Cain, D. M., and Dawes, R. M. (2006). What you don't know won't hurt me: costly (but quiet) exit in a dictator game. *Organizational Behavior and Human Decision Processes* 100(2): 193–201.

Dawkins, R. (2006). *The Selfish Gene (30th Anniversary Edition)*. New York City: Oxford University Press.

De Neve, J. E. (2011). Functional polymorphism (5-HTTLPR) in the serotonin transporter gene is associated with subjective well-being: evidence from a US nationally representative sample. *Journal of Human Genetics* 56: 456–9.

De Neve, J. E., Christakis, N. A., Fowler, J. H., and Frey, B. S. (2012). Genes, economics, and happiness. *Journal of Neuroscience, Psychology, and Economics* 5: 193–211.

Deaton, A. (2008). Income, health, and well-being around the world: evidence from the Gallup world poll. *Journal of Economic Perspectives* 22: 53–72.

Dekel, E. and Lipman, B. L. (2012). Costly self-control and random self-indulgence, *Econometrica* 80(3): 1271–302.

Dekel, E., Lipman, B., and Rustichini, A. (2001). Representing preferences with a unique subjective state space. *Econometrica* 69(4): 891–934.

Dekel, E., Lipman, B., and Rustichini, A. (2009). Temptation-driven preferences. *Review of Economic Studies* 76(3): 937–71.

DellaVigna, S. and Malmendier, U. (2002). Overestimating self-control: evidence from the health club industry, Working Paper, University of California at Berkeley and Stanford University.

Di Tella, R., Haisken-De New, J., and MacCulloch, R. J. (2010). Happiness adaptation to income and to status in an individual panel. *Journal of Economic Behavior and Organization* 76(3): 834–52.

Di Tella, R. and MacCulloch, R. J. (2006). Some uses of happiness data in economics. *Journal of Economic Perspectives* 20(1): 25–46.

Di Tella, R., MacCulloch, R. J., and Oswald, A. J. (2001). Preferences over inflation and unemployment: evidence from surveys of happiness. *The American Economic Review* 91: 335–41.

Di Tella, R., MacCulloch, R. J., and Oswald, A. J. (2003). The macroeconomics of happiness. *Review of Economics and Statistics* 85: 809–27.

Diener, E. and Chan, M. Y. (2011). Happy people live longer: subjective well-being contributes to health and longevity. *Applied Psychology: Health and Well-Being* 3(1): 1–43.

Diener, E., Lucas, R. E., and Scollon, C. N. (2006). Beyond the hedonic treadmill: revising the adaptation theory of well-being. *American Psychologist* 61(4): 305–14.

Diener, E. and Seligman, M. E. P. (2004). Beyond money: toward an economy of well-being. *Psychological Science in the Public Interest* 5(1): 1–31.

Diener, E., Tay, L., and Oishi, S. (2013). Rising income and the subjective well-being of nations. *Journal of Personality and Social Psychology* 104(2): 267–76.

Ditto, P. H., Pizzaro, D. H., Epstein, E. B, Jacobson, J. A., and MacDonald, T. K. (2006). Visceral influences on risk-taking behavior. *Journal of Behavioral Decision Making* 19: 1–15.

Duesenberry, J. (1949). *Income, Saving, and the Theory of Consumer Behavior*. Cambridge, MA: Harvard University Press.

Dynan, K. (2000). Habit formation in consumer preferences: evidence from panel data. *American Economic Review* 110: 391–406.

Easterlin, R. A. (1974). Does economic growth improve the human lot? Some empirical evidence. In P. A. David and M. W. Reder (eds.), *Nations and Households in Economic Growth: Essays in Honor of Moses Abramovitz*. New York: Academic Press, pp. 89–125.

Easterlin, R. A. (1995). Will raising the incomes of all increase the happiness of all? *Journal of Economic Behavior and Organization* 27(1): 35–47.

Easterlin, R. A. (2001). Income and happiness: towards a unified theory. *Economic Journal* 111(473): 465–84.

Easterlin, R. A. (2003). Explaining happiness. *Proceedings of the National Academy of Science* 100(19): 11176–83.

Easterlin, R. (2013). Happiness and economic growth: the evidence. Discussion Paper No. 7187, Bonn: Institute for the Study of Labor.

Easterlin, R., Mcvey, L., Switek, M., Sawangta, O., and Zweig, J. (2010). The happiness paradox revisited. *Proceedings of the National Academy of Sciences* 107(52): 22463–8.

Elster, J. (1998). Emotions in economic theory. *Journal of Economic Literature* 36: 47–74.

Epstein, L. (2006). An axiomatic model of non-Bayesian updating. *Review of Economic Studies* 73: 413–36.

Epstein, L. and Kopylov, I. (2007). Cold feet. *Theoretical Economics* 2: 231–59.

Epstein, L., Noor, J., and Sandroni, A. (2008). Non-Bayesian updating: a theoretical framework. *BE Journal of Theoretical Economics* 3(2): 193–229.

Fleurbaey, M. (2009). Beyond GDP: the quest for a measure of social welfare. *Journal of Economic Literature* 47(4): 1029–75.

Fleurbaey, M. and Blanchet, D. (2013). *Beyond GDP: Measuring Welfare and Assessing Sustainability*. Oxford: Oxford University Press.

Frank, R. H. (1988). *Passions Within Reasons: The Strategic Role of the Emotions*. New York: Norton.

Frederick, S. and Loewenstein, G. (1999). Hedonic adaptation: In D. Kahnemann, E. Diener, and N. Schwarz (eds.), *Well Being: The Foundations of Hedonic Psychology*. New York: Russell Sage Foundation Press, pp. 302–29.

Fredrickson, B. L. and Kahneman, D. (1993). Duration neglect in retrospective evaluations of affective episodes. *Journal of Personality and Social Psychology* 65: 45–55.

Freud, S. (1924). *The Ego and the Id*, translated by Joan Riviere. New York: W. W. Norton, 1962.

Frey, B. S. and Benz, M. (2008). Being independent is a great thing: subjective evaluations of self-employment and hierarchy. *Economica* 75(298): 362–83.

Frey, B. S. and Stutzer, A. (2000). Happiness, economy and institutions. *Economic Journal* 110(446): 918–38.

Frey, B. S. and Stutzer, A. (2002). What can economists learn from happiness research? *Journal of Economic Literature* 40(2): 402–35.

Frijda, N. H. and Mesquita, B. (1994). The social roles and functions of emotions. In S. Kitayama and H. R. Markus (eds.), *Emotion and Culture: Empirical Studies of Mutual Influence.*

Washington, DC: American Psychological Association.

Frijters, P., Haisken-Denew, J. P., and Shields, M. A. (2004). Money does matter! Evidence from increasing real income and life satisfaction in East Germany following reunification. *American Economic Review* 94: 730–40.

Fudenberg, D. (2006). Advancing beyond advances in behavioral economics. *Journal of Economic Literature* 44: 694–711.

Fudenberg, D. and Levine, D. K. (2006). A dual self model of impulse control. *American Economic Review* 96(5): 1449–76.

Fudenberg, D. and Levine, D. K. (2011). Risk, delay, and convex self-control costs. *American Economic Journal: Microeconomics* 3: 34–68.

Gardner, J. and Oswald, A. J. (2007). Money and mental wellbeing: a longitudinal study of medium-sized lottery wins. *Journal of Health Economics* 26: 49–60.

Gilbert, D. T., Gill, M. J., and Wilson, T. D. (2002). The future is now: temporal correction in affective forecasting. *Organizational Behavior and Human Decision Processes* 88: 430–44.

Glimcher, P. W., Camerer, C., Poldrack, R., and Fehr E. (eds.) (2009). *Neuroeconomics: Decision Making and the Brain*. London: Academic Press.

Goldie, P. (2009). *The Oxford Handbook of Philosophy of Emotion*. Oxford: Oxford University Press.

Graham, C., Eggers, A., and Sukhtankar, S. (2004). Does happiness pay? An initial exploration based on panel data from Russia. *Journal of Economic Behavior and Organization* 55: 319–42.

Gruber, J. and Koszegi, B. (2001). Is addiction "rational"? Theory and evidence. *Quarterly Journal of Economics* 116(4): 1261–303.

Gul, F. and Pesendorfer, W. (2001). Temptation and self control. *Econometrica* 69(6): 1403–36.

Gul, F. and Pesendorfer, W. (2004). Self-control and the theory of consumption. *Econometrica* 72(1): 119–58.

Gul, F. and Pesendorfer, W. (2005). The revealed preference theory of changing tastes. *Review of Economic Studies* 72: 429–48.

Gul, F. and Pesendorfer, W. (2007). Harmful addiction. *Review of Economic Studies* 74: 147–72.

Guven, C., Senik, C., and Stichnoth, H. (2012). You can't be happier than your wife. Happiness gaps and divorce. *Journal of Economic Behavior and Organization* 82(1): 110–30.

Helliwell, J. F. (2007). Well-being and social capital: does suicide pose a puzzle?. *Social Indicators Research* 81: 455–96.

Helliwell J. and Putnam R. D. (2004). The social context of well-being. *Philosophical Transactions of the Royal Society (London), Series B [Internet]* 359: 1435–46.

Inglehart, R., Foa, R., Peterson, C., and Welzel, C. (2008). Development, freedom, and rising happiness. *Perspectives on Psychological Science* 3(4): 264–85.

Jevons, W. (1905). *Essays on Economics*. London: Macmillan.

Kahneman, D., Fredrickson, B. L., Schreiber, C. A., and Redelmeier, D. A. (1993). When more pain is preferred to less: adding a better end. *Psychological Science* 4: 401–5.

Kahneman, D. and Thaler, R. H. (2006). Anomalies: utility maximization and experienced utility. *Journal of Economic Perspectives* 20(1): 221–34.

Kahneman, D., Wakker, P. P., and Sarin, R. (1997). Back to Bentham? Explorations of experienced utility. *Quarterly Journal of Economics* 112: 375–405.

Kassenboehmer, S. C. and Haisken-DeNew, J. P. (2009). You're fired! The causal negative effect of entry unemployment on life satisfaction. *Economic Journal* 119(536): 448–62.

Kenny, C. (1999). Does growth cause happiness, or does happiness cause growth? *Kyklos* 52(1): 3–26.

Knabe, A. and Rätzel, S. (2011). Scarring or scaring? The psychological impact of past unemployment and future unemployment risk. *Economica* 78(310): 283–93.

Knight, J. and Gunatilaka, R. (2012). Income, aspiration and the hedonic treadmill in a poor society. *Journal of Economic Behavior and Organization* 82(1): 67–81.

Knight, J., Song, L., and Gunatilaka, R. (2009). SWB and its determinants in rural china. *China Economic Review* 20: 635–49.

Kreps, D. M., (1979). A representation theorem for preference for flexibility. *Econometrica* 47: 565–77.

Kreps, D. and Porteus, E. (1978). Temporal resolution of uncertainty and dynamic choice theory. *Econometrica* 46: 185–200.

Krusell, P., Kuruscu, B., and Smith, A. A. (2010). Temptation and taxation. *Econometrica* 78(6): 2063–84.

Kuhn, P., Kooreman, P., Soetevent, A., and Kapteyn, A. (2011). The effects of lottery prizes on winners and their neighbors: evidence from the Dutch postcode lottery. *American Economic Review* 101(5): 2226–47.

Kunreuther, H., Ginsberg, R., Miller, L., Sagi, P., Slovic, P., Borkan, B., and Katz, N. (1978). *Disaster Insurance Protection: Public Policy Lessons*. New York: Wiley.

Laibson, D. (1997). Golden eggs and hyperbolic discounting. *Quarterly Journal of Economics* 112: 443–77.

Laibson, D. (2001). A cue-theory of consumption. *Quarterly Journal of Economics* 116: 81–119.

Layard, R. (2003). Happiness: Has Social Science a Clue? Lionel Robbins Memorial Lectures 2002/3. Lecture given at the London School of Economics, London, March 3–5.

Layard, R. (2005). *Happiness: Lessons from a New Science*. New York: Penguin Press.

Lipman, B. L. and Pesendorfer, W. (2013). Temptation. In D. Acemoglu, M. Arellano, and E. Dekel, (eds.), *Advances in Economics and Econometrics: Tenth World Congress, Volume 1*. Cambridge: Cambridge University Press.

Loewenstein, G. (1987). Anticipation and the valuation of delayed consumption. *Economic Journal* 97: 666–84.

Loewenstein, G. (1996). Out of control: visceral influences on behavior. *Organizational Behavior and Human Decision Processes* 65(3): 272–92.

Loewenstein, G. (2000). Emotions in economic theory and economic behavior. *American Economic Review* 90(2): 426–32.

Loewenstein, G. (2010). Insufficient emotion: soul-searching by a former indicter of strong emotions. *Emotion Review* 2(3): 234–9.

Loewenstein, G. and O'Donoghue, T. (2004). Animal spirits: affective and deliberative processes in economic behavior. Unpublished paper.

Loewenstein, G. and O'Donoghue, T. (2007). The heat of the moment: modeling interactions between affect and deliberation. Unpublished paper.

Loewenstein, G., O'Donoghue, T., and Rabin, M. (2003). Projection bias in predicting future utility. *Quarterly Journal of Economics* 118: 1209–48.

Loewenstein, G., Weber, E., Hsee, C., and Welch, N. (2001). Risk as feelings. *Psychological Bulletin* 127: 267–86.

Loomes, G. and Sugden, R. (1986). Disappointment and dynamic consistency in choice under uncertainty. *Review of Economic Studies* 53: 271–82.

Luechinger, S., Meier, S., and Stutzer, A. (2010). Why does unemployment hurt the employed? Evidence from the life satisfaction gap between the public and the private sector. *Journal of Human Resources* 45(4): 998–1045.

Lundborg, P. and Lindgren, B. (2004). Do they know what they are doing? Risk perceptions and smoking behaviour among Swedish teenagers. *Journal of Risk and Uncertainty* 28: 261–86.

Luttmer, E. (2005). Neighbors as negatives: relative earnings and wellbeing. *Quarterly Journal of Economics* 120: 963–1002.

Massey, D. S. (2002). A brief history of human society: the origin and role of emotion in social life. *American Sociological Review* 67(1): 1–29.

Meier, S. and Stutzer, A. (2008). Is volunteering rewarding in itself? *Economica* 75(297): 39–59.

Meshulam, M., Winter, E., Ben-Shakhar, G., and Aharon, I. (2012). Rational emotions. *Social Neuroscience* 7(1): 11–17.

Metcalfe, J. and Mischel, W. (1999). A hot/cool-system analysis of delay of gratification: dynamics of willpower. *Psychological Review* 106(1): 3–19.

Mischel, W., Ayduk, O., and Mendoza-Denton, R. (2003). Sustaining delay of gratification over time: a hot-cool systems perspective. In G. Loewenstein, D. Read, and R. F. Baumeister (eds.), *Time and Decision: Economic and Psychological Perspectives on Intertemporal Choice*. New York: Russell Sage Foundation, pp. 175–200.

Monat, A., Averill, J., and Lazarus, R. (1972). Anticipatory stress and coping reactions under various conditions of uncertainty. *Journal of Personality and Social Psychology* 24: 237–53.

Myers, D. G. (2000). The funds, friends, and faiths of happy people. *American Psychologist* 55(1): 56–67.

Noor, J. (2011). Temptation and revealed preference. *Econometrica* 79(2): 601–44.

O'Donoghue, T. and Rabin, M. (1999). Doing it now or later. *American Economic Review* 89(1): 103–24.

OECD (2001). *The Well-Being of Nations: The Role of Human and Social Capital*. Paris: OECD Centre for Educational Research and Innovation.

Oswald, A. and Powdthavee, N. (2008). Does happiness adapt? A longitudinal study of disability with implications for economists and judges. *Journal of Public Economics* 92(5–6): 1061–77.

Oswald, A., Proto, E., and Sgroi, D. (2015). Happiness and productivity. *Journal of Labor Economics* 33(4): 789–822.

Oswald, A. and Wu, S. (2011). Well-being across America: evidence from a random sample of one million U.S. citizens. *Review of Economics and Statistics* 93(4): 1118–34.

Ozdenoren, E., Salant, S., and Silverman, D. (2012). Willpower and the optimal control of visceral urges. *Journal of the European Economic Association* 10(2): 342–68.

Pavlov, I. P. (1904). Sur la secretion psychique des glandes salivaires. *Archives Internationales de Physiologie* I: 119–35.

Phelps, E. and Pollak, R. A. (1968). On second-best national saving and game-equilibrium growth. *Review of Economic Studies* 35: 185–99.

Pollak, R. A. (1970). Habit formation and dynamic demand functions. *Journal of Political Economy* 78: 745–63.

Preston, S. D. and de Waal, F. B. M. (2002). Empathy: its ultimate and proximate bases. *Behavioral and Brain Sciences* 25(1): 1–71.

Read, D. and van Leeuwen, B. (1998). Predicting hunger: the effects of appetite and delay on choice. *Organization Behavior and Human Decision Processes* 76(2): 189–205.

Redelmeier, D. and Kahneman, D. (1996). Patients' memories of painful medical treatments: real-time and retrospective evaluations of two minimally invasive procedures. *Pain* 116: 3–8.

Rode, M., Knoll, B., and Pitlik, H. (2013). Economic freedom, democracy, and life satisfaction. In J. Gwartney, R. Lawson, and J. Hall, *Economic Freedom of the World: 2013 Annual Report*. Fraser Institute, pp. 215–33.

Rolls, E. T. (2014). *Emotion and Decision Making Explained*. Oxford: Oxford University Press.

Ruhm, C. J. (2000). Are recessions good for your health? *Quarterly Journal of Economics* 115(2): 617–50.

Sacks, D. W., Stevenson, B., and Wolfers, J. (2013). Growth in subjective wellbeing and income over time. Unpublished.

Sarracino, F. (2010). Social capital and subjective well-being trends: comparing 11 Western European countries. *Journal of Socio-Economics* 39(4): 482–517.

Schneider, W. and Shiffrin, R. M. (1977a). Controlled and automatic human information processing: detection, search, and attention. *Psychological Review* 84: 1–66.

Schneider, W. and Shiffrin, R. M. (1977b). Controlled and automatic human information processing: 2. Perceptual learning, automatic attending and a general theory. *Psychological Review* 84: 127–90.

Sen, A. (1985). *Commodities and Capabilities*. Oxford: Oxford University Press.

Sen, A. (1992). *Inequality Reexamined*. New York: Russell Sage Foundation; Cambridge, MA: Harvard University Press.

Senik, C. (2014). Wealth and happiness. *Oxford Review of Economic Policy* 30(1): 92–108.

Shefrin, H. and Thaler, R. (1988). The behavioral life-cycle hypothesis. *Economic Inquiry* 26(4): 609–43.

Shiffman, S. and Waters, A. J. (2004). Negative affect and smoking lapses: a prospective analysis. *Journal of Consulting and Clinical Psychology* 72(2): 192–201.

Shiv, B. and Fedorikhin, A. (1999). Heart and mind in conflict: the interplay of affect and cognition in consumer decision making. *Journal of Consumer Research* 26: 278–92.

Sinaceur, M. and Tiedens, L. Z. (2006). Get mad and get more than even: when and why anger expression is effective in negotiations. *Journal of Experimental Social Psychology* 42: 314–22.

Slovic, P., Finucane, M., Peters, E., and MacGregor, D. G. (2002). The affect heuristic. In T. Gilovich, D. Griffin, and D. Kahneman (eds.), *Heuristics and Biases: The Psychology of Intuitive Judgment*. New York: Cambridge University Press, pp. 397–420.

Smith, D., Loewenstein, G., Jepson, C., Jankovich, A., Feldman, H., and Ubel, P. (2008). Mispredicting and misremembering: patients with renal failure overestimate improvements in quality of life after a kidney transplant. *Health Psychology* 27(5): 653–8.

Smith, K. and Dickhaut, J. (2005). Economics and emotion: institutions matter. *Games and Economic Behavior* 52: 316–35.

Stevens, J. R., Hallinan, E. V., and Hauser, M. D. (2005). The ecology and evolution of patience in two new world monkeys. *Biology Letters* 1: 223–6.

Stevenson, B. and Wolfers, J. (2008). Economic growth and subjective well-being: reassessing the Easterlin paradox. *Brookings Papers on Economic Activity* 1–87.

Stevenson, B. and Wolfers, J. (2013). Subjective well-being and income: is there any evidence of satiation? *American Economic Review: Papers & Proceedings* 103(3): 598–604.

Strotz, R. H. (1955). Myopia and inconsistency in dynamic utility maximization. *Review of Economic Studies* 23(3): 165–80.

Stutzer A. (2004). The role of income aspirations in individual happiness. *Journal of Economic Behaviour and Organization* 54(1): 89–109.

Stutzer, A. and Lalive, R. (2004). The role of social work norms in job searching and subjective well-being. *Journal of the European Economic Association* 2(4): 696–719.

Thaler, R. and Shefrin, H. (1981). An economic theory of self-control. *Journal of Political Economy* 89(2): 392–406.

Tobin, H., Logue, A. W., Chelonis, J. J., and Ackerman, K. T. (1996). Self-control in the monkey macaca fascicularis. *Animal Learning and Behavior* 24(2): 168–74.

Tooby, J. and Cosmides, L. (1992). The psychological foundations of culture. In J. Barkow, L. Cosmides, and J. Tooby (eds.), *The Adapted Mind: Evolutionary Psychology and the Generation of Culture*. New York: Oxford University Press.

Tversky, A. and Kahneman, D. (1992). Advances in prospect theory: cumulative representation of uncertainty. *Journal of Risk and Uncertainty* 5(4): 297–323.

Van Praag, B. M. S. (1968). *Individual Welfare Functions and Consumer Behavior: A Theory of Rational Irrationality*. Amsterdam: North-Holland.

Van Praag, B. M. S. (1971). *Individual Welfare Functions and Consumer Behavior—A Theory of Rational Irrationality*. Dissertation, Contributions to Economic Analysis, No. 57. Amsterdam: North-Holland Publishing Company.

Van Praag, B. M. S. and Ferrer-i-Carbonell, A. (2011), Happiness economics: a new road to measuring and comparing happiness. *Foundations and Trends in Microeconomics* 6(1): 1–97.

Varey, C. and Kahneman, D. (1992). Experiences extended across time: evaluation of moments and episodes. *Journal of Behavioral Decision Making* 5: 169–86.

Veblen, T. ([1899] 1973). *The Theory of the Leisure Class: An Economic Study of Institutions. Introduction John Kenneth Galbraith.* Boston, MA: Houghton Mifflin.

Veenhoven, R. (1991). Is happiness relative? *Social Indicators Research* 24(1): 1–34.

Veenhoven, R. (2000). Freedom and happiness: a comparative study in 44 nations in the early 1990s. In E. Diener and E. M. Suh (eds.), *Culture and Subjective Wellbeing.* Cambridge, MA: MIT Press, pp. 257–88.

Veenhoven, R. and Vergunst, F. (2013). The Easterlin illusion: economic growth does go with greater happiness, Erasmus University Rotterdam, MPRA Paper No. 43983.

Viscusi, W. K. (1990). Do smokers underestimate risks? *Journal of Political Economy* 98: 1253–69.

Vohs, K. D. and Faber, R. J. (2007). Spent resources: self-regulatory resource availability affects impulse buying. *Journal of Consumer Research* 33: 537–47.

Vohs, K. D. and Heatherton, T. F. (2000). Self-regulatory failure: a resource-depletion approach. *Psychological Science* 11(3): 249–54.

Wälde, K. (2015). Stress and coping: An economic approach. Mimeo, Gutenberg University Mainz.

Wilson, E. O. (2012). *The Social Conquest of Earth.* New York: Liveright Publishing Corporation.

Winkelmann, L. and Winkelmann, R. (1998). Why are the unemployed so unhappy? Evidence from panel data. *Economica* 65: 1–15.

Winter, E. (2014). *Feeling Smart: Why Our Emotions Are More Rational Than We Think.* New York: Public Affairs.

Winter, E., Méndez-Naya, L., and García-Jurado, I. (2014). Equilibrium and strategic emotions. Mimeo.

Wolfers, J. (2003). Is business cycle volatility costly? Evidence from surveys of subjective well-being. *International Finance* 6(1): 1–26.

PART II
BEHAVIORAL WELFARE
ECONOMICS

CHAPTER 3

Behavioral Welfare Economics

3.1 Introduction

Neoclassical welfare economics follows the liberal tradition in economics in the following sense. The primitives in the model are unobserved individual *preferences* over a set of outcomes. Observed *choices* reflect underlying preferences. In neoclassical theory, policymakers and society respect observed choices because they reflect a *considered judgment* of one's welfare. For this reason, these preferences are sometimes known as *normative preferences*. The neoclassical approach is encapsulated in *revealed preference analysis*. Individuals make choices based on normative preferences and the aim is to see if the observed choices can be rationalized by some underlying utility function (Samuelson, 1948; Houthakker, 1950; Afriat, 1967).

Neoclassical economics allows for the regulation of the behavior of individuals in some cases. In the behavioral economics literature, neoclassical paternalism is sometimes referred to as *heavy-handed paternalism* (Loewenstein and Haisley, 2008). Not everyone will agree on this terminology, but I use it simply as a convenient way of describing the neoclassical benchmark. Its main motivation is that individuals may impose externalities on others, or even on themselves, that they can be made to internalize by appropriately designed regulation or *Pigouvian taxes*.[1] Examples include compulsory helmets for drivers of two-wheelers, seat belts in cars, mandatory third party vehicle insurance, and certificates of roadworthiness of vehicles. These regulations are often justified by a lack of adequate awareness of the risks on the part of individuals, or by the externalities imposed on others from careless behavior. In other cases, individuals might not provide adequately towards a public good. In this case, the neoclassical solution is either government provision, financed by taxes, or Lindahl taxes. There are also regulations on firms in markets that depart from the perfectly competitive ideal, as encapsulated in, say, antitrust laws and environmental regulations.

The evidence from behavioral economics contests the neoclassical view that individuals always make considered judgments of their welfare. A large body of evidence suggests that there is a wedge between revealed and normative preferences. The wedge may be exacerbated by the underlying complexity of the situation, long horizons, and limited personal experience

---

[1] The interested reader can pursue these arguments in any standard book on public economics (Atkinson and Stiglitz, 1980; Stiglitz, 2000) or in microeconomic theory (Mas-Collel et al., 1995).

(Beshears et al., 2008). The relevant evidence is discussed throughout the book, so here we give only a brief outline and suppress the references as far as possible.

Individuals exhibit a range of judgment heuristics and biases that are reflected in actual choices (see Volume 5). Examples include anchoring, representativeness, law of small numbers, base rate underweighting, affect heuristic, hindsight bias, conjunction fallacy, confirmation bias, ignoring regression to the mean, and false consensus effect. In other cases, individuals might not have well-defined preferences and choices may be unduly influenced by informationally equivalent frames and contexts. Individuals might also make important decisions, such as buying consumer durables, or marriage/divorce, in an emotional hot state of the mind that they regret later, once they are in a cold state (see Chapters 1 and 2). Individuals can sometimes exhibit self-control problems on account of present-biased preferences that lead to suboptimal outcomes such as inadequate savings for retirement, obesity, procrastination, and drug use (see Volume 3). Furthermore, many individuals report that they would prefer to save more, or prefer the median portfolio to their own, and others pay to kick a bad habit, indicating that they recognize their choices to be suboptimal (Camerer et al., 2003; Beshears et al., 2008).

Data from the US shows that many individuals do not utilize the full limits of their 401(k) pension plans. There is also inadequate diversification of portfolios. For instance, individuals often use the $1/n$ heuristic to allocate their portfolio, where n is the number of options available. This skews their pension portfolios towards equities, particularly company equity, which can have adverse consequences, as it did for Enron employees. Individuals often overutilize payday loans. These are loans that are repaid when the next paycheck arrives; the short-term interest rates on these loans are excessively steep. Individuals often suffer from limited attention. For instance, they react more to sales taxes that are more salient, and there are discontinuous drops in the prices of used cars at 10K thresholds (see Volume 5).

Given this evidence, what welfare or normative significance can one attach to individual choices, and how can we modify neoclassical methods to take account of observed choices? This forms the main subject matter of this chapter.

The main thrust in *behavioral welfare economics* has been on reconstructing the *informed underlying judgment of individuals*. This has given rise to a range of suggestions under the umbrella term of *soft paternalism* that we describe in more detail below. Camerer et al. (2003) view the relaxation of normative preferences in welfare economics as a natural progression of the relaxation of other restrictive assumptions in economics, such as perfect competition, perfect information, and certainty.

We begin, in Section 3.2, by outlining a simple framework of analysis (Dalton and Ghosal, 2011, 2018; Dalton et al., 2016). Individuals derive utility from actions and psychological states. A feedback function maps actions to psychological states. Classical decision makers, who have no behavioral biases or misperceptions, take account of the feedback. However, behavioral decision makers ignore the feedback, hence, their revealed choices differ from normative choices and their welfare level is also lower. We explore a range of policy interventions that can raise the welfare levels of behavioral decision makers to the same level as neoclassical decision makers. These include *direct paternalism* (directly choosing an action for the decision maker), *indirect paternalism* (using Pigouvian taxes/subsidies), and *soft paternalism* (appropriate nudges that impose minimal costs on rational individuals but confer maximal benefits to boundedly rational individuals).

In contrast to *heavy-handed paternalism* in neoclassical economics, the generic form of paternalism in behavioral economics is known as *soft paternalism* or *light paternalism*. In Section 3.3, we consider a range of proposals that have been made under this umbrella term. These include *libertarian paternalism* (Thaler and Sunstein, 2003, 2009; Sunstein and Thaler, 2003), *asymmetric paternalism* (Camerer et al., 2003), and *light paternalism* (Loewenstein and Ubel, 2008).

At the heart of most proposals under the ambit of soft paternalism is the need to distort individual choices as little as possible, and use as little coercion as possible. The idea is that the mistakes, or misperceptions, of boundedly rational individuals will be *nudged* in the direction of a beneficial correction (as judged by their own fully informed self, acting in a cold state) by a *benevolent planner* or a *choice architect*. At the same time, the minimum intrusion associated with soft paternalism is designed to impose little or no cost on the actions of the fully rational individuals.

Let us consider an example. A *choice architect* or *benevolent planner* might arrange food items in a cafeteria in a certain order. Boundedly rational consumers, who pay inordinate attention to items placed at eye level, could benefit from the placement of healthy options at eye level; this is an example of a *nudge*. Neoclassically rational consumers are not influenced by the arrangement of items, so little cost is imposed on them. The intervention of the choice architect is a form of paternalism. However, ultimately it is the consumer who exercises choice; in this sense, the proposal respects *consumer sovereignty*, which is a form of liberalism. Hence, one is led to the term *libertarian-paternalism*. We consider the effects of several concrete policy proposals in this tradition; these include the role of default options, deadlines, and cooling-off periods.

Some have questioned these proposals and dissenting views have been given (Sugden, 2008, 2013). Under soft paternalism, the choice architect proposes welfare improving nudges to individuals, based on designing choices, *as judged best by the individuals* under perfect information, unlimited cognitive abilities, and complete self-control. While the preference for median portfolios rather than their own, and checking into rehab to kick a habit, provide tantalizing evidence of individuals judging their choices to be poor, it might not always be clear what individuals judge to be in their best interests.

To operationalize light paternalism, one needs to specify what a mistake/misperception is. Furthermore, in the light of these mistakes/misperceptions, how should we judge the outcomes of light-paternalistic policies? The latter question requires us to have some behavioral welfare criteria. The reason that a traditional welfare criterion is not suitable is that actual choices might not be indicative of an individual's best interests. Thus, we cannot directly use existing measures of welfare, such as equivalent variation and/or compensating variation, to determine the direction in which individual welfare is improving. As Loewenstein and Haisley state (p. 12): "Clearly, it doesn't make sense to assess whether someone is committing an error using a measure that is premised on the assumption that people don't commit errors."

In the typical case considered in economics, consumers have greater information about their own type, for instance, their demand for a good or their health status, relative to the firm. In Section 3.4, we consider the opposite possibility. Namely, that firms are better informed about the consumer's usage of their product, say, energy usage, perhaps because consumers exhibit limited attention (Kamenica et al., 2011). In particular, we focus on the *RECAP regulation* suggested by Thaler and Sunstein (2009). Among other things, it requires firms to improve the transmission of information to consumers about their own usage of a product.

As an example, energy firms may be required to install home power meters for their clients, allowing consumers to monitor their own usage. We show that, under exogenous prices, this regulation can reduce the expenditure of consumers, and increase their welfare. However, this regulation may also induce consumers to switch firms. If endogenous prices are allowed, it is not possible to say whether prices will increase or decrease, although intuition suggests that the switching decisions will put downward pressures on prices.

Section 3.5 considers the appropriate scope of economics. An extreme position holds that the only admissible data in economics is *choice data*, and the scope of economics is solely to infer preferences from observed choices (Gul and Pesendorfer, 2008). In this view, non-choice data, such as survey data, self-reported measures of well-being, neuroeconomic data, data based on pupil dilation or skin conductance, or pulse rates, and data generated by mouselab software, are considered outside the scope of economics. Indeed, in the most extreme view, even experimental data may be viewed as non-choice data, or at least, minimally, with great suspicion. In this view, economists should restrict themselves to observing pairs of quantities and prices, remaining agnostic about the reasons for choice. A second component of the Gul–Pesendorfer position is that the neoclassical framework is flexible enough to account for unexpected observations.

Most behavioral economists do not subscribe to the Gul–Pesendorfer position; certainly this book does not. The edited volume by Caplin and Schotter (2008) gives a range of views on this matter and we describe some selected views. Definitions are inherently subjective, and one need not subscribe to the one suggested by Gul–Pesendorfer. Furthermore, the record of non-choice data in estimating economic parameters of interest, and in illuminating diverse economic phenomena, has been impressive (Camerer, 2008). Misusing the flexibility of the neoclassical model to take account of unexpected observations by introducing ad-hoc auxiliary assumptions, produces *wacky models* (Köszegi and Rabin, 2008a; Camerer, 2008). It is possible to show that by taking account of behavioral misperceptions, one may be able to recover underlying preferences from choices (Köszegi and Rabin, 2008a,b). Experiments have been hugely influential in exploring parameter spaces that may not be observed in actual choice data, and in allowing for treatments that are difficult to observe outside the experimental lab; this has allowed for stringent testing of economic theory (Schotter, 2008).

In Section 3.6, we consider *choice-based welfare criteria* with a focus on the Bernheim–Rangel proposal (Bernheim and Rangel, 2009; Salant and Rubinstein, 2008; Rubinstein and Salant, 2012). One begins with a domain of sets of outcomes, and *ancillary conditions* or *frames*, over which individuals have preferences that need not be complete or transitive. If the domain is trimmed-down to a "welfare relevant domain," then one can define preference relations that are complete but possibly intransitive. However, intransitivity does not preclude a welfare analysis. The preference relations on the trimmed-down domain allow one to define criteria for welfare improvement. Under the assumption that each ancillary condition corresponds to a different self of the same individual, and frame-independent choices, one can relate the preference relations to the neoclassical Pareto criterion. Rubinstein and Salant (2012) depart from the Bernheim–Rangel framework by proposing a welfare criterion based on preference orderings that are frame dependent. They explain inconsistent choices by invoking switches in preference orderings between frames.

The developments in choice-based measures of welfare under behavioral biases are promising, but they also illustrate the great difficulty in making progress in this direction. For instance, in the Bernheim–Rangel model, it is not clear who will trim-down the original domain to a welfare relevant domain, or indeed how it could be done. Presumably, in order to do so, one will need to use some non-choice data or invoke some other welfare criteria, which runs into the danger of an infinite regress of welfare criteria. This has led some to make calls for advocating welfare criteria based on preferences rather than choice (Loewenstein and Haisley, 2008).

Section 3.7 takes account of *limited attention* in the choice-based approach to revealed preference (Masatlioglu et al., 2012). For instance, consumers might simply choose between the two cheapest suppliers, ignoring all others; or in choosing a car, potential buyers might first focus on a car with the best fuel efficiency, and then choose the cheapest car in this category, ignoring all others. In the Bernheim–Rangel approach, an alternative x is unambiguously preferred to y, if y is never chosen when x is available. However, under limited attention, in some choice situations, the individual might choose y simply because he does not pay attention to x. We jointly consider the twin phenomena of *revealed preference* and *revealed inattention* and propose an appropriate modification of the weak axiom of revealed preference under these conditions. We close by briefly considering the relation with related approaches (Cherepanov et al., 2013; Manzini and Mariotti, 2007).

Section 3.8 outlines the *contractarian approach* (Sugden, 2013) that draws on an older literature in normative economics (Buchanan, 1968, 1975, 1986). This approach criticizes the paternalism advocated in neoclassical economics, and under soft paternalism, because proposals addressed to a social planner lack a valid *addressee*. The contractarian approach advocates addressing recommendations directly to the individuals who exhibit the relevant biases; for instance, through a public information campaign that disseminates information about the harmful effects of smoking.

The recommendations made by a contractarian appeal to the self-interest of individuals in improving their own welfare, rather than to the general or larger interests of a group of people. Nudges are not allowed in this approach if individuals choose not to be nudged. However, providing information directly to individuals under the contractarian approach may also be viewed as one form of a nudge. Furthermore, it is not clear who will decide how the relevant information will be framed, i.e., who the relevant addressee is; this is particularly important if framing effects are important, or unclear. Thus, the contractarian approach also suffers from some of the same drawbacks that it finds wanting in other theories.

Section 3.9 continues our discussion of *behavioral public finance* from Volume 5. It considers welfare issues and public policy in the presence of behavioral factors, particularly, limited attention. Section 3.9.1 shows how one might model limited attention as a wedge between demand elasticities arising from price changes and changes in ad-valorem taxes. Section 3.9.2 considers the problem of computing the relative *tax incidence* on producers and consumers of an increase in a specific sales tax under limited attention (Chetty et al., 2009). Under limited attention, producers bear a lower burden of the tax increase and the tax incidence falls relatively more on the consumers. While the final outcome is similar to the case of a fall in the elasticity of demand, tax elasticity and limited attention have different effects that we explain.

Section 3.9.3 derives the formulae for the *excess burden* of taxation under limited attention (Chetty et al., 2009). We show that the excess burden increases with the square of a parameter, θ, such that lower values of θ denote higher inattention. When there are no income effects, then limited attention may reduce the excess burden of taxation, which is welfare improving. Finally, in Section 3.9.4, we consider some reduced-form approaches to behavioral welfare analysis. We mainly focus on models that make a distinction between *decision utility* and *experienced utility* (Mullainathan et al., 2012). We also briefly discuss other promising approaches that extend classical optimal tax theory by incorporating behavioral factors such as limited attention (Farhi and Gabaix, 2015).

3.2 Fixing basic ideas

In this section, we introduce some of the issues in behavioral welfare economics, using a simple motivating framework due to Dalton and Ghosal (2011). The conclusions are not restricted to this framework but they apply to any situations where behavioral decision makers do not take full account of some relevant aspect of the economic environment, relative to typical neoclassical decision makers.

3.2.1 *The basic framework*

Suppose that an individual chooses from the set of actions $A = [\underline{a},\overline{a}] \subset \mathbb{R}$ and experiences the set of possible psychological states $\Theta = [\underline{\theta},\overline{\theta}] \subset \mathbb{R}$. Examples of psychological states include moods, aspirations, temptations, reference points, motivations, and the degree of self-confidence.[2]

Psychological states are modeled using the theory of *reciprocal determinism* (Bandura, 1977). This implies that psychological states influence the actions of the individual, but are also, in turn, influenced by actions through a feedback function. For instance, more confident/adventurous individuals are more likely to try out a bungee jump. Once they have made the jump (action), their confidence and sense of adventure might be further increased (feedback).

Formally, we assume that the individual has well-defined preferences and the utility function is given by $u : A \times \Theta \rightarrow \mathbb{R}$; u is twice continuously differentiable in both arguments, and has continuous cross partial derivatives. The *feedback function* that maps actions to psychological states is given by $f : A \rightarrow \Theta$; f is twice continuously differentiable. We assume that:

$$\text{For all } a \in A, \exists \theta \in [\underline{\theta},\overline{\theta}] : \theta = f(a). \tag{3.1}$$

Definition 3.1 *A consistent decision state is a pair (a,θ), where $a \in A$ and $\theta \in \Theta$, such that $\theta = f(a)$.*

Thus, for any $(a,\theta) \in A \times \Theta$, the decision maker's utility is $u(a,\theta)$ and for a consistent decision state, $(a,\theta) = (a,f(a))$, utility is given by $u(a,f(a))$.

Formal models of behavioral welfare economics typically consider two kinds of decision makers. *Classical* decision makers conform to the assumptions of neoclassical economics. *Behavioral* decision makers, in most behavioral welfare models, exhibit some behavioral departures relative to classical decision makers. The main distinction between the two decision makers in the model below, is the degree of awareness of the feedback function.

Classical decision makers take account of f, and solve the following *classical decision problem* (CDP).

$$a^c \in \arg\max_{a \in A} v(a) \equiv u(a,f(a)). \tag{3.2}$$

v is a continuous function on a compact set, hence, a maximum exists, although there is no guarantee that it is unique.

Behavioral decision makers do not take account of the feedback function, f. The solution to a *behavioral decision problem* (BDP) is a pair $(a^b,\theta^b) \in A \times \Theta$ that solves two conditions.[3]

1. For a given psychological state, θ, the chosen action is optimal, i.e.,

$$a^b \in \arg\max_{a \in A} u(a,\theta). \tag{3.3}$$

u is a continuous function on a compact interval, so a maximum exists.

---

[2] The framework is easily extended to the case where A and Θ are subsets of a finite dimensional Euclidean space.

[3] For an axiomatic characterization of the choice theoretic foundations of the CDP and the BDP and their welfare implications, see Dalton and Ghosal (2018).

2. The psychological state is influenced by the feedback rule in equilibrium, i.e.,

$$\theta^b = f(a^b), \tag{3.4}$$

although this is not recognized in the BDP.

For pedagogical reasons, we assume that the global maximum lies in the interior of the set $[\underline{a},\overline{a}]$ for both kinds of decision makers. Our assumptions do not guarantee the existence of a unique equilibrium because neither u nor v are strictly concave. If there are several maxima, then the global maximum is the upper bound of this set. In the discussion that follows, we shall only be interested in the global maximum. We use the notation u_1 and u_2, respectively, for partial derivatives of $u(a,f(a))$ with respect to the first and the second arguments. First and second order partial derivatives of f are written, respectively, as f' and f''.

The first order condition for an interior optimum to the CDP, evaluated at the optimal values, is

$$u_1\left(a^c, f\left(a^c\right)\right) + u_2\left(a^c, f(a^c)\right)f'(a^c) = 0. \tag{3.5}$$

The first order condition and the equilibrium condition for an interior optimum to a BDP are given by

$$u_1\left(a^b, f(a^b)\right) = 0 \text{ and } \theta^b = f(a^b). \tag{3.6}$$

In the first order condition, the behavioral decision maker does not take account of the feedback rule between actions and psychological states. The welfare criteria is defined next.

Definition 3.2 *Let $(a_1,\theta_1),(a_2,\theta_2),(a,\theta) \in A \times \Theta$. The pair (a_1,θ_1) dominates the pair (a_2,θ_2) if $u(a_1,\theta_1) > u(a_2,\theta_2)$. A consistent decision state (a,θ) is optimal if there is no other consistent decision state that dominates it.*

Consider the solution to the BDP $\left(a^b,\theta^b\right)$ in (3.6), so $\theta^b = f(a^b)$. Using (3.5), suppose that there exists some $a' \in A$, which solves the following equation:

$$u_1\left(a', f(a^b)\right) + u_2\left(a', f(a^b)\right)f'(a^b) = 0. \tag{3.7}$$

Then, it follows that

$$u(a^b,\theta^b) < u(a', f(a^b)) \leq u(a^c, f(a^c)). \tag{3.8}$$

The first inequality in (3.8) follows from (3.7), while the second follows from the optimality (but also possibly non-uniqueness) of the optimal solution $(a^c, f(a^c))$ to the CDP. It follows that the solution to the BDP is welfare dominated by the solution to the CDP. Hence, one might think of designing policy interventions to improve the decisions taken by behavioral decision makers.

It is useful to distinguish between the following classes of policy interventions. The first two play a major role in neoclassical economics that does not take into account the existence of behavioral decision makers; yet, many such interventions appear designed for a world that has behavioral decision makers. The third plays a prominent role in behavioral welfare economics.

1. *Direct paternalism*: A third party may directly choose an action for the behavioral decision makers that forces them to take account of the feedback effect. Alternatively, the third party may make these actions legally binding. In neoclassical economics, direct paternalism takes the form of legal requirements such as wearing seat belts; minimum driving age; minimum age for various kinds of consent; prohibition on using mobile phones while driving; purchase of compulsory car insurance; and rules governing publicly observable obscene behavior.

2. *Indirect paternalism*: This takes the form of policy interventions, typically through changes in prices, that induce decision makers to internalize externalities caused to others, or to themselves. Examples are vehicle road taxes based on CO_2 emissions, emissions taxes on factories, subsidies to charitable giving, and child tax credits.

3. *Libertarian paternalism or soft paternalism*: These interventions (see Section 3.3, below) impose low costs on classical decision makers. However, a third party, typically a benevolent planner, controls the menu of options, for instance, defaults, faced by behavioral decision makers. This is a form of *nudging* and embodies various degrees of paternalism, depending on how intrusive the nudges are. The behavioral decision makers are, however, free to choose an option from the given menu. For instance, they can override the default option without the threat of legal sanctions that arises under direct paternalism. This aspect of the intervention respects individual liberty.

   Hence, these policies are said to exhibit *libertarian paternalism*. Given that individuals ultimately choose their own actions, despite facing a paternalistic third party, this class of interventions is also sometimes given the generic name of *soft paternalism*. Dalton and Ghosal (2011) use this term to include psychological therapies such as cognitive behavioral therapy and expert advice.

   In the context of the simple model used in this section, the nudge takes the form of a choice by the planner of some $\theta \in \Theta$, where θ may be thought as a reference point, or a default option.

Insofar as behavioral interventions are about making recommendations, for instance, to nudge consumers, it is worth asking who the relevant *addressee* of such recommendations is. In neoclassical economics one does not typically ask this question. In normative neoclassical economics, the addressee is a benevolent social planner. This is also the approach taken in most of modern behavioral welfare economics, for instance, under soft paternalism as well as in choice-based or revealed preference approaches; see Sections 3.6 and 3.7, below.

By contrast, Sugden (2008, 2013), in advocating the *contractarian approach* (see Section 3.8, below) questions the usefulness of the social planner benchmark on the grounds that this is a purely hypothetical construct (i.e., lacks a valid addressee). His approach is to respond to behavioral biases by identifying directly the relevant addressee, i.e., the individual who exhibits these biases. This takes the form of policy interventions that provide information "directly" to individuals who "choose" to be nudged.

Once we move away from the normative benchmark of a social planner, the relevant addressee for behavioral recommendations could be an executive agency, a regulatory body, or any policy making department in the government. Such an entity, which we simply term as a *policymaker*, might have the following two kinds of informational disadvantages, singly, or in conjunction.

Definition 3.3 (a) *Under Type 1 asymmetric information, the policymaker is uncertain about the type (classical or behavioral) of individuals. We capture this by assigning respective probabilities $\mu_1 \in [0,1]$ and $1 - \mu_1$ that the decision maker solves a CDP and a BDP.*

(b) *Under Type 2 asymmetric information, the policymaker knows the type, classical or behavioral, of the decision maker but is uncertain about the preferences of the decision maker. The policymaker assigns a probability $\mu_2 \in [0,1]$ to the correct utility function (v for a CDP and u for a BDP). But with probability $1 - \mu_2$, the policymaker has the following incorrect beliefs about the decision maker's preferences.*

(bi) *If the decision maker is classical, then the policymaker believes that preferences are given by $\tilde{v}(a) \equiv \tilde{u}(a, \tilde{f}(a))$, where $\tilde{v} : A \to \mathbb{R}$ is twice continuously differentiable in a and $\tilde{f} \neq f$.*

(ii) *If the decision maker is behavioral, then the policymaker believes that preferences are given by $\hat{u}(a, \theta)$, where $\hat{u}$ is twice continuously differentiable in both arguments and has continuous cross partial derivatives.*

We now consider the solution under various regimes.

3.2.2 Direct paternalism

Under direct paternalism, the policymaker directly chooses an action for the individual under one of the two kinds of information asymmetries in Definition 3.3. Consider first Type 1 asymmetric information. The objective function of the policymaker is

$$a_1^d \in \arg\max_{a \in A} \mu_1 u(a, f(a)) + (1 - \mu_1) u(a, \theta), \tag{3.9}$$

and the consistency requirement is

$$\theta_1^d = f(a_1^d). \tag{3.10}$$

The first order condition to the optimization problem in (3.9) is

$$\mu_1 \left[u_1 \left(a_1^d, f(a_1^d) \right) + u_2 \left(a_1^d, f(a_1^d) \right) f'(a_1^d) \right] + (1 - \mu_1) u_1(a_1^d, \theta_1^d) = 0. \tag{3.11}$$

Jointly solving (3.10) and (3.11) we get the solution $\left(a_1^d, \theta_1^d \right)$; a solution always exists because the objective function is continuous over a compact set. In the special cases of $\mu_1 = 1$, and $\mu_1 = 0$, respectively, we get the solution under CDP and BDP.

Consider Type 2 asymmetric information in which the planner believes that the decision maker solves a CDP, but is uncertain of the exact preferences (Definition 3.3(bi)). The objective function of the policymaker is

$$a_2^d \in \arg\max_{a \in A} \mu_2 u(a, f(a)) + (1 - \mu_2) \tilde{u}(a, \tilde{f}(a)), \tag{3.12}$$

subject to the consistency requirement

$$\theta_2^d = f(a_2^d). \tag{3.13}$$

The first order condition to the problem in (3.12) is

$$\mu_2 \left[u_1 \left(a_2^d, f(a_2^d) \right) + u_2 \left(a_2^d, f(a_2^d) \right) f'(a_2^d) \right] + (1 - \mu_2) \tilde{u}_1 \left(a_2^d, \tilde{f}(a_2^d) \right) + \tilde{u}_2 \left(a_2^d, \tilde{f}(a_2^d) \right) \tilde{f}'(a_2^d) = 0. \tag{3.14}$$

Jointly solving (3.13), (3.14), we get the solution $\left(a_2^d, \theta_2^d\right)$. If there is no misperception of preferences ($\mu_2 = 1$) then the solution is identical to the CDP, (a^c, θ^c).

Interventions under direct paternalism are more attractive if μ_1 is low (i.e., it is more likely that the decision maker is solving a BDP), and if μ_2 is high (the policymaker has greater knowledge of the underlying preferences). At the other extreme (high μ_1 and low μ_2), direct paternalism may do more harm than good.

3.2.3 Indirect paternalism

Under indirect paternalism, the policymaker acts like a Stackelberg leader and imposes taxes/subsidies, t, on the actions taken by the decision maker; t is also known as a Pigouvian tax. The behavioral decision maker observes t, takes it into account, and then chooses his optimal action. Thus, the BDP in this case is

$$a^i \in \arg\max_{a \in A} u(a, \theta) - ta,$$

where t is the tax ($t > 0$) or subsidy ($t < 0$) per unit of action, a, imposed by a policymaker. The solution is given by the analog of (3.6):

$$u_1\left(a^i, f(a^i)\right) - t = 0 \text{ and } \theta^i = f(a^i). \tag{3.15}$$

In the absence of any information asymmetries, the policymaker can implement the solution to the CDP. Comparing (3.5) and (3.15), and choosing

$$t = -u_2\left(a^c, f(a^c)\right) f'(a^c), \tag{3.16}$$

ensures that the solution is $\left(a^i, \theta^i\right) = (a^c, \theta^c)$. The tax/subsidy gives the correct incentives to the decision maker to internalize the own-produced externality of ignoring the feedback effect.

We now consider the presence of asymmetric information. We distinguish between two kinds of solutions. The solution that arises under asymmetric information on the part of the policymaker (the ex-ante solution) and the solution that arises when the asymmetric information is resolved (the ex-post solution). For instance, the policymaker may assign probabilities that the decision maker to be regulated is classical or behavioral (asymmetric information). Yet, once the appropriate regulations are announced, the actual decision maker, either classical or behavioral, takes actions under the given regulations (resolution of asymmetric information).

Proposition 3.1 *(Dalton and Ghosal, 2011): Consider Type 1 asymmetric information (Definition 3.3a).*

(a) *Ex-ante solution: The following level of Pigouvian tax, $t = t_1$, ensures the ex-ante solution is identical to that in the CDP, (a^c, θ^c),*

$$t_1 = (1 - \mu_1) u_1(a^c, \theta^c). \tag{3.17}$$

(b) *The ex-post solution: The ex-post solution, i.e., once the decision maker turns out to be a classical or behavioral decision maker, is not necessarily identical to (a^c, θ^c).*

Proof: (a) Consider Type 1 asymmetric information. The objective function of the policymaker is

$$a_1^i \in \arg\max_{a \in A} \mu_1 \left[u(a, f(a)) - t_1 a \right] + (1 - \mu_1) \left[u(a, \theta) - t_1 a \right] \tag{3.18}$$

subject to the consistency requirement

$$\theta_1^i = f(a_1^i). \tag{3.19}$$

The first order condition to this optimization problem is

$$\mu_1 \left[u_1 \left(a_1^i, f(a_1^i) \right) + u_2 \left(a_1^i, f(a_1^i) \right) f'(a_1^i) - t_1 \right] + (1 - \mu_1) \left[u_1(a_1^i, \theta_1^i) - t_1 \right] = 0, \tag{3.20}$$

which can be rewritten as

$$u_1 \left(a_1^i, f(a_1^i) \right) + u_2 \left(a_1^i, f(a_1^i) \right) f'(a_1^i) = \frac{1}{\mu_1} \left[t_1 - (1 - \mu_1) u_1(a_1^i, \theta_1^i) \right]. \tag{3.21}$$

Setting $t_1 = (1 - \mu_1) u_1(a^c, \theta^c)$ ensures that the RHS of (3.21) equals zero. Comparing with (3.5) and using (3.19), the solution is $\left(a_1^i, \theta_1^i \right) = (a^c, \theta^c)$, as claimed. This is the ex-ante solution, prior to the resolution of the asymmetric information faced by the policymaker.

(b) The Stackelberg leader, the policymaker, announces the Pigouvian tax given in (3.17), under uncertainty about the type of the decision maker: classical or behavioral. Having observed the tax, the decision maker, or Stackelberg follower, who privately knows his type to be either classical or behavioral, chooses an action $a \in A$. The ex-post solution, say $\left(\tilde{a}, \tilde{\theta} \right)$, is unlikely to equal (a^c, θ^c). For instance, the optimization problem of a behavioral decision maker is given by

$$\tilde{a} \in \arg\max_{a \in A} u(a, \theta) - \left[(1 - \mu_1) u_1(a^c, \theta^c) \right] a,$$

subject to the consistency condition $\tilde{\theta} = f(\tilde{a})$. A similar argument can be applied if, ex-post, the decision maker solves a CDP. ∎

The difference between the ex-ante and ex-post solutions reflects the distortions created by an indirect policy intervention. From (3.17), the size of the intervention depends on the size of μ_1. The size of the distortion diminishes as $\mu_1 \to 1$, i.e., the closer the decision maker turns out to be a classical one.

3.2.4 *Libertarian paternalism*

Under libertarian paternalism, boundedly rational individuals are *nudged* in a beneficial direction by a benevolent planner and minimum costs are imposed on the fully rational individuals. We consider a simple example that illustrates some of the implications of libertarian paternalism. Suppose that the action set $A = \{a_l, a_h\}$, where $a_l < a_h$ and a_l is the status quo. To fix ideas, think of a_l as the action "stay at home" and a_h as the action "go to college." The set of psychological states is given by $\Theta = \{\theta_l, \theta_h\}$; let us interpret these states as the aspiration levels. The utility function of the individual is given by

$$\begin{cases} u(a_l, \theta) = 0, \theta \in \{\theta_l, \theta_h\} \\ u(a_h, \theta_l) < 0, u(a_h, \theta_h) > 0 \end{cases}. \tag{3.22}$$

Thus, staying at home gives zero utility, irrespective of the psychological state. Going to college is a relatively better option under the good psychological state, but not if the psychological state is bad (e.g., the individual cannot study properly if depressed, and fails, but must pay fees and other college expenses). Denote the optimal choice of an action under libertarian paternalism by a^*.

Behavioral decision makers ignore the feedback between actions and psychological states. Hence, under the assumptions made so far, they choose as follows.

$$\begin{cases} u(a_l,\theta_l) > u(a_h,\theta_l) & \Rightarrow a^* = a_l \\ u(a_l,\theta_h) < u(a_h,\theta_h) & \Rightarrow a^* = a_h \end{cases}. \tag{3.23}$$

In contrast, classical decision makers take account of the feedback function, f. Assume that

$$\theta_l = f(a_l) < \theta_h = f(a_h). \tag{3.24}$$

A classical decision maker realizes that if he went to college, his aspiration level will be raised (see (3.24)), thus, going to college is a dominant action for such a decision maker.

By contrast, for behavioral decision makers, the decision is critically dependent on the initial aspiration levels (see (3.23)). Those who have low aspiration levels, $\theta = \theta_l$, choose not to go to college, so $a = a_l$. However, those with high aspirations, $\theta = \theta_h$, do go to college, so $a = a_h$. Since $u(a_l,\theta_l) = 0$, and $u(a_h,\theta_h) > 0$, if the initial aspiration level of a behavioral decision maker is θ_l, a nudge to the decision maker that either raises aspiration levels to θ_h, or makes going to college a *default option*, is welfare improving. This does not alter the optimal decision of the classical decision makers but improves the decision of the behavioral decision makers. This is the basic idea behind libertarian paternalism. For an interpretation of θ as aspirations in a model that explains poverty arising from aspiration failures, see Dalton et al. (2016).

3.2.5 *Effect of other policies*

In neoclassical economics, providing more information to decision makers, or expanding their set of actions typically improves the welfare of individuals. In the present framework, this need not be the case because behavioral decision makers ignore the feedback between actions and psychological states. Exercise 5 illustrates these issues.

3.3 Soft paternalism

In economics, *paternalism* may be taken as any infringement of *consumer sovereignty* that is intended to improve the well-being of economic actors. For instance, parents might choose healthy snacks for children and limit access to the TV, or the kinds of websites they can visit on the Internet. Paternalism has been viewed with suspicion in neoclassical economics. However, as Jolls et al. (1988, p. 1545) note in their *anti-antipaternalistic approach*: "No axiom demonstrates that people make choices that serve their best interests; this is a question to be answered based on evidence."

Soft paternalism is an umbrella term that is associated with several kinds of behavioral welfare frameworks that advocate limited and light interventions, for instance, the choice of default options. These interventions impose little or no costs on classically rational individuals but intend to improve the welfare of boundedly rational individuals by suggestions or *nudges*, while allowing them the liberty to choose their actions, e.g., overriding the default option.

3.3.1 *Libertarian paternalism*

The main target for soft paternalism is boundedly rational individuals. The interventions are designed to influence the choices of such individuals for the better; in this sense the interventions are *paternalistic*. Yet, the interventions do not infringe the liberty of the individuals to make the eventual choices; in this sense the interventions are liberal. Thaler and Sunstein (2003, 2009) and Sunstein and Thaler (2003) argue that their *libertarian-paternalism* proposal is not an oxymoron. In their proposal, Sunstein and Thaler take it that they are advising a *planner* or a *choice architect* whose job is to decide on the options to be presented to an individual. The planner decides on the menu of choices for individuals, based on his judgment about what options are in their best interests, as would be judged by the individuals if one could invoke their underlying rational selves.

Sunstein and Thaler (2003) note that most economists are libertarians, a position associated with respect for freedom of individual choice. They argue that the unfavorable response to paternalism in economics and law, which they call *dogmatic paternalism* (p. 1163), is based on one false assumption and two misconceptions that we describe now.

The false assumption is that (Sunstein and Thaler, 2003, p. 1163): "almost all people, almost all of the time, make choices that are in their best interest or at the very least are better, by their own lights, than the choices that would be made by third parties." A range of evidence in behavioral economics that runs contrary to this assumption is highlighted in this book; it is also briefly alluded to in the introduction. Thaler and Sunstein mainly refer to the evidence on context dependence of preferences and the instability of preferences. Within behavioral economics, this is uncontroversial. Furthermore, individual choices are influenced by the individual's psychological state and by self-control problems. Finally, the choices made by individuals are sometimes not consistent with the choices that they endorse in their role as consumers. For instance, this is the case when individuals visit a rehab center to kick a habit or prefer the median portfolio of a savings plan to their own (Sunstein and Thaler, 2003, p. 1169).

If a choice architect or planner has to act in a paternalistic manner then he needs to discover what is best for an individual. Sunstein and Thaler (2003, p. 1162) treat individuals as not acting in their best interests if they make "decisions that they would change if they had complete information, unlimited cognitive abilities, and no lack of self-control." Sugden (2008, 2013) terms this as the *informed desire criterion*. How does the choice architect figure out what is best for the individual? The choice architect could use a cost–benefit analysis or employ insights from psychology to figure out when more options will be beneficial (Sunstein and Thaler, 2003, p. 1166). Or, the choice architect could use simple rules of thumb and experiment as in automatic defaults and the Save More Tomorrow plan (Sunstein and Thaler, 2003, p. 1190).

The two misconceptions, in Thaler and Sunstein's view, are the following (Sunstein and Thaler, 2003, p. 1163). First, there is a viable alternative to paternalism. By contrast, most choices offered to individuals are already framed in some manner by someone else, so some paternalism is always implicit in most, if not all, human choice. Second, paternalism necessarily involves coercion. The behavioral biases and misperceptions of individuals show that they can potentially benefit from the "steer" provided by the choice architect (subject to the caveats about the choice architect's role discussed below). Furthermore, paternalism need not be coercive. The essence of libertarian paternalism is that the choice architect respects the freedom of choice of the individual, once a menu of choices is offered to the individual. This view is not universally agreed upon. For instance, a literature in Law and Economics defends the rationality assumption and views paternalism with suspicion on account of regulatory capture and the bounded rationality of bureaucrats (Posner, 1986).

In Thaler and Sunstein's view, a policy is paternalistic if it alters the choices of individuals in a manner which makes them "better off." The term *better off* is not formally defined. Furthermore, in this view, primacy is given to preferences rather than choices, for choice might, for a variety of reasons, not faithfully reflect preferences. If this is the case and the two misconceptions are accepted, then Thaler and Sunstein (2003, p. 175) conclude that: "we can abandon the less interesting question of whether to be paternalistic or not and turn to the more constructive question of how to choose among paternalistic options." Let us clarify these issues further with a concrete example.

Example 3.1 *(The cafeteria example; Sunstein and Thaler, 2003): The "cafeteria example" features prominently in the work of Thaler and Sunstein and nicely illustrates the essentials of libertarian paternalism. It is typically the case that the arrangement of food items (a form of framing) has a significant effect on what people choose in a cafeteria or a supermarket. For instance, people might be more inclined to choose items that are placed at "eye level" or items that are placed at the front end. Consider a cafeteria in which the manager must decide on the arrangement of food items in the store. Suppose that the cafeteria manager has the following options:*

1. *She could make choices that she thinks would make the customers best off, all things considered.*
2. *She could make choices at random.*
3. *She could choose those items that she thinks would make the customers as obese as possible.*
4. *She could give customers what she thinks they would choose on their own.*

Anti-paternalism dictates choosing option 4. However, it is difficult to determine what the consumers would choose on their own if the cafeteria manager were not to first choose one of the options. As Sunstein and Thaler (2003, p. 1164) write: "If the arrangement of the alternatives has a significant effect on the selections the customers make, then their true 'preferences' do not formally exist." Ruling out option 4, the only reasonable option is option 1. Hence, a degree of paternalism is inevitable. Furthermore, option 1 illustrates why coercion is not an inevitable part of paternalism in the following sense. The cafeteria manager simply engages in framing the choices without reducing the number of choices. This should hardly have an effect on the neoclassical fully rational consumers, so it imposes no change in their well-being. However, by perhaps placing the healthy options at eye level, the cafeteria manager may improve the well-being of boundedly rational consumers who might be subject to self-control problems and choose unhealthy snacks otherwise.

One may also think about the likely outcomes if the cafeteria manager were purely a profit maximizer (Sugden, 2008, p. 236). However, if the cafeteria manager believes that current preferences are not well formed and she anticipates that in the longer run consumers will like healthier options, then profit maximizing and welfare issues could be closely related.

In actual practice, the job description of a choice architect already exists in many domains. For instance, doctors often advise patients on a choice menu of treatments chosen by them, architects often advise clients about house designs, interior decorators often choose a subset of designs to show to clients, based on their perceived suitability, and so on. However, the strict definition of a choice architect is satisfied when the suggested interventions are designed to make individuals better off, *as judged by themselves* (Thaler and Sunstein, 2009, ch. 5). Furthermore, the choice architect does not unduly limit the freedom of choice of individuals. Hence, *nudges* are not only admissible, they are the primary means of producing outcomes from the choice architecture. Nudges are believed to be most effective when the decisions of individuals are infrequent and their decisions give rise to noisy feedback; when the choice architect has more experience and expertise; and when individual heterogeneity is low (Thaler and Sunstein, 2009, ch. 4).

In the actual practice of public policy, one observes a wide variety of nudges that could be imagined to originate from a choice architect. For instance, cash machines dispense cash only when the relevant bank card has been taken out first; nozzles for dispensing different kinds of car fuel, e.g., diesel and petrol, are often of a different size or color to prevent incorrect use of fuel; many cars produce a beeping sound if the driver is not wearing a seat belt; automatic electric switches in cars and offices are often used to conserve energy or prevent batteries from running out; default options in savings and pension plans enable people to invest better; the Save More Tomorrow plan takes account of current self-control problems to enable greater savings in the future as income grows over time (see Section 3.3.4 below); color coded labels on food (red for high fat and green for low fat) and government mandated guidelines on the number of fruit portions a day; warnings on cigarette packs; and prohibition of advertising of cigarettes.

Thaler and Sunstein (2009, pp. 102–3) give an example of a regulation called RECAP, short for *record, evaluate, and compare alternative prices,* that allows better across-firms comparability of prices. This regulation calls for a personalized electronic summary of the consumer's use of the good/service sold by the firm in a standardized form, that allows comparison of prices from alternative suppliers. This is similar, in spirit, to the practice in UK supermarkets of separately stating sticker prices of goods of different brands/sizes in standardized units, say per 100 grams, or per 100ml.

In each case, the justification for these nudges in the libertarian-paternalistic framework is that some people are making undesirable choices, as judged by themselves (Thaler and Sunstein, 2009, p. 5). Thaler and Sunstein present a range of evidence to underpin the claim that individuals would wish to be nudged in many cases. Examples include, preference for the median savings portfolios relative to the own portfolio; New Year resolutions for smoking and other addictions that often fail, or activities that involve procrastination; evidence that shows health related risks from temptation activities such as smoking, drinking, and obesity inducing foods (Thaler and Sunstein, 2009, ch. 1, 4). This evidence is certainly impressive but some have doubted if it clinches the argument that people wish to be nudged (Sugden, 2009, p. 371).

3.3.2 Asymmetric paternalism

Concurrently and independently of the development of the idea of libertarian paternalism, Camerer et al. (2003) propose the closely related concept of *asymmetric paternalism* or *paternalism for conservatives*. They define and describe the main features of asymmetric paternalism as follows (p. 1212). "A regulation is asymmetrically paternalistic if it creates large benefits for those who make errors, while imposing little or no harm on those who are fully rational. Such regulations are relatively harmless to those who reliably make decisions in their best interest, while at the same time advantageous to those making suboptimal choices."

How should alternative paternalistic policies be evaluated? Camerer et al. (2003) propose a simple cost–benefit framework. Suppose that a fraction p of the consumers are boundedly rational, while the rest are fully rational. Consider a proposed paternalistic policy that is implemented by incurring some implementation costs, I. The policy imparts some benefits $B > 0$ to the boundedly rational consumers, but also imposes some costs $C > 0$ on the fully rational consumers. Suppose that the incremental effect on the profits of the firms on account of the change in consumer behavior is $\Delta\pi$ which could be positive or negative. The proposed policy is beneficial if

$$pB - (1-p)C - I + \Delta\pi > 0. \qquad (3.25)$$

An asymmetrically paternalistic policy is characterized by a high value of B and low values of C and I. In the limit, the purest case of asymmetric paternalism arises when $C = 0$. There is still no guarantee that I will be low, although this would seem to be an important requirement of asymmetric paternalism. Asymmetric paternalism becomes more attractive as the proportion of boundedly rational consumers, p, increases. The effect on and sign of $\Delta\pi$ depends on the precise context. For instance, if bounded rationality creates errors in the direction of buying too little, then under an asymmetric paternalistic policy, $\Delta\pi > 0$; and in the converse case, $\Delta\pi < 0$. While (3.25) is useful to organize our thoughts, in actual practice, the measurement of costs and benefits in the presence of behavioral biases is a vexed one. For instance, perceived benefits, B, may depend on behavioral factors such as one's psychological state, framing, context, and status-quo bias, which may be inherently hard to measure.

The class of policies that alters "default outcomes" comes closest to satisfying the requirements of asymmetric paternalism. This is particularly the case when a status-quo bias arises, say, due to procrastination. Think, for instance, of two alternative states s_1 and s_2 with respective benefits B_1 and B_2 such that $B_1 > B_2$; the states are chosen by the individual. If the status quo is s_1 and individuals exhibit a status-quo bias that prevents them from choosing s_2 then a paternalistic policy might wish to set the default option to s_2. An example of a default option is automatic enrollment in 401(k) pension plans, which has been shown to improve participation rates (Madrian et al., 2001).

The paternalistic policy of automatic enrollment in 401(k) plans also alerts us to a careful consideration of unexpected aspects of the problem. In this case, in actual practice, the default enrollment meant choosing also the default contribution rates and the default portfolio of assets. The default rates were set quite low (2–3%) and the default portfolio was a conservative one (mostly money market funds). These defaults, however, turned out to be disadvantageous. The low default rates reduced the effectiveness of the default, while the conservative portfolio earned lower returns because stocks have traditionally outperformed bonds. This offset some of the beneficial effects of the increased enrollment rates arising from the new default option (Choi et al., 2004; Madrian et al., 2001).

A second example of unexpected outcomes comes from the detailed text that accompanies mortgage and lease contracts in the US. The detail in the text is a response to the Federal Truth in Lending Act. The text typically gives details of all costs and terms of the contract; multiple, mandatory, signatures certify that the reader has read the separate sections of the contract. Borrowers have to read the following statement and sign that they understand it: "If you obtain this loan, the lender will have a mortgage on your home. You could lose your home, and any money you have put into it, if you do not meet your obligations under the loan." This text exemplifies asymmetric paternalism because the rational types will not need to read the fine print while the boundedly rational types are expected to benefit from reading it. Furthermore, once the text is designed, the cost of producing copies is relatively low. However, a potentially unexpected outcome is that because individuals have limited attention (see Volume 5 of the book), the boundedly rational types simply ignore the fine print, in which case the policy might have limited benefits. Indeed, such individuals might have read a more abbreviated version of the text (see the relevant evidence in Volume 5). The condition in (3.25) advocates taking account of all such relevant costs.

Many existing regulations discussed in this section can be interpreted as a form of asymmetric paternalism. Indeed, it is hard to give an interpretation of these regulations on traditional grounds of efficiency when all economic agents are rational. Hence, somewhat paradoxically for neoclassical economics, one might argue that the law reflects asymmetric paternalism (Camerer et al., 2003, p. 1223).

3.3.3 *A pragmatic approach*

Loewenstein and Haisley (2008) propose a pragmatic approach, light paternalism, in which welfare judgments can be made under two main conditions that they term as *dominance* and *self-officiating.*[4] The dominance criteria comes into play if one strategy clearly dominates another, in terms of outcome or risk. For instance, full utilization of 401(k) matching programs typically dominates underutilization. Thus, light paternalism would advocate a default option that equals the maximum allowable contribution that is matched by the employers.

Self-officiating means that individuals choose their own goals and then they are provided with the necessary information and incentives to aid self-control. The choice of goals is to be made in a "cold" rather than a "hot" state (see Chapters 1 and 2 for this distinction). Consider the example of an office in which employees determine that they would be better off without a soda machine that dispenses unhealthy drinks. The self-officiating criterion allows for the removal of the machine from the premises provided that the employees make this decision in a cold state. This appears relatively heavy-handed but allows individuals to pursue their stated goals more directly.

The pragmatic approach also differs from the choice-based approach of Bernheim and Rangel (2007) in that it focuses on preferences rather than choice. Loewenstein and Haisley (2008, p. 223) capture the spirit and thrust of their approach in the following quote.

Our own opinion is that the welfare criterion for evaluating paternalistic policies should be based on preference. Much as a psychotherapist would likely take at face value a client's professed desire to become happier, more sociable, or less anxious, even if she engaged in patterns of thinking and behavior that led to the opposite result, we would argue that the economist-as-therapist should treat verbal statements of preference as useful information, even if choice is not in line with professed preference. If people express a desire to lose weight but make choices that cause them to gain weight; if they express a desire to be financially solvent, but make choices that lead to burdensome debt; if they want to stop smoking but continue to smoke; if they want to take prescription medications but fail to do so, these are all situations in which paternalistic interventions could be helpful.

---

[4] A third criterion, *clearly negative outcomes*, is also identified. However, it appears that in a broader definition this criterion can be subsumed within the dominance criteria.

3.3.4 *Some applications of soft paternalism*

We briefly consider some applications of soft paternalism. Our discussion is abbreviated because these issues have been considered in varying degrees elsewhere in the book.

THE ROLE OF DEFAULTS

The status-quo bias is a well-documented finding in behavioral economics.[5] Suppose that there are two possible actions/policies, x and y, with respective benefits to an individual equal to b_x and b_y. Suppose that the cost of changing from any action to the other is c. Then there is a status-quo bias in favor of x if (i) $b_y - b_x > c$, and (ii) the individual prefers to persist with x. Concurrently, there might be a status-quo bias in favor of y too.

Camerer et al. (2003) note several sources of status-quo bias. (1) *Loss aversion*: If a change in policy is associated with a potential loss, then the status-quo policy is preferred. (2) *Asymmetric experienced regret*: There is some evidence that people regret bad outcomes that result from their own actions as compared to bad outcomes that result purely from inaction. (3) *Hyperbolic discounting*: Current-bias might cause individuals to procrastinate in shifting to the economically more beneficial policy.

Status-quo bias opens the possibility that paternalism, in the form of default options, potentially associated with higher welfare, may be effective. The status-quo bias ensures the individuals are unlikely to override default options. The stickiness of default options has been widely documented: for instance, in decisions to donate one's organs (Johnson and Goldstein, 2003; Abadie and Gay, 2004); default options in car insurance plans (Park et al., 2000); and pension and savings plans (Thaler and Sunstein, 2009). Defaults can be viewed as a form of asymmetric paternalism because they can be set in a manner that is beneficial for a boundedly rational consumer, but impose little or no cost on the rational individuals who can easily override them.

Consider the following natural experiment that illustrates the effect of default rules for insurance policies. In New Jersey, the default was a limited right to sue the other party following an accident, while, in Pennsylvania, the default was a full right to sue. In each state, customers could switch to the other possibility by either paying more (full right to sue in New Jersey) or by receiving a discount (for a limited right to sue in Pennsylvania). Johnson et al. (1993) show that when offered a choice to alter the defaults, only 20% of drivers in New Jersey chose full rights to sue while 75% of drivers in Pennsylvania retained full rights to sue.

RETIREMENT SAVINGS AND DEFAULTS

We have shown in Volume 3 that in the presence of present-biased preferences, such as hyperbolic discounting, individuals may save insufficiently for retirement. Other behavioral factors may also reduce savings; we give two examples. (1) By reducing current consumption relative to a reference level of consumption, an individual with a mental account for consumption may suffer loss aversion. Thus, individuals might be reluctant to save more. (2) If the default is zero savings/contributions to a retirement plan, the status-quo bias could further weaken the desire to save.

The idea behind Benartzi and Thaler's (2004) SMarT ('save more tomorrow') plan is to take account of behavioral features in such a manner that encourages more savings. Essentially,

---

[5] See, for instance, Samuelson and Zeckhauser (1988), Kahneman et al. (1991), and Kahneman and Tversky (2000).

under a SMarT plan, individuals agree to save a part of their next pay increase. Since only a fraction of the pay increase in the future is used towards savings, loss aversion from a fall in consumption does not kick in sufficiently. Furthermore, since the saving is made in the future, it is not influenced by the current-bias in preferences arising through, say, hyperbolic discounting. Finally, the status-quo bias can be exploited by altering the default option to contribute rather than not-contribute. In the spirit of soft paternalism, individuals can choose to opt-out if they wish to.

Evidence supports the "savings enhancing effects" of changing the default option (Choi et al., 2004; Madrian and Shea, 2001). An alternative to using the default option is to ask employees when they begin their jobs if they would like to enroll or not. Choi et al. (2004) show that this method increases enrollment relative to the case of the opt-in option (default is not-contribute) but less relative to the opt-out option (default is to contribute).

Loewenstein and Haisley (2008) note two limitations of empirical studies that suggest a positive welfare effect of paternalistic savings policies. First, where does an increase in retirement savings come from? If other items of expenditure are compromised and there is an associated increase in credit card debt, then these factors need to be factored in. Second, a range of behavioral factors come into play in many policies. For instance, in the operation of SMarT savings plans, these factors include hyperbolic discounting, loss aversion, and status-quo bias. What is the individual contribution of each of these factors? These are pertinent questions for future research.

OBESITY

Loewenstein and Haisley (2008) report on their research on the effects of deposit contracts in countering obesity. People who express a preference to lose weight are asked to pay a deposit of $90/month, or $3 a day. Individuals are set a target of losing a pound of weight over a week. They are weighed each day against a target. If the weight is below the target, the experimenter doubles the deposit and gives the money, $6, to the subject. If the weight is greater than the target then the subject loses the deposit.

The scheme works on two behavioral principles; the various components are described in Volumes 3 and 5 of the book. First, initial overconfidence contributes to the decision to join the plan. One could also use a hyperbolic discounting argument similar to the optimistic take-up of annual versus daily offers in gym memberships. Second, a loss of the deposit money is viewed as out-of-pocket costs, which are overweighted relative to forgone-gains, on account of loss aversion. Hence, individuals are more reluctant to avoid out-of-pocket costs, which contributes to their efforts to get their weight below the target. The take-up of deposit contracts is a voluntary decision (liberalism). Rational individuals have no need for them. However, boundedly rational individuals can benefit from them (paternalism). Furthermore, the idea of respecting individually chosen goals in a cold state of the mind, and aiding in the achievement of these goals is consistent with the *self-officiating criterion* under light paternalism (see Section 3.3.3).

Wisdom et al. (2010) consider two kinds of interventions to reduce calorie intake in fast food restaurants. In the first, individuals are simply provided with information about the calorie content of their food items. This is consistent with recently proposed laws and the contractarian approach that we outline in Section 3.8. The second proposal is a form of nudge, consistent with soft paternalism, that simply makes choosing high calorie foods more inconvenient, for instance by altering the placement of items on a menu.

Both interventions were effective in reducing calorie intake. However, each intervention had drawbacks. Providing calorie information did not reduce the calorie intake of overweight people who presumably are the main target of these interventions. The nudge worked less well in a weak form as compared to a strong form. An unexpected effect of the nudge was that individuals reduced consumption of high calorie sandwiches but increased their consumption of higher calorie side orders and drinks. These results show that a combination of the two policies may work better and nudge proposals may have unexpected effects on complementary activities. Hence, careful pilot studies must precede actual policy recommendations.

COOLING-OFF PERIODS

Consumers might sometimes regret a purchase decision on account of several factors. These include: buying in an emotional hot state, or being subject to projection-bias that overstates the future need for the purchase (see Chapters 1 and 2); or present-biased preferences, arising, say, from hyperbolic discounting, that make the benefits of the current purchase salient relative to its future costs (see Volume 3). Regulation, in the form of *cooling-off periods*, protects consumers from potential future regret arising from current decisions. Cooling-off periods typically take one of two forms.

(a) Individuals are free to choose but allowed to reverse their decision within some legal time horizon, T. This typically occurs with the purchase of consumer durables and many services such as insurance products.

(b) Having made their initial decision, individuals are not free to exercise their choice until some time, $\tau > 0$, has passed. For instance, once one files for a divorce, the divorce is not granted until some time has elapsed. There might be a mandatory period of separation that precedes the divorce. Often, there is also a mandatory period (usually, a few days) between filing for a marriage request and the granting of a marriage license.

Several examples of cooling-off periods for the US, for the two cases, (a), (b) above, are given in Camerer et al. (2003). Cooling-off periods are an example of asymmetric paternalism. Rational individuals do not need such periods, and when cooling-off periods take the form in (b), a delay of a few days is probably not too costly for such people. Indeed, being rational, they would take the waiting period into account. However, for boundedly rational individuals, cooling-off periods can be welfare improving on account of the various behavioral features noted above.

DEADLINES

One implication of hyperbolic discounting is the tendency of individuals to procrastinate in the completion of some task (see Volume 3). In a multiple selves interpretation, the current self, unless fully sophisticated, typically believes that the future selves will suffer from fewer self-control problems. Hence, the current self, rationally, puts off completion of the task to some future date. If this optimism about future self-control problems is misplaced, the task might never be completed.

Deadlines can often be self-imposed. However, sometimes they are externally imposed, and are legally binding. The paternalistic aim of deadlines is to ensure the completion of a task when the planner perceives that the benefits exceed the costs, say, in the sense of (3.25). For instance, in order to contribute to the tax-exempt individual retirement account (IRA), individuals not only must respect the constraint of a given maximum amount each year, but also the deadline of April 15. Thus, if individuals procrastinate beyond this deadline, their entitlement to the maximum allowed tax allowance for the year is lost. This magnifies the effect of missing the deadline.

Presumably, this deadline should help individuals who procrastinate, to take advantage of the investment opportunity.

Ariely and Wertenbroch (2002) run the following experiment using MIT students. Students had to write three short term papers for a course and they were sorted into two groups. One of the groups was given three equally spaced deadlines for completion of the term papers (the restricted choice condition). The other group could decide to hand in their term papers any time before the end of term (the free choice condition). An identical late submission penalty applied to both groups. Few students in the free choice condition chose to impose equally spaced deadlines on themselves but most did impose some sort of deadlines on themselves. In general, students who were subjected (externally or internally) to evenly spaced deadlines performed better in terms of grades. One possible reason is that this allowed for better budgeting of time. In the absence of such deadlines, students might try to do too much, too late, lowering their grades.

3.3.5 *A critique of soft paternalism*

Recall the *informed desire criterion* in our discussion of libertarian paternalism in Section 3.3.1. Essentially, the criterion suggests that individual choices may be suboptimal, as judged by themselves, in the presence of incomplete information, limited cognitive abilities, and self-control problems. Sunstein and Thaler (2003, p. 1162) treat individuals as not acting in their best interests if they make "decisions that they would change if they had complete information, unlimited cognitive abilities, and no lack of self-control." Sugden (2008, 2013) questions the empirical usefulness of the informed desire criterion on the following grounds.

The concepts of incomplete information, limited cognitive abilities, and self-control need a formal definition. Even if one could define these concepts in a satisfactory manner, it might still be difficult to pin down human behavior if these factors were taken into account. Should we expect preferences to be consistent when we relax these constraints? For instance, a preference for status quo or anchoring might be hardwired, so the informed desired criterion might not eliminate such preferences. This is clearly an unresolved issue and should be an interesting area of research for the future. As Sugden (2008, p. 234) puts it: "Thus, while we can understand how planners might be motivated by paternalism, we are entitled to be sceptical about how far the planners' judgements about other people's well-being are justified, either objectively or inter-subjectively."

How does the choice architect figure out what is best for the individual? The suggestion in libertarian paternalism is that the planner uses cost–benefit analysis (as in (3.25)) or rules of thumb. These recommendations may appear to many readers as vague (Sugden, 2008, p. 233). Guala and Mittone (2015) propose that if it is the case that individual welfare is impossible or too costly to discover, then one may make a case for a political justification for nudging. They argue that since individual biases are likely to cause externalities to others (and to the individuals themselves), the associated social costs may justify nudging interventions on political grounds.

Soft paternalism is relatively silent about issues of political failure. Regulatory capture, where regulators are unduly influenced by special interest groups, and the bounded rationality of bureaucrats, does not ensure that paternalistic choices will be good ones (Glaeser, 2006). However, it is also true that, in a wide range of cases, government policies are the outcome of more deliberate and detailed information processing. These cases are all counterexamples to the proposition that governments functioning under imperfect information and political constraints will necessarily preclude the possibility of any beneficial paternalistic interventions.

For instance, laws on cooling-off periods, various default options, mandatory third party car insurance, compulsory seat belts in cars, and reminders to fill-in tax returns by publicly known deadlines. Furthermore, behavioral economists take great pains to stress caution, field testing, and pilot studies in the application of paternalistic policies.

Gul and Pesendorfer (2008) argue for a separation of the roles of economists as social scientists, in which they attempt to explain economic phenomena, and their roles as advisors/advocates, e.g., for public policy. Economists who do not respect the distinction between these two roles are termed by them as economist-therapists. We examine this critique in more detail in Section 3.5. Gul and Pesendorfer assign a relatively restricted role for economics and economists, a view that is not shared by all economists. Espousing the opposite view, Loewenstein and Haisley (2008, p. 9) write:

Although Gul and Pesendorfer seem to view "therapist" as a pejorative label, we see no reason to not embrace it. Therapy is, in fact, not a bad metaphor for the new types of policies that behavioral economists have been proposing...Just as the therapist endeavors to correct for cognitive and emotional disturbances that detract from the well-being of the patient, such as anxiety, depression, or psychosis, the economist/therapist endeavors to counteract cognitive and emotional barriers to the pursuit of genuine self-interest.

Klick and Mitchell (2006) argue that soft paternalism ignores the long-run costs. By this, they mean (p. 1625), costs that "offset short-run gains because of the negative learning and motivational effects of paternalistic regulations." Paternalistic policies, it is argued, interfere with the learning-by-doing process via a moral hazard argument. Individuals, because they are protected via paternalistic policies, may have a lower incentive to protect themselves against bad outcomes.

While this argument may be true in some cases, there are several counterexamples that apply in cases where learning is either very slow, feedback is poor, or where the outcomes of one's actions are known with substantial delay. For instance, if an individual saves inadequately for his retirement on account of present-biased preferences, then by the time that the outcome (low savings, post-retirement) is revealed, it is too late to learn. This critique is also silent about the forms that learning takes. For instance, suppose that learning takes place through reinforcement learning. Then, presumably, soft paternalism, which nudges the individual in the direction of actions that produce a better outcome, reinforces the use of such actions in future.

3.3.6 *A note on behavioral welfare criteria*

Given the discussion so far, what is the appropriate welfare criterion? This is a difficult question on which there appears to be no consensus. This section briefly outlines some of the issues.

One approach is to use self-reported assessments of happiness as a proxy for welfare. This approach draws on the distinction between *experienced utility* and *decision utility*. These issues have already been discussed in Section 1.9 in Chapter 1, so our discussion here will be brief. Decision utility refers to the practice in economics of inferring utility functions from the observed choices of individuals. Experienced utility is the hedonic experience associated with an outcome (Bentham, 1789; Kahneman et al., 1997).

Since experienced utility is one's subjective recollection of the satisfaction derived from a good or service in the past, its measurement can pose problems. For instance, it is well established that self-reported survey questions that report experienced utility are subjected to biases, such as *duration neglect*, and *peak-end evaluation* (Kahneman et al., 1997). However, evidence shows that subjective measures of well-being are consistent with the actual choices of the vast majority of subjects and these measures are the best predictors of choices (Benjamin et al., 2012). As shown in Section 1.9, such subjective measures successfully predict a range of phenomena such as job quits, probability of suicides, productivity, and the probability of a future divorce among couples.

The phenomenal growth in the literature on happiness economics shows that an increasing number of economists take experienced utility as an objective and useful indicator of an individual's welfare. Some have forcefully advocated the maximization of happiness as the goal of government policy (Layard, 2005). However, others continue to be skeptical (Loewenstein and Haisley, 2008). First, as noted above, the recollection of a past event could be influenced by current moods or emotions and subject to duration neglect and peak-end bias. Second, individuals might adapt to the current level of conditions in their life. For instance, once accustomed to their condition, the happiness levels of patients on dialysis were found to be very similar to a control set of healthy patients (Riis et al., 2005; Ubel et al., 2005). Many would find the resulting policy recommendation that ill-health is not an undesirable outcome to be troublesome.

If people make mistakes in their choices, then one solution is to provide them with the correct information first. Individuals can then maximize their utility in the usual manner. This is the so-called *informed utility approach*. In actual practice, government regulation tries to impart a variety of information to consumers, such as warnings on cigarette packs, content-labeling on food items, and even, in the case of the UK, daily recommended amounts of fruits and vegetables etc. Armed with the appropriate information, the resulting 'debiased choice' of individuals could then form the basis of welfare criteria.

A concern with this approach is that it does not specify the exact method of imparting information; this is important because there are potential framing effects associated with different methods of information provision. Consider the well-known example from Tversky and Kahneman (1981) in which individuals make different choices when the instructions are phrased in terms of "lives lost" rather than "lives saved" (see Volumes 1 and 5). Indeed, deciding on the appropriate frame/context within which the information is to be presented will require some welfare criteria, but this takes us back to the original problem of constructing welfare criteria in the presence of behavioral biases. A second source of concern for the informed utility approach is that while it can potentially counter mistakes that are made on account of imperfect information, it does not address the issue of mistakes (relative to the neoclassical benchmark) that are made when all information is available. For instance, individuals might have self-control problems, or they might rely on a range of judgment heuristics (see Volumes 3 and 5).

There is growing popularity of choice-based measures of welfare that correspond to decision utility (Bernheim and Rangel, 2007, 2009); see Sections 3.5 and 3.6 below. These measures assume that despite the enumeration of behavioral biases in behavioral economics, there is a strong systematic component to human behavior that is enriched by psychological considerations. Hence, choice data can be used to disentangle the systematic component. However, when choices are inconsistent as, for instance, in the evaluation of new products (see the discussion on coherent arbitrariness in Volume 5) then one may trim the existing choices to those that are well-behaved. Once trimmed of "undesirable" choices, the choice criteria retain their usefulness. However, it is not always clear how choices are to be trimmed. Bernheim and Rangel (2009) suggest using non-choice data, for instance, data from brain scans. However, reservations have also been expressed about the ability of neuroeconomic studies to determine which choices are welfare enhancing (Loewenstein and Haisley, 2008).

3.4 Regulation under imperfect self-information

In neoclassical economics, the standard assumption is that consumers have better information about their types relative to firms. In the leading textbook example of asymmetric information, from the area of health insurance, consumers are better informed than firms about their own state of health. The firm then designs clever contracts to truthfully elicit the state of health of the consumers. However, in many cases, consumers might have limited information on their usage of a product, and the usage data collected by the firm could give an informational edge to firms. This could be the case, for instance, in information collected by cell phone companies or Internet search engines.

It is pertinent to explore the effects on consumer welfare when information is provided to consumers of their own usage. Examples include power companies in Britain offering to put electricity meters in peoples' houses to enable them to monitor their usage on a continual basis. Once consumers are informed of their usage, they might wish to switch firms. Mullainathan et al. (2012) show this to be the case in a randomized field experiment in the usage of Medicare Part D prescription drug plans in the United States; 28% of the group of subjects that received a letter with personalized cost information switched their providers, as compared to 17% who switched in a comparison group.

The RECAP regulation that we considered above, highlights the welfare effects of information provision in this case. We now consider a model, due to Kamenica et al. (2011), that formalizes the effect of RECAP type regulations.

Suppose that consumers are distributed uniformly over the unit interval, $[0,1]$. Any consumer uses $x \in \{1,3\}$ units of service, per month, provided by a private firm. Half the consumers use 1 unit and the other half uses 3 units. However, consumers are imperfectly informed of their own private usage, say, due to limited attention.

Each consumer receives an iid signal, $\theta \in \{1,3\}$, of her usage. Signal accuracy is captured as follows. Let $p(x \mid \theta)$ be the conditional probability that the usage is x, conditional on the signal, θ. Then,

$$p(x \mid \theta) = \begin{cases} \lambda \in \left[\frac{1}{2},1\right] & if \quad x = \theta \\ 1 - \lambda & if \quad x \neq \theta \end{cases},$$

thus, the signal is accurate about the true usage with probability λ. We can now determine the expected usage of each consumer, conditional on the signal received, $E[x \mid \theta]$.

$$E[x \mid \theta] = x_i p(x_i \mid \theta) + x_j p(x_j \mid \theta); x_i \neq x_j \in \{1,3\}, \theta \in \{1,3\}.$$

Thus,

$$E[x \mid \theta = 1] = 3 - 2\lambda \text{ and } E[x \mid \theta = 3] = 1 + 2\lambda. \tag{3.26}$$

The utility function of each consumer, on receiving the signal, θ, is given by

$$U(\theta) = 1 - E[x \mid \theta] - E[M(\theta)], \tag{3.27}$$

where $E[M(\theta)]$ is the expected monetary payment from the consumer to the firm based on the signal received. In this reduced-form model, utility is decreasing in expected usage to reflect the fact that often when consumers are informed about their usage, they are likely to be surprised by the level of usage, and often switch providers of the service in the hope of getting a better deal.

Suppose that there are two providers of the service, A and B. Firm A charges a fixed monthly price of $P_A = 2$, irrespective of usage, thus, $E[M(\theta)] = 2$. Firm B charges a per unit price equal to $P_B = 1$, so if the usage is $x = 1$ the consumer pays 1 and if the usage is $x = 3$, the consumer pays 3.[6] Thus, if consumers knew their own usage with certainty (and had no need to rely on the signal θ), then those with $x = 3$ would prefer to buy from firm A and those with $x = 1$ from firm B.

Now suppose that consumers did not know their usage with certainty and need to rely on the signal to infer their usage. Consider consumers who receive a high usage signal, $\theta = 3$. For such consumers, we can calculate their utility from buying from firm A, $U(\theta = 3, A)$ and buying from firm B, $U(\theta = 3, B)$ as follows.

$$U(\theta = 3, A) = 1 - E[x \mid 3] - 2.$$
$$U(\theta = 3, B) = 1 - E[x \mid 3] - [3E[3 \mid 3] + E[1 \mid 3]]$$
$$= 1 - E[x \mid 3] - (1 + 2\lambda).$$

Since $\lambda \in \left[\frac{1}{2}, 1\right]$, it follows that $1 + 2\lambda \geq 2$ so $U(\theta = 3, A) \geq U(\theta = 3, B)$. Thus, consumers who receive a high signal will buy from firm A. A simple calculation shows that those who receive a low usage signal will prefer to purchase from firm B because $U(\theta = 1, B) \geq U(\theta = 1, A)$.

The expected expenditure of all consumers, given that half get a high signal and half get a low signal, is given by $Y = \frac{1}{2}P_A + \frac{1}{2}E[x \mid \theta = 1]P_B$. Using (3.26) and $P_A = 2$, $P_B = 1$, we get

$$Y = 1 + \left(\frac{3}{2} - \lambda\right). \tag{3.28}$$

The first term in (3.28) is the expected expenditure of those who receive a high signal and the second term is the expected expenditure of those who receive a low signal.

Proposition 3.2   *Consumer regulation that provides consumers information about their own usage, decreases expected consumer expenditure and increases their welfare.*

Proof: Regulation that provides consumers information about their usage is equivalent to increasing the accuracy of the signal, λ, in informing consumers of their usage. From (3.28), overall expected expenditure of consumers falls, as λ increases. From (3.27), this increases $U(\theta)$, which is a measure of consumer welfare. ∎

In actual practice, providing information to consumers under regulations such as RECAP will also alter prices, which are assumed given in the model, above. Perhaps intuition might suggest that the resulting desire of consumers to change providers may also put downward pressure on prices. However, Kamenica et al. (2011) give the following useful analogy to show that this need not be the case.

---

[6] It is possible to endogenously derive the optimality of different pricing schemes for firms; see, for instance, Piccione and Spiegler (2012).

Suppose that two firms with identical costs compete in prices under Hotelling price competition and consumers are uniformly distributed over the interval $[0, 1]$. When consumers do not know their own usage, $x \in \{1, 3\}$, and receive no signals, both firms appear identical to them. Thus, in a Bertrand equilibrium, the firms set prices equal to their marginal costs. Suppose that consumer regulation informs each consumer of their usage. Now firms can employ different pricing schemes (e.g., a fixed monthly price or a price based on usage). Based on their level of usage and traveling costs, consumers no longer find the firms to be symmetric. Firms can take advantage of this "new" market power by extracting some of the surplus. Thus, consumers may pay a higher price.

3.5 Choice and non-choice data: What is the scope of economics?

Should economics restrict itself to choice data alone, or should it also be open to the use of non-choice data? In "The case for mindless economics," Gul and Pesendorfer (2008) present an extreme case for restricting the boundaries of economics to choice data alone. Indeed, it would not be surprising if many economists hold the same views, although most behavioral economists are unlikely to subscribe to it. Hence, it is important to examine the opposing arguments in more detail. Gul and Pesendorfer's views are summarized under four main points, GP1 to GP4, below.

GP1. Non-choice data is inadmissible in economics because the scope of economics is restricted to inferring an individual's preferences from observed choices. Non-choice data, such as neuroeconomic data, or self-reported survey data, or non-incentivized experimental data, is inconsistent with the scope of welfare economics. It is not entirely clear if Gul and Pesendorfer approve of data from experiments conducted under proper incentive compatibility conditions or whether experimental data in which subjects make choices may also be classified as choice data.

Welfare and choice are identical. If an individual chooses option A over B then his welfare is higher under option A. The reasons why he chose A, for instance, impulsive buying, limited attention, free will, and biological necessity, are irrelevant to economics. They write (p. 5): "The standard definition of welfare is appropriate because standard economics has no therapeutic ambition; it does not try to improve the decision-maker but tries to evaluate how economic institutions mediate (perhaps psychologically unhealthy) behavior of agents."

Non-choice data cannot be used to invalidate neoclassical economics. In particular, data from neuroeconomics has no bearing on the validity of economic models because economic models make no assumptions about the neuroeconomic foundations of choice. They write (p. 7): "Our conclusion is that the neuroeconomic critique fails to refute any particular (standard) economic model and offers no challenge to standard economic methodology."

GP2. There is a limited role for insights from psychology in economics because the two disciplines ask different questions, and have different conventions and terms. They differentiate the scope of economics and psychology by writing (p. 10): "economics and psychology do not offer competing, all-purpose models of human nature. Nor do they offer all-purpose tools. Rather, each discipline uses specialized abstractions that have proven useful for that discipline." And on p. 22 they write: "Economics and psychology differ in the question they ask. Therefore, abstractions that are useful for one discipline will typically be not very useful for the other."

GP3. Economists are not advocates for any normative criteria, even when the "right normative criterion is unambiguous" (p. 29). They give the example of Bayes' rule, which could be advocated on normative grounds, yet economists typically do not do so. They write (p. 35): "Populating economic models with 'flesh-and-blood human' beings was never the objective of economists."

GP4. Neoclassical economics is sufficiently flexible that the observed departures from the neoclassical model can be explained by modifying the neoclassical model without changing its nature. Mistakes or biases that are highlighted in behavioral economics can be accommodated within neoclassical economics by changing the feasible strategies. They give the example of American tourists in the UK who suffer injuries and fatalities because they look to the left (Bernheim and Rangel, 2004). The solution proposed by Gul and Pesendorfer (p. 23) is as follows. The action "look right" is not in the feasible set of American tourists visiting the UK. However, if they are alerted with a sign "look right" then their feasible set changes and they will indeed "look right" eliminating the supposed mistake.

These views, and others expressed in the Gul–Pesendorfer paper, are the subject of an insightful set of contributions in the edited volume by Caplin and Schotter (2008). We mostly focus on three contributions, each with a fairly instructive title: Camerer (2008) responds under the title "The case for mindful economics." Schotter (2008) offers the views of an experimental economist under the title "What's so informative about choice?" Köszegi and Rabin (2008a) give their views under the title: "Revealed mistakes and revealed preference."[7]

GP1, GP2, and GP3 are subjectively defined boundaries of economics that are extremely narrow. Indeed, great progress has been made in behavioral economics by looking beyond these boundaries. Camerer (2008, p. 44) speaks for many behavioral economists, when, commenting on GP1 and GP2, he writes: "This argument is simply a definition of economics as inherently mindless, and there is no debating a definition. The definition simply draws a preferred boundary rather than makes an evidentiary 'case' for mindless economics." He continues (p. 59): "Much of GP's paper is linguistic gerrymandering by defining economics as the revealed preference approach, then constantly reminding the reader that anything else is, by their definition, not economics."

This leaves only GP4 as the potentially interesting argument to ponder over. In fact, this argument goes to the heart of how economists should practice their craft; for a fuller discussion, see the introductory chapter. Economists have been extremely ingenious in constructing theoretical arguments to explain empirical phenomena. Indeed, given enough freedom to make auxiliary assumptions in standard neoclassical models, one can explain almost any observed behavior. Consider, for instance, the solution suggested by Gul–Pesendorfer to the problem of mistakes made by American tourists in GP4. Their suggestion is to keep the neoclassical framework intact, but explain the observation through changes in the feasible set.

A behavioral or an experimental economist would naturally ask: "Does the data on American tourists in the UK support the proposed explanation?" Indeed, many neoclassical economists

---

[7] The reader may also wish to consult the paper by Caplin (2008) in the same volume. Since we have covered similar ground elsewhere in Volume 4 and in Chapter 1, we omit a repetition of these issues here.

would also agree with this suggestion. However, so rapid is the pace of theoretical proposals in the neoclassical tradition to explain departures from the neoclassical model that the supply of models has outstripped the supply of diagnostic data (Camerer, 2008, p. 47). In many cases, the freedom in the use of auxiliary assumptions in neoclassical economics to explain observed departures from the model, often by invoking bogus "as if" arguments, accords well with the definition of "ad-hoc" in science.

In some places, Gul and Pesendorfer (2008) appear to protect neoclassical theories from stringent diagnostic testing by suggesting that they should not be taken literally. For instance, commenting on the Kreps–Porteus explanation of a psychological phenomenon (the details are not relevant here), they write (p. 15): "While the formula is suggestive of a mental process, this suggestiveness is an expositional device not meant to be taken literally. The formula encapsulates the behavioral assumptions of the theory in a user-friendly way and thereby facilitates applications of the theory to (more complicated) economic problems."

Among some other important responses made by Camerer (2008) to the Gul and Pesendorfer framework are the following (page numbers below refer to the Camerer (2008) article). See Chapter 4 for some the details of the neuroeconomic aspects of Camerer's arguments.

1. Firms that introduce brand new products (or services), and regulators asked to formulate regulations for these products often cannot depend on existing choice data to predict consumer behavior. Hence, choice data, by itself, has limitations to make predictions in some domains. Yet, in actual practice, firms do introduce billions of dollars worth of new products every year after market research that is largely based on non-choice survey data of potential consumers. Yet, most economists will not argue that these economically significant decisions lie outside the scope of economics.

2. When there are several competing theories that explain given choices, then studying the neural basis of these theories can potentially help us to choose among competing theories. Unlike the assertion of Gul and Pesendorfer, important economic variables of interest such as the coefficient of relative risk aversion and loss aversion have been measured using neuroeconomic data (p. 49). The neural correlates of several economic variables, such as discount rates have been discovered (p. 49). Deception is correlated with pupil dilation (non-choice data), hence, it can be used as the basis for predicting the state of the world from a message (p. 51).

3. Economists can benefit by importing terms from psychology (and vice versa). Consider the following case study. Gul and Pesendorfer (2008) give an example of the term *cue* that they feel is unsatisfactory for economists because it lumps together two distinct phenomena: *complements* and *externalities* (e.g., fries might be the cue to eat hamburgers). Hence, they argue (pp. 11, 12): "The concept of a 'cue' offers a good illustration of how abstractions from psychology are inappropriate for economics and, conversely, how the corresponding economic concepts are inappropriate for psychology and neuroscience." They suggest that economists stick to defining terms in a manner that is underpinned by their own terminology and abstractions.

   Camerer (2008) argues that precisely because we do not have words in economics that describe goods/states that are complements and externality causing, importing terms such as cues is useful. He writes (p. 55): "So we could adapt the language of economics to describe 'cues' as 'dynamically adaptive, rapidly reinstateable asymmetric complements to consumption.' Or we can just learn a new vocabulary word—'cue' which summarizes certain kinds of complements."

4. Let us revisit the example of the American tourist in GP4, above. Camerer (2008) suggests, sensibly, that one can interpret the American tourist looking for cars in the UK as engaged in a *Stroop task* (see Volume 5) and his mistake in looking left and crossing a road is a *Stroop mistake*.[8] The fact that people get better at a given Stroop task with experience, i.e., commit fewer Stroop mistakes, suggests that it is not very probable that changes in the feasible set account for the mistakes of American tourists in the UK.

Schotter (2008) examines the Gul–Pesendorfer arguments from an experimental economist's point of view. We summarize some of his arguments below.

In making their case for using choice data, Gul and Pesendorfer (2008, p. 8) argue that: "Standard economics focuses on revealed preference because economic data come in this form." Schotter (pp. 73–4) does not dispute this claim or the importance of choice data; however, he argues that we should not make a virtue out of a constraint (that most economic data comes in this form). Indeed, all sorts of data that help us to test the predictions of economic models should be used.

Furthermore, it is worth asking if actual choice data materializes for the reasons assumed in neoclassical economics, say, the maximization of a well-defined utility function. What if choice data also arises from other considerations such as emotions, advice from friends, satisficing heuristics, simply following the herd, or any of a range of judgment heuristics described in Volume 5? Choice data does not reflect the reasons for choice. So, in order to test alternative theories, say, based on emotions or psychological game theory (see Volume 4), it might be unavoidable to use non-choice data, for instance, based on elicited beliefs.

In some cases, it might be important to discover why choices are made in order to test the predictions of the relevant theory. Consider the 2×2 matching pennies strategic form game shown in Figure 3.1 from Goeree and Holt (2001). First, suppose that $x = 80$ in the payoff matrix in Figure 3.1. In this case, there is a unique Nash equilibrium in mixed strategies in which each player randomizes equally between the two pure strategies. In their experiments, Goeree and Holt find that the players played each of their pure strategies with nearly equal probabilities, which is consistent with the Nash outcome.

Now let $x = 320$. This should leave unchanged the behavior of the row player because, in neoclassical theory, his choice of a probability distribution over his pure strategies is designed to make the opponent indifferent between his equilibrium pure strategies. Thus, in the mixed strategy equilibrium, corresponding to $x = 320$, the row player plays Top and Bottom with equal probabilities while the column player plays Left with probability $\frac{1}{8}$ and Right with probability $\frac{7}{8}$. However, in contrast to the predictions of classical game theory, row players now choose Top, 96% of the time.

	Left	Right
Top	x, 40	40, 80
Bottom	40, 80	80, 40

Figure 3.1 A 2×2 matching pennies game.

[8] A Stroop task is an automatic, practiced, response by System 1 (such as looking left while crossing a road) that can be incorrect (e.g., in the UK, the American tourist must look right before crossing a road). System 2, the deliberative system, may or may not be able to rein in System 1 while it is making a Stroop mistake.

When $x = 80$, the outcome is close to a Nash equilibrium, yet the choice of a Nash equilibrium is accidental in the symmetric game. A researcher who construed support for a mixed strategy Nash equilibrium based on this choice data would be misled because in the asymmetric game, the outcome differs significantly from a Nash equilibrium. It would appear that some economists view experimental data, even when subjects are properly incentivized, as non-choice data. In this strict view, only market data, say, price–quantity pairs, are admissible. Yet, if the market was mostly like the world with $x = 80$, it might not be able to refute the mixed strategy Nash equilibrium. Furthermore, this example provides a good illustration of why experiments in economics are critical.

Another example of non-choice data is the use of *mouselab software* to study the pattern of search and look ups in experimental games and infer its consistency with solution concepts in game theory, such as backward induction. For instance, in Volume 4 we considered a three period sequential bargaining game where the cake size shrinks in successive rounds (Johnson et al., 2002). The observed pattern of searches and lookups appears to be inconsistent with backward induction. For instance, subjects search forward, not backward, and only about 7% of the time is spent looking at the information in the last stage. Many subjects act as if they were playing a single stage ultimatum game in which the mean offer is about 40% of the cake size in that round. These results are valuable, despite the fact that economic theory makes no direct assumptions about the pattern of search and lookups. In a clever experimental design, Johnson et al. (2002) find that when subjects are trained in backward induction, they are more likely to search backwards, giving credence to their proposed method. This highlights why the experimental method must be critical to economics. Indeed, one might never be able to stringently test economic theory otherwise.

Survey data, another form of non-choice data, has provided a major impetus to progress in the rapidly expanding literature on happiness economics. This is discussed in more detail in Chapter 1 and other observations on survey data are made in the introductory chapter, so we omit further discussion here.

Actual choice data might be restricted to a subset of the parameter space, which might not allow for stringent tests of theory. We have already illustrated this observation above, but consider another insightful example by Schotter (2008) based on the work of Eliaz and Schotter (2010).

There are two boxes, A and B. A monetary prize is hidden in one of the boxes. The probability that the prize is hidden in box A in state $i = h, l$ is $p_i(A)$ such that $0.5 < p_l(A) < p_h(A)$. In treatment 1, there are two stages. In the first stage, the subject can pay a fee to learn the state, $i = h, l$; if no fee is paid, then the state is not learnt. In the second stage, subjects choose a box, A or B followed immediately by the payment of the prize if the correct box is chosen. In treatment 2, in the first stage, subjects choose a box, A or B. In the second stage they can pay a fee to learn the state of nature before being paid a prize if they choose the correct box.

Since $0.5 < p_l(A)$, choosing box A first order stochastically dominates choosing box B, irrespective of the state or the individual's attitudes towards risk. Thus, anyone who pays a fee has non-classical preferences. Two alternative explanations for the payment of a fee are considered. The first is the Kreps and Porteus (1978) framework that can accommodate the payment of a fee because subjects have a preference for an early resolution of uncertainty. The second explanation is the *confidence effect*; here people pay a fee just to feel happier from choosing a box that has a higher probability of a prize.

The two frameworks make different predictions. For instance, if as in Kreps–Porteus, individuals have a preference for early resolution of uncertainty, then such a preference should manifest in both treatments. However, if behavior is explained by the confidence effect, then it should have bite only in treatment 1 where subjects learn of the state before they actually make their choice of a box. The results are shown in Table 3.1 for three situations, which correspond to different combinations of the fee and the probabilities (the situation numbers, 3, 6, 12, correspond to those in Eliaz and Schotter, 2010).

Since the fraction of subjects who decide to pay the fee is so starkly different in the two treatments, the results reject the Kreps–Porteus model for the given data. Furthermore, a far higher fraction of subjects are willing to pay the fee in treatment 1, which is consistent with the confidence effect. Suppose that the real-world choice data came only from treatment 1, but never from treatment 2, then choices might suggest support for the Kreps–Porteus framework. However, appropriate experimental design allows for stringent testing of theory, leading to the opposite conclusion.

Yet another reason for looking beyond choice data comes from framing effects. A pervasive finding is that choices are sensitive to framing, hence, without considering the frame, incorrect inferences are likely to be made. Consider, for instance, the well-known problem from Kahneman and Tversky (1984) in which the same information is framed either in terms of lives saved or lives lost (see Volumes 1 and 5). The results demonstrated that individuals make choices consistent with risk averse behavior in the domain of gains and risk-loving behavior in the domain of losses. However, if the frame is not explicitly considered as a part of the description of the problem, one may make an incorrect inference about the risk preferences of individuals from the observed choices.

Köszegi and Rabin (2008a) chiefly address the issue raised in GP4. They argue (p. 198) that introducing ad-hoc auxiliary assumptions in neoclassical models can produce *wacky theories* if one is not willing to entertain the possibility that individuals may make mistakes in their choices. This is particularly disturbing when more plausible, psychologically well-founded, alternatives are available. They propose a framework, developed slightly more formally in Köszegi and Rabin (2008b), that recognizes mistakes in choices, yet attempts to recover the underlying preferences.

The supposition is that despite the propensity of people to make mistakes, there is an underlying degree of coherence to preferences. Thus, choices are not simply random and mistakes are systematic. They propose proceeding along the following lines.

1. Impose as few restrictions as possible on preferences.
2. Compare the subjective beliefs of individuals against objective probabilities. If the two tally then choices reflect welfare.
3. If subjective and objective beliefs do not tally then propose a theory in which individuals have well-defined underlying preferences but they make mistakes.

Let us consider the possibility that individuals suffer from the *gambler's fallacy* (see Volume 5 for details). Suppose that an individual observes a series of coin tosses and q is her elicited belief

Table 3.1 Fraction of subjects who pay the fee in each treatment.

Situation	Fee ($)	Probabilities		Fraction of subjects who pay fee	
		$p_l(A)$	$P_h(A)$	Treatment 1	Treatment 2
3	0.50	0.61	1	0.783	0.063
6	2.00	0.51	1	0.565	0.125
12	0.50	0.51	1	0.739	0.125

Source: Schotter (2008).

that the next toss will produce tails (T) rather than heads (H).[9] When no flips are observed, the individual chooses $q = 0.5$; when the sequence of consecutive flips $HHHHHH$ is observed, $q = 0.55$; when the sequence of consecutive flips $TTTTTT$ is observed, $q = 0.45$. One may, as in GP4, propose a neoclassical model in which the individual has a preference to bet on T after observing the sequence $HHHHHH$ and a preference for betting on H after observing the sequence $TTTTTT$; but this is a "wacky" set of preferences that is hard to justify. A more compelling argument is that the individual's subjective beliefs differ from the objective beliefs, and the individual makes a mistake that is consistent with the well-known gambler's fallacy.

Conditional on the assumption that the individual suffers from the gambler's fallacy, we give examples of inferences about preferences that we could draw from these choices.

> **Example 3.2** *Suppose that following any sequence of coin tosses, an individual is asked which of the two fruits, blueberries or strawberries, would he commit to strictly preferring, following the outcome of the next toss. When the sequence is: (i) HHHHHH, he reveals that he strictly prefers blueberries to strawberries if a T comes up on the next toss (and the converse preference if H comes up). (ii) TTTTTT, he reveals that he strictly prefers strawberries to blueberries if a T comes up on the next toss (and the converse preference if H comes up). (iii) the null sequence (no flips of the coin yet), he reveals that he is indifferent between the fruits, irrespective of the outcome on the next toss. Given that the individual exhibits the gambler's fallacy and has preferences that do not depend on coin flips, therefore, he prefers blueberries to strawberries.*

> **Example 3.3** *Consider two individuals, classical (C) and behavioral (B). They choose one of two consumption bundles (x_h, x_t) or (y_h, y_t). The first and the second elements in each bundle can be consumed if the next toss of a coin turns out to be, respectively, H and T. Individual C chooses (x_h, x_t) over (y_h, y_t) if*
>
> $$0.5u(x_h) + 0.5u(x_t) > 0.5u(y_h) + 0.5u(y_t). \tag{3.29}$$

Individual B chooses as follows. For the null history (no observed flips) B chooses in accordance with (3.29). If the history is HHHHHH, then (x_h, x_t) is chosen over (y_h, y_t) if

$$0.45u(x_h) + 0.55u(x_t) > 0.45u(y_h) + 0.55u(y_t). \tag{3.30}$$

Finally, if the history is TTTTTT, then B chooses (x_h, x_t) over (y_h, y_t) if

$$0.55u(x_h) + 0.45u(x_t) > 0.55u(y_h) + 0.45u(y_t). \tag{3.31}$$

The behavior of individual C is unproblematic for neoclassical economics. Following GP4, if one stays within the neoclassical framework, then one will need to invoke ad-hoc auxiliary assumptions to explain the choices of individual B, interpreted now as a classical individual. For instance, one could postulate that the individual has a preference for betting on changes in coin flips. However, because the classical individual does know and use objective probabilities (see (3.29)), such wacky preferences will lose money for the individual.

A simpler explanation is that individual B is not a classical individual and suffers from the gambler's fallacy. Indeed, we can identify the preferences of B from the choice data. The behavior of such an individual is consistent with being an expected utility maximizer who

---

[9] For the details of the proposed modification to the Becker–DeGroot–Marshak mechanism that may be used to produce these elicited beliefs, see Köszegi and Rabin (2008a).

suffers from the gambler's fallacy. In an apparent response to the Gul–Pesendorfer framework, Köszegi and Rabin (2008a) write (p. 201):[10] *"We admit to not really understanding why we would at all be inclined to ban the study of B from economics departments, but we are especially chagrined at that prospect in light of the fact that we can use the same powerful tools of economics to study B as C in this case. B has well-ordered and coherent preferences. She is making an error in statistical reasoning. The two can be jointly identified. It is useful to do so."*

Example 3.4   *There is one caveat to the explanation in Example 3.3. Choice behavior may indicate a mistake. However, there could be more than one competing explanation for the mistake, and the welfare implications are dependent on the chosen explanation. Consider an experiment in which pregnant women are asked, prior to going into labor, if they would ask for an epidural injection during childbirth. Suppose that most women choose natural childbirth, yet when they go into labor, they change their mind and ask for an epidural injection.*

One potential explanation of this empirically observed phenomenon is projection-bias (see Part 6) in which pregnant women underappreciate how painful their labor will be. A second explanation is hyperbolic discounting in which the present bias at the time of labor tips the scales in favor of the epidural. There is no role for commitment under projection bias. Indeed, the decision to take an epidural at the time of labor is the welfare maximizing choice for the individual. However, if the source of the mistake is hyperbolic discounting, then the individual might find it optimal to invest in a commitment technology to bind herself to the original, ex-ante, choice. In this case, one will need extra information to determine which of the two explanations is the correct one.

3.6 Choice-based behavioral welfare economics

In this section, we consider the choice-based measure of welfare of Bernheim and Rangel (2007, 2009); the basic rationale is discussed in Section 3.3.6.

In neoclassical economics, one may proceed with standard welfare analysis in one of two possible ways. One can either specify preferences and then derive a *choice function* from it. Alternatively, one can directly specify a choice function and then derive the corresponding preferences. The two methods are equivalent; for a lucid account see Chapter 2 in Kreps (1990). Bernheim and Rangel choose the second method, i.e., begin with a choice function and then derive implications for preferences.

Suppose that $\mathbf{X}$ is the set of all possible choice objects. Choice objects are not restricted, so these could, for instance, be consumption bundles, or lotteries of dated profiles of intertemporal consumption. Denote the constraint set by $X \subseteq \mathbf{X}$. The general nature of the choice set allows this framework to address static and dynamic problems under risk. An ancillary condition, A, is any set of environment conditions such as default options, status quo, anchors or other framing conditions that are not relevant to the evaluation of an individual's welfare by a social planner.

Define a *generalized choice situation* (GCS) by $g = (X, A)$. Suppose that the individual must choose from n different GCSs: $(X_1, A_1), \ldots, (X_n, A_n)$. These can be collapsed into a single GCS, $g' = (X', A')$ where $X' = \cup_{j=1}^{n} X_j$ and A' specifies how the choice is to be made from the n different GCSs. Denote by G^*, the universal set of all GCSs allowed by a theory; thus, G^* is theory-specific.

---

[10] In the quote we have replaced Fiona with individual B and Giles with individual C from the original quote.

For instance, anchors or defaults might play no role in some theories but play a central role in others. Let $G \subseteq G^*$ be a trimmed-down universal set that contains all the *welfare relevant* GCSs; G is the *welfare relevant domain* for normative analysis in which choices reveal "true objectives" of the decision maker. We discuss the issue of specifying G later.

Next, we define a choice correspondence that maps any GCS into a set of choice objects.

Definition 3.4 (*Choice correspondence*): *A choice correspondence is defined as* $C : G^* \rightarrow \mathbf{X}$ *and* $C(g) \subseteq \mathbf{X}$ *for all* $g = (X, A) \in G^*$.

We now define the set of all constraint sets, X, such that for some ancillary condition, A, the resulting GCS, (X, A) is in the welfare relevant domain, i.e.,

$$\chi = \{X : \exists A \text{ such that } (X, A) \in G\}. \tag{3.32}$$

The following two assumptions are needed to make further progress.

A1: Every nonempty finite subset of $\mathbf{X}$ is a member of the set χ, defined in (3.32).

A2: $C(g)$ (see Definition 3.4) is nonempty for all $g \in G$.

The assumptions made so far allow for intransitive choices, and choices that are influenced by irrelevant alternatives or context. The constraint sets are not required to be compact. In conjunction with the general nature of choice objects, this framework allows a very wide range of questions to be asked.

Example 3.5 (*The cafeteria problem; Sunstein and Thaler, 2003; Thaler and Sunstein, 2003*): *Consider the cafeteria example from Section 3.3.1. Suppose that there are only two choice objects: healthy snacks, h, and unhealthy snacks, u, so* $\mathbf{X} = \{h, u\}$ *and* $X = \{h, u\}$; *from assumption A2, choices from singleton sets are trivial, hence, we suppress them. The ancillary condition specifies which object is placed at eye level where it is more salient. Let the ancillary conditions* A_1 *and* A_2 *denote, respectively, healthy and unhealthy snacks placed at eye level. Let* $g_1 = (\{h, u\}, A_1)$, $g_2 = (\{h, u\}, A_2)$, *then the universal set of all GCSs is (also recall that singleton choice sets are suppressed)*

$$G^* = \{g_1, g_2\}.$$

Suppose that the welfare relevant domain is defined to be the one where the healthy snacks are always placed at eye level, so

$$G = \{g_1\}.$$

Using (3.32),

$$\chi = \{\{h, u\}, \{h\}, \{u\}\}.$$

Suppose that the choice correspondence is defined by

$$C(g_1) = \{h\}, \ C(g_2) = \{u\}. \tag{3.33}$$

The non-empty subsets of $\mathbf{X}$ *are* $\{h, u\}$, $\{h\}$ *and* $\{u\}$ *and all three sets are in* χ *so assumption A1 is satisfied. Furthermore, from (3.33), assumption A2 is also satisfied (note that we have suppressed singleton sets in (3.33)).*

Example 3.6 *(Time inconsistency): Consider an individual who suffers from time inconsistency of preferences, say, due to hyperbolic discounting. Suppose that* $\mathbf{X} = \{x, y\}$, *where x and y are time t payoffs. Two ancillary conditions, A_1, A_2, respectively, denote choices made at time $t-1$ and time t, respectively. Thus, $g_1 = (\{x,y\}, A_1)$, $g_2 = (\{x,y\}, A_2)$ and $G^* = \{g_1, g_2\}$. The generalized choice problem g_1 specifies the choice set from which the choice is made at time $t-1$; g_2 plays the corresponding role at time t. Suppose that the choices of the individual are*

$$C(g_1) = \{x\}, \ C(g_2) = \{y\}. \tag{3.34}$$

Thus, the decision maker reveals preference reversals in dated choices. Since choice-based measures can only rely on the choices made, thus, the choices in (3.34) provide conflicting guidance to the planner. One way out for the planner is to treat the welfare relevant domain either as $G = \{g_1\}$ or $G = \{g_2\}$. In this case, inconsistent choices are trimmed away. But which of the two welfare relevant domains should the planner choose?
This aspect of the framework has been criticized by Sugden (2008) and Loewenstein and Haisley (2008). Clearly, one is then forced to rely on non-choice data to discover the welfare relevant domain. But if some welfare criteria has to be employed by the planner to resolve this problem, then we are back to square one. One suggestion by Bernheim and Rangel (2009) is to use neuroeconomic data to see which of the two choices really reflects the individual's welfare. Whether advances in neuroeconomics will allow us to do so is an open question.

Let us now develop the analogs of the neoclassical weak and strong choice relations. We restrict ourselves to the welfare relevant domain, G, ignoring questions about how it might have been discovered, or whether it could ever be discovered.

Definition 3.5 *(Weak unambiguous choice): Let $x, y \in X$ and let G be the welfare relevant domain.*

(a) *We say that x is "weakly unambiguously chosen" over y, written xRy, if*

For all $(X, A) \in G$ and $x, y \in X$, if $y \in C(X, A)$ then $x \in C(X, A)$.

(b) *Let P denote the asymmetric component of R, so*

$xPy \Leftrightarrow xRy$ but not yRx.

(c) *Let I denote the symmetric component of R, so*

$xIy \Leftrightarrow xRy$ and yRx.

This means that whenever x is chosen, y is also chosen and vice versa.

Example 3.7 *Let $X_1 = \{x, y\}$, $X_2 = \{y, z\}$, $X_3 = \{x, z\}$, $X_4 = \{x, y, z\}$, $X_5 = \{x\}$, $X_6 = \{y\}$, $X_7 = \{z\}$ and $\chi = \{X_1, \ldots, X_7\}$. We ignore the singleton sets X_5, X_6, X_7 because the choice from these sets is trivial, given assumption A2. Suppose that we observe the following choices for all ancillary conditions, A_i, $i = 1, 2, \ldots, n$*

$$C(X_1, A_i) = \{x\}, \ C(X_2, A_i) = \{y\}, \ C(X_3 A_i) = \{z\}, \ C(X_4, A_i) = \{x, y\} \tag{3.35}$$

Given (3.35), we can conclude that xRy. But yRx does not hold because in the set X_1, x is chosen but y is not. Hence, xPy.

Definition 3.6 *(Strict unambiguous choice): Let $x, y \in X$ and let G be the welfare relevant domain. We say that x is "strictly unambiguously chosen" over y, written xP^*y, if*

$$\text{For all } (X, A) \in G \text{ and } x, y \in X, \ y \notin C(X, A).$$

Since the choice set is non-empty (assumption A2), thus, when $X = \{x, y\}$ then x is chosen but y is not. In general, whenever x and y are available in any constraint set then y is never chosen.

Example 3.8 *(Example 3.7 continued ...): From (3.35), we cannot conclude that xP^*y because in the set X_4, both x, y are available, yet y is also chosen. If instead $C(X_4, A_i)$ was $\{x\}$, or $\{z\}$, or $\{x, z\}$, then we would have xP^*y. Suppose that $C(X_4, A_i) = \{x\}$, while the choices in all other cases are given by (3.35). In this case, we have xPy and xP^*y, thus, P and P^* coincide*

Definitions 3.5 and 3.6 get around the problem of human choice that is coherent but not well behaved in the sense of being intransitive, or influenced by irrelevant contexts or alternatives. However, they do not get around the problem where decision makers appear to act against their own interest such as not making full use of 401(k) plans, addictions, and low aspirations; see Dalton and Ghosal (2018) for some progress in this direction.

Whenever $C(X, A)$ is unique for each $(X, A) \in G$ then P (Definition 3.5) and P^* (Definition 3.6) coincide (see Example 3.8). Otherwise they can differ. For several binary relations, P^* is the asymmetric part, as, for instance, is the case in the next definition.

Definition 3.7 *For all $(X, A) \in G$ and for all $x, y \in X$ the binary preference relation, R^*, on G is defined as follows*

$$xR^*y \Leftrightarrow \text{ not } yP^*x,$$

i.e., y is never strictly unambiguously chosen over x. So there exists some GCS such that x and y are available and x is chosen. Similarly, one may define the indifference relation I^* as follows

$$xI^*y \Leftrightarrow xR^*y \text{ and } yR^*x,$$

i.e., there is some GCS for which x is chosen when y is available and another for which y is chosen when x is available.

In the absence of ancillary conditions, the binary relations (1) R and R^* are equivalent to the standard weak revealed preference relation in neoclassical economics, and (2) P and P^* are equivalent to the standard strong revealed preference relation in neoclassical economics. Thus, the neoclassical case is subsumed within this framework.

Proposition 3.3 *(Bernheim and Rangel, 2009): For all $(X, A) \in G$ and for all $x, y \in X$, we have*

$$xP^*y \Rightarrow xPy \Rightarrow xRy \Rightarrow xR^*y,$$

so P^* is the coarsest and R^* the finest of these binary relations.

Example 3.9 *(Intransitivity of P^* and incompleteness of R): Let $X_1 = \{a, b\}$, $X_2 = \{b, c\}$, $X_3 = \{a, c\}$, $X_4 = \{a, b, c\}$, $X_5 = \{a\}$, $X_6 = \{b\}$, $X_7 = \{c\}$, and $\chi = \{X_1, \ldots, X_7\}$. There are no ancillary conditions, so the welfare relevant domain comprises the sets $X_1, \ldots, X_7$. The choices are given by (choices are trivial for singleton sets so these are not listed):*

$$C(X_1) = \{a\}, \; C(X_2) = \{b\}, \; C(X_3) = \{c\}, \; C(X_4) = \{a\}. \tag{3.36}$$

In choice sets X_1 and X_4, the options a and b are available but b is never chosen, while a is chosen from both choice sets, so aP^*b. In choice sets X_2 and X_4, options b and c are available yet c is never chosen and b is chosen once, so bP^*c. In contrast, consider choice sets X_3 and X_4 where options a and c are present. Option c is chosen from X_3 and option a is chosen from X_4. Thus, we have both cases $\sim aP^*b$ and $\sim bP^*a$, so using Definition 3.7, we have aI^*b. Thus, P^* is intransitive. From (3.36) we neither have aRc nor cRa so R is incomplete.

Example 3.10 *(Incompleteness of R when the ancillary condition varies): Consider two GCSs $(X, A), (X, A') \in G$ where $X = \{x, y\}$. Suppose that we have the following choices*

$$C(\{x, y\}, A) = \{x\} \text{ and } C(\{x, y\}, A') = \{y\}.$$

The second choice prevents xRy and the first choice prevents yRx. Thus, R is not complete in this case. In contrast, R^* is always complete.

While Example 3.9 shows that P^* is intransitive, none of the binary relations defined so far need to be transitive. The next example illustrates intransitivity of P; an exercise asks you to show that R^* is intransitive.

Example 3.11 *(Intransitivity of P and R): Consider the setup in Example 3.9 but replace (3.36) by the following choices*

$$C(X_1) = \{a\}, \; C(X_2) = \{b\}, \; C(X_3) = \{c\}, \; C(X_4) = \{a, b, c\}.$$

We have aRb but not bRa, so using Definition 3.5 we have aPb. We can analogously check that bPc. But we do not have aRc so it is not the case that aPc. Thus P is intransitive. R is also intransitive because aRb and bRc but not aRc.

Intransitivity does not prevent a welfare analysis. If a preference relation on a finite set is acyclic then a maximal element exists. The binary relation P^* is acyclic, as shown in the next proposition; however, P need not be acyclic.

Proposition 3.4 *(Bernheim and Rangel, 2009):*

(a) *Consider outcomes $x_1, \ldots, x_N$ such that $x_1 R x_2, \ldots, x_{N-1} R x_N$ and for some $1 \leq k \leq N - 1$ we have $x_k P^* x_{k+1}$. Then $\sim x_N R x_1$.*

(b) *P^* is acyclic, so for outcomes $x_1, \ldots, x_N$ such that $x_1 P^* x_2, \ldots, x_{N-1} P^* x_N$ we have $\sim x_N P^* x_1$.*

Next we give the welfare criteria for improving choices.

Definition 3.8 *(Welfare improvement):*

(a) *(Strict welfare improvement): Given any choice $x \in X$ we can "strictly improve" upon the choice if there exists some $y \in X$ such that yP^*x. When a strict improvement is impossible then x is a weak individual welfare optimum.*

(b) *(Weak welfare improvement):*
    Given any choice $x \in X$ we can "weakly improve" upon the choice if there exists some $y \in X$ such that yPx. When a weak improvement is impossible then x is a strict individual welfare optimum.

The following proposition is an implication of Definition 3.8.

Proposition 3.5 (a) *If $x \in C(X,A)$ for any $(X,A) \in G$ then it is a "weak individual welfare optimum" in X. If $x \in C(X,A)$ is unique then it is a strict welfare optimum.*

(b) *x is a weak welfare optimum in X if and only if for each $y \in X$ such that $y \neq x$ there is some GCS (X',A') in which x is chosen when y is available (although y might be chosen as well).*

Proof: (a) Since $x \in C(X,A)$ there does not exist any $y \in X$ such that yP^*x. Hence, it is not possible to strictly improve on x, so x is a "weak individual welfare optimum" in X. If x is unique then there does not exist any element y such that yPx. Thus, a weak improvement is impossible, which implies that x is a strict welfare optimum.

(b) Since there exists some GCS (X',A') in which x is chosen when y is available, we cannot have yP^*x. Thus, we cannot strictly improve welfare starting from x, so x is a weak welfare optimum. ∎

Choice sets are non-empty (assumption A2), thus there always exist some $x \in C(X,A)$. Hence, from Proposition 3.5(a), a weak individual welfare optimum always exists within any X such that $(X,A) \in G$. This is the sense in which the welfare criteria respects individual liberty because, by definition, x is voluntarily chosen. Thus, within any welfare relevant domain, G, it is not possible to improve upon individual decisions by a third party. This is not the case when we choose the universal domain of GCSs, G^*. But this is precisely the role of the choice architect under soft paternalism: to trim down the universal domain of GCSs to the welfare relevant domain. Indeed, no assumptions such as continuity and compactness are needed for this result because of our assumption of well-behaved choice correspondences.

Example 3.12 *Let us revisit Example 3.9. The choices are given in (3.36), which give rise to an intransitive P^*. In the set X_4, a is the unique choice element, so it is a strict welfare optimum (Proposition 3.5a) in X_4 while b and c are not even weak welfare optima in X_4. Also using Proposition 3.5a, in set X_1, b is not a weak welfare optimum and in set X_2, c is not a weak welfare optimum.*

In set X_3, where the unique choice is c we cannot conclude that it is the only strict welfare optimum. The reason is that since $C(X_4) = \{a\}$ when c is available, so we cannot compare a and c under P^*. Indeed we cannot affect a weak welfare improvement starting from a or c because neither aPc (c is chosen in X_3 when a is available) nor cPa (a is chosen in X_4 when c is available). Since weak improvements are not possible, thus, both a and c are strict welfare optima in the set X_3 although only c is chosen.

Different ancillary conditions may produce conflicting choices, so much so that it becomes difficult or impossible to identify weak or strong unambiguous welfare improvements. Exercise 7 illustrates this problem. On the other hand, the framework potentially solves some empirical puzzles as the next example shows.

Example 3.13 *(Iyengar and Lepper, 2000; Bernheim and Rangel, 2009): Suppose that the potential options are 29 different brands of jams; the 30th option is "choose nothing." The welfare relevant domain contains all pairs of 30 options and the entire set of 30 options but no other combinations of options. There are no ancillary conditions. In any pairwise comparison, strawberry jam (say option x) is preferred to any other jam. However, when asked to choose among all 30 alternatives in one go, the individual chooses the 30th option, i.e., choose nothing (say, option y). In the Bernheim–Rangel framework this is not problematic. Let us start with x.*

We cannot find any other option, say, z such that zP*x. Thus, a strict improvement over x is impossible and it is a weak individual welfare optimum. x is not chosen when all 30 options are presented but option y is chosen. Yet, it is not the case that yP*x. Nor is it the case that xP*y (although xP*z and yP*z for all other options z). Thus, both x and y are weak individual welfare optimum.

In Example 3.13, if one restricted the welfare relevant domain to only all pairwise comparisons of the options, but do not allow all options to be presented together, then we do get a unique choice, x. However truncating in this manner can lead to cyclicity of P^* as shown in the next example.

Example 3.14   *Consider the setup of Example 3.9 but restrict the welfare relevant domain to $X_1 = \{a,b\}$, $X_2 = \{b,c\}$, $X_3 = \{a,c\}$, leaving out $X_4 = \{a,b,c\}$. This violates assumption A1 because $G = \{X_1,X_2,X_3\}$ does not contain all finite subsets of the options a, b, and c. Hence, Proposition 3.4 need not apply. Indeed this is the case because P^* cycles: aP^*b (whenever a and b are present in a set, b is never chosen); bP^*c (whenever b and c are present, c is never chosen); cP^*a (whenever a and c are present, a is never chosen). This intransitivity of P^* makes it difficult to figure out what the choice would be (normative or positive) in the set X_4; each of a, b, and c is improvable.*

We can relate the binary choice relations P and P^* to traditional measures of welfare improvement such as Pareto optimality in the following *multi-selves interpretation*. Suppose that the welfare relevant domain G is *rectangular*, i.e., $G = \chi \times \Gamma$ where Γ is the set of all ancillary conditions. Suppose that each ancillary condition corresponds to a different self of the same individual and for each ancillary condition $A \in \Gamma$ the individual maximizes a utility function u_A; thus, preferences are well behaved for each ancillary condition. We now apply the Pareto criteria across the different selves of the individual.

Definition 3.9   *(Multiself Pareto dominance): Let $y \in X$ for some X in χ.*

   (a) x "weakly multiself Pareto dominates" y, written xMy, if $u_A(x) \geq u_A(y)$ for all $A \in \Gamma$.
   (b) x "strongly multiself Pareto dominates" y, written xM*y, if $u_A(x) > u_A(y)$ for all $A \in \Gamma$.
   (c) $x \in X$ is a weak multiself Pareto optimum if there is no $y \in X$ such that yM*x.
   (d) $x \in X$ is a strong multiself Pareto optimum if there is no $y \in X$ such that yMx.

The criteria proposed in Definition 3.9 are quite strong. For instance, a typical behavioral finding is that the choice made by an individual often changes with framing effects, which corresponds here to changes in ancillary conditions. However, the multiself Pareto criteria requires that we do not get reversal of rankings when framing changes.

The next proposition establishes the link between multiself Pareto dominance and the relations P and P^*.

Proposition 3.6   *(Bernheim and Rangel, 2009): Suppose that G is rectangular, and each $A \in \Gamma$ activates a different multiself of the same individual. Assume that for each $A \in \Gamma$, preferences are well behaved, so we can imagine that the self corresponding to $A \in \Gamma$ maximizes a utility function u_A. Then $M^* = P^*$ and $M = P$.*

Proposition 3.6 implies that saying $x \in X$ is a weak (strong) multiself Pareto optimum is equivalent to saying that $x \in X$ is a weak (strong) individual welfare optimum.

The main difficulty in operationalizing this choice-based proposal is to specify the welfare relevant domain and to deal with cases where the welfare criterion is not very helpful in narrowing down choice or choice is cyclic (as in Example 3.14). Indeed, one might need to invoke another normative criterion in this case, or use non-choice data such as data from neuroeconomics. Bernheim and Rangel (2009) make other suggestions too. For instance, one might appeal to other principles such as *preponderance* (p. 89); thus, if a decision maker typically chooses x over y but rarely y over x then the rare exceptions should be ignored.

These comments illustrate two things. First, not everyone will find the choice-based approach to be persuasive. Second, there are severe difficulties in making progress with a choice-based approach even when the choice-based approach is stretched to its limits. Indeed, the choice-based approach has been criticized on these grounds and alternatives have been proposed. For instance, Sugden (2013) proposes a contractarian approach (see Section 3.8 below) and Loewenstein and Haisley (2008) advocate welfare criteria based on preferences rather than choice. Cason and Plott (2014) show that subject misconceptions in choice problems provide poor guidance to their underlying preferences, even in relatively simple problems. Choi et al. (2014) find considerable heterogeneity among individuals in their decision making quality/ability and consistency with utility maximization. Relatively poorer decision making quality associated with lower wealth and lower educational attainment, produces choices that have lower consistency with utility maximization.

For an extension of the Bernheim–Rangel framework to an interpersonally comparable concept of well-being and the development of criteria for policy evaluation, see Fleurbaey and Schokkaert (2013). For a survey of alternative measures of GDP in the presence of interpersonal comparisons, see Fleurbaey and Blanchet (2013). Rubinstein and Salant (2008) have independently developed a choice-based framework in which the ancillary conditions in the Bernheim–Rangel framework are called *frames*. They also develop binary relations similar to P and P^*. Manzini and Mariotti (2014) give a useful discussion of the relative merits of the model-free approach, e.g., the Bernheim–Rangel framework, and the model-based approach, e.g., Masatlioglu et al. (2012) (see Section 3.7 below).

Rubinstein and Salant (2012) depart from the Bernheim–Rangel framework by giving up the choice between alternatives based on the Pareto criterion. Their argument is that as the behavioral data grows, the ability of the Pareto criterion to rank alternatives, shrinks. They propose a welfare ranking of any two alternatives even when one alternative does not Pareto dominate the other alternative. Rather than postulate that inconsistent behavior arises by changes in, say, frames, their model supposes that individuals have more than one preference ordering. Inconsistent choices arise because the individual switches between the preference orderings while making different choices.

3.7 Revealed preference under limited attention

So far, we have assumed that individuals pay attention to all alternatives. By contrast, the evidence supports *limited attention* to alternatives in many domains (see Volume 5). In this section, we consider the welfare implications of limited attention using the model of Masatlioglu et al. (2012), who also give the following useful taxonomy of limited attention, to which their framework can be applied.

1. *Choose the top N*: Examples include choosing from among the N cheapest suppliers and ignoring the rest; considering only the N most advertised products; and considering only the products advertised on the first page of results from a search engine.
2. *Top on each criteria*: One may sequentially choose among criteria (Manzini and Mariotti, 2007, 2012). For instance, a potential buyer of a car may narrow down his choices by first choosing the safest car, then choosing the most fuel efficient car from the narrower set, and then the cheapest car from the even narrower set.
3. *Most popular category*: A potential buyer of a bike might first check online the shop that offers the largest variety of bikes and then visit it to buy the bike, ignoring all other bike shops.

The proposed framework has three stages. In the first stage, the decision maker chooses to narrow down the set of alternatives to those that he desires to pay attention to (or he may simply be unaware of the existence of some alternatives). In the second stage, he has a complete and transitive preference ordering over the remaining alternatives. In the third stage, we examine the welfare implications of the first two stages.

The Bernheim–Rangel approach described in Section 3.6 is model-free because the choice function is the primitive and any choice procedure that generates the stated choices is consistent with the model. In contrast, the approach under limited attention specifies a particular choice procedure that relies on limited attention, so it is not model-free. In the Bernheim–Rangel approach, x is unambiguously preferred over y when y is never chosen if x is available (Definition 3.6). Under limited attention, by contrast, the decision maker might sometimes not pay attention to x, resulting in a choice of y. We shall see an example below where the two criteria are in conflict.

We now develop the formal model. Suppose that X is a finite set of alternatives and χ is the set of all non-empty subsets (or feasible sets) of X. Suppose that the decision maker faces the set $S \in \chi$ of alternatives. The decision maker gives attention to a non-empty subset $\Gamma(S)$ of elements in S, known as the *consideration set*.

Definition 3.10 *(Consideration set mapping)*: $\Gamma : \chi \to \chi$ *is a consideration set mapping such that for all* $S \in \chi$, $\Gamma(S) \neq \phi$ *and* $\Gamma(S) \subset S$.

If the decision maker is in the market for a new car, then S is the set of all models of all cars sold in the country where he lives. Suppose that the decision maker pays attention to a subset $\Gamma(S)$ of the cars. Consider a model of car $x \notin \Gamma(S)$ but $x \in S$. It is quite possible that the decision maker is unaware of the existence of all models in the set $S \backslash \Gamma(S)$. If now the decision maker were to face the set $S \backslash x$ then it is reasonable to assume that his consideration set would not change, so that $\Gamma(S) = \Gamma(S \backslash x)$. In other words, the decision maker is unaware that he is unaware of all the alternatives. This motivates the next definition.

Definition 3.11 *(Attention filter)*: *A consideration set mapping is an attention filter if for any S, if* $x \notin \Gamma(S)$ *but* $x \in S$ *then* $\Gamma(S) = \Gamma(S \backslash x)$.

We shall assume that the underlying preferences, $\succ$, on X are complete and transitive and the decision maker chooses a unique best element in each consideration set. We denote $\succ$ by P.

Definition 3.12 *(Choice function)*: *A choice function* $c : \chi \to \chi$ *assigns to each element of the feasible set,* $S \in \chi$, *a unique element* $c(S) \in S$.

Definition 3.13 *(Choice with limited attention, CLA): A choice function c is a choice with limited attention (CLA) if there exists a complete transitive preference $\succ$ over X and an attention filter Γ such that $c(S)$ is the $\succ$ best element in $\Gamma(S)$.*

The preferences of the decision maker $\succ$ and the attention filter used by the decision maker are not observable to a third party. Yet, we show below, that from the observed choices we can infer preferences and the attention filter used.

Example 3.15 *Let $X = \{x, y, z\}$, so $\chi = \{\{x, y, z\}, \{x, y\}, \{y, z\}, \{x, z\}\}$; we omit the singleton sets that have a trivial choice. Suppose that the choice function is given by*

$$c(x, y, z) = x, \; c(x, y) = x, \; c(y, z) = y, \; c(x, z) = z. \tag{3.37}$$

Two possible preferences, $\succ_1$ and $\succ_2$, along with the corresponding attention filters, Γ_1 and Γ_2, are given in Figure 3.2. The reader is invited to check that Γ_1 and Γ_2 satisfy Definition 3.11. Γ_2 gives full attention to all elements of all subsets of χ except $\{x, z\}$ where it ignores the element x. Γ_1 gives full attention to the sets $\{x, y\}$ and $\{x, z\}$ but limited attention to the sets $\{x, y, z\}$ and $\{y, z\}$.

The reader can easily confirm that given the attention filters, Γ_1 and Γ_2, the preferences, $z \succ_1 x \succ_1 y$ and $x \succ_2 y \succ_2 z$, are entirely consistent with the choices given in (3.37). Yet we cannot observe either the attention filters or the preferences of the individual. However, suppose that we could discover somehow that $\succ_1$ and $\succ_2$ are the only two pairs of preferences that the decision maker could have. Then, it can be shown that the individual prefers x to y on the following grounds. The decision maker gives attention to both x and y under both attention filters, whenever x and y are available in any set in χ. However, x is always chosen when both x and y are available (see (3.37)).

The observations in Example 3.15 give rise to the next definition, which is based on a fairly conservative criterion of unanimity among all pairs of preferences and attention filters. Requiring unanimity has the advantage that the criterion is not controversial, but the disadvantage is that it limits the domain of applicability of the criterion.

Definition 3.14 *Suppose that c is a CLA (Definition 3.13) and there are k different pairs of preferences and attention filters that can represent the stated choices, given by $(\Gamma_1, \succ_1)$, $(\Gamma_2, \succ_2), \ldots, (\Gamma_k, \succ_k)$.*[11] *Then*

(a) *x is revealed preferred to y if $x \succ_i y$ for $i = 1, \ldots, k$.*
(b) *x is revealed to attract attention at S if $x \in \Gamma_i(S)$ for $i = 1, \ldots, k$.*
(c) *x is revealed not to attract attention at S if $x \notin \Gamma_i(S)$ for $i = 1, \ldots, k$.*

		Attention filter			
Preference		$\{x, y, z\}$	$\{x, y\}$	$\{y, z\}$	$\{x, z\}$
$z \succ_1 x \succ_1 y$	Γ_1	xy	xy	y	xz
$x \succ_2 y \succ_2 z$	Γ_2	xyz	xy	yz	z

Figure 3.2 Two possible preferences, $\succ_1$ and $\succ_2$, along with the corresponding attention filters, Γ_1 and Γ_2.
Source: Masatlioglu et al. (2012) with permission from the American Economic Association.

---

[11] For instance, in Example 3.15, $k = 2$.

Determining revealed preference and revealed attention/inattention can get cumbersome for large k. However, there is a simpler method that we turn to.

Consider Example 3.15 and compare the two sets $S = \{x, y, z\}$ and $S' = \{x, z\}$. From (3.37), the choices given by $c(x, y, z) = x$, and $c(x, z) = z$ reveal a choice reversal. If the decision maker paid attention to x and z in both sets, then we should not expect a choice reversal. A plausible suggestion is that the removal of y from S alters the attention set; thus, the decision maker must have paid attention to y in the set S (revealed attention). If this reasoning is accepted, then the presence of y induces the decision maker to pay attention to x in the set S and the absence of y from the set S' draws attention away from x, which explains the choice $c(x, z) = z$. Since the decision maker pays attention to x and y in the set S yet chooses x we say that x is revealed preferred to y.

More generally, if the choice changes upon removing an alternative, then the original choice is preferred to the alternative that is removed. We can formally state the general idea as follows.

Definition 3.15   *Let $x, y \in X$ be two distinct elements. Then xPy (x is revealed preferred to y) if there exists a set $S \in \chi$ such that $c(S) = x$ but $x \notin c(S \backslash y)$.*

The preference relation $\succ$ on X is transitive. Thus, we if discover that xPy and yPz, then it follows that xPz although x is not directly revealed preferred from the individual's choices. Denote by P_R, the transitive closure of P. The transitive closure of a binary relation P on a set X is the minimal transitive relation P_R on X that contains P. Thus, $x_1 P_R x_n$ if there exist $x_1, \ldots, x_n \in X$ and we have $x_j P x_{j+1}$ for $1 \leq j \leq n - 1$. The next proposition directly follows from these observations.

Proposition 3.7   *(Revealed preference; Masatlioglu et al., 2012): Suppose that c is a CLA. For $x, y \in X$, x is revealed preferred to y if and only if $xP_R y$.*

In the next example we see how the predictions of this model differ from the Bernheim–Rangel framework.

Example 3.16   *Consider a supermarket that displays four products x, y, z, t, each individually packed in a box. All four products need not be available at all times. The products can be displayed in two aisles, using the following five rules:*

(1) Each aisle can carry no more than two products because the supermarket manager has determined that it would otherwise overload customers' cognitive abilities. Furthermore, none of the aisles contains only one product unless the supermarket runs out of all remaining products.

(2) x and y come packed in big boxes, which cannot be stored in the same aisle.

(3) Since the first aisle is more visible to customers, the supermarket fills it first before any products are placed in the second aisle.

(4) Due to an exclusive agreement with the manufacturers of products y and z, these products are placed in the first aisle whenever they are available.

(5) The firm deems product t to be the least popular, so it is placed in the first aisle only if there is space remaining in the aisle after displaying the remaining available products.

Suppose that a customer has privately known preferences

$$t \succ x \succ z \succ y. \tag{3.38}$$

His choice is determined as follows: He visits the first aisle and picks his most preferred item. Due to limited attention he never visits the second aisle. Let us separately consider the inferences drawn in the Bernheim–Rangel approach and the CLA approach.

I. Bernheim–Rangel approach: Suppose that products x and y are available. From rules 2 and 4, if y is available, then x is never placed in the first aisle. Suppose that x is placed in the second aisle. Since the customer only explores the first aisle due to limited attention, hence, x never gets chosen by the customer. In the terminology of Bernheim–Rangel, yP^*x, yet the individual prefers x to y, i.e., $x \succ y$. Thus, under limited attention, the Bernheim–Rangel criteria is not suitable; indeed it was never designed for limited attention.

II. The CLA approach: The five rules, given above, suggest that the consideration sets are given by

$$\Gamma(xyzt) = \{y,z\}, \Gamma(xzt) = \{x,z\}, \Gamma(xyt) = \{y,t\}, \Gamma(yzt) = \{y,z\}, \Gamma(xyz) = \{y,z\},$$

and when any two products remain we have $\Gamma(ab) = \{a,b\}$ for all $a,b \in \{x,y,z,t\}$. Suppose all four products are available. Then, by rules 2 and 4, y and z are placed in the first aisle and x and t in the second aisle. The individual picks z from the first aisle because $z \succ y$. Once y is unavailable then x is moved to the first aisle; since $x \succ z$, x is now chosen. Suppose that z is sold out. Then t is placed in the first aisle. Given $t \succ x$, the customer then chooses t. In summary, the choices are

$$c(xyzt) = z, \ c(xzt) = x, \ c(xt) = t.$$

The choice data, if available, correctly identifies the underlying preferences in (3.38).

If removing an option from a set causes a choice reversal then the decision maker must have been paying attention to the removed object (Definition 3.13). It is also possible to determine attention even if no choice reversals take place, as shown in the following example.

Example 3.17 *Suppose that a decision maker chooses y from sets S and T. Removing x from T causes a choice reversal, so the decision maker must have been paying attention to x, i.e., $x \in \Gamma(T)$. Suppose that we now consider elements in the set $A = S \cup T \setminus S \cap T$ and suppose that all of these are revealed preferred to y. Then it must be the case that elements in the set A were not under consideration when y was chosen, i.e., did not belong to $\Gamma(S)$ and $\Gamma(T)$. But then removing these elements from S and T will not change the consideration set, so*

$$\Gamma(S) = \Gamma(S \cap T) = \Gamma(T). \tag{3.39}$$

Since $x \in \Gamma(T)$, (3.39) implies that $x \in \Gamma(S)$. Thus, we can infer which elements belong to $\Gamma(S)$ without actually looking for choice reversals from the set S. The next proposition formalizes these ideas about revealed inattention (recall that P_R is the transitive closure of P).

Proposition 3.8 *(Revealed inattention; Masatlioglu et al., 2012): Suppose that c is a CLA, then:*

(a) *x is revealed not to attract attention at a set S if and only if $xP_Rc(S)$,*
(b) *x is revealed to attract attention at a set S if and only if there exists a set T such that $c(T) \neq c(T \setminus x)$, and the following two conditions hold:*
  (bi) *$yP_Rc(S)$ for all $y \in S \setminus T$*
  (bii) *$zP_Rc(T)$ for all $z \in T \setminus S$.*

Part (a) is obvious. If x is revealed preferred to all elements actually chosen then it must be the case that the decision maker does not pay attention to x. Part (b) is exemplified in Example 3.17.

Propositions 3.7 and 3.8 require that c is a CLA. We now explore how we can characterize a CLA. We first define the analog of the weak axiom of revealed preference (WARP) under limited attention. Under full attention, WARP implies that every set S has a best alternative, x^*, such that if the choice from some set T lies in S then that choice must be x^*. Under limited attention we must, in addition, ensure that the decision maker pays attention to x^*.

Definition 3.16 *The weak axiom of revealed preference with limited attention (WARP(LA)) requires that for a non-empty set S there exists $x^* \in S$ such that if $x^* \in T$ and,*

$$\text{if (i) } c(T) \in S \text{ and (ii) } c(T) \neq c(T \backslash x^*) \text{ then } c(T) = x^*.$$

The requirement $c(T) \neq c(T \backslash x^*)$ ensures that the decision maker gives attention to x^*; this is the only component in WARP(LP) that differentiates it from WARP.

Proposition 3.9 *(Characterization of CLA; Masatlioglu et al., 2012): The choice function c satisfies WARP(LA) if and only if c is a CLA.*

Proposition 3.9 shows that the characterization of CLA is simple and depends on just one behavioral axiom, WARP(LA).

The basic idea that in choosing an element from a set S, the decision maker only considers a subset $T \subset S$ plays a role in several different models. The reader might wonder how these alternative models relate to the CLA approach. For instance, Cherepanov et al. (2013) propose a model in which decision makers evaluate alternatives based on their ability to *rationalize* them. There can be several *rationales* and each rationale is a transitive binary relation, R_i. In particular, R_i need not be complete, so R_i may not be able to compare two distinct alternatives, x and y. The set of rationalizable alternatives in S, denoted by $\hat{\Gamma}(S)$, comprises alternatives that dominate all others based on at least one rationale. Thus,

$$\hat{\Gamma}(S) = \{x \in S : \text{ For some } R_i, xR_iy \text{ for all } y \in S\}. \tag{3.40}$$

It can be shown that $\hat{\Gamma}$ is not an attention filter. Furthermore, there are rationales that do not imply the CLA model and there are attention filters that do not satisfy $\hat{\Gamma}$. Hence, neither CLA implies rationalizability nor is it implied by it; an exercise invites the reader to explore this for an example.

Manzini and Mariotti (2007) propose the application of two rationales applied in a sequential and fixed manner, irrespective of the set of alternatives. The available choices are pruned by the first rationale (shortlisting) to enable the second rationale to select the final outcome. This is termed as the Rational Shortlist Method.[12] Masatlioglu et al. (2012) state that most models in this class satisfy the *Weak WARP axiom*, which states that if x is chosen from the pair of alternatives $\{x, y\}$ and from a set with a larger number of alternatives, then y cannot be chosen from a set with an intermediate number of alternatives.

Definition 3.17 *(Weak WARP; Masatlioglu et al., 2012): Suppose $\{x, y\} \subset T \subset S$. If $c(xy) = c(S) = x$, then $y \notin c(T)$.*

It is not hard to construct examples where the choice function satisfies WARP(LA) but does not satisfy Weak WARP; an exercise asks you to show this. The converse can also be shown, namely, that choice patterns that satisfy Weak WARP need not satisfy WARP(LA); see Example 3 in Masatlioglu et al. (2012).

---

[12] For a generalization of the model to accommodate more general menu dependence, see Manzini and Mariotti (2012).

3.8 The contractarian approach

In neoclassical economics, and in the soft paternalism approach, one typically advises a choice architect, a social planner, the government, or the policymaker. In the *contractarian approach*, by contrast, one advises directly the individual who suffers from behavioral biases. Sugden (2013) outlines the contractarian approach to normative economics that is based on Buchanan (1968, 1975, 1986); we consider this below.

The contractarian recommendation to any set of individuals is addressed to each individual in the set, not by appeal to the common interest, but by stressing the advantage to each individual. Appeals in the common interest may involve winners and losers, yet the losers may agree to participate voluntarily, perhaps motivated by the common good. However, this is not part of the contractarian framework. If the contractarian recommendations lead to harm to some parties, the proposal may include compensating mechanisms. However, a contractarian recommendation cannot impose net losses on anyone, say, on the grounds that the recommendation imparts high benefits to others.

A contractarian's role is similar to that of a mediator who makes suggestions that are mutually beneficial to different parties in a conflict situation. The contractarian does not advise any particular party to strategically out-think the others. Rather he advises all individuals to reach a mutually beneficial settlement, although some individuals may gain relatively more than others. Since the aim is to achieve a mutually beneficial outcome for all parties, one begins from some baseline position or the status quo. For instance, consider several buyers and a seller of an object. The baseline position is that the seller has the object and the buyer has the money and both parties expect to trade voluntarily without any incurring losses. The contractarian might now recommend a second price auction to all parties as a trading mechanism to realize gains from trade.

Those who formulate contractarian policies are required to have incentives to make the necessary recommendations to individuals. Thus, the underlying framework needs to be broad enough to capture the incentives of the relevant actors, which might include political actors or policymakers who make the recommendations.

> **Example 3.18** *Consider the recommendation to motorists approaching a roundabout to "give way to traffic from the right." This is, for instance, enshrined in the traffic laws in the UK. This rule is mutually beneficial to drivers at the roundabout by giving rise to common expectations. In any particular trip, a driver who has to wait for the vehicle from the right loses some time while the other party gains. However, on average, as one makes many car trips, the average gains and losses counterbalance each other, and drivers benefit from a smooth and less stressful flow of traffic, so all drivers benefit.*

Sugden (2013, pp. 530–1) raises an important issue about the relevant *addressee* in normative economics and in the contractarian approach: "The literary convention of addressing normative economics to a public decision-maker seems rather out of place when what are being discussed are (supposed) mistakes in decisions that are made by private individuals and that do not affect anyone else. Advising individuals on how to pursue their own interests in their private lives is a natural counterpart to advising them about how to pursue common interests through agreement. In other words, it is a natural counterpart to the contractarian approach." The next example illustrates this point further.

Example 3.19 *Suppose that an epidemiologist discovers a link between some human actions, say, eating a particular food and some human disease or illness. The contractarian approach would take the form of direct information dissemination of the findings to the public. Indeed, in the case of smoking and alcohol consumption, this has been the approach in many countries (although belatedly in the case of smoking). So while normative economics is largely addressed to a hypothetical social planner, in actual practice it is not unusual that public policy takes the form of directly informing people about their biases.*

As these examples show, the contractarian approach takes the form of recommendations made directly to individuals, once it is discovered that they exhibit some form of bias. No paternalism is allowed in the contractarian approach. In particular, the contractarian cannot choose to nudge an individual who chooses not to be nudged, no matter how much the contractarian deems the nudge to be in the individual's interest. This stands in contrast to the libertarian-paternalism approach.

Nudges recommended under soft paternalism are viewed to be paternalistic in the contractarian approach. The reason for disallowing paternalism under the contractarian approach is not because paternalism might unduly intrude into individual liberty. Rather, the reason stems from a practical concern, namely, that *paternalism lacks a valid addressee.* Sugden (2013, p. 537) writes: "Unless individuals themselves wish to license others to act as their guardians, there is no common interest in paternalism."

The contractarian approach is not without its limitations. Providing information in the contractarian approach may also be considered by some as a form of nudging. How does one know if individuals wish to be nudged, i.e., be provided with the relevant information? Since issues of the framing of information can be critical, who decides how the relevant information is to be framed? How does one determine if the same information will not be interpreted by different people in a different manner? Perhaps these concerns apply with less force in some examples rather than others, but clearly there are no simple answers to these vexed questions.

3.9 Behavioral public finance and welfare

In Volume 5, we noted the effect of limited attention on the demand for a single good under salient and non-salient taxes (Chetty et al., 2009); we assume some familiarity with this material in the discussion below. When taxes are made more salient, individuals reduce their demand for the good. In this section, we first extend this framework to consider the tax incidence and excess burden under limited attention. Then, we consider some reduced-form frameworks that are suitable to model the welfare implications of alternative policies.

3.9.1 *Limited attention and tax elasticities*

Suppose that a consumer consumes two goods, x and y, that are in perfectly elastic supply and has the utility function $U(x, y)$. The consumer has exogenous income $I > 0$. Good y is the numeraire good, whose price is normalized to 1, and it is not taxed. Let p denote the pre-tax unit price of good x that is posted on the price stickers and is directly observable to all buyers. The post-tax price of good x is $q = p(1 + t)$, where $t > 0$ is an ad-valorem, or per-unit, consumption tax. Define

$$\tau = 1 + t.$$

Under full attention, denote the solution to the consumer's optimal demand for x by $x^*(p\tau, I)$ and for y by $y^*(p\tau, I)$. We assume that all demands are continuously differentiable in the parameters p, τ, I. All feasible choices for the levels of demand must satisfy the consumer's budget constraint $p\tau x^*(p\tau, I) + y^*(p\tau, I) = I$.

Under classical public finance theory, the consumer takes account of the full post-tax price, q. However, under limited attention, the consumer may not pay full attention to taxes that are not included on the price ticket but are added at the sales register. In order to allow for this possibility, we write the optimal demands as $x^*(p, \tau, I)$ and $y^*(p, \tau, I)$.

The classical case with full attention requires $x^*(p, \tau, I) = x^*(p\tau, 0, I)$ and $y^*(p, \tau, I) = y^*(p\tau, 0, I)$. In other words one could either add the taxes directly to the ticket price (i.e., $x^*(p\tau, 0, I)$) or not add them to the ticket price and leave them to be added later at the sales register (i.e., $x^*(p, \tau, I)$). In both cases, demand should be identical. It follows that under full attention, an increase in the post-tax price, q, on account of an increase in τ, or an increase in p, has identical effects on the demands. Our main focus will be on the demand for good x, so let us write $x(p, \tau, I) \equiv D(p, \tau, I)$ to make the demand connotation salient. Letting $\epsilon_{D,q}, \epsilon_{D,p}, \epsilon_{D,\tau}$ be, respectively, the elasticity of demand with respect to q, p, τ we have that under full attention, $\epsilon_{D,q} = \epsilon_{D,p} = \epsilon_{D,\tau}$.

Now introduce the possibility of limited attention towards the sales tax. In this case, whether the sales tax is displayed on the price stickers, or imposed at the sales register, has an important effect on demand. Empirical evidence indicates that $\epsilon_{D,p} \neq \epsilon_{D,\tau}$ (Chetty et al., 2009). Indeed, if taxes added at the sales register are more salient, we expect consumers to respond more to price changes than tax changes, so that $\epsilon_{D,p} > \epsilon_{D,\tau}$ (recall that these elasticities are positive numbers). Suppose that the demand curve is of the form $D(p, \tau, I) = Ap^\beta \tau^{\theta\beta}$. This demand curve can be derived in a variety of ways.[13] Let us write $D(p, \tau, I)$ in a log-linear form (keeping I fixed).

$$\log D(p, \tau, I) = \alpha + \beta \log p + \theta\beta \log \tau; \theta > 0, \beta < 0. \tag{3.41}$$

In (3.41), $-\beta = -\frac{\partial \log D}{\partial \log p} = \epsilon_{D,p}$ and

$$\theta = \left(-\frac{\partial \log D}{\partial \log \tau} \bigg/ -\frac{\partial \log D}{\partial \log p} \right) = \frac{\epsilon_{D,\tau}}{\epsilon_{D,p}}. \tag{3.42}$$

Under classical public finance, $\theta = 1$, which ensures $\epsilon_{D,\tau} = \epsilon_{D,p}$ (unlimited attention). However the empirical evidence suggests that $\theta < 1$ because demand is less responsive to taxes, relative to changes in the price of the good, which is relatively more salient. Thus, the magnitude of θ may be taken to be a measure of inattention. While $\theta < 1$ is in agreement with the empirical evidence on consumption taxes, for other taxes, such as estate taxes, the evidence appears consistent with $\theta > 1$ (tax rates are overestimated). From (3.42), we get the relation

$$\epsilon_{D,\tau} = \theta \epsilon_{D,p} \tag{3.43}$$

---

[13] For instance by specifying a particular form of the utility function. In a working paper, that preceedes their published paper, Chetty et al. (2009), the authors derive this functional form by modeling endogenously the costs of attention and θ is the proportion of consumers who are just indifferent to paying attention or not paying attention to taxes.

that neatly summarizes the effect of inattention in terms of creating a wedge between the two elasticites.

3.9.2 *Tax incidence under limited attention*

The problem of *tax incidence* essentially involves figuring out the relative shares of the tax burden borne by producers and consumers of an increase in the tax rate. In order to ensure the log linearity of demand in p, τ in (3.41), we needed to use ad-valorem taxes. However, for the purposes of tax incidence, it is more convenient to use specific taxes. Henceforth, define a specific tax $\tau > 0$ such that the after-tax price of good x per unit is given by

$$q = p + \tau.$$

The consumer's budget constraint evaluated at the optimal consumption bundles, $x(p, \tau, I)$ and $y(p, \tau, I)$, is

$$(p + \tau)x(p, \tau, I) + y(p, \tau, I) = I \tag{3.44}$$

Let us introduce producers in a simple manner. Suppose that identical competitive firms produce good x. The cost of production faced by a representative firm is $c(n)$, where n is the number of units of the good produced by a firm, and $c' > 0$, $c'' > 0$. The profit level of the representative firm is given by $\pi = pn - c(n)$. Profit maximizing firms produce at the point where $p = c'(n)$. This equation can be solved for the optimal supply, $S(p)$, of the representative firm as a function of the price of the good. Denote the elasticity of supply by $\epsilon_{S,p} = \frac{\partial S}{\partial p} \frac{p}{S}$.

In a partial equilibrium analysis, we are interested in market clearing in the market for good x, so

$$D(p, \tau, I) = S(p). \tag{3.45}$$

Define the following two demand elasticities.

$$\epsilon_{D,q|p} = -\frac{\partial D}{\partial p} \frac{q}{D}; \epsilon_{D,q|\tau} = -\frac{\partial D}{\partial \tau} \frac{q}{D}. \tag{3.46}$$

The two elasticities in (3.46) capture the percentage change in demand divided by the percentage change in the after-tax price arising from, respectively, a change in the (i) price, p, and (ii) specific tax rate, τ.

We assume that the analogue of (3.43) holds for the elasticities in (3.46), but τ is now a specific tax. Thus, we assume that

$$\epsilon_{D,q|\tau} = \theta \epsilon_{D,q|p}; \; \theta < 1, \tag{3.47}$$

where $\theta < 1$ captures inattention, or any other factor that drives a wedge between the two elasticities, $\epsilon_{D,q|p}$ and $\epsilon_{D,q|p}$.

Implicit differentiation of (3.45) gives $\left(\frac{\partial D}{\partial p} - \frac{\partial S}{\partial p}\right) dp + \frac{\partial D}{\partial \tau} d\tau = 0$. Simplifying, using (3.45), (3.47), and the definition of supply elasticity $\epsilon_{S,p} = \frac{\partial S}{\partial p} \frac{q}{S}$, we get

$$\frac{dp}{d\tau} = \frac{\frac{\partial D}{\partial \tau}}{\frac{\partial S}{\partial p} - \frac{\partial D}{\partial p}} = -\frac{\epsilon_{D,q|\tau}}{\frac{q}{p}\epsilon_{S,p} + \epsilon_{D,q|p}} = -\frac{\theta\epsilon_{D,q|\tau}}{\frac{q}{p}\epsilon_{S,p} + \epsilon_{D,q|p}}. \tag{3.48}$$

In (3.48), the elasticities are evaluated at the optimal solution and the given values of (p, τ, I) The price per unit received by the producers is p, hence the calculation $\frac{dp}{d\tau}$ in (3.48) gives the incidence of the specific tax on producers. Consumers pay the price q, hence using the relation $q = p + \tau$, we can find the incidence of the specific tax on consumers as $\frac{dq}{d\tau} = 1 + \frac{dp}{d\tau}$. Using (3.48) and applying (3.47) to eliminate $\epsilon_{D,q|\tau}$, we can rewrite this as

$$\frac{dq}{d\tau} = \frac{\frac{q}{p}\epsilon_{S,p} + (1-\theta)\epsilon_{D,q|p}}{\frac{q}{p}\epsilon_{S,p} + \epsilon_{D,q|p}}. \tag{3.49}$$

Figure 3.3 shows the effect of tax incidence under limited attention; the pretax price is measured on the vertical axis and the quantities demanded and supplied of good x are measured on the horizontal axis. The original equilibrium at a zero tax rate is shown at point 1. The corresponding pre-tax equilibrium price is p_0 and the equilibrium quantity is x_0; since the tax rate is zero, so the pre-tax and the post-tax prices coincide, $p_0 = q_0$. Consider now an increase in the tax rate to $\tau > 0$. The increase in the tax rate shifts the demand curve inwards by $\frac{\partial D}{\partial \tau}(\tau - 0)$. At the existing equilibrium price, p_0, there is an excess supply of the good, equal to $\frac{\partial D}{\partial \tau}\tau$, where $\frac{\partial D}{\partial \tau}$ is evaluated at $p = p_0$. In order to clear the market, competition among producers ensures that the equilibrium price falls to $p = p_1$ and the equilibrium quantity falls to x_1; the new equilibrium point is labeled 3. The post-tax price, $q_1 = p_1 + \tau$ is also shown in the figure and τ is shown as the vertical distance between points 3 and 4. The total tax revenue collected by the government is τx_1.

Clearly, the change in the price $dp = p_0 - p_1 < \tau$. Thus, producers bear a part of the burden of an increase in the tax burden, shown by the area $(p_0 - p_1)x_1$. The remaining tax burden, shown as the area $dqx_1 = (q_1 - p_0)x_1$, is borne by the consumers. Thus, $\tau x_1 = (p_0 - p_1)x_1 + (q - p_0)x_1 \equiv x_1 dp + x_1 dq$ gives the split of the increased tax revenues between that paid by firms and consumers, although the tax is levied only on the consumers. Under full attention, we have

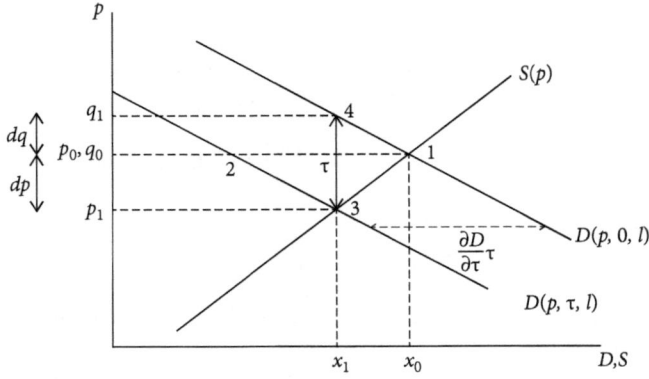

Figure 3.3 Tax incidence under limited attention.

$\theta = 1$, so $\frac{\partial D}{\partial \tau} = \frac{\partial D}{\partial p}$. Thus, in Figure 3.3, we could have shown the leftward shift in demand as $\frac{\partial D}{\partial p}\tau$, which is not the case under limited attention ($\theta < 1$); this is the only difference in Figure 3.3 relative to the standard model in public finance.

From (3.48), $\frac{dp}{d\tau}$ is directly proportional to the size of θ. In the extreme case of no attention, $\theta = 0$, we have $\frac{dp}{d\tau} = 0$, so producers do not bear any burden of the tax increase; consumers bear the entire tax burden. As θ increases, the relative tax burden borne by the producer increases, and correspondingly, the tax burden on the consumer falls. It is tempting to conclude that if consumers pay less than full attention to an increase in the tax rate, it is as if their demand is inelastic, hence, producers can pass a greater amount of the tax rate to final consumers. From (3.47) we know that $\epsilon_{D,q|\tau} = \theta\epsilon_{D,q|p}$, so a change in θ or a change in $\epsilon_{D,q|p}$ have similar effects on $\epsilon_{D,q|\tau}$, yet their effect on tax incidence is different.

To see this, suppose we have two economies, A and B, with identical supply elasticities $\epsilon_{S,p}^{A} = \epsilon_{S,p}^{B} = 0.1$. In economy A, all consumers are neoclassical and display perfect attention ($\theta^{A} = 1$), but in economy B they display limited attention ($\theta^{B} = 0.3 < 1$). Demand in economy A is inelastic ($\epsilon_{D,q|p}^{A} = 0.3$) while in economy B it is more elastic ($\epsilon_{D,q|p}^{B} = 1$). Thus, in each case we have $\epsilon_{D,q|\tau}^{A} = \epsilon_{D,q|\tau}^{B} = 0.3$. However, using (3.48), we have $\left(\frac{dp}{d\tau}\right)_{A} = -0.75$ and $\left(\frac{dp}{d\tau}\right)_{B} = -0.27$. Producers in economy A bear a larger share of the tax despite full attention. However, the limited attention in economy B allows its producers to shift a greater share of the tax to its consumers. Following an increase in the tax rate, inattention only shifts down the demand curve (as in Figure 3.3). In contrast, a lower elasticity of demand reduces the inward shift in demand and also requires a larger price cut (size of $p_0 - p_1$ in Figure 3.3) to establish the new equilibrium where demand equals supply.

From (3.48), if we hold fixed the tax elasticity of demand, $\epsilon_{D,q|\tau}$, a larger value of the price elasticity $\epsilon_{D,q|p}$ reduces the absolute value of the change $\left|\frac{dp}{d\tau}\right|$ needed to equilibrate markets. However, it is possible that the degree of attention given may also depend on the price elasticity, in which case one would need to model the covariance between θ and $\epsilon_{D,q|p}$.

3.9.3 *Excess burden under limited attention*

Let us now use the setup in Section 3.9.2 to calculate the excess burden of taxation. It is more convenient to revert back to using $x(p,\tau,I)$ instead of $D(p,\tau,I)$. We also specialize the utility function $U(x,y)$ to an additively separable function, $U(x,y) = u(x) + v(y)$. Assume that initially, the commodity tax rate is zero ($\tau = 0$). Suppose that there are constant returns to scale in production and firms are perfectly competitive, so each firm makes zero profits. Thus, welfare measurements can be equated purely with consumer welfare.

Substituting the optimal solutions $x(p,\tau,I)$ and $y(p,\tau,I)$ into the utility function, we get the indirect utility function

$$V(p,\tau,I) = u(x(p,\tau,I)) + v(y(p,\tau,I)). \tag{3.50}$$

Let $V(p,\tau_1,I)$ be the indirect utility at a price p and specific tax rate, τ_1. Let the expenditure function be denoted by $e(p,\tau_2,V(p,\tau_1,I))$; it is the minimum expenditure required to achieve the level of utility $V(p,\tau_1,I)$ when the price is p and the specific tax rate is τ_2. We denote government revenue under the specific tax by $R = \tau x(p,\tau,I)$. From (3.44), we have that the consumer budget constraint can be written as:

$$px(p,\tau,I) + y(p,\tau,I) = I - \tau x(p,\tau,I) \equiv I - R(p,\tau,I). \tag{3.51}$$

The LHS of (3.51) is the total expenditure on consumption goods, and the RHS is the total disposable income.

We now use these concepts to define the excess burden, or deadweight loss, of a consumption tax by

$$EB(\tau) = I - R(p,\tau,I) - e(p,0,V(p,\tau,I)). \tag{3.52}$$

$I - R(p,\tau,I)$ is the disposable income when the distortionary consumption tax rate is τ, and the corresponding indirect utility is $V(p,\tau,I)$. Suppose that we ask what expenditure is needed to achieve a utility of $V(p,\tau,I)$ when we remove the distortionary tax and replace it by a lump-sum tax, L? The budget constraint with a lump-sum tax is $px(p,0,I) + y(p,0,I) = I - L$. Since there are no distortions associated with a lump-sum tax, hence, the same level of utility can be achieved with a lower expenditure, $e(p,0,V(p,\tau,I))$. Thus, the RHS of (3.52) measures the extra expenditure required under a distortionary tax to achieve the same level of utility as a lump-sum tax; in other words, it is the deadweight loss associated with the tax.

An issue in most behavioral welfare analyses where people do not strictly optimize is to compute the indirect utility $V(p,\tau,I)$. The indirect utility function is obtained by substituting the optimal choices into the utility function. Suppose, as an extreme example, that an individual pays no attention to tax rates ($\theta = 0$). Then, as the tax rate changes, the individual does not choose the optimizing bundles of x, y, thus making it difficult to define an indirect utility function. In order to deal with this problem, consider two assumptions.

A1: Taxes do not directly affect the utility function. Rather, taxes only affect the utility function indirectly through changes in the demands $x(p,\tau,I)$ and $y(p,\tau,I)$. In other words, the indirect utility function is as given in (3.50).

A2: When tax-inclusive prices are fully salient, the agent chooses the same allocation as a fully-optimizing agent. Recall from Section 3.9.1 that, given our notation above, $x(p,\tau,I)$ is the consumption bundle under limited attention, and $x(p + \tau,I)$ is the consumption bundle under of a fully optimizing consumer who gives full attention to the tax rate. We require that these two consumption bundles are identical when $\tau = 0$, i.e.,

$$x(p,0,I) = x(p + 0,I). \tag{3.53}$$

The implication of (3.53) is that under limited attention, we can discover the underlying preferences of a decision maker who exhibits limited attention, if $\tau = 0$. When $\tau = 0$, there are no issues of inattention.

It is best to examine conditions under which these assumptions are violated in order to understand them better.

Assumption A1 is not likely to hold if taxes directly influence individual utility. This may happen, for instance, (1) if individuals are troubled by the fairness of the fiscal system (e.g., those individuals who feel that the tax system is unfair may evade more taxes), or (2) if individuals must expend costly cognitive effort to give more attention to taxes. In these cases, instead of (3.50), the indirect utility function may have to be written as $\tilde{V}(p,\tau,I) = u(x(p,\tau,I),\tau) + v(y(p,\tau,I),\tau)$. Assumption A2 can be violated even when in the absence of taxes, individuals do not choose the optimal consumption bundles; for instance, under *shrouded attributes* (see Volume 5).

Thus, our strategy is to first use (3.53) to compute the individual's underlying preferences, and then use the Marshallian demand functions under limited attention, $x(p,\tau,I)$ and $y(p,\tau,I)$, to compute the indirect utility function in (3.50).

Denote by $h = h(p,\tau,V)$ the Hicksian or compensated demand for good x, under limited attention. Then assumption A2, and the Slutsky equation implies

$$\frac{\partial h}{\partial p} = \frac{\partial x}{\partial p} + x\frac{\partial x}{\partial I}. \tag{3.54}$$

Demands, Hicksian or Marshallian, optimally respond to prices, so we have the usual condition $\frac{\partial h}{\partial p} < 0$. However, due to limited attention, there is no presumption that demands respond optimally to changes in the tax rate, τ. So if we define

$$\frac{\partial h}{\partial \tau} = \frac{\partial x}{\partial \tau} + x\frac{\partial x}{\partial I}, \tag{3.55}$$

then there is no presumption that $\frac{\partial h}{\partial \tau} < 0$. Using notation used above in (3.46), define the compensated elasticities of demand with respect to p and τ by $\epsilon_{h,q|p} = -\frac{\partial h}{\partial p}\frac{q}{h}$ and $\epsilon_{h,q|\tau} = -\frac{\partial h}{\partial \tau}\frac{q}{h}$.

Proposition 3.10   *(Chetty et al., 2009): Suppose that the supply curve is infinitely elastic ($\epsilon_{S,p} = \infty$), initial commodity tax rate is zero ($\tau = 0$), assumptions A1 and A2 hold, producer prices are fixed, and our measure of excess burden is given (3.52).*

(a) *Evaluating all derivatives at $(p,0,I)$, and defining the compensating attentional parameter $\theta^c = \left(\frac{\partial h}{\partial \tau}/\frac{\partial h}{\partial p}\right) = \frac{\epsilon_{h,q|\tau}}{\epsilon_{h,q|p}}$, the excess burden of introducing a small positive tax ($\tau > 0$), $EB(\tau)$, is*

$$EB(\tau) \simeq \frac{-1}{2}\tau^2\theta^c\frac{\partial h}{\partial \tau}$$
$$= \frac{1}{2}(\tau\theta^c)^2 x(p,\tau,I)\frac{\epsilon_{h,q|p}}{p+\tau}. \tag{3.56}$$

(b) *In the special case of full attention, excess burden is a special case of the formula in (3.56), with $\theta^c = 1$.*

(c) *Suppose that the initial tax is non-zero, $\tau_0 > 0$, and the tax is now increased to $\tau_0 + \Delta\tau$. Let the initial demand be x_0 and the initial price be $q_0 = p + \tau_0$. Then, the excess burden is given by the formula*

$$EB(\tau) \simeq \frac{-1}{2}\theta^c\frac{x_0}{q_0}\epsilon_{h,q|\tau}\left(\tau_0\Delta\tau + \frac{1}{2}(\Delta\tau)^2\right).$$

Two things are immediate from Proposition 3.10. First, the formula for the excess burden is a second order Taylor series approximation that ignores all higher order terms, so the approximation holds best for small tax rates only. Second, the formulae under limited attention and under full attention are identical, except for the presence of the term, θ^c.

In Figure 3.4, we show the excess burden of taxation in the special case when there are no income effects, $\frac{\partial x}{\partial I} = 0$ (e.g., underlying utility function is quasilinear). So to save on notation, we replace $x(p,\tau,I)$ by $x(p,\tau)$. The Slutsky equation in (3.54) shows that in this case $\frac{\partial h}{\partial p} = \frac{\partial x}{\partial p}$; in the presence of income effects we would have to consider Hicksian demands in Figure 3.4. In the absence of income effects, we can also replace θ^c by θ in (3.56).

Two kinds of demand curves are shown in Figure 3.4. $x(p,0)$ is the demand curve when $\tau = 0$, and it shows how optimal demand varies under limited attention when the price alone varies. Under assumption A2 it is equivalent to the marginal utility curve $u'(x)$ so it captures the marginal willingness to pay for x in the absence of taxation. The initial commodity price of good x is p_0, and $\epsilon_{S,p} = \infty$, so the supply curve is horizontal at p_0. The demand curve $x(p_0,\tau)$ shows the variation in optimal demand when price is fixed at p_0, but the tax rate, τ, varies. In the figure, we have shown $x(p_0,\tau)$ to be steeper relative to $x(p,0)$; this is consistent with the empirical evidence that consumers respond relatively less to taxes as compared to prices that are more salient.

The equilibrium when $\tau = 0$ is shown at point J and the consumer demands x_0 units at a price p_0 per unit. Now suppose that we impose a commodity tax $\tau > 0$ on x so that the post-tax price of x is $p_0 + \tau$. In response to an increase in the tax, a consumer who is attentive to the tax reduces demand from x_0 to x_1. However, at a level of demand x_1, the marginal willingness to pay is lower than $p_0 + \tau$ due to the limited attention given to taxes. Suppose that the marginal willingness is given by the vertical distance FM. Let us use as our measure of welfare, the sum of consumer surplus and government tax revenues (our assumptions ensure profits of firms are zero). Before the imposition of the tax, tax revenues are zero and consumer surplus is AGJ, so initial total welfare is AGJ. After the imposition of the tax, consumer surplus is $AKMF - BKMD = ABC - CDF$. Total government tax revenues equal $BGIFC + CDF$. Thus, total welfare after the imposition of the tax is $ABC + BGIFC$. The difference in the levels of welfare in the two cases is $AGJ - (ABC + BGIFC) = FIJ$; this is the excess burden of the tax and is shown as the shaded area in Figure 3.4.

As noted above, in the absence of income effects, $\frac{\partial x}{\partial I} = 0$, so we may write $EB(\tau) \simeq \frac{1}{2}(\tau\theta)^2 x(p,\tau,I)\frac{\epsilon_{x,q|p}}{p+\tau}$ (Proposition 3.10(a)). Thus, if $\theta = 0$ (tax changes are ignored, so extreme limited attention), then $EB(\tau) \simeq 0$. The reason is that starting from a zero tax rate, if the imposition of a positive tax rate is ignored by the individual, then there are no substitution effects, hence there is no deadweight loss either. When $\theta = 0$, the budget constraint of the consumer must nevertheless be respected on imposition of the tax. Thus, the distortionary tax under extreme limited attention ($\theta = 0$) becomes just a lump-sum tax, that leads to a choice of the first best consumption bundle. On the other hand, if $0 < \theta < 1$ then the excess burden increases with the square of θ, just as it does for the tax rate, τ. Thus, limited attention reduces

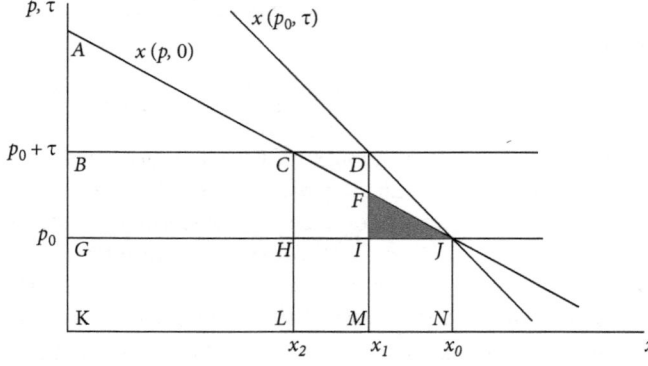

Figure 3.4 The excess burden of taxation under limited attention.

the excess burden of taxation, which is welfare improving. In classical public finance theory, it does not matter if taxes are imposed on consumers or producers. However, under limited attention, the two taxes may lead to different effects. The reason is that taxes on producers are often included in the posted price of the good, hence, they are more salient (higher θ); thus the excess burden arising from these taxes is relatively greater.

Going back to Figure 3.4, where we assumed $\frac{\partial x}{\partial I} = 0$, suppose that starting from a price of p_0, the curve $x(p, 0)$ becomes steeper (price elasticity reduces), while the curve pivots around the point J. Then the area FIJ expands, so the excess burden increases.

If there are income effects $\frac{\partial x}{\partial I} > 0$, then limited attention may increase the excess burden of taxation; this result arises even if $\theta = 0$, so the consumer pays no attention to tax, $\frac{\partial x}{\partial \tau} = 0$. When $\frac{\partial x}{\partial \tau} = 0$, we get from (3.55) that $\frac{\partial h}{\partial \tau} = x \frac{\partial x}{\partial I}$. Substitute this, and $\theta^c = \left(\frac{\partial h}{\partial \tau} / \frac{\partial h}{\partial p} \right)$, into the first line of (3.56), to get

$$EB(\tau) \simeq \frac{-1}{2}(\tau x)^2 \left(\frac{\partial x}{\partial I} \Big/ \frac{\partial h}{\partial p} \right) \frac{\partial x}{\partial I} > 0. \qquad (3.57)$$

The sign in (3.57) follows because $\frac{\partial h}{\partial p} < 0$. Thus, under complete inattention, we can get a positive excess burden of taxation when there are income effects.

To see this, consider an example in which x is the number of visits to the theater and y is food. Suppose that the government levies tax, $\tau > 0$, on theater visits and the consumer is completely inattentive to these taxes ($\theta = 0$). The budget constraint of the consumer is given by $(p + \tau)x(p, \tau, I) + y(p, \tau, I) = I$. Differentiate both sides with respect to τ to get

$$\frac{\partial x}{\partial \tau} + \frac{\partial y}{\partial \tau} = -x.$$

Thus, one method by which the budget may be balanced is that the individual ignores the effect of tax on x, i.e., sets $\frac{\partial x}{\partial \tau} = 0$. In this case, as the consumer's income goes down after paying the tax, the full effect is felt as a decrease in the consumption of food, y. Thus, the new income level, net of taxes, is not allocated efficiently between theater visits and food, which creates a deadweight loss from taxation, hence, the excess burden is positive.

Finally, note from Proposition 3.10, when tax increases are imposed on pre-existing positive tax rates, then the tax increases can have first order effects (as in the term $\tau_0 \Delta \tau$), although these effects are weakened by inattention (low values of θ^c).

3.9.4 A note on reduced-form approaches to behavioral public finance

Departures in behavior from the neoclassical benchmark can sometimes be explained by several competing behavioral explanations. Consider, for instance, the finding that individuals might buy energy inefficient lightbulbs and cause carbon externalities on others (Hausman, 1979; Allcott et al., 2014). Do individuals engage in this decision because they are present-biased (lightbulbs impose current costs, but future benefits; see Volume 3 of the book), or simply because they possess limited attention (insufficient attention to future benefits; see Volume 5 of the book)? Competing behavioral explanations of the same phenomenon are viewed by some as a drawback of behavioral economics. This is a mistake. There are almost always competing explanations of any phenomenon in any science, at least initially before empirical evidence adjudicates among the competing explanations. Even in neoclassical economics one can often explain the same phenomenon by invoking some form of asymmetric information plus auxiliary assumptions or full information plus other auxiliary assumptions. It is the role of empirical evidence in economics, as it is in science, to help us choose the correct explanation.

Reduced-form approaches to behavioral public finance seek to provide a framework that is robust to alternative behavioral explanations, within some subset of explanations. Mullainathan et al. (2012) propose a reduced-form approach that nests competing behavioral explanations that draw on the distinction between experienced utility and decision utility (see Chapter 1 and Volume 5 of the book). We now consider the basic model.

Suppose that there are n individuals indexed by $i = 1, \ldots, n$. Individual i can take a binary action $a_i \in \{0, 1\}$, for instance, buy or not buy an energy efficient product; 0 denotes *inaction*, while 1 denotes taking the *action*. The action costs p (price and other costs associated with the action). The benefit to individual i from the action, in income equivalent units, is b_i; benefits have a distribution function F in the population. By taking the action, an individual imposes an externality e on all individuals (e.g., higher carbon emissions for all when an individual buys a more polluting car). So if $m \leq n$ individuals choose to take the action, then the externality on any individual is me.

The government levies a tax t on the action taken by an individual. Hence, the post-tax price paid by an individual who chooses to take the action is $q(t)$; for instance, in the case of a specific consumption tax, $q(t) = p + t$. The government also transfers an amount T to each individual, so the government budget constraint can be written as $G(t, T) = 0$.

The initial income of each individual is Y, and each individual has an increasing and concave utility function, U, that is defined as follows.

$$U = \begin{cases} U(Y + T + (b - q(t)) - me) & \text{if} \quad a_i = 1 \\ U(Y + T - me) & \text{if} \quad a_i = 0 \end{cases}. \tag{3.58}$$

It follows that $a_i = 1$ is strictly preferred to $a_i = 0$ by a neoclassical consumer, if

$$b > q(t). \tag{3.59}$$

We can also find that $m = 1 - F(q(t))$. In contrast to (3.59), behavioral consumers, in this reduced-form approach, chose $a_i = 1$ over $a_i = 0$, if

$$b + d(b, t) > q(t), \tag{3.60}$$

where $d(b, t) \gtrless 0$ is a non-stochastic distortion term that reflects behavioral factors, and is increasing in b. We may describe the decision rule (3.60) as reflecting *decision utility* and the decision rule (3.59) as reflecting *experienced utility*. This framework applies to any situation where there is a wedge between experienced and decision utility. Clearly this does not apply to many kinds of behavioral factors such as social preferences or to the presence of reference points, where no such meaningful distinction between the two notions of utility is required.

> **Example 3.20** *(Laibson, 1997; O'Donoghue and Rabin, 1999): Suppose that the individual takes some action that involves current benefits and future costs (e.g., buying consumer durables on credit; see Volume 3 for several examples). Let $b = v - c$, where v is the current benefit and c is the future cost. Suppose that $t = T = 0$ and the price $p = p_0 + p_1$, where p_0 is the price paid now and p_1 is the price paid in the future. Suppose that $\beta \in (0, 1)$, then present-biased individuals choose to take the action if $v - \beta c - (p_0 + \beta p_1) > 0$, or*

$$v - c + (1 - \beta)(c + p_1) > p_0 + p_1.$$

Setting $d(b,t) = (1 - \beta)(c + p_1)$ and $q = p_0 + p_1$, we get the decision rule in (3.60).

Example 3.21 *(Thaler, and Sunstein, 2009): Let b denote benefits and q(t) the costs from an action. Then, the decision rule in the absence of nudges is $b > q(t)$. Suppose that there are $j = 1, 2, \ldots, k$ possible nudges that may induce (or deter) the individual to take the relevant action. Denote the jth nudge by $d_j(b, t)$. Then, using (3.60), the decision rule in the presence of the jth nudge is $b + d_j(b, t) > q(t)$.*

The main insight offered by this reduced-form approach is to show that the identity of the marginal individuals on whom policy applies in the presence and in the absence of behavioral factors is different. Suppose, for instance, that the government increases the tax rate from t to $t + \Delta t$. Prior to the tax increase, the individuals who took the action satisfied the condition

$$b > p + t - d,$$

while after the tax increase, the individuals who take the action satisfy the condition

$$b > p + t + \Delta t - d.$$

The marginal behavioral individual for small changes, $\Delta t \to 0$, is one whose benefit from the action is $b \approx p + t - d$. In neoclassical economics, the marginal individual has benefits $b \approx p + t$, which reflect the true marginal cost of taking the action. Suppose that $d > 0$ (e.g., sin goods; see Volume 3 for a framework of analysis), then for a behavioral individual, the marginal benefit, b, of the good is below the marginal cost, $p + t$. The extra tax could then dissuade this individual from undertaking the activity, which is welfare improving. In Volume 3, we report evidence, based on Canadian data, that cigarette smokers welcome an increase in the tax rate. As Mullainathan et al., (2014, p. 17.9) put it: "For many policy problems, the feature of the behavioral bias that matters most is how it affects who is marginal. This change is at the heart of our entire approach."

Farhi and Gabaix (2015) propose an ambitious research program in which they model limited attention by using the sparse max operator (see Volume 5 for the details) and develop the theory of optimal taxation with behavioral agents. They derive optimal tax formulae under these conditions for commodity taxes (the analogue of Ramsey taxes), income taxes (the analog of the Mirrlees approach to non-linear income taxation), and corrective taxes in the presence of externalities (the analog of the Pigouvian framework in classical public finance). The optimal taxes in classical public finance are often too complex relative to real-world taxes that are relatively simple. The authors exploit insights from limited attention to show that taxpayers may give even lower salience to complex tax systems, driving an even greater wedge between the private marginal cost and the private marginal benefit of a decision, making it welfare improving to design simpler tax systems.

3.10 Exercises for Part II

1. (Camerer et al., 2003) (a) Evidence shows that people are ambiguity averse (see Part 1) and have social preferences (see Part 2). Do these findings create a need for paternalism?
(b) Use asymmetric paternalism in order to evaluate the following policy proposal. A policy that requires patients to get a second opinion before undergoing surgery.
(c) Can one use asymmetric paternalism to rationalize the existing licensing regulations

in many countries for physicians (and car drivers) that bar entry into the profession if one does not have the appropriate license?

(d) How can *cooling-off periods* for consumers, advocated under soft paternalism, influence the behavior of sellers?

2. (Camerer et al., 2003) Suicide is currently illegal, which is a form of *heavy-handed paternalism*. How might you deal with the problem of suicide using soft paternalism?

3. (Camerer et al., 2003) How might one use asymmetric paternalism in order to address the problems indicated in the following empirical findings?

(a) Enron's 401(k) plan was heavily invested in the company's own stock with the result that when Enron collapsed, so did the pension plans of the employees.

(b) Evidence indicates that people vastly overestimate the chances of winning lotteries, which might account for the large participation rates in lotteries.

(c) "Rent to own" establishments lease consumer durables and furniture, typically to low-income consumers. Most US states treat these contracts as rental agreements even though 70% of the consumers buy the products they rent. This frees up firms from the regulations that cap interest rates. Consumers end up paying high interest rates.

(d) People often run up high credit card debts because they fail to fully appreciate the difference between simple and compound interest rates.

4. Derive the analog of Proposition 3.1 under Type 2 asymmetric information (Definition 3.3b).

5. (Dalton and Ghosal, 2011) Consider the framework developed in Section 3.2. Suppose that the action set is $A = \{a_1, a_2, a_3\}$ and the set of psychological states is given by $\Theta = \{\theta_1, \theta_2, \theta_3\}$. The decision maker faces payoff relevant uncertainty. There are two equally likely states of the world in which the payoffs corresponding to each action–psychological state pair are given in Tables 3.2 (for state 1) and 3.3 (for state 2).

(a) Suppose that the decision maker must choose his action before uncertainty about the state of the world resolves and that he is an expected utility maximizer. What is the

Table 3.2 Payoffs in state 2.

	θ_1	θ_2	θ_3
a_1	−1	0	0
a_2	0	3	0.5
a_3	1	4	1

Source: Dalton and Ghosal, 2011.

Table 3.3 Payoffs in state 1.

	θ_1	θ_2	θ_3
a_1	1	4	1
a_2	0.5	3	0
a_3	0	0	−1

Source: Dalton and Ghosal, 2011.

unique solution to the behavioral decision problem (BDP) and the corresponding payoff of the decision maker? Would the decision maker be better off if he had known the state of the world with certainty?

(b) Consider the payoff matrix in Table 3.4.

Suppose first that $A = \{a_1, a_2\}$ and $\Theta = \{\theta_1, \theta_2\}$, so the relevant payoff matrix is the 2×2 payoff submatrix in Table 3.4. Now expand the set of actions and psychological states such that $A = \{a_1, a_2, a_3\}$ and $\Theta = \{\theta_1, \theta_2, \theta_3\}$; the payoff matrix is given by the entire 3×3 payoff matrix in Table 3.4. Find the unique BDP solution in each case. Is the decision maker better off or worse off following an increase in the set of actions?

6. Consider the Bernheim and Rangel (2009) framework developed in Section 3.6. Consider the setup in Example 3.9 but replace (3.25) by the following choices

$$C(X_1) = \{a\}, C(X_2) = \{b\}, C(X_3) = \{c\}, C(X_4) = \{c\}.$$

Show that the binary relation R^* is intransitive.

7. (Bernheim and Rangel, 2009) Consider the Bernheim–Rangel framework in Section 3.6. Let $X_1 = \{a, b\}$, $X_2 = \{b, c\}$, $X_3 = \{a, c\}$, $X_4 = \{a, b, c\}$, and $\chi = \{X_1, X_2, X_3, X_4\}$. Suppose that we have two possible ancillary conditions A and A'. The welfare relevant GCSs are given by $G = \chi \times \{A, A'\}$. Under the ancillary condition A, b is never chosen when a is available and c is never chosen. Under the ancillary condition A', b is never chosen when c is available and a is never chosen.

(a) Are any of the alternatives, a, b, c, comparable under P or P^*?

(b) What conclusions can you draw about the set of weak and strict individual optima (see Definition 3.8).

8. (Masatlioglu et al., 2012) Consider the CLA method in Section 3.7. Show that the complete and transitive relation P in this model is acyclic if and only if the choice function c satisfies WARP(LA) given in Definition 3.16.

9. (Masatlioglu et al., 2012; Cherepanov et al., 2013) Consider the Rationalization model in Section 3.7 and the associated set of rationalizable alternatives, $\hat{\Gamma}$, given in (3.40). Construct examples to show the following.

(a) Show using an example with 3 alternatives and 2 rationales that $\hat{\Gamma}$ is not an attention filter (Definition 3.11).

(b) Show that for any rationalization, R_i, and some set S of alternatives

$$x \in \hat{\Gamma}(S) \Rightarrow x \in \hat{\Gamma}(T) \text{ for all } x \in T \subset S.$$

Table 3.4 Payoffs for each pair of actions and psychological states.

	θ_1	θ_2	θ_3
a_1	-1	0	0
a_2	0	3	0.5
a_3	1	4	1

Source: Dalton and Ghosal, 2011.

Does this property hold in the CLA model?

(c) What relationship can you conclude between the CLA model and the Rationalization model from your answers to (a) and (b)?

(d) Show that the Rationalization model is a special case of the CLA model if the rationales, R_i, were transitive and complete for all i (Note: in the Rationalization model R_i is incomplete).

10. (Masatlioglu et al., 2012) Consider the model of CLA in Section 3.7. Suppose that there are four alternatives x, y, a, b. The alternatives a and b are never chosen (unless there is no other alternative) but they alter the attention of the decision maker. The decision maker's preference is given by $y \succ x \succ a \succ b$ and she picks the best alternative using these preferences. She considers y only when either a or b is feasible, but not both, and always considers all other alternatives. Show that her consideration set mapping satisfies WARP(LA) (Definition 3.16) but it does not satisfy Weak WARP (Definition 3.17).

11. (Sugden, 2013) Thaler and Sunstein (2009), in their libertarian paternalism approach, give the example of the operation of a cash machine. The machine returns the card first, which if taken out first, triggers the delivery of cash. This prevents individuals from forgetting their card in the cash machine. Consider now the contractarian approach outlined in Section 3.8. Suppose that we are back in time when machines returned cash before the card. How would a contractarian design the appropriate intervention if it were found that people sometimes forget cards in the machine? In your answer, consider two different cases. (i) The cash machine is owned by a private firm. (ii) The cash machine is owned by a public agency that finances its operations through general taxation.

12. (Mullainathan et al., 2012) Consider the reduced-form model in Section 3.9.4. In each of the two examples below, show that the decision rule for the individual can be stated in terms of the decision utility interpretation in (3.60) and find an explicit formula for $d(b, t)$.

(a) Inattention to salient components of price (Gabaix and Laibson, 2006; Chetty et al., 2009; DellaVigna, 2009) Suppose that individuals decide to take some action for which benefits are salient. However, the individual pays limited attention to sales taxes. Inattentive individuals discount non-salient costs by the factor $\theta \in (0, 1)$. Thus, inattentive consumers think that they are paying a price $p + \theta t$, where p is the retail price per unit and t is a sales tax.

(b) False beliefs and overconfidence (Sandroni and Squintani 2007, Spinnewijn 2015) Suppose that agents misestimate or have false beliefs about the benefits from an action. For instance, the unemployed could be too overconfident of their ability to find a job, hence, searching suboptimally for a new job. Conversely, people may overweigh the benefits to taking an action, for example, when buying an inefficacious herbal medicine. Instead of taking the action when $b > q(t)$, such people take the action when $\hat{b} > q(t)$.

REFERENCES FOR PART II

Abadie, A. and Gay, S. (2004). The impact of presumed consent legislation on cadaveric organ donation: a cross country study. *Journal of Health Economics* 25: 599–620.

Afriat, S. (1967). The construction of a utility function from expenditure data. *International Economic Review* 8: 67–71.

Allcott H., Mullainathan S., and Taubinsky D. (2014). Externalities, internalities, and the targeting of energy policy. *Journal of Public Economics* 112: 72–88.

Ariely, D. and Wertenbroch, K. (2002). Procrastination, deadlines, and performance: self-control by precommitment. *Psychological Science* 13: 219–24.

Atkinson, A. and Stiglitz, J. (1980). *Lectures on Public Economics*. New York: McGraw-Hill.

Bandura, A. (1977). *Social Learning Theory*. New York: General Learning Press.

Benartzi, S. and Thaler, R. H. (2004). Save more tomorrow: using behavioral economics to increase employee savings. *Journal of Political Economy* 112: S164–S187.

Benjamin, D. J., Heffetz, O., Kimball, M. S., and Rees-Jones, A. (2012). What do you think would make you happier? What do you think you would choose? *American Economic Review* 102(5): 2083–110.

Bentham, J. (1789). *An Introduction to the Principles of Morals and Legislation*. Oxford: Clarendon Press.

Bernheim, B. D. and Rangel, A. (2004). Addiction and cue-conditioned cognitive processes. *American Economic Review* 94(5): 1558–90.

Bernheim, B. D. and Rangel, A. (2007). Toward choice-theoretic foundations for behavioral welfare economics. *American Economic Review Papers and Proceedings* 97: 464–70.

Bernheim, B. D. and Rangel, A. (2009). Beyond revealed preference: choice-theoretic foundations for behavioral welfare economics. *Quarterly Journal of Economics* 124(1): 51–104.

Beshears, J., Choi, J. J., Laibson, D., and Madrian, B. C. (2008). How are preferences revealed? *Journal of Public Economics* 92(8–9): 1787–94.

Buchanan, J. M. (1968). *The Demand and Supply of Public Goods*. Chicago: Rand McNally.

Buchanan, J. M. (1975). *The Limits of Liberty*. Chicago: University of Chicago Press.

Buchanan, J. M. (1986). *Liberty, Market and State*. Brighton: Wheatsheaf.

Camerer, C. F. (2008). The case for mindful economics. In A. Caplin and A. Schotter (eds.), *The Foundations of Positive and Normative Economics*. Oxford: Oxford University Press.

Camerer, C. F., Issacharoff, S., Loewenstein, G., O'Donoghue, T., and Rabin, M. (2003). Regulation for conservatives: behavioral economics and the case for asymmetric paternalism. *University of Pennsylvania Law Review* 151: 1211–54.

Caplin, A. (2008). Economic theory and psychological data: bridging the divide. In A. Caplin and A. Schotter (eds.), *The Foundations of Positive and Normative Economics*. Oxford: Oxford University Press.

Caplin, A. and Schotter, A. (eds.) (2008). *The Foundations of Positive and Normative Economics*. Oxford: Oxford University Press.

Cason, T. N. and Plott, C. R. (2014). Misconceptions and game form recognition: challenges to theories of revealed preference. *Journal of Political Economy* 122(6): 1235–70.

Cherepanov, V., Feddersen, T., and Sandroni, A. (2013). Rationalization. *Theoretical Economics* 8: 775–800.

Chetty, R., Looney, A., and Kroft, K. (2009). Salience and taxation: theory and evidence. *American Economic Review* 99(4): 1145–77.

Choi, J. J., Laibson, D., and Madrian, B. C. (2004). Plan design and 401(k) savings outcomes. *National Tax Journal* 57: 275–98.

Choi, S., Kariv S., Müller, W., and Silverman, D. (2014). Who is (more) rational? *American Economic Review* 104(6): 1518–50.

Dalton, P. S. and Ghosal, S. (2011). Behavioral decisions and policy. *CESifo Economic Studies* 57(4): 560–80.

Dalton, P. S. and Ghosal, S. (2018). Self fulfilling mistakes: characterization and welfare. *Economic Journal* 128(609): 683–709.

Dalton, P. S., Ghosal, S., and Mani, A. (2016). Poverty and aspirations failure. *Economic Letters* 126(590): 165–88.

DellaVigna, S. (2009). Psychology and economics: evidence from the field. *Journal of Economic Literature* 47(2): 315–72.

Eliaz, K. and Schotter, A. (2010). Paying for confidence: an experimental study of the demand for non-instrumental information. *Games and Economic Behavior* 70(2): 304–24.

Farhi, E. and Gabaix, X. (2015). Optimal taxation with behavioral agents. Manuscript under preparation.

Fleurbaey, M. and Blanchet, D. (2013). *Beyond GDP: Measuring Welfare and Assessing Sustainability.* Oxford: Oxford University Press.

Fleurbaey, M. and Schokkaert, E. (2013). Behavioral welfare economics and redistribution. *American Economic Journal: Microeconomics* 5(3): 180–205.

Gabaix, X. and Laibson, D. (2006). Shrouded attributes, consumer myopia, and information suppression in competitive markets. *Quarterly Journal of Economics* 121: 505–40.

Glaeser, E. L. (2006). Paternalism and psychology. *University of Chicago Law Review* 73: 133–56.

Goeree, J. K. and Holt, C. A. (2001). Ten little treasures of game theory and ten intuitive contradictions. *American Economic Review* 91(5): 1402–22.

Guala, F. and Mittone, L. (2015). A political justification of nudging. *Review of Philosophy and Psychology.* Online March 5, 2015.

Gul, F. and Pesendorfer, W. (2008). The case for mindless economics. In A. Caplin and A. Schotter (eds.), *The Foundations of Positive and Normative Economics.* Oxford: Oxford University Press.

Hausman, J. A. (1979). Individual discount rates and the purchase and utilization of energy-using durables. *Bell Journal of Economics* 10(1): 33–54.

Houthakker, H. S. (1950). Revealed preference and the utility function. *Economica* 17(66): 159–74.

Iyengar, S. S. and Lepper, M. R. (2000). Why choice is demotivating: can one desire too much of a good thing? *Journal of Personality and Social Psychology* 79: 995–1006.

Johnson, E. J., Camerer, C. F., Sen, S., and Rymon, T. (2002). Detecting failures of backward induction: monitoring information search in sequential bargaining. *Journal of Economic Theory* 104(1): 16–47.

Johnson, E. J. and Goldstein, D. G. (2003). Do defaults save lives? *Science* 302: 1338–9.

Johnson, E. J., Hershey, J., Meszaros, J., and Kunreuther, H. (1993). Framing, probability distortions, and insurance decisions. *Journal of Risk and Uncertainty* 7: 35–53.

Jolls, C., Sunstein, C. R., and Thaler, R. H. (1998). A behavioral approach to law and economics. *Stanford Law Review* 50: 1471–550.

Kahneman, D., Knetsch, J., and Thaler, R. (1991). The endowment effect, loss aversion, and status quo bias. *Journal of Economic Perspectives* 5: 193–206.

Kahneman, D. and Tversky, A. (1984). Choices, values, and frames. *The American Psychologist* 39: 341–50.

Kahneman, D. and Tversky, A. (eds.). (2000). *Choices, Values and Frames.* New York: Cambridge University Press.

Kahneman, D., Wakker, P., and Sarin, R. (1997). Back to Bentham? Explorations of experienced utility. *Quarterly Journal of Economics* 112: 375–406.

Kamenica, E., Mullainathan, S., and Thaler, R. (2011). Helping consumers know themselves. *American Economic Review* 101(3): 417–22.

Klick, J. and Mitchell, G. (2006). Government regulation of irrationality: moral and cognitive hazards. *Minnesota Law Review* 90: 1620–63.

Koszegi, B. and Rabin, M. (2008a). Revealed mistakes and revealed preference. In A. Caplin and A. Schotter (eds.), *The Foundations of Positive and Normative Economics.* Oxford: Oxford University Press.

Koszegi, B. and Rabin, M. (2008b). Choices, situations, and happiness. *Journal of Public Economics* 92: 1821–32.

Kreps, D. M. (1990). *A Course in Microeconomic Theory.* Princeton, NJ: Princeton University Press.

Kreps, D. M. and Porteus, E. L. (1978). Temporal resolution of uncertainty and dynamic choice theory. *Econometrica* 46: 185–200.

Laibson, D. (1997). Golden eggs and hyperbolic discounting. *Quarterly Journal of Economics* 112: 443–77.

Layard, R. (2005). *Happiness: Lessons from a New Science.* London: Allen Lane.

Loewenstein, G. and Haisley, E. (2008). The economist as therapist: methodological ramifications of "Light" Paternalism. In A. Caplin and A. Schotter (eds.), *The Foundations of Positive and Normative Economics*. Oxford: Oxford University Press.

Loewenstein, G. and Ubel, P. A. (2008). Hedaric adaptation and the role of decision and experience utility in public policy. *Journal of Public Economics* 92: 1795–810.

Madrian, B. C. and Shea, D. F. (2001). The power of suggestion: inertia in 401(k) participation and savings behavior. *Quarterly Journal of Economics* 116: 1149–525.

Manzini, P. and Mariotti, M. (2007). Sequentially rationalizable choice. *American Economic Review* 97(5): 1824–39.

Manzini, P. and Mariotti, M. (2012). Categorize then choose: boundedly rational choice and welfare. *Journal of the European Economic Association* 10(5): 1141–65.

Manzini, P. and Mariotti, M. (2014). Welfare economics and bounded rationality: the case for model-based approaches. *Journal of Economic Methodology* (21)4: 343–60.

Masatlioglu, Y., Nakajima, D., and Ozbay, E. Y. (2012). Revealed attention. *American Economic Review* 102(5): 2183–205.

Mas-Colell, A., Whinston, M. D., and Green, J. R. (1995). *Microeconomic Theory*. New York: Oxford University Press.

Mullainathan, S., Kling, J. R., Shafir, E., Vermeulen, L., and Wrobel, M. V. (2012). Comparison friction: experimental evidence from medicare drug plans. *Quarterly Journal of Economics* 127(1): 199–235.

Mullainathan, S., Schwartzstein, J., and Congdon, W. (2012). A reduced-form approach to behavioral public finance. *Annual Review of Economics* 4: 511–40.

O'Donoghue, T. and Rabin, M. (1999). Doing it now or later. *American Economic Review* 89: 103–24.

Park, C. W., Jun, S. Y., and MacInnis, D. J. (2000). Choosing what I want versus rejecting what I do not want: an application of decision framing to product option choice decisions. *Journal of Marketing Research* 37: 187–202.

Piccione, M. and Spiegler, R. (2012). Price competition under limited comparability. *Quarterly Journal of Economics* 127: 97–135.

Posner, R. A. (1986). *Economic Analysis of Law*. 3rd edition. Boston: Little, Brown.

Riis, J., Loewenstein, G., Baron, J., Jepson, C., Fagerlin A., and Ubel, P. A. (2005). Ignorance of hedonic adaptation to hemo-dialysis: a study using ecological momentary assessment. *Journal Experimental Psychology: General* 134: 3–9.

Rubinstein, A. and Salant, Y. (2012). Eliciting welfare preferences from behavioural data sets. *Review of Economic Studies* 79: 375–87.

Salant, Y. and Rubinstein, A. (2008). (A, f): choice with frames. *Review of Economic Studies* 75(4): 1287–9.

Samuelson, P. A. (1948). Consumption theory in terms of revealed preference. *Economica* 15(60): 243–53.

Samuelson, W. and Zeckhauser, R. J. (1988). Status quo bias in decision making. *Journal of Risk and Uncertainty* 1: 7–59.

Sandroni, A. and Squintani, F. (2007). Overconfidence, insurance, and paternalism. *American Economic Review* 97: 1994–2004.

Schotter, A. (2008). What's so informative about choice? In A. Caplin and A. Schotter (eds.), *The Foundations of Positive and Normative Economics*. Oxford: Oxford University Press.

Spinnewijn, J. (2015). Unemployed but optimistic: optimal insurance design with biased beliefs. *Journal of the European Economic Association* 13(1): 130–67.

Stiglitz, J. E. (2000). *Economics of the Public Sector*. 3rd edition. New York: W.W. Norton & Company.

Sugden, R. (2008). Why incoherent preferences do not justify paternalism. *Constitutional Political Economy* 19: 226–48.

Sugden, R. (2013). The behavioural economist and the social planner: to whom should behavioural welfare economics be addressed? *Inquiry: An Interdisciplinary Journal of Philosophy* 56(5): 519–38.

Sunstein, C. R. and Thaler, R. H. (2003). Libertarian paternalism is not an oxymoron. *University of Chicago Law Review* 70: 1159–202.

Thaler, R. H. and Sunstein, C. R. (2003). Libertarian paternalism. *American Economic Review: Papers and Proceedings* 93: 175–9.

Thaler, R. H. and Sunstein, C. R. (2009). *Nudge: Improving Decisions about Health, Wealth, and Happiness*. New Haven, CT: Penguin Books.

Tversky, A. and Kahneman, D. (1981). The framing of decisions and psychology of choice. *Science* 211: 453–8.

Ubel, P. A., Loewenstein, G., Schwarz, N., and Smith, D. (2005). Misimagining the unimaginable: the disability paradox and healthcare decision making. *Health Psychology* 24: S57–S62.

Wisdom, J., Downs, J. S., and Loewenstein, G. (2010). Promoting healthy choices: information versus convenience. *American Economic Journal: Applied Economics* 2(2): 164–78.

PART III
NEUROECONOMICS

CHAPTER 4

Neuroeconomics

4.1 Introduction

It is useful to begin with a definition of neuroeconomics. Camerer et al. (2015) define neuroeconomics as follows.

> Neuroeconomics is the study of the biological microfoundations of economic cognition and economic behavior. Biological microfoundations are neurochemical mechanisms and pathways, like brain regions, neurons, genes, and neurotransmitters.[1] Economic cognition includes memory, preferences, emotions, mental representations, expectations, anticipation, learning, perception, information processing, inference, simulation, valuation, and the subjective experience of reward. In general, neuroeconomic research seeks to identify and test biologically microfounded models that link cognitive building blocks to economic behavior.

Neuroeconomic insights have already begun to enrich behavioral economics, and may do so even more, in due course, but in the past they have not been massively critical. For instance, the work of Kahneman and Tversky in the 1970s that laid the seeds of behavioral economics, and much subsequent work, did not use neural foundations. The System 1 and System 2 distinction (see Volume 5) that Kahneman (2011) uses to motivate judgment heuristics is just a useful metaphor to organize behavioral insights; there is no clear cut distinction between the brain regions that correspond to these systems.

The advocates of neuroeconomics suggest several potential benefits of their research, many of which are necessarily speculative at this early stage (Glimcher et al., 2009; Glimcher and Fehr, 2014; Camerer et al., 2005; Camerer et al., 2015). The most ambitious hope is that, in due course, economic models will make joint predictions about observed choices and the neural mechanisms that give rise to these choices. Such models can then be tested using either traditional methods in economics or neuroeconomic methods, or both. Furthermore, such theories may make novel predictions that theories based on choice behavior alone might not be able to make.

Other ambitious hopes from neuroeconomic research include direct measurements of human welfare, and the use of neuroeconomic data to spur the development of newer models in

---

[1] Neurotransmitters are molecules that carry neurochemical signals from one neuron to another.

economics. The common perception is that neuroeconomics tries to identify particular brain areas for each task. However, as Camerer et al. (2015) note, the main thrust of neuroeconomics is the hope that "common patterns of [brain] circuitry will emerge which will inform debates about the computations that are performed, and suggest new theories of behavior and new predictions."

The literature on neuroeconomics, and the neuroscience that it draws on, is already quite vast. This chapter gives a brief account of a few selected topics from this literature. We make no pretense at being complete, comprehensive, or balanced. One justification for this brevity is that several excellent accounts written by the leaders in the field are already available (Glimcher et al., 2009; Glimcher, 2011; Glimcher and Fehr, 2014; Camerer, 2013; Camerer et al., 2015). We choose to focus only on a few studies that explore the neural foundations of some of the human behavior outlined in the book: behavioral decision theory, social preferences, time preferences, and strategic behavior. The hope is to give the readers a flavor of the methods and results, so as to stimulate their interest in a fuller exploration of the issues from more authoritative sources.

We omit a range of standard topics in neuroeconomics that can be more fully pursued in the references. These include estimation techniques and computational methods in neuro-economics, and the neuroeconomics of learning and emotions. We also omit a discussion of the debate between those who argue that economics should only consider choice data and others who argue for a broader view of economics; the thrust of these issues has already been considered in Chapter 3. In the most restrictive view of economics, all non-choice data is inadmissible, particularly neuroeconomic data; this position is most starkly outlined in Gul and Pesendorfer (2008). For a view offering strong support for a broader view of economics, particularly encompassing neuroeconomic data, see Camerer (2008).[2] Several key arguments offered by Camerer such as the ability of neuroeconomic data to predict human choice and estimate behavioral parameters of interest are illustrated in this chapter.

The first two sections give an introduction to the basics. Section 4.2 gives a brief introduction to brain areas and regions of interest to neuroeconomists. Section 4.3 gives an introduction to alternative methods of measuring brain activity and identifying neural circuitry responsible for economic decisions. Each method has its own advantages and disadvantages, hence, a more complete picture typically emerges by comparing the results from different complementary techniques. We separate the techniques into two classes: *Measurement techniques* and *manipulation techniques*, and evaluate them on the following three criteria. *Temporal resolution* (time frequency of recording of brain activity), *spatial resolution* (precision with which one can narrow down brain activity to a particular area), and the *degree of invasiveness*.

Measurement techniques typically establish correlations between economic behavior and brain activity. This can take the form of single unit recording of neuronal activity, or forming 2D or 3D images of brain activity. We mainly discuss *single-neuron recording, electroencephalography* and *magnetoencephalography*, *positron emission tomography* (PET), and *functional magnetic resonance imaging* (fMRI). Manipulation techniques alter activity (either increase or inhibit it) in a part of the brain and then study the resulting change in human behavior. The three main manipulation techniques that we describe are: *repeated transcranial magnetic stimulation* (rTMS), *transcranial direct current stimulation* (tDCS), and studies of *brain lesion patients*.

Section 4.4 considers the neuroeconomics of risky decisions with a focus on prospect theory. We begin in Section 4.4.1, with a brief discussion of the neural correlates of value and probability (Glimcher, 2011; Fehr and Rangel, 2011). We ask if the brain computes something like a utility

---

[2] See also Bernheim (2008) who offers a constructive view on the role of neuroeconomics.

from simple outcomes that is decisive in choosing among the outcomes. The bulk of the studies that answer this question have been performed using simple food items or simple tasks such as judging the quality of an item. It is not always clear if these results will carry over to more complex economic decisions such as portfolio choice (Camerer, 2013). The distinction that we drew in Volume 5 between *decision utility* and *experienced utility* turns out to be of critical importance in these experiments and is shown to have a good neural basis. Decision utility appears to be associated with the ventromedial prefrontal cortex while experienced utility is associated with the orbitofrontal cortex and the nucleus accumbens (these and other brain regions are described in more detail in Section 4.2). We also comment very briefly on the neural basis of mean variance utility, and the axiomatic approach to modeling brain activity.

Section 4.4.2 considers reference dependence. The amygdala has been implicated in fMRI studies of framing effects that are consistent with reference dependence (De Martino et al., 2006; Roiser et al., 2009). However, contrary to these claims, amygdala lesioned patients also exhibit framing effects (Talmi et al., 2010). In another implication of reference dependence— the WTA/WTP disparity—the neural correlates of WTA and WTP lie, respectively, in the ventromedial prefrontal cortex and the lateral orbitofrontal region (Knutson et al., 2008; De Martino et al., 2009). Section 4.4.3 considers loss aversion. Tom et al. (2007) find that in mixed lottery experiments, there is increased activity in the ventromedial prefrontal cortex, medial orbitofrontal cortex, and the anterior cingulate cortex when subjects face increased gains. However, when they face increased losses there is simply reduced activity in the same brain areas. Furthermore, when activity in the relevant brain area is fitted against gains/losses, the slope of the best fitting line is greater in absolute value for losses (where the slope is negative) as compared to gains; this is a form of *neural loss aversion*.

In particular, risky losses do not induce activity in the expected brain areas such as the amygdala and the insula, which are associated with fear, anxiety, and emotions. However, contrary to these results, patients with brain lesions in the amygdala show no loss aversion (De Martino et al., 2010). Several reasons may account for this difference, which include the range of losses used in the experiments, and the role of the amygdala as an intermediate output area (Jenison et al., 2011). Finally, Section 4.4.4 considers non-linear probability weighting. Prominent brain regions that appear to be associated with non-linear probabilities are the striatum and the cingulate gyrus (Paulus and Frank, 2006; Berns et al., 2008; Hsu et al., 2009).

Section 4.5, the longest section in this chapter, considers the neural foundations of social preferences. Section 4.5.1 considers the neural circuitry associated with social rewards. There appears to be a common neural activation for private and social rewards (Izuma et al., 2008; Smith et al., 2010). Based on identical underlying tasks, in private and social rewards treatments, areas of ventromedial prefrontal cortex and the ventral striatum, encode signals for both kinds of rewards (Lin et al., 2012). Section 4.5.2 shows that inequity averse preferences have strong neural foundations (Tricomi et al., 2010). Indeed the *neural strength* of these preferences appears to be greater than the *behaviorally observed* inequity averse preferences in a sense that we make precise. The ventral striatum and the ventromedial prefrontal cortex are important brain areas that appear to encode these preferences. Neural data can also differentiate between inequity averse preferences that arise from cases where the income distribution is generated from endogenous or exogenous effort (Cappelen et al., 2014).

Section 4.5.3 considers the neural basis of social punishment and trust. In a trust game with punishment that varied intentions and punishment costs, brain activity in the caudate nucleus under free punishment predicted the level of punishment when it was costly (De Quervain et al., 2004). Furthermore, the punishment decision involved a trade-off between reduction in personal rewards and the satisfaction arising from punishing. Hence, it activated the median orbitofrontal cortex, which has been implicated in similar trade-offs. These results speak to an important puzzle in classical game theory that arises from the empirical results from public goods games with punishment: Why do people punish when bygones are bygones? The neural answer is simply that people derive satisfaction from the act of punishing norm offenders; such punishment activates the brain's reward circuits, hence, punishment confers hedonic benefits. Players who are treated unfairly in ultimatum games show increased activation of the emotional regions of the brain such as the anterior insula (Sanfey et al., 2003). Thus, unfair offers appear to elicit an emotional or affective response.

The differing neural responses in punishing ingroup and outgroup members provide a neural basis for *parochial altruism* (Baumgartner et al., 2012). In punishing outgroup members there is activation in the right orbitofrontal gyrus, right lateral prefrontal cortex, and the right dorsal caudatus. However, in punishing ingroup members, subjects must generate rationales for mitigating punishments. The neural circuitry that is activated in this case is the temporoparietal junction that is often implicated in neural research on the *theory of the mind*, i.e., mentalizing about the motives, strategies, and beliefs about others. Brain manipulation techniques show that disrupting the right lateral prefrontal cortex reduces rates of rejection in ultimatum games (Knoch et al., 2009). Individuals with lesions in the ventromedial prefrontal cortex exhibit different social preferences relative to non-lesioned subjects (Koenigs and Tranel, 2007; Krajbich et al., 2009). The amygdala has also been implicated in the evaluation of fairness in ultimatum games (Koscik and Tranel, 2011; Gospic et al., 2011). The size of the amygdala is also correlated with the size of one's social network (Bickart et al., 2011).

Section 4.5.4 considers the neural basis of selected human virtues. Neural activity in deceptive and honest players is markedly different when they play the same game. Activity in the anterior cingulate cortex and the right inferior frontal gyrus in an anticipation task can successfully predict the extent of deception that an individual will engage in (Baumgartner et al., 2009). Section 4.5.5 shows that there is a neural basis to some of the constructs used in psychological game theory (see Volume 4), such as the feeling of *guilt* in trust games when receivers return low amounts to trustors (Chang et al., 2011).

Section 4.6 considers the neuroeconomics of time preferences. Support is found for two different models of time discounting considered in Volume 3, (β, δ) or quasi-hyperbolic discounting (Laibson, 1997), and the planner–doer models (Thaler and Shefrin, 1981; Fudenberg and Levine, 2006). Separate areas of the brain are activated when subjects express a preference for immediate rewards (β-areas), relative to delayed rewards (δ-areas). β-areas include nucleus accumbens, subgenual cingulate cortex, and medial orbitofrontal cortex, while δ-areas include posterior cingulate cortex, posterior parietal cortex, and the insula (McClure et al., 2004, 2007). However, these results have been questioned by contrary empirical evidence (Glimcher et al., 2007, Kable and Glimcher, 2007). In the planner–doer models, fMRI evidence indicates that the dorsolateral prefrontal cortex plays the role of a patient long-run planner (Hare et al., 2009). Temporary disruption of the dorsolateral prefrontal cortex using brain manipulation techniques leads subjects to choose more immediate rewards, which is consistent with the planner–doer approach (Figner et al., 2010).

Section 4.7 considers the neuroeconomics of strategic interaction. A major thrust of this literature is to uncover neural activity that illuminates how players develop and use a theory of the mind. In other words, how do players infer the likely strategies, beliefs, and mental models of others? One method of revealing a theory of the mind is to check for the contrast when humans play against human opponents and against computers. Different neural circuits appear to be engaged in the human–human and human–computer pairings (Gallagher et al., 2002; McCabe et al., 2001; Coricelli and Nagel, 2009).

Another issue is the differing neural activity of 'equilibrium types' who play in accordance with classical equilibrium strategies, and the 'behavioral types' who play non-equilibrium strategies (e.g., level-k players). Since beliefs and choices are aligned for equilibrium types, their brain activity occurred in largely similar areas, but brain activity was more dispersed for the behavioral types (Bhatt and Camerer, 2005). Within level-k subjects, differing neural activity has been found among high level reasoners (high k) and low level reasoners in a p-beauty game; decisions of high level reasoners were associated with relatively greater activity in the medial prefrontal cortex (Coricelli and Nagel, 2009). Two brain areas were particularly highlighted for high level reasoners; one is associated with taking a third person perspective while the other is involved in thinking about the strategies of like-minded other people. However, results from other studies have not always supported these conclusions (Kuo et al., 2009). Finally, we consider the neural basis of deception that is of critical importance in game theory. Emerging evidence supports level-k reasoning in simple, two-player, buyer–seller bargaining experiments where deception is possible (Bhatt et al., 2010, Bhatt et al., 2012).

Finally, in Section 4.8, we briefly touch upon the expanding literature on the pharmacology of economic and social decision making. The main aim of this research is to interfere with the body's *neuromodulator systems* by altering the levels of neuromodulators (dopamine, serotonin, norepinephrine), or hormones such as testosterone and oxytocin. We focus exclusive attention on the role of oxytocin as an illustration of this line of research. Readers interested in an authoritative and accessible survey can consult Crockett and Fehr (2014). Oxytocin has been shown to increase the level of trust that trustors place in trustees in trust games. However, the effect of oxytocin is very selective in influencing only the trust level of trustors; it does not alter the general level of optimism, risk perception, moods, or social trust (Kosfeld et al., 2005). Subsequent studies have enriched our understanding of oxytocin by examining the effects of interpersonal relations, generosity, cooperation, perceptions of trustworthiness, attractiveness, approachability, attachment, and socio-emotional responses such as envy and social aversion (Bartz et al., 2011). In the trust game, it is payoff improving for both parties if the trustor trusts more, hence, oxytocin plays a positive role. However, in other contexts, oxytocin may reduce the ability to recognize deceptive behavior and reduce one's payoffs (Israel et al., 2014).

4.2 A brief introduction to the brain

In this section, we briefly review some features of the human brain that are useful in the study of neuroeconomics; for an authoritative source for economists, see Glimcher and Fehr (2014). *Modularity* refers to the idea that the brain is composed of discrete parts that perform their own specific computations and then pass on the results to other brain areas for further processing and analysis (Gazzaniga, 2009). *Plasticity* refers to the ability of the brain to evolve and learn as the environment changes. *Automaticity* refers to the idea that we engage in certain behaviors/deliberations without being consciously aware that we are doing so.

We might often be unaware of the cause of our own behavior on account of automaticity. As Camerer et al. (2004) put it: "the human brain is like a monkey brain with a press secretary, which puts a coherent spin, and sometimes a wrong one, on what the monkey brain did." The brain is sometimes "too good" for its own good at *sense making*. Experimental evidence, reviewed elsewhere in the book, indicates that people claim to spot regularity in completely random patterns such as stock market prices. Elsewhere, hot hands in basketball, the gambler's fallacy, the hindsight bias, and regression to the mean may also, perhaps, be guided by a similar desire for sense making even when the underlying data does not support these inferences based on classical statistics (see Volume 5).

The flip side of these features is that the brain allocates attention selectively, which protects capacity limits in perception and cognition by biasing/prioritizing salient or relevant representations over others; recall, for instance, the phenomenon of confirmation bias discussed in Volume 5. In an interesting paper by Simons and Chabris (1999) with the title "Gorillas in our midst: Sustained inattentional blindness for dynamic events," subjects watch a video of six individuals playing basketball. The experimental task is to count the number of passes made by each team that wears a different jersey color. Within a minute, a gorilla walks into the center of the game and stays there for 9 seconds. At the end of the experiment, half the subjects in the experiment have no recollection of seeing a gorilla in the video clip; their attention was taken up by counting the number of passes.

When humans departed from their nearest primate relatives about 6 million years ago, the human brain was not redesigned from scratch. Evolution, because it is inherently conservative and cautious, added neural regions imparting significant cognitive ability to humans, such as the prefrontal cortex, on top of the existing brain structures. Going back even further into evolutionary history, at the core of the human brain is a primitive mammalian brain, the limbic system, that controls emotions such as fear, anger, disgust, etc. Thus, experiments conducted on other mammals are of potential value for an understanding of the human brain, particularly those conducted on our nearest primate relatives. For instance, rats become addicted to almost all the substances that humans become addicted to (Camerer, 2007). Wrapped around this primitive mammalian brain is the neocortex (also called the cerebral cortex, which corresponds to people's perception of gray matter) that accounts for about 5/6 of the human brain. The neocortex is responsible for human cognition, language, and speech. For instance, it allows humans, unlike other animals, to think about the longer-term consequences of their actions.

With this brief introductory background, let us consider the various brain regions that are important in neuroeconomics.[3] The four main regions of the brain are shown in Figure 4.1. Each of the four lobes is responsible for functions that are either independent or overlapping. The *frontal lobe* is associated with cognition and logic. The *parietal lobe* is associated with recognition and movement; the *occipital lobe* with the processing of visual information; and the *temporal lobe* with memory and auditory stimuli. Neuropsychological studies of aphasia (a term used for a collection of speech disorders) suggest that speech production and comprehension might be attributed to distinct frontal and temporal substrates. The lobes come in pairs, one on each side of the brain; language is associated with the left hemisphere of the brain. The lobes are connected by neurons that enable the brain to simultaneously engage its various parts to generate a composite response to external stimuli.

Example 4.1 *(Camerer et al., 2004): "When an automated insurance broker calls and says, 'Don't you want earthquake insurance? Press 1 for more information' the occipital lobe 'pictures' your house collapsing; the temporal lobe feels a negative emotion; and the frontal lobe receives the emotional signal and weighs it against the likely cost of insurance. If the frontal lobe 'decides' you should find out more, the parietal lobe sends signals to your finger to press 1 on your phone."*

---

[3] For textbook treatments see Breedlove et al. (2014) and Bear et al. (2007). For a brief and clear introduction, see Glimcher and Fehr (2014).

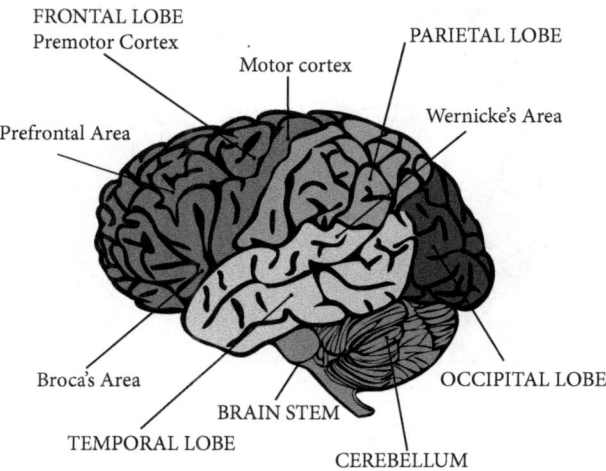

BRAIN FUNCTION

FRONTAL LOBE
Premotor Cortex

Motor cortex

PARIETAL LOBE

Prefrontal Area

Wernicke's Area

Broca's Area

OCCIPITAL LOBE

BRAIN STEM

TEMPORAL LOBE

CEREBELLUM

Figure 4.1 A classification of the brain into four lobes: frontal, parietal, occipital, and temporal. © Shutterstock

The following terminology is useful in identifying various brain regions; see Figure 4.2. We quote the following description from Zak (2004, p. 1739): "Terms for locations of brain regions include: dorsal (top, from the Latin for back); ventral (bottom facing the central axis, from the Latin for belly) or basal; rostral (front, from the Latin for beak) or anterior; caudal (back, from the Latin for tail) or posterior; superior (towards the top); inferior (towards the bottom); medial/mesial (middle); lateral (away from midline); and orbital (above the eyes, from the Latin orbital meaning eye sockets)." In evolutionary terms, ventral brain regions are typically phylogenetically older in comparison to dorsal and rostral regions.

It is sometimes helpful to separate the brain into three divisions. These are the forebrain or *telencephalon*, midbrain or *mesencephalon*, and the hindbrain or *brainstem*; see Figure 4.3. The focus in neuroeconomic research has been on the telencephalon. In turn, the telencephalon is typically divided into three main regions. These are the *cerebral cortex, thalamus* (Figure 4.3), and the *basal ganglia* (Figure 4.4). Our main focus will be on the cerebral cortex and the basal ganglia. Of these, in evolutionary terms, the cerebral cortex is the most recently evolved structure, while the basal ganglia is the oldest (recall that the more ventral structures are typically phylogenetically older).

The two regions in the basal ganglia, *caudate* and *putamen*, together comprise the *striatum*, an important brain region in neuroeconomics. The striatum, an input area of the basal ganglia, receives inputs from the frontal cortex and mainly sends its inputs to the output areas in the basal ganglia, the *globus pallidus* and the *substantia nigra pars reticula*. Another area in the basal ganglia that plays an important role in neuroeconomics is the dopaminergic system that is comprised of neurons that release dopamine in the *ventral tegmental area* and the *substantia nigra par compacta*.

The brain is covered with an outer layer of neural tissue called the *cerebral cortex*; in common usage this is also referred to as *gray matter*. Dense axons under the gray matter are sometimes known as *white matter*. The most recent evolutionary part of the cerebral cortex is the neocortex,

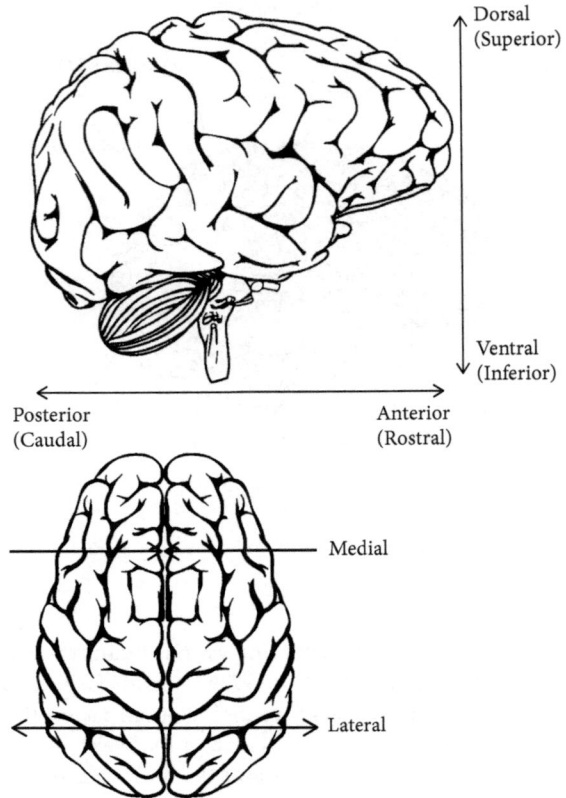

Figure 4.2 A convenient classification of brain regions. © Shutterstock

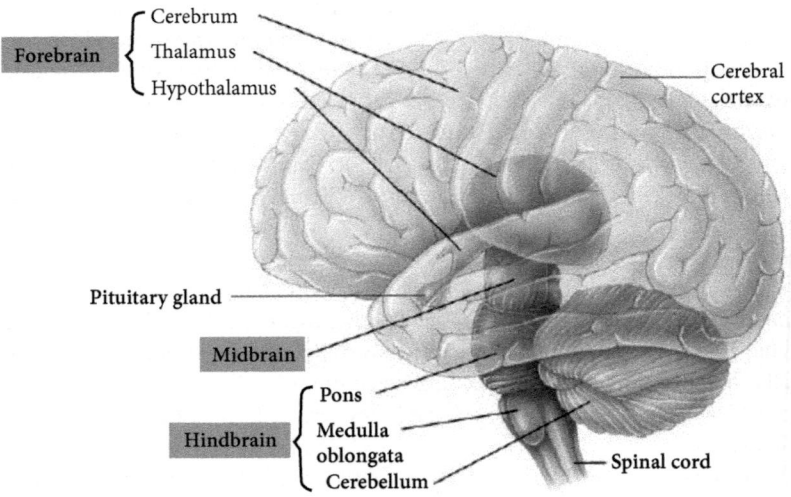

Figure 4.3 A classification of the brain into three regions: forebrain, midbrain, and hindbrain.

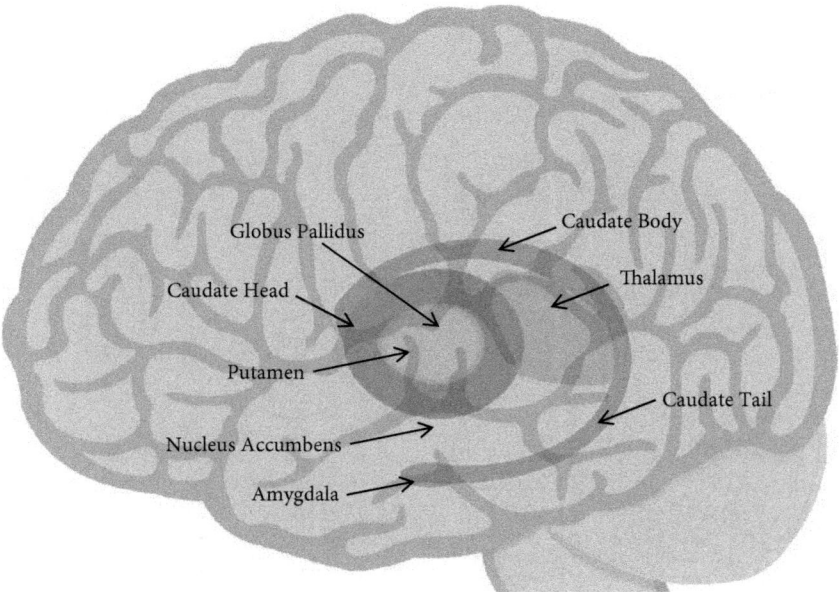

Figure 4.4 Structure of the basal ganglia and the approximate position of its various parts. © Shutterstock

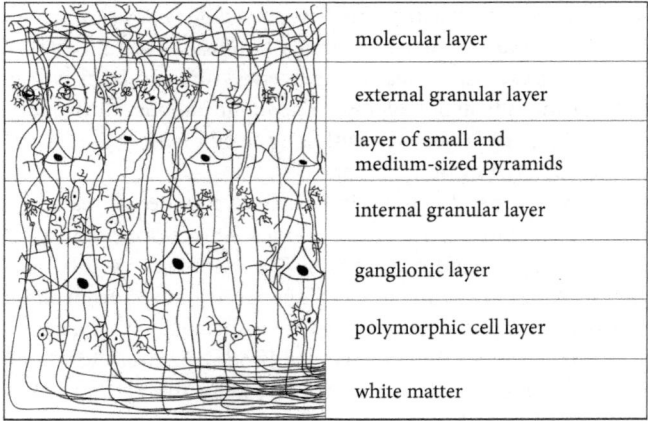

Figure 4.5 Different layers of the cerebral cortex. © Anna Hine, Shutterstock

which is a six layered structure shown in Figure 4.5. Each layer can have different kinds of neurons, and has its own functional specialization, but overall the neocortex is fairly uniform. For instance, layer 4 (the internal granular layer) is typically an input region in the cortex and layer 5 comprises mainly the pyramidal neurons that connect, through their axons, with other regions in the cortex. The phylogenetically more ancient part of the cerebral cortex is the hippocampus, which is a three layered structure. In order to increase surface area within the confines of the skull, the cerebral cortex is folded; ridges are known as gyri (singular gyrus) and grooves are known as sulci (singular sulcus).

THE LIMBIC SYSTEM

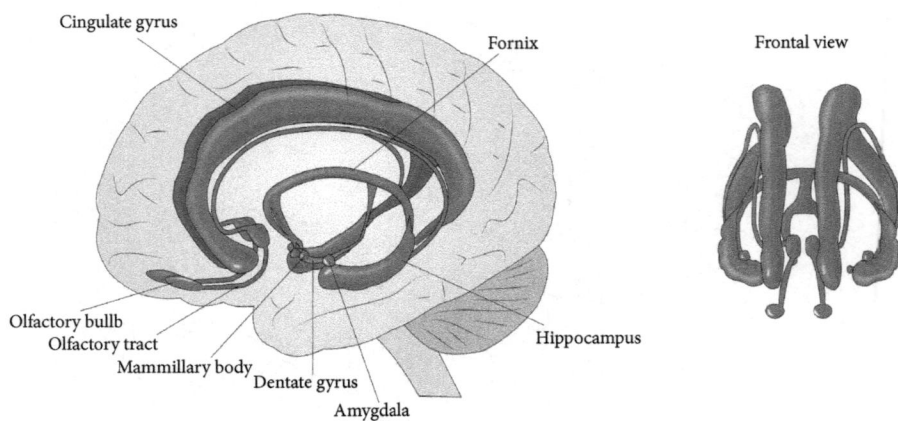

Figure 4.6 The limbic system of the brain. © Shutterstock

Figure 4.6 shows a sketch of the limbic system, which is a part of the forebrain; some of the important limbic structures for neuroeconomic research are the hippocampus, amygdala, fornix, mammillary body, and cingulate gyrus. The amygdala is a part of the telencephalon, yet it is not considered to be a part of the basal ganglia or of the cerebral cortex. The amygdala is activated when individuals experience fear or a perceived threat; it receives inputs from several sensory areas and feeds into the hypothalamus. The hippocampus, a three layered structure, is a part of the ancient cortex; it is associated with long-term memory and plays a central role in neuroeconomic studies of learning and memory.

Korbinian Brodmann classified the brain into distinct, numbered, regions based on the differences in neuronal architecture between these regions. This classification, published originally in 1909, is shown in Figure 4.7 (Brodmann, 1909). The Brodmann areas typically perform well-defined and discrete tasks. Some Brodmann regions receive inputs from the eyes and ears, so they are referred to as *sensory areas*, while others are associated with the control of movement, so they are known as *motor areas*. We can use the Brodmann areas to identify an important region of interest for neuroeconomists, the *prefrontal cortex*, abbreviated as PFC; this is neither a sensory, nor a motor, area and is sometimes referred to as an *association area*. The PFC comprises the following three regions. *Dorsolateral prefrontal cortex* abbreviated as dlPFC (areas 9, 46); *ventromedial prefrontal cortex*, abbreviated as vmPFC (area 45); *orbitofrontal cortex* OFC (area 10).

Different parts of the brain communicate with each other through special cells called *neurons* or *nerve cells*. There are many kinds of neurons in the human body. For instance, the motor neurons receive information from the spinal cord and are responsible for muscle contractions. The sensory neurons respond to the senses, e.g., touch, and transmit signals to the spinal cord. Figure 4.8 shows two neurons and the basic structure of a neuron; multiple arrows represent the direction of the flow of information.

The bulbous cell body, or *soma*, encloses the nucleus; different structures inside the cell body process sugars and oxygen to provide the energy that powers the neuron. Several thin structures

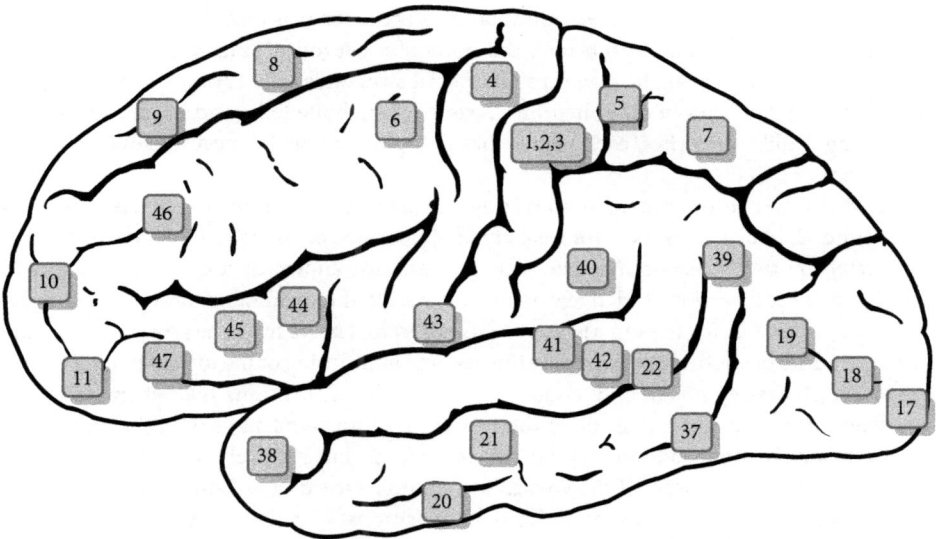

Figure 4.7 Brodmann areas of the human brain.

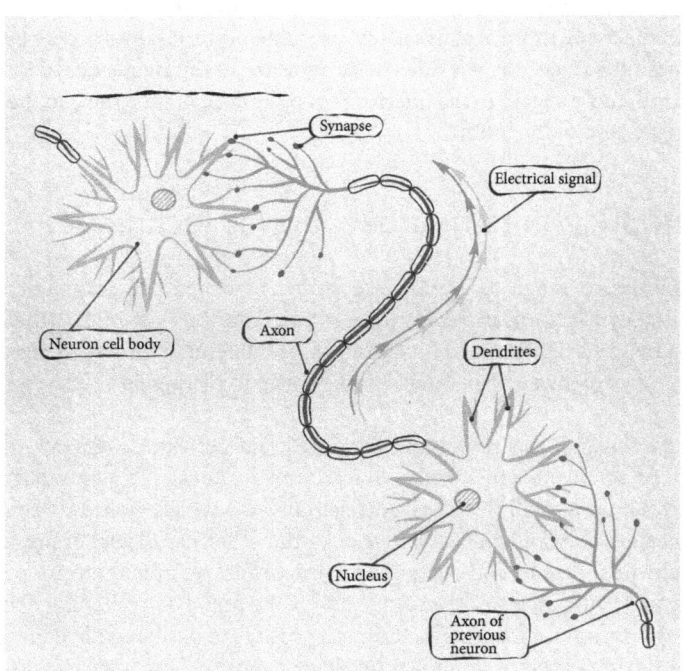

Figure 4.8 The structure of a neuron. © Shutterstock

that can branch several times, called *dendrites*, emanate from the soma; these are the input structures of the neuron and receive information from other neurons. A single, thin, output structure, the *axon*, originates from each cell body of a neuron. It transmits electrochemical information to a neighboring neuron through special structures called *synapses* that come into contact with the dendrites of other neurons. Axons can be quite long, and in rare cases, up to a meter long. Unlike dendrites, each neuron has a single axon, which nevertheless can branch several times.

Signals between neurons are sometimes known as *action potentials* or simply *spikes*. Neurons are surrounded, like all cells, by a thin *membrane* impermeable to water-based chemicals that is perforated by tiny tubes or *channels*. These tubes, also known as ion channels, allow for the exchange of sodium ions (relatively abundant outside the membrane) and potassium ions (relatively abundant inside the soma). *Neurotransmitters* that move from the synapse of one axon onto the dendrite of another axon regulate the opening and closing of the ion channels. Neurons have an electric resting potential of about -70 microvolts. This means that when the neuron is not sending any signals, the inside of the neuron is 70 microvolts less than the outside and there are relatively more sodium ions outside the neuron but relatively more potassium ions inside. Action potentials occur if the voltage in a neuron exceeds a certain threshold, typically around -50 microvolts caused by inputs from other neurons. This allows the ion channels in the membranes of neurons to be activated. Depending on the type of the neuron, the baseline firing rates vary from a few spikes per second to about a hundred spikes per second.

We shall sometimes report activity in an area of the brain by its (x, y, z) coordinates; most software packages use the Montreal Neurological Institute (MNI) coordinates. Camerer et al. (2015) succinctly explain these coordinates: "A higher positive value of y is further forward, or more anterior, in the brain; more negative values are more posterior toward the back of the brain. Similarly, x values range from the left side (most negative) to the right side (most positive), and z-values range from most negative (the inferior part or bottom of the brain) to the most positive (the superior part or top of the brain)."

4.3 An introduction to neuroeconomic techniques

Neuroeconomics uses a range of methods to gather evidence and form inferences.[4] Many methods of neuroeconomic measurement aim to measure the flow of electrochemical information between neurons. Different techniques measure different aspects of neural activity with varying degrees of accuracy and precision. It might help to distinguish between two categories of techniques.

Measurement techniques measure some form of brain activity using, say, neuronal firing rates, or metabolic activity, when subjects in experiments engage in some relevant economic choice. Such techniques typically establish correlation, but not causation, between brain activity and human decisions. *Manipulation techniques*, on the other hand, alter some aspect of brain function, typically temporarily, and observe the causal effect on human decisions. It is possible to alter the neuronal firing rates in a selected region of the brain, or to alter the neurotransmitter levels in a transient manner. In animal studies, it is possible to permanently damage brain tissue and then observe which aspects of animal behavior change. Human subjects may have *brain*

---

[4] For an excellent and concise introduction, see Ruff and Huettel (2014) that we draw upon below.

lesions caused by infections or by accidents that are also used in manipulation techniques. There is a degree of complementarity between the two techniques because measurement techniques may identify brain areas that can be manipulated later to establish causality.

4.3.1 *Criteria for evaluating neuroeconomic measurement techniques*

Alternative methods of measuring brain activity have their pros and cons. Hence, alternative techniques play a complementary role in building a richer picture of the relation between brain activity and economic decisions. Neuroeconomic methods of measurement may be evaluated on the following three main criteria.

(1) *Temporal resolution* is the frequency with which brain activity is recorded. The best techniques that measure neuronal activity directly, by measuring the flow of ions in brain tissue (electrophysiological measurements), achieve millisecond precision. Indirect measures of neuronal activity, such as measuring changes in blood oxygen levels in the brain, have intermediate temporal resolution that ranges from seconds to minutes. Brain manipulation techniques, say, drug induced temporary damage to brain tissue, have the lowest precision that ranges from minutes to days (the exception is event-related transcranial magnetic stimulation).

(2) *Spatial resolution* is the precision with which one can narrow down brain activity to a particular region of the brain. Naturally, techniques that place electrode sensors directly in the brain, typically in animals, achieve the highest spatial resolution and may measure activity directly for a particular neuron. Functional neuroimaging techniques that are extremely popular (see below) achieve spatial resolution of millimeters to centimeters. Finally, techniques that measure electrical signals of brain activity non-invasively, say, by measurements taken on the skull, achieve the poorest spatial resolution that ranges from centimeters to the entire brain.

(3) *Degree of invasiveness* refers to the extent to which one may have to interfere with brain processes in order to measure brain activity. Examples include knocking-out areas of the brain temporarily or permanently; the latter is typically possible only with animals. In humans, invasive techniques may be used prior to neurosurgery.

Our focus is not on the estimation and computation techniques of neuroeconomics. The interested reader can begin with Busemeyer and Diederich (2014) and follow the references therein.

The older methods measure *psychophysical* activity, i.e., the involuntary reaction to stimuli. These methods include, for instance, pupil dilation, skin conductance, and the heart rate. We now focus on some of the modern methods of measurement.

4.3.2 *Single unit recording*

Using fairly invasive methods, one can measure the electrical activity in a single targeted neuron. An electrode, typically a very thin insulated wire, is inserted in the neural tissue surrounding a single neuron; this is able to measure the neuron's electrical activity. Such techniques are quite invasive because they involve the opening of the skull, hence, they are typically used only on animals. However, they are also sometimes used on humans, who for some medical reasons, e.g., epilepsy, need to have an electrode inserted in their brain. Since animals share the affective rather than the deliberative faculties of the brain with humans, this evidence speaks more to the emotional rather than cognitive aspects of behavior. The advantage of these techniques is that they can target their location very precisely.

Most neurons are extremely small, so it might not always be possible to distinguish the firing rate of a neuron from other neurons in close proximity. However, improvements in techniques have reduced this problem. Single unit recording has very high temporal and spatial resolution, hence, it has enabled the identification of some of the core brain functions. Since the method is highly targeted at specific neurons, and neurons differ in their firing rates and their responses to different inputs, it helps to build a picture of brain functions that is unmatched in comparison to the other methods. The main drawback of the technique is the degree of invasiveness, and the rate of data collection is very slow because data is collected for a single neuron at a time. Animal colonies for experimental purposes are costly to maintain, so the technique is relatively expensive. Finally, the technique is also not very suitable when analyzing complex brain functions that involve interactions among several parts of the brain or neural coding at the population level.

4.3.3 *Electroencephalography and magnetoencephalography*

The *electroencephalogram* (EEG) measures brain activity, externally, say, by electrodes positioned on the scalp, or positioned internally, while subjects make some decisions. EEG at the scalp measures changes in the polarity of synchronously firing populations of neurons. The advantages of this technique are as follows. (i) It measures brain activity directly, rather than using some proxy such as blood flow or the level of metabolism. (ii) It has a high temporal resolution that allows one to study dynamic processes in the brain. (iii) It is relatively inexpensive in terms of equipment, say, relative to the cost of an MRI scanner (although the set-up time to position the electrodes correctly on the scalp is high). The disadvantage is that it has low spatial resolution, i.e., it measures aggregate brain activity in some region of the brain and cannot always localize the source of that activity.

An alternative to measuring electrical activity is to measure the magnetic fields associated with electrical activity in the neurons; this technique is known as *magnetoencephalography*. It has similarly high temporal resolution as electroencephalography but does not suffer from the problem of weakening of the electrical signal on passing through the skull, which is the case with electroencephalography. However, the magnetic fields are relatively weak and the equipment is relatively expensive, hence, not many studies in neuroeconomics have used it.

4.3.4 *Positron Emission Tomography*

Positron Emission Tomography (PET) relies on early work done in the 1950s and falls within the ambit of *functional neuroimaging*, i.e., producing 2D or 3D maps of brain activity. The method is to inject a weak, short-lived, radioactive isotope into the body of a subject in the experiment. Once enough time has been given for the solution to permeate the tissue of interest, the radioactive solution decays and emits positrons. The emitted positrons collide with electrons within a short distance and emit gamma rays. A *PET scanner* records the gamma rays and assigns to them a likely region of origin in the brain; this gives rise to a *PET image*.

The disadvantages of this technique are that it is invasive, relatively expensive, and its temporal resolution is relatively low (it shows average brain activity over an entire experiment), while its spatial resolution is intermediate. However, there are some advantages over other functional neuroimaging techniques such as fMRI, which relies on blood flow to correlate with neural activity. For instance, PET provides a more direct indicator of neural activity and, by creating customized molecules that are attached to radioactive isotopes, it can provide fairly precise chemical information.

4.3.5 *Functional magnetic resonance imaging*

Magnetic resonance imaging (MRI) is a body imaging technique that is about 35 years old. It can provide detailed information about any part of the human body in any plane. The idea is to expose the body to a powerful magnetic field so that the protons in human cells line up with the direction of the magnetic field. A second electromagnetic field is then switched on which enables the protons to absorb the energy of this field. When this secondary electromagnetic field is switched off, the protons emit the energy that they have absorbed. MRI contrasts are then created based on the speed with which protons realign with the magnetic field once the radio frequency pulse offsets. Protons from different tissues in the body emit energy in different ways, allowing the researcher to form detailed internal images of the body.

A newer version of the MRI is the *functional magnetic resonance imaging* technique (fMRI) that has been developed since the early 1990s and is very popular.[5] Electrical activity in the brain requires the firing of neurons. However, neurons do not have their own internal source of energy. Hence, when neurons need to fire, they absorb oxygen from the surrounding blood stream. This increases the blood flow towards those neurons (a process called as *hemodynamics*) after a delay of between 1–5 seconds. The response of oxygenated blood to a magnetic field is different from that of deoxygenated blood; this is known as the blood-oxygenation-level-dependent (BOLD) contrast. The BOLD contrast allows a magnetic field to pick out the neurons that are firing (say, in response to some stimuli). The fMRI interface modifies the MRI technique by installing an MRI-compatible monitor or a head mounted display, which subjects use to register their choices and decisions by using a joystick or pressing buttons. Arguably the biggest distinction between fMRI and MRI is that fMRI measures changes in the BOLD signals while MRI produces high resolution structural images of the brain's shape and structure.

The advantage of the fMRI technique is that it is non-invasive (like the EEG) and it has good spatial resolution (3–6 millimeters). The disadvantage, relative to the EEG, is that it has poorer temporal resolution (several seconds), although it is still relatively good. This is because, while the EEG measures electrical activity, fMRI measures the differential response of oxygenated and deoxygenated blood. Other shortcomings of fMRI are that (1) it is relatively expensive, (2) subjects face many repeated trials to uncover the underlying brain processes, even for essentially static games, and (3) the MRI scanner is loud and it presents a confined environment. The unit of measurement in fMRI trials is typically a *voxel* that localizes brain activity using three-dimensional coordinates. The typical fMRI voxels are $27\,mm^3$, i.e., a cube whose sides are of 3 mm length. Each voxel can have more than a million brain cells.

The fMRI technique allows one to correlate an external stimulus with hemodynamic activity in a certain part of the brain. It does not directly establish causality, although it can do so indirectly by running more than one treatment. One can use observations on neural activity from some treatment, and then make predictions of neural activity that will arise in another treatment, also known as "out of treatment forecasting." Fehr and Camerer (2007) give the following examples (p. 423): "For example, individual differences in caudate nucleus activation when punishment is costless for the punisher can be used to predict how much individuals actually pay for punishment when it is not costless. Likewise, individual differences in striatal activity in the condition in which donations are forced can be used to predict subjects' willingness to donate money to charities in the condition in which donations are voluntary."

---

[5] For a textbook treatment of the technique, see Huettel et al. (2009).

4.3.6 *Manipulation techniques*

The techniques discussed above, establish correlation between human decisions and activity in specific regions of the brain. This does not establish causality (unless one uses out of treatment forecasting). We now consider *manipulation techniques* that either temporarily or permanently disable a brain area or heighten activity in that area, and then study the resulting behavioral implications. Brain lesions and neuropharmacological interventions provide an opportunity to apply these techniques in humans. The basic principles have been understood for a long time, initially by using invasive studies for animals (Fritsch and Hitzig, 1870) and humans (Penfield and Rasmussen, 1950).

Most studies nowadays use non-invasive methods; the two most popular methods are *transcranial magnetic stimulation* and *transcranial direct current stimulation*. These studies take a step towards establishing causality but none of the methods, on their own, can conclusively establish causality. A great difficulty in establishing causality in neuroeconomic studies is that the same brain region is typically activated in a range of economic situations. Given the current state of knowledge in neuroeconomics, it is very difficult to establish causality from an activation of a brain region (Poldrack, 2006). One typically uses other supporting evidence to increase faith in the degree of causality; this includes moods, skin conductance measures, and response times; see Hutzler (2014) for a view that is more sympathetic to the ability of neuroscience data to establish causality.

TRANSCRANIAL MAGNETIC STIMULATION

Transcranial magnetic stimulation (TMS) is a non-invasive manipulation method.[6] As noted above, neurons have an electric resting potential of −70 microvolts. TMS takes the form of stimulating areas in the brain by using the principle of electromagnetic induction. A weak electrical current is induced in the neurons belonging to a selected part of the brain by rapidly changing magnetic fields. This is achieved by placing a looped copper coil on the part of the scalp directly over the brain region that is intended to be stimulated; not all locations in the brain are equally easy to stimulate.

Modern studies typically use repetitive TMS (rTMS) pulses separated by only a few milliseconds to achieve high temporal resolution. One may apply rTMS pulses in one of two ways: in an *online fashion* or in an *offline fashion*. When applied in the offline fashion, rTMS is applied at low temporal frequency for several minutes just prior to subjects' participation in the actual experimental task. This induces lowered cortical excitability in a particular brain region that lasts for 10–30 minutes. When applied in the online fashion, rTMS pulses serve to heighten cortical activity. If part X of the brain is thought to perform some task T, then TMS can be used to momentarily enhance or knock out part X. If this affects performance on task T, then it is suggestive of the causality of brain region X for task T.

A major advantage of the TMS technique is that it is non-invasive and has high spatial and temporal resolution. A disadvantage is that it is more difficult to be precise in targeting a specific brain area, particularly the deeper brain areas. In the offline studies, it is not always clear how long the rTMS pulse should be applied, prior to the experiment. Furthermore, some subjects might find the procedure noisy and uncomfortable.

---

[6] See Wassermann et al. (2008) for a book length treatment.

TRANSCRANIAL DIRECT CURRENT STIMULATION

Under *transcranial direct current stimulation* (tDCS), two electrodes are placed on the scalp and an electric current is passed through them. This affects the voltage in the membranes of the neurons along the path of the current and, thus, their firing rates, which can be measured. One of the electrodes is positively charged (anodal) and the other is negatively charged (cathodal).

There are two main types of tDCS simulations. Under *anodal* tDCS, the neurons are upregulated, or stimulated, while under *cathodal* tDCS, they are downregulated. A third kind of simulation, *sham simulation*, applies only a momentary current for the same length of time as the other two simulations; subjects are not told that they are in a sham simulation treatment, hence, this acts as a placebo or control treatment.

The advantages of tDCS are that it is relatively inexpensive, not noisy, and unlike TMS, it does not have unpleasant tactile sensations. One can run tDCS experiments simultaneously with a group of subjects (not possible under many other methods, such as fMRI). This feature is very useful in running a wider range of experiments, particularly those that involve social preferences.

BRAIN LESION STUDIES

One may study individuals who exhibit behavioral deficits following damage to some area of the brain (brain lesions); this is part of the subject matter of *neuropsychology*. The classic study is based on a grievous accident suffered by a Vermont Railway worker, Phineas Gage, in 1848.[7] In an injury caused by a dynamite explosion, a tamping iron rod went through the side of his face, through the back of his left eye and broke the top of his skull; see Figure 4.9.

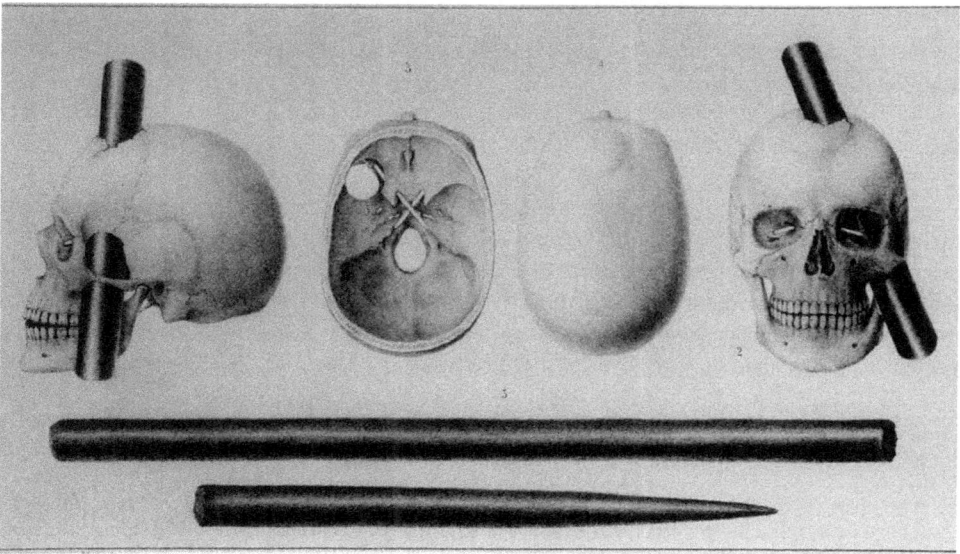

Figure 4.9 A drawing showing the skull of Phineas Gage, after a tamping iron went through it. © Everett Collection Historical/Alamy Stock Photo

---

[7] An excellent account of the incident can be found on the wikipedia page: http://en.wikipedia.org/wiki/Phineas_Gage.

Phineas Gage survived the accident but the destruction to his left prefrontal cortex significantly altered his behavior. Post-accident, he exhibited lack of foresight, fickle changes of mind, bad temper, impulsiveness, and several kinds of emotion deficits that were previously absent in his behavior (Harlow, 1868).[8] A case study of this accident contributed significantly to an understanding of the causal role of the prefrontal cortex.

Brain lesions can occur in many ways, for instance, surgical removal of tumors, brain infections such as meningitis or encephalitis, and exposure to neurotoxins such as excessive alcohol. The challenge is to pinpoint, as accurately as possible, the exact location of the brain lesion. In *double disassociation studies*, one establishes that two groups of patients with different brain lesions perform differently in two distinct tasks. This is an important component in establishing causality. Brain lesion studies are subject to two disadvantages. First, one typically does not have data on patients prior to their brain lesions. Second, as the brain reorganizes in the period following the brain lesion, as it appears to have done in the later years of Phineas Gage's life, one needs to separate two different effects: Those arising from the original brain lesion and those arising from brain reorganization. In animals, brain lesion studies involve more direct and invasive intervention in which the targeted brain tissue is either permanently or temporarily disabled. In a control group, an identical surgery is performed but the relevant brain areas are not disabled; clearly this is not possible with human subjects.

4.4 The neuroeconomics of risky decisions

Volume 1 considered alternative theories of risk, uncertainty, and ambiguity. The behavioral evidence indicates that among the available behavioral theories, prospect theory is currently the most satisfactory alternative. For this reason, this section focuses mainly on the neural evidence on prospect theory.

4.4.1 *Neural basis of value and risk*

There is a large literature on the neural encoding of value for simple binary tasks that differ in the quantity or quality of a reward. For instance, choosing between a higher and lower quantity of apples, or choosing between a more or less tasty variety of apple. The aim is to show that the brain computes something like the utility of an outcome. While there is substantial merit in understanding the correlates of neural activity for simple choice tasks, it is not clear if the insights gained from this analysis carry over to more complex tasks such as deciding among complex

---

[8] Here is the full quote from Harlow (1868, pp. 13–14), who was the doctor who treated him using pioneering methods: "The equilibrium or balance, so to speak, between his intellectual faculties and animal propensities, seems to have been destroyed. He is fitful, irreverent, indulging at times in the grossest profanity (which was not previously his custom), manifesting but little deference for his fellows, impatient of restraint or advice when it conflicts with his desires, at times pertinaciously obstinate, yet capricious and vacillating, devising many plans of future operations, which are no sooner arranged than they are abandoned in turn for others appearing more feasible. A child in his intellectual capacity and manifestations, he has the animal passions of a strong man. Previous to his injury, although untrained in the schools, he possessed a well-balanced mind, and was looked upon by those who knew him as a shrewd, smart business man, very energetic and persistent in executing all his plans of operation. In this regard his mind was radically changed, so decidedly that his friends and acquaintances said he was 'no longer Gage.'"

portfolios of stocks, or among alternative pension plans (Camerer, 2013). For this reason, our discussion will be brief. The interested reader can consult several references for more details.[9]

A typical experiment in this literature proceeds as follows. The subjective value assigned by subjects to an object is elicited, using standard behavioral economics experiments. For instance, subjects might be asked to bid for an item under institutional rules such as second price auctions, which predict that bids and valuations for the item will be identical. While placing the bids, the brain activity of subjects is measured, say, using fMRI techniques, or single neuron recordings. One could then ask, which brain regions are particularly active, or what brain circuitry is implicated when individuals choose high value items? The items used in the analysis are typically simple food items such as snacks (Plassmann et al., 2007). The main result from these experiments indicates that value is encoded in the vmPFC. Experiments using gambles, charitable contributions, and delayed monetary rewards also support this result (Levy et al., 2010; Kable and Glimcher, 2007; Hare et al., 2009).

An important insight in this literature is to address the observed choice between options by individuals; a choice that appears apparently stochastic. For instance when individuals are repeatedly asked to make a choice between two close options, A and B, or we use a between-subjects design to study the choice between these two options, there is an element of stochasticity to the choices. One way of modeling stochasticity in choices is to use random utility models (see Appendix B in Volume 4). An alternative, and intriguing, possibility is that this stochasticity reflects noise in underlying cognitive processing (Glimcher, 2011; Woodford, 2014).[10] Thinking of options A and B as two external stimuli, the choice made by an individual depends on the number of spikes produced by different populations of neurons, each tuned to respond differentially to the two stimuli. The number of spikes, in turn, is drawn from an underlying probability distribution that could be common to the two options. For binary choice data, Clithero and Rangel (2013) show that when response times are taken into account, the out of sample predictions based on such a model (the drift-diffusion model) outperform the predictions from the standard logistic model.

Recall the distinction between *decision utility* and *experienced utility* that we made in Volume 5; the evidence indicates that this distinction has a neural basis. A quick summary of the literature is as follows.

(1) *Decision utility*, or *subjective expected value*, arises at the time of making choices. Different choice options give rise to different *stimulus values* (SV), which are compared to determine the option with the highest SV (Wallis, 2007; Kable and Glimcher, 2009; Rangel et al., 2008; Rangel and Hare, 2010; Rushworth et al., 2009). Furthermore, fMRI evidence shows that SV signals have been found in the vmPFC (Chib et al., 2009; Hare et al., 2008, 2009; Kable and Glimcher, 2007; Padoa-Schioppa, 2009; Plassmann et al., 2007; Plassmann et al., 2010; Tom et al., 2007). The vmPFC also appears to encode value from *appetitive goals* (e.g., tempting food when hungry) and *aversive* goals (e.g., an electric shock) (Litt et al., 2010; Plassmann et al., 2010). Single neuron studies in monkeys show that decision value signals exhibit *range adaptation*, i.e., the neuronal firing rate is a linear function of the range of values given (Padoa-Schioppa, 2009; Padoa-Schioppa and Assad, 2006). If these findings apply to humans, they could violate the standard assumption of independence of irrelevant alternatives.

---

[9] For a book length treatment, see Glimcher (2011); for a survey for economists, see Fehr and Rangel (2011); and for a critical and insightful commentary on this literature, see Camerer (2013).

[10] For a theoretical exploration of the relation between the two approaches, see Webb (2015).

(2) *Experienced utility* is the *experienced subjective value* (R) at the time of consumption. While the vmPFC is activated in the case of decision utility, as described above, experienced utility appears to be associated instead with the orbitofrontal cortex and the nucleus accumbens (Blood and Zatorre, 2001; de Araujo et al., 2003; McClure et al., 2004). The initial price of a product may signal the quality of a product, hence, it could also influence the experienced utility from the product. Plassmann et al. (2008) varied the original price for an identical wine after which subjects received squirts of the wine inside a fMRI scanner. They found that experienced utilities were positively influenced by the initial price and higher experienced utility was associated with greater activity in the orbitofrontal cortex.

(3) *Prediction error* (PE) is the difference between decision utility and experienced utility. PE is used to update stimulus values in models of reinforcement learning. The main brain region associated with PE in human fMRI studies is the ventral striatum (Delgado et al., 2000; Berns et al., 2001; Yacubian et al., 2006; Hare et al., 2008).

Many models in finance use mean-variance utility analysis. Evidence suggests that different brain areas encode the mean and variance of rewards. Mean rewards are correlated with activity in the striatum (Preuschoff et al., 2006) while variance of rewards, since it reflects risk, activates the insula (Mohr et al., 2010). The greater activation of the insula when presented with higher risks suggests that there is an *affective response* to risk that is consistent with the *risk as feelings* hypothesis of Loewenstein et al. (2001) (see Chapter 1). tDCS studies show that stimulation of the right dlPFC increases risk aversion (Fecteau et al., 2007) and disrupting the dlPFC increases risk seeking (Knoch et al., 2006).

An alternative approach to studying neural activity is to propose axioms related to the neural encoding of rewards and prediction errors (differences between decision and experience utilities). This approach has been used, for instance, to test the *dopaminergic reward prediction error hypothesis* (DRPE) (Caplin and Dean, 2008; Caplin et al., 2010). The DRPE hypothesis relates to the responsiveness of dopamine release (a neurotransmitter) from dopamine neurons as various external stimuli, such as rewards or probabilities are manipulated. An advantage of the axiomatic approach is that it makes very precise and testable predictions. The axiomatic approach also allows for a more direct and stringent test of the DRPE hypothesis because one can dispense with auxiliary assumptions based on reinforcement learning that alternative approaches have relied upon. Camerer (2013, Section 4.1) critically evaluates the axiomatic approach relative to the alternative approach of fitting ever improving functional forms as the understanding of a phenomenon improves. Camerer's (2013, p. 1167) own assessment of the axiomatic approach, at this relatively early stage, is that: "I agree that there is an added dimension of 'rigour' ... but there is not a big leap in knowledge."

4.4.2 Reference dependence

One implication of reference dependence is the identification of differences in behavioral patterns in the domains of gains and losses. De Martino et al. (2006) exploit this implication to study the neurobiological basis of reference dependence. Twenty subjects initially received an endowment of £50 and were then asked to choose between risky options of the form $(x, p; -y, 1-p)$ and a sure option $(z, 1)$, where x, y, z are positive monetary amounts and $p > 0$ is a probability. The sure outcome, z, was either framed as a gain or as a loss. For instance, in the *gain frame*, the sure option could take the form "keep £20 of the £50." In the *loss frame*, the equivalent sure option is described as "lose £30 of the £50." Subjects chose the risky option in 42.9% of the cases in the gain frame and 61.6% of the cases in the loss frame; these proportions are different from 50% at the 5% significance level. Thus, as expected under prospect theory, decision makers are risk averse in the gain frame and risk seeking in the loss frame (the authors do not check for the *fourfold classification of risk* under prospect theory; see Volume 1).

Decisions between lotteries were made inside an fMRI scanner. Thus, brain activity was monitored when in the gains frame subjects chose the sure option (G_{sure}) or the risky option (G_{gamble}). Likewise in the loss domain they were monitored when they chose either the sure option (L_{sure}) or the risky option (L_{gamble}). The main contrast was between activation in brain areas when subjects chose in accordance with their predominant behavioral tendency ($G_{sure} + L_{gamble}$) or against it ($G_{gamble} + L_{sure}$).

The main results are shown in Figure 4.10. Panel A shows activation in the amygdala when subjects choose according to their predominant behavioral tendencies (sure outcome in gains and risky outcome in losses). Panel B shows the percentage signal change for peaks in the right amygdala; a positive change is observed when choosing according to their behavioral tendencies and a negative change when they do not choose according to it. When subjects choose contrary to their behavioral tendencies (risky outcome in gains and sure outcomes in losses) the fMRI scan in Panel C shows activation mainly in the ACC and to a lesser extent in the dlPFC. In Panel D, one can observe relatively increased activation in the ACC when subjects make choices contrary to their behavioral tendencies.

Subjects who resisted framing effects (gains and losses are the two frames) showed relatively greater activation in the orbitomedial prefrontal cortex (omPFC). The authors interpret

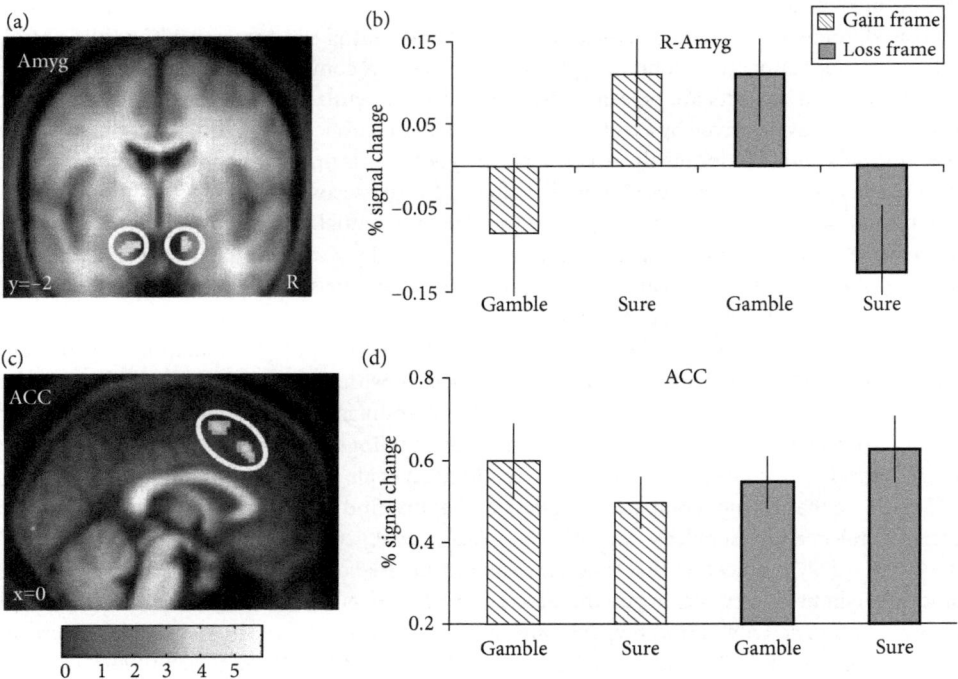

Figure 4.10 fMRI results for the gain and loss frames.

Source: From De Martino, B., Kumaran, D., Seymour, B., and Dolan, B. J. (2006). "Frames, biases, and rational decisionmaking in the human brain. *Science* 313: 684–7. Reprinted with permission from AAAS.

activation in the amygdala when subjects are susceptible to framing effects as driven by an affect heuristic (p. 686). Furthermore, they argue (p. 687) that "As such, our findings support a model in which the omPFC evaluates and integrates emotional and cognitive information, thus underpinning more rational (i.e., description-invariant) behavior."

These results were replicated in the study by Roiser et al. (2009) who showed that subjects who had a specific genetic neurotransmitter variant were more influenced by framing effects. But when this genetic variant was absent, subjects appeared to show no framing effects. However, Talmi et al. (2010) found that amygdala lesioned subjects continued to exhibit framing effects of the sort studied in De Martino et al. (2006). This makes it difficult to implicate the amygdala conclusively in framing effects. In related neuroeconomic studies of the disparity between WTP and WTA (for which reference dependence is a necessary condition) a correlation has been found between (i) WTP and activation in the vmPFC, and (ii) WTA and activation in the lateral orbitofrontal region (Knutson et al., 2008; De Martino et al., 2009).[11]

4.4.3 *Loss aversion*

Tom et al. (2007) examine the neural correlates of loss aversion. They presented subjects with a range of choices between accepting or rejecting lotteries of the form $(x, p; -y, 1-p)$, where $x > 0$ and $y > 0$. In order to ensure that subjects would never be out of pocket, they were given an endowment of money larger than the maximum loss that they could incur. Subjects were asked to rate the strength of their acceptance or rejection on a four point scale.

The median loss aversion was found to be 1.93. Other things fixed, as the size of gains increased, there was increased activation in dorsal and ventral striatum, vmPFC, vlPFC, ACC, OFC, and dopaminergic midbrain regions. There are two competing hypotheses about brain activation when subjects are presented with increased potential losses. One hypothesis is that loss aversion may be driven by a fear response that is caused by activation of brain regions such as the amygdala and anterior insula. An alternative hypothesis is that gains and losses are mediated by a single system. In this study, support is found for the second hypothesis. No brain region is found to be additionally activated when the size of potential loss in gambles increased. The same brain areas involved in the computation of expected rewards for gains showed decreased activity when potential losses are increased; these areas are the striatum, vmPFC, ventral ACC, and medial OFC. In particular, there was hardly any activity in the amygdala and the insula. Thus, it appears that there is a single brain system involved in the computation of gains and losses. Increased activity in the striatum that is associated with gains and decreased activity in the striatum associated with losses is consistent with the findings from some other studies (Breiter et al., 2001; Delgado et al., 2003). Replications of these findings also showed up decreased activity in the vmPFC when losses are increased (Cunningham et al., 2009; Plassmann et al., 2010).

So how do these results compare with other studies that find activation in the amygdala and the insula in the evaluation of lotteries with losses (Kahn et al., 2002; Kuhnen and Knutson, 2005)? Tom et al. (2007) conjecture that their experiments focused on decision utility, while the other studies might have been picking up the effects of prediction errors. De Martino et al. (2006) find a correlation in activity in the amygdala and an increase in risk. However, risk and loss aversion are different concepts. Furthermore, Tom et al. (2007) identify a form of *neural loss aversion*. The positive slope which reflects the increase in activity in the striatum and the vmPFC for gains

---

[11] For more details, the interested reader can pursue Louie and De Martino (2014).

is found to be smaller than the absolute value of the negative slope that measures a decrease in activity for losses in the same brain areas. Thus, these results provide support for a core component of prospect theory—loss aversion—a feature that humans share with close primate relatives such as capuchin monkeys (see Volume 1 for the details on the empirical evidence).

Yacubian et al. (2006) consider the neural correlates of positive and negative expected values of lotteries using fMRI data. Let $x < 0 < y$, and consider choices over lotteries of the form $(x, p; y, 1 - p)$. Then the expected value EV can be written as $EV = EV^+ + EV^-$, where $EV^+ = y(1 - p)$ and $EV^- = xp$. The prediction error is given by $PE = R - EV$, where R is the actual outcome, x or y. EV^+ was found to be correlated with activity in the ventral striatum; in particular, the bilateral ventral striatum was activated as the reward magnitude or its probability increased. EV^- was correlated with activity in the bilateral amygdala.

An alternative method of discovering brain areas associated with loss aversion is to study patients with brain lesions. De Martino et al. (2010) study the behavior of two subjects with lesions in the amygdala. Subject SM, a 43-year-old woman, had lesions in the entire amygdala region, while subject AM's lesions were confined to 50% of the amygdala. Both subjects were endowed with $50 cash and then asked to accept or reject a series of mixed gambles in which gains ranged from $20 to $50 and losses ranged from −$20 to −$50. The decisions of each subject were compared to a set of six subjects, comparable in terms of education, age, income, and gender; these subjects played the role of control subjects.

Both lesioned subjects exhibit no loss aversion relative to their respective control groups; this finding echoes the spirit of studies with other primates in which amygdala lesioned monkeys approach stimuli that are rejected by non-lesioned monkeys (Mason et al., 2006). In contrast, the loss aversion parameter found in the control group in each case is close to the previous findings. However, both lesioned patients satisfy a basic consistency requirement by preferring larger gains and smaller losses; these results are consistent with evidence from other primate studies (Murray et al., 1996). The more lesioned patient, SM, exhibited a slight loss seeking behavior while the less lesioned patient, AM, was loss-neutral.

Clearly, these results on the role of the amygdala differ from those in the fMRI study by Tom et al. (2007). One possible reason is that the De Martino et al. (2010) study uses a larger range of losses. For smaller losses, the BOLD signal in the amygdala might not be detectable using existing fMRI techniques. A second possibility is that in the evaluation of mixed lotteries, the amygdala might contribute vital inputs to other brain regions (e.g., the striatum) involved with the processing of synaptic processing that is picked up by the BOLD signal. This possibility is confirmed in Jenison et al. (2011) who recorded 16 amygdala neurons whose spike is particularly associated with a WTP task for three subjects. Of these 16 neurons, 9 showed a negative correlation with the WTP and 7 showed a positive correlation. Thus, it is quite likely that in fMRI studies, the neuronal signals from the amygdala cancel out, yet the amygdala may play an important role in providing inputs during mixed lottery decision tasks.

De Martino et al. (2010) were able to distinguish between risk aversion and loss aversion. Loss aversion implies an aversion to mixed gambles because losses are weighted more heavily than gains. In contrast, in gambles with all gains or all losses, loss aversion does not have bite. For such gambles, the spread of outcomes can be varied to test for risk aversion. It turns out that the risk aversion of amygdala lesioned patients is no different from the respective control groups. Thus, amygdala damage seems to lower loss aversion while keeping fixed the level of risk aversion; indeed separate neural systems could be responsible for loss aversion and risk aversion.

The behavioral evidence shows that loss aversion can be reduced in some cases by asking subjects to think like traders and combine gains and losses (Sokol-Hessner, Delgado, et al., 2009).

The neural correlates of such manipulation have been shown to be a reduction in activity in the amygdala and increased activity in the dlPFC (Sokol-Hessner, Hsu, et al., 2009).

4.4.4 *Non-linear probability weighting*

Under expected utility theory, probabilities enter into the objective function in a linear manner. In contrast, in the main behavioral alternatives such as rank dependent utility and prospect theory, individuals weight objective or subjective probabilities in a non-linear manner. In particular, inverse S-shaped probability weighting is the most common empirical finding, at least for probabilities bounded away from the endpoints of the probability interval $[0,1]$; see Volume 1 for the details on these assertions. There are many alternative probability weighting functions, but the most satisfactory is the Prelec (1998) function; it is axiomatically founded, and consistent with the empirical evidence.[12] The one parameter form of the Prelec function is $w(p) = e^{-(-\ln p)^{\alpha}}$, where $\alpha > 0$ is the single parameter, $p \in [0,1]$ is the probability, and w is the probability weight.

Most probability weighting functions are relatively flat in the middle range of probabilities. Hence, in order to detect non-linear probability weighting, one needs to use lotteries with probabilities that are dispersed over the range $[0,1]$. Neural responses to probabilities have been found in the striatum and the cingulate gyrus (Paulus and Frank, 2006; Berns et al., 2008). A PET study by Takahashi et al. (2010) found a negative correlation between dopamine D_1 receptor binding in the striatum and the degree of non-linear probability weighting (relative to the benchmark of linear weighting).

Hsu et al. (2009) allow for a suitably large range of probabilities; we consider their work, next. In their experiments, on the first screen, subjects observed a lottery $L_1 = (x_1, p_1)$ (x_1 is an outcome and p_1 is a probability) without the confounding influence of a comparison between two lotteries. On the second screen, subjects were asked a question to test their understanding of the lottery (x_1, p_1) (e.g., is the probability lower than or greater than p?). On the third, and final, screen, subjects were asked to choose between two lotteries, $L_1 = (x_1, p_1)$ and $L_2 = (x_2, p_2)$, where (x_2, p_2) is another outcome–probability pair. The first experiment (first two screens) revealed the brain areas involved in *reward anticipation*, while the second experiment (third screen) revealed brain areas involved in *choice*. Probabilities were chosen from the set $\{0.01, 0.1, 0.3, 0.5, 0.8, 0.95\}$ and outcomes, all positive, were chosen from the set $\{10, 20, 50, 100\}$.

In order to separate the objective function into a linear and a non-linear component, the objective function under prospect theory for lottery $L = (x, p)$ can be written as $PT(L) = \pi(p, \alpha)v(x)$, where $\pi(p, \alpha)$ is the decision weight under prospect theory (α is the parameter of the one-parameter Prelec function) and $v(x)$ is the utility function under prospect theory (see Volume 1 for the details). We can rewrite the objective function as

$$PT(L) = \pi(p, \alpha)v(x) = pv(x) + \Delta(p, \alpha)v(x), \text{ where } \Delta(p, \alpha) = \pi(p, \alpha) - p. \qquad (4.1)$$

In the parametric estimation, v is assumed to take the power form $v(x) = x^{\gamma}$, $\gamma > 0$.[13]

---

[12] For three different axiomatic foundations, see Prelec (1998), Luce (2001), and al-Nowaihi and Dhami (2006). For empirical support for the Prelec function, see Stott (2006).

[13] The power form of utility is supported by the evidence (Kahneman and Tversky, 1979; Tversky and Kahneman, 1992; Stott, 2006). For an axiomatization of the power form of utility under prospect theory, see al-Nowaihi et al. (2008).

In the first experiment that involved reward anticipation, the BOLD signal in the brain is regressed on the two terms on the RHS of (4.1), $pv(x)$ and $\Delta(p,\alpha)v(x)$. If humans only take account of linear probability weighting, as under expected utility, then the BOLD signal should not be correlated with the non-linear term $\Delta(p,\alpha)v(x)$; in constructing $\Delta(p,\alpha)$ the group mean value of $\alpha = 0.77$ was used.

A non-parametric method was also employed to correlate brain activity with the behavioral shape of the Prelec function.[14] Each of the probabilities is assigned a dummy variable, $d(p_i)$ (e.g., $d(p_i) = 1$, $d(p') = 0$ for $p_i \neq p'$). Letting z be the BOLD response in the brain, captured by the fMRI evidence, the relation

$$z = a + \beta_i d(p_i)v(x) + \varepsilon \tag{4.2}$$

was estimated; ε is a noise term and a, β_i are the parameters to be estimated. Each β_i (for each of the 6 probabilities) is then rescaled by dividing with the slope of the regression coefficient of the linear term in a regression of z on the linear and the deviation $(\pi(p,\alpha) - p)$ terms.

The results are as follows. In the parametric model, the brain regions that correlated with the linear term $(pv(x))$ in the first experiment (anticipated reward case) are the striatum, cerebellum, motor areas, and the median prefrontal cortex. These results are consistent with the identification of similar areas in related tasks. Activation in the following regions was correlated with the non-linear term $(\Delta(p,\alpha)v(x))$: striatum, cingulate gyrus, motor cortex, and the cerebellum. The areas of the brain that were equally activated by the linear and non-linear terms are striatum, motor cortex, and the cerebellum. The activation of the striatum for the reward anticipation task is consistent with the results from other studies on reward anticipation/reward processing (Knutson et al., 2000; O'Doherty et al., 2004). This region has also been found responsive to a multiplicative combination of probabilities and reward magnitudes (Tobler et al., 2007).

The coefficient β in the non-parametric model (4.2) is shown for various probabilities as the dots in Figure 4.11 for the left and right striatum, separately. The BOLD signal activation is

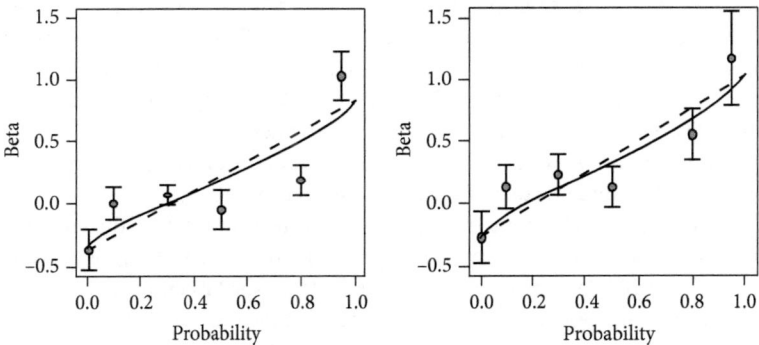

Figure 4.11 The rescaled coefficient β in (4.2) (shown as the dots) for the left striatum (left panel) and the right striatum (right panel) for different probabilities. The behavioral Prelec function for the group average value of $\alpha = 0.77$ is shown as the continuous curve.

Source: Hsu et al. (2009).

---

[14] Note that the inverse S-shape of the Prelec function arises for $\alpha < 1$ but not for $\alpha > 1$, which is also admissible under the axioms that lead to the Prelec function; see al-Nowaihi and Dhami (2006).

non-linear in probabilities; it is overweighted relative to the behavioral Prelec function for low probabilities and underweighted for high probabilities.

4.5 The neuroeconomics of social preferences

The incorporation of social preferences into economics has led to a huge increase in our understanding of a wide range of phenomena. Volume 2 of this book is devoted to a study of social preferences. In this section, we study the neural basis of some aspects of human sociality.

4.5.1 *Computation of social rewards in the brain*

Most of the studies mentioned in Section 4.4.1 on the neural correlates of private rewards, use non-social rewards such as juice, food, or money. In this section, we ask the question: Which are the neural correlates of social rewards? Are the same regions and neural processes that are involved in private rewards, also implicated in the processing of social rewards? Izuma et al. (2008) found that acquiring a good reputation (a social reward) activates the same brain areas as in the case of monetary rewards. They conclude that there is a common neural currency for private and social rewards, which is supported by other neuroeconomic evidence (Zink et al., 2008; Smith et al., 2010).

We focus now on Lin et al. (2012) who consider identical tasks that can lead to either private or social rewards. The task is shown in Figure 4.12. In the private/monetary and social rewards conditions, individuals chose between two slot machines, each of which produced three possible outcomes, positive ($1), neutral ($0), and negative (−$1); subjects had to learn the probability distribution over outcomes produced by each of the slot machines. In each stage, the choice was between a neutral slot machine (represented by six circular dots) which had a uniform distribution over the three outcomes, and one of two other slot machines (see top two machines in panel (b) in Figure 4.12).

If the outcome is positive, then (i) under social rewards, individuals see a smiley face and hear emotionally matched words such as excellent, bravo, and fantastic, and (ii) under monetary rewards subjects simply received $1. If a negative outcome arises, then (i) under social rewards, subjects see an angry face and hear words such as stupid, moron, and wrong, and (ii) under monetary rewards, $1 was subtracted from their endowments. Finally, in the case of a neutral outcome, (i) under social rewards, subjects see a neutral face and hear neutral words such as desk and paper, and (ii) under monetary rewards they receive $0.

As one would expect in such a simple task, participants learnt to choose the positively valanced slot machine after a few trials (the machine in the middle row in panel (b)); see panels (c) and (d) in Figure 4.12. The fMRI data for subjective value (SV), reward magnitude (R), and prediction error (PE) for the social, monetary, and a combined condition are shown for various regions of the brain in Figure 4.13. In the monetary and social conditions, the SV on the slot machines was correlated with the vmPFC and additionally with the mid-cingulum, superior frontal gyrus, and angular gyrus. Thus, the neural circuitry for computing SV is similar in the monetary and social rewards tasks. In the monetary condition, activation in the caudate and putamen was correlated with PE, while there were no statistically significant correlations, at the chosen threshold, in the social task. Finally, reward magnitudes (R) are correlated with activation in the vmPFC for social and monetary conditions; in the monetary condition there was also activation in the insula, occipital cortex, cingulate gyrus, and the superior frontal gyrus. The authors conclude (p. 280):

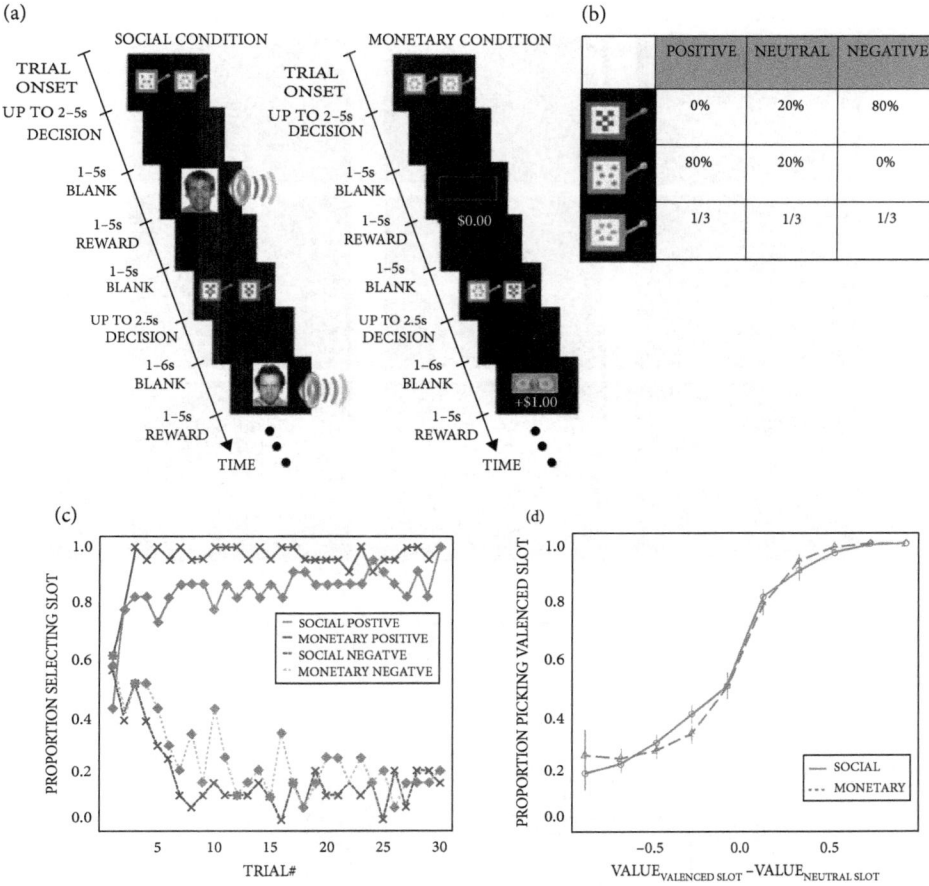

Figure 4.12 Panel (a): Each choice involved choosing from a neutral or valenced slot machine. The decision and rewards time intervals are shown. Panel (b): Probability distributions over rewards of the three slot machines, each represented by a different pattern. Panels (c) and (d): Choices of subjects by disaggregated and aggregated treatment effects.

Source: Lin et al. (2012).

"Together with other recent findings ... our results provide increasing support that overlapping areas of vmPFC and ventral striatum encode value signals for both types of rewards."

4.5.2 *The neural basis of inequity averse preferences*

We have discussed *models of inequity aversion* in Volume 2 (Fehr and Schmidt, 1999; Bolton and Ockenfels, 2000). However, several explanations that were traditionally based on inequity aversion were sought to be supplanted later by concerns for social image (Andreoni and Bernheim, 2009) as well as reciprocity considerations (Falk et al., 2008; Rabin, 1993). In this section, we report neural evidence, based on fMRI tests, that establishes neural networks in the brain, which encode inequity averse preferences in a simple model.

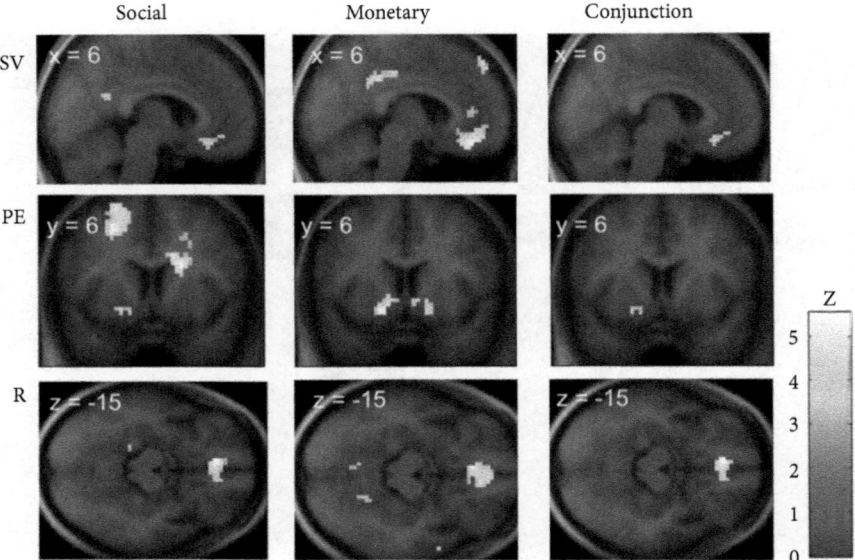

Figure 4.13 Activation of various brain regions correlated with SV (first row), PE (second row), and R (third row).

Source: Lin et al. (2012).

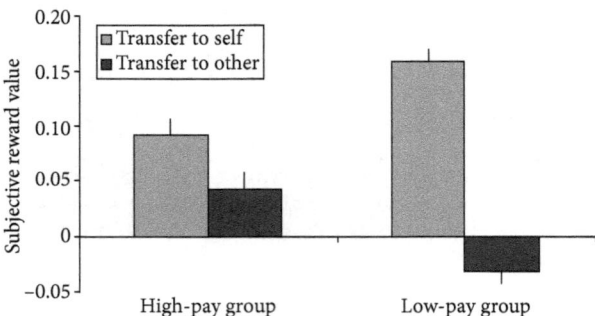

Figure 4.14 The behavioral evidence. Vertical bars denote standard errors of the mean.

Source: Reprinted by permission from Macmillan Publishers Ltd. *Nature* 463: 1089–91 (25 February 2010). "Neural evidence for inequality-averse social preferences," Elizabeth Tricomi, Antonio Ranger, Colin F. Camerer and John P. O'Doherty.

In Tricomi et al. (2010), the data is based on 20 pairs of unacquainted males who were given a baseline pay of \$30. Half were then randomly selected and given \$50 (high-pay group), while the other half was given nothing extra (low-pay group). Individuals in both groups then had to rate an incremental transfer between \$0 and \$50 to themselves and to their partner in the group by assigning a number from a ratings set $\{-5, -4, \ldots, 0, \ldots, 5\}$.

Figure 4.14 shows the regression coefficient obtained by regressing ratings on the amount transferred to themselves and to others. Both groups rated own-transfers positively. Now consider transfers to the partners. Members of the high-pay group rated transfers to the low-pay partner positively (advantageous inequity), because such transfers narrowed the income gap. By contrast, members of the low-pay group rated transfers to the high-pay partner negatively (disadvantageous inequity), because such transfers widened the income gap. Thus, the behavioral data is consistent with the Fehr–Schmidt (1999) model of inequity aversion.

fMRI data shows that in the case of own-transfers, there was a statistically significant correlation in the activation of the vmPFC and ventral striatum with the magnitude of transfers. This is not surprising. The same areas are known to be activated in the case of private rewards; see Section 4.4.1.

The authors next considered a statistic, which is the contrast of the fMRI response for own-transfers relative to partner-transfers for both groups. Figure 4.15 shows the resulting effects on the ventral striatum while Figure 4.16 shows the corresponding effects on the vmPFC. For each

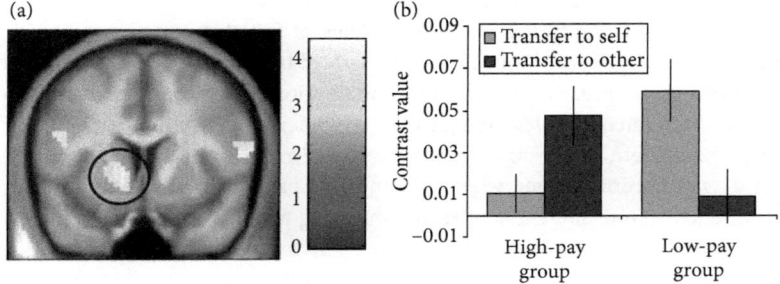

Figure 4.15 The fMRI evidence on activation of the ventral striatum for the contrast between own-transfers relative to partner-transfers for both groups. (a) Activation in the ventral striatum (circled); contrast was significantly higher for low-pay group. (b) Contrast values for both groups. Vertical bars denote standard errors of the mean.

Source: Reprinted by permission from Macmillan Publishers Ltd. *Nature* 463: 1089–91 (25 February 2010). "Neural evidence for inequality-averse social preferences," Elizabeth Tricomi, Antonio Ranger, Colin F. Camerer, and John P. O'Doherty.

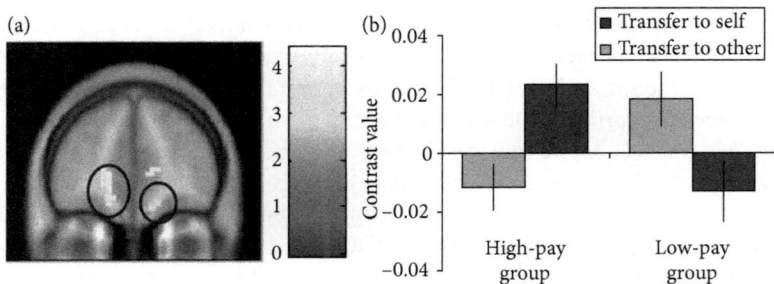

Figure 4.16 The fMRI evidence on activation of the vmPFC for the contrast between own-transfers relative to partner-transfers. (a) Activation in the vmPFC (circled); contrast was significantly higher for low-pay group. (b) Contrast values for both groups. Vertical bars denote standard errors of the mean.

Source: Reprinted by permission from Macmillan Publishers Ltd. *Nature* 463: 1089–91 (25 February 2010). "Neural evidence for inequality-averse social preferences," Elizabeth Tricomi, Antonio Ranger, Colin F. Camerer, and John P. O'Doherty.

of the two groups, there is activation in both the regions and the contrast statistic is significantly higher for the low-pay group. For the low-pay group, the activation of both regions is greater for own-transfers as compared to partner-transfers. For the high-pay group, we get the opposite result, i.e., relatively more activation for partner-transfers relative to own-transfers. The results hold even when wealth effects and prediction errors are controlled for.

Comparing Figure 4.14 with Figures 4.15 and 4.16 for the high-pay group, one notices a discrepancy between the behavioral and the neural results. In the behavioral results, one rates an own-transfer relatively higher than a partner-transfer while the reverse is true for the neural data. The authors note (p. 1090): "basic reward structures in the brain may reflect even stronger equity considerations than is necessarily expressed or acted on at the behavioral level. These findings raise the possibility that even when basic reward responses reflect strong equity considerations, in some cases additional factors may intercede to moderate the influence of such equity judgements on behavior, such as strategizing . . . or the engagement of self-serving biases such as judgements of deservingness or need." This is an example where neural data enriches understanding of human behavior relative to a consideration of behavioral data alone.

Cappelen et al. (2014) study the neural correlates of inequity aversion when individuals evaluate different income distributions that are generated by an input of endogenous effort. The behavioral data suggests a preference for income distributions in which incomes are proportional to effort. Thus, individuals are less inequity-averse when inequity arises from the input of endogenous effort. There was a significant activation in the striatum whenever the income distribution deviated from the one where incomes are proportional to effort. In competitive environments, such as tournaments between competing agents, workers, or athletes, winning is considered more personally rewarding. In such environments, winning is correlated with increased activity in the vmPFC and the striatum, which are also activated in the case of private rewards (Bault et al., 2011).

4.5.3 *Neural basis of social punishment and trust*

Classical game theory predicts that bygones are bygones, so we should not observe players imposing costly punishments on others. Yet, the empirical findings of costly punishment in a range of games, precisely when bygones should be bygones, is puzzling. A prominent example is the data from public goods games with punishment (Fehr and Gächter, 2002; see Volume 2 for details). In other contexts, one observes costly punishment meted out to others, including third parties, for violating social norms; this is sometimes known as *altruistic punishment* or *indirect reciprocity*. Indeed, such reciprocal behavior appears to have been critical to the survival of traditional societies, prior to the establishment of a formal state, and it has evolutionary foundations.[15] In this section, we consider the neurobiological foundations of such behavior.

De Quervain et al. (2004) consider a *trust game* between player A (the trustor) and player B (the trustee) that allows for punishment of the trustee for betrayal of trust. Players A and B are endowed with 10 MUs (experimental unit of currency). Player A sends an amount, x MUs, to B that the experimenter quadruples and passes on to B. Player B then has an opportunity to repay this trust by choosing to send back one of two amounts: 0 MUs or $\frac{1}{2}(10 + 4x)$ MUs. On observing the amount sent back by B, player A is given 1 minute to deliberate and then decide on the level

---

[15] See Volumes 2, 6 for the details. Several excellent references are available. These include Boyd et al. (2003), Bowles and Gintis (2004, 2011), Fehr and Gachter (2002), Fehr et al. (2002), and Fehr and Fischbacher (2003).

of punishment to impose on B. Different treatments vary the cost of punishment on both players. During the 1 minute that player A deliberates, his brain is scanned using positron emission tomography (PET). In order to reduce the exposure of radioactive substances, the authors scan in only those cases where player B sends back nothing; we report these results below.

Four different treatment conditions were considered, depending on the cost of punishment; these are IC, IF, IS, and NC. The first letter in any name of treatment captures the intentionality (I) or non-intentionality (N) of the decision made by B. Under N, a random device makes the decision on behalf of player B, while under I, player B directly makes the decision. The second letter of the treatment name determines if the punishment is costly (C), free (F), or purely symbolic (S). Under C, player A gives up 1 MU to reduce the payoff of player B by 2 MUs, while under F, there is no cost to player A. Under S, there is no cost to either of the players.

The four treatments provide the necessary contrasts to evaluate the relevant hypotheses. Player A should have an incentive to punish player B whenever B intentionally chooses the action of sending back nothing (the only case considered below). When punishment is symbolic, player A has the intention to punish but not the means to do so, hence, he might not get any satisfaction in this case. The contrast IF−IS captures the satisfying aspect of punishment. If punishment is satisfactory in the treatment IF, then provided punishment is not too costly, we expect players to also punish in the IC treatment, although the punishment might be reduced. Indeed, brain areas that are involved in the calculation of such trade-offs may come into play.

One might expect that subjects with the greatest activation in the reward areas in the brain in the IF treatment might engage in the greatest punishment in the IC treatment. If so, then this would contribute to the ability of neuroeconomics to make successful predictions. When the decision by player B is non-intentional, then player A should not derive any pleasure from punishing player B. The combined contrast (IC + IF) − (IS + NC) is also useful. In the treatments IC and IF, there is a desire and opportunity to punish while in treatment IS there is no opportunity to punish and in treatment NC there is no desire to punish.

Player A is asked to rank the perceived unfairness of player B and the desire to punish player B on a seven-point *Likert scale* from −3 to +3. A Likert scale is a bipolar scale in which subjects indicate a positive and a negative response, with 0 denoting indifference. The behavioral results are shown in Figure 4.17 for each of the four treatments. Maximal perceived fairness is indicated

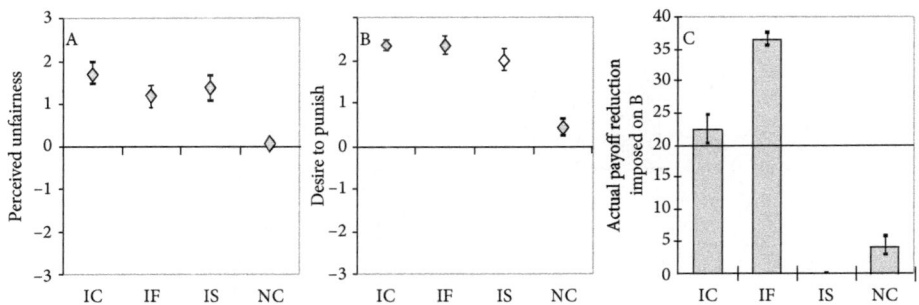

Figure 4.17 Mean responses by player A when player B returns 0 MUs, and the actual payoff reduction of player B in various treatments.

Source: "The neural basis of altruistic punishment." Dominique J.-F. de Quervain, Urs Fischbacher, Valerie Treyer, Melanie Schellhammer, Ulrich Schnyder, Alfred Buck, and Ernst Fehr, *Science* (27 August 2004) 305 (5688): 1254–8. Reprinted with permission from AAAS.

by −3 and maximum perceived unfairness by +3. The maximal desire to punish is indicated by +3 and the maximal desire to reward by −3.

Mean perceptions ± standard errors are shown in the two leftmost panels in Figure 4.17. When the choices of B are unintentional (treatment NC) there is no perceived unfairness (leftmost panel), desire to punish is very small (middle panel), and the payoff of player B is reduced very little through punishment, possibly on account of inequity-aversion (rightmost panel). In the other three treatments, the intentional choices of B are perceived as unfair, there is desire to punish, and actual punishment takes place. The highest punishment takes place when it is free (treatment IF).

Consider the contrasts (IC + IF) − (IS + NC), IF − IS, IC − IS, IF − NC, IC − NC. In these contrasts, the PET results show that the highest activation is achieved in the caudate nucleus and this activation is particularly significant in the contrasts (IC + IF) − (IS + NC) and IF − IS. The MNI coordinates of this brain area are [6, 22, 4]. A secondary area that was activated in these contrasts is the thalamus.

Figure 4.18 shows the peak blood-flow increase in the caudate nucleus in each treatment, relative to the average level of activation. The greatest activation was in the IC and IF treatments where there is a desire and an opportunity to punish, relative to the other two cases. The caudate nucleus has been found to be associated with the brain's reward circuits in brain lesion studies in rats, single neuron studies in non-human primates (Hollerman et al., 1998) and neuroimaging studies in humans (Knutson et al., 2001; Delgado et al., 2000). The thalamus too has been implicated in the processing of rewards in neuroimaging studies in humans (Delgado et al., 2000). Thus, it appears that the act of punishing an unfair act by player B is hedonically rewarding to player A.

An important step is taken in establishing causality by first identifying the 16 subjects in their roles as player A who exhibit the highest caudate activation in the IF condition when they punish player B. These players are also the ones who punish maximally in the IC condition when punishment is costly. Thus, the PET study appears to clearly identify those players who derive the greatest pleasure from punishing norm violation by player B; these players behave exactly as predicted in the IC condition. Costly punishments involve a trade-off. On the one hand, punishment is satisfying, but on the other hand, punishment imposes a personal cost.

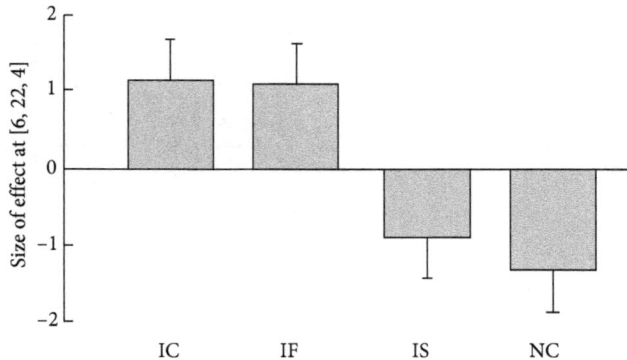

Figure 4.18 Peak activation in the caudate nucleus relative to the mean level in all four treatments.
Source: de Quervain et al. (2004).

In this case, the PET data shows activation also in the mOFC, which is typically engaged in making difficult choices.

Empathy allows individuals to share the emotions, pain, and suffering of others. Neural evidence shows that similar brain regions are highlighted when one experiences painful events or suffering, or observes others experiencing these events with whom one has empathy. These brain areas are typically the anterior insula (AI), front-insular cortex (FI), and the anterior cingulate cortex (ACC) (Wicker et al., 2003; Keysers et al., 2004; Singer et al., 2004; Morrison et al., 2004). One might wonder how empathy towards others varies, depending on how favorably one views them. This question is addressed by Singer et al. (2006) and is the one that we consider next.

They play a modified trust game that they call a sequential prisoner's dilemma. Subjects in their roles as first movers could send an amount of money to a second player who then chooses to either send back a low, seemingly unfair, amount or a high, seemingly fair, amount. The second player is a confederate of the experimenter in the sense that he/she chooses a fair or an unfair amount in accordance with the experimenter's instructions. First movers were then asked to rate the fairness, agreeableness, or likeability of the second player; they rated the second player positively on these traits if they sent a fair amount, and negatively otherwise.

Once first movers had rated the second players, fMRI was used to monitor their empathetic responses when a painful stimulus was applied to them (self-condition) and to the other players who were fair or unfair (others-condition). Consistent with the earlier literature on empathy, in the self-condition, the activated brain areas were AI and ACC, extending into the FI and brainstem. There was also a high correlation between empathy scores in behavioral tasks and activation of the relevant brain areas associated with empathy. The others-condition gives rise to two main results. First, less brain empathy is generated, measured by the activation of the relevant brain areas in fMRI data, when the partner is unfair, relative to being fair. Second, there is a significant gender difference. Measured by peak brain activity, there was little or no empathetic response in the fMRI data of men when the partner was unfair. In contrast, women still showed a significant empathetic brain response to unfair partners, although lower as compared to fair partners.

In an early study, Sanfey et al. (2003) showed that players who were treated unfairly in ultimatum games (offered a low amount by the proposer) exhibited activation in the emotional regions of the brain, such as the anterior insula. Thus, rejection of unfair offers may be associated with a negative emotional response. Tabibnia et al. (2008) argue that it is not clear if the brain responds to a lower monetary offer or a lower perceived fairness of the offer. They disentangle these two effects in which all players, in their roles as responders, play two ultimatum games. There were no proposers in the game, although the responders were told that proposers had already made offers that they were to respond to and actual payments would be made to the hypothetical proposers, whose pictures were shown to them.[16]

Consider, for instance, the offers in ultimatum games shown in Figure 4.19. An offer of $7 out of $15 may be deemed as fair but so is an offer of $0.50 out of $1. Hence, one may vary the monetary amount but maintain the same degree of fairness. Figure 4.19 also shows that depending on the base amounts, two different monetary payoffs, one higher than the other, may be deemed to be unfair (7 out of 23 is unfair but 0.50 out of 1 is fair).

---

[16] Experimenters in economics often argue strongly for eliminating deception from experiments (Houser and McCabe, 2014, p. 27). The experiments reported here could possibly be construed as borderline deception.

		Material payoffs	
		High	Low
Fairness	High	$7 out of $15	$0.50 out of $1
	Low	$7 out of $23	$0.50 out of $10

Figure 4.19 Different offers in an ultimatum game that signify varying levels of fairness. Source: Tabibnia et al. (2008).

In the behavioral results, self-reported happiness of responders is significantly higher for fairer offers and self-reported contempt was significantly higher for unfair offers. The main areas of brain activity revealed by fMRI data that were activated in the fair versus unfair offers contrast were vmPFC, ventral striatum, and the amygdala. The activation of the amygdala is interesting because one typically associates it with a fear response. However, it has also been implicated in reward processing in other studies also.[17] One potential limitation of this study is that the authors only included matched pairs of data in which the same amount was rejected in one case and accepted in the other (see p. 342). Hence, as Fehr and Krajbich (2014, p. 206) note, the "high > low fairness contrast is essentially the same as contrasting accepted > rejected offers."

Baumgartner et al. (2012) explore the neural basis of *parochial altruism*, which is a form of altruism that is particularly directed at ingroup members only; see Volume 2 for issues of social identity. The authors give a very clear definition (p. 1453): "Parochial altruism constitutes a persuasive psychological phenomenon which is qualified by a preference for altruistic behavior towards the members of one's ethnic, racial, or any other social group, combined with a tendency for indifference, mistrust, or even hostility toward outgroup members." Parochial altruism has played a critical role in norm compliance not only over human evolution but also in modern times; see Volumes 2 and 6 for details. Such norm compliance often takes the form of third party punishment of norm violators. Third parties are typically not harmed by observed opportunistic behavior between other parties, yet they are willing to engage in costly punishments that do not give them any direct benefits. The authors conjecture that such behavior, which is the product of human evolution, might also have given rise to specialized neural structures that support it.

The setting for the social identity experiments used by the authors has already been discussed in Chapter 3 in Volume 2 (Goette et al., 2006). Swiss army recruits are randomly assigned to platoons over a four week training course. The behavioral results are consistent with the social identity view that own-platoon members are considered as ingroups relative to other-platoon members. A simultaneous move prisoner's dilemma is conducted with two players A and B in the third or fourth week of training. A and B are given 20 points; the points can be exchanged for money with the experimenter at a known exchange rate. Under cooperation, C, the players can simultaneously transfer 20 points to the other player, which the experimenter doubles before transferring to the other player. So if both players transferred their entire endowments to the

---

[17] The interested reader can look up the references in Tabibnia et al. (2008).

other player, each gets 40 points. The players can also choose not to transfer (defection, D) and simply exchange their endowment for money with the experimenter at the end of the game. Since decisions are made simultaneously, the four outcomes or *conditions* are CC, CD, DC, and DD. Thus, for instance, in condition DC, player A plays the strategy defect (D) and player B plays the strategy cooperate (C).

A third player, player C (not to be confused with the strategy C) observes the results of these experiments within five days and must decide on the level of punishment. He can only punish one of the two players. The identities of the players are so arranged that player C can only punish player A, who could be a ingroup or an outgroup member. Punishment costs 1 point but allows for a deduction of 3 points from the target. While engaging in punishment, fMRI data was collected from player C, whose behavior will be our main focus of attention.

There are three main groups/constellations, each with three players. In group ABC, all three players are from the same platoon; in group AC, players A and C are from the same platoon, but B belongs to another platoon; in group BC, players B and C are from the same platoon, but A belongs to another platoon. To summarize:

$$\begin{cases} \text{2 player Conditions/Strategy profiles chosen by players A, B:} & \{\text{CC, CD, DC, DD}\} \\ \text{3 player Groups/Constellations listing ingroup members only:} & \{\text{ABC, AC, BC}\} \end{cases}$$

Consider the condition DC in which player A defects and player B cooperates. In the constellation BC, player A is an outgroup member, while in the constellation AC, A is an ingroup member. Parochial altruism arises if player C punishes A more in the constellation BC (where A is an outgroup member) as compared to the constellation AC (where A is an ingroup member).

In the case of two-player punishment games, the brain regions involved in the punishment of norm violators are the right lateral prefrontal cortex (rlPFC) (Knoch et al. 2006, 2008; Sanfey et al. 2003), and the dorsal caudatus (de Quervain et al. 2004; Seymour et al. 2007). The calculations in third party punishment games are similar to the case of two-player punishment games. One has to trade off the loss in personal material payoff with the desire to punish norm violators; indeed such punishment offers personal satisfaction (de Quervain et al., 2004). Hence, we might expect similar brain regions to be activated in third party punishment.

However, the introduction of third party punishment in a social identity experiment introduces other issues. Third parties will need to engage *mentalizing processes* that justify why punishment meted out to ingroup members should be lower as compared to outgroup members for the same norm violation. Such mentalizing might take the form of mitigating factors to justify norm violations of ingroup members. Neural evidence indicates that the brain regions associated with this type of mentalizing are the dorsomedial prefrontal cortex (dmPFC) and the bilateral temporoparietal junction (TPJ). A range of studies have implicated the TPJ in suggesting *a theory of the mind*, i.e., the ability of an individual to take on the perspective of another person (Decety and Lamm, 2007; Frith and Frith, 2007; Van Overwalle, 2009).

The main condition of interest that we now focus on is DC (because in the conditions CC, CD, and DD, player A behaves no worse than player B so there would appear to be no desire to punish). Two main brain contrasts were used in the condition DC. (1) Constellation BC (player A belongs to the outgroup) minus the constellations (AC + ABC) (player A belongs to the ingroup). (2) The constellation (AC + ABC) minus the constellation BC. The first contrast allows us to examine if there is increased brain activity when one punishes an outgroup norm violator. The second contrast allows one to test if there is increased activity in the mentalizing network when one reduces punishment of ingroup norm violators.

A special software (MarsBaR) is used to identify the *regions of interest* (ROI analysis) during fMRI imaging.[18] This is based on maximum observed voxel activity in these regions during third party punishment. Furthermore, Physio-Physiological Interaction (PPI) analysis was used to determine interaction between brain regions that goes towards establishing causality of one brain region in modulating activity in other brain regions.

The behavioral results confirm the classical results in social identity theory. There is punishments of norm violators, which arises most starkly in the condition DC (relative to the conditions CC, CD, and DD). Furthermore, there is a statistically strong effect of group membership on punishment; outgroup members belonging to other platoons are punished much more strongly than ingroup members for the same norm violation.

The fMRI results are as follows. Consider first the outgroup effects as captured by the contrast between the constellation BC minus the constellations (AC + ABC); see Figure 4.20 for the results. Here the third party punishes outgroup members who violate norms against ingroup members who follow norms. The expected brain areas involved in punishment decisions showed increased activity in this case. These included the right orbitofrontal gyrus (rOFG), rlPFC and the right dorsal caudatus (rdCau). In order to establish the connectivity across these brain regions, a PPI analysis reveals that greater activity in rOFC is associated with greater connectivity of neural activity between rlPFC and the right caudatus. This suggests that the three regions are part of a functionally connected neural network that determines punishment behavior.

The results for the second brain contrast, the constellation (AC + ABC) minus the constellation BC, that captures ingroup effects is shown in Figure 4.21. The main brain activity in the contrast took place in those regions of the brain that have already been implicated in the mentalizing

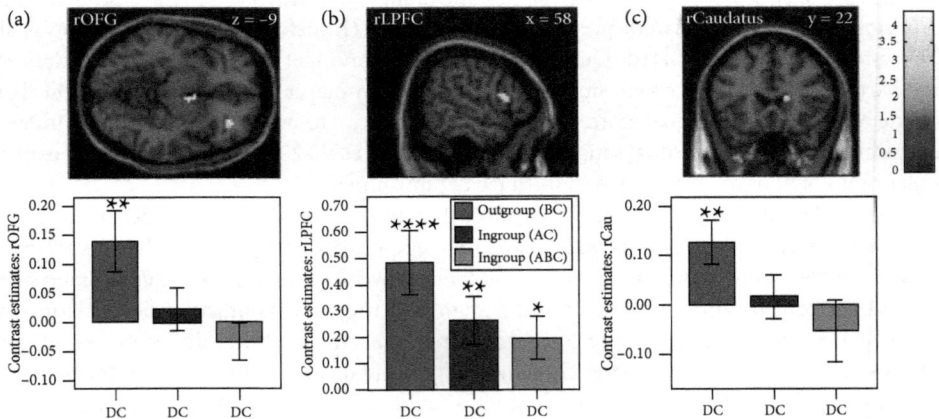

Figure 4.20 Outgroup effects captured by third party punishment of outgroup members who play opportunistically against ingroup members who cooperate. All data shown is for the condition DC. The first row shows activation in the three main brain regions of interest using fMRI data. The second row shows the contrast estimates, relative to a baseline, in the three brain regions, for three different constellations BC, AC, and ABC. Bars denote standard errors of mean.

Source: Baumgartner, T., Götte, L., Gügler, R., and Fehr, E. (2012). "The mentalizing network orchestrates the impact of parochial altruism on social norm enforcement." *Human Brain Mapping* 33: 1452–69. With permission from John Wiley and Sons. Copyright © 2011 Wiley-Liss, Inc.

---

[18] Other programs can also be used to define ROI on the basis of anatomical or functional criteria, e.g., SPM and MRIcro.

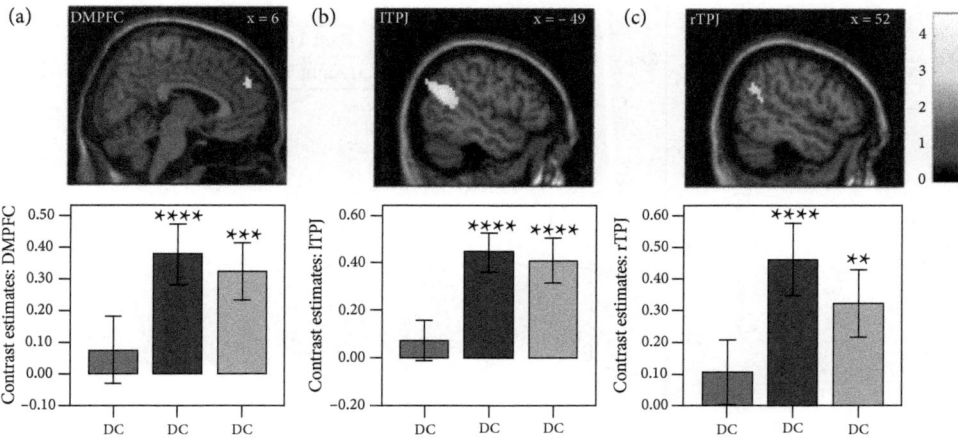

Figure 4.21 Ingroup effects captured by third party punishment of ingroup members who play opportunistically against outgroup members who cooperate. All data shown is for the condition DC. The first row shows activation in the three main brain regions of interest using fMRI data. The second row shows the contrast estimates, relative to a baseline, in the three brain regions, for three different constellations BC, AC, and ABC. Bars denote standard errors of mean.

Source: Baumgartner, T., Götte, L., Gügler, R., and Fehr, E. (2012). "The mentalizing network orchestrates the impact of parochial altruism on social norm enforcement." *Human Brain Mapping* 33: 1452–69. With permission from John Wiley and Sons. Copyright © 2011 Wiley-Liss, Inc.

network; these regions are dmPFC and the temporoparietal junction (TPJ) (Gallagher and Frith, 2003; Rilling et al., 2004a). In Figure 4.21, the ROI analysis revealed the left and right parts of the TPJ, respectively lTPJ and rTPJ, as being active in this contrast. Interestingly, the stronger the interaction between these two regions of the mentalizing network, the lower is the punishment of ingroup members for defecting. A PPI analysis showed that activity in the lTPJ modulates the connectivity between dmPFC and areas in the OFC and rlPFC. These areas, thus, appear to form a mentalizing network that shades punishment of ingroup members.

Neural findings suggest that disrupting the right dlPFC through repeated transcranial magnetic stimulation (rTMS) reduces the rejection rates of subjects (termed deviant subjects) in ultimatum games. Such disruption does not influence the ability of the deviant subjects to judge the fairness of offers (Knoch et al., 2006; Knoch et al., 2008; Wout et al., 2005). However, when rTMS is applied to the left dlPFC, it produces no differences in rejection rates relative to a sham treatment.

Baumgartner et al. (2011) combine fMRI methods with rTMS in order to reduce the limitations of these methods when they are applied separately. In their experiments, subjects play an ultimatum game. The proposer has an endowment of CHF 20 and he proposes a split to the responder. The offers are restricted to the set $\{4, 6, 8, 10\}$, so 4 is the most unfair offer and 10 the most fair because it results in an equal share of the pie for both players. Low frequency, 1Hz, rTMS is applied for 15 minutes to the right or left dlPFC of responders, prior to their decision to reject or accept offers (offline rTMS). This disrupts the functioning of the dlPFC; deviant subjects whose right dlPFC is disrupted are expected to reject unfair offers less frequently.

The results are shown in Figure 4.22. The rejection rates increase when the proposers make smaller offers. Disruption of the right dlPFC by rTMS leads to a much lower rate of rejection, which is consistent with the earlier results. Overall, the percentage rejection rates for offers of

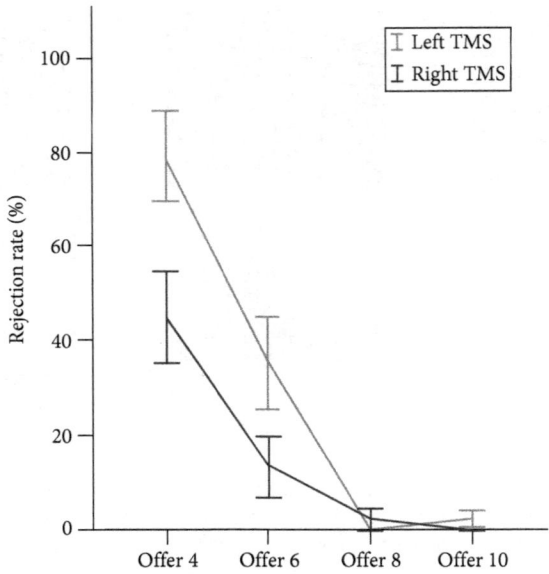

Figure 4.22 Mean rejection rates ± s.e.m. for different treatment groups and for different offers.

Source: Reprinted by permission from Macmillan Publishers Ltd. *Nature Neuroscience* 14: 1468-74. Baumgartner, T., Knoch, D., Hotz, P., Eisenegger, C., and Fehr, E. (2011). "Dorsolateral and ventromedial prefrontal cortex orchestrate normative choice."

4, 6, 8, and 10 were, respectively, 62, 25, 1, and 1. The percentage rejection rates for the unfair offers of 4 and 6, under right rTMS, were 45 and 13, while the corresponding figures for left rTMS were 79 and 35. The differences are statistically significant.

Several empirical studies report the following findings. (1) In the processing of unfair offers, two main brain regions, the anterior insula and the dACC, are reported to be activated (Sanfey et al., 2003; Tabibnia et al., 2008). (2) These brain regions are also known to be involved in the processing of negative emotions and in modulating conflict between cognitive and behavioral tasks (Baumgartner et al., 2009; Herwig et al., 2007).

The empirical evidence shows that disrupting the left dlPFC does not reduce rejection rates but disrupting the right dlPFC does reduce rejection rates; see Figure 4.22. So the regions listed in (1) and (2) above, are expected to be activated in the contrast between these two disruption treatments when evaluating fair and unfair offers. However, no differential activation of these regions is found in the two treatments. The only brain region that is differentially activated in the two treatments in the fair/unfair contrast is the posterior vmPFC, a region typically associated with positive stimuli. However, unfair offers are negative stimuli. This suggests that distinct areas in the pvmPFC are associated with the processing of positive and negative stimuli, a result that is confirmed by the authors.

Knoch et al. (2009) examine if disruption of the right lateral prefrontal cortex (rlPFC) by rTMS alters behavior in a 15 period repeated trust game in two treatment conditions. Trustees could either transfer back nothing, or transfer a quarter, or equalize payoffs by their back transfer. In the anonymous condition, the trustor does not learn of the trustee's past behavior. However, in the reputation condition, he can observe their behavior in the last three periods. The results are shown in Figure 4.23 for the following three cases. (i) Disruption of right dlPFC. (ii) Disruption of left dlPFC. (iii) A sham condition.

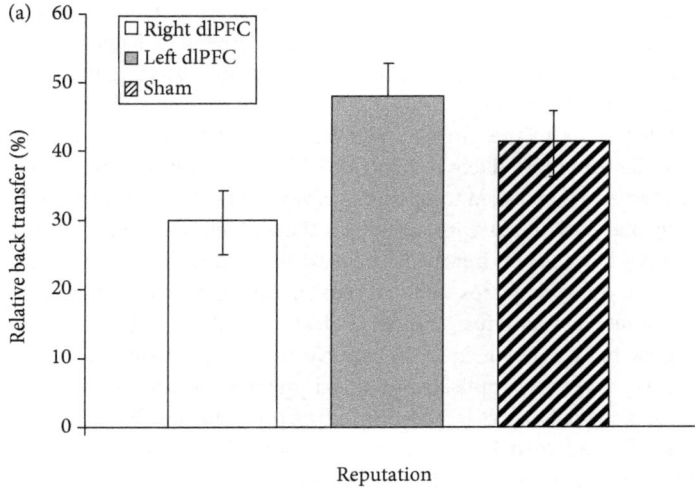

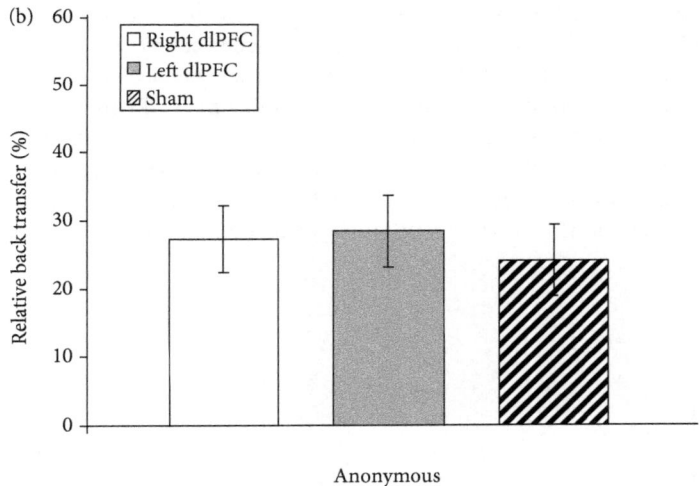

Figure 4.23 Relative back transfers in the two treatment conditions with varying degrees of brain function disruption.

Source: Knoch, D., Schneider, F., Schunk, D., Hohmann, M., and Fehr, E. (2009). "Disrupting the prefrontal cortex diminishes the human ability to build a good reputation." *Proceedings of the National Academy of Sciences* 106: 20895–9.

In the anonymous condition, there are no differences in the back transfers by the trustee in the three cases because there is no incentive to build a reputation. However, in the reputation condition, disruption to the right dlPFC causes lower back transfers relative to the other two cases. Such disruption appears to increase the temptation to reap current rewards relative to investing in one's reputation. It turns out that trustees who engaged in reputation building ended up with relatively higher payoffs. For instance, trustees who always chose to equalize payoffs, faced a 71% chance of getting a 10 point investment from the trustor, while the corresponding probability for those who returned nothing was less than 6%. It is important to note that disruption to the right dlPFC did not alter the fairness judgments of subjects. This was inferred from questions that subjects were asked immediately after the experiment to judge the fairness of alternative levels of back transfers.

Individuals with lesions to the vmPFC have been found to be more sensitive to fairness concerns because they are more likely to reject unfair offers in ultimatum games (Koenigs and Tranel, 2007). However, when asked to respond to hypothetical unfair offers, their answers are very similar to normal individuals without lesions (Leland and Grafman, 2005; Krajbich et al., 2009). Individuals with lesions in the vmPFC also exhibit diminished social preferences in their roles as proposers in dictator games, and trustees in trust games (Krajbich et al., 2009). The difference in hypothetical and actual choices indicate that the vmPFC is not involved in the detection of fairness, but it is involved in the expression of social preferences.

The amygdala has also been implicated in social preferences. For instance, individuals who have lesions in the amygdala react less to untrustworthy behavior (Koscik and Tranel, 2011). The amygdala also plays a role in determining punishments for different crimes (Buckholtz et al., 2008). In an ultimatum game, administration of a benzodiazepine that lowers amygdala activity also reduced the rejection rates (Gospic et al., 2011).

The size of the amygdala has been found to be associated with the size of one's social network and social behavior in nonhuman primates (Lewis and Barton, 2006). Bickart et al. (2011) conduct a similar analysis for humans. The regression results are shown in Figure 4.24, using two alternative but highly correlated measures of social networks. These are the number of people in the social network and the number of embedded networks (the number of distinct groups of contacts). Amygdala volume is measured using MRI data. Since the amygdala volume decreases with age, it is controlled for in the empirical analysis. Linear regression lines for both measures of social networks are plotted in Figure 4.24, and the regression coefficient is shown as the number B. A significantly positive relation between amygdala volume and social networks

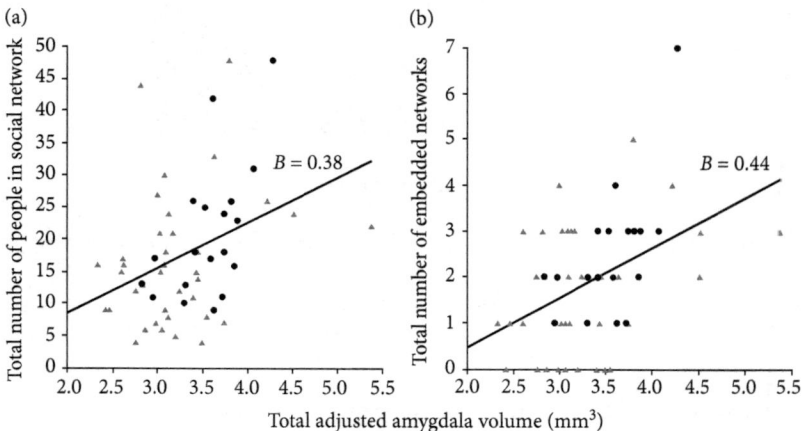

Figure 4.24 Two different measures of social networks plotted against amygdala size for two age groups: young participants (black circles) and older participants (gray triangles).

Source: Reprinted by permission from Macmillan Publishers Ltd. *Nature Neuroscience* 14: 163–4 (2011), "Amygdala volume and social network size in humans," Kevin C. Bickart, Christopher I. Wright, Rebecca J. Dautoff, Bradford C. Dickerson, and Lisa Feldman Barrett.

was found using both measures. Bickart et al. (2014) show that different parts of the amygdala are responsible for different aspects of social behavior.

Altruistic behavior has been observed in a wide range of other human activities. For instance, one may be slightly more altruistic when being observed by others. There is some evidence that there is increased activity in the left ventral striatum when one's charitable donations are observed by others (Izuma et al., 2010). Hsu et al. (2008) consider trade-offs between equity and efficiency. They find that a brain area, the putamen, responds to efficiency considerations while the insula responds to inequity considerations. Zaki and Mitchell (2011) also provide behavioral and neural support to efficiency considerations. They implicated the OFC in efficiency choices. The activation of the insula in equity considerations, which is also found in several other studies, indicates that fairness in behavior has a basis in emotional processing. Indeed, the very first fMRI study of ultimatum games found increased activity in the anterior insula and the ACC in the fair/unfair offers contrast (Sanfey et al., 2003). In redistribution of wealth from rich to poor individuals, increased activity was observed in the lateral frontal gyrus and the anterior insula (Dawes et al., 2012). However, when expressing egalitarian preferences, only the insular cortex activations were observed.

4.5.4 *Human virtues and the brain*

Chapter 3 in Volume 2 is devoted to the study of human virtues. Is there a neural basis for human virtues? Consider, for instance, the act of making a promise and keeping it, even at a cost in terms of material payoffs. This is considered to be a virtuous act in most cultures, yet it is at odds with a model based purely on self-regarding preferences. Indeed, oral and non-binding promises might have been the precursor of modern legally enforceable contracts that underpin economic exchange. However, the presence of enforceable contracts has not diminished the importance of promises in creating favorable expectations, and a great deal of modern commerce and exchange is possibly based on oral promises. In repeated games, promises can be motivated by reputational concerns. However, we know from Volume 2 that promises and other human virtues can also be motivated by intrinsic considerations (Charness and Dufwenberg, 2006; Vanberg, 2008); we explore the neural basis of some of these considerations now.

Baumgartner et al. (2009) consider a modified two-player trust game in which the trustor (player A) can send any or part of an endowment of 2 MUs to a trustee (player B); B has no endowment. The experimenter multiplies the amount sent by A by a factor of 5 and passes it on to player B. Player B then sequentially decides to send back either half of the MUs to A, or nothing. Each set of players play three consecutive trust games. In one set of trials, player B cannot make an upfront promise on his back transfers (before A makes his decision). In another set of trials, B can choose the *strength of his promise*, i.e., promise upfront that he will send back half the MUs to A *always*, *mostly*, *sometimes*, or *never*. Almost all players choose their promise with the maximum strength, i.e., "always."

The data revealed two clusters of players among those who had originally promised to send back a transfer. The first cluster does not send back any MUs (dishonest subjects), while the second cluster keeps its promise of sending back half the MUs (honest subjects). These clusters behaved in an identical manner, irrespective of whether the trials allowed a promise to be made or not. Thus, honest player Bs returned half their MUs to A, irrespective of having made a promise or not, while the dishonest player Bs never returned any MUs to A. An additional feature of these experiments relative to the earlier literature on deception in neuroscience studies is the introduction of an anticipation stage.[19]

Once player B has made a promise, there is a time interval of a few seconds that creates an anticipation in the mind of player B if player A will trust him. During the anticipation period, useful brain data can be gathered. Player Bs who intend to break their promise are likely to exhibit different brain activity relative to those who make a sincere promise that they intend to keep. This is because dishonest players may face emotional conflict from making a promise that they do not intend to keep.

An important aim of this study is to be able to predict whether player Bs will subsequently honor their promise by looking at their brain activity at the time of making their decision. In other studies, such emotional conflict has led to increased activity in the anterior cingulate cortex (ACC) and the amygdala (Botvinick et al., 1999; Phillips et al., 2003; Sanfey et al., 2003). Furthermore, is the anticipation period for dishonest player Bs more uncertain and stressful as revealed by their fMRI scans? Finally, when dishonest player Bs break their promise, they may fear the negative consequences if their dishonesty is discovered. In previous studies, such deception has led to increased activation of the ACC.[20]

These anticipated results are largely confirmed. In the anticipation stage, dishonest player Bs exhibited relatively greater brain activity in the right anterior insula and right inferior frontal gyrus (IFG), as compared to a baseline condition. In the decision stage, when player A makes his decision, dishonest player Bs exhibited relatively greater brain activity in the ACC as compared to a baseline condition. In another decision stage just prior to the decision of player Bs to honor their promise, when they are reminded of their original promise, dishonest player Bs show relatively greater activity in the left amygdala.[21] Using brain activity at the time of making a promise, activation in the anterior insula, ACC, and IFG, can successfully predict if player B intends to break his promise subsequently.

4.5.5 *Neural interplay of guilt and social preferences*

Prosocial behavior may be caused by feelings of *guilt* that arise from antisocial behavior. We have considered formal models of guilt in Volume 4 of the book, in the section on psychological game theory. Here, we consider the neural correlates of guilt by describing the experiments of Chang et al. (2011), who collect fMRI data from individuals who play the trust game. They give a useful definition of guilt (p. 560): "Guilt can be conceptualized as a negative emotional state associated with the violation of a personal moral rule or a social standard (Haidt, 2003) and is particularly salient when one believes they have inflicted harm, loss, or distress on a relationship partner, for example when one fails to live up to the expectations of others (Baumeister et al., 1994)."

Using the notation of Volume 4, let b_A^1 be the first order beliefs of the trustor (player A) about the amount of money that the trustee (player B) will return to him. The trustee's second order beliefs about b_A^1 are denoted by b_B^2 and his payoff is given by

---

[19] For a survey of earlier neuroscience studies of deception that do not allow for promises made under free will or issues of anticipation, see Spence et al. (2004) and Sip et al. (2008).

[20] For a focus on the neural systems underlying the trustors' behavior in trust games see Delgado et al. (2005), King-Casas et al. (2005) and Krueger et al. (2007). van den Bos et al. (2009) show that player Bs who abuse the trust of player As in trust games, typically show enhanced activity in the vmPFC and the posterior cingulate cortex (PCC).

[21] In this and the previous sentence, the world "relatively" captures statistical significance either at the 5% or the 1% level, based on the treatments.

$$\pi_B = \begin{cases} m_B - \theta\left(b_B^2 - r\right) & \text{if } r \leq b_B^2, \\ m_B & \text{if } r > b_B^2, \end{cases}$$

where m_B is the final monetary amount in the ownership of player B at the end of the game, r is the amount returned by B to A, and $\theta > 0$ is a guilt-aversion parameter. Notice that guilt arises if B's action (r) falls short of the second order beliefs of B about the action (b_B^2). Player B chooses r in order to maximize his utility. Furthermore, the beliefs are endogenous and, in equilibrium, they must concur with the actions. If the guilt-aversion parameter is high enough, in the sense that $\theta > 1$ and $r < b_B^2$, then by making an extra unit of back transfer relative to keeping it, the trustee increases his own payoff. Hence, guilt aversion may enhance prosocial behavior. On the other hand, if guilt aversion is low ($\theta < 1$) the trustee does not send back anything.

Participants in the experiments played the one-shot trust game multiple times. The first and second order beliefs of players were also elicited before they made their respective decisions. The trustees underwent fMRI scans while they made their decisions. The behavioral results are in line with the typical trust game experiments. Some amount of money was always sent by the trustors. The trustees were typically able to predict the expectations of the trustors fairly accurately. The actual amounts returned by them, r, were close to these expectations, which is consistent with the guilt-aversion hypothesis.

The fMRI results are as follows. The main contrast is between two groups of trustees for whom $r = b_B^2$ and $r < b_B^2$, respectively. When $r = b_B^2$, there is increased activity in the insula, supplementary motor area (SMA), dorsal anterior cingulate (dACC), dorsolateral prefrontal cortex (DLPFC), and the temporal parietal junction (TPJ). In contrast when $r < b_B^2$, there is increased activity in the ventromedial prefrontal cortex vmPFC, bilateral nucleus accumbens (NAcc), and dorsomedial prefrontal cortex (dmPFC).[22] The individual differences between the players also give interesting insights. Trustees who reported that they would have felt guilty if they had returned less money showed more activity in the insula and in the SMA when they contributed the expected amount ($r = b_B^2$). By comparison, participants who said that they would not feel guilty by returning less than the expected amount, showed increased activity in the NAcc when they contributed lower amounts ($r < b_B^2$). Thus, activity in the insula appears to be correlated with fairer choices.

4.6 The neuroeconomics of time preferences

Animals, even primates, who are most closely related, find it difficult to delay gratification (unless the animal is pre-programmed to do so, e.g., seasonal food storage among squirrels). As Loewenstein et al. (2008) describe: "Even after long periods of training, our nearest evolutionary relatives have measured discount functions that fall in value to nearly zero after a delay of about one minute. For example, Stevens et al. (2005) report that cotton-top tamarin monkeys are unable to wait more than eight seconds to triple the value of an immediately available food reward." In humans, individuals whose prefrontal cortex is damaged, say, by accident or surgery, are influenced more by the availability of immediate reward (Lhermitte et al., 1986). In particular, damage to the mPFC and the extent of the damage are both positively correlated with the choice

---

[22] Trustees in trust games who abuse trust show greater activity in the vmPFC and in the posterior cingulate region; see van den Bos et al. (2009).

of immediate over later rewards (Sellitto et al., 2010). These observations provide clues to the potential neural basis of intertemporal choice.

Let $\mathbf{c}_0 = (c_0, c_1, \ldots, c_T)$ denote the *temporal consumption profile* of the individual at time $t = 0$. Under the (β, δ) form of hyperbolic discounting, or quasi-hyperbolic discounting (see Volume 3), the temporal stream $(c_0, c_1, \ldots, c_T)$ is evaluated in the following manner (Laibson, 1997):

$$U^0(c_0, c_1, \ldots, c_T) = u(c_0) + \beta \sum_{t=1}^{T} \delta^t u(c_t), \; 0 < \beta < 1, \delta > 0. \tag{4.3}$$

By a multiplicative scaling, (4.3) can be written as

$$V^0 = \left(\frac{1}{\beta} - 1\right) u(c_0) + \sum_{t=0}^{T} \delta^t u(c_t). \tag{4.4}$$

The first and the second terms in (4.4) can be thought of as describing, respectively, the β system and the δ system.

McClure et al. (2004) measure brain activity when participants in their experiments make a set of intertemporal choices between a smaller–earlier reward (\$$s$ with a time delay d) and a larger–later reward (\$$L$ with a time delay D); $L > s$ and $D > d$. Values of $d = 0$ (immediate gratification) and $d > 0$ were considered, while the rewards ranged from \$5 to \$40. The authors hypothesize that the limbic system is driven relatively by immediate rewards rather than future rewards while the anterior and dorsolateral regions of the prefrontal cortex are driven relatively more by future rewards.

In terms of the (β, δ) preferences of quasi-hyperbolic discounting, McClure et al. (2004) hypothesized that β is controlled by the limbic system, while δ is controlled by the prefrontal cortex. It turned out that when the choice (s, d) was made, parts of the limbic system, which the authors call β-areas, the ventral striatum, orbitofrontal cortex and the medial prefrontal cortex, were disproportionately activated. In contrast, when difficult intertemporal choices are given, the δ-areas, such as the prefrontal and parietal cortex are disproportionately activated. This is because difficult choices are evaluated using the cognitive system. The δ-areas were also disproportionately activated when individuals chose the (L, D) option. The frontal and parietal cortex is activated for all (s, d) and (L, D) options; these are regions responsible for abstract planning and cognition.

In the McClure et al. (2004) experiments, the rewards were gift certificates, so one potential drawback of the approach was that gift certificates did not necessarily represent immediate rewards. This criticism was addressed in a later study by McClure et al. (2007) that we now describe. Subjects in their experiments abstained from drinks for 3 hours prior to the experiment. A choice between dated rewards was offered; the rewards being squirts of juice or water. The typical choice was of the following form. Choose (x, D) or (x', D'), where x and x' are both either squirts of juice or squirts of water and D, D' were, respectively, time delays expressed in minutes. In the experiments, the values of (x, x') used were $(1, 2)$, $(1, 3)$, and $(2, 3)$ while the values of (D, D') used were $(0, 1)$, $(0, 5)$, $(10, 11)$, $(10, 15)$, $(20, 21)$, $(20, 25)$.

The behavioral data is shown in Figure 4.25, where the vertical axis is the probability of choosing the earlier reward, x, and D is the earlier time. The probability of choosing the earlier reward is always higher when the early time, D, is closer to the present; these results are consistent with models of present-biased preferences such as hyperbolic discounting. In the right hand side

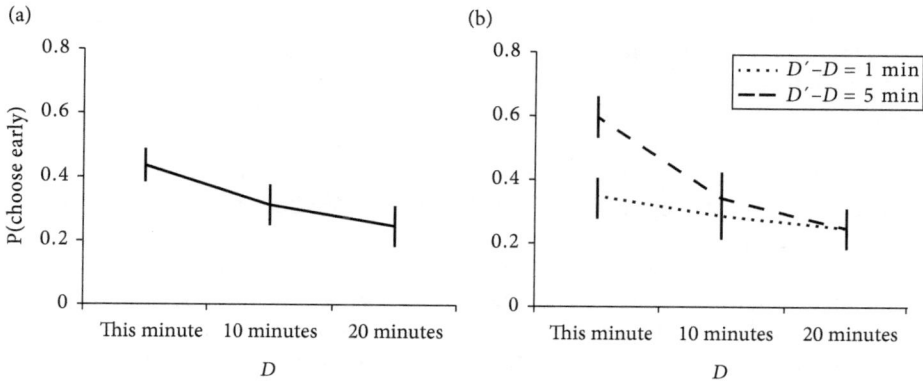

Figure 4.25 The behavioral data.

Source: McClure, S. M., Ericson, K. M., Laibson, D. I., Loewenstein, G., and Cohen, J. D. (2007). "Time discounting from primary rewards." *Journal of Neuroscience* 27: 5796–804.

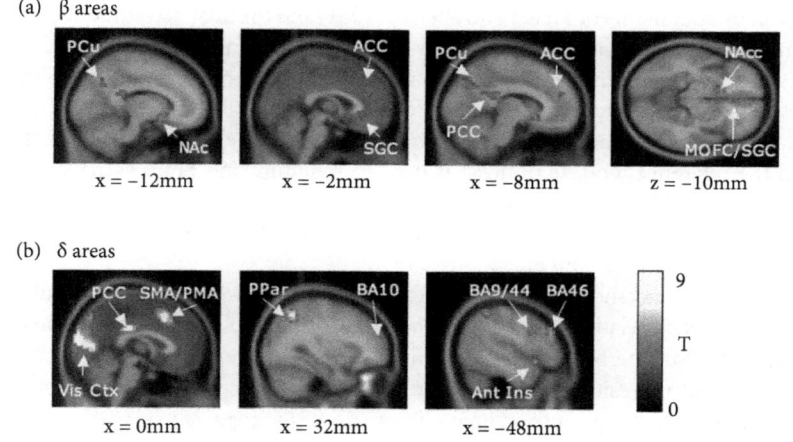

Figure 4.26 Activation in the β areas and the δ areas in the brain as rewards with varying delays are presented to the subjects.

Source: McClure, S.M., Ericson, K.M., Laibson, D. I., Loewenstein, G., and Cohen, J. D. (2007). "Time discounting for primay rewards." *Journal of Neuroscience* 27: 5796–804.

panel in Figure 4.25, it is clear that the results are mainly driven by the cases where the time delay difference $D' - D$ is 5 minutes; there is a smaller effect when $D' - D$ is 1 minute.

The fMRI data is shown in Figure 4.26. It is not based on a region of interest analysis, but rather on a whole brain analysis in which the BOLD signal measure in each voxel is regressed on a number of variables such as the reward magnitude and time delay. The brain regions that were most activated when subjects chose the earlier option were classified as the β areas (top panel of Figure 4.26). These brain regions include the nucleus accumbens (NAcc), subgenual cingulate cortex (SGC), medial orbitofrontal cortex (mOFC), posterior cingulate cortex (PCC), and precuneus. As in McClure et al. (2004), these regions lie within the limbic system and the paralimbic cortex. In contrast, the brain regions that are correlated with the larger–later choices, the δ areas (bottom panel of Figure 4.26), include regions associated with higher-level cognitive functions such as the posterior cingulate cortex (PCC), bilateral areas in the posterior parietal cortex (pPar), bilateral areas in the anterior insula (Ant Ins), and several regions in the dorsolateral prefrontal cortex (dlPFC) (Brodmann areas 9, 44, 46, and 10). Other areas that were activated included primary visual and motor cortex areas, possibly because subjects made choices by looking at a visual display. In comparing the results in McClure et al. (2004) and McClure et al. (2007), there is a greater match between the two in the δ-areas, but a lower match in the β-areas, suggesting that the β-areas might be context and task dependent.

Other studies have questioned the findings of McClure et al. (2004, 2007). Glimcher et al. (2007) do not find increased activation of the limbic and paralimbic systems in the case of immediate rewards. Kable and Glimcher (2007) find that the β-areas in McClure et al. (2007) are activated when the delayed reward, x', changes, thus, they question if these areas are exclusively associated with immediate rewards. For some possible explanations for these contrary findings, see Loewenstein et al. (2008).

A second class of models that explains the choice between immediate and delayed rewards invokes conflict between two brain systems for control. Two main types of models in this class are the planner–doer model of Thaler and Shefrin (1981) and the dual-selves model of Fudenberg and Levine (2006); see Volume 3 and Chapter 2 (this Volume) for the details. Hare et al. (2009) confront subjects with 50 different kinds of foods and ask them to rate them on health and taste. This allows the identification of a reference food for each subject that is neutral on taste and health grounds. In a second task, subjects are asked to choose between each of the 49 food items and the reference food item; fMRI is used to monitor their brain activity as they make their choices. The subjects were then classified into two groups. Self-controllers (SC) use health and taste criteria to make choices while the non self-controllers (NSC) decided on the basis of taste alone.

The behavioral results show that the subjects in the SC group were more successful in avoiding liked-unhealthy foods relative to the NSC group. The SC group also chose liked-healthy foods more frequently than the NSC group. The dlPFC shows greater activity in the choices of SC subjects who avoid unhealthy foods and also shows greater activity when the reference food item is chosen over the tempting food items. Thus, the dlPFC appears to play the role of a patient long-run planner. This interpretation is supported in the results of Figner et al. (2010) who find that temporary disruption of the dlPFC by TMS induces greater impatience in subjects. Relative behavioral impulsivity in adolescents is also associated with slower development of the neural brain circuitry in the prefrontal cortex (Sowell et al., 2003; Casey et al. 2008). This provides some neural basis for why younger people might make more impatient choices, which has economic implications for them such as higher car insurance premiums.

4.7 The neuroeconomics of strategic interaction

In this section, we consider the neural evidence on strategic interaction. The direct cognitive evidence from eyetracking studies, typically using the MOUSELAB software, that supports level-k and cognitive hierarchy (CH) models is considered in Volume 4 and is not repeated here (Crawford, 2008; Wang et al., 2010).

In Bhatt and Camerer (2005), subjects play eight, two-player, dominance solvable games with 2–4 strategies. Players engage in three tasks in random order. In the *choice task* (*C*), they choose their own strategy. In the *first order belief task* (*B*), they guess the strategy choice of the opponent. In the *second order belief task* (*2B*), they guess the opponent's first order beliefs about them. In the classical game theoretic equilibrium, choices, first order beliefs, and second order beliefs, should align, i.e., beliefs should be confirmed in equilibrium and choices should be optimal given beliefs. Bhatt and Camerer hypothesize that when subjects play according to equilibrium, neural activity in the three tasks *C*, *B*, and *2B* should be similar. However, when the choices of subjects are not in equilibrium, say, because they follow level-k or CH reasoning (see Volume 4), then dissimilar areas of the brain are likely to be activated. For instance, nonstrategic or level-0 players might not spend much time in forming beliefs. Consistent with these predictions, the authors find that in task *C*, when subjects were out of equilibrium, there is relatively greater activity in the mPFC and dlPFC. In contrast, for equilibrium subjects, brain activity was confined largely to similar brain areas, except for a small area in the ventral striatum.

In game theory, it is critical to determine what *theory of the mind* players have about others, i.e., how players believe others feel, believe, and choose. One line of research seeks to identify such *mentalizing* on the part of players by comparing their behavior when they play against other humans, relative to playing against computer programs. The hypothesis is that humans may need to mentalize against other humans, but not computers; this is confirmed in several neuroeconomic studies (Gallagher et al., 2002; McCabe et al., 2001; Coricelli and Nagel, 2009).[23]

In Coricelli and Nagel (2009), subjects play a *p*-beauty contest. They simultaneously choose a number in the interval [0, 100] and the winning individual's guess is closest to *p* times the average guess of all individuals. For *p* < 1, in a Nash equilibrium, all subjects are predicted to choose 0. By contrast, a level-k individual chooses $p^k 50$, $k = 0, 1, 2, \ldots$ (see Volume 4 for details). For instance, when $p = \frac{2}{3}$, the optimal guess of a (i) level-0 individual is 50, (ii) level-1 individual is $\frac{2}{3} 50 = 33.3$, (iii) level-2 individual is $\left(\frac{2}{3}\right)^2 50 = 22.2$, and so on. In the 'human condition' subjects were matched with other humans and in the 'computer condition' they were matched with computers who were pre-programmed to choose a number in the interval [0, 100]. Various values of *p* were used.

Figure 4.27 shows the results (the letter *M* in the figure is to be read as the probability *p*). The behavioral results are shown in panel (a) for a representative individual in each category— low level of reasoning (level-1 against a human opponent) and a high level of reasoning (level-2 against a human opponent) for varying values of *p* (data shown by filled-in dots). Although their behavior was different against human opponents, both types chose to behave like level-1 individuals against the computer opponent (data shown in triangles). The level-1 prediction is shown as the dotted line with triangles and the level-2 prediction as the dotted line with dots; in panel (a), below *p* = 1, the dotted line with dots is below the dotted line with triangles, and above *p* = 1, the line with triangles cross over. The data for the two types of individuals for a particular value of $p = \frac{2}{3}$ is shown in the bottom figure in panel (b). Overall, across all individuals, the majority of choices were consistent with level-1 to level-3 players and only 5% of the players were higher than level-3.

Panel (b) in Figure 4.27 shows the fMRI data. In the human versus computer contrast, enhanced activity was found in the mPFC, rostral anterior cingulate cortex (rACC), superior temporal sulcus (STS), posterior cingulate cortex, and bilateral temporoparietal junction (TPJ). However, the crucial finding came from comparing the data for low and high level reasoning

---

[23] One may conjecture that humans need to mentalize against computers too because humans wrote the software that determines the computer's choices. However, whether humans do so or not is an empirical question.

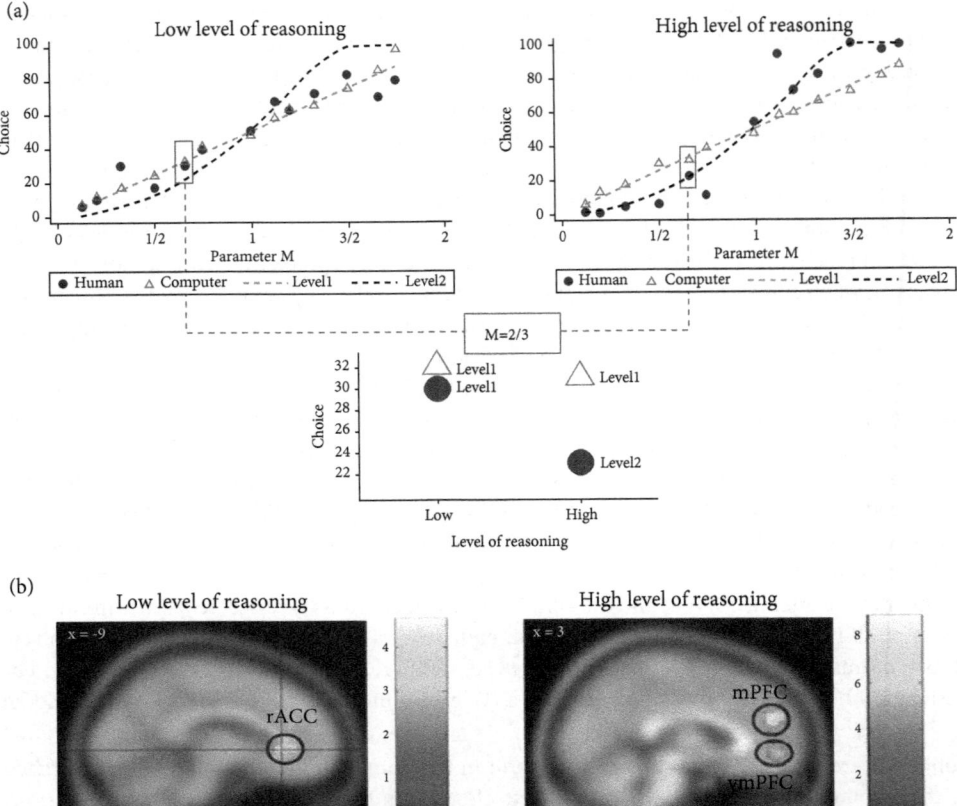

Figure 4.27 Results in the p-beauty contest game. Behavioral results (panel a) and fMRI results (panel b). *M* is to be read as the probability *p*.

Source: Coricelli, G. and Nagel, R. (2009). "Neural correlates of depth of strategic reasoning in medial prefrontal cortex." *Proceedings of the National Academy of Sciences* 106(23): 9163–8.

subjects. In this case, in the contrast between the human and the computer treatments, activity in the mPFC was found in the high level reasoners but not in the low level reasoners. Two areas in the mPFC stood out. A more dorsal area with coordinates $(x, y, z) = (0, 48, 24)$ and a more ventral area with coordinates $(x, y, z) = (9, 48, -6)$. The area $(0, 48, 24)$ has been found to be important when humans take a third person perspective (Amodio and Frith, 2006; D'Argembeau et al., 2007) and the area $(9, 48, -6)$ has been found important in thinking about like-minded other people (Mitchell et al., 2005; Mitchell et al., 2006; Jenkins et al., 2008). While the p-beauty contest is a simultaneous move game, the mPFC has also been implicated in a theory of the mind when players make sequential choices (Hampton et al., 2008).

In contrast, the fMRI evidence indicates that the main brain area engaged in the decisions of low level reasoners appears to be the rACC that has been implicated in self-referential thinking in social cognitive tasks (Moran et al., 2006). Two areas of the brain showed increased activity, irrespective of the level of reasoning of the players; these are the TPJ and the superior temporal sulcus. The TPJ has been implicated in a theory of the mind in other studies (Saxe and Wexler, 2005), while the superior temporal sulcus has been implicated in assigning intentions to the actions of others and establishing causality (Brunet et al., 2000; Castelli et al., 2000). However, several other empirical studies do not necessarily support the conclusions arrived at here. For instance, Kuo et al. (2009) show that in other contexts, the mPFC does not correlate with steps of reasoning in others. Similarly, the TPJ has been implicated in other studies in tasks that are unrelated to the theory of the mind (Decety and Lamm, 2007; Mitchell, 2008).

Bhatt et al. (2010) consider issues of deception or *management of social image* as with poker players who are engaged in bluffing. They use a two-player bargaining environment in which players must form first and second order beliefs about models of the mind. In the experiments, a buyer and a seller play 60 rounds of a bargaining game. At the beginning of each round, the buyer's private valuation, $v \in \{1, 2, \ldots, 10\}$, is privately revealed to the buyer. The buyer then suggests a price to the seller, s, who is free to ignore the suggestion if he wishes to. Finally, the seller asks for a price, p. If $v \geq p$, then trade takes place with respective payoffs to the seller and the buyer equal to p and $v - p$. Otherwise, no trade takes place and both parties receive 0. Since the interests of the two parties are completely non-aligned, the prediction of standard economic analysis is that the buyer will babble and the seller will pay no attention to the suggestions.

A regression of the suggested price, s, on the buyer's valuation, v, reveals three kinds of buyers. *Conservatives* play with their cards close to their chest and their suggestions do not reveal valuations; their behavior is closest to the standard game theoretic prediction. *Incrementalists* demonstrated a strong positive correlation between v and s; this behavior is potentially efficiency enhancing if believed by the seller. Finally, *strategists* reveal a significant negative correlation between v and s. This behavior is consistent with buyers who are level-2 players who believe that the seller is level-1.[24]

As compared to the other types, there is relatively greater activity in the dlPFC of strategists when they make their suggestions. Furthermore, when their realized value, v, is higher, strategists need to bluff the most (because v and s are strongly negative correlated); in this case they exhibit greater activity in the superior temporal sulcus (STS). In a later paper, Bhatt et al. (2012) show that the absolute gap between the actual price asked by the seller, p, and the buyer's suggested price, s, reflected the degree of suspicion that sellers have about the suggestions. There was relatively greater activation in the amygdala when more suspicious sellers choose prices.

4.8 Pharmacoeconomics: an application to social effects of oxytocin

There has been much interest in studying the economic effects of *neuromodulator systems*. In classical synaptic transmission, described in Section 4.2, information is transmitted from a single neuron to another neuron. In a different kind of information transmission, a small group of neurons can secrete neuromodulators in a wide and diffuse area of the brain, simultaneously influencing information transmission to many neurons; these effects can be long lasting. Examples of neuromodulators include neurotransmitters such as *dopamine, serotonin, norepinephrine*, as well as hormones such as *testosterone* and *oxytocin*. Crockett and Fehr (2014) provide an

---

[24] Level-1 sellers will look at the past history in judging current suggestions; if strategists behaved like conservatives, then a low suggestion will be interpreted as a bluff, hence, level-2 strategists will mix their suggestions.

excellent and accessible survey on the economic effects of these neuromodulators. In this section, we confine ourselves to a brief outline of some of the social effects of oxytocin.

In their seminal study using a trust game experiment, Kosfeld et al. (2005) gave one group of subjects a single dose of intranasal oxytocin, while the other group received a placebo. Both players were initially endowed with 12 MUs. The trustor/investor could pass on any amount from the set $\{0, 4, 8, 12\}$ to the trustee; the experimenter tripled the amount before it was received by the trustee. The aim was to examine the effect of oxytocin on the behavior of trustors and trustees. In a second set of experiments, the risk experiments, trustees played against an inanimate random mechanism. This random mechanism replicated the trustees' decision in trust experiments, say, by randomly choosing from the distribution of back transfers in the trust game.

The transfers in the trust and risk experiments are shown, respectively, in panels a and b in Figure 4.28. Filled-in bars and blank bars represent, respectively, subjects who were given oxytocin and the placebo. In the trust experiments, subjects who are given oxytocin make, on average, 17% higher transfers relative to the placebo group. The maximum transfer of 12 MUs was made by 45% of the subjects in the oxytocin group and 6% in the placebo group. At the bottom end of transfers, 21% of the oxytocin group made transfers less than 8 MUs while 45% of the placebo group made similarly low transfers.

The authors then engage in an exemplary experimental design that further illuminates the role of oxytocin. Do the trustors transfer more in the oxytocin group because they perceive "lower risk in a social interaction" or just "lower risk"? The risk experiments that do not involve

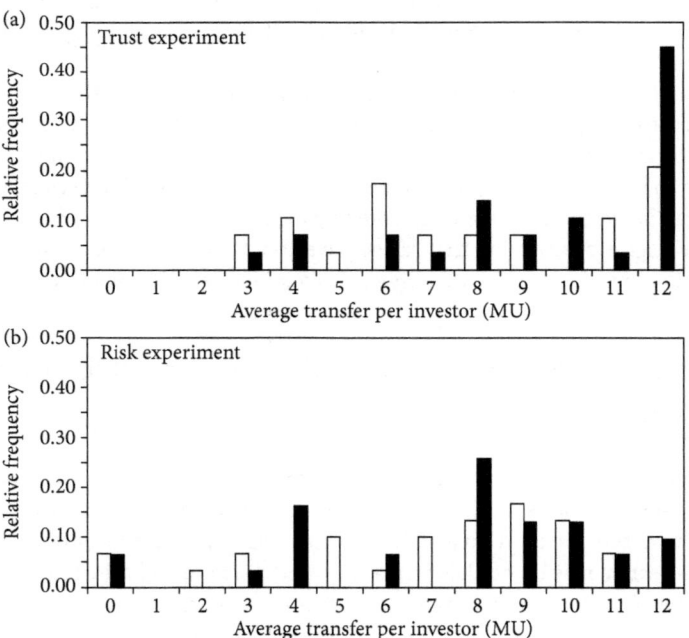

Figure 4.28 Transfers in the trust experiments (panel a) and risk experiments (panel b). Filled-in bars represent subjects who were given oxytocin and the blank bars represent subjects who were given a placebo.

Source: Reprinted by permission from Macmillan Publishers Ltd. *Nature* 435: 673–6. Kosfeld, Michael, Markus Heinrichs, Paul J. Zak, Urs Fischbacher, and Ernst Fehr (2005). "Oxytocin increases trust in humans."

any social interaction are able to answer this question. In the risk experiments, there is no significant difference in the transfers made between the oxytocin and placebo groups. Thus, oxytocin appears to enhance trust only in social interactions. Could the results be caused by other factors such as moods and calmness differences? In order to test this, measures of moods and calmness were taken before and after the administration of oxytocin but no significant differences were found. Does oxytocin cause a general increase in prosocial behavior? In order to test this, one can examine the back transfers of trustees, which were not found to be statistically different among the oxytocin and the placebo groups. Thus, oxytocin does not lead to a general increase in prosocial behavior, but, specifically, an improvement in trusting behavior. Is the observed effect of oxytocin caused by a general increase in optimism? In order to test this, the beliefs of trustors about the back transfers of trustees in the oxytocin and placebo groups are elicited but no differences are found in these beliefs. Thus, the results are not driven by an increase in optimism.

Subsequent research has examined several social effects of oxytocin. In addition to trusting behavior, these include interpersonal relations, generosity, cooperation, perceptions of trustworthiness, attractiveness, approachability, attachment, and socio-emotional responses, such as envy and social aversion; the interested reader can look up the associated references in the meta-study by Bartz et al. (2011). Bartz et al. (2011) also note that the overall social effects of oxytocin are small and heavily context dependent. Their solution is to advocate greater recognition of heterogeneous frames and contexts as well as individual-level heterogeneity. For instance, the prosocial effects of oxytocin are moderated, disappear, or reverse if one's opponents are portrayed as untrustworthy or are perceived to be outgroup members (Mikolajczak et al., 2010; Declerck et al., 2010; De Dreu et al., 2010).

Israel et al. (2014) examine the effect of oxytocin on the ability to detect deception, based on facial expression, body language, tone of voice, and other non-verbal clues. Two groups of subjects are shown clips of the game show "Friend or Foe" in which two individuals engage in a non-binding discussion prior to playing a prisoner's dilemma type of game; each player in the game has two strategies, friend (cooperate) or foe (defect). The clip is paused just before the outcome is revealed and subjects are asked to guess the outcome. One group is exposed to oxytocin and the second group is exposed to a placebo. Oxytocin subjects were more likely to be deceived as compared to placebo subjects, i.e., their accuracy in predicting deception was lower. However, oxytocin and placebo subjects made guesses of similar accuracy when predicting the cooperative behavior of others. Placebo subjects, but not oxytocin subjects, were able to predict the decisions of the contestants better than chance. Thus, oxytocin appears to reduce social vigilance that can reduce their payoffs.

REFERENCES FOR PART III

al-Nowaihi, A., Bradley, I., and Dhami, S. (2008). A note on the utility function under prospect theory. *Economics Letters* 99(2): 337–9.

al-Nowaihi, A. and Dhami, S. (2006). A simple derivation of Prelec's probability weighting function. *Journal of Mathematical Psychology* 50(6): 521–4.

Amodio, D. M. and Frith, C. D. (2006). Meeting of minds: the medial frontal cortex and social cognition. *Nature Reviews Neuroscience* 7: 268–77.

Andreoni, J. and Bernheim, B. (2009). Social image and the 50–50 norm: a theoretical and experimental analysis of audience effects. *Econometrica* 77: 1607–36.

Bartz, J. A., Zaki, J., Bolger, N., and Ochsner, K. N. (2011). Social effects of oxytocin in humans: context and person matter. *Trends in Cognitive Sciences* 15(7): 301–9.

Bault, N., Joffily, M., Rustichini, A., and Coricelli, G. (2011). Medial prefrontal cortex and striatum mediate the influence of social comparison on the decision process. *Proceedings of the National Academy of Sciences* 108: 16044–9.

Baumeister, R. F., Stillwell, A. M., and Heatherton, T. F. (1994). Guilt: an interpersonal approach. *Psychological Bulletin* 115: 243–67.

Baumgartner, T., Fischbacher, U., Feierabend, A., Lutz, K., and Fehr, E. (2009). The neural circuitry of a broken promise. *Neuron* 64: 756–70.

Baumgartner, T., Goette, L., Gügler, R., and Fehr, E. (2012). The mentalizing network orchestrates the impact of parochial altruism on social norm enforcement. *Human Brain Mapping* 33: 1452–69.

Baumgartner, T., Knoch, D., Hotz, P., Eisenegger, C., and Fehr, E. (2011). Dorsolateral and ventromedial prefrontal cortex orchestrate normative choice. *Nature Neuroscience* 14: 1468–74.

Bear, M. F., Connors, B. W., and Paradiso, M. A. (2007). *Neuroscience: Exploring the Brain*. Lippincott Williams and Wilkins.

Bernheim, B. D. (2008). Neuroeconomics: a sober (but hopeful) appraisal. NBER Working Paper No. 13954.

Berns, G., Capra, C., Chappelow, J., Moore, S., and Noussair, C. (2008). Nonlinear neurobiological probability weighting functions for aversive outcomes. *NeuroImage* 39: 2047–57.

Berns, G. S., McClure S. M., Pagnoni G., and Montague P. R. (2001). Predictability modulates human response to reward. *Journal of Neuroscience* 21: 2793–8.

Bhatt, M. and Camerer, C. F. (2005). Self-referential thinking and equilibrium as states of mind in games: fMRI evidence. *Games and Economic Behavior* 52: 424–59.

Bhatt, M., Lohrenz, T., Camerer, C., and Montague, R. (2010). Neural signatures of strategic types in a two-person bargaining game. *Proceedings of the National Academy of Sciences* 107(46): 19720–5.

Bhatt, M., Lohrenz, T., Camerer, C., and Montague, R. (2012). Distinct contributions of the amygdala and parahippocampal gyrus to suspicion and uncertainty in a repeated bargaining game. *Proceedings of the National Academy of Sciences* 109(22): 8728–33.

Bickart, K. C., Dickerson, B. C., and Barrett, L. F. (2014). The amygdala as a hub in brain networks that support social life. *Neuropsychologia* 63: 235–48.

Bickart, K. C., Wright, C. I., Dautoff, R. J., Dickerson, B. C., and Barrett, L. F. (2011). Amygdala volume and social network size in humans. *Nature Neuroscience* 14: 163–4.

Blood, A. J. and Zatorre, R. J. (2001). Intensely pleasurable responses to music correlate with activity in brain regions implicated in reward and emotion. *Proceedings of the National Academy of Sciences USA* 98: 11818–23.

Bolton, G. E. and Ockenfels, A. (2000). ERC: a theory of equity, reciprocity, and competition. *American Economic Review* 90(1): 166–93.

Botvinick, M., Nystrom, L. E., Fissell, K., Carter, C. S., and Cohen, J. D. (1999). Conflict monitoring versus selection-for-action in anterior cingulate cortex. *Nature* 402: 179–81.

Bowles, S. and Gintis, H. (2004). The evolution of strong reciprocity. *Theoretical Population Biology* 65: 17–28.

Bowles, S. and Gintis, H. (2011). *A Cooperative Species: Human Reciprocity and Its Evolution*. Princeton, NJ: Princeton University Press.

Boyd, R., Gintis, H., Bowles, S., and Richerson, P. J. (2003). Evolution of altruistic punishment. *Proceedings of the National Academy of Sciences USA* 100: 3531–5.

Breedlove, S. M., Watson, N. V., and Rosenzweig, M. R. (2014). *Biological Psychology: An Introduction to Behavioral, Cognitive and Clinical Neuroscience*. Sinauer Associates, Inc. Publishers.

Breiter, H. C., Aharon, I., Kahneman, D., Dale, A., and Shizgal, P. (2001). Functional imaging of neural responses to expectancy and experience of monetary gains and losses. *Neuron* 30: 619–39.

Brodmann, K. (1909). *Vergleichende Lokalisationslehre der Grosshirnrinde* (in German). Leipzig: Johann Ambrosius Barth. English translation by Gary, L. (1999). *Brodmann's Localisation in the Cerebral Cortex*. Imperial College Press: World Scientific Publishers.

Brunet, E., Sarfati, Y., Hardy-Bayle, M. C., and Decety, J. (2000). A PET investigation of the attribution of intentions with a nonverbal task. *NeuroImage* 11: 157–66.

Buckholtz, J. W., Asplund C. L., and Dux, P. E. (2008). The neural correlates of third-party punishment. *Neuron* 60(5): 930–40.

Busemeyer, J. R. and Diederich, A. (2014). Estimation and testing of computational psychological models. Chapter 4 in P. W. Glimcher and E. Fehr (eds.), *Neuroeconomics*. Elsevier Inc.

Camerer, C. F. (2007). Neuroeconomics: using neuroscience to make economic predictions. *Economic Journal* 117: C26–C42.

Camerer, C. F. (2008). The case for mindful economics. In A. Caplin and A. Schotter (eds.), *The Foundations of Positive and Normative Economics*. Oxford: Oxford University Press.

Camerer, C. F. (2013). Review essay about *Foundations of Neuroeconomic Analysis* by Paul Glimcher. *Journal of Economic Literature* 51(4): 1155–82.

Camerer, C. F., Cohen, J., Fehr, E., Glimcher, P., and Laibson, D. (2015). Neuroeconomics. In J. Kagel and A. Roth (eds.), *Handbook of Experimental Economics*. Forthcoming.

Camerer, C. F., Loewenstein, G., and Prelec, D. (2004). Neuroeconomics: why economics needs brains. *Scandinavian Journal of Economics* 106: 555–79.

Camerer, C. F., Loewenstein, G., and Prelec, D. (2005). Neuroeconomics: how neuroscience can inform economics. *Journal of Economic Literature* 43: 9–64.

Caplin, A. and Dean, M. (2008). Axiomatic neuroeconomics. In P. W. Glimcher, C. F. Camerer, E. Fehr, and R. A. Poldrack (eds.), *Neuroeconomics: Decision Making and the Brain*. London and San Diego: Elsevier, Academic Press, pp. 21–32.

Caplin, A., Dean, M., Glimcher, P. W., and Rutledge, R. B. (2010). Measuring beliefs and rewards: a neuroeconomic approach. *Quarterly Journal of Economics* 125(3): 923–60.

Cappelen, A. W., Eichele, T., Hugdahl, K., Karsten Specht, K., Sørensen, E. Ø., and Tungodden, B. (2014). Equity theory and fair inequality: a neuroeconomic study. *Proceedings of the National Academy of Sciences* USA 111(43): 15368–72.

Casey, B. J., Getz, S., and Galvan, A. (2008). The adolescent brain. *Development Review* 28: 62–77.

Castelli, F., Happe, F., Frith, U., and Frith, C. (2000). Movement and mind: a functional imaging study of perception and interpretation of complex intentional movement patterns. *NeuroImage* 12: 314–25.

Chang, L. J., Smith, A., Dufwenberg, M., and Sanfey, A. G. (2011). Triangulating the neural, psychological, and economic bases of guilt aversion. *Neuron* 70(3): 560–72.

Charness, G. and Dufwenberg, M. (2006). Promises and partnership. *Econometrica* 74(6): 1579–1601.

Chib, V. S., Rangel, A., Shimojo, S., and O'Doherty, J. P. (2009). Evidence for a common representation of decision values for dissimilar goods in human ventromedial prefrontal cortex. *Journal of Neuroscience* 29: 12315–20.

Clithero, J. A. and Rangel, A. (2013). Combining response times and choice data using a neuroeconomic model of the decision process improves out-of-sample predictions. Unpublished manuscript.

Coricelli, G. and Nagel, R. (2009). Neural correlates of depth of strategic reasoning in medial prefrontal cortex. *Proceedings of the National Academy of Sciences* 106(23): 9163–8.

Crawford, V. P. (2008). Look-ups as the windows of the strategic soul: studying cognition via information search in game experiments. In A. Caplin and A. Schotter (eds.), *The Foundations of Positive and Normative Economics.* New York: Oxford University Press, pp. 249–80.

Crockett, M. J. and Fehr, E. (2014). Pharmacology of economic and social decision making. In P. W. Glimcher and E. Fehr (eds.), *Neuroeconomics.* Elsevier Inc, pp. 259–79.

Cunningham, W. A., Kesek, A., and Mowrer, S. M. (2009). Distinct orbitofrontal regions encode stimulus and choice valuation. *Journal of Cognitive Neuroscience* 21, 1956–66.

D'Argembeau, A., Ruby, P., Collette, F., et al. (2007). Distinct regions of the medial prefrontal cortex are associated with self-referential processing and perspective taking. *Journal of Cognitive Neuroscience* 19: 935–44.

Dawes, C. T., Loewen, P. J., Schreiber, D., et al. (2012). Neural basis of egalitarian behavior. *Proceedings of the National Academy of Sciences USA.* 109(17): 6479–83.

de Araujo, I. E., Rolls, E. T., Kringelbach, M. L., McGlone, F., and Phillips, N. (2003). Taste-olfactory convergence, and the representation of the pleasantness of flavour, in the human brain. *European Journal of Neuroscience* 18: 2059–68.

De Dreu, C. K., Greer, L. L., Handgraaf, M. J., et al. (2010). The neuropeptide oxytocin regulates parochial altruism in intergroup conflict among humans. *Science* 328: 1408–11.

De Martino, B., Camerer, C. F., and Adolphs, R. (2010). Amygdala damage eliminates monetary loss aversion. *Proceedings of the National Academy of Sciences USA* 107: 3788–92.

De Martino, B., Kumaran, D., Holt, B., and Dolan, R. J. (2009). The neurobiology of reference-dependent value computations. *Journal of Neuroscience* 29: 3833–42.

De Martino, B., Kumaran, D., Seymour, B., and Dolan, R. J. (2006). Frames, biases, and rational decision-making in the human brain. *Science* 313: 684–7.

Decety, J. and Lamm, C. (2007). The role of the right temporoparietal junction in social interaction: how low-level computational processes contribute to meta-cognition. *Neuroscientist* 13: 580–93.

Declerck, C. H., Boone, C., and Kiyonari, T. (2010). Oxytocin and cooperation under uncertainty: the moderating influence of incentives and social information. *Hormones and Behavior* 57: 368–74.

Delgado, M. R., Frank, R. H., and Phelps, E. A. (2005). Perceptions of moral character modulate the neural systems of reward during the trust game. *Nature Neuroscience* 8: 1611–18.

Delgado, M. R., Locke, H. M., Stenger, V. A., and Fiez, J. A. (2003). Dorsal striatum responses to reward and punishment: effects of valence and magnitude manipulations. *Cognitive, Affective, and Behavioral Neuroscience* 3(1): 27–38.

Delgado, M. R., Nystrom, L. E., Fissell, C., Noll, D. C., and Fiez, J. A. (2000). Tracking the hemodynamic responses to reward and punishment in the striatum. *Journal of Neurophysiology* 84: 3072–7.

De Quervain, D., Fischbacher, U., Treyer, V., et al. (2004). The neural basis of altruistic punishment. *Science* 305(5688): 1254–8.

Falk, A., Fehr, E., and Fischbacher, U. (2008). Testing theories of fairness and reciprocity—intentions matter. *Games and Economic Behavior* 62(1): 287–303.

Fecteau, S., Knoch, D., Fregni, F., Sultani, N., Boggio, P., and Pascual-Leone, A. (2007). Diminishing risk-taking behavior by modulating activity in the prefrontal cortex: a direct current stimulation study. *Journal of Neuroscience* 27: 12500–5.

Fehr, E. and Camerer, C. F. (2007). Social neuroeconomics: the neural circuitry of social preferences. *Trends in Cognitive Sciences* 11: 419–27.

Fehr, E. and Fischbacher, U. (2003). The nature of human altruism. *Nature* 425: 785–91.

Fehr, E., Fischbacher, U., and Gächter, S. (2002). Strong reciprocity, human cooperation, and the enforcement of social norms. *Human Nature* 13(1): 1–25.

Fehr, E. and Gächter, S. (2002). Altruistic punishment in humans. *Nature* 415: 137–40.

Fehr, E. and Krajbich, I. (2014). Social preferences and the brain. Chapter 11 in P. W. Glimcher and E. Fehr (eds.), *Neuroeconomics.* Elsevier Inc.

Fehr, E. and Rangel, A. (2011). Neuroeconomic foundations of economic choice–recent advances. *Journal of Economic Perspectives* 25(4): 3–30.

Fehr, E. and Schmidt, K. M. (1999). A theory of fairness, competition and cooperation. *Quarterly Journal of Economics* 114(3): 817–68.

Figner, B., Knoch, D., Johnson, E. J., et al. (2010). Lateral pre-frontal cortex and self-control in intertemporal choice. *Nature Neuroscience* 13: 538–39.

Firth, C. D. and Frith, U. (2007). Social cognition in humans. *Current Biology* 17: R724–R732.

Fritsch, G. and Hitzig, E. (1870). Ueber die elektrische Erregbarkeit des Grosshirns [On the electical excitability of the cerebrum]. *Archiv für Anatomie und Physiologie* 37: 300–32.

Fudenberg, D. and Levine, D. (2006). A dual self model of impulse control. *American Economic Review* 95: 1449–76.

Gallagher, H. L. and Frith, C. D. (2003). Functional imaging of "theory of mind." *Trends in Cognitive Science* 7: 77–83.

Gallagher, H. L., Jack, A. I., Poepstorff, A., and Frith, C. D. (2002). Imaging the intentional stance in a competitive game. *NeuroImage* 16: 814–21.

Gazzaniga, M. S. (2009). *The Cognitive Neurosciences*. Cambridge, MA: MIT Press.

Glimcher, P. (2011). *Foundations of Neuroeconomic Analysis*. Oxford: Oxford University Press.

Glimcher, P. W., Camerer, C. F., Fehr, E., and Poldrack, R. A. (2009). *Neuroeconomics*. Academic Press, Elsevier Inc.

Glimcher, P. W. and Fehr, E. (eds.). (2014). *Neuroeconomics*. Elsevier Inc.

Glimcher, P. W., Kable J., and Louie, K. (2007). Neuroeconomic studies of impulsivity: now or just as soon as possible? *American Economic Review* 97: 142–7.

Goette, L., Huffman, D., and Meier, S. (2006). The impact of group membership on cooperation and norm enforcement: Evidence using random assignment to real social groups. *American Economic Review* 96: 212–16.

Gospic, K., Mohlin, E., Fransson, P., Petrovic, P., Johannesson, M., and Ingvar, M. (2011). Limbic justice: amygdala involvement in immediate rejection in the ultimatum game. *PLoS Biology* 9(5): e1001054.

Gul, F. and Pesendorfer, W. (2008). The case for mindless economics. In A. Caplin and A. Schotter (eds.), *The Foundations of Positive and Normative Economics*. Oxford: Oxford University Press.

Haidt, J. (2003). The moral emotions. In R. J. Davidson, K. R. Scherer, and H. H. Goldsmith (eds.), *Handbook of Affective Sciences* Oxford: Oxford University Press, pp. 852–70.

Hampton, A., Bossaerts, P., and O'Doherty, J. (2008). Neural correlates of mentalizing-related computations during strategic interactions in humans. *Proceedings of the National Academy of Sciences* 105(18): 6741–6.

Hare, T., Camerer, C., and Rangel, A. (2009). Self-control in decision-making involves modulation of the vMPFC valuation system. *Science* 324: 646–8.

Hare, T. A., O'Doherty, J., Camerer, C. F., Schultz, W., and Rangel, A. (2008). Dissociating the role of the orbitofrontal cortex and the striatum in the computation of goal values and prediction errors. *Journal of Neuroscience* 28: 5623–30.

Harlow, J. M. (1868). Recovery from the Passage of an Iron Bar through the Head. *Publications of the Massachusetts Medical Society* 2: 327–47. Reprinted as Recovery from the Passage of an Iron Bar through the Head (David Clapp and Son, 1869).

Herwig, U., Baumgartner, T., Kaffenberger, T., et al. (2007). Modulation of anticipatory emotion and perception processing by cognitive control. *Neuroimage* 37: 652–62.

Hollerman, J. R., Tremblay, L., and Schultz, W. (1998). Influence of reward expectation on behavior-related neuronal activity in primate striatum. *Journal of Neurophysiology* 80(2): 947–63.

Houser, D. and McCabe, K. (2014). Experimental economics and experimental game theory. Chapter 2 in P. W. Glimcher and E. Fehr (eds.), *Neuroeconomics*. Elsevier Inc.

Hsu, M., Anen, C., and Quartz, S. R. (2008). The right and the good: distributive justice and neural encoding of equity and efficiency. *Science* 320: 1092–5.

Hsu, M., Krajbich, I., Zhao, C., and Camerer, C. F. (2009). Neural response to reward anticipation under risk is nonlinear in probabilities. *Journal of Neuroscience* 29(7): 2231–7.

Huettel, S. A., Song, A. W., and McCarthy, G. (2009). *Functional Magnetic Resonance Imaging*. 2nd edition. Sunderland, MA: Sinauer Associates.

Hutzler, F. (2014). Reverse inference is not a fallacy per se: cognitive processes can be inferred from functional imaging data. *NeuroImage* 84(1): 1061–9.

Israel, S., Hart, E., and Winter, E. (2014). Oxytocin decreases accuracy in the perception of social deception. *Psychological Science* 25(1): 293–5.

Izuma, K., Saito, D. N., and Sadato, N. (2008). Processing of social and monetary rewards in the human striatum. *Neuron* 58: 284–94.

Izuma, K., Saito, D. N., and Sadato, N. (2010). Processing of the incentive for social approval in the ventral striatum during charitable donation. *Journal of Cognitive Neuroscience* 22: 621–31.

Jenison, R. L., Rangel, A., Oya, H., Kawasaki, H. and Howard, M. A. (2011). Value encoding in single neurons in the human amygdala during decision making. *Journal of Neuroscience* 31(1): 331–8.

Jenkins, A. C., Macrae, C. N., and Mitchell, J. P. (2008). Repetition suppression of ventromedial prefrontal activity during judgments of self and others. *Proceedings of the National Academy of Sciences USA* 105: 4507–12.

Kable, J. W. and Glimcher, P. W. (2007). The neural correlates of subjective value during intertemporal choice. *Nature Neuroscience* 10: 1625–33.

Kable, J. W. and Glimcher, P. W. (2009). The neurobiology of decision: consensus and controversy. *Neuron* 63: 733–45.

Kahn, I., Yeshurun, Y., Rotshtein, P., Fried, I., Ben-Bashat, D., and Hendler, T. (2002). The role of the amygdala in signaling prospective outcome of choice. *Neuron* 33(6): 983–94.

Kahneman, D. (2011). *Thinking Fast and Slow*. New York: Farrar, Strauss, Giroux.

Kahneman, D. and Tversky, A. (1979). Prospect theory: an analysis of decision under risk. *Econometrica* 47: 263–91.

Keysers, C. et al. (2004). A touching sight: SII/PV activation during the observation and experience of touch. *Neuron* 42: 335–46.

King-Casas, B., Tomlin, D., Anen, C., Camerer, C. F., Quartz, S. R., and Montague, P. R. (2005). Getting to know you: reputation and trust in a two person economic exchange. *Science* 308: 78–83.

Knoch, D., Nitsche, M. A., Fischbacher, U., Eisenegger, C., Pascual-Leone, A., and Fehr, E. (2008). Studying the neurobiology of social interaction with transcranial direct current stimulation: the example of punishing unfairness. *Cerebral Cortex* 18: 1987–90.

Knoch, D., Pascual-Leone, A., Meyer, K., Treyer, V., and Fehr, E. (2006). Diminishing reciprocal fairness by disrupting the right prefrontal cortex. *Science* 314: 829–32.

Knoch, D., Schneider, F., Schunk, D., Hohmann, M., and Fehr, E. (2009). Disrupting the prefrontal cortex diminishes the human ability to build a good reputation. *Proceedings of the National Academy of Sciences* 106: 20895–9.

Knutson, B., Adams, C. M., Fong, G. W., and Hommer, D. (2001). Anticipation of increasing monetary reward selectively recruits nucleus accumbens. *Journal of Neuroscience* 21: RC159(1–5).

Knutson, B., Westdorp, A., Kaiser, E., and Hommer, D. (2000). FMRI visualization of brain activity during a monetary incentive delay task. *NeuroImage* 12: 20–27.

Knutson, B., Wimmer, G. E., Rick, S., Hallon, N. G., Prelec, D., and Loewenstein, G. (2008). Neural antecedents of the endowment effect. *Neuron* 58: 814–22.

Koenigs, M. and Tranel, D. (2007). Irrational economic decision-making after ventromedial prefrontal damage: evidence from the ultimatum game. *Journal of Neuroscience* 27(4): 951–6.

Koscik, T. R. and Tranel, D. (2011). The human amygdala is necessary for developing and expressing normal interpersonal trust. *Neuropsychologia* 49: 602–11.

Kosfeld, M., Heinrichs, M., Zak, P. J., Fischbacher, U., and Fehr, E. (2005). Oxytocin increases trust in humans. *Nature* 435: 673–6.

Krajbich, I., Adolphs, R., Tranel, D., Denburg, N., and Camerer, C. (2009). Economic games quantify diminished sense of guilt in patients with damage to the prefrontal cortex. *Journal of Neuroscience* 29(7): 2188–92.

Krueger, F., McCabe, K., Moll, J., et al. (2007). Neural correlates of trust. *Proceedings of the National Academy of Science USA* 104: 20084–9.

Kuhnen, C. M. and Knutson, B. (2005). The neural basis of financial risk taking. *Neuron* 47: 763–70.

Kuo, W. J., Sjöström, T., Chen, Y. P., Wang, Y. H., and Huang, C. Y. (2009). Intuition and deliberation: Two systems for strategizing in the brain. *Science* 324: 519–22.

Laibson, D. (1997). Golden eggs and hyperbolic discounting. *Quarterly Journal of Economics* 112(2): 443–78.

Leland, J. W. and Grafman, J. (2005). Experimental tests of the somatic marker hypothesis. *Games and Economic Behavior* 52(2): 386–409.

Levy, I., Snell, J., Nelson, A. J., Rustichini, A., and Glimcher, P. W. (2010). The neural representation of subjective value under risk and ambiguity. *Journal of Neurophysiology* 103(2): 1036–47.

Lewis, K. P. and Barton, R. A. (2006). Amygdala size and hypothalamus size predict social play frequency in nonhuman primates: a comparative analysis using independent contrasts. *Journal of Comparative Psychology* 120: 31–7.

Lhermitte, F., Pillon, B., and Serdaru, M. (1986). Human anatomy and the frontal lobes. Part I: Imitation and utilization behavior: a neuropsychological study of 75 patients. *Annals Neurology* 19: 326–34.

Lin, A., Adolphs, R., and Rangel, A. (2012). Social and monetary reward learning engage overlapping neural substrates. *Social Cognitive and Affective Neuroscience* 7(3): 274–81.

Litt, A., Plassmann, H., Shiv, B., and Rangel, A. (2010). Dissociating valuation from motivation, attentional, and arousal signals during decision-making. *Cerebral Cortex* 21: 95–102.

Loewenstein, G., Rick, S., and Cohen, J. D. (2008). Neuroeconomics. *Annual Review of Psychology* 59: 647–72.

Loewenstein, G., Weber, E. U., Hsee, C. K., and Welch, N. (2001). Risk as feelings. *Psychological Bulletin* 127: 267–86.

Louie, K. and De Martino, B. (2014). The neurobiology of context dependent valuation and choice. Chapter 24 in P. W. Glimcher and E. Fehr (eds.), *Neuroeconomics.* Elsevier Inc.

Luce, R. D. (2001). Reduction invariance and Prelec's weighting functions. *Journal of Mathematical Psychology* 45(1): 167–79.

McCabe, K., Houser, D., Ryan, L., Smith, V., and Trouard, T. (2001). A functional imaging study of cooperation in two-person reciprocal exchange. *Proceedings of the National Academy of Sciences of the United States of America* 98(20): 11832–5.

McClure, S. M., Ericson, K. M., Laibson, D. I., Loewenstein, G., and Cohen, J. D. (2007). Time discounting for primary rewards. *Journal of Neuroscience* 27: 5796–804.

McClure, S., Laibson, D., Lowenstein, G., and Cohen, J. (2004). Separate neural systems value immediate and delayed monetary rewards, *Science* 306: 503–7.

Mason, W. A., Capitanio, J. P., Machado, C. J., Mendoza, S. P., and Amaral, D. G. (2006). Amygdalectomy and responsiveness to novelty in rhesus monkeys (Macaca mulatta): generality and individual consistency of effects. *Emotion* 6: 73–81.

Mikolajczak, M., Gross, J. J., Lane, A., Corneille, O., de Timary, P., and Luminet, O. (2010). Oxytocin makes people trusting, not gullible. *Psychological Science* 21: 1072–4.

Mitchell, J. P. (2008). Activity in right temporoparietal junction is not selective for theory-of-mind. *Cerebral Cortex* 18: 262–71.

Mitchell, J. P., Banaji, M. R., and Macrae, C. N. (2005). The link between social cognition and self-referential thought in medial prefrontal cortex. *Journal of Cognitive Neuroscience* 17: 1306–15.

Mitchell, J. P., Macrae, C. N., and Banaji, M. R. (2006). Dissociable medial prefrontal contributions to judgments of similar and dissimilar others. *Neuron* 50: 655–63.

Mohr, P. N. C., Biele, G., and Heekeren, H. R. (2010). Neural processing of risk. *Journal of Neuroscience* 30: 6613–19.

Moran, J. M., Macrae, C. N., Heatherton, T. F., Wyland, C. L., and Kelley, W. M. (2006). Neuroanatomical evidence for distinct cognitive and affective components of self. *Journal of Cognitive Neuroscience* 18: 1586–94.

Morrison, I., Lloyd, D., di Pellegrino, G., and Roberts, N. (2004). Vicarious responses to pain in anterior cingulate cortex: is empathy a multisensory issue? *Cognitive, Affective and Behavioral Neuroscience* 4: 270–8.

Murray, E. A., Gaffan, E. A., and Flint, R. W., Jr. (1996). Anterior rhinal cortex and amygdala: dissociation of their contributions to memory and food preference in rhesus monkeys. *Behavioral Neuroscience* 110: 30–42.

O'Doherty, J. P. (2004). Reward representations and reward-related learning in the human brain: insights from neuroimaging. *Current Opinion in Neurobiology* 14: 769–76.

Padoa-Schioppa, C. (2009). Range-adapting representation of economic value in the orbitofrontal cortex. *Journal of Neuroscience* 29: 14004–14.

Padoa-Schioppa, C. and Assad, J. A. (2006). Neurons in the orbitofrontal cortex encode economic value. *Nature* 441(7090): 223–6.

Paulus, M. P. and Frank, L. R. (2006). Anterior cingulate activity modulates nonlinear decision weight function of uncertain prospects. *Neuroimage* 30: 668–77.

Penfield, W. and Rasmussen, T. (1950). *The Cerebral Cortex of Man: A Clinical Study of Localization of Function*. Oxford: Macmillan.

Phillips, M. L., Drevets, W. C., Rauch, S. L., and Lane, R. (2003). Neurobiology of emotion perception I: the neural basis of normal emotion perception. *Biological Psychiatry* 54: 504–14.

Plassmann, H., O'Doherty, J., and Rangel, A. (2007). Orbitofrontal cortex encodes willingness to pay in everyday economic transactions. *Journal of Neuroscience* 27: 9984–8.

Plassmann, H., O'Doherty, J., and Rangel, A. (2010). Appetitive and aversive goal values are encoded in the medial orbitofrontal cortex at the time of decision making. *Journal of Neuroscience* 30: 10799–808.

Plassmann, H., O'Doherty, J., Shiv, B., and Rangel, A. (2008). Marketing actions can modulate neural representations of experienced pleasantness. *PNAS* 105(3): 1050–4.

Poldrack, R. A. (2006). Can cognitive processes be inferred from neuroimaging data? *Trends in Cognitive Science* 10(2): 59–63.

Prelec, D. (1998). The probability weighting function. *Econometrica* 66(3): 497–527.

Preuschoff, K., Bossaerts, P., and Quartz, S. R. (2006). Neural differentiation of expected reward and risk in human subcortical structures. *Neuron* 51: 381–90.

Rabin, M. (1993). Incorporating fairness into game theory and economics. *American Economic Review* 83: 1281–302.

Rangel, A., Camerer, C., and Montague, P. R. (2008). A framework for studying the neurobiology of value-based decision making. *Nature Reviews Neuroscience* 9: 545–56.

Rangel, A. and Hare, T. (2010). Neural computations associated with goaldirected choice. *Current Opinion in Neurobiology* 20: 262–70.

Rilling, J. K., Sanfey, A. G., Aronson, J. A., Nystrom, L. E., and Cohen, J. D. (2004). The neural correlates of theory of mind within interpersonal interactions. *NeuroImage* 22: 1694–703.

Roiser, J. P., De Martino, B., Tan, G. C. Y., et al. (2009). A genetically mediated bias in decision making driven by failure of amygdala control. *Journal of Neuroscience* 29(18): 5985–991.

Ruff, C. C. and Huettel, S. C. (2014). Experimental methods in cognitive neuroscience. Chapter 6

in P. W. Glimcher and E. Fehr (eds.), *Neuroeconomics*. Elsevier Inc.

Rushworth, M. F., Mars, R. B., and Summerfield, C. (2009). General mechanisms for making decisions? *Current Opinion Neurobiology* 19: 75–83.

Sanfey, A. G., Rilling, J. K., Aronson, J. A., Nystrom, L. E., and Cohen, J. D. (2003). The neural basis of economic decision-making in the ultimatum game. *Science* 300: 1755–8.

Saxe, R. and Wexler, A. (2005). Making sense of another mind: the role of the right temporoparietal junction. *Neuropsychologia* 43: 1391–9.

Seymour, B., Singer, T., and Dolan, R. (2007). The neurobiology of punishment. *Nature Reviews Neuroscience* 8: 300–11.

Sellitto, M., Ciaramelli, E., and Pellegrino, G. D. (2010). Myopic discounting of future rewards after medial orbitofrontal damage in humans. *Journal of Neuroscience* 30: 16429–36.

Simons, D. J. and Chabris, C. F. (1999). Gorillas in our midst: sustained inattentional blindness for dynamic events. *Perception* 28: 1059–74.

Singer, T., Seymour, B., O'Doherty, J., Kaube, H., Dolan, R. J., and Frith, C. D. (2004). Empathy for pain involves the affective but not sensory components of pain. *Science* 303: 1157–62.

Singer, T., Seymour, B., O'Doherty, J. P., Stephan, K. E., Dolan, R. J., and Frith, C. D. (2006). Empathic neural responses are modulated by the perceived fairness of others. *Nature* 439: 466–9.

Sip, K. E., Roepstorff, A., McGregor, W., and Frith, C. D. (2008). Detecting deception: the scope and limits. *Trends in Cognitive Sciences* 12: 48–53.

Smith, D. V., Hayden, B. Y., Truong, T. K., Song, A. W., Platt, M. L., and Huettel, S. A. (2010). Distinct value signals in anterior and posterior ventromedial prefrontal cortex. *Journal of Neuroscience* 30: 2490–5.

Sokol-Hessner, P., Delgado, M. R., Hsu, M., Camerer, C. F., and Phelps, E. A. (2009). Thinking like a trader: cognitive re-appraisal and loss-aversion. *Proceedings of National Academy of Sciences* 106: 5035–40.

Sokol-Hessner, P., Hsu, M., Delgado, M. R., Camerer, C., and Phelps, E. A. (2009). Getting some perspective: neural correlates of regulation during decision-making. Program No. 102.20, Society for Neuroscience.

Sowell, E. R., Peterson, B. S., Thompson, P. M., Welcome, S. E., Henkenius, A. L., and Toga, A. W. (2003). Mapping cortical change across the human life span. A. W. *Nature Neuroscience* 6(3): 309–15.

Spence, S. A., Hunter, M. D., Farrow, T. F., et al. (2004). A cognitive neurobiological account of deception: evidence from functional neuroimaging. *Philosophical Transactions of the Royal Society of London. Series B, Biological Sciences* 359: 1755–62.

Stevens J. R., Hallinan E. V., and Hauser M. D. (2005). The ecology and evolution of patience in two New World monkeys. *Biology Letters* 1: 223–26.

Stott, H. P. (2006). Choosing from cumulative prospect theory's functional menagerie. *Journal of Risk and Uncertainty* 32(2): 101–30.

Tabibnia, G., Satpute, A. B., and Lieberman, M. D. (2008). The sunny side of fairness: preference for fairness activates reward circuitry (and disregarding unfairness activates self-control circuitry). *Psychological Science* 19(4): 339–47.

Takahashi, H., Matsui, H., Camerer, C. F., et al. (2010). Dopamine D1 receptors and nonlinear probability weighting in risky choice. *Journal of Neuroscience* 30: 16567–72.

Talmi, D., Hurlemann, R., Patin, A., and Dolan, R. J. (2010). Framing effect following bilateral amygdala lesion. *Neuropsychologia* 48: 1823–7.

Thaler, R. H. and Shefrin, H. M. (1981). An economic theory of self-control. *Journal of Political Economy* 89(2): 392–406.

Tobler, P. N., O'Doherty, J. P., Dolan, R. J., and Schultz, W. (2007). Reward value coding distinct from risk attitude-related uncertainty coding in human reward systems. *Journal of Neurophysiology* 97(2): 1621–32.

Tom, S. M., Fox, C. R., Trepel, C., and Poldrack, R. A. (2007). The neural basis of loss aversion in decision-making under risk. *Science* 315: 515–18.

Tricomi, E., Rangel, A., Camerer, C. F., and O'Doherty, J. P. (2010). Neural evidence for inequality-averse social preferences. *Nature* 463: 1089–91.

Tversky, A. and Kahneman, D. (1992). Advances in prospect theory: cummulative representation of uncertainty. *Journal of Risk and Uncertainty* 5(4): 297–323.

van den Bos, W., van Dijk, E., Westenberg, M., Rombouts, S. A. R. B., and Crone, E. A. (2009). What motivates repayment? Neural correlates of reciprocity in the Trust Game. *Social Cognitive & Affective Neuroscience* 4: 294–304.

Van Overwalle, F. (2009). Social cognition and the brain: a meta-analysis. *Human Brain Mapping* 30(3): 829–58.

Vanberg, C. (2008). Why do people keep their promises? An experimental test of two explanations. *Econometrica* 76(6): 1476–80.

Wallis, J. (2007). Orbitofrontal cortex and its contributions to decision-making. *Annual Reviews in Neuroscience* 30: 31–56.

Wang, J. T., Spezio, M., and Camerer, C. F. (2010). Pinocchio's pupil: using eyetracking and pupil dilation to understand truth telling and deception in sender-receiver games. *American Economic Review* 100(3): 984–1007.

Wassermann, E. M., Epstein, C. M., Ziemann, U., Walsh, V., Paus, T., and Lisanby, S. H. (eds.). (2008). *The Oxford Handbook of Transcranial Stimulation*. Oxford: Oxford University Press.

Webb, R. (2015). The dynamics of stochastic choice. Unpublished manuscript.

Wicker, B. et al. (2003). Both of us disgusted in my insula: the common neural basis of seeing and feeling disgust. *Neuron* 40: 655–64.

Woodford, M. (2014). Stochastic choice: an optimizing neuroeconomic model. *American Economic Review* 104(5): 495–500.

Wout, M. van't, Kahn, R. S., Sanfey, A. G., and Aleman, A. (2005). Repetitive transcranial magnetic stimulation over the right dorsolateral prefrontal cortex affects strategic decision-making. *NeuroReport* 16: 1849–52.

Yacubian, J., Glascher, J., Schroeder, K., Sommer, T., Braus, D. F., and Buchel, C. (2006). Dissociable systems for gain- and loss-related value predictions and errors of prediction in the human brain. *Journal of Neuroscience* 26: 9530–7.

Zak, P. J. (2004). Neuroeconomics. *Philosophical Transactions of the Royal Society B* 359: 1737–48.

Zaki, J. and Mitchell, J. (2011). Equitable decision making is associated with neural markers of subjective value. *Proceedings of the National Academy of Sciences USA* 108: 19761–6.

Zink, C. F., Tong, Y., Chen, Q., Bassett, D. S., Stein, J. L., and Meyer-Lindenberg, A. (2008). Know your place: neural processing of social hierarchy in humans. *Neuron* 58: 273–83.

PART IV

A Guide to Further Reading

CHAPTER 5

A Guide to Further Reading

5.1 Introduction

In this chapter, we consider some recent and important developments in the subject that took place since the submission of the book manuscript for Dhami (2016) in 2015.[1] Of the three topics in this volume, our discussion is predominantly focused on behavioral welfare economics. Of the ten sections in this chapter, seven are on behavioral welfare economics, two on emotions, and one on neuroeconomics. There are three reasons for this uneven attention. First, some of the important topics in emotions in this book are discussed within the ambit of psychological game theory in Volume 4, which has already outlined the recent advances in the area. Second, and as noted in Chapter 4, the treatment of neuroeconomics in this book was never intended to be authoritative and comprehensive, given the many excellent sources for it and the author's lack of research competence in this area. Third, traditionally welfare economics is one of the most important areas in economics.

A description of this chapter is as follows. Section 5.2 considers issues of self-control, persistent temptation (defined in Section 5.2), and the optimal timing of self-control and commitment decisions (Houser et al., 2018).

Section 5.3 considers further evidence for projection bias that comes from early/late ordering of food (VanEpps et al., 2016); the accuracy of self-reported satisfaction from life events (Odermatt and Stutzer, 2019); and the effect of the current environmental conditions, e.g., weather/pollution on consumer purchase decisions (Busse et al., 2015).

Section 5.4 gives a classification of public policy, based on Loewenstein and Chater (2017), that recommends a more holistic approach to the use of policy instruments in behavioral welfare economics. The argument is that soft paternalism alone, such as nudges, cannot be relied on to resolve all important economic problems such as climate change and obesity. Behavioral economists must also be open to traditional policy instruments that are based on hard paternalism, such as taxes and subsidies. While this idea should be uncontroversial, the popular debate in behavioral welfare economics focuses almost entirely on the instruments of

[1] I am very grateful to Ali al-Nowaihi, Junaid Arshad, Kinjal Ahir, and Narges Hajimoladarvish for comments on an earlier draft of this chapter.

soft paternalism, such as nudges. Thaler and Sunstein (2009) themselves never recommended an exclusive reliance on nudges in resolving all economic problems.

Section 5.5 considers some recent evidence that highlights the positive role played by nudges, particularly reminders and also the form taken by reminders. Section 5.6 considers several situations where nudges have unexpected or possibly unforeseen effects. Spillover effects on other actions/policies may cause nudges to crowd out other beneficial actions/policies. Negative effects of nudges might arise from, say, the triggering of negative emotions in those responsible for harmful action; we consider attempts to quantify such effects. Nudges might also have different effects and command different levels of support from different groups in society—contributory factors include one's ethnic, political, religious, and national affiliation.

In Section 5.7 we first present a theoretical model of individual actions in the presence of default options, a fixed cost of default, and heterogeneity in default costs (Carroll et al., 2009; Bernheim et al., 2015). We then show how the insights of this model can be used to explain some of the empirical findings from online charitable contributions that offer defaults and codonation options (Altmann et al., 2018).

In Section 5.8 we use a model of quasi hyperbolic discounting to explains why delays in the take-up of default options might take place on account of the present bias of individuals. The setup of the model is taken from Blumenstock et al. (2018) to make predictions corresponding to their empirical design. But unlike these authors, we derive the perception-perfect strategies (see Volume 3 for details) for three types of unawareness of future self-control problems (time consistents, sophisticates, and naifs). Our method of solution and predictions are different from theirs. We then consider their impressive empirical evidence which shows that defaults and incentives both matter in the take-up of a voluntary savings plan in Afganistan; the effects are similar to those observed with Western subjects. Furthermore, the resulting effects are long-lived.

Section 5.9 continues our discussion of behavioral public finance (see Section 3.9 in Chapter 3). We heuristically explain how limited attention may lead to the violation of a monotonicity property in optimal taxation and how the deadweight loss from taxation increases when taxes become salient (Taubinsky and Rees-Jones, 2018). We then consider the deadweight losses from taxation that take account of the externalities and internalities from the consumption of sugary drinks (Allcott et al., 2019a,b).

A great deal of the thrust in the modern behavioral welfare economics literature has been on trying to purify observed preferences and infer the latent and consistent underlying preferences of an individual that are context independent (e.g., Section 3.6 in Chapter 3). The latent preferences are typically assumed to tally with those of the textbook neoclassical economic actor. One can then conduct normative analysis on these underlying, but unobserved latent preferences. Section 5.10 outlines the work of Infante et al. (2016) and Sugden (2017, 2018) which argues that this practice is questionable and not intellectually satisfying. This underlying dual-selves framework is not directly refutable and there is no presumption that the latent preferences, if at all they exist, are either context independent or consistent with evolutionary accounts of human nature. We go on to consider the implications for soft paternalism, particularly nudges. This criticism does not overturn the case for soft paternalism, but questions if nudges can be justified on the grounds that an individual chooses the best options, as judged for by himself (the *informed desire criterion* in Section 3.3.1 in Chapter 3). We examine a response (Sunstein, 2018) and some of the relevant implications for nudge theory such as cases where this critique does not apply and the difference between the ex-ante and ex-post evaluation of welfare.

The final section, Section 5.11, considers some of the recent advances in neuroeconomics. This is a relatively short section and we point the reader in the direction of several recent surveys of the literature. We consider the exemplary empirical study of Frydman and Camerer (2016a) that shows how neuroeconomics can be used to directly infer the emotion of regret in human financial choices. Using fMRI signals of regret as their predictor, the authors show that it can explain the *repurchase effect* in finance (defined in Section 5.11). Furthermore, this is correlated with the disposition effect (see Volumes 1 and 5), suggesting a common neural mechanism for both effects. We also consider some of the effects of the neuropeptide, arginine vasopressin (AVP) on cooperative choices made in stag hunt games (Brunnlieb et al., 2016).

5.2 Temptation, commitment, and self-control

In the presence of persistent temptation, and self-control costs, individuals may choose commitment devices. Commitment can take many forms that we have considered in this book. Examples include removing tempting choices from the menu (Volume 6), accepting deadlines (Volume 3), and committing to personal rules of behavior. The choice of the commitment device, and its timing, depends on the cost of the commitment device and also the temporal pattern of self-control costs. *Persistent temptation* means that an individual repeatedly faces a tempting choice and (1) either gives in to the temptation at some point in time, or (2) invests in a commitment device that permanently removes the temptation. As time progresses, and the individual resists the temptation, self-control costs may increase because self-control is likely to be a scarce and exhaustible resource.[2] Timing issues of this sort have been considered in a dual-selves model by Fudenberg and Levine (2012). We first outline their framework, through an example in Houser et al. (2018), and then consider the experimental evidence.

Consider a risk neutral individual who lives for 3 time periods $t = 1, 2, 3$ and has an initial endowment of 1 unit. We consider the consumption-saving choices of the individual over the 3 periods (there is no production). The initial endowment of 1 unit doubles every period and the individual must consume only once over the 3 periods. Thus, the three possible profiles of consumption, denoted by I, II, III, are

$$(c_1, c_2, c_3) = \begin{cases} (1,0,0) & : I \\ (0,2,0) & : II \\ (0,0,4) & : III \end{cases}. \tag{5.1}$$

The individual has a patient long-run (LR) self who cares about utility over the 3 periods, and a sequence of 3 short-run (SR) selves who are myopic and care only about current utility. Each period t is divided into the following two subperiods. In the first subperiod, the LR self can take a costly action, interpreted as self-control, that can influence the preferences of the subsequent SR selves. In the second subperiod, the SR self makes the actual decision for that period.

The discount factor of the long-run self is $\delta = 0.8$. The self-control cost, which can be exercised only once in a period, is $a_1 = 0.05$ per unit of foregone utility in the period when it is first exercised. The second time that self-control is exercised, it costs $a_2 = 0.20$ per unit of foregone utility in that period. Thus, self-control costs are increasing, perhaps due to depleting willpower, and this plays an important role in the analysis. Self-control costs do not need to be exercised

---

[2] We have already considered evidence in Chapter 2 that exerting cognitive load depletes willpower, making individuals more likely to choose a tempting option.

more than twice because the earliest these costs could be exercised is at $t = 1$ and if consumption has not taken place by $t = 3$, then it will certainly take place at $t = 3$ so no self-control needs to be exerted at $t = 3$. The commitment cost, should a one-off commitment option be used, is 0.3. This option eliminates the desire of any of the subsequent myopic SR selves to consume (other than at $t = 3$). Denote the utility of the LR self from the consumption profile $j = I, II, III$ in (5.1) by U_j. We now consider three different regimes, A, B, C.

In each regime, in the absence of any actions by the LR self, the optimal action of the myopic SR self is to consume immediately. However, the LR self may try to influence the actions of the SR self through self-control or through commitment.

A. In the absence of any self-control costs, and using $\delta = 0.8$, the utility of the LR self from the three consumption profiles in (5.1) is given by

$$\begin{cases} U_I^* = 1 \\ U_{II}^* = 0.8(2) = 1.6 \\ U_{III}^* = (0.8)^2\, 4 = 2.56 \end{cases} \qquad (5.2)$$

Thus, the LR self prefers to wait and consume at $t = 3$.

B. Now consider the possibility of self-control costs, but no commitment. The utility to the LR self from the three different consumption profiles in (5.1) is given by

$$\begin{cases} U_I^{SC} = 1 \\ U_{II}^{SC} = 0.8(2) - 0.05(1-0) = 1.55 \\ U_{III}^{SC} = (0.8)^2\, 4 - 0.05(1-0) - 0.20(0.8)(2-0) = 2.19 \end{cases} \qquad (5.3)$$

To enjoy the doubling of endowment to 2 at $t = 2$, the LR self must ensure that the SR self at $t = 1$ defers consumption in period 2. The cost of exerting this self-control is $a_1 = 0.05$ per unit of foregone utility by the SR self, which equals $1 - 0 = 1$. Analogously, to defer consumption to $t = 3$, an additional self-control cost of $a_2 = 0.20$ per unit of foregone utility for the SR self at $t = 2, 2 - 0 = 2$, needs to be incurred.

C. Consider the possibility of both self-control and commitment. Commitment can take place at $t = 1$ or $t = 2$ (as noted above, there is no point of commitment at $t = 3$ because conditional on having reached period 3, it is optimal to consume anyway). Suppose that commitment is exercised in $t = 1$ at the commitment cost of 0.3. This eliminates the incentives of the SR selves at $t = 1$ and $t = 2$ to consume. Thus, consumption occurs at $t = 3$, which is the preferred outcome for the LR self. In this case, the utility of the LR self is

$$U_{III}^{C_1} = (0.8)^2\, 4 - 0.3 = 2.26.$$

The other possibility is that the LR self practices self-control in $t = 1$ and then commitment in $t = 2$. This too allows consumption to take place at $t = 3$. The utility of the LR self in this case is given by

$$U_{III}^{SC_1 + C_2} = (0.8)^2\, 4 - 0.05(1-0) - (0.8)0.3 = 2.27$$

It follows that $U_{III}^{SC_1 + C_2} > U_{III}^{C_1}$. However, this relies on the assumption that the SR self at $t = 2$ will find it optimal to engage in commitment. Let us now check for the incentive of the SR self at

$t = 2$. The utility of the SR self from (i) immediate consumption is 2, (ii) exerting self-control at $t = 2$ (deferring consumption by 1 period) conditional on self-control having been used once at $t = 1$ is $(0.8)4 - 0.2(2 - 0) = 2.8$, and (iii) exerting commitment at $t = 2$ is $(0.8)4 - 0.3 = 2.9$. The highest utility arises from commitment at $t = 2$. Thus, the choice of self-control at $t = 1$ and commitment at $t = 2$ is time consistent.

This is one of the central insights of the paper by Fudenberg and Levine (2012). Namely, in the presence of increasing costs of self-control and under perfect foresight, commitment may be used and it might be optimally delayed. However, if the costs of self-control are not increasing but are, say, constant, then this result need no longer hold.

Houser et al. (2018) consider the case of constant costs in their experiments. Their justification is that the time horizon in experiments is too compressed and most subjects will wait until $t = 3$ to consume 4. So, they choose a different experimental design in which subjects had to perform a tedious repetitive task to earn rewards (counting the number of 1s in a series of 9 digits that are zero or one within 15 seconds) in the presence of a temptation (surf the Internet for free). Individuals could eliminate the temptation at a cost and so commit to the counting task for the rest of the session, or exert their own unobserved willpower or self-control and continue to count in the presence of the temptation. Under constant costs, the prediction of the Fudenberg and Levine model is that (i) individuals will either immediately commit or give in to the temptation to surf the Internet, or (2) if self-control costs are low enough, resist the temptation till the end of the experiment. This prediction is confirmed for the majority of the subjects. However, and as the authors themselves point out, other models too can make this prediction. This includes the Gul–Pesendorfer model and the quasi-hyperbolic discounting model.

Consider a quasi-hyperbolic discounting model with multiple selves. The current self may wish to limit the choices of future selves through some form of commitment if it is expected that future selves will pick a detrimental option (see Volume 3). For instance, the current self might invest in illiquid assets (commitment) to limit the extent of wasteful consumption that future selves could indulge in. On the other hand, the model predicts that there is no demand for commitment if the current self does not expect future selves to succumb to temptation. By contrast, in the Gul and Pesendorfer (2001) model (see Section 1.7), even if an individual does not expect to succumb to temptation, he might still demand a commitment device. The reason is that not succumbing to temptation requires the exercise of costly willpower (a feature found in many models) and removing the tempting option improves utility regardless of whether one will succumb to the temptation. Thus, removal of the temptation might have even larger welfare effects if we took account of these savings in self control costs.

Toussaert (2018) exploits this difference in predictions between the quasi-hyperbolic model and the Gul–Pesendorfer model and designs experiments to test them. Subjects in the experiment were exposed to a tedious attention task that resulted in a monetary reward. However, they were tempted to read a sensational story for which no payment is received. Of particular interest are subjects who would prefer to remove the temptation from the menu of choices, yet would not choose the tempting option if given a choice from the full menu. Such subjects are called *self-control types*; while their existence is not predicted under the quasi hyperbolic model it is predicted in the Gul–Pesendorfer model. In the entire sample, 23%–36% of the subjects can be classified as self-control types. Such subjects have beliefs that they will be able to resist temptation if offered the full menu and their beliefs turn out to be correct, except for one subject. On the other hand, only 2.5% of the subjects exhibited commitment preferences consistent with the quasi hyperbolic model (remove a commitment when they correctly perceive that they will not be able to resist the temptation).

This does not mean, however, that the quasi hyperbolic model is not useful because (i) not all self-control problems take the form of temptation preferences as in the Gul–Pesendorfer model, and (ii) commitment devices often have limited availability. Alternatively, these results could be interpreted as an argument for expanding the range of commitment devices that should be made available. However, would such commitment devices be taken up? This is an issue we consider next.

Suppose that individuals make time inconsistent choices. A key determinant of the demand for commitment devices then is that they are aware of the future time inconsistency. Otherwise, they would not demand such devices. The weak demand for commitment devices has been noted before. For instance, Laibson (2015, 2018) examines this question and provides a theoretical model to argue that demand for commitment may be weak due to high costs of commitment and environmental uncertainty which creates a tradeoff between flexibility and commitment (see also Section 1.8 above). These explanations do not, however, have a bearing on the issue of unawareness of future time inconsistency problems.

Empirical studies show a positive correlation between the degree of dynamic inconsistency and the demand for commitment devices. Kaur et al. (2015) find that data entry workers in the Philippines who commit to an agreement that penalizes low output, increase their performance by 6%. Ashraf et al. (2006) offer a commitment device to savers in the Philippines that restricts access to savings. Of those who were offered the device, 28.4% accepted; more patient individuals, as measured by the rate of time preference, were more likely to accept. Large savings effects were found for individuals who chose the commitment device; these effects were also found 12 months after the individuals signed up to the commitment device, suggesting long-run effects. Augenblick et al. (2015) find little time inconsistency in monetary choices (in line with the earlier literature). However, they find time inconsistency in effort choices that determine consumption. Whether time inconsistency is more likely to be found in evolutionary salient choices (e.g., money is not evolutionary salient, but consumption is) requires further investigation.

Time inconsistent individuals are more likely to choose a commitment device. Commitment devices have also been shown to improve gym attendance (Milkman et al., 2013; Royer et al. 2015); induce a reduction in smoking (Giné et al., 2010); improve student grades (Patterson, 2018); and improve grades and completion rates of degrees (Himmler et al., 2019). Ariely and Wertenbroch (2002) show that commitments that took the form of self-imposed deadlines do not necessarily lead to early task completion and externally imposed deadlines (also a form of commitment) are more conducive to task completion. Schilbach (2019) gives cycle-rickshaw drivers in Chennai choices between receiving payments for remaining sober (requires a daily alcohol check) and higher unconditional payments. A third of the drivers chose the sobriety payments over the unconditional payments suggesting a demand for a commitment device to reduce alcohol consumption. The labour supply, productivity, and earnings of those who chose the commitment device are not higher, but their savings are higher. This ties in with other work that shows that alcohol consumption increases the present-biasedness of individual decisions, which in turn reduces savings (see Volume 3). Casaburi and Macchiavello (2019) show that when milk producers have a choice between frequent (say, daily) and infrequent (say, monthly) payments for milk that is delivered daily, they pick the infrequent payment. This arises even when the frequent payment results in a higher price per unit of milk. The authors interpret this result as a willingness to pay for a commitment device although other factors such as the transaction costs of collecting small, and daily, payments from a large number of customers while selling a perishable item might also be at play.

This evidence is suggestive of the hypothesis that people who have a lack of awareness of future self-control problems may also not adequately demand commitment devices. Using lab studies, a weak positive correlation between unawareness and commitment devices was found by Augenblick and Rabin (2019), although John (2019) found no correlation between the two.

Sadoff et al. (2019) reexamine the relation between "time inconsistency unawareness" and commitment using a food delivery service in Chicago and in Los Angeles. The study was conducted over four weeks. In the first week, subjects were given a budget and asked to order items to be delivered a week later. However, when the items were delivered, an option was given to the subjects to exchange some of the items for other items. The new food basket does not contain any items that were not available to order a week earlier. If subjects do engage in such item exchanges, they reveal time inconsistency of choices. Once this stage of the experiment concludes, subjects are again given an opportunity to order food items to be delivered a week later in week 3. A similar choice is given for week 4. However, for both these deliveries (for weeks 3, 4) subjects are asked to make a choice between making exchanges at the delivery (as in week 2) or making a commitment at a cost to not make exchanges.

The results are as follows. In the absence of commitment (week 2 delivery) 46% of the subjects exchanged at least one item; their choices are dynamically inconsistent in this sense. Furthermore, the exchanges replace healthy food items such as fruits and vegetables for unhealthy ones that had high calorie and fat content. When a commitment option is available (week 3, 4), 53% of the subjects take up the option to not exchange previously ordered items. One of the most interesting results is that only 40% of the subjects whose delivery choices in week 2 were dynamically inconsistent chose the commitment option as compared to 60% whose choices were consistent. Thus, the bulk of the commitment demand does not come from those who might need it the most. This is suggestive of a lack of awareness of self-control problems. Indeed, this might be an important factor for the low observed take-up of commitment devices.

5.3 Additional evidence on projection bias

In Section 1.6 we considered the phenomenon of projection bias, namely that individuals use their current states to determine estimates of their utility from future states. VanEpps et al. (2016) provide further evidence for projection bias by looking into the correlation between the timing of food orders and the healthiness of food, as measured by its calorie content. The growing use of online ordering which provides the opportunity to place temporally advance orders, say, for food items, provides a real-world context to this problem. Their motivation is the following quote from Schelling (1978, p. 290): "I have heard of a corporate dining room in which lunch orders are placed by telephone at 9:30 or 10:00 in the morning: no food or liquor is then served to anyone except what was ordered at that time, not long after breakfast, when food was least tempting and resolve was at its highest."

Projection bias predicts that the closer is the order to the intake of food, the more unhealthy will be the food that is ordered. The reason is that one is more hungry closer to a meal, and so likely to project the current hungry state to the future, thereby anticipating greater/unhealthier food consumption. Since hunger is a visceral influence (see Section 1.2) one may also invoke *hot-cold empathy gaps* (overprojecting the current visceral state in estimating a future visceral state) to explain such behavior. A final explanation for this behavior also arises from invoking *temporal construal theory* (Trope and Liberman, 2000, 2003). The basic idea is that people take account of different factors in deciding on temporal options that differ in their delay to an outcome.

For instance, in ordering a meal well in advance, one considers broader, more abstract, issues such as the healthiness of a meal and longer-term goals such as losing weight. By contrast, when the meal options are considered closer to the time of meal, more specific and less abstract factors come to the fore. Such factors include the tastiness of the meal, even at a cost to longer-term health goals. These explanations may also provide the necessary microfoundations for more popular models in behavioral economics such as quasi hyperbolic discounting.

VanEpps et al. (2016) consider both naturally occurring time delays in ordering meals (Study 1) and also experimentally manipulated delays (Study 2) in ordering meals. In each case, greater time delays reduce the number of calories in the food orders, typically arising through reduced fat and saturated fat content. The reduction in calories is relatively small on average, about 30 calories, but the difference is significant. In both Study 1 and Study 2 there is a time gap of 30 minutes between the immediate ordering of the meals and obtaining the meals. In Study 3 that is not directly comparable with the first two studies; this time gap is reduced from 30 minutes. Yet, a larger effect of a reduction of about 100 calories is found from pre-ordering of the meals relative to immediate ordering. Self-reported hunger did not turn out to be an important factor in explaining the reduction in calories in food choices. This suggests that an explanation based on visceral influences might be less persuasive relative to one that is based on quasi hyperbolic discounting. Similar findings come from other subject pools and contexts such as from online grocery store orders (Milkman et al., 2008) and from lunchtime meals of school children when ordered in advance and at mealtime (Hanks et al., 2013).

Odermatt and Stutzer (2019) consider differences in predicted and actual life satisfaction arising from various events, using the German Socio-Economic Panel. Participants are asked about their current life satisfaction and their predictions of life satisfaction in five years' time. Data is used from 1991–2004 and contains 180,000 observations. Significant prediction errors are found when the relevant events are unemployment, disability, and widowhood. The greatest prediction errors arise in the case of widowhood. There are no systematic prediction errors for separation and divorce. A potentially confounding factor for many of these events, say, for widowhood, is that prediction errors might arise from either (1) incorrect beliefs about finding new partners, or (2) underestimation of adaptation to widowhood. The authors try to control for this confound by considering individuals whose status did not change over the five years. For such individuals, the prediction errors, for widowhood, unemployment, and disability, arise from underestimation of the adaptation to the events (which the data confirms) rather than pessimistic beliefs. By contrast, for marriage, people are overly optimistic about future levels of life satisfaction. Data based on the German Socio-Economic Panel also reveals a young/old divide. Younger people are more optimistic about future life satisfaction while older people are more pessimistic, an explanation consistent with projection bias (Lang et al., 2013; Schwandt, 2016).

The weather at the time of a purchase decision might influence one's longer-term purchase of a consumer durable (Conlin et al., 2007). Busse et al. (2015) show that the current weather also influences the type of car (a long-term investment) that individuals purchase. Consumers who are not subject to projection bias should not base their long-term purchase decisions on the immediate weather. The authors study data on 40 million new and used car transactions in car dealerships in the US. When the temperature is 10 degrees Fahrenheit higher than normal (i.e., an abnormal high), then the sales of convertibles increases by 2.7%. On the other hand, snowstorms of approximately 10 inches increase sales of four-wheel drive vehicles by 6% over the next few weeks. This evidence is consistent with projection bias. Other environmental events also influence purchases. For instance, Chang et al. (2018) show that the level of pollution in any given day significantly influences the number of health insurance contracts sold on that day.

5.4 The need for a holistic approach to behavioral public policy

In thinking about behavioral public policy, the emphasis in Volume 7 has been mainly on soft paternalism, particularly on nudges. But this is not necessarily true of the other book volumes. In Volume 1, we considered deterrents to tax evasion, such as audit rates and penalties. Using the terminology in Volume 7, this would be classified as heavy-handed paternalism, and not nudges. In Volume 2 we pointed out the effects that legal institutions such as referenda have on the extent of anti-social public goods punishments (heavy-handed paternalism). In Chapter 3 of Volume 3, we considered the role of optimal sin taxes (heavy-handed paternalism) in curbing the consumption of sin goods, such as smoking.

Thus, an important message of the book is that behavioral public policy is multifaceted and requires the joint consideration of a variety of policy instruments. This includes traditional economic policy instruments such as taxes, subsidies, and regulation. But it also includes, simultaneously or separately, behavioral nudges as outlined in Thaler and Sunstein (2009). We have noted in this volume that nudges have been highly successful in many domains, particularly, but not solely, in their roles as default options for pensions, savings, and organ donations. In these domains, nudges often have effects that are quantitatively comparable or superior to taxes and subsidies. Yet, nudges by themselves, do not constitute the entire domain of behavioral public policy instruments, nor was this intended/claimed by its originators.

Loewenstein and Chater (2017) have recently argued along these lines, while also considering important policy applications. We now consider some aspects of their work. Begin with Figure 5.1, which is a slight modification of their Table 1 on page 29. For the moment, we stick to the specific example of smoking cigarettes, which is dealt with in several of these book volumes. Let us, for the moment, ignore the last row and the last column in Figure 5.1.

Rationale for Intervention	Type of Intervention		
	NEOCLASSICAL (taxes, subsidies, regulation)	BEHAVIORAL (soft-paternalism)	HYBRID (combination of hard and soft paternalism)
NEOCLASSICAL (externalities, adverse selection)	A Smoking externalities (taxes)	B Smoking externalities (nudges)	C Smoking externalities (bans on smoking in public places) +
BEHAVIORAL-SELF (internalities, bounded rationality)	D Smoking internalities (taxes)	E Smoking internalities (nudges)	F Smoking internalities (bans on cigarette displays in store) +
BEHAVIORAL-OTHERS (firms exploiting individual biases)	G Smoking externalities (regulation, e.g., ban advertising)	H Smoking internalities (graphic warnings on cigarette packs)	I Successive bans on advertising on TV, in press, on billboards, in shops, on packaging

Figure 5.1 A classification of public policy and rationales for intervention, with particular emphasis on smoking, based on Loewenstein and Chater (2017).

In neoclassical economics (second row of Figure 5.1), the typical motivation for public policy is externalities (e.g., the effect of smoking on others, or passive smoking) and information asymmetries (e.g., health costs of smoking). In neoclassical public economics, this is typically dealt with by *Pigouvian taxes* on consumers to counter externalities and information disclosure requirements on firms, such as health warnings on cigarette packs (second column in Figure 5.1). The main problem highlighted in behavioral economics is the self-inflicted *internalities* by an individual from smoking (e.g., future health consequences) and the bounded rationality of consumers (e.g., procrastination in giving up smoking; taking up smoking due to peer pressure without calculating future costs/benefits). This is the third row of Figure 5.1 labeled Behavioral-Self because the actions have consequences for one's own future selves, as in models of multiple selves. The behavioral solution to the problem of externalities and internalities is nudges of various sorts such as graphic warning labels on cigarette packs (third column in Figure 5.1 labeled Behavioral (soft-paternalism)).

The possibility that individuals have behavioral biases relative to the neoclassical model may lead firms to try to exploit such biases in order to increase profits. Public policy has a powerful role to play in this regard. Indeed, it has played such a role, although belatedly, in the case of cigarette smoking. The final row in Figure 5.1, labeled Behavioral-Others, refers to such exploitative practices by an external agent. Cigarette firms have faced successive bans from advertising, their output subject to taxes (externality control) and they have been required by law to put graphic warnings on cigarette packs (to internalize externalities caused by individuals on their own future selves). Most public policies are hybrids of this sort, a combination of hard and soft paternalism (last column in Figure 5.1). The 'plus sign' in the last column refers to the fact that these policies are used in conjunction. Indeed, it would be hard to argue that nudges alone could solve the problem of addiction to smoking. The various policies in conjunction (taxes, regulation, nudges) have been successful in reducing adult smoking rates; for instance, in the US the smoking rate declined from 42% to 17% over the period 1965–2014.

Loewenstein and Chater raise two further important points

1. Underlying structural factors. Obesity has often been explained in behavioral economics by an appeal to present biased preferences. Individuals with these preferences do not fully internalize the consequences of a bad diet and/or bad lifestyle on their own future selves. One possible nudge solution is to raise awareness of the number of calories in food and label them clearly by using traffic-light symbols (e.g., a red light is the worst in terms of calories or fat content), and to advise firms that tempting high calorie foods not be placed at eye level in grocery stores.

   High rates of obesity is a relatively new problem in the US and it does not appear to have been caused by a sudden increase in impatience but by several structural factors (Cutler et al., 2003; Brownwell et al., 2010). These factors include the relative prices of packed and fresh foods; changed lifestyles that reduce the time available for cooking fresh food; snacking habits and portion sizes; recruitment of prominent scientists by fizzy drinks companies to argue that the problem is lack of exercise and not high sugar content; and attempts to put salt and sugar in unhealthy foods that help develop a taste and habit for them. Public policy that relied only on nudges to counter the obesity problem and ignored the underlying structural issues is likely to have limited success. Indeed, it would appear that nudges combined with taxation of unhealthy foods (e.g., the fat tax, which was not successful in Denmark due to cross-border shopping in Germany) and regulation of junk food companies (e.g., banning/regulating the use of harmful triglycerides) may be the more promising options.

2. Is soft paternalism too soft? There is no presumption that all behavioral biases relative to the neoclassical benchmark could be eliminated simply by nudges (neither did Thaler and Sunstein make this claim). As a case study, Loewenstein-Chater compare the pension savings figures for the US and for Australia. In the US, one can withdraw from pension funds before retirement, at no penalty. Clearly, within a model of multiple selves and in the presence of present bias, such actions could lead to inefficient withdrawals. By contrast, such actions are legally forbidden in the Australian system and withdrawals are only possible after retirement. Furthermore, in Australia, employers are required to contribute 9% of their salary to the pension pot and employees make a mandatory contribution of 3% of their salary. Such mandatory requirements are not nudges, yet they are very effective. The US population is 14 times larger, but the pension pot is not even double that of Australia. The upshot of this analysis is that one might need to augment nudges with some form of hard paternalism to have the desired effect.

Loewenstein-Chater make a similar point about climate change. Behavioral economics has so far considered several kinds of nudges to induce people to reduce their energy consumption (e.g., smart electricity meters and energy consumption comparisons with the average consumption of the neighborhood), but these are unlikely to be sufficient to counter the problem of global climate change. What is needed here is a variety of strong regulations on firms/consumers and a taxation policy that aligns individual incentives with social needs, in conjunction with behavioral solutions.

5.5 More on the effectiveness of nudges

Altman and Traxler (2014) conduct a field study at a German dentist and explore the role of reminders relative to a control condition where no reminders were sent. The reminders were about preventive checks for periodontal disease. The expectation was that in the absence of the reminders, individuals might pay limited attention to the checks, or procrastinate in setting up an appointment, or simply be unaware of the potential benefits of the checkup. Three kinds of reminders were given. (i) Simple reminders without any further information. (ii) Reminders with information on the benefits of a preventive health checkup. (iii) Reminders that were framing positively and negatively. Relative to the control condition with no reminders, reminders doubled the fraction of individuals who contacted the dentist for a checkup (19.3% up from 8.9%). The fraction of individuals who actually visited the dentist is also 10 percentage points higher relative to the control group. However, the form of the reminder had little effect on preventive checkups.

There is now a growing literature on the positive effect of reminders on individual actions. This includes the effect of reminders for charitable giving (Huck and Rasul, 2010; Sonntag and Zizzo, 2015); gym attendance (Calzolari and Nardotto, 2017); individual savings (Karlan et al., 2016); take-up of social benefits (Bhargava and Manoli, 2015); medical treatment (Altmann and Traxler, 2014); and the take-up of contraceptives in Kenya (McConnell et al., 2018). Defaults such as reminders can produce effects that exceed those from conventional economic policies (Sunstein, 2016, 2017).

Czap et al. (2018) consider an upstream-downstream situation in which an upstream farmer chooses between two actions. The first action is environmentally friendly, but the second causes negative externalities to a downstream farmer. There are no underlying property rights, so this game is similar to a dictator game. Two types of nudges are considered—financial nudges and empathetic nudges that highlight empathy. A variety of empathetic nudges are considered. An example is the following appeal made by the downstream farmer to the upstream farmer before the upstream farmer makes his decision: "Before choosing your decision, please understand my situation better by imagining how your decision looks from my perspective." Financial nudges which take the form of a subsidy payment to the upstream farmer have only a moderate effect on behavior. Males exhibit no effect of empathetic nudges, while females exhibit a significant effect. A combination of financial and empathetic nudges are potent for both genders, but particularly for females.

Marx and Turner (2019) consider loan offers in offer letters to students wishing to gain admission into community colleges in the US. Colleges have discretion on including non-binding loan offers to students. In the field study, in three different treatments, students were offered loans of $0, $3500, and $4500. Students could override these defaults and choose any level of the loan. However, students who were made strictly positive default offers (of $3500 and $4500), were 40% more likely to borrow relative to those offered a $0 default. Those who took up the loan also exhibited, on average, 30% higher grades and GPAs. These effects persist even when measured after two years. Thus, contrary to the practice of the federal government that discourages borrowing and also the actions taken by colleges to limit borrowing out of a concern for loan repayment, the loans have a net positive effect on attainment.

5.6 A consideration of unexpected effects of nudges

Nudges might have unexpected effects on the welfare of the individual, and some, but not all, of these effects could be negative. This is not surprising. Undergraduate students in economics are taught that the partial equilibrium effects of a policy may need to be modified when general equilibrium considerations are taken into account. The imperative of conducting appropriate pilots before implementing nudges in order to understand more fully the effects of nudges has been stressed from the beginning. There has been an explosion in the literature in recent years that has highlighted some of the unexpected effects of nudges. We explore this below.

Thunström (2018) considers the possible negative effects of calorie menu labeling that informs consumers of their food calorie values. The idea behind calorie labeling is that it should nudge those who are boundedly rational or have low self-control in eating towards healthier eating—perhaps by providing the necessary information, or by making it salient. It should have no effect on those whose self-control is high enough so that they are not tempted. Hence, calorie menu labeling is consistent with the definition of a nudge. In earlier work it had been shown that calorie information evokes negative emotions among people who have high self-control problems by reminding them of the unhealthiness of their food (Thunström et al., 2016).

Negative emotions from nudges might also be invoked in other contexts, for instance, graphic warnings on cigarette packs. Glaeser (2006) terms nudges as a form of emotional tax but his arguments that such emotional taxes do not raise revenues and do not increase utility are debatable. If, for instance, nudges in the form of graphic warnings reduce smoking and, by implication, the health costs to a public health system, the tax revenues freed up, as a result, are entirely on account of the nudge. Furthermore, the argument that such emotional taxes do not increase utility is not supported by the empirical evidence from smokers in Canada who supported sin taxes on cigarettes, or people who voluntarily check into rehab centers (see Volume 3).

The asymmetric paternalism framework in Section 3.3.2 can then be invoked to derive some implications. Suppose that the nudge is not effective in reducing food calorie consumption. Then, among those who have low self-control but experience emotional costs from calorie labeling, the nudge imposes a net cost; such individuals are unlikely to feel positive about the nudge. However, if the nudge is successful in reducing calorie intake, then the net benefit for such individuals could well be positive. The emotions experienced by the subjects are self-reported and the underlying experiment presents a hypothetical scenario.

The results in Thunström (2018) are as follows. Overall, averaged across the subjects, the nudge has a positive effect in reducing calorie intake. A significant percentage, 37%, report no emotions from the nudge; 42% report positive emotions, and 21% report negative emotions. Subjects who are found to have low self-control adjust their calorie intake less, value the nudge less, and are more likely to report negative emotions than those who are found to have high self-control.

Cronqvist et al. (2018) examine if the effects of nudges are long-lived. Sweden introduced, in the year 2000, the Premium Pension Plan, which incorporated defined contributions for its entire population of a little over 7 million. It allowed relatively free entry of mutual funds (456 mutual funds were available in the plan), freedom to choose the options, and competition among the mutual funds to advertise and sell their financial products. Two competing plan options were available to the plan participants. (1) Choose a default fund (called AP7) which consisted of a preselected set of mutual funds. (2) Choose your own portfolio of mutual funds. This was backed by extensive government advertising for the second option to highlight individual choice. Let us call individuals who chose the default option as Delegators and those who chose to design their own portfolio as Choosers.

In the initial year, 2000, 66.6% of the plan participants were Choosers. The expensive government advertisement campaign to highlight the second option probably induced many to override the default option in the initial period. From the government's point of view, advertising was particularly cost effective in the initial year because all 4.4 million Swedes, then in the workplace, enrolled in the plan. In subsequent years, the advertising expenditure was much more modest and fewer people were left over to enroll in the plan every year. The result has been that the percentage share of Choosers has massively fallen over successive years; it was 11.95% for the next 6 years and only 2.37% in the next 10 years. Thus, the vast majority of people in the following years chose the default option.

Over a period of 16 years, 2000–2016, 27.4% of the Delegators switched to become Choosers. Institutional factors favored this direction of switch as compared to the opposite direction (about 3% made the opposite switch). For instance, for the first 8 years, Choosers could not switch to being Delegators. Most of these switches occurred in the first 10 years and were probably caused on account of third party nudging by private mutual funds who could switch individuals from Delegators to Choosers by acting on behalf of their clients. In any case, 72.6% of the Delegators never switched. About 97% of the Choosers also never switched either despite massive changes in risk and default possibilities that should have induced a switch in mutual funds. Thus, in this sense, the initial nudge to either be a Delegator or a Chooser had long-lasting effects.

A growing literature considers spillover effects of nudges, such as the crowding out of traditional policy instruments or of other actions; see Truelove et al. (2014) for a review of environmental issues. Spiegler (2015) provides suggestive theoretical models in which the partial equilibrium effect of a nudge is positive but the general equilibrium effect is negative. The models are too stylized to be taken as serious descriptions of economic phenomena, but they perform a useful role in alerting the behavioral economics profession of the importance of general equilibrium effects. Indeed, these observations are as true of behavioral economics, as they are of neoclassical economics. As a concrete empirical example, nudges used to decrease water consumption increased the consumption of electricity (Tiefenbeck et al., 2013). The explanation lies in a reduction in the perceived immorality of an action following a moral action.

Green nudges such as default options to enroll in more energy efficient choices and reminders of the average energy consumption of a relevant reference group of individuals have been shown to be effective (Allcott, 2011; Hedlin and Sunstein, 2016). However, it is well recognized that climate change cannot be countered with nudges alone and traditional economic policy instruments such as regulation and taxes are also required (Loewenstein and Chater, 2017). Hagmann et al. (2019) consider the spillover effect of green nudges to counter climate change on other policy instruments such as support for carbon taxes. They consider a range of treatments (or Studies), all with hypothetical scenarios, that tease out the various spillover effects. We now describe these below.

In Study 1A there is the possibility of a nudge that defaults consumers to a renewable energy plan and a \$40/ton carbon tax. Subjects could either face (1) the tax alone, or (2) a combination of the tax and the nudge. A total of 70% and 55% of the participants supported the carbon tax in the two cases, respectively. The difference is statistically significant, so nudges crowd out support for the carbon tax. In Study 1B, the tax was framed so that the tax costs reflected (1) low pain, and (2) high pain, in terms of foregone utility. In this case, 72% and 46% of the participants, respectively, supported the carbon tax in the two cases. Thus, crowding out of taxes is more severe, the more painful are the perceived consequences of a tax. The crowding out effect occurs only when the nudge (e.g., a green nudge) is related to the carbon tax but not if the nudge is unrelated, e.g., a nudge to take up a more efficient pension product (Study 2). Similarly, a nudge to improve retirement savings reduces support for a social security tax; the reduction in magnitude is similar to the reduction in the support for a carbon tax due to a green energy nudge (Study 3).

Study 4 examines the important question of what causes the crowding out effect. Here participants are asked to give their support for the carbon tax, and the green nudge. The four treatments here are as follows. (1) Tax First in which subjects state their support for the tax, followed by their support for the nudge. (2) Nudge First, which requires subjects to state their support for the nudge first, followed by support for the tax. (3) Nudge Ineffective in which subjects are told that the nudge is not very effective and then they state their support for the nudge and the tax, in that order. (4) Tax Attractive in which subjects are told that the cost of the tax is low and then they state their support for the nudge and the tax, in that order.

The results are shown in Figure 5.2. The percentage of subjects who support the nudge in the 4 treatments (right panel of Figure 5.2) does not vary much between the treatments and the pairwise differences are statistically insignificant. However, support for the carbon tax in the left panel varies significantly across the treatments. A simple reordering of the tax and nudge policy instruments (Treatments 1 and 2) changes support for the tax by 10% points, which is significant only at the 10% level. However, in the Nudge Ineffective treatment, support for the carbon tax increases to 72%, which is significantly different from the 60% support in Treatment 2 at the 5% level. Similarly, the difference between Treatments 2 and 4 is statistically significant. Thus, crowding out is influenced by the perceived effectiveness of the nudge and the costliness of the tax. These findings suggest that public information along these lines can either make nudges more or less effective.

Pe'er et al. (2019) argue that aggregating societal views about nudges may hide important group level differences. For instance, minorities may have different ideological and religious views relative to the general population which could induce different views towards nudges (e.g., towards default options in organ donations). In particular, they consider two minority groups

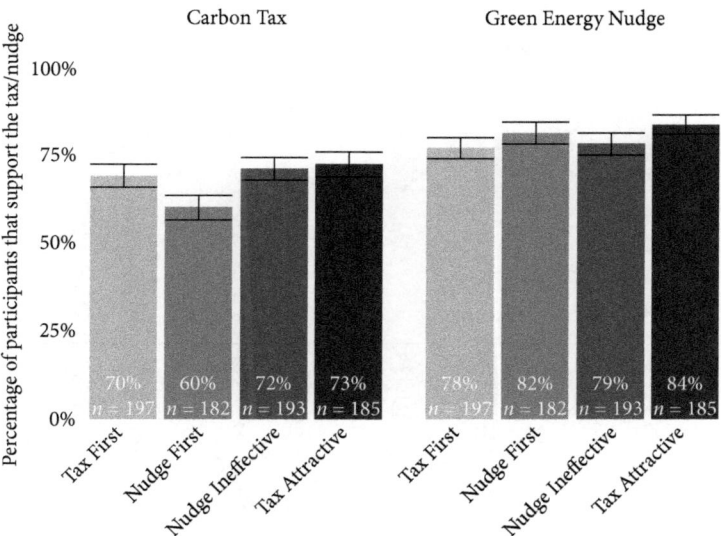

Figure 5.2 Percentage of subjects who support the carbon tax (left panel) and the green energy nudge (right panel). Error bars show ± one standard error.

Source: Reprinted by permission from Springer Nature. *Nature Climate Change*. Nudging out support for a carbon tax. Hagmann, D., Ho, E.H, and Lowenstein, G., © Springer Nature 2019.

in Israel, Israeli Arabs and Ultra-Orthodox Jews. They elicited attitudes towards 17 different hypothetical nudges (organ donation registration defaults, graphic warnings on cigarette packs, no exam-cheating pledge, automatic enrollment for donations in wills, health signals on food items capturing healthiness of food, credit limit alerts warning account holders who are about to go into the red, pre-appointments/reminders for medical tests, distancing candy nudges that require placing tempting candies away from checkouts, . . .).

The results are shown in Figure 5.3; the names of the nudges are self-explanatory. The three most supported nudges across the population were pre-appointments, credit limit alerts, and health signals. The three least supported nudges are honesty pledges, distancing candy, and organ donation registration defaults. Of the majority Jews, 59.13% supported organ donation defaults, while the corresponding percentages for Israeli Arabs and Ultra-Orthodox Jews were, respectively, 35.29% and 12% only. Except organ donation, Israeli Arabs expressed the lowest support among the three groups for all other nudges. Ultra-Orthodox Jews were more supportive of some other nudges relative to majority Jews. These include automatic muting of messages while driving (Ultra-Orthodox Jews drive much less than others); health signals, credit limit alert; self-breathalyzer tests before driving; distancing from candy. By contrast, majority Jews gave higher support for pre-appointments for medical exams; two-sided printing defaults; and privacy settings in posting social media content.

Why do these differences arise? The authors then classify nudges into two groups based on a classification in Hagman et al. (2015). Pro-social nudges are those that benefit other members of society. These include organ donor registration, voting reminders (automatic texts, one day before voting), two-sided printing, and no exam-cheating pledge. The rest are categorized as pro-self nudges. The hypothesis is that minority groups, who might have a lower national attachment,

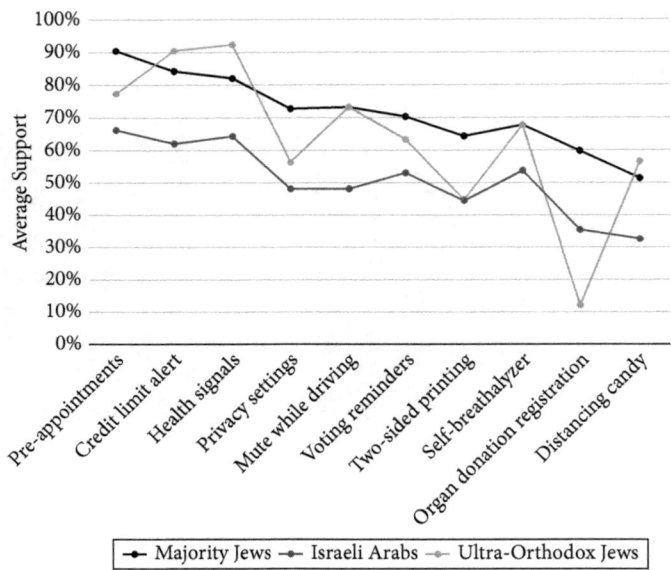

Figure 5.3 Average support for various nudges, disaggregated by majority and minority groups.

Source: Pe'er, E., Feldman, Y., Gamliel, E., Sahar, L., Tikotsky, A., Hod, N., and Schupak, H. (2019). Do minorities like nudges? The role of group norms in attitudes towards behavioral policy. *Judgment and Decision Making* 14(1): 40–50. Published under a Creative Commons CC-BY-3.0 licence.

would be more receptive to pro-self nudges relative to pro-social nudges, as compared to the majority Jews. This was indeed found to be the case. The most extreme and significant difference in the receptiveness towards the two categories of nudges was found for Ultra-Orthodox Jews (even when the organ donation nudge was excluded), followed by Israeli Arabs. Thus, support for nudges depends on the social and cultural norms within one's own group and there can be substantial heterogeneity in support for various forms of nudges.

Tannenbaum et al. (2017) show that the framing of nudges is an important factor in their acceptance. When framed and supported with examples that are consistent with their political affiliation in the US (Republicans or Democrats), subjects are more likely to accept nudges. Cornwell and Krantz (2014) show that framing of nudges matters. The support is higher when nudges are framed in more general terms as applicable to the population at large rather than to the individual posed with the nudge. The sensitivity of nudges to framing should not surprise readers of this book and we have covered elsewhere several examples, such as the sensitivity to whether the questions are framed as gains or losses. There are also cross-country differences with the Swedes found to be more supportive of nudges as compared to Americans (Hagman et al. 2015).

Jung and Mellers (2016) examine the correlation between support for nudges (drawn from Sunstein, 2013) and a variety of psychological variables. They find that more *empathetic individuals* (empathy is measured using the Interpersonal Reactivity Scale, due to Davis, 1983) gave greater support for nudges particularly when nudges highlighted social benefits and costs. This is perhaps because the target for many nudges is to help individuals achieve personal and social goals. *Reactant individuals* are those who vigorously resist the imposition of goals on them by outsiders. Measuring reactance by a scale, due to Hong and Page (1989), they find that more reactant individuals are more likely to oppose nudge, particularly those nudges that appear to engage System 1 (such as default options, changes in the placement of items in a grocery store, or smaller servings of meals). *Individualist individuals* (measured by using the Cultural Cognition Scale, due to Kahan et al. (2009), Kahan et al. (2011)) trust humans to independently pursue their own welfare, while *communitarians* believe that governments can be trusted to secure collective welfare. Individualists (in contrast to communitarians) and *conservatives* (in contrast of individuals classified as *liberals*) are more likely to oppose nudges. The authors find that System 2 nudges (e.g., warning signs, calorie labels) that require greater cognitive effort, are supported more as compared to System 1 nudges. However, the distinction between nudges that can be classified as belonging to any of the two systems is a matter of subjective judgment and it is hard to give objective definitions.

The positive effect of nudges in the form of contrasting information on own energy consumption and that of a relevant reference group, e.g., neighbors, has been shown to reduce energy consumption (Schultz et al., 2007; Nolan et al., 2008; Goldstein et al., 2008; Alcott, 2011); for a meta-study of 156 field studies, see Delmas et al. (2013). Costa and Kahn (2013) extend this literature by studying the effects of political affiliation in experiments using data from a Californian utility that sends households their home energy report and a comparison with their neighbors. The authors classify energy users into two types. (1) Political liberals: members of Democrats, Greens, and the Peace and Freedom parties who also contribute to environmental causes and live in a liberal community. (2) Political conservatives: members of Republican, American, and Libertarian parties who do not contribute to environmental causes and live in a conservative community. The home energy report reduces energy consumption by 3.6% among the political liberals (who already consume lower energy to begin with) and by 1.1% among the political conservatives. The latter are also more likely to opt out of receiving the home energy reports. One policy recommendation that follows from this study is to target the home energy report to the specific partisan affiliation of energy users.

Allcott and Kessler (2019) argue that the beneficial effects of nudges are overestimated because they do not take account of the costs of adopting the nudge. For instance, if an energy related nudge reduces demand for energy, then costs could include the associated inconvenience of reduced energy usage (and the benefits which the authors do not consider, such as the warm glow from doing something for the planet). Other examples include graphic warnings on cigarettes that could impart an emotional cost to smokers; children could feel guilty from receiving body fat report cards; and energy nudges could have associated time costs in managing the new energy efficient technology. If such costs exist, then the typical practice of evaluating the effectiveness of nudges, say green nudges, by the energy saved net of the implementation costs, could be an underestimate. In order to take account of such costs they consider a program of providing home energy reports (HER) to 10,000 users in upstate New York.

The recipients received the HERs for free in the first year. However, to receive the reports in the second year, they were asked to state their willingness to pay (WTP) for the reports and this was implemented in an incentive compatible manner; $WTP < 0$ is allowed to include the possibility that consumers do not wish to receive the reports or that the net benefits of the report to them are negative. The average WTP was $3, which was about 57% of the retail energy savings. The cost savings are relatively small relative to the much stronger effects of nudges in other areas such as pensions and savings. The authors interpret this figure to mean that the neglected costs of the adoption of the nudge were 43% of the savings and need to be subtracted from the gross benefits of the nudge to arrive at a welfare measure. For 34% of the people, $WTP \leq 0$, i.e., they would not like to receive the HER, even if it were free.

Damgaard and Gravert (2018) highlight the effect that nudges might have on opting out of a program altogether. They conduct a field study on charitable donations. The main finding is that a request for charitable contributions to a cause (to be made within 10 days) increases charitable donations significantly by two thirds. However, an unintended consequence is that it leads more people to unsubscribe from the mailing list.

5.7 Nudges and costs of overriding defaults

What is the role played by nudges when individuals have to incur a cost to override a default option? How do changes in default options in this case influence the aggregate of actions across all individuals? Altmann et al. (2018) consider these sorts of questions. They employ a simple, but instructive, theoretical model and empirical data drawn from betterplace.org, a non-profit organization, which is Germany's largest online platform for making charitable donations to about 6000 different projects in Germany and worldwide. Data is collected on 680,000 donation page visits and 23,000 donations that totalled €1.17 million.

The default options are varied in two dimensions.

1. Level of donations: Three possible default contributions are chosen, € 10, 20, 50. These correspond to the 25th, 50th, and 75th percentile of donations during the previous 6 months on this online platform (the experiment was conducted in 2012–13). We also allow for the possibility of the absence of a default option.
2. Codonations: These are extra donations which cover the costs of the non-profit organization. Amounts range from 5% to 25% in increments of 5% or "other amount" that can be voluntarily chosen. Potential contributors pick any of these amounts, which are added to their chosen donations.

We first construct a simple theoretical model of optimal donations in the presence of costs of overriding donations (as in Carroll et al., 2009; Bernheim et al., 2015), followed by the empirical results.

5.7.1 *Theoretical model*

Consider the following simple model of charitable contributions in the presence of a default option, a fixed cost of default, and heterogeneity in default costs.

The utility function from charitable contributions, x, in the absence of default options is given by

$$u(x,\theta) = \theta x - \frac{x^2}{2}; \ \theta \geq 0, \ x \in \mathbb{R}_+. \tag{5.4}$$

The first order condition is necessary and sufficient for a unique solution, which is given by

$$x^* = \theta. \tag{5.5}$$

Thus, the observed distribution of actual contributions in the absence of a default option directly reveals the underlying distribution of the parameter θ.

Let us now consider optimal contributions in the presence of contribution defaults and let $x = d$ be the contribution default. Consider two types of individuals.

Ungenerous individuals have the utility function $u(x,0)$ i.e., $\theta = 0$. Thus, they optimally choose $x_1^* = 0$. In particular, x_1^* is not influenced by the default contribution d.

Generous individuals have $\theta > 0$, and are further divided into two distinct subtypes depending on whether they have strictly positive or zero costs from deviating from the default option.

1. A fraction $1 - \lambda_1, \lambda_1 \in [0,1]$, have the following utility function

$$U(x,\theta,c) = \begin{cases} u(d,\theta) & \text{if} \quad 0 < x = d \\ u(x,\theta) - c & \text{if} \quad 0 < x \neq d \,,\, c > 0, \theta > 0, \overline{u} > 0, \\ -\overline{u} & \text{if} \quad x = 0 \end{cases} \qquad (5.6)$$

where u is defined in (5.4); $c > 0$ is the cost of deviating from the default contribution in either direction; and $-\overline{u} < 0$ is the disutility from not contributing, which possibly captures costs arising from emotions such as guilt or shame.

2. The remaining fraction λ_1 has the utility $U(x,\theta,0)$ (i.e., zero costs), where $U(x,\theta,c)$ is defined in (5.6).

Let the binary variable $z = 1$ if an individual belongs to the fraction $1 - \lambda_1$ and $z = 0$ if the individual belongs to the fraction λ_1. There is a distribution of c, conditional on z that is given by

$$F(c \mid z = 1) = \begin{cases} 1 - e^{-\lambda_2 c} & c \geq 0 \\ 0 & c < 0 \end{cases}, \lambda_2 > 0.$$

Thus, an increase in λ_2 increases the probability weight on lower costs.

Conditional on an individual being a generous type individual, $\theta > 0$, there is a distribution of the utility cost, $\overline{u}$, of choosing $x = 0$ given by

$$G(\overline{u} \mid \theta > 0) = \begin{cases} 1 - e^{-\lambda_3 \overline{u}} & \overline{u} \geq 0 \\ 0 & \overline{u} < 0 \end{cases}, \lambda_3 > 0.$$

An increase in λ_3 increases the probability mass on lower values of $\overline{u}$. The three parameters, $\theta, c, \overline{u}$ are distributed independently of each other.

From (5.6), if $0 < x \neq d$ (middle row), then the optimal choice is $x^* = \theta$ given in (5.5). Thus, the optimal choice of generous individuals, x^G, when they belong to the fraction $1 - \lambda_1$ of the population is given by

$$x^G = \begin{cases} d & \text{if} \quad (i) \, u(d,\theta) > u(\theta,\theta) - c, \, (ii) \, u(d,\theta) > -\overline{u}. \\ \theta & \text{if} \quad (i) \, u(\theta,\theta) - c > u(d,\theta), \, (ii) \, u(\theta,\theta) - c > -\overline{u}.. \\ 0 & \text{if} \quad Max\{u(d,\theta), u(\theta,\theta) - c\} < -\overline{u} \end{cases} \qquad (5.7)$$

A simple calculation shows that

$$\Delta(\theta,d) \equiv u(\theta,\theta) - u(d,\theta) = \frac{\theta^2 + d^2}{2} - \theta d > 0. \qquad (5.8)$$

The sign follows because θ is the maximizing choice, hence, $u(\theta,\theta) > u(x,\theta)$ for all $x \in \mathbb{R}_+$, and in particular for $x = d$.

Proposition 5.1 *(a) Consider individuals who belong to the fraction λ_1 and have $c = 0$. Such individuals always choose $x^{**} = \theta$.*
(b) Consider individuals who belong to the fraction $1 - \lambda_1$ and have $c > 0$.
(bi) If $u(d,\theta) < -\bar{u}$ and $u(\theta,\theta) - c < -\bar{u}$, then the optimal choice of contributions is $x^G = 0$.
(bii) Let $u(d,\theta) > -\bar{u}$ and $u(\theta,\theta) - c > -\bar{u}$. Also let

$$\Delta(\theta,d) \equiv \hat{c},$$

where $\Delta(\theta,d)$ is defined in (5.8). If $c > \hat{c}$ then $x^G = d$ and if $c < \hat{c}$ then $x^G = \theta$. In particular, if $\theta > \frac{d}{2}$ then individuals either pick $x^G = d$ or $x^G = \theta$.
(biii) if $\theta > d$ then $\frac{\partial \hat{c}}{\partial \theta} > 0$ and $\frac{\partial \hat{c}}{\partial d} < 0$, but if $\theta < d$ then $\frac{\partial \hat{c}}{\partial \theta} < 0$ and $\frac{\partial \hat{c}}{\partial d} > 0$.

Proof of Proposition 5.1: (a) Set $c = 0$ in the second row of (5.7) and check that both conditions are satisfied. Condition (i) requires $\frac{\theta^2 + d^2}{2} - \theta d > 0$, which is true from (5.8). Condition (ii) requires that $u(\theta,\theta) = \frac{\theta^2}{2} > -\bar{u}$, which is true. Hence $x^{**} = \theta$ is the optimal choice.

(b) Consider individuals who belong to the fraction $1 - \lambda_1$ of the population who have $c > 0$. For such individuals, the optimal choice x^G is given by (5.7).

(bi) Let $u(d,\theta) < -\bar{u}$ and $u(\theta,\theta) - c < -\bar{u}$. From the third row of (5.7), the optimal choice in this case is $x^G = 0$.

(bii) Let $u(d,\theta) > -\bar{u}$ and $u(\theta,\theta) - c > -\bar{u}$. Then, in each of the first two rows of (5.7), condition (ii) is satisfied, so we need to consider only condition (i) to determine if the optimal choice should be d or θ. It is given that $\Delta(\theta,d) \equiv \hat{c}$. Thus, it follows from (5.8) that if $c > \hat{c}$ then $x^G = d$. If $c < \hat{c}$ then $x^G = \theta$. The second part of the claim follows because if $\theta > (d/2)$ then $u(d,\theta) > -u$, hence, such contributors never choose $x^G = 0$.

(biii) Differentiating $\hat{c}$ with respect to θ, d we get

$$\frac{\partial \hat{c}}{\partial \theta} = \theta - d; \; \frac{\partial \hat{c}}{\partial d} = -(\theta - d).$$

Thus, it follows that if $\theta > d$ then $\frac{\partial \hat{c}}{\partial \theta} > 0$ and $\frac{\partial \hat{c}}{\partial d} < 0$, but if $\theta < d$ then $\frac{\partial \hat{c}}{\partial \theta} < 0$ and $\frac{\partial \hat{c}}{\partial d} > 0$. ∎

Discussion of Proposition 5.1: From part (a), the fraction λ_1 of contributors who face zero costs of deviating from the default, do deviate and pick their most preferred contribution, $x^{**} = \theta$. This is identical to the contribution of individuals who do not face a default option (recall $x^* = \theta$). Consider now contributors with $c > 0$. From part (bi), if the cost c is too high, or the valuation for the contribution θ is too low, or the default d is too distant from the optimal choice $x^* = \theta$, then it is possible that the individual decides not to contribute anything. From part (bii) if $\theta > \frac{d}{2}$, i.e., the individual is sufficiently generous, then zero contributions can always be ruled out. In this case, the individual chooses either the default contribution or the most preferred contribution $x^* = \theta$.

Which of these cases arises depends on the critical value of cost, $\hat{c}$. If the cost exceeds the critical value $c > \hat{c}$, then individuals always pick up the default option. Deviating from the default is too costly in this case. For sufficiently low costs of deviating from the default ($c < \hat{c}$), the individual chooses $x^* = \theta$. Finally, Proposition 5.1(biii) tells us how the critical cost, $\hat{c}$, is affected by the parameters of the model. If $\theta > d$, then an increase in d to a new default value reduces $\hat{c}$. This increases the range of values of cost for which the new default option is chosen. Conversely, if $\theta < d$ then an increase in d to a new default value reduces the range of values of cost for which the new default option is chosen.

5.7.2 *Empirical results*

The empirical results are as follows (all figures in Euros). Contribution defaults have a major effect on actual donations. The modal contribution for each of the default levels 10, 20, 50, is the default level of the contributions. For instance, when the default is €10, in three different treatments corresponding to different codonation amounts, the modal contribution of €10 is made by 22.9%, 22.8%, and 21.7% of the contributors. By contrast, when the defaults are 20 and 50, only 12–14 percent of the contributors choose €10. A Kolgomorov–Smirnov test shows that the distribution of contributions for the levels of defaults 10, 20, 50, and the no defaults case differ significantly from each other ($p < 0.001$ in all pairwise tests of differences). However, fixing the level of default, variation in codonations does not produce significantly different distributions of contributions (only 1 out of 12 pairwise comparisons is significant in this case). When the level of default is varied, then the contributions distributions for different levels of codonations differ significantly ($p < 0.001$ in all pairwise tests of differences using a Kolgomorov–Smirnov test).

In response to the second question posed at the beginning of this section, there is very little difference in average contributions across the different treatments. Thus, the level of defaults does not have an effect on average contributions. When no defaults are given, the average contribution is 1.69. The average contributions under the default levels 10, 20, 50 are, respectively, 1.70, 1.68, 1.77.[3] The reason is that some people are induced to donate more when defaults increase while other reduce contributions (see, e.g., Proposition 5.1(bii) for the two cases $\theta > d$ and $\theta < d$). When the default is the highest, 50, there is also an extensive margin effect. Some people opt out of donating anything at a high default. In terms of the theoretical model above, when defaults are too far away from the desired contribution level, θ, we are more likely to get the case $u(d, \theta) < -\overline{u}$ and $u(\theta, \theta) - c < -\overline{u}$ (Proposition 5.1(bi)) so that optimal contributions are zero. These results suggest that a policy of increasing charitable contributions simply through raising the default level of contributions may not be effective.

The estimate of λ_1 is 0.89. This means that 89% of the individuals simply ignore the effect of defaults on their contribution levels (Proposition 5.1(a)). Relative to the case of no defaults, under various levels of default, there was an increase of 5–10% of individuals who contributed the default amount. Thus, defaults are effective for some individuals, but leave the behavior of the vast majority of the subjects unchanged. But we do know that defaults are quite effective in other contexts. One possibility is that the current experimental design does not involve a time element, so no procrastination, a major factor in default choices, is involved. Restricting attention to the remaining 11% subjects (the fraction $1 - \lambda_1$), the estimates of λ_2 and λ_3 indicate that the probability is high that default override cost, c, and the opt out cost, $-\overline{u}$, are high. Thus, such individuals are likely to be unduly influenced by the default.

5.8 Default nudges and present biased preferences

Blumenstock et al. (2018), in conjunction with Roshan, Afganistan's largest mobile phone operator, devised a new phone-based savings account (M-Pasandaz or "mobile savings") with 949 employees of the company. Previously, all employees were paid their salaries into their mobile

---

[3] These results are in line with some other results that allow the default levels to vary where they find either no effects (Fiala Noussair, 2017) or weak positive effects (Goswami and Urminsky, 2016).

phone banking account. In the first phase of the 2×3 design, the employees are randomly assigned to two default treatments—either 0% or 5% of their salary automatically contributed towards a savings account. The interest rate on the savings is zero. However, the financial incentive to save is that the employees are randomly assigned to three groups—an employer match of 0%, 25%, and 50%.

The employees make monthly contributions for 6 months and the matching contributions, if any, accrue over time, but all benefits are paid at the end of the 6-month period. Employees could withdraw their money prior to the end of the 6-month period, but all matching contributions are lost in this case. Employees were also free to change their contribution rates at any time during the 6 months (irrespective of which default category, 0% or 5%, they were drawn into) to be any rate between 0%–10%. The changed rate was then applied to the remaining 6-month period. The change could be made by simply visiting or calling the HR department in their firm.

One can then compare the (i) benchmark case (0% default) with the case of 5% default to study the effect of defaults, and (ii) the benchmark case (0% matching contributions) with the case of positive matching contributions (25%, 50%) to study the effects of financial incentives. This allows for a study of the effects of defaults and incentives within the same study, with an identical group of subjects.

The structure of the remaining section is as follows. We first present a theoretical model of default enrollment and matching contributions that closely matches the structure described above but simplified for pedagogical convenience.[4] Furthermore, the theoretical model is based on the preferred explanation of the authors in explaining their data, which is a model of present biased preferences with multiple selves in which individuals might procrastinate to sign up for the savings plan. We shall employ quasi-hyperbolic preferences to model present bias. The general framework with present biased preferences in the presence of multiple selves is outlined in Sections 3.2.2 and 3.5 in Volume 3. We assume familiarity with this material.

While the underlying problem in our theoretical model is identical to the one in Blumenstock et al. (2018) and it employs present biased preferences with multiple selves, nevertheless our solution concept is completely different from theirs.[5] We use the standard concept of a *perception-perfect strategy* that we outline in Section 3.5 in Volume 3, due to O'Donoghue and Rabin (1999). As such, there is some novelty in the fully solved model that we present below.

5.8.1 *Theoretical Model*

An employee considers joining the M-Pasandaz program and finds himself in the 50% default match group. The fixed cost of joining the program is $\theta \geq 0$ and the interest rate is zero. The employee considers making a £2 per month contribution towards the savings program for 6 months, $t \in T = \{1, 2, \ldots, 6\}$. The benefits from the program accrue at $t = 7$. Once the employee is enrolled into the program he stays in the program till the end and makes no further

---

[4] For instance, in the model, once an employee picks a contribution level, it stays the same over the 6-month period. Also, we fix the matching contribution rate to be 50% only and each individual who chooses to be enrolled, contributes a fixed amount of £2 per month.

[5] This model is available as an online appendix in Blumenstock et al. (2018). In particular, the authors do not articulate which equilibrium concept they are using to find an equilibrium to a sequential game under full information. For this reason, it is difficult to evaluate the theoretical contribution that the authors make. The predictions of our theoretical model do not always tally with the authors' results.

switches to different levels of contributions. All monetary amounts (costs and benefits) are measured in dollars. The model can be easily extended to any default match group and any monthly contribution level. The employee has quasi hyperbolic $(\beta, \delta) = (\beta, 1)$ preferences, where $0 < \beta < 1$, is the discount factor that shrinks all future levels of utilities and costs (see Volume 3).

Suppose that an employee signs up for the program in period $t \in T$. Then, the variable cost of the investment of the employee is $2(7 - t)$ (including contributions made at t). Since the employer matches half the contribution level, the match amount is $(7 - t)$; this is the only return on the individual's investment. Thus, the total benefit of contributions to the employee at t is $3(7 - t)$.

Suppose that the employee joins the program at some time $\tau \in T$. Then, the undiscounted gross benefit from the contributions (available at $t = 7$) is

$$v_\tau = 3(7 - \tau). \tag{5.9}$$

The *present discounted value* of the cost at time $\tau \in T$, when the employee enrolls at time τ is

$$c_\tau(\tau) = \theta + 2 + 2\beta(6 - \tau). \tag{5.10}$$

In (5.10), θ is the one time fixed cost, 2 is the current variable cost at time τ and $2\beta(6 - \tau)$ is the discounted value of the future costs (2 every period) until the end of period $t = 6$.

The undiscounted value of costs at time $t \in T$ when the individual enters into the default option at a future time $\tau \in T : \tau > t$ is

$$c_t(\tau) = (\theta + 2 + 2(6 - \tau)), \tau > t. \tag{5.11}$$

Since $\delta = 1$, the time difference $\tau - t$ plays no role on the RHS of (5.10, 5.11). Note that the costs in (5.10) are discounted but the costs in (5.11) are undiscounted. This is to ensure that we can define utility in the standard form in (5.12) below.

We use the same utility function for the employee as we used in Section 3.5 in Volume 3 for $(\beta, 1)$ preferences. Preferences of the employee at time $t \in T$ are given by

$$U_t(\tau) = \begin{cases} \beta v_\tau - c_\tau(\tau) & \text{if} \quad \tau = t \\ \beta(v_\tau - c_t(\tau)) & \text{if} \quad \tau > t \end{cases}, \tag{5.12}$$

where v_τ is defined in (5.9), current discounted costs $c_\tau(\tau)$ are defined in (5.10) and undiscounted future costs $c_t(\tau)$ in (5.11). The utility function in (5.12) is the *current costs, future benefits* type that would be familiar to readers of Volume 3. So if the savings program is entered into at date $\tau = t$, then the current utility is given in the first row of (5.12). If however, the entry into the savings program occurs at some future date $\tau > t$, then the same discount factor, β, is applied to benefits and costs (since $\delta = 1$, it does not matter exactly which future period the savings program is entered into). The outside option of the employee is normalized to zero.

Using (5.9), (5.10), (5.11) we can calculate the first and the second rows in (5.12), respectively,

$$\beta v_\tau - c_\tau(\tau) = \beta(9 - \tau) - \theta - 2. \tag{5.13}$$

$$\beta(v_\tau - c_t(\tau)) = \beta(7 - \theta - \tau); \tau > t. \tag{5.14}$$

In (5.14), the right hand side is independent of the difference $\tau - t$ (as noted above, this follows because $\delta = 1$). Thus, irrespective of which future self (at $\tau > t$) enters into the default program, the utility to the current self (at t) is unchanged.

Employees have present biased preferences and each period is populated by a different self of the same employee. The impatience parameter of the current self of the employee is given by β (see (5.12)). However, the current self must estimate the impatience parameter of the future selves. There are three possibilities (we omit here partial naifs; see Volume 3). (1) Time consistents (or exponential discounters) have $\beta = 1$ and estimate $\widehat{\beta} = 1$. Indeed with $(\beta, \delta) = (1, 1)$ preferences, there is no present-bias at all. (2) Sophisticates are characterized by $0 < \beta = \widehat{\beta} < 1$, i.e., they are present biased and forecast, correctly, that their future selves will also have an identical degree of present bias. (3) Naifs exhibit $0 < \beta < \widehat{\beta} = 1 - \epsilon$, where $0 < \epsilon < \frac{1}{3}$ is a infinitesimally small number, so $\lim_{\epsilon \to 0} \widehat{\beta} = 1$. Thus, for small ϵ, naifs recognize that they are present biased but forecast incorrectly that their future selves will have (almost) no present bias. Let us now consider the optimal choices of these three types of individuals.

We now define *perception-perfect* strategies, which is a slight modification of subgame perfection; for the details see Chapter 3 in Volume 3. This requires individuals to choose their current action given their beliefs about how their future selves will behave. An individual's strategy is a complete contingent plan of action for each of the 6 selves. Denote a strategy by $\mathbf{s}^i = (s_1^i, s_2^i, \ldots, s_6^i)$, where s_t^i is the action of self t, and the type of the player is indexed by $i = c, s, n$ for, respectively, time consistents, sophisticates, and naifs. Any $s_t^i \in \{Y, N\}$, where Y denotes "enter into the savings program" and N denotes "do not enter into the savings program."

> **Definition 5.1** A "*perception-perfect strategy*" for a type $i = c, n$ (respectively, time consistent, and naif) player is a strategy $\mathbf{s}^i = (s_1^i, s_2^i, \ldots, s_6^i)$ that satisfies $\forall t < 6$, $s_t^i = Y$, if and only if, $U_t(t) > U_t(\tau)$ for all $\tau > t$ and $U_t(t) > 0$. At $t = 6$, $s_6^i = Y$, if $U_6(6) > 0$, otherwise $s_6^i = N$.

The definition of a perception-perfect strategy for time consistents and naifs is identical because both believe that all future selves will behave like time consistent individuals. The difference is that the beliefs of naifs are mistaken

> **Definition 5.2** A perception-perfect strategy for a sophisticate is a strategy $\mathbf{s}^s = (s_1^s, s_2^s, \ldots, s_6^s)$ that satisfies $\forall t < 6$, $s_t^s = Y$, if and only if, $U_t(t) > U_t(\underline{\tau})$ where $\underline{\tau} = \min_{\tau > t} \{\tau \mid s_\tau^s = Y\}$ and $U_t(t) > 0$. At $t = 6$, $s_6^s = Y$, if $U_6(6) > 0$, otherwise $s_6^s = N$.

A sophisticate (Definition 5.2) is aware that future selves will have identical self-control problems, hence, several future selves might succumb to temptation. The current self only needs to know the earliest future self that will succumb, because the activity is undertaken only once. By contrast, time consistents and naifs (Definition 5.1) believe that all future selves have no self-control problems, so the plans that they make are time consistent. Hence, they only need to know if it is optimal to do it now, or later. The method of solution is by backward induction. We first determine the optimal action of self 6; then, the optimal action of self 5, conditional on the beliefs of self 5 about the future action of self 6, and so on. We summarize the results for the three types of employees in separate propositions below.

> **Proposition 5.2** Suppose that there exists at least one $\tau \in T$ for which $\beta v_\tau - c_\tau(\tau) > 0$. Time consistents ($\beta = \widehat{\beta} = 1$) enter into the savings program at time $t = 1$, i.e., there is immediate enrollment.

Proof of Proposition 5.2: Since there is no discounting with $(\beta, \delta) = (1,1)$ preferences, such individuals pick the period which has the highest current value of benefits net of cost, $v_\tau - c_\tau(\tau)$. In other words they pick a value of $\tau \in T$ for which $v_\tau - c_\tau(\tau)$ is maximized; the outside option of 0 guarantees that this value of $\tau \in T$ is optimal. Setting $\beta = 1$ in (5.13), $v_\tau - c_\tau(\tau) = (9 - \tau) - \theta - 2$, which is decreasing in τ. Thus, the optimal enrollment choice of the decision maker is $\tau = 1$, i.e., immediate enrollment. The assumptions (i) that there exists at least one $\tau \in T$ for which $\beta v_\tau - c_\tau(\tau) > 0$, and (ii) that $v_\tau - c_\tau(\tau)$ is a maximum, in conjunction with (5.13) ensure that $v_1 - c_1(1) > 0$. Thus, any perception-perfect strategy of consistents must have $s_1^c = Y$. Since a strategy must prescribe a complete contingent plan of action, for any $t = 2, \dots, 6$, $s_t^c = Y$ if $v_t - c_t(t) > 0$ and $s_t^c = N$ otherwise. ∎

From Proposition 5.2, there is never any procrastination by time consistents. Thus, if we observe any procrastination in the take up of the savings plan for an employee, then the employee cannot be a time consistent employee. Next we consider the case of sophisticates. In this case, general results are not very enlightening, so we also give more specific results for the following numerical values $(\beta, \theta) = (0.5, 0.4), (0.5, 0.7)$.

Proposition 5.3   *Consider sophisticated individuals ($0 < \beta = \widehat{\beta} < 1$).*
(a) Suppose that there exists some self $\widehat{\tau} \in T$ who chooses to enter into the default program, i.e., $s_{\widehat{\tau}}^s = Y$. Then all higher selves $\tau' \in T : \tau' > \widehat{\tau}$, if any, choose not to enter, i.e., $s_{\tau'}^s = N$. If $\widehat{\tau} = 1$ then $s_1^s = Y$ and $s_2^s = \dots = s_6^s = N$.
(b) Let $\widehat{\tau} > 1$. (bi) If $\theta < \frac{3\beta - 2}{1 - \beta}$ then the optimal strategy is $s_1^s = \dots = s_{\widehat{\tau}}^s = Y$ and $s_{\widehat{\tau}+1}^s = \dots = s_6^s = N$. (bii) If $\theta > \frac{3\beta - 2}{1 - \beta}$, then no general results can be given. Procrastination may lead to entry into the savings program in any $t \in T$
(ci) Let $\beta = 0.5$ and $\theta = 0.4$. The perception-perfect strategy is $s_1^s = s_4^s = Y$ and $s_2^s = s_3^s = s_5^s = s_6^s = N$.
(cii) Let $\beta = 0.5$ and $\theta = 0.7$. The perception-perfect strategy is $s_3^s = Y$ and $s_j^s = N$ for all $j \neq 3$ and $j \in T$.

Proof of Proposition 5.3: (a) Using (5.13), and successively working downwards from times $6, 5, \dots, 1$, let $\widehat{\tau} \in T$ be the first self such that $\beta v_\tau - c_\tau(\tau) = \beta (9 - \widehat{\tau}) - \theta - 2 > 0$ or

$$\theta < \beta (9 - \widehat{\tau}) - 2. \tag{5.15}$$

Furthermore, for any $\tau' \in T : \tau' > \widehat{\tau}$, we have $\beta (9 - \tau') - \theta - 2 < 0$, so $s_{\tau'}^s = N$; such a $\widehat{\tau}$ may or may not exist. If $\widehat{\tau} = 1$ then the solution is trivial, $s_1^s = Y$ and $s_2^s = \dots = s_6^s = N$.
(b) Suppose that $\widehat{\tau} > 1$.
Now consider the problem of the self in the previous period, $\widehat{\tau} - 1$. Using (5.12), self $\widehat{\tau} - 1$ chooses to enter into the default program if

$$U_{\widehat{\tau}-1}(\widehat{\tau} - 1) > U_{\widehat{\tau}-1}(\widehat{\tau}) \Leftrightarrow \beta v_{\widehat{\tau}-1} - c_{\widehat{\tau}-1}(\widehat{\tau} - 1) > \beta (v_{\widehat{\tau}} - c_{\widehat{\tau}-1}(\widehat{\tau})) \tag{5.16}$$

Using (5.13) and (5.14) we can rewrite (5.16) as

$$\beta (9 - (\widehat{\tau} - 1)) - \theta - 2 > \beta (7 - \theta - \widehat{\tau})$$

or

$$\theta < \frac{3\beta - 2}{1 - \beta}. \tag{5.17}$$

If (5.17) holds, then $s^s_{\hat\tau-1} = Y$. Since (i) (5.17) is independent of $\hat\tau$, and (ii) a sophisticate considers the earliest future self who chooses Y, it follows that selves $\hat\tau - 2, \hat\tau - 3, \ldots 1$ will also face the condition (5.17) to enter into the savings program and also choose Y, so all lower types $\tau' \in T$: $\tau' < \hat\tau$ enter into the savings program, i.e., $s^s_{\hat\tau-j-1} = s^s_{\hat\tau-j-2} = \ldots = s^s_1 = Y$. Thus, the optimal strategy is $s^s_1 = \ldots = s^s_{\hat\tau} = Y$ and $s^s_{\hat\tau+1} = \ldots = s^s_6 = N$.

If condition (5.17) is violated then self $\hat\tau - 1$ optimally chooses $s^s_{\hat\tau-1} = N$. Now consider the problem of self $\hat\tau - 2$ who realizes that $s^s_{\hat\tau} = Y$, $s^s_{\hat\tau-1} = N$. Hence, self $\hat\tau - 1$ chooses to enter into the savings program if

$$U_{\hat\tau-2}(\hat\tau - 2) > U_{\hat\tau-2}(\hat\tau) \Leftrightarrow \beta v_{\hat\tau-2} - c_{\hat\tau-2}(\hat\tau - 2) > \beta(v_{\hat\tau} - c_{\hat\tau-2}(\hat\tau)) \qquad (5.18)$$

Using (5.13) and (5.14) we can rewrite (5.18) as

$$\beta(9 - (\hat\tau - 2)) - \theta - 2 > \beta(7 - \theta - \hat\tau)$$

which simplifies to

$$\theta < \frac{4\beta - 2}{1 - \beta}. \qquad (5.19)$$

If condition (5.19) holds, then self $\hat\tau - 2$ chooses $s^s_{\hat\tau-2} = Y$. If this condition is violated (i.e., $s^s_{\hat\tau-2} = N$), then simple calculations show that $s^s_{\hat\tau-3} = Y$ if

$$\theta < \frac{5\beta - 2}{1 - \beta}, \qquad (5.20)$$

otherwise $s^s_{\hat\tau-3} = N$.

This pattern of iteration leads to the following conclusions. The sequence of conditions for participation in the savings plan if any self finds that all higher selves up to but not including self $\hat\tau$ have chosen N instead of Y (see (5.17), (5.19), (5.20)), is: $\theta < \frac{3\beta-2}{1-\beta}, \theta < \frac{4\beta-2}{1-\beta}, \theta < \frac{5\beta-2}{1-\beta}, \ldots$. We can rewrite these in the following form which makes clear the self to which they apply:

$$\theta < \theta_{\hat\tau-1} \equiv \frac{(2+1)\beta - 2}{1 - \beta}, \theta < \theta_{\hat\tau-2} \equiv \frac{(2+2)\beta - 2}{1 - \beta}, \ldots, \theta < \theta_{\hat\tau-(\hat\tau-1)} \equiv \frac{(2+\hat\tau-1)\beta - 2}{1 - \beta}, \qquad (5.21)$$

where the subscript on the θ identifies the relevant self. Suppose that $\theta_{\hat\tau-j} < \theta < \theta_{\hat\tau-j+1}$, where $\theta_{\hat\tau-j}$ belongs to the sequence in (5.21), and (5.15) is satisfied (so $s^s_{\hat\tau} = Y$). Then it follows that $s^s_{\hat\tau-1} = \ldots = s^s_{\hat\tau-j+1} = Y$ but $s^s_{\hat\tau-j} = N$. If $j = \hat\tau - 1$, then we are done. Suppose $j > \hat\tau - 1$. Self $\hat\tau - j - 1$ knows that the earliest future self who will enter into the savings program is self $\hat\tau - j + 1$. So self $\hat\tau - j - 1$ enters into the savings program if

$$\theta_{\hat\tau-j-1} < \frac{4\beta - 2}{1 - \beta}.$$

If this condition holds then $s^s_{\hat\tau-j-1} = Y$. If $\hat\tau - j - 1 = 1$ then we are done and there are no more selves to consider. If not, then we need to consider the decision of self $\hat\tau - j - 2$ following the same template as above. This gives the method of solution, but depending on the size of θ one can get enrollment into the savings plan in any period.

(ci) Let $\beta = 0.5$ and $\theta = 0.4$. Then condition (5.15) can be written as $\theta = 0.4 < 0.5\,(9 - \widehat{\tau}) - 2$. It follows that $\widehat{\tau} = 4$ and $s_4^s = Y$. Self 3 now participates in the savings program if $\theta < \frac{3\beta - 2}{1 - \beta} = -1$, which is false, so $s_3^s = N$. Self 2 participates if $\theta < \frac{4\beta - 2}{1 - \beta} = 0$ which is false, so $s_2^s = N$. Self 1 participates if $\theta < \frac{5\beta - 2}{1 - \beta} = 1$, which is true so $s_1^s = Y$. So the perception-perfect strategy in this case is $s_1^s = s_4^s = Y$ and $s_2^s = s_3^s = s_5^s = s_6^s = N$. There is no procrastination in this case because the self at $t - 1$ immediately enrolls into the plan.

(cii) Let $\beta = 0.5$ and $\theta = 0.7$. Then condition (5.15) gives $\theta = 0.7 < 0.5\,(9 - \widehat{\tau}) - 2$, so $\widehat{\tau} = 3$ and $s_3^s = Y$. Self 2 and 1 now both choose N (because, respectively, $0.7 > -1$ and $0.7 > 0$). The perception-perfect strategy in this case is $s_3^s = Y$ and $s_j^s = N$ for all $j \neq 3$ and $j \in T$. ∎

From Proposition 5.3, sophisticates may procrastinate before entering into the savings program, or perhaps procrastinate indefinitely. The numerical examples indicate that an increase in the fixed cost of enrollment, θ, increases the delay in enrollment.

Next we consider naifs who overestimate their future self control ($0 < \beta < \widehat{\beta} = 1 - \epsilon$, where $0 < \epsilon < \frac{1}{3}$). The actual problem solved by their future selves is different from the perception of the current self about the problem solved by the future selves. Furthermore, the empirical evidence reviewed in Volume 3 indicates that $\beta < \frac{2}{3}$. We make use of this empirical evidence in the next proposition which shows that naifs will never choose to enter into the savings program but will forever be hopeful that all their future selves will choose to enter into the program.

Proposition 5.4   *Consider naifs ($0 < \beta < \widehat{\beta} = 1 - \epsilon$, where $0 < \epsilon < \frac{1}{3}$). Assume that $\beta < \frac{2}{3}$ and $\theta > 0$. In every period $t = 1, \ldots 5$ the period t self believes that all future selves will enter into the savings program. The optimal choice of action is $s_t^n = N$ for all $t \in T$.*

Proof of Proposition 5.4: Consider time period $t = 6$. Using (5.13), self 6 enrolls into the default program if $\beta\,(9 - 6) - \theta - 2 > 0$ or

$$3\beta > \theta + 2 \Leftrightarrow \theta < 3\beta - 2. \tag{5.22}$$

By contrast, self 5 estimates the β value for self 6 to be $\widehat{\beta} = 1 - \epsilon$, where $0 < \epsilon < \frac{1}{3}$, so self 5 believes that self 6 will enroll into the default program if

$$3\,(1 - \epsilon) > \theta + 2 \Leftrightarrow \theta < 1 - 3\epsilon. \tag{5.23}$$

Suppose that (5.23) holds so that self 5 believes self 6 will enroll. Then, self 5 enrolls into the default program if

$$U_5\,(5) > U_5\,(6) \Leftrightarrow \beta v_5 - c_5(5) > \beta\,(v_6 - c_5\,(6)) \tag{5.24}$$

Using (5.13) and (5.14) we can rewrite (5.24) as

$$\beta\,(9 - 5) - \theta - 2 > \beta\,(7 - \theta - 6).$$

or

$$\theta < \frac{3\beta - 2}{1 - \beta}. \tag{5.25}$$

If the upper bound on fixed costs, θ, given in (5.25) holds then self 5 enters into the default program. Otherwise, self 5 procrastinates and does not enter into the default program forecasting incorrectly that self 6 will enter into the program.

Now consider the decision of self 4 who believes that selves 5 and 6 have $\widehat{\beta} = 1 - \epsilon$. If (5.23) holds then self 4 believes that self 6 will choose the default program. Since $\widehat{\beta} = 1 - \epsilon$, self 4 incorrectly perceives condition (5.25) to be

$$\theta < \frac{1 - 3\epsilon}{\epsilon}. \tag{5.26}$$

Since $0 < \epsilon < \frac{1}{3}$, $\lim_{\epsilon \to 0} \frac{1-3\epsilon}{\epsilon} = \infty$, thus, condition (5.26) always holds for sufficiently small ϵ. Thus, if (5.23) also holds, then self 4 believes that both selves 5 and 6 will enter into the savings program. The perception-perfect strategy now requires that self 4 enroll into the default program if the following two conditions hold.

$$U_4(4) > U_4(5) \Leftrightarrow \beta v_4 - c_4(4) > \beta(v_5 - c_4(5)) \tag{5.27}$$

$$U_4(4) > U_4(6) \Leftrightarrow \beta v_4 - c_4(4) > \beta(v_6 - c_4(6)) \tag{5.28}$$

(5.27) implies that

$$\beta(9 - 4) - \theta - 2 > \beta(7 - \theta - 5). \tag{5.29}$$

(5.28) implies that

$$\beta(9 - 4) - \theta - 2 = \beta(7 - \theta - 6). \tag{5.30}$$

From (5.29), (5.30), the two critical conditions for self 4 to enter into the default program now are

$$(i)\ \theta < \frac{3\beta - 2}{1 - \beta}.\ (ii)\ \theta < \frac{4\beta - 2}{1 - \beta}. \tag{5.31}$$

Self 3 misperceives the conditions in (5.31) as

$$(i)\ \theta < \frac{1 - 3\epsilon}{\epsilon}.\ (ii)\ \theta < \frac{2 - 4\epsilon}{\epsilon}. \tag{5.32}$$

Since $0 < \epsilon < \frac{1}{3}$, condition (5.32) always holds. If, in addition, condition (5.23) holds (like self 4, self 3 also believes that (5.26) always holds), then self 3 believes that all future selves will enter into the default program. The pattern of recursion is now set. Self 3 will then enter into the default program if three conditions, analogous to (5.31) "jointly" hold. These are:

$$(i)\ \theta < \frac{3\beta - 2}{1 - \beta}.\ (ii)\ \theta < \frac{4\beta - 2}{1 - \beta}.\ (iii)\ \theta < \frac{5\beta - 2}{1 - \beta}. \tag{5.33}$$

If any of the conditions in (5.31) fails, then self 3 will prefer one of the future selves to enter into the savings program but choose not to enter into the program herself. Self 2 misperceives these conditions to be

$$(i) \ \theta < \frac{1 - 3\epsilon}{\epsilon}. \ (ii) \ \theta < \frac{2 - 4\epsilon}{\epsilon}. \ (iii) \ \theta < \frac{3 - 5\epsilon}{\epsilon}, \tag{5.34}$$

which hold because $0 < \epsilon < \frac{1}{3}$. If in addition, condition (5.23) holds then self 2 believes all future selves will enter into the default program. Self 2 will then enter into the default program if 4 conditions, analogous to (5.31) "jointly" hold. These are:

$$(i) \ \theta < \frac{3\beta - 2}{1 - \beta}. \ (ii) \ \theta < \frac{4\beta - 2}{1 - \beta}. \ (iii) \ \theta < \frac{5\beta - 2}{1 - \beta}. \ (iv) \ \theta < \frac{6\beta - 2}{1 - \beta}. \tag{5.35}$$

Self 1 misperceives these conditions to be

$$(i) \ \theta < \frac{1 - 3\epsilon}{\epsilon}. \ (ii) \ \theta < \frac{2 - 4\epsilon}{\epsilon}. \ (iii) \ \theta < \frac{3 - 5\epsilon}{\epsilon}. \ (iv) \ \theta < \frac{4 - 6\epsilon}{\epsilon}, \tag{5.36}$$

which hold true because $0 < \epsilon < \frac{1}{3}$. Self 1 will now enter into the default program if if the following 5 conditions "jointly" hold

$$(i) \ \theta < \frac{3\beta - 2}{1 - \beta}. \ (ii) \ \theta < \frac{4\beta - 2}{1 - \beta}. \ (iii) \ \theta < \frac{5\beta - 2}{1 - \beta}. \ (iv) \ \theta < \frac{6\beta - 2}{1 - \beta}. \ (v) \ \theta < \frac{7\beta - 2}{1 - \beta}. \tag{5.37}$$

The conditions in (5.25), (5.31), (5.33), (5.35), (5.37) jointly fail because $\beta < \frac{2}{3}$ and $\theta > 0$. However, each of the conditions in (5.26), (5.32), (5.34), (5.36) hold because $\epsilon > 0$ is infinitesimally small. Hence, each self believes that all future selves will enroll into the program. ∎

From Proposition 5.4, naifs procrastinate the most. For such individuals, compulsory deadlines could be effective.

Having established that a range of misperceptions about one's future self control problems might lead to different degrees of procrastination in enrolling into the savings plan, we now consider the empirical evidence next.

5.8.2 *Empirical results*

We now consider the empirical results in Blumenstock et al. (2018). A little over half, 51.7%, of the employees never changed their default savings plan (they could change their contributions between 0% − 10% at any time during the 6-month period). In particular, despite the availability of the matching contribution from their employer, 39% of the employees who were defaulted into the 0% savings plan, never actively chose to contribute a strictly positive amount. In effect, they left money on the table. Most of the voluntary changes in the contribution rates, away from the default option, occurred during the first three weeks of the 6-month study.

Defaults not only made a significant difference to contributions, the estimated effects of defaults are similar to those observed in data from Western subjects. For instance, those who participated in the 5% default savings plan were 40 percentage points more likely to make a positive savings contribution relative to those who participated in the 0% default plan. This increased their average monthly contributions by about 10% of the median monthly wage.

Matching employee contributions also had a significant effect on participation rate. In the three matching treatments with a match of 0%, 25%, and 50%, the respective participation rates were 1%, 27%, and 57%. Thus, savings respond to incentives. How effective are defaults relative to matching contributions in terms of participation rates? It turns out that the effects of defaults are equivalent to a matching contribution of 50%.

Once successfully defaulted into the savings program, employees exhibit longer-term effects. At the end of the 6 months, once the default option and the matching contribution rates are removed, employees were asked if they would like to contribute a portion of their future salary to the M-Pasandaz account. The desire to participate was stronger among those who participated in the earlier savings program at the 5% default rate, relative to the 0% default rate. Furthermore, 45% of those approached indicated a desire to participate despite there being no matching employer contributions. This suggests an explanation based on internalizing the self-control mechanism that such contributions are able to provide. When followed up two years later, the employees who had participated in the savings program reported greater financial security and higher savings. This is suggestive of the role of savings habits in influencing future savings choices.

What accounts for these empirical results? Two separate factors stand out—present bias and cognitive limitation. First, the authors separately elicit several measures of present bias based on both hypothetical and incentivized studies. Employees who exhibit greater present bias (lower values of β in the $(\beta, 1)$ framework) in these studies are also the ones who were more likely to stick to their default options. This probably arose because they procrastinated switching to another plan, particularly those employees who were defaulted into the 0% default plan. Second, of the several interventions that were used to encourage the take-up of default options, the most successful intervention consisted of clearly informing employees how much they would save under different actions. This is suggestive of cognitive limitations of employees in not being able to perform the relevant calculations in making their decisions. Other possible factors such as limited attention, employer endorsement effects, and salience effects can be ruled out by the construction of the experiments. Repeated text messages and other attempts to make default options salient, and text messages to make the savings program salient had no effect on participation. It was emphasized that the savings program does not carry employer endorsement and this understanding was successfully tested among the employees in follow up questions.

5.9 Behavioral public finance

In Section 3.9 we considered various aspects of behavioral public finance. In particular, following the work of Chetty et al. (2009) we outlined how issues of tax incidence and excess burden of taxation are modified in the presence of limited attention to non-salient taxes. In particular, all individuals are assumed to be homogenous with respect to their degree of limited attention. Taubinsky and Rees-Jones (2018) extend this framework to heterogeneity in limited attention among individuals. We give a heuristic discussion of their two main theoretical contributions below.

First, they show that a sorting property might be violated, which leads to even larger efficiency losses from taxation than are predicted by a model of homogenous individuals. When individuals are homogenous, following a change in sales tax, and in the presence of limited attention, it is still the case that individuals who value a good higher, also consume the good. This monotonicity property might break down in the presence of heterogeneity. Suppose that two individuals,

1 and 2, have unit demands for a good whose price is p, and the ad-valorem sales tax is τ.[6] The valuations of individuals 1 and 2, respectively, for the good are v_1, v_2 and $0 < v_1 < v_2$. Suppose that individual 2 pays attention to the tax but individual 1 does not. Then we could have the case $v_2 - p(1 + \tau) < 0$ and $v_1 - p > 0$. In this case, individual 1 who has a lower valuation wishes to consume the good but individual 2 does not. This breaks the efficient sorting property that arises in the case of homogenous individuals.

Second, they argue that an increase in taxes makes taxes more salient. Continuing the previous example, if the tax rate increases to $t > \tau$, it is possible that both individuals pay attention to taxes. The excess burden of taxes increases with the square of the tax rate (see for example (3.56)). However, for individual 2, the increase in tax is not $t - \tau$ but rather $t - 0$ because τ was not salient. Since $t > t - \tau$ the change in the excess burden of taxes is increasing in t^2 and not $(t - \tau)^2$, which gives rise to a larger deadweight loss of taxation.

Conducting an online experiment with sales taxes for US consumers, the authors show that: (1) For low levels of taxes, on average, consumers treat the tax only worth 25% of what it actually is. However, when the tax is tripled, consumer attention to the tax increases and they treat the tax as if it were 50% of what it actually is. (2) Heterogeneity in consumer attention leads to efficiency costs of taxation that are 200% higher.

Alcott et al. (2019a) consider the welfare effects of a tax on sugary drinks, a form of *sin taxes* (see Volume 3). We outline below the simpler exposition in Alcott et al. (2019b). Taxes on sugary drinks are widespread; Table 2 in Alcott et al. (2019b) lists 39 countries that subscribe to such a tax. While increased public campaigns have been successful in reducing the consumption of sugary drinks, there is a concern with the potentially regressive nature of such sin taxes because sugary drinks are disproportionately consumed by the poor. In the US, data for the period 2009–16 shows that households whose annual income is lower than $25,000 consume 200 calories/day from sugary drinks, but households above $75,000 consume 117 calories/day from these drinks. The US dietary guidelines recommend not consuming more than 10% of calories from sugars in all food and drinks (not just sugary drinks alone). By contrast, Americans, on average, take about 7% of their calories from sugary drinks alone, which is 3–4 times higher than the world average. This is likely to contribute to three major health issues: weight gain, type 2 diabetes, and cardiovascular disease. Hence, this is a relatively serious problem.

We consider below the welfare effects of consuming sugary drinks in terms of *externalities* (increased cost on the health care system), and *internalities* (the negative effect on one's own future health). By contrast, the classical analysis focuses only on externalities. Figure 5.4 shows the demand and supply curves in a competitive market for sugary drinks. S_1 is the pre-tax supply curve and D_P is the (observed) private demand curve that captures the marginal private benefit from having an extra sugary drink. Suppose that the average monetary value of the per unit externality created on others from sugary drinks is $e > 0$ (assumed constant for all levels of demand, but this is only for simplicity). Moving D_P downwards by e units results in the curve D_S, which captures the social marginal benefit. Suppose that the government now levies a specific tax at the rate $t > 0$ on sugary drinks. This is equivalent to an increase in the marginal cost of the perfectly competitive firm. The post-tax supply curve is shown by S_2. The pre-tax price quantity

---

[6] Here we focus only on taxes in reducing consumption of, say, sugary drinks. However, there are other methods that also work. For instance, a nudge at MacDonald's that moved Coca-Cola to the last position on the menu screen and Zero-Coke to the third position, reduced consumption of Coca-Cola at the expense of Zero-Coke (Schmidtke et al., 2019).

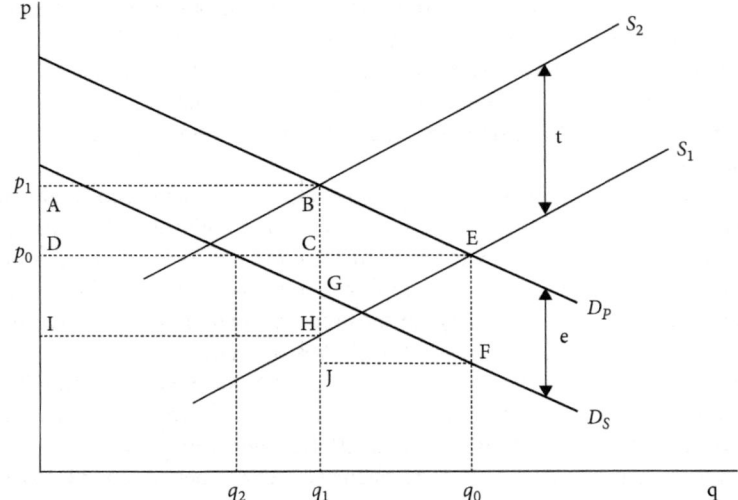

Figure 5.4 Social costs and benefits of a tax in the presence of externalities.

pair is (p_0, q_0) and the post-tax price quantity pair is (p_1, q_1). Notice that the price does not go up by the full amount of the tax. The tax burden is shared between the producers and the consumers.

The tax has the following effects on consumer welfare; competitive firms make zero profits, so we abstract from a consideration of producer welfare. Relative to the pre-tax equilibrium (p_0, q_0), the consumer surplus from sugary drinks falls by the area ABED at the post-tax equilibrium (p_1, q_1). The area ABCD (which formed a part of the pre-tax consumer surplus) is transferred from the consumers to the government as tax revenues. The area DCHI is transferred from the producers to the government as tax revenues. Thus, total tax revenues transferred to the government equal the area ABHI.

The triangular area BEC is the traditional measure of the deadweight loss of tax—it is a reduction in consumer surplus that is not offset by any additional government tax revenues. However, note that at the pretax equilibrium, (p_0, q_0), and for the quantity $q_0 - q_1$, the net social cost (externality) on consumers who do not consume the sugary drink is

$$\int_{q_1}^{q_0} [D_S - D_P]\, dq = e(q_0 - q_1) = area\ \text{BEFG}$$

$$= area\ \text{CEFG} + area\ \text{BEC}.$$

Let us assume that the externality reduction $e_0(q_0 - q_1)$ translates into an equivalent increase in government revenue (perhaps on account of reduced public health costs for those who are afflicted by health problems from sugary drinks). To this, if we add the tax revenues from the consumers to the government tq_1, then the total extra monetary transfer from the consumers to the government equals

area ABCD + *area* CEFG + *area* BEC.

Thus, in addition to the classical deadweight loss from taxes, area BCE, we have a 'deadweight gain' from taxes, *area* CEFG +*area* BEC. The net deadweight gain is the *area* CEFG. We have argued above that this area corresponds to a monetary gain for the government. In order to evaluate this gain, we need to evaluate the marginal loss of a dollar from a consumer against the marginal gain of a dollar by the government. The answer depends on the social weight that we put on different individuals. If the money flows mainly from poorer individuals who disproportionately consume sugary drinks, then the social value of a dollar is likely to be lower. This would scale down the sum of areas CEFG and BEC.

The sum of areas CEFG and BEC depends on three main factors. First, if the average elasticity of demand is higher, then the term $q_0 - q_1$ is higher. Second, if the average externality is high, then the term e is high. Both these factors increase $e(q_0 - q_1) \equiv area$ BEFG. Third, if there is a high covariance between those who create a greater externality and those who reduce their demand the most following an increase in tax, then the social benefits of a tax are higher.

As noted above, a distinguishing feature of the consumption of sugary drinks is that it creates internalities on those consuming it. There are no internalities in Figure 5.4. To take account of internalities, we could draw a figure similar to Figure 5.4 but reinterpret the per unit externality e, as an internality, i, which need not be the same as e. In this redrawn figure, the area BEFG may be considered as a gain to one's own future selves. It can, of course, offset future health costs and a monetary value imputed to it (as was the case with externalities). However, since it is the poorer individuals who disproportionately consume sugary drinks, this reduces the regressivity of the tax on sugary drinks. Furthermore, if the tax revenues that are collected by the government are earmarked to benefit poorer individuals more, then the regressivity argument against taxes on sugary drinks might be weakened further. Finally, as noted in Figure 5.4, the burden of taxation is shared by producers and consumers. Insofar as producers share a larger burden (which depends on the relative elasticities of the demand and the supply curves), and the consumption of sugary drinks is disproportionately geared towards the poor whose tax dollars have greater social value, this reduces the welfare costs of the tax.

5.10 Some fundamental issues in behavioral welfare economics

In an important critique of behavioral welfare economics, Sugden (2017, 2018) and Infante et al. (2016), which has Sugden as one of the co-authors, raise foundational issues in behavioral welfare economics. Infante et al. (2016) argue that a significant part of the modern literature on behavioral welfare economics presupposes the following imaginary construct.[7] An individual acts as if he/she had a dual self which is characterized by an inner, unobserved, *rational self*, and an outer, observed, *psychological self*. The rational self is taken to have well defined and consistent preferences that are context/frame independent; such preferences may be termed as *latent preferences* in contrast to the *psychological preferences* of the psychological self.

The rational self might be taken to be similar to an economic agent in a neoclassical economics course. The psychological self, on the other hand, acts in the manner of a typical economic agent in a course in behavioral economics, so it may have context/frame dependent preferences

---

[7] Included in this modern literature are a range of papers, many of which we have reviewed in this book volume (Bernheim and Rangel, 2007, 2009; Köszegi and Rabin, 2007, 2008b; Salant and Rubinstein, 2008; Bordalo et al., 2013; Bleichrodt et al., 2001; Li et al., 2011). Also included in this list would be some of the papers that were published subsequently (Bernheim et al., 2015; Bernheim, 2016; Bernheim and Taubinsky, 2018; Benkert and Netzer, 2018).

and exhibit biases relative to the neoclassical benchmark (or what we have described as the *Bayesian rationality benchmark* in Volume 5). The challenge, and the agenda in this behavioral welfare economics literature, is to recover the unobserved underlying latent preferences and base normative analysis on such preferences. The difference in the behavior of the rational self and the psychological self is then ascribed to mistakes and errors. Psychological preferences, thus, need to be purified of these mistakes for welfare analysis; this the authors term as the *preference purification agenda*.

As an illustration of how one may 'interpret' a rational self and a psychological self, explicitly or implicitly, in much of the literature that uses revealed preference arguments in modern behavioral welfare economics, consider some examples. We note that the original models are not necessarily couched in the language of a rational self and a psychological self.

1. Consider the discussion of Bernheim and Rangel (2007, 2009) in Section 3.6. Individuals choose from a set of objects and face a set of framing and context factors (ancillary conditions). Together, the objects and the ancillary conditions constitute a generalized choice situation, GCS. For instance, in the cafeteria problem (Example 3.1 in Chapter 3), the food items and a particular display of the food objects (ancillary condition), together constitute one GCS. Roughly speaking, a social planner then respects the individual's revealed preferences if these are not influenced by the ancillary conditions. In a stronger form of their criterion, the authors propose to eliminate the problematic GCSs where the individual's choices are influenced by ancillary conditions. One can now use the data, purified of behavioral anomalies, and then the use of revealed preference over the purified data is postulated to be the normative object of interest for a social planner. In particular, the purified data is context independent. The purified data may be taken to be the latent preferences and the raw data may be taken to be the psychological preferences.

2. Consider the model of Bordalo et al. (2013). Here choices are made over goods that are represented by bundles of characteristics or attributes. The rational self maximizes a utility function that linearly weights these attributes. However, the psychological self may be hampered by limited attention and give disproportionate weight to those attributes that are more salient, i.e., stand out from the average attributes in the set. For this reason, the psychological self maximizes a salience weighted non-linear set of attributes. Further assumptions in the paper ensure that with the accumulation of sufficient data, the underlying latent preferences can be recovered.

3. Bleichrodt et al. (2001) and Li et al. (2014) postulate that the underlying latent preferences are consistent with expected utility theory and the psychological preferences reflect prospect theory preferences. The authors suggest recovering the underlying latent preferences by conducting face to face interviews with individuals and confronting them with choices that are inconsistent with their latent preferences. Köszegi and Rabin (2007, 2008) postulate that under risk, the rational self prefers more money to less and a higher probability of winning a higher prize to a lower probability. If the individual choices are consistent with these postulates, then the data is acceptable for welfare analysis. If the individual acts in a manner that is inconsistent with these postulates (psychological self), say, on account of a gambler's fallacy (see Section 3.5 in Chapter 3), then the beliefs of the individual can be purified by calculating individual choices if the postulates had been respected.

The assumption that there exists such a dual model in which the rational self conforms to the axioms of neoclassical economic theory is directly non-falsifiable. The behavior of the rational self is certainly not observable, separate from the behavior of the psychological self. There is also no presumption that, if the rational self corresponds in some sense to System 2 (see Volume 5 for the System 1 and System 2 distinction), then evolution would have shaped it to conform to the axioms of neoclassical economic theory. What if a rational self does exist but acts as if it were context dependent, or indeed possessed some of the same psychological features that characterize the psychological self? This would make it difficult, if not impossible, to sustain many of the conclusions of behavioral economic theory that depends on these assumptions.

It is worth noting that the arguments above, for or against a dual model, do not refute arguments for paternalism. Indeed, Sugden (2017) is careful to state this point. He contests, however, one of the key assertions in the work of Thaler and Sunstein (2009) that we have outlined in Section 3.3.1 in Chapter 3, namely, the *informed desire criterion*. Essentially, this refers to the aim of nudges to make people better off *as judged by themselves*, and not as judged by someone else, say, the choice architect who designs the nudges. Sugden interprets this as another example of the dual model (although this is not how Thaler and Sunstein frame their discussion). Namely, that the psychological self makes errors or mistakes due to, say, cognitive load; or has limited attention; or exhibits present biased preferences. Cleverly designed nudges then allow the rational self to eliminate or minimize the biases of the psychological self (such as those listed above, or any additional biases that could be added to the list). In this sense, the rational self is better off after the nudge, *as judged by the rational self*.

If, however, the dual framework based on rational and psychological selves is suspect, or lacks adequate foundations, as argued above, then, argues Sugden (2017), the "as judged by themselves to be in their best interests" criterion cannot be defended. Consider, for instance, Bill, who eats unhealthily and is obese but he suffers no symptoms of ill health. However, he could suffer a future heart attack and over the years he must have been exposed to public information that warned of the potential consequences. Yet he continues to eat unhealthily. In the framework suggested above, his behavior would be termed as an error or mistake. He is nudged to eat healthily and complies. Should we now infer that he took the action as "judged to be in his best interest" given that he has not had a heart attack yet? It might be so, but it is unclear if such an inference by an outside observer is watertight. This is the crux of the criticism raised by Sugden. Notice that this criticism does not question the paternalism implicit in offering a nudge to improve health in the first place.

Sunstein (2018) replied to this criticism, which elicited a reply from Sugden (2018). Our own reading of the evidence and this debate is as follows.

Nudges are often provided in cases where the underlying preferences are not context dependent. However, the individual might suffer from limited attention or procrastinate. In these cases, nudges in the form of reminders, text messages, or information disclosure may actually help the individual to take an appropriate action. Thus, one may legitimately argue that it is acceptable for an outside observer to infer that individuals take an action as judged to be in their best interests. Consider the following three examples from Sunstein (2018, pp. 3–4) where this is indeed the case.

1. Luke has heart disease, and he needs to take various medications. He wants to do so, but he is sometimes forgetful. His doctor sends him periodic text messages. As a result, he takes the medications. He is very glad to receive those messages.
2. Meredith has a mild weight problem. She is aware of that fact, and while she does not suffer from serious issues of self-control, and does not want to stop eating the foods that she enjoys, she does seek to lose weight. Because of a new law, many restaurants in her

city have clear calorie labels, informing her of the caloric content of various options. As a result, she sometimes chooses low-calorie offerings—which she would not do if she were not informed. She is losing weight. She is very glad to see those calorie labels.

3. Edna is a professor at a large university, which has long offered its employees the option to sign up for a retirement plan. Edna believes that signing up would be a terrific idea, but she has not gotten around to it. She is somewhat embarrassed about that. Last year, the university switched to an automatic enrollment plan, by which employees are defaulted into the university's plan. They are allowed to opt out, but Edna does not. She is very glad that she has been automatically enrolled in the plan.

Examples where there are no clear ex-ante latent preferences, or possibly even no latent preferences at all, are more problematic. In this case, one needs to make a distinction between an ex-ante and an ex-post evaluation of welfare. Consider two examples of this case from Sunstein (2018).

1. Thomas has a serious illness. The question is whether he should have an operation, which is accompanied by potential benefits and potential risks. Reading about the operation online, Thomas is not sure whether he should go ahead with it. Thomas' doctor advises him to have the operation, emphasizing how much he has to lose if he does not. He decides to follow the advice. In a parallel world (a lot like ours, but not quite identical), Thomas's doctor advises him not to have the operation, emphasizing how much he has to lose if he does. He decides to follow the advice.

2. George cares about the environment, but he also cares about money. He currently receives his electricity from coal; he knows that coal is not exactly good for the environment, but it is cheap, and he does not bother to switch to wind, which would be slightly more expensive. He is quite content with the current situation. Last month, his government imposed an automatic enrollment rule on electricity providers: People will receive energy from wind, and pay a slight premium, unless they choose to switch. George does not bother to switch. He says that he likes the current situation of automatic enrollment. He approves of the policy and he approves of his own enrollment.

Consider first the case of Thomas. He appears to have no latent preferences. In two different contexts, he follows the opposite advice. Furthermore, suppose that Thomas accepts the advice to have an operation but on the way to the operation theater, he is offered the contrary advice. What if he now accepts the contrary advice? This makes it difficult to accept the argument that there is an underlying rational self that has context independent preferences. It is quite likely that Thomas is happy ex-post with each of the two decisions. In these cases, particularly when there are no latent preferences, it is tempting to argue that nudges help to construct one's preferences. Indeed, one's own latent preferences might change in the presence of the information provided by the nudge, and one's experiences after the decisions to accept the nudge. George, in contrast to Thomas, could be construed to have either a latent preference for the environment relative to saving money, or the other way around.

An important question is which of the relevant nudges to choose in these cases, particularly in the case of Thomas. This is a difficult question and in this case the informed consent criterion has little bite. There is no reason why behavioral economics should restrict itself to criteria that are based on narrowly defined individual interests rather than broader societal goals. For instance, the human race has an obligation to save the planet and climate change is one of the topical and important human concerns. Suppose that it is somehow revealed that George's latent preference is money over the environment; in this case, there is a conflict between individual preferences and social preferences. From a societal point of view it is clear which nudge ought to be given in this case. However, this argument invokes a stronger form of paternalism that goes beyond nudges. We have already noted that there might be no getting away from stronger forms of paternalism and soft paternalism has limitations of scope in certain situations (as correctly noted in some of Sugden's concerns).

The 'as judged best for themselves' criterion has greater bite in an ex-post sense in some cases. If individuals who are given an opportunity to be voluntarily nudged, choose a nudge, and report ex-post satisfaction with their choice, then they could be said to have made a choice as judged best for themselves. After all, they could have chosen not to follow the nudge (this is built into the 'liberalism' feature of nudges). In all the examples above, except for Thomas's, the individual is satisfied, or not, for a unique action. However, Thomas is likely to report being satisfied with both options, ex-post. The fact that the ex-post action that is judged to be in Thomas's best interest, as judged by him, is not unique appears no more serious than many cases where one has multiple equilibria in economics. Should an ex-post criterion be used, then behavioral economics has to be prepared to live with this possibility. Prior to introducing a nudge, policymakers might have informed guesses, but no more, of what percentage of the population will accept the nudges and be happy with their choice. Perhaps pilot experiments and other social goals may guide their intuition further.

Nudges play a powerful role when individuals are subjected to self control problems, as in default options. Sugden's (2017) views are that the domain of such problems is narrow. Sunstein's (2018) offers the uncontroversial view that the narrowness of domains is an empirical question. He also reports preliminary research that suggests that this is an important domain. Sunstein et al. (2019) find strong majority support for 15 nudges in 5 countries (Belgium, Denmark, Germany South Korea, and the US). Support for the nudges was correlated with trust in public institutions. Several of these nudges arguably influence decisions in the presence of procrastination. Admittingly this is indirect evidence, and more direct lab evidence that takes account of the degree of present-bias in preferences and one's degree of awareness of such bias will add usefully to the evidence base.

5.11 Some new findings in neuroeconomics

As noted in the introduction to Chapter 4, the scope of our discussion on neuroeconomics is limited to only selected aspects. For this reason, our discussion in this section is relatively brief. Several informative and useful surveys have appeared in recent years in the area of neuroeconomics that we refer the interested reader to. In a review essay, Camerer and Mobbs (2017) survey the existing evidence to argue that real and hypothetical rewards in experiments have different effects. (1) The intensity of neural activation differs. (2) Different neural circuits might be activated in both cases. While the evidence is not always conclusive, this suggests that subjects in experiments should receive real rewards, as far as possible. For a review essay on social neuroeconomics (the intersection of social psychology and neuroscience) with potential applications for economics, see Alós-Ferrer (2018). For an accessible survey of the literature on the neuroeconomics of financial decision making that covers the neural correlates of many of the empirical findings in Chapter 3 of Volume 6 (Behavioral Finance), see Frydman and Camerer (2016b). For a general survey of neuroeconomics, see Serra (2019). Nave et al. (2015) survey the evidence on the positive link between the neuropeptide oxytocin (OT) and trust and conclude

(p. 772) that "the cumulative evidence does not provide robust convergent evidence that human trust is reliably associated with OT."

Regret has been invoked in several applications in finance. This includes two effects that we have already considered in Volume 6. (i) Individuals may not be willing to sell an asset that is currently priced below the purchase price to avoid regret (*disposition effect* in Shefrin and Statman, 1984). (ii) Narrow framing of options in which the outcomes of current financial decisions are not integrated with the returns from other assets does not provide a risk hedging role and may lead to regret (Barberis et al., 2006). There is a third effect that we have not yet mentioned in the book. (iii) Suppose that an investor has sold a stock, then the probability of repurchasing it is lower if the current price is higher in order to avoid the regret from selling it too early (*repurchase effect* in Strahilevitz et al., 2011).

In an exemplary contribution that illustrates the power and usefulness of neuroeconomics, Frydman and Camerer (2016a) study the role of regret in making alternative choices. Regret may be defined as the foregone utility, or negative hedonic utility, that arises from comparing the foregone payoff from an alternative action with the current payoff. This requires measuring an individual's neural activity exactly at the point where the current payoff is realized. The authors do this through fMRI data, and using this as their measure of regret they successfully predict an individual's subsequent trading behavior.

Subjects in the experiment are given an initial endowment of $350 and must initially buy 1 unit each of three stocks, each costing $100. The subjects then make asset purchase/sale decisions over two sessions, where each session has 108 trials indexed by t. For $t \leq 9$, individuals cannot trade but can see the price of stocks being updated in each trial to get an idea of how prices evolve. For trials $t > 9$, each trial has two stages, a (i) price update stage (price of one of the 3 shares, randomly chosen, is updated by choosing a random price increment, positive or negative, from the set $\{5, 10, 15\}$), and (ii) a trading decision stage in which one of the three stocks is chosen at random, and subjects can choose to buy/sell that stock. The buy/sell decision can take one of two forms. Either the subject can sell a unit of stock, if he has it; or he can buy a unit, if he does not have it. Thus, short selling is not allowed.

The price of stocks is governed by an underlying Markov process that has two states—a good state and a bad state. The stock returns are positively autocorrelated. The initial state, good or bad, is randomly chosen. In any trial t, the stock whose price is chosen to be randomly updated stays in the same state as it was in trial $t - 1$ with probability 0.8, and switches state with probability 0.2. Thus, if prices are high (low) they are very likely to stay high (low). The prices of other stocks do not change at t. All participants are provided this information.

Consider the following two scenarios.

(i) Scenario 1: Following the sale of an asset, suppose that the price of a stock has increased recently, then because it is likely to increase in price in the future (positive autocorrelation) it is likely to lead to capital gain.

(ii) Scenario 2: Following the sale of an asset, suppose that the price of a stock has decreased recently, then it is likely to decrease in price in the future (positive autocorrelation) so it is likely to lead to capital loss.

A Bayesian investor is likely to repurchase the asset in Scenario 1 and unlikely to repurchase in Scenario 2. Now consider a subject who is subject to the repurchase effect. In Scenario 1, buying an asset at a higher price might lead to regret from thinking about the alternative strategy of not selling the asset in the past. Such an individual is less likely to repurchase the asset in order to avoid regret. In Scenario 2, the subject is likely to feel elation (the opposite of regret) from buying the asset at a lower price. Hence, he is more likely to repurchase it. Thus, the predictions for a

Bayesian investor and one who is subject to the repurchase effect are opposite in each scenario, and this can be tested.

The empirical findings are as follows.

1. Relative to a Bayesian investor, 92% of the subjects exhibit a repurchase effect (i.e., over and above what would be observed following the optimal investment strategy of a Bayesian investor).

2. In Scenario 1, the neural activity of subjects is consistent with feelings of regret. In each scenario, the signal of a price change alters the present value of utility from investing in the asset. This is termed as *reward prediction error* (RPE) in the neuroeconomics literature. The ventral striatum, a part of the basal ganglia, has been implicated in the operation of RPE by past research. The authors hypothesize that in Scenario 1, the news of a price increase generates a RPE that reflects the regret from selling the stock too early. The fMRI activity in the ventral striatum is consistent with the repurchase effect. As price increases, the regret from buying the asset also increases, reducing the RPE, hence, reducing the activity in the ventral striatum. The vmPFC has been shown to encode decision values, or the subjective expected utility from repurchasing the stock. An individual who is subject to the repurchase effect should experience a fall in the decision value in Scenario 1, and hence is predicted to show lower vmPFC activity. This too is confirmed by the fMRI data.

3. Those subjects who exhibit greater regret-consistent neural activity following Scenario 1, also exhibit a greater repurchase effect. Thus, the regret signal helps to explain the between-subjects trading behavior. This evidence, coupled with the evidence in Chapter 4, is important to counter the accusation that neuroeconomics does not provide us with causal factors that can influence economic decisions (notice that the signal is measured first, followed by observations on trading activity).

4. Subjects who exhibit a greater repurchase effect also exhibit a greater disposition effect. These two departures from Bayesian rationality are thus likely to be governed by similar psychological mechanisms.

Brunnlieb et al. (2016) considers the effects on human cooperation of the neuropeptide, arginine vasopressin (AVP), which is a neurotransmitter and a hormone. It has been shown to influence several brain regions (PFC, amygdala, hippocampus) and it also interacts with the brain's reward circuits. Based on existing research, the authors conjecture that AVP levels influence the degree of cooperation. The authors consider the following two-player stag-hunt game, where $S > 0$.

	Stag	Rabbit
Stag	$200, 200$	$0, S$
Rabbit	$S, 0$	$160, 160$

The two pure strategy Nash equilibria are where both players play either Stag or Rabbit. Both play Stag is the Pareto dominant and the *payoff dominant equilibria* and both play Rabbit is the *risk dominant equilibrium*; see Appendix A in Volume 4 for an explanation of these terms. Intuitively speaking, playing Stag gives high payoffs if the opponent also plays Stag, but it is risky if the opponent plays Rabbit. However, playing Rabbit is less risky. The payoff S is varied and the percentage of players who play the two strategies is observed. Individuals in one treatment are administered a dose of AVP, and those in the control treatment are administered a placebo. As S increases, the percentage of players who play Rabbit increases, as expected, in both treatments (the safe strategy becomes safer). However, the percentage who play Rabbit is significantly higher for the control group at each level of S. AVP administered subjects are more likely to play Stag at each level of S. These results are robust to controlling for social preferences and moods.

The beta-blocker *propranolol* diminishes the amygdala's influence, which has been implicated in loss aversion. Sokol-Hessner et al. (2015) find that propranolol reduces loss aversion in a baseline treatment (that depends on the initial level of loss aversion). Furthermore, the effect is dose dependent in that, other things constant, smaller individuals (lower BMI) are more effected relative to larger individuals (higher BMI). Importantly, they find that there was no effect of propranolol on risk aversion or on choice consistency.

REFERENCES FOR PART IV

Allcott, H. (2011). Social norms and energy conservation. *Journal of Public Economics* 95(9–10): 1082–95.

Allcott, H., and Kessler, J. B. (2019). The welfare effects of nudges: a case study of energy use social comparisons. *American Economic Journal: Applied Economics* 11 (1): 236–76.

Allcott, H. Lockwood, B. B., and Taubinsky, D. (2019a). Regressive sin taxes, with an application to the optimal soda tax. *Quarterly Journal of Economics* 134(3): 1557–1626.

Allcott, H., Lockwood, B. B., and Taubinsky, D. (2019b). Should we tax soda? An overview of theory and evidence. *Journal of Economic Perspectives* 33 (3): 202–27.

Alós-Ferrer, C. (2018). A review essay on social neuroscience: can research on the social brain and economics inform each other? *Journal of Economic Literature* 56(1): 234–64.

Altmann, S., Falk, A., Heidhues, P., Jayaraman, R. and Teirlinck, M. (2018). Defaults and donations: evidence from a field experiment. *Review of Economics and Statistics* 101(5): 1–15.

Altmann, S. and Traxler, C. (2014). Nudges at the dentist. *European Economic Review* 72(C): 19–38.

Ariely, D., and Wertenbroch, K. (2002). Procrastination, deadlines, and performance: self-control by precommitment. *Psychological Science* 13(3): 219–24.

Ashraf, N., Karlan, D., and Yin, W. (2006). Tying Odysseus to the mast: evidence from a commitment savings product in the Philippines. *Quarterly Journal of Economics* 121(2): 635–72.

Augenblick, N., Niederle, M. and Sprenger, C. (2015). Working over time: dynamic inconsistency in real effort tasks. *The Quarterly Journal of Economics*, 130(3): 1067–115.

Augenblick, N. and Rabin, M. (2019). An experiment on time preference and misprediction in unpleasant tasks. *The Review of Economic Studies* 86(3): 941–75.

Barberis, N., Huang, M. and Thaler, R. (2006). Individual preferences, monetary gambles, and stock market participation: a case for narrow framing. *American Economic Review* 96(4): 1069–90.

Benkert, J.-M. and Netzer, N. (2018). Informational requirements of nudging. *Journal of Political Economy* 126(6): 2323–55.

Bernheim, B. D. (2016). The good, the bad, and the ugly: a unified approach to behavioral welfare economics. *Journal of Benefit Cost Analysis* 7(1): 12–68.

Bernheim, B. D., Fradkin, A., and Popov, I. (2015). The welfare economics of default options in 401 (k) plans. *American Economic Review* 105(9): 2798–837.

Bernheim, B. D. and Rangel, A. (2007). Toward choice-theoretic foundations for behavioral welfare economics. *American Economic Review Papers and Proceedings* 97: 464–70.

Bernheim, B. D. and Rangel, A. (2009). Beyond revealed preference: choice theoretic foundations for behavioral welfare economics. *The Quarterly Journal of Economics* 124(1): 51–104.

Bernheim, B. D. and Taubinsky, D. (2018) Behavioral public economics. *NBER Working Paper* No. 24828.

Bhargava, S., Manoli, D. (2015). Psychological frictions and the incomplete take-up of social benefits: evidence from an IRS field experiment. *American Economic Review* 105(11): 3489–529.

Bleichrodt, H., Pinto, J.-L., & Wakker, P. (2001). Making descriptive use of prospect theory to improve the prescriptive use of expected utility. *Management Science* 47(11): 1498–1514.

Blumenstock, J., Callen, M., and Ghani, T. (2018). Why do defaults affect behavior? Experimental evidence from Afghanistan. *American Economic Review* 108(10): 2868–901.

Bordalo, P., Gennaioli, N., and Shleifer, A. (2013). Salience and consumer choice. *Journal of Political Economy* 121(5): 803–43.

Brownell, K. D., Kersh, R., Ludwig, D. S., Post, R. C., Puhl, R. M., Schwartz, M. B., and Willett, W. C. (2010). Personal responsibility and obesity: a constructive approach to a controversial issue. *Health Affairs* 29(3): 379–87.

Brunnlieb, C., Nave, G., Camerer, C. F., Schosser, S., Vogt, B., Münte, T. F., and Heldmann, M. (2016). Vasopressin increases cooperative behavior. *Proceedings of the National Academy of Sciences* 113(8): 2051–6.

Busse, M. R., Pope, D. G., Pope, J. C., and Silva-Risso, J. (2015). The psychological effect of weather on car purchases. *The Quarterly Journal of Economics* 130(1): 371–414.

Calzolari, G. and Nardotto, M. (2017). Effective reminders. *Management Science* 63(9): 2915–32.

Camerer, C. and Mobbs, D. (2017) Differences in behavior and brain activity during hypothetical and real choices. *Trends in Cognitive Sciences* 21(1): 46–56.

Carroll, G. D., Choi, J. J., Laibson, D., Madrian, B. C., and Metrick, A. (2009). Optimal defaults and active decisions. *Quarterly Journal of Economics* 124(4): 1639–74.

Casaburi, L. and Macchiavello, R. (2019). Demand and supply of infrequent payments as a commitment device: evidence from Kenya. *American Economic Review* 109(2): 523–55.

Chang, T. Y., Huang, W., and Wang, Y. (2018). Something in the air: pollution and the demand for health insurance. *The Review of Economic Studies* 85(3): 1609–34.

Chetty, R., Looney, A., and Kroft, K. (2009). Salience and taxation: theory and evidence. *American Economic Review* 99(4): 1145–77.

Cornwell, J. F. and Krantz, D. H. (2014). Public policy for thee, but not for me: varying the grammatical person of public policy justifications influences their support. *Judgment and Decision Making* 9(5): 433–44.

Costa, D. L. and Kahn, E. (2013). Do liberal home owners consume less electricity? A test of the voluntary restraint hypothesis. *Journal of the European Economic Association* 11(3): 680–702.

Cronqvist, H., Thaler, R. H., and Yu, F. (2018). When nudges are forever: inertia in the Swedish Premium Pension Plan. *American Economic Association Papers and Proceedings* 108: 153–8.

Cutler, D. M., Glaeser, E. L., and Shapiro, J. M. (2003). Why have Americans become more obese? *The Journal of Economic Perspectives* 17(3): 93–118.

Czap, N. V., Czap, H. J., Khachaturyan, M., and Burbach, M. E. (2018). Conforming to or defying gender stereotypes? Empathy nudging vs. financial incentives in environmental context. Papers in Natural Resources. 981. University of Nebraska-Lincoln. https://digitalcommons.unl.edu/natrespapers/981.

Damgaard, M. T. and Gravert, C. (2018). The hidden costs of nudging: experimental evidence from reminders in fundraising. *Journal of Public Economics* 157: 15–26.

Davis, M. H. (1983). A multidimensional approach to individual differences in empathy. *Journal of Personality and Social Psychology* 44(1): 113–26.

Delmas, M. A., Fischlein, M., and Asensio, O. I. (2013). Information strategies and energy conservation behavior: a meta-analysis of experimental studies from 1975 to 2012. *Energy Policy* 61(C): 729–39.

Dhami, S. (2016). *The Foundations of Behavioral Economic Analysis*. Oxford: Oxford University Press.

Fiala, L. and Noussair, C. (2017). Charitable giving, emotions, and the default effect. *Economic Inquiry* 55 (4):1792–1812.

Frydman, C. and Camerer, C. F. (2016a). Neural evidence of regret and its implications for investor behavior. *Review of Financial Studies* 29(11): 3108–39.

Frydman, C. and Camerer, C. F. (2016b). The psychology and neuroscience of financial decision making. *Trends in Cognitive Sciences* 20(9), 661–75.

Fudenberg, D. and Levine, D. K. (2012). Timing and self-control. *Econometrica* 80, 1–42.

Giné, X., Karlan, D., and Zinman, J. (2010). Put your money where your butt is: a commitment contract for smoking cessation. *American Economic Journal: Applied Economics* 2(4): 213–35.

Glaeser, E. L. (2006). Paternalism and psychology. *University of Chicago Law Review* 73(1): 133–56.

Goldstein, N. J., Cialdini, R. B., and Griskevicius, V. (2008). A room with a viewpoint: using social norms to motivate environmental conservation in hotels. *Journal of Consumer Research* 35(3), 472–82.

Goswami, I. and Urminsky, O. (2016). When should the ask be a nudge? The effect of default amounts on charitable donations. *Journal of Marketing Research* 53(5): 829–46.

Gul, F. and Pesendorfer, W. (2001). Temptation and self-control. *Econometrica* 69(6): 1403–36.

Hagmann, D., Ho, E. H., and Loewenstein, G. (2019). Nudging out support for a carbon tax. *Nature Climate Change* 9: 484–9.

Hagman, W., Andersson, D., Västfjäll, D., and Tinghög, G. (2015). Public views on policies involving nudges. *Review of Philosophy and Psychology* 6(3): 439–53.

Hanks, A. S., Just, D. R., and Wansink, B. (2013). Preordering school lunch encourages better food choices by children. *Journal of the American Medical Association Pediatrics* 167(7): 673–4.

Hedlin, S. and Sunstein, C. (2016) Does active choosing promote green energy use? Experimental evidence. *Ecology Law Quarterly* 43(1): 107–41.

Himmler, O., Jäckle, R., and Weinschenk, P. (2019). Soft commitments, reminders, and academic performance. *American Economic Journal: Applied Economics* 11(2): 114–42.

Hong, S.-M. and Page, S. (1989). A psychological reactance scale: development, factor structure and reliability. *Psychological Reports* 64(3, Pt 2): 1323–6.

Houser, D., Schunk, D., Winter, J. K., and Xiao, E. (2018). Temptation and commitment in the laboratory. *Games and Economic Behavior* 107: 329–44.

Huck, S. and Rasul, I. (2010). Transaction costs in charitable giving. *B.E. Journal of Economic Analysis and Policy* 10(1): 31.

Infante, G., Lecouteux, G., and Sugden, R. (2016). Preference purification and the inner rational agent: a critique of the conventional wisdom of behavioural welfare economics. *Journal of Economic Methodology* 23(1): 1–25.

John, A. (2019). When commitment fails: evidence from a field experiment. Forthcoming *Management Science*. https://doi.org/10.1287/mnsc.2018.3236.

Jung, J. Y. and Mellers, B. A. (2016). American attitudes toward nudges. *Judgment and Decision making* 11(1): 62–74.

Kahan, D. M., Braman, D., Slovic, P., Gastil, J., and Cohen, G. (2009). Cultural cognition of the risks and benefits of nanotechnology. *Nature Nanotechnology* 4(2): 87–91.

Kahan, D., Jenkins-Smith, H., and Braman, D. (2011). Cultural cognition of scientific consensus. *Journal of Risk Research* 14(2): 147–74.

Karlan, D., McConnell, M., Mullainathan, S., and Zinman, J. (2016). Getting to the top of mind: how reminders increase saving. *Management Science* 62(12): 3393–411.

Kaur, S., Kremer, M., and Mullainathan, S. (2015). Self-control at work. *Journal of Political Economy* 123(6): 1227–77.

Köszegi, B. and Rabin, M. (2007). Mistakes in choice-based welfare analysis. *American Economic Review* 97(2): 477–81.

Köszegi, B. and Rabin, M. (2008). Choices, situations, and happiness. *Journal of Public Economics* 92(8–9): 1821–32.

Laibson, D. (2015). Why don't present-biased agents make commitments? *American Economic Review Papers and Proceedings* 105(5): 267–72.

Laibson, D. (2018). Private paternalism, the commitment puzzle, and model-free equilibrium. *American Economic Review Papers and Proceedings* 108: 1–21.

Lang, F. R., Weiss, D., Gerstorf, D., and Wagner, G. G. (2013). Forecasting life satisfaction across adulthood: benefits of seeing a dark future? *Psychology and Aging* 28(1): 249–61.

Li, C., Li, Z., and Wakker, P. (2014). If nudge cannot be applied: a litmus test of the readers' stance on paternalism. *Theory and Decision* 76(3): 297–315.

Loewenstein, G. and Chater, N. (2017). Putting nudges in perspective. *Behavioral Public Policy* 1(1): 26–53.

Marx, B. M. and Turner, L. J. (2019). Student loan nudges: experimental evidence on borrowing and educational attainment. *American Economic Journal: Economic Policy* 11 (2): 108–41.

McConnell, M., Rothschild, C. W., Ettenger, A., Muigai, F., and Cohen, J. (2018). Free contraception and behavioural nudges in the postpartum period: evidence from a randomised control trial in Nairobi, Kenya. *British Medical Journal: Global Health* 3:e000888.

Milkman, K. L., Minson, J. A., and Volpp, K. G. M. (2013). Holding the hunger games hostage at the gym: an evaluation of temptation bundling. *Management Science* 60 (2): 283–99.

Milkman, K. L., Rogers, T., and Bazerman, M. H. (2008). I'll have the ice cream soon and the vegetables later: a study of online grocery purchases and order lead time. *Marketing Letters* 21(1): 17–35.

Nave, G., Camerer, C., and McCullough, M. (2015). Does oxytocin increase trust in humans? Critical review of research. *Perspectives on Psychological Science* 10(6): 772–89.

Nolan, J. M., Schultz, P. W., Cialdini, R. B., Goldstein, N. J., and Griskevicius, V. (2008). Normative social influence is underdetected. *Personality and Social Psychology Bulletin* 34(7): 913–23.

O'Donoghue, T. and Rabin, M. (1999). Doing it now or later. *American Economic Review* 89(1): 103–24.

Odermatt, R. and Stutzer, A. (2019). (Mis-) Predicted subjective well-being following life events. *Journal of the European Economic Association* 17(1): 245–83.

Patterson, R. W. (2018). Can behavioral tools improve online student outcomes? Experimental evidence from a massive open online course. *Journal of Economic Behavior and Organization* 153: 291–321.

Pe'er, E., Feldman, Y., Gamliel, E., Sahar, L., Tikotsky, A., Hod, N., and Schupak, H. (2019). Do minorities like nudges? The role of group norms in attitudes towards behavioral policy. *Judgment and Decision Making* 14(1): 40–50.

Royer, H., Stehr, M., and Sydnor, J. (2015). Incentives, commitments, and habit formation in exercise: evidence from a field experiment with workers at a fortune-500 company. *American Economic Journal: Applied Economics* 7 (3): 51–84.

Sadoff, S., Samek, A., and Sprenger, C. (2019). Dynamic inconsistency in food choice: experimental evidence from two food deserts. Forthcoming in *The Review of Economic Studies*.

Salant, Y. and Rubinstein, A. (2008). (A, f): choice with frames. *Review of Economic Studies* 75 (4): 1287–96.

Schelling, T. C. (1978). Egonomics, or the art of self-management. *American Economic Review* 68(2): 290–4.

Schilbach, F. (2019). Alcohol and self-control: a field experiment in India. *American Economic Review* 109:4: 1290–1322.

Schultz, W., Nolan, J., Cialdini, R. B., Goldstein, N., and Griskevicius, V. (2007). The constructive, destructive, and reconstructive power of social norms. *Psychological Science* 18(5), 429–34.

Schmidtke, K. A., Watson, D. G., Roberts, P., and Vlaev, I. (2019). Menu positions influence soft drink selection at touchscreen kiosks. *Psychology & Marketing* 36(10): 964–70.

Schwandt, H. (2016). Unmet aspirations as an explanation for the age u-shape in wellbeing.

Journal of Economic Behavior & Organization 122(C): 75–87.

Serra, D. (2019). Neuroeconomics and modern neuroscience. CEE-M Working Paper 2019–12.

Shefrin, H. and Statman, M. (1984). Explaining investor preference for cash dividends. *Journal of Financial Economics* 13(2): 253–82.

Sokol-Hessner, P., Lackovic, S. F., Tobe, R. H., Camerer, C. F., Leventhal, B. L., and Phelps, E. A. (2015). Determinants of propranolol's selective effect on loss aversion. *Psychological Science* 26(7): 1123–30.

Sonntag, A. and Zizzo, D. J. (2015). On reminder effects, drop-outs and dominance: evidence from an online experiment on charitable giving. *PLoS ONE* 10(8): e0134705 08.

Spiegler, R. (2015). On the equilibrium effects of nudging. *Journal of Legal Studies* 4(3): Article 5.

Strahilevitz, M., Barber, B. M., and Odean, T. (2011). Once burned, twice shy: how naive learning, counterfactuals, and regret affect the repurchase of stocks previously sold. *Journal of Marketing Research* 48: 102–20.

Sugden, R. (2017). Do people really want to be nudged towards healthy lifestyles? *International Review of Economics* 64(2): 113–23.

Sugden, R. (2018). 'Better off, as judged by themselves': a reply to Cass Sunstein. *International Review of Economics* 65(1): 9–13.

Sunstein, C. R. (2013). *Simpler: The Future of Government*. New York: Simon and Schuster.

Sunstein, C. R. (2016). The council of psychological advisers. *Annual Review of Psychology* 67(1): 713–37.

Sunstein, C. R. (2017). Default rules are better than active choosing (often). *Trends in Cognitive Sciences* 21(8): 600–6.

Sunstein, C. R. (2018) "Better off, as judged by themselves": a comment on evaluating nudges. *International Review of Economics* 65(1): 1–8.

Sunstein, C. R., Reisch, L. A., and Kaiser, M. (2019). Trusting nudges? Lessons from an international survey. *Journal of European Public Policy* 26(10): 1417–43.

Tannenbaum, D., Fox, C. R., and Rogers, T. (2017). On the misplaced politics of behavioural policy interventions. *Nature Human Behaviour* 1, Article number 0130.

Taubinsky, D. and Rees-Jones, A. (2018). Attention variation and welfare: theory and evidence from a tax salience experiment. *Review of Economic Studies* 85(4): 2462–96.

Thaler, R. H. and Sunstein, C. R. (2009). *Nudge: Improving Decisions about Health, Wealth, and Happiness*. New Haven, CT: Penguin Books.

Thunström, L. (2018). Incidence of an emotional tax: the case of calorie menu labeling. Available at SSRN: https://ssrn.com/abstract=3272036.

Thunström, L., Nordström, J., Shogren, J. F., Ehmke, M., and van 't Veld, K. (2016). Strategic self-ignorance. *Journal of Risk and Uncertainty* 52(2): 117–36.

Tiefenbeck, V., Staake, T., Roth, K., and Sachs, O. (2013). For better or for worse? Empirical evidence of moral licensing in a behavioral energy conservation campaign. *Energy Policy* 57: 160–71.

Toussaert, S. (2018). Eliciting temptation and self-control through menu choices:

a lab experiment. *Econometrica* 86(3): 859–89.

Trope, Y. and Liberman, N. (2000). Temporal construal and time-dependent changes in preference. *Journal of Personality and Social Psychology* 79(6): 876–89.

Trope, Y. and Liberman, N. (2003). Temporal construal. *Psychological Review* 110(3): 403–21.

Truelove, H. B., Carrico, A. R., Weber, E. U., Raimi, K. T., and Vandenbergh, M. P. (2014). Positive and negative spillover of pro-environmental behavior: an integrative review and theoretical framework. *Global Environmental Change* 29: 127–38.

VanEpps, E.M., Downs, J.S., and Loewenstein, G. (2016). Calorie label formats: using numbers or traffic lights to reduce lunch calories. *Journal of Public Policy and Marketing* 35(1): 26–36.

NAME INDEX

SUBJECT INDEX